HISTORICAL DICTIONARY OF AMERICAN RADIO

HISTORICAL DICTIONARY OF AMERICAN RADIO

Edited by
Donald G. Godfrey
and Frederic A. Leigh

GREENWOOD PRESS
Westport, Connecticut • London

Library of Congress Cataloging-in-Publication Data

Historical dictionary of American radio / edited by Donald G. Godfrey
   and Frederic A. Leigh.
      p.   cm.
   Includes bibliographical references and index.
   ISBN 0-313-29636-7 (alk. paper)
    1. Radio broadcasting—United States—History—Dictionaries.
   2. Radio—United States—History—Dictionaries. I. Godfrey, Donald
   G. II. Leigh, Frederic A.
   PN1991.2.H57   1998
   384.54′0973—dc21   97–33140

British Library Cataloguing in Publication Data is available.

Library of Congress Catalog Card Number: 97–33140
ISBN: 0-313-29636-7

First published in 1998

Greenwood Press, 88 Post Road West, Westport, CT 06881
An imprint of Greenwood Publishing Group, Inc.

Printed in the United States of America

The paper used in this book complies with the
Permanent Paper Standard issued by the National
Information Standards Organization (Z39.48–1984).

10 9 8 7 6 5 4 3 2 1

Contents

Preface

In accordance with the dictionary definition of a "dictionary," this alphabetical listing of terms comprehensively treats the various branches of knowledge relating to the specific subject of American radio history. Readers will find entries on almost every subject related to the topic of radio.

It is acknowledged at the outset that there are limitations to the work. The obvious omissions are the technical and personality aspects of radio: Detailed scientific concepts are left to engineering and technical publications; personalities, to other publications. That does not mean that all discussions of these aspects of radio are eliminated. It means, rather, that this work focuses on topics as they relate to the general history of radio.

Intended for an interdisciplinary audience in college, university, institutional, and public library settings, this publication presumes no prior knowledge of radio, and each definitional entry stands independently. This reference publication is intended to assist those interested in research. It is a quick, ready reference to a wide variety of topics. Our goal is to provide a series of reference-styled entries organized alphabetically, A to Z.

The editors began this project by compiling a list of potential entries. The list was constructed by assimilating the indexes and tables of contents from a variety of broadcast history books; it was edited to accommodate a historical radio focus; and topics from scholarly journals were added to extend the list, which became a working document for the dictionary.

Once the list of terms was completed, contributors were solicited through the various academic organizations; most notably, the Broadcast Education Association (BEA) provided mailing lists for several of its Interest Divisions, including history, news, and production. This list was extended through the American Journalism History Association and the Association for Education in Journalism and Mass Communication, and a call was also distributed at the BEA National Convention. An interest form and a list of topics were mailed to potential contributors, who were then organized according to their expressed interests. Specific scholars were also invited to contribute entries where their published research/experience/expertise was well known. All were asked to contribute original entries. At this point, the contributors were asked for their input in regard to the list of topics, and as a result, a number of new subjects were added.

In general, the subject entries consist of the term heading, followed immediately by a clear definition or identification of the subject. General narrative, if needed, follows and provides an expanded definition or narrative development related to the historical background, precedents, and the relative environmental contexts within which the term occurs. The editors requested a purely factual writing. Following general narrative, there are often several references the author felt most important in directing the reader to further information. The author's name ends each individual entry.

In compiling the entries from the contributors, the editors worked to maintain the integrity of the original. Each author is responsible for his or her own original entry, as edits were made only to clarify the topic, eliminate redundancy, and set the entry to publication form. The editors have edited repetitive suggested readings. The single source cited most often was the work of Christopher H. Sterling and John M. Kittross, *Stay Tuned: A Concise History of American Broadcasting*. The reader is directed to this and the following key works cited throughout this publication:

Erik Barnouw, *The Golden Web: A History of Broadcasting in the United States, 1933–1953* (Oxford: Oxford University Press, 1968).

Erik Barnouw, *A Tower in Babel: A History of Broadcasting in the United States to 1933* (New York: Oxford University Press, 1966).

Sydney W. Head, Christopher H. Sterling, Lemuel Schofield, Thomas Spann, and Michael McGregor, *Broadcasting in America: A Survey of Electronic Media,* 8th ed. (Dallas: Houghton Mifflin, 1998).

Lawrence W. Lichty and Malachi C. Topping, *American Broadcasting: A Source Book on the History of Radio and Television* (New York: Hastings House Publishers Inc., 1975).

Robert W. McChesney, *Telecommunications, Mass Media and Democracy: The Battle for the Control of U.S. Broadcasting, 1928–1935* (New York: Oxford University Press, 1993).

Christopher H. Sterling and John M. Kittross. *Stay Tuned: A Concise History of American Broadcasting* (Belmont, Calif.: Wadsworth, 1990).

Including the above, the reader will note additional references following many entries. Caution should be given to the Web site references as they are dynamic and constantly changing. Please note that the editors updated the Web citations in the Select Bibliography as this book went to press so some may not be as they appear in the original entry.

The editors are indebted to many who made this publication possible: Dr. Ronald Garay and the editors of Greenwood, who extended the invitation to create the dictionary; the invited scholars who contributed their time and expertise, and all of our contributors; Janet Soper and Mary Fran Draisker of the Publication Assistance Center, College of Public Programs, Arizona State University; and all of our colleagues at the Walter Cronkite School of Journalism and Telecommunication, Arizona State University.

Introduction: A Brief History of "The Whispering Gallery of the Skies"

"Science has made a whispering gallery of the skies," declared Senator Henry F. Amherst as he marveled at the new technology called radio.[1] The evolution of radio began well over 120 years ago. It was not the invention of a single person but the evolution of a technology influenced by people, their environment, big business, and big government. Radio was the invention of pioneers who had engineering and entrepreneurial skills. It has a history of people interacting with people and their environments.

Radio Pioneers

The roots of radio broadcasting extend back to the Industrial Age, the last half of the nineteenth century. During the mid-1800s, the telegraph transmitted coded signals, providing the world's first instantaneous news service. Once success with the telegraph had been achieved by Samuel Morse, the next step was to send voice messages. Alexander Graham Bell created the necessary technology when he invented the telephone. Bell completed his first successful voice transmissions by wire in 1874.[2]

The telegraph and the telephone were critical inventions in the history of American electronic communication. But the real challenge was to develop a method of sending coded and voice messages without wires. James Clerk Maxwell, a Scottish physicist, was the first to publish a theory that a spectrum of electromagnetic energy beyond visible light exists.[3] In 1888, a German physicist named Heinrich Hertz proved Maxwell's theory by demonstrating the existence of invisible electromagnetic waves in his laboratory.[4] Hertz played an important part in the birth of wireless communication because he demonstrated that electromagnetic waves carry electrical energy. He didn't envision radio as we know it today, but his experiments laid the groundwork for the next critical invention in radio history: the wireless telegraph. The technology for a device that would send coded messages without wires was developed by Guglielmo Marconi, an Italian inventor and entrepreneur.[5] Marconi took Maxwell's theories and Hertz's lab experiments and put them into practice. He created the first radio transmitter and receiver—devices that used the electromagnetic spectrum to send bursts of radio energy. In 1901, he succeeded in sending a wireless telegraph signal across the Atlantic Ocean.[6]

Marconi realized the commercial value of his inventions and established corporations to market them, first in Great Britain, then in the United States, Canada, and Italy. Shortly after his transatlantic transmissions, he began to build radiotelegraphy stations along the Atlantic coast of the United States with a primary purpose of ship-to-shore communication. The Marconi Companies developed quickly into a dominant force in maritime communication, a force that lasted until after World War I.

While Marconi was building his radiotelegraph empire, a Canadian scientist named Reginald Fessenden was experimenting with wireless voice transmission.[7] Sending voice signals on the radio spectrum was a more complicated process than that of coded transmission. Fessenden had to develop a device that would generate a continuous radio wave. He also had to develop a method of modulating the human voice onto the radio wave so that it would carry the message to a receiver. Using a telephone microphone to modulate a continuous radio wave, Fessenden broadcast the first wireless voice transmission on Christmas Eve in 1906.[8] His audience consisted primarily of radiotelegraph operators aboard ships off the Atlantic coast that evening. They were amazed to hear a human voice and even music in their headphones for the first time!

Two years after Fessenden made the first voice broadcast, another radio pioneer broadcast voice and music on radio waves. Lee de Forest's radio broadcasts came a bit later in history, but he utilized a revolutionary device called the audion.[9] It was essentially a vacuum tube that used three electrodes to amplify electrical signals passing through it. This was a critical invention for broadcasting because earlier voice transmissions were quite weak and could only be heard faintly on headphones. De Forest's audion allowed signals to be amplified many times to a level that could be heard on a loudspeaker, a basic component of radio receivers designed for home listening.[10]

Radio Corporations

Radio in the first decade of the twentieth century was primarily used for point-to-point communication, as were the telegraph and telephone. It was a maritime ship-to-shore and ship-to-ship communications tool. The concept of broadcasting, using radio to communicate with the general public, had not yet emerged.

The significance of the radiotelegraph in ship-to-shore communication was dramatically demonstrated in 1912 when the *Titanic* struck an iceberg in the north Atlantic. Even though there was another ship near the *Titanic* that night, its wireless operator was not on duty to receive a distress call. By the time the call was received by other ships, it was too late. Nearly 1,500 people were drowned, and reports of the disaster focused the nation's attention on the potential power of radio. The *Titanic* disaster demonstrated the need for regulation of the radio spectrum. The *Radio Act of 1912* was the U.S. government's response to the disaster. Two years earlier, the *Wireless Ship Act* had been passed, but it simply required large passenger ships to have radio equipment aboard. The new law also was designed for ship-to-shore wireless but required licensing of transmitters through the secretary of commerce. It also specified radio frequencies to be used, assigned call letters, and prioritized the transmission of distress signals. The *Radio Act of 1912* was the first comprehensive piece of legislation dealing with radio, but it would later prove to be inadequate as broadcasting emerged in the 1920s.[11]

The corporations that would play major roles in developing broadcasting were in place at the turn of the century. These included General Electric (GE), AT&T, Westinghouse,[12] and the Marconi Companies.[13] Each of their companies held specific patents on radio components and had the financial resources necessary to make broadcasting a commercially viable medium.

As World War I approached, business and industry were nationalized and focused on war production. These changes affected radio as a business, and when the United States entered the war in 1917, all wireless stations were shut down. When they were signed on again, they were under the control of the navy. One of the most important results of the navy's controlling radio was the consolidation of patents. The corporations involved in producing radio parts held a variety of patents independent of one another. Marconi had attempted to build a global monopoly on radio by acquiring patents from competitors and holding strict control of his own. But the war effort forced manufacturers to pool their patents, allowing significant technological advances to be made during this time.

After the war, the navy, which was nervous about the control of radio by a foreign entity, namely, the Marconi Companies, proposed that radio communication remain under government control.[14] But significant corporate pressure on the government resulted in wireless stations being returned to private ownership. The patent pool was released to the control of a new company: the Radio Corporation of America (RCA).[15] Established in 1919, RCA was created to take over the holdings of the American Marconi Company. A young Marconi Company radio-telegraph operator named David Sarnoff would rise to the presidency of the new company.[16]

Under the new corporate agreement, GE would manufacture radio receivers and RCA would market them. AT&T would manufacture radio transmitters for use in the radiotelephone business. The remaining radio corporate player, Westinghouse, joined RCA along with its patents in 1921 in exchange for RCA stock. This ended the patent rivalries and established the corporate base for the emergence of a new radio industry: broadcasting.

As radio entered the 1920s, it was still primarily a wireless telegraph industry. However, the corporate partners of RCA were experimenting with radio stations that were designed to broadcast to the general public. Fessenden and de Forest made radio broadcasts to anyone who might have been listening but never established radio stations with regular program schedules. The stations generally cited as the first broadcasting stations were Westinghouse's KDKA, Pittsburgh, and CFCF, Montreal.

KDKA grew from the experiments of a Westinghouse engineer named Frank Conrad.[17] In 1920, he began evening broadcasts from his garage. Rather than just talking, Conrad played phonograph records and was surprised to get music requests by letter from regular listeners. Conrad's broadcasts began to affect record sales and drew the attention of a local department store. The store began to market radio receivers to people who were interested in listening to Conrad's station and were happy to furnish more records for the programming. Soon, executives at Westinghouse saw the opportunity to sell receivers as well and licensed KDKA. The station's first official broadcast was coverage of the 1920 elections. Other pioneering stations have claimed to have been first, but according to Baudino and Kittross, KDKA is the oldest of the four claimants in the United States.[18] Westinghouse and KDKA were the first to move decisively into commercial broadcasting, and KDKA was the first commercially licensed station in the United States.[19]

CFCF radio grew from experiments conducted by the Canadian Marconi Company. On May 20, 1920, before anything comparable had been heard in the United States, members of the Royal Society of Canada assembled to observe Canada's first wireless operation. It was the first public demonstration of commercial radio in Canada, marking CFCF's claim to the title "North America's oldest broadcasting station."[20] The results from this broadcast were immediate, as "people were lining up at the counters of electrical shops to buy home receivers." In the movie theaters where receiving equipment was on display, "these events drew larger billings than the motion picture."[21]

Many other radio stations followed KDKA's and CFCF's precedents, the most prominent being those established by the major companies: AT&T, RCA, and GE. These corporations each established key stations and were to play major roles in developing radio networks in the 1920s. The AT&T station, WEAF, was different from the others in its mission: It was operated as a "radio telephone booth" that could be used to send messages to the public for a toll.[22] In this manner, WEAF sold the first radio advertising and aired the first radio commercials. AT&T considered the sale of radio time for "tolls" to be its exclusive right, and as a result, other radio stations did not sell airtime. AT&T also reserved the right to interconnect stations, so it is credited with another first in radio history: network broadcasting.

Network Broadcasting

AT&T's practice of selling airtime was widely criticized as too commercial for a public medium like radio. One of the critics was David Sarnoff, who proposed that radio should be supported by philanthropy like libraries and museums. Even some members of Congress were threatening legislation that would ban advertising on radio.[23] WEAF continued the practice, and by the end of the decade, selling radio advertising was accepted as the principal means of financing the industry.

At the same time, a corporate battle for control of the new radio broadcasting industry was growing. Within the structure of RCA, there were basically two groups: the Radio Group and the Telephone Group. The Radio Group, led by David Sarnoff, envisioned the radio medium as a source of information and entertainment for the general public.[24] The Telephone Group, led by AT&T, considered broadcasting to be a "common carrier," like the telephone. It was simply providing a medium for public use without providing programming. It soon became obvious, however, that if radio stations were going to attract listeners, entertaining programs would have to be offered.

The first weekly advertiser on WEAF was Browning King, a clothing manufacturer that sponsored a regular program of music featuring the "Browning King Orchestra." The concept allowed advertisers to attach their company name to programs but did not include commercials promoting products. The radio commercials, as we know them today, would emerge later, but stations in the 1920s adopted AT&T's sponsorship concept.

Now, AT&T, a government-regulated monopoly, found itself in the awkward position of programming a radio station and selling airtime. This position, seen by critics as a conflict of interest, would eventually lead to the withdrawal of AT&T from the broadcasting business. But not before AT&T established the first radio network. The company already had telephone lines across the country, so the interconnection of radio stations seemed a logical step. AT&T set up the first experimental connection between New York and Boston in 1923. By the next year, it had a regular network or "chain" of six stations established.

The Radio Group of RCA also wanted to establish its own network of stations. However, AT&T would not lease telephone lines to other networks; instead, David Sarnoff had to use Western Union telegraph lines to connect stations to his flagship station WJZ. The quality of the telegraph lines was not as good as the telephone lines, so Sarnoff's network was at a disadvantage. This generated more criticism of AT&T, and by 1926, it gave in to pressure to get out of the broadcasting business. AT&T sold its flagship station, WEAF, and its network to David Sarnoff at RCA, but AT&T retained the rights to lease telephone lines for station and network interconnection, a practice that it continued for many years.

With the acquisition of the AT&T station and access to interconnection, David Sarnoff established a new network under the RCA umbrella: the National Broadcasting Company (NBC). The inaugural NBC broadcast aired across the country on November 15 ,1926.[25] The next year, RCA divided NBC into two networks: NBC Red, the WEAF-based network purchased from AT&T, and NBC Blue, the original RCA network with WJZ as its flagship station. Although the two networks would become similar in size during the mid-1930s, NBC Red was the dominant network with the programming and advertising revenue developed by AT&T.[26]

Competition for NBC was not long in coming. The United Independent Broadcasters (UIB) network debuted in 1927, the creation of a talent promoter and a music business manager. The network was intended to provide an alternative to NBC for music performers. After a major investment from the Columbia Phonograph Company, that company's name was attached to the network's name.[27] The phonograph company soon changed its mind about network ownership and sold its interest to one of the network's major advertisers, William Paley. Paley, vice president of his father's cigar company, negotiated for the right to retain the network name, Columbia. He dropped the phonograph part, and it became the Columbia Broadcasting System (CBS) in 1928.[28]

William Paley, an experienced businessman, started a campaign to build CBS affiliates to compete with NBC. Perhaps the most significant contribution Paley made to network broadcasting was the foundation of modern affiliate contracts. He offered affiliates a certain number of network program hours each week. These "sustaining" programs were offered free of charge to affiliates that he paid to broadcast "sponsored" programs. In exchange, the affiliates gave the network commercial time for network advertisers and an exclusive outlet for network programs. This affiliate contract was later adopted by NBC and remains the basis for network contracts today.

Other radio networks followed NBC and CBS. Some failed, but others were able to compete with the big two during the 1930s. The most significant of these was the Mutual Broadcasting System (MBS).[29] In contrast to NBC and CBS, Mutual was not developed from a flagship station and had no studios. It was a cooperative venture built around program sharing by a series of independent radio stations. The new network's most famous program, *The Lone Ranger,* was introduced in 1933 on WXYZ, Detroit. MBS has survived to this day as a radio network, but never made the transition to television as did NBC, CBS, and the American Broadcasting Company (ABC).

ABC emerged in the 1940s after NBC was forced by a Federal Communications Commission (FCC) ruling to sell off one of its two networks.[30] After a court battle against the FCC rule prohibiting the operation of two or more simultaneous radio networks, NBC sold its weaker Blue Network in 1943. The new owner was Edward Noble, the Life Savers candy mogul, who changed the network name to ABC.

Radio Broadcasting Legislation

As more stations signed on the air during the 1920s, frequency interference became a major problem. The assignment of broadcast station frequency was still being made by the secretary of commerce under the *Radio Act of 1912.* As noted earlier, this radio act was designated for radiotelegraphy, point-to-point wireless communication. It was inadequate for the expanded frequency demands of commercial radio broadcasting.

By 1923, there were more than 500 radio stations licensed for broadcasting.[31] The secretary of commerce was required to license radio stations under the act, but the legislation gave him little power to regulate frequency assignments. As a result, radio stations were interfering with each other, using the same frequency, changing frequencies, and varying their power levels. By 1926, interference problems and complaints to the secretary had increased dramatically. It was obvious that new legislation was needed. An opinion of the U.S. attorney general confirmed that fact.[32]

The first legislation designed specifically for commercial radio was passed by Congress in 1927. The *Radio Act of 1927* recognized broadcasting as a distinct service apart from radiotelegraphy, and it established the "public interest, convenience, and necessity" standard for station licensing.[33] It created a temporary agency, the Federal Radio Commission, to institute regulations and frequency assignments. Stations would be licensed for a period of three years and operate in the public interest. After one year, the responsibility for radio regulation was to return to the secretary of commerce.

The Federal Radio Commission continued until 1934. That year, President Franklin D. Roosevelt recommended to Congress that new legislation was necessary to regulate both wireless and wired communication. The regulatory power of the Federal Radio Commission and the Interstate Commerce Commission would be combined in a new agency, the FCC. Much of the philosophical framework of the *Radio Act of 1927* was reenacted in the *Communications Act of 1934*. The public interest standard remained; public ownership of the airwaves, equitable distribution, license eligibility standards, First Amendment protection, and the right to challenge governmental regulations were all retained in the 1934 act. With a number of amendments accommodating growth, new technology, and a changing environment, the act served as the primary electronic media legislation until it was replaced by the *Telecommunications Act of 1996.*

Radio Programming

Programming on the early radio networks consisted primarily of music performed live in the studio by the networks' own orchestras. Large studios were designed for live music and musicians dressed in formal attire even though they could not be seen. In 1927, musical variety accounted for 30 percent; light music, 8 percent; and concert music, 39 percent of radio programming time, with the remainder devoted to news, sports, and other information programming.[34]

As the country entered the Great Depression in the 1930s, network radio programming began to expand. Vaudeville performers who were forced out of work by the growth of movies found radio a good outlet for their talents. Their mix of music and comedy routines became the basis for network radio's variety programming. The first series to draw large audiences was *Amos 'n' Andy,* a program about a taxicab company in the ghetto. The African-American characters were played by white comedians Charles Correll and Freeman Gosden. Introduced on NBC in 1929, the program had become the top network show in the 1930s. The idea of white actors playing black characters was considered racist by some critics even at that time, but the program was so popular that it stopped traffic and even movies in progress when it aired. *Amos 'n' Andy* moved to CBS television in the 1950s with African-American actors.

Dramatic adaptations of stage plays on radio appeared in the early 1920s. The networks also developed their own series including mystery programs like *The Shadow* and *Lights Out* and weekly anthologies like *Lux Radio Theater.* Perhaps the most famous drama aired on a radio network was "War of the Worlds," Orson Welles's adaptation of H. G. Wells's Martian invasion of Earth story. The program, presented live on Halloween evening in 1938, caused a panic among listeners on the East Coast, where the Martians supposedly had landed.[35]

Welles adapted the story for radio as live news coverage of an actual event. Even though listeners were informed several times during the program that it was not real, many listeners thought it was actually happening. Because listeners had come to rely on radio to bring them news of the faltering economy and the threat of war in Europe, many were emotionally charged and ready to believe newscasters. The producers of "War of the Worlds" and the radio networks in general were widely criticized by the public. The networks were warned by the FCC that such misleading programs were not to be broadcast in the future. Nevertheless, the program demonstrated the tremendous power of the networks in the late 1930s.

As drama and comedy grew on the networks, music programming declined. During the 1930s, the percentage of music programming on network evening schedules dropped drastically.[36] Mystery and adventure programs were generally scheduled during the evening, but the daytime hours offered a new type of radio program: the soap opera.[37] Two of the most popular soap operas on radio were *Helen Trent* and *Mary Noble, Backstage Wife*. Radio programming matured during the 1930s, a period that came to be known as "the Golden Age of Radio."

Radio News Emerges

News and information programming during the 1920s and early 1930s consisted primarily of what today might be considered special event coverage: speeches, political debates, religious sermons, and celebrations. President Roosevelt used the radio for his famous *Fireside Chats* in which he projected an intimate personality that listeners came to trust during the Depression.[38]

The NBC Blue Network initiated nightly newscasts with Lowell Thomas in 1930.[39] It was obvious that radio could offer something that newspapers could not: immediacy. Newspaper owners realized this and attempted to stall radio news by forcing the wire services to withhold news from radio networks and stations.[40]

Under an agreement between radio networks and newspapers, a Press-Radio Bureau was established in 1933 to supply news to radio. Radio newscasts could not be scheduled until after the morning and evening papers had been distributed. News commentary was not included in the agreement, so radio network newscasters became news commentators. By 1935, one of the news wire services, United Press (UP), broke the agreement and began to distribute news to radio networks. The Associated Press and the International Press Service followed UP's lead soon after, and the Press-Radio Bureau was dead by 1938.

Radio news matured during World War II.[41] Radio had become a consumer medium during the Depression. Listeners had come to depend on radio for entertainment and, increasingly, news. Radio could bring news of a war across the sea into listeners' living rooms with immediacy and drama. Among the most notable of the network newscasters during WWII was Edward R. Murrow, who reported from London on CBS.[42] He brought listeners reports on the bombing of London complete with the sounds of the battlefield. For the first time, listeners actually heard the events of war unfolding live.[43] Radio brought listeners the first news of the bombing of Pearl Harbor and of America's entry into the war in 1941.[44] World

War II marked the beginning of a new era in radio and television.[45] The foundations were laid in those news reports, "live" from the battlefield. Radio and television today continue to reflect those patterns.

Frequency Modulation: FM

During the 1930s, engineers (Farnsworth working for Farnsworth Radio and Television[46] and Zworykin working for RCA)[47] were already working on the technology for a new medium: television. Another engineer and friend of David Sarnoff, Edwin Howard Armstrong, had taken on one of the most difficult challenges of radio technology at the time: the elimination of static from the radio signal. Armstrong discovered a new method of modulating sound onto a radio wave by varying the frequency rather than the amplitude. This method of modulation, introduced in 1933, eliminated the static in the resulting radio signal, but it required an entirely new system of radio broadcasting with different transmitters and receivers.[48] This would not be acceptable to David Sarnoff and RCA.

Sarnoff told his friend Armstrong that he could not support FM as a replacement for AM (amplitude modulation). Rather, he saw it as a new technology that would enhance television sound. However, Armstrong persisted in his position that FM should replace AM radio. This was the beginning of a long and bitter battle between the two men for control of the new technology. Armstrong went ahead on his own with the development of FM radio on a network of stations on the East Coast. The FCC approved the commercial operation of FM stations in 1941.

Following WWII, David Sarnoff convinced the FCC to reassign FM to a different part of the spectrum. This delayed FM's development. In 1945, FM was assigned to 88–108 megahertz (MHz), where it resides today. The move, at the time, meant that all of Armstrong's FM stations and receivers would be obsolete. Thus, the initial interest in FM fostered by Armstrong's stations began to wane. AM station owners did apply for FM frequencies, but most FM signals simply became simulcasts of AM stations. In the late 1940s, there was not enough demand for the higher quality of FM, and the industry excitement was being generated by television's potential. Armstrong continued to fight for FM radio for the rest of his troubled life. He finally took his life in despair in 1954. He died not knowing that little more than a decade later FM would begin a rise to dominate radio broadcasting and threaten to eliminate AM.

Post-WWII

Radio broadcasting emerged from WWII at the peak of its popularity. By 1945, it had become the most popular medium for both entertainment and news. Network programs and their stars were well established, listenership was at an all-time high, and advertising support was plentiful. All of this was to change dramatically within the next decade. The changes were due to a new electronic medium that threatened the very future of radio: television.

Television technology had been introduced to the public by Farnsworth in 1934[49] at the Benjamin Franklin Institute and by RCA at the New York World's Fair in 1939,[50] but the U.S. entry into the war in 1941 brought a temporary halt to the development of television. Following the war, the networks renewed their efforts in TV development, and many predicted the death of radio at that time.

Beginning in the late 1940s, popular radio network programs began to make the transition to television. As radio network-program schedules diminished, local stations began to drop their network affiliations. The loss of network affiliation resulted in a significant drop in national advertisers. In fact, by 1958, the average radio station earned about half of the advertising income it had in 1948.[51] Fortunately, radio station owners recognized the strengths of their medium and turned to more localized programming and advertising support.

Formats Emerge

The radio music program had originated in the 1920s on the *Grand Ole Opry* and later on *Your Hit Parade.*[52] By the late 1940s, recorded music had become more prevalent on radio stations. Recorded music programs were relatively inexpensive to produce, and as a result, these programs were common on independent stations that could not depend on network programming. As network radio stations began to lose programming to television, they turned to recorded music to fill the gaps. Stations used announcers to introduce pieces of music and the "disc jockey" (DJ) was born.

Some station owners held on to the notion that they could still attract mass audiences, but most recognized that they would do better attracting segments of the radio audience with a particular style of music. This was the philosophy of radio formats or formulas: People watch television programs, but they listen to radio stations.

It was not until the advent of a new music style that format radio really emerged as a major programming force. In the early 1950s, new music was emerging that would take teenagers by storm: rock 'n' roll.[53] The term is thought to have been used first by Cleveland disc jockey Alan Freed, who was inspired by an old blues lyric, "My baby rocks me with a steady roll."[54] As radio stations came to depend more on music, the time was right for the new and popular form of music to develop on radio. Rock 'n' roll appeared on radio in the form of the first format: top 40. Two radio pioneers are usually credited with the creation of top 40: Todd Storz and Gordon McClendon. In Omaha, Nebraska, in the early 1950s, Storz saw the jukebox as the inspiration for a new format. He noticed that people tended to play the same popular songs over and over again. He wondered whether a radio station could be programmed in the same way: a rotation of the most popular songs repeated throughout the day. At about the same time, Gordon McClendon was beginning to program his Dallas radio station with a top-40 format. He also developed a rotation system for the music, but he added heavy on-air promotion and personalities to the mix. Disc jockeys on top-40 formats became an important part of the sound and, in fact, achieved celebrity status as a result. Not only was the timing right for radio and rock 'n' roll to come together, but the target audience for the format was the teenager, a portion of the population that was growing rapidly. Teens flocked to rock 'n' roll music in droves and became devoted listeners to top-40 radio.

FM Finally Emerges

By 1960, it was clear the radio would survive—but not as a network-dominated medium serving mass audiences. Radio's future was in formats geared to localized target audiences. With the development of transistors, radio receivers had become more mobile and personalized. This was something that television could not offer, so radio receivers became more common in automobiles. With the success of the top-40 format, station owners were inspired to experiment with other formats designed for special segments of the population.

Much of the growth in format radio continued to be on AM stations up until the mid-1960s. Even though FM technology had been in existence since the 1930s, the demand for better sound quality on radio did not materialize until much later. By the middle of the 1960s, the FCC had recognized the need to foster the growth of FM radio. In 1961, the agency had approved stereo broadcasting on the FM band. By this time, the recording industry was offering stereophonic records, and music lovers were more interested in higher-quality recordings. Because FM already had an advantage of being static free, the availability of stereo sound made it even more attractive. Specialized formats, such as classical and easy-listening, began to appear on FM stations.

In 1962, the FCC placed a freeze on new AM applications because the AM portion of the electromagnetic spectrum was becoming saturated. This encouraged FM applications, but a third FCC ruling in the 1960s had the most significant effect on the growth of FM. In 1965, the FCC ruled that AM and FM station combinations (operated by the same owner) in cities of 100,000 or more population could not duplicate programming more than half of the broadcast day. Before this ruling, many of these stations had been simulcasting (duplicating the entire day) on the AM and FM bands. The new FCC ruling, requiring different programming for one of the stations for part of the day, encouraged the development of new formats on FM.

By 1966, nearly 50 percent of homes in the United States had FM radio receivers, and this would increase to 93 percent by 1975.[55] With the growth of FM stations came further experimentation with new radio formats. The improved sound quality of FM and stereo signals also encouraged new music formats. Contemporary music was expanding and changing in the 1960s as well. New music formats such as AOR (album-oriented rock) and progressive rock reflected these changes. In the AOR format, longer album cuts were played rather than the hits heard on the top 40, and DJ styles were more mellow. As more and varied music formats became available on FM, listeners began to shift away from AM stations. By the middle 1970s, FM radio's share of the audience had reached 40 percent. Even though AM radio still had the larger share of advertising dollars, the trend was clear: FM would surpass AM in music format audiences. AM station owners were already exploring different formats that would be competitive in the 1980s and beyond.

As the 1980s began, FM domination of radio markets was complete with more than 50 percent of the audience. FM stations now offered a variety of music formats geared to different demographic or population groups. FM stations programmed popular formats like top 40, AOR, adult contemporary, and oldies as well as "niche" formats like alternative, jazz, New Age, and classical. As AM stations lost listeners to FM, they turned to information formats like news, sports, and talk that did not require the signal quality of FM.

Radio in the 1990s

By the middle of the 1990s, there were nearly 12,000 radio stations on the air in the United States. The FM share of the audience had risen to about 75 percent, with nearly 60 percent listening exclusively to FM.[56] Contemporary radio is characterized by intense competition among stations for their fragment of the audience. The largest listener shares were held by adult contemporary stations, but that prize was taken by country stations in 1994. News/talk formats, particularly in large radio markets, have grown in popularity throughout the decade. Growth formats include urban contemporary, Spanish, modern rock, and jazz.

Another prominent current trend in contemporary radio is group ownership. The *Telecommunications Act of 1996* under Title II, Section 202, has removed ownership limits on radio stations owned by groups. This prompted a frenzy of station buying and selling, particularly in large radio markets. As of 1997, the largest radio station group owner was Chancellor/Capstar, which owned 325 stations across the country. Ownership limits for radio stations in one market or city were also raised. One individual or company can now own up to 8 radio stations in a single market (5 in one service, AM or FM). This means that group owners will try to control a format by buying all the country stations or adult contemporary stations in a market.

Radio networks have enjoyed a resurgence in the 1990s. Satellite networks now deliver 24-hour music and talk formats to radio stations all over the country. The networks have been particularly successful in medium and small radio markets where stations cannot afford expensive on-air and programming personnel. Satellites also will deliver national radio stations directly to the listener as the new millennium arrives. These stations will offer compact disc (CD)–quality, digital sound via satellite to your home or vehicle. But radio in the year 2000 and beyond will continue to build on its strengths as a local, mobile, and personal medium.

Frederic A. Leigh
Donald G. Godfrey

Notes

1. C. C. Dill, "Traffic Cop for the Air," *American Review of Reviews* 75 (February 1927): 191.

2. For a survey of radio's prehistory, see Elliot N. Sivowitch, "A Technological Survey of Broadcasting's Pre-History, 1876–1920," *Journal of Broadcasting* 15 (1) (winter 1970–1971): 1–20.

3. Andrew F. Inglis, *Behind the Tube: A History of Broadcasting Technology and Business* (Boston: Focal Press, 1990), p. 6.

4. Inglis, pp. 6–7. See also Erik Barnouw, *A Tower in Babel: A History of Broadcasting in the United States to 1933* (New York: Oxford University Press, 1966), pp. 9–11.

5. Degna Marconi, *My Father, Marconi* (New York: McGraw-Hill, 1962). See also Barnouw, *A Tower in Babel,* pp. 12–15; and Christopher H. Sterling and John M. Kittross, *Stay Tuned: A Concise History of American Broadcasting* (Belmont, Calif.: Wadsworth, 1990), pp. 25–27.

6. *New York Times,* December 15, 1901, pp. 1–2.

7. Helen Fessenden, *Fessenden: Builder of Tomorrows* (New York: Coward-McCann, 1940; reprint, with a new index, New York: Arno Press, 1974). See also Inglis, p. 49; Barnouw, pp. 19–21; and Sterling and Kittross, pp. 27–29.

8. Sterling and Kittross, pp. 33–34.

9. Lee de Forest. *Father of Radio: The Autobiography of Lee de Forest* (Chicago: Wilcox and Follett, 1950). See also Sterling and Kittross, pp. 33–34; Barnouw, *A Tower of Babel,* pp. 21–27; and Inglis, p. 13.

10. Sterling and Kittross, p. 29.

11. Public Law 264, 62nd Congress, August 13, 1912. See Frank J. Kahn, ed., *Documents of American Broadcasting* (Englewood Cliffs, N.J.: Prentice-Hall, latest edition).

12. Inglis, p. 55.

13. "History of the American Marconi Company," *Old Timer's Bulletin* 13 (1) (June 1972): pp. 11–18. See also the papers of the Canadian Marconi Company, Public Archives of Canada. These papers provide a glimpse into the radio industries of the time and their diversification.

14. Gleason L. Archer, *History of Radio to 1926* (New York: American Historical Society, Inc., 1938), pp. 63, 376–380.

15. Archer, pp. 162, 169, 177–189. See also Barnouw, *A Tower in Babel,* pp. 57–61; Sterling and Kittross, pp. 52–58; and Inglis, pp. 98–99.

16. Kenneth Bilby, *The General: David Sarnoff and the Rise of the Communications Industry* (New York: Harper & Row, 1986).

17. Sterling and Kittross, pp. 42, 59–60; and Barnouw, *A Tower in Babel,* pp. 67–72.

18. Joseph E. Baudino and John M. Kittross, "Broadcasting's Oldest Stations: An Examination of Four Claimants," *Journal of Broadcasting* 21 (1) (winter 1977): 61–83.

19. History of Broadcasting and KDKA Radio, Public Relations Department, Westinghouse Broadcasting Company, news release, n.d., pp. 1–34; cited in Lawrence W. Lichty and Malachi C. Topping, *American Broadcasting: A Source Book on the History of Radio and Television* (New York: Hastings House Publishers Inc., 1975), pp. 102–110.

20. "Concert by Wireless," *London Times,* May 20, 1920, p. 14.

21. "CFCF Canada's First Station" (unpublished station manuscript, Multiple Access Ltd., n.d.), p. 3. See also Donald G. Godfrey, "Canadian Marconi: CFCF the Forgotten First," *Canadian Journal of Communication* 8 (4) (1982): 56–71.

22. For the script of WEAF's first commercial continuity see Archer, pp. 397–398.

23. *Congressional Record* 67 (2) (1926): 2309.

24. Archer, pp. 110–113, 189; part of Archer's story is questioned by Bilby in *The General* and by Louise Benjamin. See Louise M. Benjamin, "In Search of the Sarnoff 'Radio Music Box' Memo," *Journal of Broadcasting and Electronic Media* 37 (3) (summer 1993): 325–335.

25. Sydney W. Head, Christopher H. Sterling, and Lemeul B. Schofield, *Broadcasting in America: A Survey of Electronic Media,* 7th ed. (Boston: Houghton Mifflin, 1994), p. 37.

26. For a history of the networks, see Federal Communications Commission, *Report on Chain Broadcasting* (Commission Order No. 37, Docket 5060, May 1941), pp. 5–20.

27. *Report on Chain Broadcasting,* pp. 21–25.

28. William S. Paley, *As It Happened: A Memoir* (Garden City, N.Y.: Doubleday, 1979).

29. *Report on Chain Broadcasting,* pp. 26–28.

30. See *Report on Chain Broadcasting.* Also see Sterling and Kittross, pp. 210–211.

31. See Sterling and Kittross, p. 632. Also see Frank J. Kahn, ed., *Documents of American Broadcasting* (New York: Appleton-Century-Crofts, 1968), p. 17.

32. See Kahn, 1968, p. 27, for a copy of the attorney general's opinion.

33. See Kahn, 1968, p. 35, for a copy of the *Radio Act.*

34. Sterling and Kittross, p. 642.

35. Hadley Cantril, *The Invasion from Mars: A Study in the Psychology of Panic* (Princeton, N.J.: Princeton University Press, 1940).

36. Sterling and Kittross, pp. 118, 642–643.

37. George A. Willey, "End of an Era: The Daytime Radio Serial," *Journal of Broadcasting* 5 (2) (spring 1961): 97–115.

38. Hadley Cantril and Gordon W. Allport, *The Psychology of Radio* (New York: Harper & Brothers, 1935; reprinted New York: Arno Press, 1971), pp. 7–17.

39. Irving E. Fang, *Those Radio Commentators!* (Ames: Iowa State University Press, 1977) pp. 65–83.

40. Giraud Chester, "The Press Radio War: 1933–1935," *Public Opinion Quarterly* 13 (summer 1949): 263.

41. Donald G. Godfrey, "CBS World News Roundup: Setting the Stage for the Next Half Century," *American Journalism* 7 (3) (summer 1990): 164–172.

42. Alexander Kendrick, *Prime Time: The Life of Edward R. Murrow* (Boston: Little, Brown, 1969). See also Edward Bliss, Jr., ed., *In Search of Light: The Broadcasts of Edward R. Murrow, 1938–1961* (New York: Alfred A. Knopf, 1967); Stanley Cloud and Lynne Olsen, *The Murrow Boys: Pioneers on the Front Lines of Broadcast Journalism* (New York: Houghton Mifflin, 1996).

43. Milo Ryan, *History in Sound* (Seattle: University of Washington Press, 1963).

44. Ernest D. Rose, "How the U.S. Heard about Pearl Harbor," *Journal of Broadcasting* 5 (4) (fall 1961): 285–298.

45. Paul W. White, *News on the Air* (New York: Harcourt, Brace & Co., 1947).

46. George Everson, *The Story of Television: The Life of Philo T. Farnsworth* (New York: W. W. Norton, 1949). See also Elma G. Farnsworth, *Distant Vision: Romance and Discovery on an Invisible Frontier* (Salt Lake City: Pemberly-Kent Publishers, 1989).

47. Albert Abramson, *Zworykin: Pioneer of Television* (Chicago: University of Illinois Press, 1995).

48. Lawrence Lessing, *Man of High Fidelity: Edwin Howard Armstrong* (Philadelphia: J. B. Lippincott, 1956).

49. "Tennis Starts Act in New Television," *New York Times,* August 25, 1934, sec. 14, p. 4.

50. Erik Barnouw, *Tube of Plenty: The Evolution of American Television* (New York: Oxford University Press, 1975), pp. 86, 89–92.

51. Head, Sterling, and Schofield, p. 37.

52. Reed Bunzell, "Filling the Magic Box," *Broadcasting* 121 (supp.) (December 1, 1991): 28.

53. David T. MacFarland, "Up from Middle America: The Development of Top-40," in Lichty and Topping, pp. 399–403.

54. Edd Routt, James B. McGrath, and Fredric A. Weiss, *The Radio Format Conundrum* (New York: Hastings House, 1978), p. 19.

55. Routt, McGrath, and Weiss, p. 8. For the number of stations licensed during this same period, see also Sterling and Kittross, pp. 632–633. For the figures regarding ownership of receivers, see Sterling and Kittross, pp. 656–657.

56. "Riding Gain," *Broadcasting and Cable* 127 (3) (January 20, 1997): 46.

Radio Chronology

1837

Samuel F. B. Morse applied for first patent on telegraph system (received 1840).

1844

Morse patent granted, and he sends first official message: "What hath God wrought?"

1873

James Clerk Maxwell puts forth modern concept of electromagnetic energy.

1876

Alexander Graham Bell applies for first telephone patent.

1887

Heinrich Hertz discovers he can project a magnetic field into the air.

1892

Nathan B. Stubblefield begins broadcasting speech and music.

1895

Guglielmo Marconi begins experimenting on his father's farm; sends a signal approximately one mile.

1897

Marconi forms the Wireless Telegraphy and Signal Company in England.

1899

Marconi Wireless Company of America formed.

1900

British Marconi Company founded.
U.S. Weather Bureau hires Reginald A. Fessenden.

1901

Marconi sends signal across the Atlantic, from St. Johns, Newfoundland, to Cornwall, England.

1902

Fessenden forms his own company, National Electric Signaling Company.
Lee de Forest creates his De Forest Wireless Telegraphy Company.

1903

First world radio conferences conducted in Berlin to discuss control of broadcasting.

1906

Fessenden transmits the human voice.
Lee de Forest patents the audion tube.
Second world radio conference conducted in London.
David Sarnoff hired as office boy working in Marconi stations.

1907

De Forest begins broadcasting in New York.

1908

De Forest broadcasts recorded music from Eiffel Tower in Paris and is heard five miles away.

1910

First *Wireless Ship Act* passed; requires passenger vessels carry radio equipment.

1911

Marconi contracted with Wanamaker in New York and Philadelphia to install wireless.

1912

S.S. Titanic sinks, and the value of wireless is proven.
Radio Act of 1912 passes; places secretary of commerce in charge of regulating radio; station licenses now required; secretary to assign wavelengths.

1913

De Forest sells patents to AT&T.
Feedback circuit developed by Edwin H. Armstrong.

1915

San Francisco World's Fair features demonstrations of de Forest radio.
Charles D. Herrold's broadcasts received from San Jose.

1916

De Forest broadcasts the first presidential election returns in New York.

1917

The United States enters World War I; as a result, the navy takes over all wireless installations; brings experimentation with radio temporarily to an end; wireless stations closed, and radio is placed under administration of the navy.

1919

Following the war, the navy returns control of radio to private sector.
General Electric (GE) forms the Radio Corporation of America (RCA) to protect against a foreign monopoly in radio (Marconi).

RCA acquires the rights/assets of American Marconi; enters into cross-licensing agreements with GE.

1920

Westinghouse radio KDKA, the first commercially licensed radio station in the United States, broadcasts Cox-Harding election returns.

CFCF, Canadian Marconi station, broadcasts historic program.

AT&T goes into a cross-licensing radio group.

American Marconi corporation dissolved.

WWJ, Detroit, a new station, signs on the air.

1921

Westinghouse joins patent pool group. In cross-licensing agreements, GE and Westinghouse have the exclusive right to manufacture radio receiving sets; RCA, the right to sell the sets; AT&T, the right to make, lease, and sell transmitters.

WBZ, KYW, WJZ, and WHA sign on the air.

1922

Herbert Hoover conducts first Radio Conference.

The AT&T station WEAF broadcasts first commercial program called a "toll broadcast."

Inventor Edwin H. Armstrong demonstrates superheterodyne receiver.

Department of Commerce runs out of three-letter call-letter-assignment combinations and begins assigning four letters.

ASCAP (American Society of Composers Authors and Publishers) wants music royalties for music used on the air.

1923

Hoover conducts second Radio Conference.

National Association of Broadcasters (NAB) formed to fight rising royalty payments to ASCAP.

First network experiment links AT&T stations together.

Federal Trade Commission (FTC) begins radio patent and monopoly investigations.

Wallace H. White drafts first radio bill.

KFKB signs on as Dr. John R. Brinkley station.

Everready (batteries) launches radio program, *Everready Hour.*

1924

AT&T experiments with first national network hookup linking 26 stations to broadcast a speech by President Calvin Coolidge.

Competition between AT&T stations and the Radio Group (RCA, GE, and Westinghouse) stations becomes heated.

Hoover conducts third Radio Conference.

FTC issues report critical of AT&T, RCA, GE, Westinghouse, and United Fruit radio monopoly.

1925

Hoover conducts fourth Radio Conference.

Department of Commerce records show more than 1,400 station authorizations.
Scopes Trial broadcast by WGN.

1926

Congress begins serious debate on radio legislation.
Zenith Radio Corporation challenges Hoover's regulatory authority.
U.S. Attorney Donovan suggests Hoover seek new legislation.
AT&T withdraws from the business of broadcasting, and RCA purchases radio
    interests.
RCA forms two networks: NBC Blue, based on its former stations, and NBC
    Red, based on stations purchased from AT&T.
NBC inaugural broadcast conducted.
WEAF carries Jack Demsey–Gene Tunney fight.
Father Charles Coughlin begins his radio career.

1927

Radio Act of 1927 becomes first comprehensive commercial radio legislation;
    established basic regulatory standards; declared public ownership of airwaves
    and government's right to regulate.
Federal Radio Commission (FRC) created to regulate radio.
United Independent Broadcasters (UIB) organized to supply talent at a network
    level; UIB struggles and seeks financial assistance from Columbia Records,
    thus creating the Columbia Phonograph Broadcasting System.

1928

William S. Paley family comes to the aid of the struggling Columbia system;
    CBS is created.
Radio becomes a mass medium.

1929

Great Lakes case declares balanced-programming requirement.
Quality Network begins (later to become Mutual).
NBC signs contract with Floyd Gibbons.
Walter Winchell begins with CBS.
Amos 'n' Andy begins on NBC.
Stock market crash leads to global depression.

1930

Lowell Thomas begins first daily news and commentary programs on NBC Blue.
H. V. Kaltenborn joins CBS.
RCA unification takes over GE radio engineering and manufacturing interests.
Census reports 14 million receiving sets.
Average family radio listening reported at 3.9 hours per day.
Boake Carter begins broadcasting with WCAU, Philadelphia.
Raymond "Gram" Swing begins his broadcast career with the British Broadcast-
    ing Corporation.
Radio-ratings system begins.
David Sarnoff appointed president of RCA.
The Federal Radio Commission denies station license of Dr. Brinkley.

1931

Gabriel Heatter begins on station WMCA.

NBC reports having 1,359 employees.

CBS has 408 employees.

CBS begins series *The March of Time.*

1933

Press-Radio War begins as press restricts radio news.

President Franklin D. Roosevelt begins *Fireside Chats,* the first dealing with the national banking crisis.

Vaudeville comes to radio programming.

Hitler comes to power in Germany.

RCA sees Armstrong's demonstration of FM.

1934

Communications Act of 1934 replaced the FRC with the Federal Communications Commission; powers of the commission are extended beyond radio to include wire and wireless communications, both interstate and foreign.

Philo Taylor Farnsworth conducts first public demonstration of electronic television at Franklin Institute in Philadelphia.

Mutual Broadcasting System begins operations.

Jack Benny begins on radio.

Upton Close first appears on NBC.

1935

Armstrong demonstrates FM at Radio Engineers Convention.

Press-Radio War ends as the Associated Press and United Press International agree to provide stations with news service.

The first recording device is demonstrated at the German Annual Radio Fair, the magnetophone.

Edward R. Murrow joins CBS as director of talks and education.

Audimeter first appears as radio research tool.

1936

NBC hires Dorothy Thompson to help cover Democratic National Convention.

Mutual's WOL starts the radio career of Fulton Lewis, Jr.

CBS begins the program *Columbia Workshop.*

1937

The American Bar Association, in reaction to chaotic radio coverage of the Lindbergh kidnaping trials, issues press guidelines, Canon 35.

NBC Symphony orchestra formed.

Norman Corwin's *Fall of a City* airs on CBS.

Mae West in trouble for "Adam and Eve" broadcast.

1938

Orson Welles's famous "War of the Worlds" program creates panic.

Mutual Broadcasting System requests investigation of radio monopoly.

Armstrong establishes first FM station, W2XMN, in New Jersey.

Elmer Davis begins broadcasting just before the Germans march into Poland.

Norman Corwin's *The Plot to Overthrow Christmas* airs.

Columbia Records purchased by CBS.

CBS radio inaugurates CBS News Roundup as fighting escalates in Europe.

1939

Broadcast Music Incorporated (BMI) formed as a competitor to ASCAP.

RCA inaugurates regular television programming at New York World's Fair.

Armstrong establishes FM station in New York.

1940

Census figures indicate 44 million radios in America (1935 figures indicated 33 million radio homes).

Listening hours reported at five hours per day.

One world versus isolationism becomes the focus of radio discussion.

1941

FCC issues *Chain Broadcasting Report;* NBC forced to give up one of its networks.

FCC authorizes commercial FM operations and issues first "Mayflower Decision," which forbids station editorializing.

FDR's declaration of war produces an audience of 90 million, 79 percent of all American homes.

Howard K. Smith, Charles Collingwood, and Cecil Brown join the CBS network.

1942

Office of Censorship opens; censorship to be voluntary to assist in war efforts.

Elmer Davis heads the Office of War Information.

Radio manufacturing turns to manufacturing war communications materials.

American Armed Forces Radio begins.

1943

RCA Blue Network purchased by E. J. Noble (becomes the American Broadcasting System, 1945).

Wire recorders used in reporting war efforts.

1944

Disc jockey programming begins appearing.

1945

Edward R. Murrow reports from Buchenwald, a German concentration camp.

Audience hears funeral of FDR via radio.

Radio set manufacturing begins again as war ends.

FCC reassigns FM broadcasting to 88–108 MHz, where it remains today.

1946

FCC issues a memorandum entitled, "Public Service Responsibility of Broadcast Licensees," more commonly called the Blue Book.

Dr. Frank Stanton become president of CBS.

Tape recorder appears.

1948

CBS offers NBC talent differing contract and succeeds in "talent raid" on the competing network.

FCC issues a freeze on all applications, needing time to study issues of frequency allocation, interference, education, and television development.

Fred Allen program ratings at high of 28.7.

Vinyl records, 33⅓ and 45 rpm, appear.

First African-American radio stations established.

1949

FCC declares lotteries illegal.

FCC issues second "Mayflower Decision," reversing first decision and providing guidelines for station editorials; the document, *In the Matter of Editorializing by Broadcast Licensees,* became known as the Fairness Doctrine.

Todd Storz buys KOWH Radio in Omaha, Nebraska, and programs it with a rotation of popular songs that evolves into the top-40 format of the 1950s.

1950

Murrow begins new *Hear It Now* radio series.

1951

Cold War leads to blacklisting.

1952

FCC issues *Sixth Report and Order* ending the freeze; channels set aside for educational broadcasting, and allocation of frequencies established.

1953

FCC approves RCA standards for color television.

1955

Popular evening radio programming disappearing rapidly as television evolves.

1960

FCC issues statement of Programming Policy to replace Blue Book.

1961

FCC approves stereo broadcasting on FM.

Newton Minow becomes chair of the FCC.

1962

FCC places a freeze on new AM applications, thus encouraging FM applications.

1963

Martin Luther King's "I Have a Dream" speech broadcast on radio and television.

1965

FCC rules that AM and FM combinations in cities with populations of 100,000 or more could not duplicate programming more than one half of the broadcast day; the rule encourages the development of new formats on FM.

1966

Nearly half of the homes in the United States have FM radio receivers.

1967

Carnegie Report helps establish public radio and television.

1968

ABC organizes four radio networks.

1971

FCC bans advertising of cigarettes.

1976

Congress passes new *Copyright Act.*

1977

Congress begins working on new communications legislation rewrites.

1979

FM becomes the dominant force in radio, exceeding AM national radio audience figures.

1981

Era of radio deregulation begins as license periods are extended.

1982

FCC approves AM stereo broadcasting but does not designate a standard system.

1990

Digital audio broadcasting is introduced at the NAB Convention.

1996

New *Telecommunications Act* passed; eliminates national ownership limits on radio; market size determines ownership limits; extends radio license to eight years; eases license renewal process.

CBS/Group W/Infinity becomes the largest radio group in the United States with 82 stations reaching more than 2.5 million listeners (average quarter-hour listeners).

1997

FCC approves satellite radio stations.

A

ABC (AMERICAN BROADCASTING COMPANY) was formed in 1943 from the sale of the NBC Blue Network, which had been formed after the Red Network in 1927. It was programmed with secondary content such as unsponsored and public service programs.

In 1941 the Federal Communications Commission (FCC) ordered the sale to eliminate the possibility of a radio monopoly. This produced an independent network firmly entrenched in third place. By the mid-1960s, ABC Radio had developed an innovative response to the competition of television. It began offering specialized services to affiliates (see **ABC News Networks**). A companion television network was started in 1948, and it, too, was a third-place network.

The 1953 merger of ABC and United Paramount Theaters brought money and new resources. By the fall season of 1955, programming from Warner Brothers was on ABC-TV. Three hour-long programs, based on successful Warner's features, made their debut. *Cheyenne* was the only series to endure. It also spawned the westerns that dominated all networks for several seasons.

Another profitable Hollywood connection was Walt Disney. Disneyland was under construction, and he needed capital to finish the project. The result was money for Disney and programming for ABC: the weekly *Disneyland* and daily *Mickey Mouse Club*. In the 1970s, Fred Silverman made ABC television an equal force with CBS and NBC. Today, ABC is an attractive financial property. It has had two recent ownership changes: Capital Cities Communications acquired American Broadcasting Companies in 1985, and a merger with Disney in 1995 made ABC the largest entertainment corporation.

Quinlan, Sterling. *Inside ABC: American Broadcasting Company's Rise to Power.* New York: Hastings House, 1979.

William F. Lyon

ABC NEWS NETWORKS. In 1943, the government forced RCA to sell one of its two networks. The Blue Network was purchased by candy magnate Edward J. Noble, and it became ABC. By 1968, competition from television had reduced the national radio networks to providing news on the hour, plus occasional sports reports and features. ABC's management decided to create four radio networks.

The radio networks paid for full-time access to AT&T long-distance lines connecting them to their affiliates, even though during some hours they transmitted no more than 10 minutes of programming. Managers at ABC reasoned that multiple networks could be fed simply by assigning certain portions of each hour's transmission time to each of four networks. Thus, on January 1, 1968, ABC split the radio network into four segments: (1) the Contemporary Network brief news reports with content appealing to young people; (2) the Entertainment Network news and features with an emphasis on personalities for middle-of-the-road stations; (3) the FM Network 4 minutes of news on the hour; and (4) the Information Network hourly 5-minute news reports plus extended newscasts, commentary, and sports. ABC signed up affiliates, and soon it was common to find two or more ABC Radio affiliates in a community.

One major advantage ABC enjoyed was its longtime relationship with Paul Harvey, who became the most listened-to newscaster in the country. In 1982, ABC created other subnetworks when its transmission network was switched to satellite, permitting concurrent transmissions on different transponders.

Quinlan, Sterling. *Inside ABC: American Broadcasting Company's Rise to Power.* New York: Hastings House, 1979.

Phillip O. Keirstead

ACID ROCK, a form of rock music developed in the mid-1960s and remaining popular through the early 1970s. Also known as *psychedelic rock* or the *San Francisco sound.* The purpose of the music was to mimic or recreate the effects of psychoactive or mind-expanding drugs.

The music made great use of electronically produced sound effects, extended improvisationals, and the introduction and use of Middle Eastern music and Indian ragas.

Acid rock, first appearing in the Haight-Ashbury district of San Francisco, was played by such artists as Jefferson Airplane, Terrazzo Brothers, The Charlatans, Quicksilver Messenger Service, The Electric Prunes, The Grateful Dead, The Strawberry Alarm Clock, and a host of others.

The venues for the artists and their music were large pavilionlike buildings where people could dance as well as listen to the music. Places like the Fillmore West (San Francisco), the Fillmore East (New York City), the Aragon (Chicago), the Electric Factory (Philadelphia), and Ludlow's Garage (Cincinnati) became almost as popular and as well known as the artists themselves.

Acid rock was popular primarily with listeners in their teens and early twenties, but they had difficulty in finding the music on radio. Many stations would not play music that seemed to advocate drug use or was reminiscent of drug-induced experiences. In addition, the lengths of most selections did not fit into tightly formatted radio station playlists. In later years, acid rock became more acceptable and more mainstream and thereby received more airplay. Acid rock gave rise to the progressive rock movement.

Marsh, Dave, and Kevin Stein. *The Book of Rock Lists.* New York: Dell Publishing, 1981.
Pareles, Jon, and Patricia Reminisce, eds. *The Rolling Stone Encyclopedia of Rock & Roll.* New York: Summit Books, 1983.
Ward, Ed, Geoffrey Stokes, and Ken Tucker. *Rock of Ages: The Rolling Stone History of Rock & Roll.* New York: Summit Books, 1986.

Regis Tucci

A. C. NIELSEN COMPANY, founded by Arthur C. Nielsen, one of the major pioneers in radio audience research (see **Crossley, Archibald Maddock; Hooper [C. E. Hooper Company]**). A graduate of the University of Wisconsin in electrical engineering, Nielsen developed a successful market research firm in the early 1930s targeting grocery and drug sales. In 1936 he purchased the rights to an electromechanical device called the Audimeter from two professors at the Massachusetts Institute of Technology (MIT). This device measured and recorded radio usage information in the home by determining when the receiver was turned on and to which station it was tuned. Nielsen spent the next eight years developing, improving, and testing the device and, in 1942, began offering the Nielsen Radio Index (NRI) based on information provided by Audimeters. This meter service was sold to radio networks and advertisers and successfully competed with the Crossley and Hooper services that used phone call and diary sampling. NRI geographical coverage and the number of subscribers increased through the second half of the 1940s, displacing the Crossley service. By 1949 Nielsen was able to provide acceptable national radio ratings. In 1950 Nielsen's company purchased Hooper's national radio and television ratings services. In 1954 Nielsen began offering the Nielsen Station Index (NSI), which provided additional demographic information, not available in the NRI, obtained through the use of personal diaries. Because of the difficulty of measuring radio listening outside the home accurately, the great number of new radio stations along with decreased listening, and declining advertiser interest in radio, Nielsen discontinued the radio services in 1963. Nielsen's television ratings services, however, continued to prosper and have become preeminent. Nielsen died in 1980. The A. C. Nielsen Company merged with Dun & Bradstreet in 1984.

Beville, Hugh Malcolm, Jr. *Audience Ratings: Radio, Television, and Cable.* Rev. ed. Hillsdale, N.J.: Lawrence Erlbaum Associates, Publishers, 1987.
Dominick, Joseph R., Barry L. Sherman, and Gary A. Copeland. *Broadcasting/Cable and Beyond: An Introduction to Modern Electronic Media.* 3rd ed. New York: McGraw-Hill, 1996.

Steven C. Runyon

ADI (AREA OF DOMINANT INFLUENCE), a classification used by the Arbitron Company to define a radio or television market for ratings purposes. Each county in the United States is placed in one, and only one, ADI. These markets are ranked in size by the number of television households in the ADI. The top three ADIs are New York, Los Angeles, and Chicago. There are other classification formulas used for television and radio ratings (see also **metropolitan statistical area [MSA]; total survey area [TSA]**.

Webster, James G., and Lawrence W. Lichty. *Ratings Analysis: Theory and Practice.* Hillsdale, N.J.: Lawrence Erlbaum Associates, 1991.

Donald Diefenbach

ADULT CONTEMPORARY (AC), radio format incorporating contemporary music targeted to an adult audience ranging from ages 25 to 54. Musical playlists include popular artists also heard on contemporary-hit-radio or top-40 formats. AC formats generally do not include hard rock or rap music, and on-air personalities cater to adult audiences. Variations of the AC format include soft AC, light AC, hot AC, and mainstream AC. The format is often targeted to women in the age group 25 to 49.

Radio Today. New York: Arbitron, 1995.

Frederic A. Leigh

ADVERTISING, the sale of time on the air for the placement of commercial messages. From the first appearance of radio, there was great excitement for that medium's potential to inform, persuade, and educate. It was only natural that entrepreneurs and businesses sought to declare the virtues of their products and services on the air. Commercials on radio came at a time when advertising itself had begun to boom, in the 1920s. Radio advertising started modestly, carefully, and at first it was not even allowed during the evening hours when most people were doing their relaxed listening. Revenues from advertising made radio one of the most successful of all media during the 1940s and 1950s. Locally, it continues to be one of the top forms of advertising.

Many of those involved in developing radio never foresaw the role of advertising as its base of economic support. Indeed, the self-declared "Father of Radio," Lee de Forest, denounced radio advertisers as "vulgar hucksters [who] continue to enslave and sell for quick cash the grandest medium which has yet been given to man to help upward his struggling spirit." But when advertising agencies began to place commercials in programs offered on networks, paying local affiliates for carrying the program, advertising took a firm hold in radio. Network advertising surpassed even strong local advertising at that time. Today, network advertising comprises only about 4 percent of radio advertising, with national spot advertising another 18 percent, and the largest share being local spot, at about 78 percent.

During the 1940s and 1950s, radio commercials, together with their jingles and repeated slogans, became not only highly effective product sellers but also a part of popular culture.

Radio and its advertising were greatly affected by television advertising in the 1950s and today have much different functions, following different listening patterns. For example, the highest patterns of radio listening occur on car radios while people are driving to and from work. This "drive time" captures the highest advertising rates. Daytime radio listening is often done in the workplace setting, eliciting advertising directed toward workers. Evening listening is split, with either youth-oriented programming or adult-oriented talk, news, and sports, each with its respective advertising targeting specific kinds of listener demographics.

Advertising agencies. A central role in national spot and network advertising is played by the advertising agency, which serves the advertising client by creating the ads (sometimes reassigned to production houses to produce the commercials) and placing the ads in the various media, including radio. To design the ads for the consumers most likely to buy, the agency conducts marketing research, including information about which demographic characteristics are held by those using each medium. In radio, an agency must know which kinds of listeners are tuned to which stations. The agency, when it makes an agreement to place advertising on a specific radio station, will get a commission, usually 15 percent of gross media expenditures (time, talent, facilities, etc.) and about 17 percent of net advertising production expenses.

Advertising, beer and wine. In recent years, advertising beer and wine products has come under fire because of the social problems associated with alcohol abuse. Does advertising these products play a role in promoting the associated social evils? Among those who answer affirmatively, there has been a move to eliminate such advertising or to impose warnings in the ads. However, broadcasters eager to demonstrate responsibility in the matter have promoted public service announcements ("Don't drink and drive," and so on) to offset such criticism. Radio advertising of these products remains controversial, and some members of Congress introduce, from time to time, legislation mandating warning labels or prohibiting the advertising, as was done in 1970 when Congress eliminated advertising cigarettes on radio and television.

Advertising, in children's programming. Radio reaches its listeners as segmented groups (or audiences or markets), including children and youth. However, advertising found in children's programming has been especially sensitive and controversial. Some observers feel that advertising simply should not be directed toward children, who might not have the discretion or finances to make intelligent purchasing choices. Others see advertising directed toward children as legitimate, as long as they are not the targets of products that cannot be used legally by them, such as beer. Most radio advertisers today have strict sanctions against such advertising.

Advertising, cigarettes. Advertising cigarette and tobacco products was a central part of radio advertising during the 1930s through the 1960s. In the mid-1960s the U.S. surgeon general's report disclosed medical research showing a causal relationship between smoking and a number of health problems. Antismoking groups said the controversy surrounding the claims was strong enough so that stations carrying cigarette commercials ought to be subject to the Fairness Doctrine and be forced to carry antismoking messages to offset the ads. In 1970, Congress passed the *Cigarette Smoking Act of 1969,* which banned advertising cigarettes on radio and TV after 1971. Many broadcasters were displeased, both because they lost revenue and because such prohibitions did not cover other nonbroadcast media, which continue to carry such ads.

Advertising, codes on. Because radio demonstrated itself as a powerful and persuasive advertising medium, some groups moved to limit the amount of time devoted to advertising, then outlined the kinds of products and services that should not be advertised (see **codes of ethics**). In 1929, there were ads during the daytime but not in the evening. By 1937, the National Association of Broadcasters (NAB) Code allowed a maximum of 9 minutes of commercial material per daytime hour and only 6 minutes each evening hour. In 1970, the Radio Code permitted twice that much—18 minutes per hour, day or night. Today, there are no time restrictions.

The code did not allow advertising such things as gambling, fortune-telling, spiritualism, astrology, personal products, and hard liquor. In 1982, a federal court found that the Codes of Good Practice of the National Association of Broadcasters violated antitrust laws, and the NAB dropped them. Today, most restrictions have been lifted to whatever the marketplace (consumers) will bear.

Advertising, as financing source. Early in broadcasting, it was believed that the sale of radio receivers would pay for the broadcasting service. Many early stations were actually owned by manufacturers. In other cases, stations were operated by organizations, such as religions or colleges, without a great interest in making money. After the first runs at advertising, it was apparent that there was money to be made by combining this new medium with advertising. Growth during the 1930s fed such a notion, and radio established itself as a major medium of advertising, first, in local advertising, then in both national and local, and now primarily in local.

Advertising, institutional. Institutional advertising is that which promotes an organization or institution and helps enhance its image, as opposed to selling the specific products or services it provides.

Advertising, participating. When a commercial announcement is placed within a program, as opposed to an ad between different programs, it is participating. This was a strong distinction when network programs contained commercials, and stations carrying the program were expected to carry commercials as well, since this was the payment source to stations.

Advertising, piggyback. As the practice of commercial placement evolved, standards dictated that there be a limited number of commercial "interruptions." Some advertisers, however, anxious to advertise more than one of their products, would "piggyback" one product with another in the same advertising time slot. At first this practice was frowned upon, but later it came to be common practice.

Advertising, public broadcasting and. Earlier in radio's history, when only AM stations existed, many were operated by educational institutions and were basically noncommercial. As they struggled to survive, some became commercial. But there were basically no noncommercial frequencies or channels set aside; noncommercial stations operated that way by choice. When FM frequencies were developed in the 1940s, the Federal Communications Commission (FCC) set aside 20 frequencies (channels) to be used without any commercialization. Many of these "educational" stations struggled but were helped somewhat by the *Public Broadcasting Act of 1967*, which provided some federal funding for noncommercial "public" stations. The struggling continued, and many of these stations elicited funding by giving brief one-phrase recognition to underwriting/sponsoring organizations. Such over-the-air references to financial support were considered a kind of advertising.

Advertising rates. *Rates* are simply the amount charged for a specified-length advertisement. The rates a station may charge for its commercials are affected by many factors: number of listeners, which may be affected by the time of day; the amount any one advertiser buys; whether the ads are placed in specified programs or simply rotated throughout the day by the station; and whether it participates with another advertiser in a dual "co-op ad." Normally, the rate does not include production costs, the music, special voices, comedy dialogue, and so on. Rates are sometimes laid out on rate cards that may list the prices or rates with the previously identified variables.

Advertising, spot. Traditionally, a *spot* refers to radio time purchased from an independent station, as opposed to network advertising. If a national advertiser buys time on various stations, perhaps concentrating on certain markets or cities, such ads might be referred to as *national spot* advertising, as distinguished from either network or local advertising. Usually, spot advertising is separate from program sponsorship, although spots may be purchased adjacent to or within programs.

Val E. Limburg

ADVERTISING, HISTORY OF. Radio advertising got its start in August 1922 on WEAF, an AT&T-owned radio station in New York. It began a practice for the medium that continues today. When radio station KDKA signed on the air in 1920, its parent corporation Westinghouse was interested in its own wares and paid the expenses to promote Westinghouse products. This changed as the sale of commercial time began. WEAF called the sale of commercial time *toll broadcasting,* similar to that of telephone long-distance toll calls. The first radio advertisement was for an apartment complex in New York City. The advertiser paid $50 for a 10-minute speech but never mentioned the cost of the apartment.

By 1923, advertisers were beginning to support radio programs and performers. WEAF featured the first weekly advertiser. *The Browning King Orchestra,* named for the clothing manufacturer who bought the time, performed an hour of music without mentioning the specific product—clothes. The name of the manufacturer was mentioned each time the band was introduced. The first commercially sponsored program series was also a WEAF program, *The Everready Hour.* It was handled by the J. M. Mathes Agency.

The concept of advertising sponsorship grew in the late 1920s. Advertising agencies produced the spots and eventually gained control over the entire show. Each program served as a vehicle for the sponsor. By 1928, overall radio advertising had grown from its WEAF beginning to $14.1 million in national revenues.

Irving Settel wrote in *A Pictorial History of Radio,* "Radio created one of the most extraordinary new product demands in the history of the United States. From all over the country, orders for radio receiving sets poured into the offices of manufacturers." With this boom came an increase in radio advertising. Advertising agencies and copywriters adjusted their style of writing for this new medium. Instead of the longer print advertisements, radio ads were catchy slogans and sayings, written for consumers who were listening, not looking. These new advertisements introduced a racier, vaudeville style quite different from the staid print style.

According to *The Mirror Makers,* Stephen Fox's history of advertising, cigarette advertisers were the first to cash in on the radio market. First came Lucky Strike, then its competition, Camel. There was also a *Chase & Sanborn Hour* and the *Kraft Music Hall.* Jack Benny and the *Jell-O Variety Show* scored big for both the artist and the product. "Jell-O again. This is Jack Benny speaking" was the slogan for the show. Other famous stars of the day were pitching for major advertising agencies, including Kate Smith for Calumet Baking Powder and Swansdown Flour and Arthur Godfrey for Lipton's Tea.

In the early 1930s, following the crash of the stock market, radio continued to thrive, emerging as the preeminent advertising medium. The 1930s began with 612 stations and 12 million sets and ended with 814 stations and 51 million sets. Optimism was high during these early commercial years, but radio was still only a small part of the national advertising picture. Of the $61.9 million in advertising revenue reported for 1932, only 5 percent went to radio.

The 1930s also introduced using "station representatives" for geographic buys, and thus national spot radio began. The spot announcements were easily produced and distributed throughout the country via electrical transcription. This provided an alternative to network advertising as the station representative worked with individual stations in different markets across the nation to purchase national spot time. National spot sales in 1935 were reported at $14 million, and by 1940, they had grown to $42.1 million.

Things began to change in businesses across America with the beginning of World War II in Europe, and the advertising industry as a whole was affected. It was only logical that radio advertising, like its print counterpart, would become part of the war effort.

A new organization was conceptualized only days before the bombing of Pearl Harbor and formalized only days after. Dubbed the War Advertising Council (WAC), this organization worked within the newspaper, magazine, and advertising communities to change the methods of advertising and promotion in the United States. From mid-1942 until the end of the war on September 2, 1945, the WAC helped government and business produce advertising. In the process, it dictated policy, form, and content of advertisements to corporations and advertising agencies across the country.

With the end of the war and the beginning of television, radio stations and hence radio advertising began a decline. Many radio stations now had sister television stations, and these outlets provided competition in both staffing and audiences. By 1951, more than 10 million television sets had replaced the console radio's honored place in American living rooms, according to Sterling and Kittross. To adapt, radio producers focused on radios in automobiles, while programmers shifted radio's "prime-time" hours and focus to morning and evening "drive time," when commuters were preparing for and driving to work. Music formats replaced the hour-long shows and "soap operas," and advertisers focused more on the demographics of the new audience. The famous advertiser-supported radio shows were now on television, but advertisements on radio continued to be short and catchy, written for the ear. While there was a decline at first, the radio advertising market stabilized.

Radio advertising continues to be a value unsurpassed by print and television. According to Kleppner's Advertising Procedure, with more than 550 million radios in use, there is virtually no American without a radio today. The Radio Advertising Bureau reported that there are 5.6 radios per household and that 79 percent of all adults are reached weekly by radio. Ninety-five percent of all cars have radios.

Radio listeners are like magazine subscribers in that they are habitual listeners, at predictable times, to stations with narrowly targeted formats. They are loyal, identifiable, and cheaper for the advertiser to reach.

Fox, Stephen. *The Mirror Makers: A History of Advertising and Its Creators.* New York: Random House, 1984.
Settel, Irving. *A Pictorial History of Radio.* New York: Grosset & Dunlap, 1967.

Ginger Rudeseal Carter

AFFILIATION. *See* **network affiliation.**

AFTERNOON-DRIVE TIME is the term used to describe the late afternoon hours when many people listen to their car radios while driving home from work. Most programmers consider afternoon-drive time as 4 p.m. to 6 p.m. During these hours, music radio stations frequently program faster-paced music and announcers than during the midday hours. These elements are often supplemented with short, concise newscasts. Because this time period is usually the second-most-listened-to daypart (after morning-drive time), listeners also hear more commercials. Music stations usually attempt to project a lively, informational image, but with less talk than morning-drive time.

Kenneth D. Loomis

AIR CHECK is a recorded sample of on-air performance by an announcer. Air checks are included in applications for on-air jobs in radio and television and are usually about three minutes long. Career opportunities that require air checks are: disc jockey, news, talk, interview, or freelance announcing positions.

Air checks are also used by talent to improve on-air work. These air checks are recorded as the announcer is actually performing on-air duties and critiqued after the program.

Hyde, Stuart. *Television and Radio Announcing.* 7th ed. Boston: Houghton Mifflin, 1995.
O'Donnell, Lewis B., Carl Hausman, and Philip Benoit. *Announcing: Broadcast Communicating Today.* Belmont, Calif.: Wadsworth, 1996.

Mary E. Beadle

ALEXANDERSON, ERNST FREDRIK WERNER (1878–1975) was an engineer-inventor whose most significant contribution to radio technology was the high-frequency radio alternator.

Born in Uppsala, Sweden, in 1878, Alexanderson studied engineering at the Royal Institute of Technology in Stockholm and at the Koenigliche Technische Hochschule in Germany, where he studied electromagnetic theory and technology under Adolf Slaby. After completing his schooling in 1901, Alexanderson immigrated to the United States to pursue his career in an environment he perceived would afford greater opportunity and individual freedom. By 1902, Alexanderson worked for General Electric (GE), where he would remain until his retirement in 1948. He worked his way up to director of the prestigious department of consulting engineers. For a brief period between 1920 and 1923, Alexanderson split his duties between GE and the newly formed RCA, where he was chief engineer. He continued at RCA as the chief consulting engineer from 1924 to 1930, when a consent decree forced a separation of the two companies.

In 1900, Reginald Fessenden asked General Electric to build a high-frequency alternator for wireless transmission. Fessenden was pursuing two objectives: increase the distance that wireless signals could travel and make possible wireless telephony. Fessenden believed that the only way to do this was through a continuous-wave technology such as an alternator that could operate at radio frequencies. General Electric accepted the project, and by 1904, Alexanderson was designing the 100 kilohertz (kHz) alternator that would eventually come to be known as the Alexanderson alternator. Fessenden and Alexanderson would continue to collaborate until Fessenden's withdrawal from the radio field in 1910. Although Fessenden had fully demonstrated the superiority of the continuous-wave broadcasting system, it would be several years before the importance of the alternator was fully realized.

The significance of Alexanderson's alternator went beyond the advent of sound transmission to play a role in international politics and commerce. In 1914, American Marconi decided to install an alternator instead of a spark transmitter in its new transatlantic station in New Brunswick, New Jersey. British Marconi ultimately secured an agreement with GE for exclusive rights to purchase the alternator for its vast system of radio transmission service. After the war, the U.S. Navy worried that foreign interests would control American radio and therefore interceded to convince General Electric to buy up interests in American Marconi and create a new American-controlled radio company called the Radio Corporation of America. Marconi could still buy alternators but could not use them in the American market. The Alexanderson alternator, which was one of only two continuous-wave technologies available at the time, gave GE a very strong position in reorganizing the radio industry to American advantage.

Alexanderson continued to work on improving the alternator until it was supplanted by vacuum-tube technology in the early 1920s. He worked on hundreds of other projects throughout his long career, including the magnetic amplifier, radio facsimile, mechanical television, and many war-related technologies. He was awarded over 340 U.S. patents and was responsible for many advances in the field of electrotechnology.

Brittain, James E. *Alexanderson: Pioneer in American Electrical Engineering.* Baltimore: Johns Hopkins University Press, 1992.

Christina S. Drale

ALLEN, FRED (1892–1956), a popular radio comedian of the 1930s and 1940s, was known for his acerbic wit and grating voice. He billed himself as the world's worst juggler and a latter-day Mark Twain. His radio program was described as the most literate comedy on air. Born John F. Sullivan in Cambridge, Massachusetts, in 1892, he worked as a stack boy in the Boston Public Library, got a book on juggling, and began to practice. He entered amateur contests and toured movie houses. He changed his name to Fred St. James and added patter to his juggling act. He dropped the "Saint" and became known as Fred James.

He spent 1914 and 1915 appearing in vaudeville in Australia, Tasmania, New Zealand, and Honolulu. He returned to America and changed his name to Fred Allen. His act became more monologue than juggling. By the 1920s, he had moved up to revues on Broadway and wrote vaudeville acts, sketches, articles, and film shorts. During this time he married Broadway performer Portland Hoffa.

In 1932 on CBS, Allen began his radio career with *The Linit Bath Club Revue,* followed in 1933 by *The Salad Bowl Revue* for Hellman's Mayonnaise and in 1934, *Town Hall Tonight* for Bristol Meyer.

He initiated a famous "feud" with Jack Benny in 1936 for publicity. Allen insulted Benny's violin playing, and after that, they traded insults over the air and occasionally appeared on each other's shows. Allen cosponsored a contest asking listeners to end the sentence "I hate Jack Benny because . . . ." He was overwhelmed with mail. When the two of them faced off on Benny's show, the listening audience was said to be second only to one of Roosevelt's *Fireside Chats.* As testimony to their enduring friendship, Allen's last guest on his radio show in 1949 was Jack Benny.

He was best known for *Texaco Star Theater,* which debuted on CBS in 1940. He created Allen's Alley and the Mighty Allen Art Players. High-blood pressure forced him off the air in 1944, but he returned to NBC in the fall of 1945. He waged war with a group of NBC censors through the 1940s. The public finally forced the network to back off, but his scripts were still carefully reviewed.

His television debut in 1950 was on the *Colgate Comedy Hour,* but his style did not translate well to television. It was reported he told humorist Goodman Ace: "I should have done exactly what George Burns did then I could've had a television career" (Burns, p. 243). In 1953, he hosted a quiz show *Judge for Yourself* that was to be filled with his witty ad-libbing with amateur talent, but it failed. A heart attack forced him into semiretirement. He took a job as panelist on *What's My Line,* which he held until his death in 1956.

Allen, Fred. *Much Ado about Me.* Boston: Little, Brown, 1956.
Allen, Fred. *Treadmill to Oblivion.* Boston: Little, Brown, 1954.
Burns, George, with David Fisher. *Gracie: A Love Story.* New York: G. P. Putnam's Sons, 1988.
Havig, A. *Fred Allen's Radio Comedy.* Philadelphia: Temple University Press, 1990.

Mary E. Beadle

ALLEN, GRACIE (1905–1964), played the scatterbrained wife of George Burns as part of the comedy team Burns and Allen. She performed in vaudeville, radio, television, and film. Gracie was born in San Francisco about 1905 and joined her father's act when she was 3½ years old. At 13, she and her three older sisters performed in vaudeville as Irish dancers. She joined the Larry Reilly Dance Company but left after a disagreement over billing. She became a stenographer in New York and met Burns backstage in 1922 through her roommate who was doing an act at the same theater as George. George's act with Billy Lorraine was breaking up, and George asked Gracie to team with him. At first Gracie asked the questions and George gave the comedy answers, but he soon realized it was better the other way around. In 1926, they married in Cleveland. In 1931, Eddie Cantor asked if Gracie could appear with him on his radio show. She stole the show, and the next day Burns and Allen had a radio contract. She and George adopted two children and lived in Beverly Hills their entire lives.

Gracie became a national symbol of misunderstanding and ineptitude. The federal government even created a safety campaign that warned "Don't Be Gracie Allen" (Burns, p. 160). *The Burns and Allen Show* ran for 17 years. She rarely saw a script ahead of time and read it once before rehearsal, once during rehearsal, and once on the air. Gracie had microphone fright, and they did the show without an audience for a few years. For publicity she appeared on numerous other shows looking for her imaginary lost brother George. National concern was so high that her real brother had to hide out until the stunt was over. In 1940, she ran for president as a candidate of the Surprise Party. She urged Americans to be proud of our debt because it was the biggest in the world. She received 50,000 votes. She also ran for governor of the State of Coma. She appeared with George in a number of movies, was a painter of surrealism, and even had an exhibition in 1938 in a Manhattan art gallery.

In 1950, their famous radio show aired on television (CBS) as a biweekly series. For a short time, they continued to do both the radio and television shows. Television was a tremendous amount of work and was done live. Gracie often would have 26 pages of dialogue out of a 40-page script that needed to be memorized. Her health was poor; she suffered from migraines and severe angina. After nearly 50 years in show business, she was ready to retire, and finally, in 1958, she did. After 6 years of retirement, Gracie died in 1964.

Blythe, Cheryl, and Susan Sackett. *Say Goodnight, Gracie!* New York: E. P. Dutton, 1986.
Burns, George, with David Fisher. *Gracie: A Love Story.* New York: G. P. Putnam's Sons, 1988.

Mary E. Beadle

ALLEN, MEL (1913–1996), from Alabama, was one of the great voices of baseball broadcasting. He broadcast New York Yankees baseball for most of his 58 years as a sports broadcaster. From baseball's World Series and All Star games to college football and boxing, Allen "did it all." His signature phrase, by which he set himself apart from the other broadcasters, was "How about that?!" But he was best known for applying his Alabama drawl to Yankee baseball broadcasts and as the voice of the weekly syndicated sports show *This Week in Baseball.* He covered the Yankee greats Babe Ruth, Joe DiMaggio, and Mickey Mantle, among others, during his years behind the Yankee microphone. Allen aspired to be a baseball player in his youth but was cut from the University of Alabama team. He turned instead to broadcasting the game. Allen was elected to the Baseball Hall of Fame. He had open heart surgery in 1989 and suffered from an undisclosed illness for some years before dying on June 15, 1996, in Greenwich,Connecticut.

Allen, Mel. Obituary. *The Phoenix Gazette,* June 18, 1996.

ElDean Bennett

ALLEN, STEVE (1921–), a multitalented entertainer who became famous as the first host of television's *Tonight Show.* Allen quit the Arizona State Teachers' College (now Arizona State University) to take his first radio job. After his discharge from the service in WWII, he returned to Phoenix and worked as an announcer, writer, pianist, and producer at KOY. There he began developing his comedy repertoire. After three years at KOY, he headed to Los Angeles and persuaded the Mutual Broadcasting Company to air a five-nights-a-week comedy show, *Smile Time.* Two years later, he moved to KNX, the CBS-owned station in Los Angeles. His show on KNX actually became the prototype for his move into TV and the *Tonight Show.*

Allen's lengthy list of television credits includes: The *Steve Allen Show,* which ran opposite *Ed Sullivan* on Sunday night from 1956 to 1960; a comedy hour on ABC for two years; *I've Got a Secret* for three years; and a weekly comedy show with his wife Jayne Meadows. In 1976, he reunited his old *Tonight Show* gang for a weekly 90-minute show, *Laughback.* From 1977 to 1981, his award-winning *Meeting of Minds* appeared on the Public Broadcasting Service (PBS). This "talk show" featured discussions with historical figures such as Socrates, Karl Marx, and Cleopatra.

While Allen is best known for his TV and comedy work, his greatest skill is likely his composition of music. He has written more than 5,000 songs and recorded more than 40 albums. He also found the time to write 43 books. He continues to write and perform today.

Allen, Steve. http://www.dove.org/allenbio.htm

Max Utsler

ALL-NEWS FORMAT features consistent news programming including international, national, and local newscasts, sports, weather, and traffic. The all-news format is most often found in large markets. News-talk, the combination of news and talk segments, is more common on stations that program information rather than music (see **news-talk formats**).

Frederic A. Leigh

ALL-TALK FORMAT. "Talk" has been a central ingredient in radio telephony from its inception, but *all-talk format* refers to the broad genre of radio station programming that relies on a variety of nonmusical forms of information and entertainment. Talk radio has repeatedly demonstrated its appeal to listeners and is an important program format in most medium- and large-radio markets, with some radio markets having competing all-talk stations. Since the higher fidelity of FM stations is better suited to musical programs, talk-radio formats are more frequently associated with standard or AM radio stations. Often these talk formats include both one-way discussions by radio personalities and two-way interaction with call-in listeners whose comments constitute a vital part of the format. Over 80 percent of all AM radio stations include some form of the talk format in their regular broadcast day.

Historians have traced the roots of contemporary all-talk formats to the early telephone-quiz shows of the 1930s when radio program hosts would call listeners in the audience to ask questions. At first, only the announcer's portion of the conversation was heard, but by the 1940s, both portions were broadcast with a periodic high-pitched tone or "beep" to identify for listeners that it was a telephone conversation on a tape delay. At least one historian states that the first contemporary all-talk format was started by radio station KABC, Los Angeles, in 1963. However, a number of other stations across the U.S. lay claim to this distinction, including a second Los Angeles outlet, KNX.

By the mid-1960s, the all-talk format was experiencing wide success as listeners sought an opportunity to express their own views on topics of public interest. As specialized radio formats continued to evolve, the all-talk stations began to develop "subformats" to attract specific segments of the listening audience who identified with the interests and personalities of the talk-radio hosts. There were talk-show hosts whose on-air styles ranged across the entire spectrum from the antagonistic Joe Pyne to political satirist Mort Sahl.

For nearly a decade the politics and social unrest that accompanied America's involvement in the Vietnam War afforded an ample array of lively topics regardless of one's own perspective or affiliation, but as the years passed, the format appeared to be growing stale. Demographic studies revealed that the more loyal listeners were growing older and were becoming less attractive to commercial advertisers. The all-talk format needed an infusion of new vitality, and it arrived at the Storer Broadcasting station, KGBS-AM, in Los Angeles in 1971. In an attempt to reach women in the 18–34 age demographic during midday, Storer programmers brought over their all-night disc jockey from KGBS-FM to host the newly created *Feminine Forum*. Bill Balance invited female listeners to call the station and share their most intimate secrets, desires, and fantasies. The response was overwhelming, as the daytime audience doubled within a single ratings period. The program was soon syndicated, and a new all-talk subformat was born "topless" or "sex-talk" radio. As the number of stations that adopted the sex-talk format increased, so did the number of complaints to the Federal Communications Commission (FCC). On April 11, 1973, the commission issued a notice of apparent liability to Sonderling Broadcasting, licensee of WGLD in Oak Park, Illinois. The radio industry took the FCC's notice as a strong warning and moved to tone down the incidents of obscene, indecent, or profane language, but audience ratings had given clear evidence of what many listeners wanted to hear.

By the late 1980s, all-talk radio had become firmly established in the mainstream of public discourse. Talk radio had become the subject of a successful play in New York City, a Hollywood movie, and a highly rated network television series. In Denver, talk-radio host Alan Berg had been gunned down by two members of a neo-Nazi group, and in Salt Lake City a white supremacist had inaugurated an

"Aryan Nations" talk-radio program. News was being broken regularly by guests appearing on the shows of such popular talk-radio hosts as Larry King and Tom Snyder, and listeners from the political left and right were being either outraged or entertained by such radio-talk personalities as Rush Limbaugh and Howard Stern. New subformats were being developed and refined, including the controversial radio-talk psychologists, often referred to as psych jocks or talk shrinks. The success of the all-talk radio format had launched the television talk-show careers of such celebrities as Judith Kuriansky and Sally Jessy Raphael, and it seemed certain that the format was destined to survive well into the twenty-first century.

Avery, Robert K. "Talk Radio: The Private-Public Catharsis." In *Talking to Strangers: Mediated Therapeutic Communication,* edited by Gary Gumpert and Sandra L. Fish (pp. 87–97). Norwood, N.J.: Ablex Publishing, 1990.

Avery, Robert K., Donald G. Ellis, and Thomas W. Glover. "Patterns of Communication on Talk Radio." *Journal of Broadcasting* 22 (1) (winter 1978): 5–17.

Carlin, John C. "The Rise and Fall of Topless Radio." *Journal of Communication* 26 (winter 1976): 31–37.

Robert K. Avery

ALL THINGS CONSIDERED, National Public Radio's (NPR's) signature afternoon newsmagazine, was the nascent noncommercial network's first journalistic program when it debuted on May 3, 1971. NPR's first program director, William Siemering, envisioned *ATC* as an innovative news broadcast in which the voices of ordinary people were as important as those of politicians and officials, in which interpretation of the day's events was as important as hard news, and in which producers could experiment with the aural medium. After a rocky infancy, *ATC* found its voice and developed a loyal organization audience, helping to establish NPR as a major national news organization. An early inside joke was "We cover the news a day late and call it analysis"; but over the years, NPR increased its worldwide news gathering capabilities and became a primary news source for many listeners, which resulted in fewer quirky features (such as host Susan Stamberg's mother's Thanksgiving recipe for cranberry relish) and less experimentation with sound.

In 1979, NPR built upon the success of *ATC* in launching a morning news program, *Morning Edition. ATC* was expanded from 90 minutes to two hours in 1995, including "cut-in" opportunities for NPR affiliates to insert local news.

Looker, Thomas. *The Sound and the Story: NPR and the Art of Radio.* Boston: Houghton Mifflin, 1995.

Stavitsky, Alan G., and Timothy W. Gleason. "Alternative Things Considered: A Comparison of National Public Radio and Pacifica Radio News Coverage." *Journalism Quarterly* 71 (4) (winter 1994): 775–786.

National Public Radio Online. http://www.npr.org

Alan G. Stavitsky

ALTERNATIVE RADIO. A number of radio stations around the country play a format that is designed to push the edges of the music industry. These stations are generally noncommercial and licensed to colleges or not-for-profit community organizations. They have created what is known as the "alternative sound," a musical mix that would not be heard over popular, commercial radio outlets. These stations serve as outlets for musical experimentation and new musicians.

The alternative music sound had roots in the punk rock of the mid-1970s. The sound was devised as a rebellion against hard rock and hippies music. The Ramones and Iggy Pop and the Stooges were early performers of this new style. The group that is generally considered to have defined the alternative sound, however, is R.E.M. Their sound caught on at college radio stations around the country in the early 1980s, and these stations felt bonded by an "underground" sound fueled by independent producers and noncommercial radio programmers.

The alternative sound became more mainstream in time, with albums from groups like Nirvana going platinum. "Mainstream alternative" emerged with heavy play on Music Television (MTV) and even on some commercial rock outlets. Alternative purists, including many college radio stations, have worked against mainstreaming by taking off the air those groups that get too "popular" and by allowing new groups to further push the limits of the alternative sound. Groups currently working in the alternative realm include Weezer, Beck, and Oasis.

Arnold, Gina. *Route 666: On the Road to Nirvana.* New York: St. Martin's Press, 1993.
CMJ New Music Report. Great Neck, N.Y.: College Media, Inc., 1996.

Jeffrey M. McCall

ALTERNATOR, a generator that produces alternating current (AC) rather than direct current (DC). A generator is a device that converts mechanical energy into electrical energy using the principle of electromagnetic induction. A mechanical power source such as a turbine or engine spins a conducting coil between the poles of a magnet or electromagnet. This induces an electric current in the coil that passes into an external circuit. When used for radio transmission, the alternator must generate a current at high enough frequencies to be in the radio frequency range (.3 kilohertz [kHz]–3,000 gigahertz [gHz]). Electromagnetic waves radiate from a metal antenna when the radio frequency current runs through it. First used for radio by Reginald Fessenden in 1906, the newly developed Alexanderson alternator made continuous-wave sound transmissions possible for the first time.

Aitken, Hugh G. J., ed. *The Continuous Wave: Technology and American Radio, 1900–1932.* Princeton, N.J.: Princeton University Press, 1985.
Macaulay, David. *The Way Things Work.* Boston: Houghton Mifflin Company, 1988.

Christina S. Drale

AM ALLOCATIONS AND CLASSES. As far back as the *Radio Act of 1912,* the federal government has attempted to define, assign, and control broadcast stations in the United States. The changing rules concerning allocations and classes of AM radio stations since 1912 are complicated, extensive, and significantly beyond the scope of this reference work. They have been addressed in later legislation as well as specific Federal Communications Commission Rules and Regulations.

AM broadcast stations are allocated a channel in the AM broadcast band (535–1,705 kilohertz [kHz]) and a class defining the station's power limits, operating hours, and service area parameters. Channels are designated 10 kHz apart, beginning at 540 kHz, and have a 10-kHz bandwidth. The 540 kHz channel, for instance, has a bandwidth from 535 kHz to 545 kHz. There are a total of 117 channels within the band. AM broadcast channels are divided into three types: *Clear channel* stations assigned to these channels serve wide areas and have primary service areas protected from objectionable interference and, depending on the class of station, protected secondary service areas; *regional channel* stations assigned to these channels serve a principal center of population and its adjacent area; and *local channel* stations assigned to these channels serve a community and the immediate surrounding area.

There are four classes of AM broadcast stations. A "Class A" station is an unlimited-time station, operating on a clear channel, and designed to render primary and secondary service over an extended area and at relatively long distances from its transmitter. The station's primary service area is protected from same- and adjacent-channel interference. The station's secondary service area is protected from same-channel interference. This class of station can have an operating power between 10 kilowatts (kW) and 50 kW. A "Class B" station is an unlimited-time station designed to provide service only over a primary coverage area and is assigned to a clear or regional channel. Class B stations operate with a power between .25 kW and 50 kW unless licensed to a channel between 1,605 and 1,705 kHz, in which case they are limited to a maximum operating power of 10 kW. A "Class C" station is an unlimited-time station operating on a local channel and designed to render service only over a primary service area. Class C stations can have operating powers between .25 kW and 1 kW. A "Class D" station operates either daytime, limited time, or unlimited time on a clear or regional channel. Nighttime operations of Class D stations are not afforded protection and must protect all Class A and Class B operations during nighttime hours. Class D stations can have an assigned daytime power from .25 kW to 50 kW but must limit their nighttime operating power to no more than .25 kW.

Code of Federal Regulations. Title 47, Part 73, Sections 14–30. Washington, D.C.: U.S. Government Printing Office, 1996. Published by the Office of the Federal Register, National Archives and Records Administration as a special edition of the Federal Register.

Steven C. Runyon

AMERICAN FEDERATION OF TELEVISION AND RADIO ARTISTS. *See* **unions.**

AMERICAN PUBLIC RADIO. *See* **Public Radio International (PRI).**

AMERICAN SOCIETY OF COMPOSERS AUTHORS AND PUBLISHERS. *See* **ASCAP (American Society of Composers Authors and Publishers).**

AMERICA'S TOWN MEETING OF THE AIR, America's first radio forum for debate and audience talk, aired on the NBC Blue Network on May 3, 1935, at Town

Hall in New York City. The radio-talk show was created by George V. Denny, Jr., associate director of the League for Political Education, and NBC vice president Richard C. Patterson. Denny proposed broadcasting the league's regular debates in order to improve the nation's political discourse. The first *America's Town Meeting of the Air* was entitled "Which Way: America Fascism, Communism, Socialism or Democracy?" Following arguments by speakers, such as Wendell Wilkie, the microphone was open to audience members, which produced a talk show popular on radio for 21 years. It was broadcast on Thursday evenings over NBC Blue from 1935 to 1945, then on ABC until 1956, shifting to Tuesday and finally Saturday nights.

Dunning, John. *Tune in Yesterday: The Ultimate Encyclopedia of Old-time Radio 1925–1976.* Englewood Cliffs, N.J.: Prentice-Hall, 1976.

Gregg, Robert L. *America's Town Meeting of the Air 1935–1950.* London: University Microfilms International, 1961.

Lackman, Ron. *Same Time—Same Station: An A-Z Guide to Radio from Jack Benny to Howard Stern.* New York: Facts on File, Inc., 1996.

William R. Davie

AMOS 'N' ANDY. *See* **Correll, Charles, and Freeman Gosden.**

AMPEX CORPORATION. Alexander M. Poniatoff formed the Ampex Electric and Manufacturing Co. in 1944 in San Carlos, California. The concept of transferring voice to a storage medium was first demonstrated in 1898 by Valdemar Poulsen, a Dane, who devised the first wire recorder. During World War II, Germany developed advanced magnetic recording technology in order to broadcast Adolf Hitler's speeches. Ampex acquired an example of the German magnetophone, which was seized by U.S. troops at the end of the war. Ampex produced its first audiotape recorder in 1948. The new technology was promptly adopted by the new American Broadcasting Company radio network for time zone delays. Ampex became the preeminent manufacturer of stationary audiotape recorders for use by American radio stations and networks.

Phillip O. Keirstead

AMPLIFICATION is the process of increasing the voltage, current, or power of an electrical or electronic signal. Amplification made radio practical by boosting audio signals to a level where they could be manipulated and transmitted, increasing transmitter power so that effective distances could be reached, strengthening the weak radio frequency signal received by a radio, and magnifying the audio signal in a radio to a level where it could be listened to on headphones or speakers.

Lee de Forest's audion tube was the first practical, successful, and recognized audio amplifier. Originally, vacuum tubes were used for amplification in radio. Now solid-state components have replaced vacuum tubes in most applications.

Steven C. Runyon

AM RADIO, amplitude modulation, was called "standard broadcasting" by the Federal Communications Commission (FCC) until 1978. AM radio uses a carrier wave modulated to reflect an input signal by varying the intensity, or amplitude, of the wave, while the frequency of the carrier wave remains constant. In the United States, the band of frequencies designated for AM radio is located in the medium-frequency range and is divided into 117 channels, with stations transmitting on carrier frequencies spaced 10 kilohertz (kHz) apart, with sidebands extending 5 kHz above and below the center. The band is located from 535 to 1,705 kHz, with the top 100 kHz added in 1988 by an act of the International Telecommunications Union. The FCC has reserved the frequencies in this expanded band for existing licensees in order to ease spectrum congestion and reduce interference. AM was surpassed in audience ratings by FM radio in the late 1970s. Since then, some AM broadcasters have struggled to maintain financial viability, whereas others have prospered through innovative programming, including news-talk and niche-music formats. The technical definition of AM is "a system of modulation in which the envelope of the transmitted wave contains a component similar to the wave form of the signal to be transmitted."

Code of Federal Regulations. Title 47, Part 73, Section 681. Washington, D.C.: U.S. Government Printing Office, 1996. Published by the Office of the Federal Register, National Archives and Records Administration as a special edition of the Federal Register.

Mark J. Braun

ANDERSON, EDDIE (1906–1977), an African-American actor, portrayed a major comic figure on radio during the late 1930s and 1940s, a time when few black actors held starring roles. He is best remembered as "Rochester," the witty, raspy-voiced butler and chauffeur on the immensely popular *Jack Benny Show.* Anderson's Rochester became one of radio's most popular black characters, and he was the first African-American performer to be featured regularly on a network radio show. In the 1920s, 1930s, and 1940s, Jim Crowism (segregation laws/rules restricting the employment of blacks) often prevented African Americans from performing on radio, and their presence was limited to sporadic occasions. Eddie Anderson first appeared on the *Jack Benny Show* in one of those occasional roles for black actors. But Anderson did not just fall into this role. He was an excellent performer trained by his entertainer parents and allowed to hone his skills as a teenaged dancer, singer, and actor on the black theater circuit. Anderson had great comedic timing and delivery, and he made excellent use of his distinctive, attention-grabbing, gravelly voice. So in 1937, when Anderson was cast in a minor role on the *Jack Benny Show* as a slow but jovial Pullman porter, listeners instantly liked him and favorably responded to the chemistry between Anderson and Benny. Anderson was called back to the show, and Jack Benny encouraged the show's writers to expand the role. The porter eventually became Rochester, Benny's valet/chauffeur. By the early 1940s, Anderson's Rochester had grown so popular that he enjoyed star billing with Benny.

Yet early on, Anderson's Rochester reflected the negative, stereotypical portrayal of black men of that day. Rochester was, in true minstrel tradition, an uneducated, irresponsible womanizer who lied, drank, and gambled. In one episode,

Anderson's Rochester even compared himself to the "lazy and shiftless" black character known as Stephen Fetchit. Over the course of the show's long run, however, Anderson was able to add more depth to Rochester, downplaying many of the role's more blatant stereotypes. And as Eddie Anderson's Rochester became a valued member of the regular *Jack Benny Show* cast, the show's writers eliminated some of the stereotypes associated with Rochester like the drinking and gambling. In many ways, Anderson's Rochester was afforded the same ability to humorously criticize his boss's penny-pinching, arrogant ways as the show's white characters. Rochester and Jack Benny maintained a great comic tit-for-tat that was not the norm between most black and white performers of that era, especially since Rochester clearly got the best of Benny and had the last word on many exchanges. While there were definite race-based limits to Rochester's ability to razz his boss, Eddie Anderson's comic-acting sense and popularity enabled him to evolve into one of the more outspoken black comic servant figures on radio, thereby breaking away from some of the stereotypes prescribed for African-American male performers of that period.

Black Radio: Telling It Like It Was. A 13-part radio documentary series with Lou Rawls. Washington, D.C.: Radio Smithsonian; Smithsonian Productions, 1996. (Series tapes are available for research at the Archives of African American Music and Culture, Indiana University, Bloomington and the Museums of Radio and Television in Los Angeles and New York.)

Boskin, Joseph. *SAMBO: The Rise and Demise of an American Jester.* New York: Oxford University Press, 1986.

Watkins, Mel. *On the Real Side: Laughing, Lying and Signifying the Underground Tradition of African American Humor that Transformed American Culture, from Slavery to Richard Pryor.* New York: Touchstone, 1994.

Sonja Williams

ANTITRUST LAW (CROSS-OWNERSHIP). The primary antitrust statutes in U.S. law are the *Sherman Antitrust Act of 1890* and the *Clayton* and *Federal Trade Commission Acts of 1914.* These laws are designed to control the exercise of private economic power by preventing monopolies and protecting competition. In radio and television broadcasting, the objectives of the antitrust statutes have been fostered by a series of ownership restrictions.

As early as 1938, the Federal Communications Commission (FCC) adopted a strong presumption against granting licenses that would create duopolies—that is, the common ownership of more than one station in the same service in a particular community. In June 1940 this became an absolute prohibition when the commission adopted rules governing FM service. These rules also contained the commission's first restrictions on ownership based not on the location of the broadcasting stations but, rather, simply on the number of stations under common ownership. The FCC adopted a "six-station rule" prohibiting ownership of more than six FM stations. The television industry was regulated by a similar set of rules in 1940, but the limit on the number of stations under common ownership was set at three. The commission extended its FM rules to AM in 1946 by creating a de facto limit of seven. In 1953, the commission formally adopted a seven-station limit for AM, raised the existing six-station limit for FM to seven, and retained the existing five-station TV limit. Within a year, the TV limit was raised to seven, no more than five of which could be VHF.

Through the 1980s, the commission gradually eased the restrictions on ownership, first by raising the number of stations any one owner could hold from 7 to 12. In 1989, the commission relaxed the radio duopoly rule and permitted a single owner to own up to 2 AM and 2 FM stations in the same market. The commission further relaxed its radio ownership rules in 1992 by increasing the national ownership cap to 30 AM and 30 FM stations nationwide. At the same time, using a tiered approach based on number of stations in a market, the commission increased the local ownership limits for radio. This tiered approach was codified by Congress in the *Telecommunications Act of 1996,* which further raised the limits for both radio and television. There is no longer a national ownership cap for radio.

In addition to the ownership limits, there have been rules prohibiting ownership across media. In 1970, the FCC adopted a rule that prohibited the owner of a television station from also holding radio stations in the same market. The commission began to relax that rule in 1975 and has since permitted AM/FM/TV combinations in the top 25 markets. Additionally, since 1975, the owners of daily newspapers are prohibited from holding the licenses of either radio or television stations within their markets. The *Telecommunications Act of 1996* retains both of these rules.

Antitrust. Code of Federal Regulations. Title 47, Part 73, Section 3555. Washington, D.C.: U.S. Government Printing Office, 1996. Published by the Office of the Federal Register, National Archives and Records Administration as a special edition of the Federal Register.

Gellhorn, Ernest. *Antitrust Law and Economics in a Nutshell.* 3rd ed. St. Paul: West Publishing, 1986.

USCA 47 Section 533 (a) 65 RR 2d 1676. *Amendment of Section 73.3555 of the Commission's Rules,* The Broadcast Multiple Ownership Rules, 1989.

USCA 47 Section 533 (a) 70 RR 2d 903. *In re* Revision of Radio Rules and Policies, 1992.

Antitrust Law. http://www.commlaw.com

Marianne Barrett

AOR FORMAT, album-oriented rock, encompasses secondary songs off a hit CD or album that do not get much airplay on the pop stations. Developed in the 1970s, AOR became an alternative format for listeners who were tired of hearing the same hit songs on the radio being played over and over. AOR took as its premise that top-selling CDs and albums contain good songs that are too "hard-edged" for the top-40 audience but are nonetheless desirable for a more narrow audience of 18- to 34-year-old males; this audience has become AOR's target demographic.

Heuton, Cheryl. "Radio Formats Now Total More than 50." *Mediaweek* 5 (43) (November 13, 1995): 12 (1).

Keith, Michael C., and Joseph M. Krause. *The Radio Station.* 3rd ed. Boston: Focal Press, 1993.

"Radio Formats." *Mediaweek* 5 (33) (September 4, 1995): 95 (1).

Robert McKenzie

ARBITRON is the largest supplier of radio audience ratings producing ratings for more than 200 markets (see **diary**).

Lawrence W. Lichty

ARCHIVES, RADIO. Broadcast programming has been preserved by both institutions and private individuals. The Library of Congress began to collect and preserve some programming in 1949 in its role as the U.S. copyright depository, and the National Archives collected and preserved programming from governmental sources and received donated event and news materials from stations and networks.

Serious recording and collecting of radio programs by individuals on home tape-recording equipment began around 1950, after some 20 companies introduced an effective, reasonably priced reel-to-reel recorder to the consumer market. This material, along with Armed Forces Radio Service discs that were produced to bring radio programs to our troops during WWII and a few network and syndicated discs, composed the starting base of material that began to be traded privately in the 1960s.

In the 1960s, small groups began to form to exchange material, information, and sources on both the East and West coasts. More material became available as people gained access to electrical transcriptions as stations began disposing of their stored material, and programs from other sources were discovered.

Newsletters on radio program collecting also began to circulate in the late 1960s. The leading newsletter today is *Hello Again* by Jay Hickerson, which began publication in 1970. Information can also be found on the Internet about old-time radio, or OTR.

Godfrey, Donald G. *Reruns on File: A Guide to Electronic Media Archives.* Hillside, N.J.: Lawrence Erlbaum Associates, 1992.
Hickerson, Jay. *Hello Again Newsletter;* and *What You Always Wanted to Know About Circulating Old-time Radio Shows,* 1986. (Box 4321, Hamden, Conn. 06514).

Marvin R. Bensman

ARMED FORCES RADIO SERVICE (AFRS). Part of the Armed Forces Radio and Television Service (AFRTS), Armed Forces Radio is a Department of Defense field activity under the authority of the assistant secretary of defense for public affairs. It provides a broad range of information and entertainment programming to military personnel and their dependents stationed in foreign countries and aboard U.S. Navy vessels at sea. Its purposes are (1) to enhance the morale, readiness, and well-being of military personnel and (2) to provide U.S. military commanders worldwide with a unique means to communicate unclassified internal information directly to military personnel and their families. Armed Forces Radio does not compete for audiences with commercial or foreign radio outlets. Nor does it endorse any commercial product or service. American commercial programming, such as newscasts, syndicated top-40 countdown shows, and music genre formats, are dubbed for rebroadcast. Commercial material is edited out, and military information is added to the programs. AFRS has no political mission in foreign countries. It is designed solely for the benefit of military personnel and their families. There is a spillover effect, however, given the worldwide popularity of American popular culture. AFRS programming received in various foreign countries has a loyal audience among the local citizenry in those countries.

Management and Operation of Armed Forces Radio and Television Service. DOD 5120.20-R. Washington, D.C.: Office of the Assistant Secretary of Defense (Public Affairs), February 1988.

Robert G. Finney

ARMSTRONG, EDWIN (1890–1954), is recognized as the inventor of FM radio. He also invented the regenerative circuit, which enhanced the audion tube's ability to amplify and transmit signals, and the superheterodyne, which improved tuning so that a single dial could be used. This constitutes the basic receiver in most radios today.

During World War I, Armstrong served in the signal corps and invented a small, lightweight radio to carry in airplanes. After the war, Lee de Forest, who claimed prior invention of the regenerative circuit, renewed a lawsuit. In 1934, the lawsuit was resolved in de Forest's favor. Armstrong tried to return the medal given him in 1918 by the Institute of Radio Engineers for the invention, but they refused.

Another invention, the superregenerative circuit, made him a millionaire. RCA paid him $200,000 and 60,000 shares of stock (later adding 20,000 shares of stock), making him the largest stockholder in RCA. Through his association with RCA, he met his wife, who was David Sarnoff's secretary. His wedding present to her was the first portable superheterodyne radio. He held a chair of electrical engineering at Columbia, although he taught no courses, and was paid $1 a year.

In 1933, Sarnoff came to Columbia to witness a demonstration of FM, and although impressed, he considered it a threat to the already established AM business and the developing television system. However, Sarnoff permitted Armstrong to use RCA space on top of the Empire State Building for tests, which were successful. Then in 1935, RCA asked him to remove his equipment from the Empire State Building to make room for its television equipment. Armstrong decided to build his own FM network and received permission from the Federal Communications Commission (FCC) to build his own experimental station at Alpine, New Jersey. This and other successful experiments began to increase demand for FM receivers. The FCC held hearings on the status of FM and announced commercial operations would begin on January 1, 1941.

RCA offered to pay Armstrong $1 million outright for his FM patents, but he would receive no royalties. He refused the offer. Although World War II halted development of television, FM had been approved for television sound. In 1944, the FCC changed the FM bandwidth allocation, making all prewar receivers and transmitters obsolete. Armstrong fought this decision until 1948. RCA claimed its own development of FM and refused to pay him royalties for television sets using FM sound receivers. In 1948, Armstrong filed suit against RCA. As his legal fees mounted, his income from royalties decreased. In 1953, his health deteriorated and his wife left him. On January 31, 1954, Armstrong, fully dressed in scarf, hat, overcoat, and gloves, jumped out of his apartment window to his death. He was 64 years old. The lawsuit was eventually settled in his favor in 1967.

Empire of the Air: The Men Who Made Radio. PBS Documentary. Producer, Ken Burns. Narrator, Jason Robards. Air date, January 28, 1992.

Lessing, Lawrence. *Man of High Fidelity: Edwin Howard Armstrong.* Philadelphia: J. B. Lippincott, 1956.

Lewis, Thomas S. W. *Empire of the Air: The Men Who Made Radio.* New York: HarperCollins Publishers, 1991.

Mary E. Beadle

ARMSTRONG, JACK. *See Jack Armstrong, the All-American Boy.*

ASCAP (AMERICAN SOCIETY OF COMPOSERS AUTHORS AND PUB-LISHERS) licenses, collects, and distributes royalties derived from the public performance of members' copyrighted works. Royalties are distributed to members based on surveys of performances of their works. ASCAP is the oldest of the two major American performing rights organizations, with a membership of more than 68,000 composers, songwriters, lyricists, and music publishers.

Composer Victor Herbert and several other music composers organized ASCAP in 1914 as a response to the growing popularity of sheet music and piano-roll sales. The *Copyright Act of 1909* gave composers and publishers a right to protect their works, but it was impossible for copyright holders to negotiate with and license their works to all of those interested in performing them. Copyright holders also found it difficult to detect unauthorized use of their works. ASCAP was founded to serve as a clearinghouse for those who create and utilize music.

In the 1920s, ASCAP became concerned that the new medium, radio's use of recorded music, had stimulated record sales and caused a decline in revenue from sheet music sales. ASCAP demanded that radio stations obtain a performance license for recorded music broadcast; however, most stations refused to enter into a licensing arrangement and dropped ASCAP works from their playlists. In 1923, broadcasters banded together to oppose ASCAP licensing of radio stations. This group became known as the National Association of Broadcasters (NAB). The efforts of the NAB were not successful, and radio stations eventually began paying ASCAP royalties for the broadcast of recorded music.

By the late 1930s, ASCAP was collecting the major portion of its income from the issuance of radio music performance licenses. When ASCAP raised its rates to radio stations in 1937, broadcasters, through the NAB, responded by creating a music licensing agency of their own. In 1939, broadcasters established Broadcast Music Incorporated (BMI), and in 1940, broadcasters ended their contracts with ASCAP. For a brief period, no popular music was broadcast on radio.

Although some artists switched affiliations from ASCAP to BMI, ASCAP still retained the most viable catalog of music. Slowly stations began to pursue licensing arrangements with ASCAP, and ASCAP compromised its demand for higher rates. By late 1941, many stations had negotiated new contracts with ASCAP, and popular music returned to the airwaves.

The result of this dispute between the NAB and ASCAP was a loss of revenue and the creation of a competitor in the music licensing business, BMI. ASCAP operates under a consent decree issued by the Department of Justice in 1960. Under this decree, ASCAP's general operation, handling of grievances, and the formulas used to determine royalty distribution are reviewed. Tensions between ASCAP and broadcasters over licensing rates continue to exist and surface regularly when licensing contracts come up for renewal.

Halloran, Mark, ed. *The Musician's Business and Legal Guide.* 4th ed. Englewood Cliffs, N.J.: Prentice-Hall, 1991.
About ASCAP. http://www.ascap.com (October 10, 1996)

Kenneth C. Creech

ASCERTAINMENT. *See* **Deregulation.**

ASSOCIATED PRESS. *See* **wire services: AP and UPI.**

AT&T (AMERICAN TELEPHONE AND TELEGRAPH COMPANY). *See* **Bell Laboratories; patent pools; WEAF (New York City); Western Electric.**

ATWATER KENT. The Atwater Kent (AK) Manufacturing Company was one of the early leading radio manufacturers. Arthur Atwater Kent (1873–1949), a technical genius who invented the Unisparker ignition system used in virtually every automobile from 1920 to 1970, turned his talents in 1920 to designing and manufacturing "breadboard"-type radio sets (components affixed to a base). While his AK Manufacturing Company was not first with several key radio innovations, AK was preeminent in quality and promotion.

Atwater Kent put its radios in cabinets in 1924 and spent $500,000 to advertise them. In 1926, AK model 30 offered one-dial tuning, combining receivers' three previous dials into one. Instead of heavy, leaky storage batteries, AK model 36 was able to use household AC electrical current in 1927. AK dominated the radio receiver market until 1929. In its *Saturday Evening Post* ad of May 26, 1928, AK claimed an installed base of more than 1.6 million receivers. AK did much to transform radio from a hobbyists' enthusiasm to a central feature of the American home. Atwater Kent receivers were recognized as the "Cadillac" of early radios, the best components in the best cabinetry.

The company's emphasis on quality also extended to program sponsorship. Beginning in October 1925, an estimated one half of the country's radio audience heard fine music, even opera, on Sunday nights' *The Atwater Kent Radio Hour.* This was the first major radio "package" show, prepared, managed, and sold as a unit to an advertising agency.

The Great Depression shifted radio buyers' emphasis from quality to affordability, and Philco took Atwater Kent's place as one of the world's leading radio manufacturers. The Atwater Kent Manufacturing Company shut its doors in 1936.

DeLong, Thomas A. *The Golden Age of Musical Radio: The Mighty Music Box.* Los Angeles, Calif.: Amber Crest Books, 1980.
Douglas, Alan. *Radio Manufacturers of the 1920's.* Vol. 1. New York: Vestal Press, 1988.

Michael Woal

AUDIENCE FRAGMENTATION, the breaking down into segments of the mass audiences attracted to early network radio programs and later expanded by network television. As network programs shifted from radio to television in the 1950s, radio turned to formats designed to appeal to smaller segments or audience fragments identified by demographic or psychographic research.

Frederic A. Leigh

AUDIENCE RESEARCH, the systematic investigation of the needs and wants of radio listeners. Audience research is conducted or commissioned to study changes in viewing or listening patterns. Audience research is used by broadcasters and cablecasters to help shape programming and to determine what to charge advertisers for commercials. Audience research remains heavily demographic (numbers oriented) but has become somewhat more psychographic (attitude oriented) over the last decade.

Demographic research investigates facts about the audience. The most important demographic categories traditionally have been age and gender. Other demographic categories include dwelling, level of education, religion, and race. The "glamour" demographic desired by radio and TV stations is the audience with the most disposable income, the 35–54 age bracket. Demographic research about radio listeners is purchased mostly from Arbitron, a company that uses diaries and phone interviews to gather data from sampled audience members and then produce ratings. Nielsen (which provides TV ratings) and Arbitron translate demographic data into two key statistical constructs: the share and the rating. The *share* is that percentage of a demographic (e.g., females 18–34) tuned into a particular program, out of all the audience members in that demographic who were tuned into TV or radio programs over a specific duration of time. The *rating* is that percentage of a demographic tuned into a particular program, out of all the audience members (all the demographics) available, regardless of whether they were tuned into a TV or a radio program or whether they were not tuned into any programs. The share is always a higher number than a rating. Comparing the share with the rating over time indicates whether TV/radio use is becoming lighter, remaining the same, or becoming heavier.

Psychographic research investigates attitudes, feelings, values, and lifestyles of audiences. Psychographic research uses smaller samples of viewers and listeners to gather data than demographic research because the emphasis is on probing an attitude or lifestyle in a way that gets at a detailed, individualistic description. For example, quotes from the audience member are often gathered as psychographic data. Psychographic research data are sometimes used to divide the audience into qualitative categories such as "sports fanatics," "achievers," "belongers," and other such lifestyle descriptors. Psychographic research is conducted by the Roper Organization, the Stanford Research Institute (producing the VALS data—values, attitudes, and lifestyles), and other research companies. Psychographic research data (e.g., sports fans) are often linked back to demographic data (e.g., men, age 18–34) by TV and radio planners for the purpose of scheduling lifestyle-oriented advertisements where they are most likely to impact the target audience (for example, scheduling a beer commercial during a broadcast of a National Football League [NFL] football game). Some traditionally minded broadcasters and cable-casters are skeptical of psychographic research findings because they believe the sample sizes of audience members taking part in the study are too small to warrant valid inferences about the larger audience.

Audience research, particularly psychographic, is increasingly being conducted in-house by radio and TV stations. The main methods of in-house research include focus groups, call-out surveys, and auditorium sampling. Focus groups involve monitoring discussions among a group of 7 to 15 audience members selected according to predefined categories (e.g., working females, ages 18–35) who ostensibly represent a larger audience. Group discussions are led by a "facilitator," a person who "throws out" topics for discussion, but remains impartial to the value judgments batted around during the discussion. Generally the focus group is permitted to take the discussion where it wants. Meanwhile, the discussion is video- or audiotaped for subsequent analysis. Focus groups are frequently used to test pilot ideas for programming before officially presenting the programming to the general audience. Call-out surveys involve a random sampling of listeners or viewers conceivably part of the larger audience. Questions are posed over the phone to the respondent, and sometimes "hooks" (15 or so seconds of a song) are played to elicit a reaction. Auditorium research involves bringing likely audience members into a large room, where audio or video hooks are played and survey questions about those hooks are administered. Respondents are normally asked to indicate their reaction to the audio or video hooks by pressing a button at their seat or by checking an answer on a questionnaire.

Audience research must stay current to match a station's programming to the constantly changing audience compositions and tastes and to determine what to charge for on-air advertising time. Therefore, audience research is an ongoing and competitive enterprise for broadcasters and cablecasters.

Cooper, Roger. "The Status and Future of Audience Duplication Research: An Assessment of Ratings-Based Theories of Audience Behavior." *Journal of Broadcasting and Electronic Media* 40 (1) (winter 1996): 96–116.

Lindlof, Thomas R., ed. *Natural Audiences.* Norwood, N.J.: Ablex Publishing Company, 1987.

Schillmoeller, Edward A. "National Television Measurement Quality Priorities." *Journal of Advertising Research* 33 (3) (May–June 1993): RC10(3).

Robert McKenzie

AUDIMETER, Nielsen Media Research company's name for several generations of the metering device used to record set tuning. Claude Robinson, while a student—later a partner with George Gallup in public opinion research—at Columbia University in 1929, patented a device to "provide for scientifically measuring the broadcast listener response by making a comparative record of . . . receiving sets . . . tuned over a selected period of time" (Webster and Lichty, p. 75) The patent was sold to NBC's parent, the Radio Corporation of America, but nothing more came of the device at this time.

In his 1935 Ph.D. dissertation at Ohio State University, Frank Stanton, later the president of CBS, built and tested 10 recorders to "record [radio] set operations for as long as 6 weeks" (p. 75). Others experimented with similar devices, including Robert Elder of MIT and Louis Woodruff, who field tested a device in the Boston area.

University of Wisconsin electrical engineering graduate Arthur C. Nielsen, who was in the consumer survey business, heard a speech by Elder, who called his device an "Audimeter." Nielsen sought permission to use the Robinson-RCA device, redesigned it, and began tests in Chicago and North Carolina. In 1942, the company launched a "radio index" based on 800 homes equipped with the device, which recorded tuning on a paper tape. While the basic purpose of the machine was unchanged, it later recorded tuning on 16-mm motion picture film. Nielsen no longer reports on radio audiences, but TV viewing is recorded by an all-electronic Audimeter and reported directly to company computers via phone line.

Webster, James G., and Lawrence W. Lichty. *Ratings Analysis: Theory and Practice.* Hillsdale, N.J.: Lawrence Erlbaum Associates, 1991.

Lawrence W. Lichty

AUDIO CDS. *See* **compact disc recording.**

AUDION was the first vacuum tube capable of amplifying weak electrical signals. The audion was composed of three elements: a negatively charged electron-emitting cathode, a positively charged anode, and a mesh "grid" between the two. Its inventor, Lee de Forest, discovered a small change in the electrical charge on the grid resulted in a large change in the electron flow between cathode and anode: amplification. The audion could be made to detect and amplify weak radio signals; later, it was found that the device could generate radio signals when wired as an oscillator. The 1906 invention of the audion was critical to most developments in electronics prior to the invention of the transistor (see **de Forest, Lee**).

Lewis, Thomas S. W. *Empire of the Air: The Men Who Made Radio.* New York: HarperCollins Publishers, 1991.
RCA Receiving Tube Manual. Harrison, N.J.: Radio Corporation of America, Electron Tube Division, 1961.

Tom Spann

AUDION TUBE. *See* **De Forest, Lee.**

AUDITORIUM MUSIC TESTING. *See* **audience research.**

AUTOMATIC FREQUENCY CONTROL (AFC) is electronic circuitry that keeps transmitters and receivers accurately tuned to a specific frequency by compensating for frequency fluctuations. AFC often works with the electronic tuning circuits of modern radios. AFC has been especially important in keeping FM radio receivers locked onto a specific station, eliminating drifting to a station on an adjacent frequency, and stereo receivers exactly on frequency, eliminating distortion and fading. The introduction of this circuitry made FM radio more competitive with AM radio.

Steven C. Runyon

AUTOMATION, RADIO PROGRAMMING, refers to programming that is produced by automatic machinery without the real-time intervention of a human operator. A hybrid form known as "live-assist" uses a live announcer who is interspersed with other elements that are cued and run by the system.

The earliest radio automation systems were based around record-changing mechanisms from jukeboxes and were thus only able to play standard phonograph records. Later, a system was developed for inserting announcements recorded on reel-to-reel tape, and although it could simulate a simple record show, the rerecording of the single, linear tape was cumbersome and time-consuming.

In the early 1960s, radio's rapid adoption of the endless-loop tape cartridge for short program elements such as commercials, promos, and jingles resulted in the development of multiple-cartridge players. These "cartridge jukeboxes" became the essential device in modern automation, and many automation systems were sold in the decade between 1965 and 1975. The simplest of them linked several multiple-cartridge players to a sequential switcher that started each machine in a predetermined order, then eventually repeated the pattern. More sophisticated random-access systems took advantage of the ability to play any desired cartridge upon command from a computer, so that certain program elements could be repeated more often than others. Systems were even developed to automatically fade the music recorded on one cartridge while an announcer's voice-track comments played from another, just as in live radio.

At many stations today, satellite-delivered shows have replaced much locally produced, automated programming because of lesser expense, greater reliability, and national promotion.

David T. MacFarland

AUTOMOBILE RADIO. Factory-installed car radios were not common until the 1930s. In its first year of featuring car radio statistics, the 1936 *Automobile Facts and Figures* reported 1.1 million units installed in 1935 models. Comparing this figure to the 4.4 million radios sold for home use that year illustrates the rapid surge in car radio interest. Total auto sets in use numbered 3 million in 1935. Coping with the Great Depression, many families were willing to pay the price for a radio presence in their cars.

By 1950, 64 percent of cars contained a radio, 75 percent by 1954. Further impetus was added by transistors and highway building. Transistor radios were lighter, compact, and more durable and required less power than vacuum-tube models. The *Federal-Aid Highway Act of 1956* triggered the massive interstate highway construction program. More people would spend more time in cars equipped with more durable, reliable radios.

In 1963, 62 percent of new cars had factory-installed radios. This figure rocketed to 85 percent in 1967. The Chilton Company began reporting tape-player installations in 1967 in *Automotive Industries,* listing 138,000 (2 percent of new cars).

FM would have its impact. In 1974, Pulse, Inc. reported more than 85 percent of all autos had radios, and about one fourth of all new auto radios featured FM.

In the 1980s, AM-FM stereo was establishing a solid presence, installed in 46 percent of new cars by 1986. AM-only units were dropping precipitously, installed in just 15 percent of cars in 1983, and by 1986 in just 5 percent. *Ward's Automotive Yearbook* omitted AM-only statistics after 1990.

This period also saw increased installation of AM-FM stereo with cassette, at 26 percent (1.6 million) in 1983 models, 42 percent (3.5 million) in 1986. By 1990, the percentage was 66 percent (4.6 million), and in 1993, 76 percent (5.2 million).

By 1993, elaborate options existed for "sound systems," including AM stereo, compact-disc players, amplifiers, equalizers, and specially designed speakers. The next major advance, nationwide reception of one station via satellite delivery, makes commercial radio stations available anywhere in the country.

Charles F. Aust

AUTRY, GENE. *See* **Golden West Broadcasters.**

AVAIL, or availabilities, is a part of the media buy that determines availability of time. According to Kleppner's Advertising Procedure, avail is determined by a number of factors, including a client's total advertising investment, willingness to pay for a spot, and willingness to place commercials across a programming day. For instance, an infrequent advertiser might want to purchase a spot on a top-rated national radio program. The spot desired, however, may not be available to that advertiser without a broader or more frequent purchase. Each station and network spreads out choice advertising time among the top advertisers, but advertisers don't always get the spots they want.

Ginger Rudeseal Carter

AVERAGE QUARTER HOUR (AQH) is the estimated number of station listeners for a minimum of five minutes within a given quarter hour. The *average quarter-hour persons* is based on the average reported listening in the total number of quarter hours the station was on the air during a reported time period. The *average quarter-hour rating* represents a percentage of the universe for a given station in the metro area or the area of dominant influence (ADI). The *average quarter-hour share* represents a percentage of the listeners for a given station for the metro only.

Max Utsler

AWAY FROM HOME LISTENING, an estimate reported for a listening location outside of the home, could identify listening taking place either in a car or some other place.

Arbitron. *A Guide to Understanding and Using Radio Audience Estimates.* New York: Arbitron Company, 1995.

Frederic A. Leigh

AYLESWORTH, MERLIN HALL "DEAC" (1886–1952), was the first president of the NBC Network. Born in Cedar Rapids, Iowa, son of a clergyman, Aylesworth graduated from Denver University Law School in 1908 and practiced for several years in the Denver area. He served as the appointed chairman of the Colorado Public Utilities Commission from 1914 to 1918. For a year, he was an official with Utah Power and Light before moving to New York in 1919 to become managing director of the National Electric Light Association. In the latter position, he became widely known in industry circles.

He was approached by Owen D. Young and Gen. James Harbord of the Radio Corporation of America (RCA) in mid-1926 about becoming the first president of the then-developing National Broadcasting Company (NBC). He was the type of business-career man that RCA leaders felt was needed to get the new radio network off the ground. When appointed on August 19, Aylesworth did not even own a radio. The network was incorporated on September 9, and a general public announcement was issued on September 13, 1926. The first broadcast, a four-hour extravaganza on November 15 featuring remotes from several cities, began with a five-minute talk on the network's future by Aylesworth.

He served as NBC's president for a decade and helped to shape the design and operation of commercial network radio broadcasting, including program decisions, relations with advertisers, and relations with the Federal Radio Commission (FRC) and the Federal Communications Commission (FCC). He oversaw the January 1927 opening of a second network, NBC Blue, worked with the prestigious advisory council of national leaders, and helped to shape the flow of initial radio network publicity. He was a widely quoted spokesperson for radio, especially on the role of advertising in supporting broadcast operations.

Aylesworth resigned as NBC president at the end of 1935 but remained vice chairman of the NBC board until September 1936, thus completing a decade of NBC leadership. He devoted his energies to the Radio-Keith-Orpheum (RKO) film studio (for which he had been serving as a board member) until mid-1937. He then served as publisher of *New York World Telegram* from 1938 to 1940. During World War II, he consulted for the Coordinator of Inter-American Affairs.

Archer, Gleason L. *Big Business and Radio.* New York: American Historical Company, Inc., 1939.

Aylesworth, Merlin Hall. "What Broadcasting Means to Business," "Who Pays for Broadcasting," and "The Listener Rules Broadcasting." *Little Books on Broadcasting,* Nos. 1, 5, 11. New York: National Broadcasting Co., 1927–1929.

Christopher H. Sterling

B

BABY SNOOKS was a children's character created by Fanny Brice of *Ziegfeld Follies* fame. The character was introduced on radio on the "Follies" show of February 29, 1936. The first appearance of Baby Snooks came as Fanny Brice was doing a baby routine for vaudeville in 1912. Some researchers pinpoint the birth of Snooks at a party in 1921 when Brice was asked to entertain and trotted out her impersonation of a little girl—a seven-year-old brat.

Brice premiered Baby Snooks for the nation on a radio broadcast called the *Ziegfeld Follies of the Air.* It was on CBS and only lasted a short time. In December 1937, Brice joined NBC in another musical/comedy extravaganza, *Good News of 1938.* Snooks became a regular part of that program and was a radio fixture for the next 14 years.

The *Good News* show was continued through 1939, but in March 1940, it was cut to 30 minutes. Known as the *Maxwell House Coffee Time,* it was split into 15-minute segments—the first with comedian Frank Morgan, and the other 15 minutes were skits of Snooks. In 1944 Brice emerged again on CBS with her own half-hour *Baby Snooks Show.* It was sponsored by Post Cereals in 1944–1945, and Sanka Coffee in 1945–1946. In 1949, Brice took Snooks to NBC Tuesday nights. In 1959, Fanny Brice suffered a cerebral hemorrhage, and five days later she was dead at the age of 59.

Dunning, John. *Tune in Yesterday: The Ultimate Encyclopedia of Radio Programs: 1930–1976.* Englewood Cliffs, N.J.: Prentice-Hall, 1976.

ElDean Bennett

BACK ANNOUNCING, the practice of announcing song titles and artist information after a music selection has been played. Back announcing tends to be most prevalent in jazz and classical/fine arts radio formats.

Frederic A. Leigh

BANDWIDTH, in reference to radio, is the frequency range or channel within which a station is assigned and limited. AM broadcast stations have a bandwidth of 10 kilohertz (kHz) with the assigned carrier frequency at the center of the channel (for instance, a bandwidth of 735–745 kHz having an assigned frequency at 740 kHz). FM radio stations have a bandwidth of 200 kHz (for instance, a station whose carrier frequency is 90.3 megahertz [MHz] would have a bandwidth of 90.2–90.4 MHz). Sometimes bandwidth refers to the actual range of frequencies used to accommodate a specific modulated signal, which should be no greater than the assigned channel frequency range.

Steven C. Runyon

BARTER is an exchange of program time for advertising between a radio station and an advertising agency or sponsor. According to Kleppner's Advertising Procedure, barter is a way for an advertiser or agency to buy media below the rate card price. For example, a barter agency might approach a radio station and offer a nationally syndicated radio program. In return, the station would reserve from three to four minutes of advertising time for the agency's advertisers. The advertisements receive prime slots on the program, and the station receives the popular show. The exchange can be cash plus barter, or no money may exchanged be in the deal. According to a 1993 report by the International Reciprocal Trade Association, advertisers, their agencies, and media outlets exchanged or bartered more than $7.02 billion in goods and services.

Ginger Rudeseal Carter

BASIE, COUNT, JAZZ ORCHESTRA, first heard nationwide on a live remote broadcast from Kansas City's Reno Club over W9XBY, an experimental high-frequency AM station operated by First National Television School. Born in Red Bank, New Jersey, August 21, 1904, Bill Basie began playing piano as a child and eventually played clubs in Harlem. He toured the Midwest with Theater Owners' Booking Association (TOBA), joined the Blue Devils, and eventually landed in Kansas City. Basie's first broadcasts probably were with Bennie Moten's Kansas City orchestra, on KMBC. Basie temporarily took over the band after Moten's untimely death in 1935 but soon formed his own group. He also had a regular solo jazz organ program on Kansas City's WHB.

Basie recalled there was no contract for playing on radio then; the band was glad to have the publicity. Basie on W9XBY was heard in the Midwest, the South, and on the East Coast. Basie once was quoted saying he was dubbed "Count" by a W9XBY announcer on a 1935 Reno Club broadcast because other jazz leaders used names like Duke and King; however, in his autobiography Basie said he had used the name earlier but that the band's name, Barons of Rhythm, did originate on W9XBY. Once, when not all tunes had titles, a W9XBY announcer urged Basie to name his last song of the evening. Basie said he glanced at the clock and told the announcer to call it "One O'Clock Jump." Thereafter it was Basie's theme song and the number best associated with the band.

Important people responded to the Basie sound on W9XBY, including Lester Young, who left Chicago to be Basie's tenor sax player. Others in the Reno Club orchestra included Professor Smith, Jack Washington, Tatti Smith, Joe Keys, Lips

Page, and Jo Jones and singers Jimmy Rushing and Hattie Noels. John Hammond, *Down Beat Magazine* music critic who brought Bessie Smith and Benny Goodman to national prominence, heard Basie's W9XBY broadcast on his car radio in Chicago one evening in 1936. He traveled to Kansas City to meet Basie. Basie later said his fame began with Hammond's Kansas City visit. Hammond recommended Basie to Decca Records, then to Brunswick, and eventually to Columbia Records. Hammond also introduced Basie to Willard Alexander, who signed Basie with Music Corporation of America and booked him for Chicago and East Coast gigs. Like other big bands of the era, Basie appeared on late-night radio. The Basie orchestra played at the 1939 World's Fair and went on to international fame, performing with such jazz greats as Ella Fitzgerald, Frank Sinatra, Sarah Vaughn, Oscar Peterson, and Sammy Davis, Jr. Acknowledging his contributions to the radio, TV, and recording industries, in 1959 he was invited to perform at a national convention of radio and TV disc jockeys in Miami. Basie died on April 26, 1984.

Basie, Count, as told to Albert Murray. *Good Morning Blues.* New York: Random House, 1985.
Shapiro, Nat, and Nat Henthoff, eds. *Hear Me Talkin' to Ya'.* New York: Rinehart, 1955.

William James Ryan

BBC RADIO. The British Broadcasting Company (BBC) began regular scheduled broadcasting in Britain in 1922. By 1925, a national radio network had been established. In 1927, the name was changed to the British Broadcasting Corporation, a quasi-government entity, overseen by 12 governors appointed by the queen on the recommendation of the prime minister. The corporation engaged in noncommercial broadcasting, referred to as "public service broadcasting," receiving its base funding from a tax on receivers.

BBC Radio developed an array of services, described by names such as Radio 1 or Radio 3. Each had a distinct character, based on the type of programming it transmitted. For decades local BBC transmitters were primarily used to carry network programming. Local listeners paid little attention to local stations' names, dialing instead on the basis of network service the station carried. News programming was centralized in the radio newsroom at Broadcasting House, just off Oxford Circus in Central London.

Development of independent (commercial) radio after World War II led to enhancement of BBC local stations as sources of local programs and news. The level of competition locally and nationally was considerably increased by the *Broadcasting Act 1990,* which made provision for added commercial stations and networks.

In the mid-1990s, radio news and current affairs were moved to a centralized venue in West London, where the radio and television newsrooms could engage in more joint efforts. This was part of an effort to move the BBC's funding base away from taxation (licenses) and toward alternate revenue sources but not commercials.

Keirstead, Phillip O., and Sonia-Kay Keirstead. *The World of Telecommunication: Introduction to Broadcasting, Cable, and New Technologies.* Boston: Focal Press, 1990.

Tunstall, Jeremy. *The Media in Britain.* London: Constable, 1983.

Phillip O. Keirstead

BEA. *See* **Broadcast Education Association (BEA).**

BEAUTIFUL MUSIC, radio programming format characterized by the presentation of instrumental and soft vocal interpretations of works selected from the standard and contemporary-popular music repertoire. The term originated in the late 1960s with the introduction of a program service produced and syndicated to FM stations by Jim Schulke's Stereo Radio Productions (SRP). SRP producers carefully matched the tempo and timbre of the instrumental recordings selected for airplay, interspersing occasional choral and vocal selections to vary the sonic texture. This formula effectively attracted and held the attention of upscale, mature listeners who had become radio's disenfranchised silent majority.

Although initially a large-market phenomenon, beautiful music filtered into the medium and smaller markets during the 1970s as competing syndicators emulated the SRP approach. Bonneville Broadcast Consultants, Peters Productions, KalaMusic, and other programmers marketed variations of the format, primarily to FM stations. During this decade, a shift in programmer preference away from the utilization of commercially released recordings began to emerge. Following the deaths of several noted orchestra leaders, including Mantovani, Percy Faith, Andre Kostelanetz, and Bert Kaempfert, the supply of fresh, contemporary-sounding instrumental recordings diminished. As a result, several of the larger syndicators, notably SRP and Bonneville, shifted to reliance on custom-recorded programming. Both syndicators commissioned studio-based musicians to perform instrumental cover versions of pop music selections to augment their record libraries.

With this influx of new material, the popularity of beautiful music accelerated to its peak in 1979, when Arbitron declared it the nation's highest-rated format. Interest in this style of musical presentation diminished during the 1980s as listeners and advertisers defected to formats targeting the baby-boomer generation. Beautiful music stations today attract approximately 1 percent of the nationwide radio audience.

"Hard Times for Easy Listening." *Broadcasting* 116 (November 28, 1988): 122.

Lanza, Joseph. *Elevator Music: A Surreal History of Muzak, Easy-Listening, and Other Moodsong.* New York: St. Martin's Press, 1994.

Routt, Edd, James B. McGrath, and Fredric A. Weiss. *The Radio Format Conundrum.* New York: Hastings House, 1978.

Bruce Mims

BELL, ALEXANDER GRAHAM (1847–1922), educator, inventor, scientist, philanthropist. Although he is best known as the inventor of the telephone, Alexander Graham Bell always stated his profession as teacher of the deaf, a skill he learned from his father. Bell emigrated with his parents from his native Scotland to Canada and eventually took a job at the Boston School for the Deaf. During this period, Bell took what he knew about sound, hearing, and tuning forks and began to experiment with electrical circuits. By March 1876, he and Thomas Watson had developed a model of the device that became the basis for the entire telephone industry.

In 1877, Bell began a series of experiments in wireless telephony using both the earth and bodies of water as natural conductors, much as Morse had done. Working with John Trowbridge of Harvard, he eventually attained a distance of four miles along and across the Potomac River, but the sounds of the human voice were too indistinct.

Bell had much greater success with his photophone, receiving the first patent for wireless telephony in 1880. With a diaphragm connected to a delicately balanced mirror, a person speaking into the transmitter would modulate a reflected beam of light. At the receiver, the light struck a piece of selenium, a photoelectric element, which converted the light to an electrical signal that a telephone could decode. A later version substituted simple lampblack for the exotic and expensive selenium. Although the photophone was never more than a novelty, an 1882 variation was named the radiophone, marking the first use of the term *radio* to describe a wireless communication device.

Soon thereafter, Bell gave all his AT&T stock to his wife as a wedding gift, moved his family back to Canada, and reverted to his chosen profession as a teacher of the deaf. In his later years, Bell turned his inventive interests to airplanes and speedboats, founded the journal *Science,* and rescued the National Geographic Society from the brink of bankruptcy.

Bell, Alexander Graham. "Upon the Production of Sound by Radiant Energy." *American Journal of Science* 21 (1884): 463–490.

Fagen, M. D., ed. *A History of Engineering and Science in the Bell System: The Early Years (1875–1925).* New York: Bell Telephone Laboratories, 1975.

Robert H. Lochte

BELL LABORATORIES, formerly AT&T's Bell Telephone Laboratories, Bell Laboratories is the research and development arm of Lucent Technologies. Bell Labs is the largest and most successful communications research facility in the world, boasting more than 26,000 patents and inventions. Many modern-day communications technologies including the transistor, communications satellite, and sound-motion pictures were developed at Bell Labs. Formed by Theodore Vail in 1925 as the successor to the Western Electric Research Laboratories, Bell Labs was created to integrate the various research and engineering programs of AT&T in one division. Under Frank B. Jewett, its first president, Bell Labs quickly developed key communications inventions that would modernize the communications industry and point to future development interests for the labs. Sound-motion pictures, television network transmission technology, and the negative-feedback circuit (which was important for the development of high-fidelity sound and long-distance telephony) were some inventions that came out within its first three years of operations.

During the next decade, Bell Labs invented stereophonic sound, speech synthesis, and the first electronic digital computer. As World War II approached, its efforts were directed toward helping the U.S. military solve problems in wireless telephony and radar. Later inventions and developments included coaxial cable, microwave relay, cellular telephony, and the Unix computer-operating system. While Bell Labs is probably best known for the development of the transistor, which ushered in the solid-state communications and computer eras, its inventors and scientists have developed an impressive list of modern communications technologies such as the charge-coupled device (CCD), used in most television cameras today; and electronic system switching, which made direct-distance dialing, 800 numbers, and call forwarding possible. Laser technology, developed in 1958, has revolutionized communications, helping to make the information age possible.

Seven Bell Labs scientists have been awarded the Nobel Prize, and five have received the National Medal of Science. Breakthrough basic research points to the fact that Bell Labs has been blessed with brilliant researchers and has cultivated an environment supporting important basic research. Nobel Prize winner Karl Jansky is credited with being the father of radio astronomy, Claude Shannon originated a new area of mathematical inquiry called "information theory," and Arno Penzias and Robert Wilson are credited with detecting background radiation supporting the "Big Bang" theory. In 1985, President Ronald Reagan recognized the achievements of Bell Labs when it became the only U.S. laboratory ever to be awarded the National Medal of Technology.

During its early years, Bell Labs funding was split between revenues generated by AT&T as a regulated monopoly and those derived from its patents used in various manufacturing sectors. However, as a result of the 1956 Consent Degree, AT&T was barred from exploiting technologies not directly related to its core business as a telephone company. Many of the laboratories' innovations such as Unix, a popular computer-operating system, were not able to be marketed as a result. With the 1984 breakup of AT&T, Bell Labs was freed of the Justice Department constraints and was able to market its inventions and license its technology. Though some scientists and government policy makers expressed concern that without telephone tariff subsidies AT&T would be unable to afford to continue its tradition of funding basic research, AT&T chairman Robert A. Allen pledged to continue funding Bell Labs with a view toward long-term development. In 1996, as part of a massive restructuring of AT&T, Bell Labs became a subsidiary of Lucent Technologies, currently under the leadership of Dan C. Stanzione. Bell Laboratories employs 25,000 people located in eight states and 21 countries.

Today, Bell Labs has focused its research into three areas related to the information age: microelectronics technology, photonics, and advanced-software systems. The lab is also involved in high-definition television (HDTV) and super-conductivity research. Though critics say that expenditures are out of proportion to the value of its commercial developments, Bell Labs is widely regarded as the finest private research organization in the world.

Baida, Peter. "Breaking the Connection." *American Heritage* 36 (5) (June–July 1985): 65–80.

Bernstein, Jeremy. *Three Degrees above Zero: Bell Labs in the Information Age.* New York: Charles Scribner, 1984.

Kleinfield, Sonny. *The Biggest Company on Earth.* New York: Holt, Rinehart, and Winston, 1981.

Oslin, George P. *The Story of Telecommunications.* Macon, Ga.: Mercer University Press, 1992.
"Why Own One of the Wonders of the World." *Economist* (July 13, 1991): 87–88.
Bell Laboratories. http://www.bell-labs.com/

Fritz Messere

BELL SYSTEM. *See* **Bell, Alexander Graham; Bell Laboratories; Gardner Hubbard; Western Electric.**

BENNY, JACK (1894–1974), was an early radio comedian. His career covered 40 years and he was known for his masterful sense of timing. John J. O'Connor, in the *New York Times,* called Benny the most enduring and astonishingly shrew creation of radio. For listeners in the 1930s and 1940s, Sunday night at 7 meant Jack Benny and the gang. His program aired on radio for 23 years, first on NBC, then on CBS.

He was born Benjamin Kubelsky in Chicago, on St. Valentine's Day, in 1894. He spent his childhood in Waukegan, Illinois, where his Jewish father, Meyer Kubelsky, who had immigrated from Russia, owned a store.

As Jack Benny, he was known to work hard and earnestly to be funny. He rarely deviated from a script, although he had a keen sense of ad-libbing. Two of the items in Benny's repertoire were silence and a violin. The hallmark of his program was his hackneyed rendition of "Love in Bloom."

Contrary to his radio persona, Benny played the violin quite well. He began playing the violin at the age of 8 and gave concerts at a local theater. He quit school in the ninth grade to pursue his music as a violinist virtuoso. At 18, he went into vaudeville, playing his violin with a pianist. During an appearance, he told a joke and the audience laughed. He later said that the laughter ended his days as a vaudeville musician.

During World War I, he served in the navy with "The Great Lakes Road Show." In 1926, he had a part on Broadway, in *The Great Temptation.* His career got a jumpstart after he became master of ceremonies at the Palace Theatre. He then went to Hollywood, where he found his niche radio. In 1932, he had a guest appearance on the *Ed Sullivan Show.* Within a year, Benny had his own program on NBC. He led in the popularity polls from 1934 to 1936 and subsequently continued to be ranked in the top-10 radio programs for many years. Several of his competitors were other veterans of vaudeville who had made it into radio: Eddie Cantor, Al Jolson, Ed Wynn, Phil Baker, and George Burns and Gracie Allen.

In 1948, Benny left NBC to go to CBS. The radio show folded in 1955. Meanwhile, Benny continued on television. The show's first telecast was on October 28, 1950. His television show lasted until 1965, but he continued to make guest appearances on radio and television in his retirement. He played nightclubs, The Sahara in Las Vegas and The Waldorf-Astoria in New York. In his retirement years, he reportedly raised $5 million on behalf of musical causes through appearances at benefit concerts.

Benny used self-deprecating one-liners that mirrored the failings people recognized in themselves. According to his obituary in the *New York Times,* he was the most consistently funny of America's funnymen, although other comedians told funnier jokes.

Other attributes his comedic character was known for include tightfistedness and pomposity. As John O'Connor said in the *New York Times,* the radio medium worked so well for Benny's penny-pinching character because his old Maxwell auto sputtered and coughed, the many locks on his bank vault squeaked and clanked, and the pay telephone and cigarette machine in his living room noisily consumed coins.

He expressed frustration by resting his chin in his hand, staring like a martyr while he unblinkingly said, "Well!" If he were unmercifully teased, he might express his exasperation by saying, "Now cut that out!"

The *New York Times* cites one of his most frequent routines. A bandit holds him up and demands, "Your money or your life." After a prolonged period of silence, punctuated only by the laughter of the audience, Jack Benny says, "I'm thinking. I'm thinking."

Reportedly, in one of his last television appearances, which was on the Anne Bancroft show (called *Annie and the Hoods*), he brought down the house by not saying a word. He played the part of a psychiatrist listening to the silly prattle of a patient.

His friendship with George Burns, who was also a Jewish immigrant, lasted more than 50 years. Benny was said to be a notorious pushover for Burns's pranks. Benny apparently laughed at all of Burns's jokes. However, Burns reportedly disliked his best friend's wife, Sadie Marks, known as Mary Livingstone on the Benny broadcasts. After Burns began to fade from the show business spotlight and his radio career, he made occasional appearances on Jack Benny's TV show, where Livingstone played Benny's wife.

Rumors say Benny and Burns competed with each other on how many women they could score with. According to one story, every time Gracie Allen caught George Burns cheating, he bought her a more expensive gift. "I wish he would do it more often," she reportedly said. "I could use another tea service."

Like Burns, Benny appeared in a number of Hollywood films, especially through the 1930s, including the *Hollywood Review of 1929, Chasing Rainbows, The Medicine Man, It's in the Air, College Holiday, Artists and Models, Transatlantic Merry-Go-Round, Buck Benny Rides Again, Charlie's Aunt, To Be or Not to Be, George Washington Slept Here, The Meanest Man in the World,* and *The Horn Blows at Midnight.*

Jack Benny died of cancer at the age of 80 on December 28, 1974, at his home in Beverly Hills, California. Comedians Bob Hope and George Burns delivered his eulogy at Hillside Memorial Cemetery in Culver City, Calif., before mourners who included his wife, whom he married in 1927; Don Wilson, announcer; and Eddie Anderson, who played the role of Rochester, his valet on the program; and funnymen Danny Kaye, Jack Lemmon, Johnny Carson, George Jessel, and Walter Matthau.

Ironically, it was the death of Jack Benny that made George Burns a reborn celebrity. Benny was supposed to play an aging Jewish vaudevillian in the film version of Neil Simon's *The Sunshine Boys,* opposite Walter Matthau. When Benny died, the comedian's role went to Burns, who had last appeared in films in 1939 in the MGM film *Honolulu.* Burns won the Academy Award as the best supporting actor for his role in *The Sunshine Boys* in 1976. At age 79, Burns found himself labeled with the moniker "movie star." He went on to make more films, as well as to make frequent appearances on the media until his death at the age of 100 in March 1996. With Burns's death, the torch carried previously by Jack Benny, of elder statesman of radio comedy, passed from Burns to Bob Hope, 92.

The Museum of Television & Radio in Beverly Hills has a Radio Listening Room, where one can hear Jack Benny and others on five channels, as well as view clips on the long-standing feud between Jack Benny and Fred Allen.

Butters, Pat. "The Last Vaudevillian: Burns's Not-Always-Funny 100 Years." *Washington Times* (January 28, 1996), sec. B, p. 87.

O'Connor, John J. "A National Institution" *New York Times* Biographical Service (December 1974): 1672–1673.

Shepard, Richard F. "Jack Benny, 80, Dies of Cancer on Coast." *New York Times* Biographical Service (December 1974): 1670–1672.

Whitcomb, Dan. "Friends and Family Bid George Burns Farewell." Reuters, March 12, 1996, Newsbank CD.

Beverly G. Merrick

BENTON, WILLIAM (1900–1973), best known as an assistant secretary of state during the presidency of Harry Truman, was important to radio as a leader in the advertising industry and as one of the founders of educational broadcasting. His series of educational radio broadcasts produced at the University of Chicago during World War II garnered numerous honors, including the 1944 Peabody Award.

Benton grew up in Minnesota and later studied at the Harvard Law School. During the 1920s Benton commenced a successful career in advertising, having started as a copywriter with the firm Lord and Thomas before advancing to the firm later known as Batten, Barton, Durstine and Osborn (BBD&O). In 1929, with partner Chester Bowles, Benton founded the ad agency Benton and Bowles, which in 1932 landed the advertising account of the giant General Foods corporation. By the mid-1930s, Benton and Bowles was the largest coordinator of radio advertising, with $18 million in annual billings. From his role at Benton and Bowles, Benton was considered significant in radio's so-called Golden Age.

A former classmate of a figure named Robert Hutchins, Benton was invited to the University of Chicago to begin a series of educational radio broadcasts after Hutchins was named that school's president in the late 1930s. Two of Benton's best-known broadcast educational ventures, heard all over the country, were called *Round Table* and *The Human Adventure.* In 1945, the final year of World War II, Benton's educational programs on radio examined radar, the atomic bomb, and Einstein's theory of relativity. These same ventures increasingly assumed a popular appeal and some won advertiser support. Also at the University of Chicago, Benton developed an interest in audiovisual education, and he set about to augment his radio fare with educational programs on the new medium of television. In his later years, Benton would help advance educational television.

Largely on the notoriety gained from the radio programs, Benton was appointed to several influential positions in the American foreign service after World War II. He was considered an expert in Anglo-American trade relations. Among Benton's advisers in the State Department post were Ralph McGill, editor of the *Atlanta Constitution,* John Hay Whitney, editor of the *New York Herald-Tribune,* and Harold Lasswell, a noted political science professor with research interests in radio. In 1945 Benton joined the State Department as the head of overseas public affairs and in that capacity steered the Voice of America, a European radio network that had begun during World War II as a small series of shortwave transmitters.

In his later years, Benton had duties with the United Nations and wrote widely in popular magazines. Through the 1960s he remained a frequent contributor to network and local radio programs.

Hyman, Sydney. *The Lives of William Benton.* Chicago: University of Chicago Press, 1969.

Craig M. Allen

BERG, GERTRUDE (1899–1966), was the creator and the lead actress of *The Goldbergs.* The daughter of immigrants, Berg was the married mother of two when, in the early days of 1929, she obtained her first radio job. Her early duties included translating commercials into Yiddish and reading recipes over the air. Eventually, though she had little experience, she tried her hand at scriptwriting. Her first creation, *Effie and Laurie,* had its one and only airing on CBS in mid-1929. She created *The Goldbergs* quickly thereafter, and it premiered on NBC on November 20, 1929. *The Goldbergs* was the story of the home life of a Brooklyn-based Jewish family: mother Molly (played by Berg), husband Jake, children Rosalie and Sammy, and live-in uncle David.

A hybrid of comedy and gentle human drama, the series was originally serialized like a soap opera. Eventually, episodes became self-contained, and the melodrama lessened in order to greater emphasize the fun and gossipy nature of Mother Molly chatting with her neighbors and the humorous appeal of Molly's troubles with the English language. Over the years, Molly's misconstrued statements ("Enter whoever!"; "I'm putting on my bathrobe and condescending the stairs") became one of the trademarks of the series, as did her opening cry to her next-door neighbor, "Yoohoo, Mrs. Bloom!" But Molly was never too tongue-tied to offer homespun advice to her children (and to her listeners): "Better a crust of bread and enjoy it than a cake that gives you indigestion."

Successful nearly from its first broadcast, *The Goldbergs* quickly gained a sustaining sponsor, Pepsodent; a loyal audience in the thousands; and it spawned a comic strip and several vaudeville skits. Berg, who wrote and acted in every single episode, over 10,000 programs, eventually parlayed her success into writing for the movies (*Make a Wish*) and other radio series (*Kate Hopkins*).

The first incarnation of *The Goldbergs* on radio ended in 1934 when Berg took the series and its cast on a nationwide tour. Berg returned in a new, self-written, self-starring series, *House of Glass,* at NBC in 1935. Set in a Catskill Mountain resort (based on some of Berg's childhood memories), the series drew poor reviews and never found an audience; eventually it ended in its first year.

In 1938, Berg was offered a $1 million contract to revive *The Goldbergs*. Berg did and the new *Goldbergs,* again with Berg as star and writer, aired until March of 1945. In 1948, after a successful bow on the Broadway stage in a play based on *The Goldbergs,* Berg took the series to television, where it aired, in various incarnations, on network and in first-run syndication, from 1949 to 1955. Berg was the first winner of TV's Emmy Award for Best Actress.

Berg, Gertrude. *Molly and Me.* New York: McGraw-Hill, 1961.
O'Dell, Cary. *Women Pioneers in Television: Biographies of Fifteen Industry Leaders.* Jefferson, N.C.: McFarland, 1996.
Seldes, Gilbert. "The Great Gildersleeve." *Saturday Review* (June 2, 1956): 26.

Cary O'Dell

BERLE, MILTON(1908–), a well-known radio and television performer, was born Milton Berlinger on July 12, 1908, in New York City. Berle's comedic style, which included audience interaction, was much more suited to the visual medium of television than radio. On radio he hosted *Let Yourself Go* and *The Milton Berle Show,* which began in the 1947 season. He appeared in numerous other radio programs as a guest from 1936 to 1948, including *Gillette's Community Sing, Stop Me If You've Heard This One,* and *Kiss and Make Up,* a radio quiz show (MacDonald, p. 145). MacDonald notes how Berle focused on specific areas, "comically saluting" on *The Milton Berle Show* in 1947–1948 "health, Christmas, women, literature, public service, and communications" (p. 97).

His career began at age five under the direction of his mother Sandra. Berle said of her, "She forged me and she worked on me like a son of a gun. Every place I ever appeared, whether it was vaudeville, theaters, nightclubs or TV, she was in the audience being a one-woman flack for me. I can still hear her tremendous big laugh on the kinescopes" ("TV's First Star," p. 108). His mother took him to Hollywood, where his silent film career began in 1914. He appeared in over 50 silent movies, making appearances with Charlie Chaplin and Mary Pickford.

In 1931, he was master of ceremonies at the Palace Theater in New York City, and he once performed at the Cotton Club in Chicago and appeared in vaudeville with Ziegfeld Follies. After his retirement from the *Texaco Star Theater* in 1959, Berle made guest appearances on television programs such as *Jack Benny,* the *Lucy Show, F-Troop, Get Smart, The Love Boat,* and *Love American Style,* and recently, *Beverly Hills, 90210* (Atherton and Scott).

Berle was also featured in Stanley Kramer's *Mad, Mad, Mad, Mad World* and also appeared in *The Bell Boy* starring Jerry Lewis and *Let's Make Love* with Marilyn Monroe. Berle received a television Emmy award for his role in *Doyle against the House.*

Berle is most remembered for his appearances on television as the host of the *Texaco Star Theater,* which NBC began broadcasting on June 8, 1948. The television show was an immediate hit. The October 19, 1948, show received a 63.2 Hooper rating, a 92.4 television audience share, still the largest ever in radio and television history (MacDonald, p. 146). Berle signed a lifetime contract with NBC after the third season of the show, reported to be six figures per year ("TV's First Star," p.

108). Most recently, October 28, 1996, Berle, affectionately called "Uncle Miltie," received the first lifetime achievement award from the New York Television Academy. *M*A*S*H* cocreator Larry Gelbart calls Berle the "founding father" of television. "In a fairer world, Berle would have received a royalty on every TV set ever sold. It was the enjoyment he supplied that helped create the demand" (p. 108). Berle is quoted as saying, "One of the biggest thrills I ever got was having my picture and story on the cover of *Time* and *Newsweek* in the same week [May 16] in 1949. That was the first time that ever happened for a comedian. When I hit, I just busted right through" (p. 108).

Berle married Joyce Matthews in 1941, and they later divorced. His second marriage to Ruth Cosgrove in 1953 lasted until her death. Berle has two adopted children, Vicki and William. He married Lorna Shaw in 1991. An interesting note concerns a humidor that Berle presented to President John Kennedy on Kennedy's Inauguration Day with the words "Good Health good smoking" engraved on top. It was auctioned off during Sotheby's auction of Jacqueline Onassis's possessions in April 1996 for $574,500 (Barron, p. A1).

Atherton, Ray, prod., and Lee Scott, dir. *Mr. Entertainment: Milton Berle, a Biography.* Omnivision Films, Inc., 1995. Distributed by Simitar Entertainment, Plymouth, Minn.
Barron, James. "So What to Do with Souvenirs of Camelot?" *New York Times,* April 24, 1996, p. A1.
MacDonald, J. Fred. *Don't Touch That Dial!: Radio Programming in American Life, 1920–1960.* Chicago: Nelson-Hall, 1979.
"TV's First Star and Favorite Uncle." *Broadcasting & Cable* (October 28, 1996): 108.

Arthur Thomas Challis, Jr.

BIG BAND ERA, a period roughly from 1935 to 1945, signified by bands with 10 or more members divided into instrumental sections organized by instruments and a rhythm section. During its heyday, Big Band music—also referred to as "swing"— was a staple of radio programming.

Big Band had its roots in jazz and was characterized by the tight coordination of the various sections, harmonized riffs, and repeated figures, with section leaders providing the improvisation. The result was a softer, moodier, more gentle, and more danceable sound than the "Roaring Twenties." The Big Band Era also marked the acceptance of jazz into white America. That led to a huge jump in record production and record sales. In the early 1940s record companies might introduce 20 singles a week. By the end of the decade, they were releasing as many as 100 per week.

Bandleaders such as Benny Goodman, Glenn Miller, Artie Shaw, Kay Kyser, Sammy Kay, Guy Lombardo, Duke Ellington, Woody Herman, Harry James, and Tommy and Jimmy Dorsey soon became household names. Many unknown singers also rose to fame through the Big Bands singers such as Frank Sinatra, Helen O'Connell, Dick Haymes, Peggy Lee, Bing Crosby, Perry Como, and Ella Fitzgerald.

Radio, America's prime-time entertainment medium of the 1930s and 1940s, helped the bands grow in popularity and sell records. After WWII the popularity of Big Band music began to fade. It was caused in part by a financial conflict between the American Society of Composers Authors and Publishers (ASCAP) and the radio industry but also by a declining interest in ballroom dancing.

Owen, Billy. *The Big Broadcast: 1920–1950.* New York: Viking Press, 1972.
Settel, Irving. *A Pictorial History of Radio.* New York: Grosset & Dunlap, 1967.
Big Band.
>   http://alvo.kqed.org
>   http://conct.com/home/mlp/bigbands.html
>   http://www.flash.net/rdreagan/duke.shtml
>   http://www.flash.net/rdreagan/index.shtml

Max Utsler

BILLBOARD is the international news weekly of music and home entertainment. A chronicle of American pastime culture, it began on November 1, 1894. It was devoted to the interests of bill posters and advertisers, rose with the popularity of radio and recorded music, and became the self-proclaimed bible of the music industry by the end of the twentieth century. The weekly covers business activity in the music, video, and home entertainment fields. Long noted for its peerless music charts, the magazine tracks radio airplay and electronically scans cassette and CD sales at various retailers, reporting the results in a rainbow of formats from rock to rap, country to classical, and every hue in between.

In the early 1990s, the magazine launched *Billboard Airplay Monitors,* tailored for radio station music programmers and disc jockeys. Four separate publications cover the "Top 40," "Country," "Rock," and "Rhythm and Blues" music genres. These editions showcase music charts (sales and airing) and provide a platform for record companies to expose new releases through glossy advertisements.

The larger, more expensive parent magazine *Billboard* includes the same charts, coupled with critical reviews of new singles and albums for use by radio music programmers, record distributors, and the jukebox industry. Throughout the history of rock 'n' roll, these pristine reviews helped to embed a written culture of the movement. Music historian Philip Ennis notes that this vocabulary was created by crisp, two-line reviews of new releases observing, "[T]he shrewd reviewers of those papers were masters at identifying for each record its musical style, its ancestors and influences, the merit of its performance, and the likelihood of its commercial success."

Beyond records, the magazine rounds out its home entertainment coverage using reporters in four bureaus in the United States, one in London, and one in Tokyo. In February 1997, *Billboard Bulletin* daily fax began to provide rapid industry news on topics ranging from radio station mergers to marketing, legal, and technical issues.

Ennis, Philip H. *The Seventh Stream: The Emergence of Rock 'n' Roll in American Popular Music.* Hanover, N.H.: University Press of New England, 1992.
Billboard. http://www.Billboard.com

B. William Silcock

BILTMORE AGREEMENT, the treaty of the Press-Radio War between networks, newspapers, and wire services, was drawn at the Biltmore Hotel in New

York City on December 16, 1933. Publishers negotiated the agreement to protect newspapers from radio competition by requiring that CBS close its bureau and NBC not open one. The networks agreed to broadcast only the Press-Radio Bureau's five-minute summaries twice a day after 9:30 A.M. and 9:00 P.M., which would protect early and late editions of newspapers. In defiance of this agreement, an "outlaw" Trans Radio bureau was formed in 1934 to transmit news to radio stations. United Press and International News Services eventually gave in to advertisers who wanted to sponsor network newscasts using wire stories. The Associated Press lifted its ban on providing news briefs to radio in 1939.

Bliss, Edward, Jr. *Now the News: The Story of Broadcast Journalism.* New York: Columbia University Press, 1991.
Lott, George E. "The Press-Radio War of the 1930s." *Journal of Broadcasting* 14 (3) (summer 1970): 275–286.

William R. Davie

BILTMORE HOTEL, the site of the meeting between print and broadcast representatives to resolve the ongoing Press-Radio War, attended by representatives of the American Newspaper Publishers Association (ANPA), the wire services Associated Press (AP), United Press (UP), and International News Service (INS), executives from CBS and NBC, and the National Association of Broadcasters (NAB) (representing the various independent stations) (see **Press-Radio War**). The meeting was held December 11–12, 1933, in New York City, and after two days of negotiations, a "gentleman's agreement" was reached that would allow radio to continue to carry news broadcasts while protecting the financial and institutional interests of the print media. The Biltmore Agreement, as the plan became known, was not a formal document but rather an attempt at a workable solution to an increasingly complex problem (see **Press-Radio Bureau [PRB]**). Gwenyth Jackaway notes there was no formal document signed because the legal counsel for the print media associations felt it might constitute an unfair agreement to restrain trade. The lack of a formal document, the extreme restrictions placed on network radio news, the reluctance of independent stations to agree to the restrictions, and increasing competition to provide news to radio all led to the ultimate demise of the Biltmore Agreement and the evolution of radio news.

Jackaway, Gwenyth L. *Media at War: Radio's Challenge to the Newspapers, 1924–1939.* Westport, Conn.: Praeger, 1995.

Michael D. Casavantes

BLACK DRAMA. Dramatic programs written, produced, and/or performed by African Americans were an important, though relatively rare, occurrence on radio during its early days. Jim Crow discrimination (laws/rules restricting the employment of blacks) prevented many African-American performers from being on air. The radio networks also maintained that they were constrained by the reluctance of program sponsors to finance all-black or racially mixed programs because they feared that such shows might alienate white listeners. African Americans were occasional musical guests on network variety shows, or they were represented by stereotypical comic-"minstrel" roles typified by national hits like *Amos 'n' Andy* and *The Bealuh Show.*

Yet there were sporadic presentations of African Americans in a more positive dramatic light. One of the earliest was the 1933 CBS series *John Henry, Black River Giant.* Also, from the early to mid-1930s, New York City stations WMCA and WJZ aired weekly black dramas written by and performed by African Americans. In the early 1940s, *Freedom's People,* an eight-part series developed by a black employee of the federal government's Office of Education, aired monthly on the NBC network. *Freedom's People* featured dramatic vignettes about the contributions of African Americans to American history, including such famous personalities as actor/singer Paul Robeson, fighter Joe Louis, and labor leader A. Philip Randolph. Also during World War II, the radio networks sporadically sponsored half-hour dramatic programs, such as "They Call Me Joe"(CBS) or "Dorie's Got a Medal" by noted CBS producer Norman Corwin, which paid tribute to African-American soldiers. Perhaps one of the most powerful dramatic programs that CBS produced was "An Open Letter on Race Hatred," a rather hard-hitting dramatic assessment of the causes and consequences of the Detroit race riot of 1943. On a nonnetwork level, there were several significant dramatic programs written and performed by African Americans during the 1940s. In 1944, African-American writer Roi Ottley developed a weekly half-hour radio series called *New World u Comin'* based on his book of the same title. Via docudramas and live broadcasts, the series took a progressive look at a wide range of issues including racism, fascism, and black culture. The series aired on New York's WMCA and uniquely lasted in some form until the late 1950s.

In the Chicago of the mid-1940s, another gifted black writer, Richard Durham, developed the first African-American radio soap opera, called *Here Comes Tomorrow.* But Durham is best known for his *Destination Freedom* weekly series, which aired on Chicago's WMAQ from June 1948 to August 1950. *Destination Freedom* was a powerful half-hour presentation of dramatic sketches about a wide range of African-American history makers, including baseball's Jackie Robinson, renowned surgeon Dr. Daniel Hale Williams, and journalist/activist Ida B. Wells. *Destination Freedom* was notable for its dignified presentation of African Americans and for Durham's brilliant and politically outspoken scripts. Unfortunately, many of these and subsequent black dramatic series were short-lived, since they failed to find the long-term sponsors or consistent funding sources that could sustain them.

Black Radio: Telling It Like It Was. a 13-part radio documentary series with Lou Rawls. Washington, D.C.: Radio Smithsonian, Smithsonian Productions, 1996. (Series tapes are available for research at the Archives of African American Music and Culture, Indiana University, Bloomington; and the Museums of Radio and Television in Los Angeles and New York.)

MacDonald, J. Fred. *Don't Touch That Dial!: Radio Programming in American Life, 1920–1960.* Chicago: Nelson-Hall, 1979.

MacDonald, J. Fred, ed. *Richard Durham's Destination Freedom: Scripts from Radio's Black Legacy, 1948–50.* New York: Praeger Publishers, 1989.

Sonja Williams

BLACK FORMATS. During the latter half of the 1940s, WDIA in Memphis, Tennessee, became the first station in the country to devote all of its programming to African Americans. Prior to this point, there were no all-black-oriented stations in the country, and racial segregation kept most blacks off the air on a regular basis (notable exceptions include Chicago *Black Appeal* and disc jockeys (DJs) Jack L. Cooper and Al Benson). In the 1940s, audiences and advertisers also were flocking to an exciting new medium called television, and radio station owners had to find ways to maintain listeners and generate revenue.

In 1947, WDIA owners Bert Ferguson and John Pepper fought bankruptcy by trying many different types of programming formats before they settled on the previously untapped creative and commercial "Negro" market. During the latter part of 1948, a WDIA black music program hosted by Nat D. Williams, known as the "Mid-South's First Black DJ," became so popular among Memphis' nearly 40 percent black population that Ferguson and Pepper experimented with expanding the show. Their gamble paid off, and they eventually transformed WDIA into a "black-appeal" station, the nation's first radio station programmed entirely by and for African Americans. WDIA's programming mainstay was the popular rhythm and blues (R&B) and gospel music of the day, hosted by a personable DJ staff that included Nat D., Riley B. King (blues great B. B. King), R&B singer Rufus Thomas, and Martha Jean "The Queen" Steinberg. WDIA's commercial spots were often hilarious and attention grabbing, and white advertisers, who were initially reluctant to deal with an all-black station, soon saw the lucrative economic potential of the African-American consumer. Eventually, WDIA became the first Memphis station to earn a million dollars from advertising, and the station jumped to the top of the city's popularity charts.

Known as "The Goodwill Station," WDIA's successful music and information programming and commercial appeal inspired hundreds of other stations to develop all-black formats, and in 1949, WERD in Atlanta, Georgia, became the first African-American owned-and-operated "black-appeal," or black-formatted, station. During the next 40 years, African-American formatted stations evolved, continuing to be driven by powerful black music, public affairs programs, and DJs with flashy names like "Hot Rod," "Doctor Daddy-O," "Jacko," "Doctor Hep Cat," and "Chattie Hattie." Some of these DJs, with their hip language and colorful, talkative personalities, became almost as popular as the artists they played, and thus their stations' ratings skyrocketed.

Black-formatted stations developed trendsetting music-intensive programming concepts like "Soul Radio," "The Total Black Experience in Sound," and "The Quiet Storm," some of which are still used today. For example, "The Quiet Storm's" soothing mixture of love songs and mellow tunes as developed by Howard University's WHUR during the 1970s is still programmed by some black stations today. In the 1990s, most black-formatted stations are music driven and are labeled "urban contemporary." These stations tend to target specific, narrow demographic segments of the black community, unlike the wider demographic appeal of stations during black-formatted radio's early days.

Black Radio: Telling It Like It Was. a 13-part radio documentary series with Lou Rawls. Washington, D.C.: Radio Smithsonian, Smithsonian Productions, 1996. (Series tapes are available for research at the Archives of African American Music and Culture, Indiana University, Bloomington; and the Museums of Radio and Television in Los Angeles and New York.)

Cantor, Louis. *Wheeling on Beale: How WDIA-Memphis Became the Nation's First All-Black Radio Station and Created the Sound that Changed America.* New York: Pharos, 1992.

George, Nelson. *The Death of Rhythm & Blues.* New York: Plume, 1988.

Sonja Williams

BLUE BOOK. *See* **codes of ethics; programming; and regulation.**

BLUEGRASS MUSIC, a style of country music developed in the mid-1940s by Bill Monroe and his Bluegrass Boys, is notable by its use of acoustic guitars, mandolins, banjos, and high tenor singing. Never a widely popular radio format, it is notable for its long-lasting niche success in selected dayparts by small-town radio stations throughout the South and by public radio stations in urban areas where transplanted southerners have moved, such as Washington, D.C.

Rosenberg, Neil V. *Bluegrass: A History.* Urbana, Ill.: University of Illinois Press, 1985.

Smith, Richard D. *Bluegrass.* Chicago: Cappella, 1995.

Douglas Gomery

BLUE NETWORK. The idea of linking radio stations together to share common programming was formalized in 1927 when RCA organized its stations into a subsidiary, National Broadcasting Company (NBC) and formed two groups, a Red Network and a Blue Network, with different programming serving each set of stations. In 1941, the Federal Communications Commission (FCC) adopted regulations restricting ownership of "chain broadcasting." The results were that NBC divested its Blue Network in 1943 to a candy manufacturer, Edward Noble, who changed its name to American Broadcasting Company (ABC), thus beginning one of the main competing national radio networks.

Val E. Limburg

BLUES MUSIC, a style of African-American popular music that takes its name from the term applied to a melancholy state of mind. The lyrics, which usually express feelings of loneliness and depression, are crucial to the structure of blues, which relies underlying chord sequences of 8, 12, and 16 bars (see **rhythm and blues**).

Sadie, Stanley, with Alison Latham, eds. *Brief Guide to Music.* 2nd ed. Englewood Cliffs, N.J.: Prentice-Hall, 1990.

Frederic A. Leigh

BMI (BROADCAST MUSIC INCORPORATED) is a nonprofit music-licensing organization representing more than 180,000 publishers and songwriters. BMI distributes royalties to its affiliates for the public performance and digital home copying of their works. BMI was established in 1939 by broadcasters as an alternative music-licensing agency to the American Society of Composers Authors and Publishers (ASCAP). ASCAP had proposed a major increase in rates charged to radio stations to license music to be played on the air, so broadcasters banded together to fight this increase and formed BMI. Eventually, the dispute between broadcasters and ASCAP was resolved; however, BMI remained as a second music-licensing organization in the United States. In the 1940s, BMI built its own catalog and established its own publishing company, which was later sold when the number of independent publishers serving BMI songwriters reached a sufficient number.

BMI has since surpassed ASCAP in the number of writers and publishers affiliated with the organization, but ASCAP realizes a larger gross income. Although BMI affiliates represent all forms of music, historically they have tended to be songwriters and publishers from rock, rhythm and blues, country, jazz, and gospel. Similarly, ASCAP members come from the entire spectrum of the music industry, but musical theater and motion picture publishers, songwriters, and lyricists tend to favor ASCAP membership.

BMI operates subject to a consent decree issued by the Department of Justice in 1966. This decree provides oversight of BMI's general operation, formulas for determining disbursement of royalties, and provisions for handling grievances filed by affiliates (see **ASCAP [American Society of Composers Authors and Publishers]; NAB**).

Baskerville, David. *Music Business Handbook & Career Guide.* 6th ed. Thousand Oaks, Calif.: Sage, 1996.
Fink, Michael. *Inside the Music Industry.* 2nd ed. New York: Schirmer Books, 1996.
BMI.Com. http://bmi.com/index.html (October 24, 1996).

Kenneth C. Creech

BONNEVILLE INTERNATIONAL CORPORATION (BIC) is a private corporation holding the interests of the Church of Jesus Christ of Latter-day Saints (Mormon) in one TV and 20 radio stations. The church began broadcasting in 1922 with KZN-AM (Salt Lake City), one of the first commercial radio stations. It separated KZN from its newspaper, the *Deseret News,* and in 1924 placed it in a separate company. A year later, the call sign changed to KSL.

KSL programmed commercially but carried the church's biannual conference proceedings. For 67 years, it has aired a Sunday morning broadcast featuring the Mormon Tabernacle Choir. It became a pioneer 50,000 watt, clear channel AM licensee, added an FM station, and joined the CBS Radio Network prior to 1946. Three years later, it started KSL-TV, a CBS affiliate.

In 1964, BIC was formed under the direction of church leaders and board members, with Arch Madsen as president. BIC began acquiring radio and TV stations, now owning AM and FM stations in New York City, Los Angeles, Chicago, Dallas, San Francisco, Phoenix, and Kansas City. It owns an AM/FM combination in Seattle but in 1994 sold a Seattle TV station. Dr. Rodney H. Brady succeeded

Madsen, and most recently, Bruce Reese became president and chief executive officer of BIC.

BIC owns two production companies (Video West and Third Avenue), LDS Radio Network, and Bonneville Entertainment Company. Before selling it in the 1980s, it owned a program-consulting firm (Bonneville Broadcast Consultants), which provided turnkey, automated beautiful music programming.

"Bonneville International Corporation." *Encyclopedia of Mormonism.* Vol. 1. New York: Macmillan Publishing Company, 1992.

Bonneville International Oral History Series. Conducted by Heritage Associates, W. Dee Halverson. Salt Lake City: Bonneville International Corporation, 1992.

Brady, Rodney H. *Bonneville International Corporation: A Values-Driven Company Composed of Values-Driven People.* New York: Newcomen Society of the U.S., 1994.

Godfrey, Donald G., Val Limburg, and Heber G. Wolsey."KSL Salt Lake: 'At the Crossroads of the West.'" In *Television in America: Local Station History from Across the Nation,* edited by Michael D. Murray and Donald G. Godfrey (pp. 338–352). Ames: Iowa State University Press, 1997.

Wolsey, Heber G. "The History of Radio Station KSL from 1922 to Television." (Ph.D. dissertation, Michigan State University, 1967).

J. R. Rush

BRAINARD, BERTHA, a broadcast executive at NBC, she was one of the highest paid women in the United States in the 1930s. She had held jobs as an ambulance driver, hotel manager, and journalist. She had listened to station WJZ in Newark, New Jersey, and decided to try for a job in radio. The first time she tried, the station wouldn't even let her in. The second time she came to the station, in 1922, she said that she had come to write a story about the station and she was welcomed. Once inside, she sold them her program idea, a weekly drama review of Broadway, *Broadcasting Broadway.* She brought in the Broadway stars for radio appearances and later was assigned to radio plays. Brainard was put in charge of the New York office for WJZ when it was opened, and when the main studio moved to New York, she was made assistant manager of the station. When NBC took over WJZ in 1926, Brainard became eastern program manager for the network. By 1937, she was one of the five top-salaried women in the United States.

One of her duties as program manager was to join her supervisor, John Royal, NBC vice president in charge of programs, dancing with advertising executives on Saturday mornings. They would, for example, go and test the Lucky Strike Orchestra. President of American Tobacco, George Washington Hill, spent much of his time increasing sales of Lucky Strike cigarettes. Hill had the advertising agency executives and NBC executives join him at rehearsals testing the danceability of the Lucky Strike Orchestra's foxtrot. Hill was known to have said that America should defeat the depression by dancing its way out.

Brainard recognized that radio offered equal opportunities to men and women, whoever had the initiative, the ideas, talent, and perseverance to make money for the station. Women made up the audience during the day and the stations hired women to program to them. However, she also noted that women's voices were not made for announcing. "The very qualities that make a woman's speaking voice pleasant: its softness, nuances, inflections and medium pitch are against her in announcing," said Bertha Brainard in 1926, as assistant broadcasting manager at WJZ in New York City. She encouraged women to go into programming, research, and the business side.

Marzolf, Marion. *Up from the Footnote: A History of Women Journalists.* New York: Hastings House, 1977.

Margot Hardenbergh

BRANLY, [DESIRÉ] EDOUARD (1844–1940), French physicist; inventor of first successful wireless detector. Son of a professor, Branly was a brilliant student at the École Normal Supérieure in Paris and later at the Lyceum de St. Quentin where his father taught. He earned his doctorate in physics at the Sorbonne and was later appointed a professor at the Institut Catholique in Paris. His initial interest in medicine and his study of nerves and how they carried messages led to his conceptualization of a wireless detector. While many of the basic features of his wireless detector originated with others, Branly was the first to develop a workable radio conductor (later termed a "coherer" by Oliver Lodge).

Branly demonstrated his detector idea before the French Academy in 1891. The device worked on the basis that applying voltage to metal plates on either side of a glass tube caused iron filings between the plates to cohere, thus indicating the presence of lower electrical resistance because of a signal (as in a dot or dash of Morse code). He experimented for some time before settling on iron conductors as the most efficient for his device. Any mechanical vibration—even loud sounds—could affect a coherer's operation. Further, until Marconi's work in the late 1890s, coherers were thought useful only in laboratory situations with very limited range. Others developed varied means, some automatic, of tapping the tube to make the iron filings "decohere," thus "restoring" the device to detect the next signal.

Branly continued to improve his device into the early 1900s, developing a tripod detector that was much more sensitive to weak wireless signals and could be more easily decohered. For roughly a decade, Branly's coherer (or variations of it) was the standard means of wireless detection in all countries. Only after about 1905 was it largely replaced by more sensitive and efficient electrolytic detectors developed by others. Branly continued scientific work into the early twentieth century but died at 96 in Paris, described as "a lonely, misunderstood, frustrated man."

"Edouard Branly Inventor of the Coherer." In *Radio's 100 Men of Science,* edited by Orrin E. Dunlap, Jr. (pp 76–79). New York: Harper, 1944.

McNicol, Donald. *Radio's Conquest of Space: The Experimental Rise in Radio Communication.* New York: Murray Hill Books, 1946. Reprinted by Arno Press, 1974.

Phillips, V. J. *Early Radio Wave Detectors.* London: Peter Peregrinus, 1980.

Christopher H. Sterling

BREAKOUT is the music industry term used to describe the rapid upward movement of a song or instrumental in the industry's tracking charts. In broadcasting, the term refers to a song or an instrumental that is receiving increased airplay either due to requests from listeners or because of a swift rise in the music charts.

The term is applied also to a particular selection on an album that is gaining popularity or attention rapidly. The term is applied to new artists as well as to established artists. The origin of the term is unknown.

Regis Tucci

BRINKLEY, JOHN R.(1885–1942), the case of, answered fundamental questions concerning how far the Federal Radio Commission (FRC) could go in denying station licenses by determining what programming is or is not in the public interest.

Brinkley's KFKB began with 500 watts, at 1050 kilocycles, in 1923, licensed to the Brinkley-Jones Hospital Association, Milford, Kansas, to help his hospital patients convalesce. By 1928, at 5 kilowatts, KFKB was one of North America's most powerful stations. Programming was live and typical of the era.

Nationally known as the "goat-gland doctor" for his rejuvenation operations, Brinkley began his own half-hour radio "health course" or *Medical Question Box* about 1929. From listener mail, he diagnosed unseen patients' symptoms, giving advice on radio, and prescribing medication by a code known only to his network of pharmacists. The audience mushroomed. In 1930, KFKB received *Radio Digest's* Golden Cup award as most popular station in the United States and Canada.

In 1930, following American Medical Association attacks and *Kansas City Star* reports, the FRC denied KFKB's license renewal, maintaining KFKB operated in Brinkley's *private* interest and that *Medical Question Box* was "inimical to public health and safety." One commissioner apparently believed Brinkley was doing no more than corporations do when promoting their products over their own stations.

The Kansas Medical Society challenged Brinkley's use of radio for medical diagnoses and remedies and revoked his medical license in September 1930. The next year, Brinkley sued the *Kansas City Star* for libel and appealed the FRC decision.

The U.S. Court of Appeals of the District of Columbia upheld the FRC, February 2, 1931, saying (1) that radio should operate in the public interest; (2) that serving the public interest, convenience, and necessity is a prerequisite for license renewal; radio should not operate as a mere adjunct of a business; (3) that applicants must show how the public will be served; (4) that character and quality of service must be judged; (5) that an applicant's past conduct is a factor in determining license renewal; and (6) when public interest, convenience, or necessity is not served, license denial is not censorship under the *Radio Act of 1927*.

Meanwhile, Brinkley introduced radio to Kansas political campaigning, almost winning a close three-way gubernatorial race as a write-in candidate in 1930, KFKB's last year. In 1934 he broadcast paid-political messages on local stations in the GOP primary but lost soundly to incumbent Alf Landon.

After losing his U.S. license, Brinkley temporarily broadcast by telephone line from Milford to Mexican superstation XER, then moved his radio studio to Texas. He died in Del Rio of a heart attack at age 56 on May 26, 1942.

Carson, Gerald. *The Roguish World of Doctor Brinkley.* New York: Holt, Rinehart & Winston, 1960.

Wood, Clement. *The Life of a Man, a Biography of John R. Brinkley.* Kansas City: Goshorn Publishing Co., 1934.

William James Ryan

BRITISH BROADCASTING COMPANY. *See* **BBC Radio.**

BROADCAST EDUCATION ASSOCIATION (BEA), formed in 1955, is an international organization of university professors and electronic media professionals working together to promote "educating tomorrow's electronic media professionals." BEA facilitates interaction between academicians, the industry, and students; publishes the *Journal of Broadcasting and Electronic Media,* the *Journal of Radio Studies,* and *Feedback;* and sponsors an annual convention and exhibition in conjunction with the National Association of Broadcasters. Headquartered in Washington, D.C., its purpose is to "improve education in electronic media."

Donald G. Godfrey

BROADCASTING & CABLE, a trade journal covering the broadcast and cable industries with features on radio, television, cable, and satellite. The journal, originally to have been titled *The Fifth Estate,* was established in 1931 by Sol Taishoff and Martin Codel. It was published by the Taishoff family until 1986, when it was purchased by the *Times Mirror.* The current publisher, Cahners Publishing, bought the journal in 1991.

"The First Sixty Years." *Broadcasting & Cable* 121 (24) (supp. December 9, 1991).

Frederic A. Leigh

BROADCAST MUSIC INCORPORATED. *See* **BMI (Broadcast Music Incorporated).**

BUCHENWALD. One of the most well-known German concentration camps liberated during World War II, it was the subject of a CBS Radio report by renowned war correspondent Edward R. Murrow. In his broadcast of April 15, 1945, Murrow vividly described firsthand the horrendous conditions in the camp on April 12, just one day after the camp had been liberated by the U.S. Third Army. In excerpts from his report, as it appears in *In Search of Light: The Broadcasts of Edward R. Murrow,* Murrow told listeners what he experienced as he entered the camp: "There surged around me an evil-smelling horde. Men and boys reached out to touch me; they were in rags and the remnants of uniform. Death had already marked many of them, but they were smiling with their eyes." He went on to describe the tattooed numbers on the arms of the camp's children: "In another part of the camp they showed me the children, hundreds of them. Some were only six. One rolled up his sleeve, showed me his number. . . . The others showed me their numbers; they will carry them till they die." Murrow could not describe all of Buchenwald's horror: "I pray you to believe what I have said about Buchenwald. I have reported what I saw and heard, but only part of it. For most of it, I have no words." According to *The Buchenwald Report,* during the next few months, Buchenwald became the focus of an intense publicity campaign by the United States and Great Britain to publicize German atrocities.

Bliss, Edward, Jr., ed. *In Search of Light: The Broadcasts of Edward R. Murrow, 1938–1961.* New York: Alfred A. Knopf, 1967.
Hackett, David. A., trans. *The Buchenwald Report.* San Francisco: Westview Press, 1995.

Erika Engstrom

BULLARD, ADMIRAL WILLIAM H. G., director of naval communications in 1919, convinced General Electric (GE) officials to form the Radio Corporation of America (RCA), thus starting American domination of radio communication in the twentieth century. Admiral Bullard graduated from the Naval Academy at Annapolis in 1886. In 1907, he established the department of electrical engineering at the Naval Academy, serving until 1911, when he became commandant at the San Francisco Naval Base.

Admiral Bullard became superintendent of the Naval Radio Service in 1912. He served in that capacity until 1916, when he commanded the battleship *Arkansas*. When serving as director of naval communications immediately following the war, the dependence of this country upon foreign-controlled radio patents had became apparent. GE held key patents adaptable to radio. But the American subsidiary of British Marconi was the leading factor in wireless transmission and reception in the country.

In 1915, one of GE's radio engineers, Dr. E. F. W. Alexanderson, perfected a machine generating a high-frequency signal. Marconi came to the United States to arrange for exclusive rights. Before the agreement could be concluded, Marconi returned to Italy to serve in World War I.

In 1917, GE installed a 50-kilowatt Alexanderson generator at Marconi's station at New Brunswick, New Jersey. The navy took over the New Brunswick station for war use from June 1918, five months before the armistice, until March 1, 1920, when it was restored to its owners. It carried the largest share of radio traffic between the United States and Europe because of its reliability and power. In March 1919, British Marconi sent representatives to finalize the exclusive rights to the Alexanderson alternator. GE insisted upon a royalty for the rights, causing some delay in the negotiations.

During this delay, Commander S. C. Hooper, chief of the Radio Division of the Navy Bureau of Engineering, went to Admiral Bullard, newly assigned as director of naval communications, and objected to the negotiations. The naval radio chiefs then met and asked the officers of GE on patriotic grounds to not make it impossible for an American radio communication company to enter the field on a fair competitive basis with foreign radio companies.

The pleading aroused GE officials to break off their negotiations to work out the formation of a company controlled wholly by Americans. The American Marconi stations were purchased as a nucleus and their personnel hired.

The Radio Corporation of America was organized by GE in October 1919, and Admiral W. H. G. Bullard was named the government representative to the board of directors. In 1921, Bullard served as commander of the Yangtse River patrol force of the Asiatic fleet until his retirement on September 30, 1922. In 1923 he was named a delegate to the International Safety-at-Sea Conference in London. He also worked for RCA obtaining radio concessions in China. President Coolidge then appointed him as chairman of the newly created Federal Radio Commission, which had been signed into law on February 24, 1927. Some six months after returning to the United States, on November 24, 1927, Admiral Bullard died.

"Bullard, Radio Chief, Faces a Difficult Task." *New York Times,* April 17, 1927, sec. VIII, p. 22:1.

Howeth, Captain L. S. *History of Communications–Electronics in the United States Navy.* Washington, D.C.: Government Printing Office, 1963.

Marvin R. Bensman

BURNOUT, MUSIC. Music played on the radio is said to be "burned" or suffering from "burnout" when a significant number of listeners polled by a given station say that they are tired of hearing a particular song.

Music rotations, and especially power rotations, which purposely play certain songs more often than others, are one of the major causes of burnout, but overexposure of a certain artist or too much concentration on one style of music can also cause it. The amount of burnout suffered by a popular record varies from city to city because of differences in the frequency of plays by stations in different markets. It also varies by demographic groups, with heavy listeners tending to burn out sooner than occasional listeners. That usually means that new music burns out sooner with teenagers than with any other group.

Most songs do not stay "burned." Records that drop out of a power rotation are often rested for a while, or are put back on the air as "recurrents." Later, they will usually reappear regularly as "gold" (oldies). But because oldies are used by most stations, and there are classic or oldies formats in many markets, even the oldies have to be tested for burnout.

David T. MacFarland

BURNS, GEORGE (1896–1996), was a performer for 93 years and a comedy headliner for more than 70 in vaudeville, radio, television, and movies. His most successful professional years were spent with his wife and partner, Gracie Allen: The *Burns and Allen* comedy show ran on CBS radio and television from 1932 until 1958.

Born Nathan Birnbaum on New York's Lower East Side, Burns had little formal education and began singing and dancing on the streets at age 5. Into his midtwenties he had a modest vaudeville career (including at one time a performing seal act), specializing in singing, dancing, and comic patter. He hit the big time after partnering with Gracie Allen, starting in 1923; they married in 1926. Their routines were a variation on the vaudeville staple of repartee between a wisecracking man and a scatterbrained woman. Burns, who wrote most of their early material, quickly altered the standard format to give Gracie all the punch lines, developing for himself a distinctive straight-man persona. For 35 years they regularly found comedy in the interplay between Gracie's "illogical logic," as Burns called it, and his bemused responses. (GEORGE: "Did the maid ever drop you on your head when you were a baby?" GRACIE: "Don't be silly. We couldn't afford a maid. My mother had to do it.") Even as a straight man, Burns knew how to get a laugh. (GRACIE: "A funny thing happened to my mother in Cleveland." GEORGE: "I thought you were born in Buffalo.")

Burns and Allen first appeared on radio during a tour of England in 1929–1930. Back in the United States they did guest spots, appeared in movies like *The Big Broadcast* and *International House,* and became regulars on Guy Lombardo's CBS program, doing their segments via telephone from Los Angeles to the studio in New York. Their own CBS program began in 1932, *The Adventures of Gracie,* soon renamed *The George Burns and Gracie Allen Show.* Though they now employed comedy writers, Burns continued to take an active role in developing their routines. When their top ratings declined between 1939 and 1941, Burns realized that the pair were too old for their boy-girl "street-corner act," so he switched formats to a domestic situation comedy set in Beverly Hills. Essentially playing themselves, George and Gracie drew supporting talent from the Hollywood community, including Gale Gordon, Mel Blanc, and Bea Benadaret. The show was top-rated throughout the 1940s. Beginning in 1950, the same format was used on television, ending only with Gracie's retirement in 1958 due to poor health.

After a two-decade career slump, Burns roared back in his eighties, winning an Oscar for *The Sunshine Boys* (1977), a part he inherited after the death of his best friend Jack Benny. Now a national institution, Burns continued making movies, television appearances, and club performances into his late nineties. But failing health forced him to cancel a planned Las Vegas engagement on his hundredth birthday, and he was unable to participate in the widespread celebrations of the date. He died 48 days later (see **Allen, Gracie**).

Burns, George, with David Fisher. *Gracie: A Love Story.* New York: G. P. Putnam's Sons, 1988.
Gottfried, Martin. *George Burns: The Hundred-Year Dash.* New York: Simon & Schuster, 1996.
Wertheim, Arthur Frank. *Radio Comedy.* New York: Oxford University Press, 1979.

Glen M. Johnson

BUSINESS NEWS NETWORK (BNN) is a syndicated news and financial information network. It was formed as the Business Radio Network (BRN) in 1988 but underwent a name change with the arrival of new owners in 1995. BNN distributes its programming 24 hours a day, seven days a week via satellite, and targets its format toward listeners with an interest in continuous business and financial news. In essence, it is the radio equivalent of cable television's financial news networks. BNN supplements its numerous market reports and analysis with call-in talk shows offering financial advice and opinion, as well as shows dealing with the traditional talk-show topics of politics and public policy. Also offered are programs featuring information about travel, technology, and recreational activities. As with other talk-oriented formats, BNN provides regular newscasts in its program mix. The network claims its typical listeners are professional decision makers, highly educated, and in their peak earning years. BNN affiliates have the option of carrying the entire network schedule or selecting various shows to serve as supplements to preexisting local formats. Most full-time BNN affiliates are AM stations. BNN's corporate office is in Washington, D.C.; programming office, Colorado Springs, Colorado; sales office, New York; and affiliate relations office, Providence, Rhode Island.

Kenneth D. Loomis

C

CABLE RADIO, radio programming delivered on cable television systems as digital or analog signals, then received through cable converters and amplified through subscribers' home stereo speakers. Radio programming on cable channels began in the 1970s and 1980s, providing better reception of local FM or AM radio signals. These were processed through cable TV antennas and head-ends and heard as background music for local origination cable channels.

During the mid-1980s, cable TV operators experimented with made-for-cable radio programming. Digital Cable Radio (DCR) began offering to subscribers for a fee several channels of high-fidelity radio programs in varying formats. Its investors were Jerrold Electronics and Comcast Cable.

As a variant of cable radio, some cable TV operators create local origination programs by simulcasting live video coverage of news, talk, and entertainment programming taken from local radio stations. For example, CSPAN arranged to cable-cast radio programming of Washington, D.C., and Atlanta, Georgia, stations.

Most recently, digital audio programming has been targeted for expansion by DCR, DMX, and Digital Planet, all firms focusing on the sale of digital-cable-radio feeds to cable operators. Two major music recording firms, Sony Software and MCA Recording, have purchased interests in DCR or DMX, each of which also have as investors large cable TV firms. These companies like the potential for reaching the CD music-buying audiences with CD-quality cable radio. For cable subscribers, the appeal of cable radio is the high-fidelity sound and the many, varied channels of high-quality music.

Brown, R. "Time Warner Takes Stake in Cable Radio." *Broadcasting* 123 (6) (February 8, 1993): 31.

Vizard, Frank. "Good Morning, Cable Radio." *Popular Mechanics* 170 (5) (May 1993): 118–119.

Vizard, Frank. "The Return of Digital Radio on Cable." *Broadcasting* 118 (26) (June 25, 1990): 50–52.

J. R. Rush

CALL LETTERS are combinations of alphabetic letters used to legally identify a radio station. In the early 1920s, three-letter combinations (WHO) were used, but this quickly changed to four-letter groupings (WEAF) as the number of radio stations increased. The type of station, AM or FM, is often tacked on the end of the call letters. Stations choose their own call letters, subject to some restrictions, as long as they do not duplicate any existing ones. According to custom and Federal Communications Commission (FCC) ruling, stations west of the Mississippi River use an initial letter of "K" and stations east of the Mississippi River utilize call letters beginning with a "W." However, one pioneer radio station (KDKA, Pittsburgh) didn't follow this convention. Call letter combinations must be in good taste and are subject to FCC approval. Stations also use call letters for promotional purposes and often choose combinations that are pronounceable (KISS, WACK, or KAAT) or easily remembered (KQKQ or WZZZ). Other call letters origins have a special significance, such as geographic location (KICY), format programmed (WJZZ), or station ownership (KCBS).

Peterson, Alan. "WILD, WAKY, KRZY Call Letter Combos." *Radio World* (December 27, 1995): 34.

Strak, Phyllis. "Stations Spell Out Tradition." *Billboard* (March 13, 1993): 14+.

David E. Reese

CANON 35. This guideline of the American Bar Association's (ABA's) Code of Judicial Conduct was instituted in 1937 and effectively served to forbid broadcast coverage of courtrooms for years to come. The ABA rule became a catalyst for debating the sometimes-conflicting interests of a free press and the rights of the accused to receive a fair trial.

The canon was instituted in response to media excesses at the 1935 trial of Bruno Hauptmann, who was accused of kidnapping and murdering the baby of national hero and aviator Charles Lindbergh. The judge found it difficult to control members of the media during the trial. Reporters from both the print and broadcast media moved about the courtroom, taking photographs and generally disrupting the proceedings.

To eliminate such press abuses, the ABA moved to ban photographic and broadcast coverage. Canon 35 stated that the presence of photographic and broadcast equipment compromised the dignity of legal proceedings, degraded the court, distracted participants in the trial, and created misconceptions in the mind of the public. While the ABA ban did not have the direct power of law, the guidelines were largely adopted in state statutes around the nation.

The ban on photographic and broadcast coverage of trials was put to a constitutional test in a 1965 Supreme Court decision. The case under appeal involved Billie Sol Estes, who was convicted in Texas of swindling. Texas was a state that occasionally allowed electronic coverage of trials. Cameras and microphones were allowed during the Estes trial, and like the Hauptmann trial years earlier, the media presence was distracting to the proceedings. In a 5–4 decision, the Supreme Court overturned the conviction, ruling that Estes had been denied a fair trial because of the presence of cameras and microphones. Justice Tom Clark, while acknowledging the importance of press freedoms in a democracy, wrote that the decision was based on preserving "absolute fairness in the judicial process."

The Supreme Court later, however, largely removed the constitutional barrier of the Estes decision in a 1981 ruling. As a result of improved television technology and journalists' assurances of responsible judgments in covering trials, some states, including Florida, began to again allow experimentation with cameras in the court. The *Chandler* decision involved two Miami police officers accused of conspiracy. They appealed their conviction solely on the basis that the judge had allowed electronic media coverage of the trial. A unanimous Supreme Court ruled that the mere presence of cameras and microphones in the court does not automatically make the trial unfair. While indicating that such media coverage could raise questions of fairness, Chief Justice Warren Burger wrote that there was insufficient empirical data to support a universal ban.

The effect of the *Chandler* decision has been to open up all but a handful of state courts to camera and microphone coverage. Federal courts are now open to electronic coverage only at the appellate level, with trial and Supreme Court proceedings still restricted. Thus, decades after the approval of Canon 35, the nation still debates whether the interests of media access and public awareness of court proceedings outweigh the possible unfairness to the participants that such coverage might bring.

Chandler v. Florida, 449 U.S. 560 (1981)
Estes v. Texas, 381 U.S. 532 (1965).

Jeffrey M. McCall

CAPEHART, HOMER E. (1897–1970), established the Automatic Phonograph Corporation in 1927, which later became the Capehart Corporation, Fort Wayne, Indiana. It had the reputation for making expensive but well-manufactured radio receivers. Capehart served as founder and president from 1927 to 1932. The depression took its toll on the corporation, but during the depression, he persuaded the Wurlitzer Company to produce the first jukeboxes. This investment helped make him a millionaire. He was vice president of the Wurlitzer Company from 1933 to 1940. The Capehart Corporation itself was sold in 1938 to the Farnsworth Radio and Television Corporation, which was banking on the Capehart reputation to assist in its manufacture of radio and television receivers. Homer E. Capehart left the business world to run for the Senate, where he served from 1944 to 1963.

Pickett, William B. *Homer E. Capehart: A Senator's Life.* Indianapolis, Ind.: Indiana Historical Society, 1990.

Donald G. Godfrey

CAPITAL CITIES COMMUNICATION is a media company that began as Hudson Valley Broadcasting, expanded its broadcast holdings, changed its name, diversified into publishing, and in 1986, acquired the American Broadcasting Company. Ten years later, Capital Cities/ABC was purchased by the Disney Corporation.

In 1957, Hudson Valley Broadcasting of New York purchased a Raleigh, North Carolina, broadcasting station and went public as Capital Cities Communication. Capital Cities' founder Frank Smith bought and sold radio and TV stations and publications for the company until his death in 1966, but it was Thomas Murphy who operated the company. Thomas Murphy had been hired by Hudson Valley Broadcasting in 1954 to bail out a financially troubled television station in Albany, New York. Murphy earned a degree in mechanical engineering from Cornell, served in the navy, and graduated from the Harvard Business School in 1947. Under Murphy's leadership, Capital Cities Communication diversified. In 1968, Capital Cities purchased Fairchild Publications. Other publication purchases and sales followed. Capital Cities also purchased cable systems, which it sold in 1986 as it merged with ABC. With its acquisition of ABC, the publishing group included the *Kansas City Star,* the *Fort-Worth Star-Telegram,* a major business publisher in Mexico, farming journals, and medical news publications such as *Aches & Pains.*

Many attribute the success of Capital Cities to Murphy's leadership style. He endorsed both cost control and local control, giving each property the opportunity to prosper by responding to its community and business climate. With 1982 revenues of $663 million, for example, the company's corporate overhead was just $7 million, and its New York headquarters had only 31 employees. He kept company overhead low by not having a corporate jet, legal department, or public relations staff. He employed those whose abilities he admired, regardless of their education or experience, and he rewarded them. At one point, 17 percent of the company's outstanding shares originated in stock options or stock purchase plans. Many executives served the company for 20 years or more.

In 1986, Capital Cities Communication acquired the much larger American Broadcasting Company (ABC) in a $3.5 billion deal. Warren Buffett's Berkshire Hathaway assisted in completing the purchase. Once Capital Cities/ABC purchased some shares, Berkshire Hathaway held 13 percent of the stock. Capital Cities/ABC was organized into several operating units, including Capital Cities Media, Capital Cities Media Inc. Fairchild Books and Visuals, Capital Cities Media Inc. Fairchild Publications Division, Capital Cities/ABC Inc. ABC Cable and International Broadcast Group, Capital Cities/ABC Inc. ABC Entertainment, Capital Cities/ABC Inc. ABC News, Capital Cities/ABC Inc. ABC Radio, Capital Cities/ABC Inc. ABC Sports, Capital Cities/ABC Inc. NILS Publishing Co., Capital Cities/ABC Inc. Shore Line, and Capital Cities/ABC Video Publishing Inc. On February 9, 1996, the Walt Disney Company acquired Capital Cities/ABC, Inc., creating the biggest media company in the world.

Hoover's Handbook of American Business. 2 vols. Austin: Hoover's Business Press, Inc., 1996.

Mirabile, Lisa, ed. "Capital Cities/ABC Inc." *International Directory of Company Histories.* Vol. 2. Chicago: St. James Press, 1990.

Sherman, Stratford P. "Capital Cities' Capital Coup." *Fortune* 112 (1) (April 15, 1985): 51–52.

Larry L. Jurney

CARLIN, GEORGE (1937–), comedian whose monologue on "filthy words" was broadcast on a New York City radio station in 1973. The broadcast of sexually oriented words generally considered unsuitable for radio and television resulted in a test case of the Federal Communications Commission (FCC) rules on indecent language. In 1978, the Supreme Court ruled that the FCC could require broadcast stations to "channel" indecent language to a time when children were least likely to be listening or viewing (see also **indecency; obscenity**).

Pember, Don R. *Mass Media Law.* Dubuque, Iowa: Brown & Benchmark, 1996.

Frederic A. Leigh

CARNEGIE COMMISSION. The Carnegie Commission on Educational Television grew out of recommendations from the First National Conference on Long-Range Financing of Educational Television in December 1964 and eventually had an important, though indirect, impact on the development of public radio. The commission was financed by a $500,000 grant from the Carnegie Corporation as a "blue ribbon" committee whose 15 members were appointed by President Lyndon B. Johnson. Credited with creating the term "public television," the Carnegie Commission released its report, *Public Television: A Program for Action,* on January 26, 1967. Included in the 12 recommendations set forth by the commission were enhanced funding for noncommercial educational television at all levels—federal, state, and local—and the creation of a nonprofit, nongovernmental corporation by an act of Congress that would disburse public and private funds to the stations. Encouraged by the quality and strength of the commission's report, President Johnson followed quickly with his own proposal to Congress based largely on the commission's recommendations. Senate and House bills resulting directly from these actions led to the passage of the *Public Broadcasting Act of 1967,* which included explicit provisions for public radio. While public radio was indeed added to this landmark legislation almost as an afterthought, educational radio would have remained an undernourished, hidden medium had it not been for the Carnegie Commission's leadership in calling for a strengthening of America's public television system.

Burke, John E. "The *Public Broadcasting Act of 1967:* Part I: Historical Origins and the Carnegie Commission." *Educational Broadcasting Review* 6 (April 1972): 105–119.

Carnegie Commission on Educational Television. *Public Television: A Program for Action.* New York: Bantam Books, 1967.

Robert K. Avery

CARTER, BOAKE R. (1903–1944). Born Harold Thomas Henry Carter, conservative CBS Radio news commentator in the 1930s. Carter was born in Baku, Russia, the son of an English oil firm official, who soon moved the family back to Britain. Carter enlisted at age 15 with the Royal Air Corps' coast patrol in World War I, then attended a private boy's school in Tonbridge, Kent. He began his journalism career at the *London Daily Mail* in the summer of 1921, then followed his father to a number of Latin American locations, working as a newspaper reporter. He settled in Philadelphia in the early 1920s and married a society editor of the *Philadelphia*

Evening Bulletin, where he also worked. Carter began working at WCAU in 1930 and a year later took on the name "Boake" (an old family name). He had a regular, sponsored five-minute newscast twice a day by 1931.

Carter reached the height of his fame with his 1932–1935 coverage of the Lindbergh kidnapping and later trial. He was on CBS on weeknights until mid-1938, sponsored by Philco Radio. Carter was known for his rapid-fire pace and use of metaphor and clichés to create imagery in listeners' minds. President Roosevelt was referred to as "the Boss." But Carter's commentary both on the air and in a parallel newspaper column became increasingly conservative in tone, attacking labor and the New Deal with considerable vigor. Yet he remained highly popular, judging from published ratings. He authored several quickly written books arguing against American meddling in world affairs, reflecting widespread American support for an isolationist outlook. His popularity helped pave the way for other, often more serious and soundly based commentary on the air.

By early 1938, however, substantial questions had arisen concerning the basis for Carter's attacks on the administration (and other targets), which were often more a matter of innuendo and misinformation than serious reporting. Complaints flooded into both CBS and Carter's sponsors with the result that in April 1938 he was taken off the air.

Although his newspaper column continued, he was never able to gain a consistent radio berth after 1938. Despite a history of support for isolationism, he became a booster of the war effort after the Pearl Harbor attack. Still, many of his commentaries were increasingly bizarre and reflected his own changing religious views. Some observers (not all of them critics) felt that he suffered from mental strain, evident in his sometimes odd pronouncements. Carter died of a heart attack, largely forgotten, just six years after leaving network radio.

Culbert, David H. "Boake Carter: Columbia's Voice of Doom." In *News for Everyman: Radio and Foreign Affairs in Thirties America* (pp. 34–66). Westport, Conn.: Greenwood, 1976.

Fang, Irving E. "Boake Carter." In *Those Radio Commentators!* (pp. 107–119). Ames: Iowa State University Press, 1977.

Christopher H. Sterling

CASH BOX is the international music record magazine. Launched in 1941 for the coin-machine industry, this weekly magazine matured in the 1950s to become a trade publication for music artists and their promoters. Mirroring its more famous big brother *Billboard, Cash Box* publishes competing national music charts used by radio stations to determine local playlists of current music. A lively mix of music surveys, feature stories, and reviews of new music results in an average weekly circulation of 20,339. Publisher George Albert markets the magazine as a trade publication to record company executives. Radio programmers, music artists and publishers, and talent and booking agents read it regularly. Albert bought the magazine in 1950 from its cofounder Joseph Orleck, an early force at *Billboard* magazine and a semipro baseball and basketball player.

The corporate headquarters moved from Manhattan to Los Angeles in 1971. It did so as much of the music industry launched West Coast operations. The magazine's weekly editorials served as cheer sections for the maturation of the rock 'n' roll industry. A January 11, 1969, editorial argued the irrelevancy of trying to justify rock, declaring that "Those who create or admire rock need no longer apologize for it."

   Cash Box pioneered coverage of the international popular music industry. A January 9, 1960, editorial urged readers to "recognize the foreign market as a major area for record sales." Rock music historian Philip Ennis describes this editorial as a flash of recognition for a worldwide audience. "One straightforward voice educating the parochial leaders of the vending industry came from George Albert, *eminance grise* of *Cash Box*," Ennis writes. "His message about the one world market may have seemed premature. There were, however, already indications that the specific pop stream traffic between London and New York was quickening."

   Cash Box, like *Billboard,* is an important cycle in the food chain of popular music. It tracks a tune from its release through exposure on radio, music television formats, in discos and on jukeboxes, to sales consumption by the worldwide music audience. Its pages form the press needed to propel the artists and their music successfully through the commercial cycle.

Ennis, Philip H. *The Seventh Stream: The Emergence of Rock 'n' Roll in American Popular Music.* Hanover, N.H.: University Press of New England, 1992.
"Irrelevant Justification." *Cash Box* (January 11, 1969): 3.
"Orleck, Joseph P." *New York Times,* February 6, 1997, sec. B, paid death notices, col. 1, p. 13.
"World Market–1960." *Cash Box* (January 9, 1960).
Cash Box. http://www.cashbox.com

                                                                                                    B. William Silcock

CAVALCADE OF AMERICA, a series of dramatized history sponsored by E. I. Dupont de Nemours & Company, broadcast on radio from 1935 to 1952 and on television from 1952 to 1955. It won many awards for "best educational series," and its broadcasts were used by high school teachers as home assignments. The series won considerable prestige. Such writers as Maxwell Anderson, Stephen Vincent Benet, Carl Sandburg, and Robert Sherwood were at times found willing to accept a special commission, but most scripts were the work of radio writers of the time little known to the general public—such as Arthur Arent, Peter Lyon, Norman Rosten, and Arthur Miller. The last mentioned was frequently represented on *Cavalcade of America* until his Broadway successes propelled him into world fame.

   Most programs were biographical, but accounts of scientific achievement such as *Rocky Mountain Spotted Fever,* dramatizing the struggle to find a vaccine, were also frequently used. From the start the commercials spoke of the sponsor's dedication to "better things for better living," to which the words "through chemistry" were soon added—a linkage reminding audiences of the rapid rise of nylon and other plastics.

   The launching of *Cavalcade of America* and its editorial emphases were strongly influenced by 1935 Senate hearings chaired by Senator Gerald P. Nye of North Dakota on World War I munitions profits. These revealed that Dupont had made 40 percent of the explosive powders used by the Allies, yielding war profits of $237,908,339,64 and sending Dupont stock from $125 to $593. These findings gave currency to the phrase "merchants of death." Immediately after the hearings, Dupont's advertising agency, Batten, Barton, Durstine and Osborn (BBD&O), recommended that the company undertake a radio series on American history, emphasizing humanitarian progress—especially improvements in the life of women—and avoiding war exploits. Bruce Barton, BBD&O partner, considered a master strategist in corporate public relations, was credited with formulating this policy. It made its mark on the series. From the start the sound of gunfire was taboo on *Cavalcade*. The name Dupont was henceforth to be associated, especially by the young, with humanitarian progress rather than war.

The "no-shooting" rule did not trouble writers; on the contrary, it attracted to the series young writers of pacifist and even socialist bent. Arthur Miller and Norman Rosten had both attended the University of Michigan, where many students had signed the "Oxford Pledge" never to go to war. Thus, the social concerns of young writers coincided, for the moment, with Dupont public relations interests. Research studies during the following years indicated that public opinion improved significantly by the end of the 1930s—a turnaround that Bruce Barton ascribed to nylon and *Cavalcade*.

The series acquired other taboos besides war. Like many other sponsors, Dupont was anxious to avoid race and labor issues. For over a decade, biographies commissioned for the series included no blacks. BBD&O warned that this would become a serious public relations liability. In 1948, when *Cavalcade* finally presented the career of a black, the choice fell on Booker T. Washington, who wanted blacks to be patient until better educated.

Cavalcade scripts were reviewed for BBD&O by Yale University historian Frank Monaghan, who sometimes worked closely with writers to ensure historic accuracy. Most of the scripts, considered individually, were punctilious in this respect. Yet the series as a whole, in its choice of topics, reflected a highly selective treatment of American history.

Erik Barnouw

CBS NEWS. The CBS News Network was a freestanding company formed by William S. Paley as part of the Columbia Broadcasting System. Paley began CBS's focus on news in 1930 when he hired Edward Klauber of the *New York Times* to be his executive vice president and Paul White as news editor.

In the 1920s and 1930s, network news consisted primarily of "events" coverage, including presidential speeches and election results. The first information broadcasts were done by "commentators" such as world traveler and raconteur Lowell Thomas. The 1932 kidnapping of Charles Lindbergh's baby forced the infant network news departments to respond quickly to breaking news. CBS was nudged into news activism when newspaper publishers pressured the Associated Press, United Press, and the International News Service agencies into not providing copy to broadcasters. A 10-year fight between publishers and broadcasters came to a head in 1933 when the press agencies cut off service to the networks. Paul White at CBS responded by setting up Columbia News Service bureaus in New York, Washington, Chicago, and Los Angeles. In 1934 a truce was signed, and CBS gave up its news service, agreeing to use news summaries the press associations provided free of charge.

William Paley sent Cesar Saerchinger to London to line up people to be interviewed on foreign affairs topics. The move positioned CBS News to cover the Spanish Civil War and World War II. In 1935 Edward R. Murrow joined CBS as director of talks and education. Three years later Murrow was in Europe. Murrow's broadcasts from London during the Blitz have no comparison.

World War II created a national appetite for news on radio and led to the creation of formal newsgathering organizations at CBS, NBC, and Mutual. ABC was in its formative stages.

Edward R. Murrow returned from London in 1946 to head CBS News. By then, radio news was broadcast hourly. Creative war correspondents had developed a new style of reporting, which relied on conversational language and on-scene audio.

CBS News began transmitting brief television news broadcasts in 1941 over New York station WCBW. Douglas Edwards anchored a television news program in 1947, and in August 1948, Edwards began appearing as anchor of the *CBS-TV News,* a 15-minute weekday evening broadcast. The anchor seat passed to Walter Cronkite in 1962, and the evening news was expanded to 30 minutes the following year.

Cronkite became the point man for a large, highly expert news organization with bureaus in key world capitals and a solid domestic infrasture of bureaus, owned stations, and affiliates. Walter Cronkite reached the pinnacle of his influence in 1968, when he visited Vietnam during the devastating North Vietnamese Tet offensive. Cronkite broadcast a rare commentary and suggested the United States negotiate a peace in Vietnam. A month later, a stunned President Lyndon Johnson called for peace talks and buried his plans to run for reelection.

CBS News underwent management and philosophic changes in the 1980s, during turmoil at the top of CBS Inc., and later suffered draconian budget and personnel cuts as Laurence Tisch wrested control of CBS Inc. from William Paley in 1985 and 1986. The news organization lost supremacy to NBC and ABC in the late 1980s and early 1990s. It was no longer the jewel of William Paley's "Tiffany Network" or the showplace for superior talent.

Bliss, Edward, Jr. *Now the News: The Story of Broadcast Journalism.* New York: Columbia University Press, 1991.
Boyer, Peter J. *Who Killed CBS? The Undoing of America's Number One News Network.* New York: Random House, 1988.
Godfrey, Donald G. "CBS World News Roundup: Setting the Stage for the Next Half Century." *American Journalism* 7 (3) (summer 1990): 164–172.
Paley, William S. *As It Happened: A Memoir.* Garden City, N.Y.: Doubleday, 1979.

Phillip O. Keirstead

CENSORSHIP. The Universal Declaration of Human Rights (UDHR) and the major international human rights treaties all guarantee freedom of expression as a basic right of human beings. Article 19 of the UDHR states: "Everyone has the right to freedom of opinion and expression; this right includes freedom to hold opinions without interference and to seek, receive and impart information and ideas through any media and regardless of frontiers."

While various regional organizations as well as United Nations bodies have been created to promote the compliance with the regional and international human rights treaties, the pressing challenge has been to find an effective means to encourage states to implement the basic human rights standards to which they have committed over the years.

Censorship, in the sense of interference with free expression, is the rule, not the exception, throughout the world. It is not a new phenomenon. Rather, censorship has been part of human communication vis-à-vis government in varying degrees.

Numerous legal and extralegal methods of censorship are used to suppress freedom of the press. According to Leonard R. Sussman, former executive editor of Freedom House, eleven "weapons of the state" are used against the press and individual journalists in various countries. The censorship weapons can be physical, psychological, editorial, legal, financial, or technical.

Outright murder is one of the more often used types of physical violence against journalists. The Inter-American Press Association in December 1996 reported that 164 journalists were killed between October 1988 and October 1996 for doing their work in North and South America.

In the past, the state was more likely to be behind assassination or kidnapping of journalists. In recent years, however, nongovernmental organizations more often turn to murder as the ultimate censor of their critical news reporting. In June 1996, for example, reporter Veronica Guerin was apparently shot dead by drug traffickers for her dogged investigative reporting of the drug world in Ireland.

One of the physical weapons of the state against the media is to jam broadcasts from abroad. The Cuban government's jamming of Radio Marti and TV Marti is a good illustration. China and other communist countries jam foreign shortwave broadcasts from abroad.

The state employs several editorial weapons against journalists by setting news guidelines or controlling domestic news agencies. The Korean government under President Chun Doo Hwan (1980–1987) issued daily "press guidelines" to regulate the media coverage of news events. Using such terms as "possible," "impossible," and "absolutely impossible," the Korean government controlled how its press reported particular incidents.

Access to the place where government news is released is regulated by maintaining the "press clubs" of government and journalists. International communication specialist Robert Stevenson notes that the Japanese press clubs in close cooperation with the government officials decide what to report and what not to report and how to play it.

In almost every country, the news media are subject to legislative requirements. Media licensing and registration is statutorily recognized in many countries. This is particularly the case with broadcasting media. Governmental licensing of journalists, which is still accepted in Latin American and the Caribbean, has been ruled by the Inter-American Court of Human Rights as a violation of freedom of expression. Libel laws are used to create a chilling effect on freedom of the press. Indeed, in the United States, libel is the "most common type of legal danger" that can befall the news media. Of all libel suits, more than 70 percent are filed against the mass media.

Some countries have invoked their restrictive libel laws to restrict foreign media. A Singapore judge awarded former Prime Minister Lee Kuan Yew of Singapore and two others a $678,000 damage award against the *International Herald Tribune* for libel relating to an editorial-page column about the "dynastic politics" in the island nation. In April 1996, the High Court of Singapore awarded Lee $71,000 in libel damages for an op-ed article by American professor Christopher Lingle. The article, which appeared in 1994 in the *International Herald Tribune,* implied that Lee used the compliant courts in Singapore as a tool of his repressive politics. The *Tribune* already paid $214,000 to Lee for the article, while Lingle returned to the United States from the National University of Singapore where he taught as a lecturer.

Censorship is not always imposed from outside. Self-censorship is becoming more of a modus operandi among transnational Western media. In July 1995, the *Guardian* in London did an extensive edit of William Safire's syndicated column "Honour for Singapore's PM Raises Storm," for legal reasons. CNN's willingness to accommodate the Singapore Cable Vision's wish to control its programming content is another good testimony to the prevailing atmosphere of self-censorship among global news media.

In a nutshell, censorship is imposed by governmental and nongovernmental entities upon freedom of speech and the press legally and illegally. It is invoked to protect the right of others, national security, public order, confidentiality agreements, and sources. Censorship is also employed to punish sedition and violence. Further, censorship is resorted to during states of emergency and war. Equally important, self-censorship is accepted by journalists and news media for professional and personal reasons.

Article 19. *Information, Freedom and Censorship: World Report 1991.* Chicago: American Library Association, 1991.

Sussman, Leonard R. *Power, the Press and the Technology of Freedom: The Coming Age of ISDN.* New York: Freedom House, 1989.

Kyu Ho Youm

CENSORSHIP, OFFICE OF. The U.S. Office of Censorship (OC) was created by President Roosevelt on December 19, 1941, in preparation for America's participation in World War II. Newspaperman Byron Price was named as OC director. Price subsequently appointed radio station owner J. Harold Ryan to head the OC's Broadcasting Division.

The Broadcasting Division's initial order was to develop a censorship code whose objective was to curtail either deliberate or coincidental use of radio programming as a means of conveying information useful to America's enemies. Enforcement of what became the Code of Wartime Practices was voluntary.

The OC also was responsible for investigating foreign-language broadcasts originating from U.S. radio stations and for determining whether enemy agents might be associated with such broadcasts. A special Federal Communications Commission (FCC) wartime unit, the Radio Intelligence Division, worked with the OC to monitor samples of domestic foreign-language radio programs throughout the duration of World War II.

The voluntary nature of media censorship bridged two opposing views on the matter. Some persons in the Roosevelt administration had insisted that the president invoke provisions of the *First War Powers Act,* signed into law on December 18, 1941, that authorized him to censor radio programming in order to protect national security. Radio industry leaders, fearful that the government indeed might assume such draconian authority, argued that First Amendment guarantees of free expression should be protected even in wartime.

President Harry Truman declared "voluntary censorship of the domestic press and radio at an end" on August 15, 1945, and the Office of Censorship itself was abolished by executive order three months later.

Koop, Theodore. *Weapon of Silence.* Chicago: University of Chicago Press, 1946.
Office of Censorship. *A Report on the Office of Censorship.* Historical Reports on War Administration. Series 1. Washington, D.C.: U.S. Government Printing Office, 1945.
Price, Byron. "Governmental Censorship in War-Time." *American Political Science Review* 36 (October 1942): 837–849.

Ronald Garay

CHAIN BROADCASTING, REPORT ON. On March 18, 1938, the Federal Communications Commission (FCC) undertook a comprehensive investigation to determine whether special regulations applicable to radio stations engaged in chain broadcasting were required in the "public interest, convenience and necessity." The *Communications Act of 1934* defined chain broadcasting as the "simultaneous broadcasting of an identical program by two or more connected stations." The commission directed inquiry into the number of stations licensed to or affiliated with networks, and the amount of time used or controlled by networks; contractual rights and obligations of stations under their agreements with networks; scope of network agreements containing exclusive affiliation provisions and restricting the network from affiliation with other stations in the same area; rights and obligations of stations with respect to network advertisers; nature of the program service rendered by stations licensed to networks; network policies with respect to character of programs, diversification, and accommodation to the particular requirements of the areas served by the affiliated stations; extent to which affiliated stations exercise control over programs, advertising contracts, and related matters; nature and extent of network program duplication by stations serving the same area; extent to which particular networks have exclusive coverage in some areas; competitive practices of stations engaged in chain broadcasting; effect of chain broadcasting upon stations not licensed to or affiliated with networks; practices or agreements in restraint of trade, or in furtherance of monopoly, in connection with chain broadcasting; and scope of concentration of control over stations, locally, regionally, or nationally, through contracts, common ownership, or other means. On May 2, 1941, the commission issued its *Report on Chain Broadcasting,* setting forth its findings and conclusions on the matters explored in the investigation, together with an order adopting the regulations. In its *Report,* the commission characterized the regulations as "the expression of the general policy we will follow in exercising our licensing power." Each specific regulation was directed at a particular practice found by the commission to be detrimental to the "public interest." In general, the regulations provided that no licenses were to be granted to stations or applicants having specific relationships with the networks. On October 11, 1941, the commission issued a supplemental report, together with an order amending three regulations. On October 30, 1941, suits were filed against the commission by the National Broadcasting Co., Inc., the Columbia Broadcasting System, and others to enjoin the enforcement of the regulations. The suits were eventually appealed to the U.S. Supreme Court. In *National Broadcasting Co., Inc. et al. v. United States et al.,* 319 U.S. 190, the Court found in favor of the FCC, concluding that "the *Communications Act of 1934* authorized the Commission to promulgate regulations designed to correct the abuses disclosed by its investigation of chain broadcasting." In its decision, the Court noted, "An important element of public interest and convenience affecting the issue of a license is the ability of the licensee to render the best practicable service to the community reached by his broadcasts" and that "in essence, the Chain Broadcasting Regulations represent a particularization of the Commission's conception of the 'public interest.'"

Documents in American Broadcasting. FCC Docket 5060 (May 1941).
Federal Communications Commission. *Report on Chain Broadcasting.* Washington, D.C.: U.S. Government Printing Office, 1941. Reprint, New York: Arno Press, 1974.
Kahn, Frank J., ed. *The Network Case.* 4th ed. Englewood Cliffs, N.J.: Prentice-Hall, 1984.

Marianne Barrett

CHARTS, MUSIC, lists posted each week by *Billboard* and other magazines that reflect the popularity of a particular song or album. The charts reflect a record's sales in relation to other popular songs, its up or down movement, and the number of weeks it has been on the list. *Billboard* lists its "Hot 100" each week. The charts serve as one of the "gatekeepers" in the music radio business.

Other chart publications include: *Cash Box, The Gavin Report, The Walrus,* and *The Friday Morning Quarterback.*

Charts, Music. http://www.yahoo.com/entertainment/music/charts

Max Utsler

CHENAULT, GENE. *See* **Drake, Bill.**

CHILDREN'S PROGRAMMING. *See* **Golden Age of Radio; World War II and Radio.**

CHRISTIAN MUSIC contains Christian themes whether used for praise and worship or for encouragement and evangelism. It may take any one of a variety of musical forms, including gospel, rock, country, or urban. In its gospel form, it is older than the nation. In its more modern form, contemporary Christian music (CCM) embraces popular-style melodies, expressions of personal faith, and the business of music.

During the 1960s and 1970s, secular rock lyrics reflected the feelings of young people rebelling against established morality and politics in America. Christian leaders condemned secular rock music; Christian young people were discouraged from performing or even listening to it. Consequently, Christian young people felt "locked out" of secular music, according to Jay Howard. They needed their own music. One alternative was country music; its narrative ballads and sense of patriotism readily lent themselves to the positive themes and Christian messages of early CCM. As CCM developed, it embraced the adult contemporary style with artists such as Amy Grant and Michael W. Smith. It also expanded into the more youth-oriented music forms of rap, heavy metal, and alternative. Lyrics expressed the personal faith of the artists and ranged from songs of praise to social criticism. By the early 1990s, CCM was a successful business. CCM had been outselling classical and jazz for several years. Artists were crossing over from CCM to other charts. Major music labels were purchasing CCM publishers or beginning their own Christian music divisions. National companies were beginning to support CCM. Target Stores, for instance, helped promote the Dove Awards, and Disney World's "Night of Joy," a Christian music concert, became a weeklong series of activities. Z Music, a Christian music video channel, joined TNN as a part of Gaylord Broadcasting. Regarding the broadening scope of CCM, Debbie Arkins, vice president of publishing for Word, said, "I look for lyrics that reflect the struggles of the culture we live in and give hope to our society." As the slogan says, It's not just for Sundays anymore.

Howard, Jay. "Contemporary Christian Music: Where Rock Meets Religion." *Journal of Popular Culture* 26 (1992): 123–130.

Price, Deborah Evans. "Country and Christian Pubs Love Their Neighbors." *Billboard* (April 20, 1996): 44–47.

Larry L. Jurney

CITIZEN GROUPS AND BROADCASTING. Congress, through the *Communications Act of 1934* and the current *Telecommunications Act,* has directed the Federal Communications Commission (FCC) to award licenses and regulate the broadcasting industry according to its responsibility to act in the public interest, convenience, and necessity. Citizen groups have seized upon this mandate to exert pressure regarding programming, employment practices, and granting licenses.

In 1933, Mrs. George Ernst of the Fox Meadow Parent-Teachers Association of Scaridae (New York) led a campaign that called for an end to the so-called *Ether Bogeyman* that was causing nightmares among young children. Ernst's group conducted a survey of 40 popular children's radio programs and found only 5 that were acceptable; all others, including *Betty Boop* and *Little Orphan Annie,* failed due to varying degrees of violence and suspense. These undesirable elements were said to cause overexcitement and anxiety in children, who then could not sleep at night.

Although the parents' protest had little direct effect on radio programming, such citizen actions did catch the attention of the FCC. After a preliminary investigation the commission formed the Federal Radio Education Committee, which initiated several research projects to study the effects of radio programming on children. In 1939, the FCC issued a memorandum that outlined 14 types of programming, including cliff-hanger children's shows, astrology, and other fake-science shows, that the commission warned might warrant punitive action for failure to program according to broadcasters' public interest obligation. The proposed sanctions ranged from warnings and fines to license revocation.

So began the FCC's attention to citizen advocacy groups regarding programming issues. During the 1960s, citizens groups protested overt references to drug usage and sexual activity in popular music, a movement that actually led to a change of some lyrics before they could be broadcast. Later the FCC issued a memorandum that did not prohibit the broadcast of drug-related lyrics but suggested that broadcasters must be aware of the content of the songs they played and any possible negative effects.

In 1985, the Parents Music Resource Center, led by Tipper Gore, lobbied Congress and the music industry to label records containing sexually explicit and violent lyrics. Although the Recording Industry Association of America agreed to voluntary music labeling, record companies were provided with no standard guidelines, leading to the use of inconsistent criteria throughout the industry.

Concerns over drug lyrics resurfaced recently as citizen groups turned their attention to music played on rap and alternative stations. In 1995, a citizen advocacy effort headed by former Education Secretary William Bennett and C. Dolores Tucker, chair of the National Political Congress of Black Women, called for more corporate responsibility among record labels and radio stations that played gangsta rap and alternative music. They claimed that much of the music in these formats promoted drug use and the rape, torture, and murder of women.

The renewal of broadcast licenses is another area in which citizen advocacy groups have been active. In 1969, the courts officially recognized the rights of ordinary citizens to participate in broadcast regulation, especially during the license renewal stage. The decision also led to the formation of numerous watchdog groups that work actively to hold broadcasters to their obligation to operate in the public's interest. Citizen groups, such as the Media Access Project, National Citizens Committee for Broadcasting, and the Citizens Communications Center, have argued successfully that a community has an interest in the diversity of radio formats and that the FCC should consider the impact on program diversity when reviewing proposed station sales. These groups have also participated in the FCC's rule-making process regarding the requirement and availability of program logs and public file material, as well as the equal employment opportunity rules for stations.

Haight, Timothy R., ed. *Telecommunications Policy and the Citizen*. New York: Praeger Publishers, 1979.
Prowitt, Marsha. *Guide to Citizen Action in Radio and Television*. New York: Office of Communication, United Church of Christ, 1971.

Cynthia A. Cooper

CITIZENS-BAND (CB) RADIO (Class D), operating at 27 megahertz (MHz), was established by the Federal Communications Commission (FCC) in September 1958. The service was intended to provide low-cost, short-range, two-way voice radio service for both personal and business communications with simplified licensing requirements. CB worked well until the 1970s when fuel shortages resulted in a 55-miles-per-hour national speed limit. Millions of frustrated motorists began communicating the locations of law enforcement officers via CB radio. CB quickly degenerated into a service characterized by gross technical and operating violations, making communication difficult. CB popularity faded as speed limits increased, and citizens interested in reliable mobile communications migrated to cellular telephones.

Buckwalter, Len. *ABC's of Citizen Band Radio*. Indianapolis: Howard W. Sams & Co., Inc., 1966.

Tom Spann

CLARK, DICK (1929–). Clark was born on November 30, 1929, as Richard Wagstaff Clark. His career as a radio and television host, as well as producer, made a significant impact on the American music industry. As host of *American Bandstand* for more than 30 years, Clark was an influential figure, introducing artists to millions of Americans. Clark began his on-air career in radio broadcasting while he was a student at Syracuse University on WAER, the campus radio station. He advanced to commercial radio at WOLF, then to television as a newscaster for WKTV, Utica. Clark moved to Philadelphia in 1952 and joined the staff of WFIL radio, where he hosted the program *Caravan of Music*. Clark remained with the station until 1956, at which time he took the position as host of the TV dance program *Bandstand*. Local artists lip-synced their songs for a studio audience of teenagers and included various interludes such as Record Revue, which allowed the studio audience to rate songs and assign them a numerical score. The show featured many Philadelphia-based artists including Chubby Checker, Fabian, and Frankie Avalon. Due to the program's tremendous success in Philadelphia, ABC distributed the program nationally the very next year, changing the title to *American Bandstand*. It remained a daily-run program until 1964, when it changed to a weekly format. *American Bandstand* served as a powerful launching platform for new artists, a single appearance often propelling an album into the top 10, and Dick Clark personally auditioned many acts. Clark's influential role for *American Bandstand* made him a target during congressional hearings investigating the practice of "payola," when disc jockeys receive money or gifts in exchange for playing certain songs. Clark testified in Washington in 1960 and was cleared of any wrongdoing. After the hearings, however, Clark divested himself of holdings in a number of music-related investments. Clark hosted *American Bandstand* until 1989, then other television programs including *$25,000 Pyramid* and *TV's Bloopers and Practical Jokes*. Clark built a substantial entertainment enterprise and in 1977 formed Dick Clark Productions, Inc. As the principal stockholder, he is creatively active in many of the company's projects, which include television series, specials, motion pictures, and even a restaurant called "Dick Clark's American Bandstand

Grill." Dick Clark, nicknamed "America's oldest teenager," is still active in on-air radio, currently hosting the weekly radio program *Dick Clark's Rock, Roll & Remember.*

Clark, Dick, and Richard Robinson. *Rock, Roll & Remember.* New York: Crowell, 1976.

Donald Diefenbach

CLASSIC ROCK format plays the hits of the late 1960s and 1970s; some stations today also incorporate tunes from the 1980s. According to Michael Keith in *Radio Production: Art and Science,* the focus of classic rock is on the more upbeat or harder rock of the 1960s and 1970s era. The first classic rock station hit the airwaves in July 1983 when Fred Jacobs started the format on WFAA-FM in Dallas, Texas. Classic rock formats feature the works of Jimi Hendrix, Led Zeppelin, The Doors, second-wave British invasion groups such as Pink Floyd, and San Francisco groups like Creedence Clearwater Revival and The Steve Miller Band. Classic rock stations could also play Journey, Ozzy Osbourne, and Van Halen of the late 1970s and 1980s. One distinction is that most classic rockers would play the Rolling Stones but not many of the Beatles hits. Many stations using this format will also play new rock sounds to update the adult audience it attracts. Classic rockers also play new music produced by its core artists.

According to consultant Dennis Constantine, a balance of old to new music is the key to the classic rock and adult alternative rock stations of the future. He stresses that each market is different and classic rock, adult-oriented rock stations must "understand [that] the heritage of rock music in each specific market will help stations relate to adult rockers" (Alexander, p. 80).

Michael Keith classifies classic rock as a part of the vintage rock area that includes oldies and classic hits formats. Classic rock, a fringe format, does feature vintage hard rock music and is also associated with adult-oriented rock and album-oriented rock, or AOR, because these stations will play album cuts of familiar artists.

R&R, the industry's newspaper, doesn't include a classic rock chart of the most popular hits but does recognize classic rock as a format. It includes active rock, alternative, and adult alternative charts used by many of these stations to formulate their playlists.

Although some foresee the death of classic rock, others believe the music format will continue to obtain strong ratings. John Bradley forecasts the end of classic rock, making way for the adult alternative stations to become stronger with older rock audiences. But Katz Radio Group's analysis indicates that classic rock stations are up a tenth of a point from the previous year. The *DeMers Dispatch* calls the death of classic rock a myth and adds that Arbitron rates the format share 12+ higher now than in the past two years. Forty-eight of the nation's top 50 markets currently have classic rock stations. The classic rock, audience-age demographic is between 25 and 54, depending on the music selection station to station.

Guy Zapoleon has created a rock music spectrum from soft, older appeal to hard, younger appeal. The spectrum illustrates how classic rock/AOR stations play some of the same sounds that the Hot AC (adult contemporary) formats might play as the rock audience of 15 years ago continues to age. The alternative music of the late 1960s and early 1970s is today's classic rock.

Alexander, Shawn. "What Is the State of the Format?" *R&R: The Industries Newspaper,* January 19, 1996, p. 80.
DeMers Dispatch (Exton, Penn.). October 1996, pp. 1–4.
Keith, Michael C. *Radio Production: Art and Science.* Boston: Focal Press, 1990.
Stuessy, Joe. *Rock & Roll: Its History and Stylistic Development.* Englewood Cliffs, N.J.: Prentice-Hall, 1990.
Zapoleon, Guy. "Jeremy's Spoken . . . 'The New Rock Revolution Is Here.'" *Radio Ink* (August 21–September 3, 1995): 30–31.

Arthur Thomas Challis, Jr.

CLASSIFICATION, STATION. There are about 12,000 radio stations operating on a limited number of channels (100 FM, 117 AM) in the United States. The method by which the Federal Communications Commission (FCC) is able to allow broadcast channels to be used by more than one station without creating interference is by classifying stations and channels, then regulating such factors as power and antenna height according to classification.

FM stations are classified A, B1, B, C3, C2, C1, and C, with the station's power and antenna height influencing its contour area, defined as coverage area at a specific signal strength and thus its class. Class A stations have the smallest contour distance (28 kilometers, about 18 miles) and Class C stations the largest (92 kilometers, about 60 miles). These station classes are assigned to geographic zones. Zone A is located in all or parts of 18 more densely populated northeastern states. Zone 1–A is the southern four fifths of California (below the 40th parallel) plus the District of Columbia, Puerto Rico, and the Virgin Islands. Zone II is the rest of the country. Generally speaking, more powerful Class C stations may operate only in Zone II, while the other classes are restricted to the more populous Zones 1 and 1–A. Low-power (10-watt), noncommercial educational stations are Class D, but the FCC ceased granting these licenses in 1978 and forced those existing stations to move or to raise power.

AM stations are classified according to three classes of service or coverage area: primary (ground wave), intermittent (ground wave beyond the primary area and therefore subject to fading or interference), and secondary (served by the station's sky wave and also subject to fading). AM stations are also classified according to level of protection from other stations creating interference by operating at the same frequency or on an adjacent frequency. In addition to AM station classification, AM channels are also classified as clear, regional, and local channels. The 60 North American clear channel AM stations (36 in the United States, 8 shared, 16 foreign) are classified as A, B, or D. The 41 regional channel stations can be Class B and D stations, while the 6 local channel stations are Class C. Expanded band (from 1,605–1,705 kilohertz [kHz]) are Class B by definition. Class A stations are dominant, clear channel stations operating at high power (50 kilowatts). Class B stations are on clear or regional channels and must defer to clear channel Class A stations. Class B stations are "unlimited-time" stations, with service areas determined by their frequency, power, and location. Class C stations are local channels with just primary service areas, lower power, and only daytime (ground wave) protection. Class D stations can be on clear or regional channels but are not protected during the nighttime.

Smith, F. Leslie, Milan Meeske, and John W. Wright II. *Electronic Media and Government: The Regulation of Wireless and Wired Mass Communication in the United States.* White Plains, N.Y.: Longman, 1995.

Mark J. Braun

CLASSICAL FORMAT. *See* **fine arts/classical formats.**

CLEAR CHANNEL is the Federal Communications Commission (FCC) classification used to designate AM stations that are permitted to dominate their assigned frequency by transmitting with up to 50,000 watts of power. Their ground wave signal is thus protected from objectionable interference within their primary service area, between 100 and 200 miles. Their secondary service can reach as far away as 750 miles at night because their sky waves reflect off the Kennelly-Heaviside layer of the ionosphere and return to earth, unlike during the day, when they travel into space. For a list of clear channel stations that can be received this way at night see **sky wave** and **Kennelly-Heaviside layer**.

Charles F. Aust

CLOCKS, TOP-40. *See* **top-40.**

CLOSE, UPTON (1894–1960), his real name Josef Washington Hall, the NBC radio personality was best known for his conservative radio reports in the 1930s. Close also wrote and traveled extensively and was considered along with Boake Carter, Fulton Lewis, Jr., and Father Coughlin as a pioneer of the right-wing radio political commentary.

Close was born on an Indian reservation along the Columbia River in Washington state. After studying at Washington Missionary College and then receiving a B.A. from George Washington University, Close, in 1915, married the first of his five wives. His spouse encouraged him to embark on a series of travels in Asia. After establishing residence in China, and beginning a series of articles for the *Shanghai Weekly Review,* he concluded one of his columns with the words "Up close." After an editor ran this phrase as the man's byline, although by changing "Up" to "Upton," the name stuck and, at NBC, would be his signature through the rest of his career.

Returning to the United States as a writer for the *Chicago Tribune,* Close joined NBC in Chicago in 1934 and appeared initially as a news correspondent, then later after the outbreak of World War II as an expert on the Far East. His best-known broadcast, heard on Sunday afternoons and delivered from the NBC studios in Hollywood, was called *Close-Ups of the News.* His sponsor was the Sheaffer Pen Company. Although based on the West Cost, Close traveled widely across the United States and frequently originated his broadcast from wherever he happened to be. Close's technique for traveling to different cities and reporting from them began a trend in radio news.

Throughout his radio career, Close was a vigorous opponent of the Roosevelt and Truman administrations. He opposed American involvement in World War II and had helped found "America First," an isolationist organization; Close and aviation pioneer Charles Lindbergh were two of its renown members. Many of his radio broadcasts contained direct appeals urging the Roosevelt administration to withdraw from World War II. Close went on to accuse President Harry Truman of having connections to the Ku Klux Klan.

Although Close had an audience that numbered only about 6 percent of total radio users, these listeners were fiercely loyal, particularly during World War II. Both in total listeners and in advertiser support, Close's broadcasts reached their peak of prominence in 1942 and 1943, midway through the war. After the war, however, Close's vitriolic reactionary style lost favor, and many demanded he be taken off the air. Finally, in 1945, NBC dropped Close, who for a short time continued his conservative commentaries on the Mutual Network. In 1946, Close retired from radio and moved to Mexico. Fourteen years later, he was killed in an automobile accident in the Mexican city of Guadalajara.

Craig M. Allen

CNN RADIO, founded in 1982 by Ted Turner, is a 24-hour network radio news service. Originally part of the Cable News Network family-owned by Turner, CNN Radio's founding followed the 1980 establishment of CNN and the 1981 debut of *CNN Headline News.* The radio network was the only radio affiliate broadcasting live audio when the space shuttle *Challenger* exploded in January 1986. CNN Radio, pairing with its parent CNN television, also provided around-the-clock coverage of the conflict in the Persian Gulf in January 1991.

Now called CNN Radio News and offered through Westwood One Radio Networks, this network offers a format similar to that of CNN's *Headline News.* According to information from Westwood One, CNN Radio is gathered by a separate radio division at the CNN headquarters in Atlanta, Georgia. Using the resources of CNN television, including global satellite connections, fast-breaking national and international news, in-depth financial, political, and sports coverage, CNN Radio is now sold to radio stations to suit individual station needs.

Features on the CNN Radio Network parallel the offerings on CNN and *Headline News.* Daily feature offerings include *On Screen, Healthwatch, Your Money, Earth Matters, CNN Computer Technology,* and *Science and Technology Today.* The CNN NewsLink also airs the president's radio address and opposition party's address. David Hull is CNN Radio's news anchor, having joined the network in 1984.

Ginger Rudeseal Carter

COATS, GEORGE A., was a promoter who was instrumental in establishing the Columbia Broadcasting System (CBS) in partnership with Arthur Judson. Before entering the radio business, Coats worked as a promoter and salesman for the Good

Road Equipment Company in Philadelphia. His first encounter with the radio industry seems to have come through his friendship with L. S. "Hap" Baker in New York. In 1926, Baker was a secretary to the executive chairman of the recently formed National Association of Broadcasters (NAB was at that time embroiled in a dispute with the American Society of Composers Authors and Publishers [AS-CAP] over royalties for copyrighted material). Coats came to New York to visit his friend just as NAB was preparing for its fourth annual convention. Coats knew something about the issue at hand, so Baker asked him to say a few words at the meeting. Coats spoke against the idea of paying royalties to ASCAP and in the course of the discussion suggested forming a radio program bureau to unite performers as a power bloc for the purpose of putting pressure on composers and publishers.

George Coats then joined forces with Arthur Judson, a manager for the Philadelphia Symphony and the New York Philharmonic, who was well connected with many artists in the area. Judson and Coats formed the Judson Radio Program Corporation on September 20, 1926. After a failed attempt to interest David Sarnoff of RCA in their services, Judson, in a moment of pique, declared that they would start their own radio network.

By January 1927, Coats and Judson established a new company called United Independent Broadcasters (UIB), a paper network without stations or capital. Coats set out to find affiliates and investors. He first signed WCAU of Philadelphia owned by Leon and Isaac Levy. Leon Levy convinced Coats that he could expect no better than a contract that guaranteed the station $500 per week for carrying 10 hours of network broadcasting. Coats agreed, and this became the standard for future contracts. Coats signed contracts with 16 stations in the first year of operation, with WOR in Newark, New Jersey, as the key station.

Coats was also responsible for breaking through an impasse with AT&T for securing long lines to network the affiliated stations. AT&T had stonewalled, but Coats used his connections in the Interstate Commerce Commission to persuade AT&T to be more cooperative. At the same time, Coats was working to find a corporate investor who could bring badly needed cash to the venture. He negotiated with Atwater Kent, Paramount, and Victor Talking Machine Company and finally was able to sign a contract with the Columbia Phonograph Company, which lent its name to the new broadcasting company. After losing money on the venture, Columbia terminated its contract with UIB. Millionaire Jerome H. Louchheim bought the company, but he too tired of losing money and pulled out. Coats began to withdraw at this point, having completed most of the promotional work he set out to do. By September 1928, young William S. Paley bought the network, completely restructured it, and took over all executive functions. George Coats eventually left the radio business and moved on to other promotional projects.

Archer, Gleason L. *Big Business and Radio.* New York: American Historical Company, Inc., 1939.

Christina S. Drale

CODE OF WARTIME PRACTICES, AMERICAN BROADCASTERS', was issued by the U.S. Office of Censorship (OC) on January 15, 1942. The code's purpose was to provide radio station managers with guidelines for voluntarily censoring program content throughout the duration of World War II. It was modeled after a similar Wartime Guide distributed by the National Association of Broadcasters to its member stations in December 1941. The OC's code also instructed broadcasters on handling programming that directly or indirectly might assist the enemy. The code was revised five times during the war in order to address evolving wartime conditions.

The code advised specific prohibition of such things as weather reports, information about Allied troop positions and deployments, military fortifications, shipping arrivals and departures, and battlefield strengths and casualties. The code also urged prohibition of audience participation and musical request programs. Moreover, radio station managers were required to monitor the content of all foreign language programming and to remove announcers found using such programming either to assist or to promote the enemy's cause.

OC personnel spot-checked radio network programs for any violations. Local radio station managers were expected to police their own stations and, only occasionally, were they required to submit postbroadcast program copy for OC review.

Generally, the code proved an effective tool for guiding voluntary censorship. There were few security breaches attributed to American radio during World War II, and what breaches did occur were deemed accidental and inconsequential.

Koop, Theodore. *Weapon of Silence.* Chicago: University of Chicago Press, 1946.
Office of Censorship. *Code of Wartime Practices for American Broadcasters.* Washington, D.C.: U.S. Government Printing Office, June 15, 1942, and subsequent editions.
Summers, Robert. *Wartime Censorship of Press and Radio.* Vol. 15, No. 8. New York: H. W. Wilson, 1942.

Ronald Garay

CODES OF ETHICS are voluntary guidelines agreed upon by members of the profession, in this case broadcasters, as to the rules governing their professional conduct not addressed by law. In order to ensure responsible broadcasting, the industry, through its National Association of Broadcasters (NAB), outlined voluntary measures that would limit amount of advertising time, approaches and content of the commercial messages, and themes in programming. For years this was referred to as the NAB Code. By the early 1980s, this code became elaborate and detailed and was challenged in court on the basis of violating antitrust laws. The general NAB Code was dismantled with the idea that each broadcasting licensee would have its own code of ethics.

In 1929, almost as soon as broadcasting became recognized as a business that was national in scope, and with all the earmarks of a profession, station licensees organized themselves into an association that eventually became known as the National Association of Broadcasters (NAB) that developed a Code of Good Practice. NAB's president stated that establishing the code "was based on keeping radio on a high ethical and moral plane." The plan was to keep out government regulation, which was growing rapidly at the time, in preference for *self*-regulation.

At its onset, the NAB Code consisted of eight rules. Four of the eight rules governed the use of radio for advertising purposes and revealed concern over the problem of overcommercialization. The code reminded broadcasters of their obligation in addressing persons of all ages with various religious and social beliefs. Anything that could not be mailed should also not be broadcast: material that was "fraudulent, deceptive or obscene." Broadcasters were advised to screen their clients so that dangerous or dishonest advertisers would not be allowed access to the public through radio. Another rule explained fair business practices with the competition. A final rule warned that any violation of the code of ethics would be investigated and notified. Obviously, any real penalty with enforcement powers was not to be part of a *voluntary* code of ethics.

About half of that early code was devoted to advertising practices. The first concern had to do with limitation of commercial time. During evenings, when most people listened, there were few, if any, commercials. According to the 1929 Code: "Time before 6 P.M. . . . may be devoted in part, at least, to broadcasting programs of a business nature; while time after 6 P.M. is for recreation and relaxation, and commercial programs should be of the good-will type. Commercial announcements, as the term is generally understood, *should not* be broadcast between 7 and 11 P.M."

As pressures for advertising the economic support of radio grew, the limits of the number of minutes remained specifically identified. Moreover, the distinction between evening hours and daytime hours remained in place. The pattern of maximum time allowed grew through the years:

1937: daytime, 9 minutes; evening, 6 minutes
1952: daytime, 12 minutes; evening, 7 minutes
1970: 18 minutes, daytime or evening

Through the 1970s and 1980s, commercialization became so extensive that many listeners turned their radio dials away from the "clatter" of the ads. As ratings dropped, stations began to realize the earlier virtue of nonobtrusive broadcasting and "more-music" formats were established on the premise that less advertising might be more attractive to listeners.

Another part of the code addressed the issue of what could be advertised: no fortune-telling, astrology, mind-reading; no hard liquor; no tip sheets or publications giving odds in betting or lotteries; no dramatized statement by those purporting to be doctors, dentists, nurses. Also, constraint was to be used when advertising to children, when promoting premiums, offers, and contests, and in beer and wine ads.

Programming codes included honoring the sanctity of marriage and the home, being sensitive to all people, and "enrich[ing] the experience of living through the advancement of education and culture. . . . In . . . any element of crime, mystery, or horror, proper consideration should be given to the possible effect on all members of the family." There were also careful guidelines recommending avoidance of profanity, obscenity, smut, and vulgarity, including slang that may be considered derisive.

Moreover, in 1946, the Federal Communications Commission (FCC) put forth some definitive programming guidelines in its Blue Book (*Public Service Responsibility of Broadcast Licensees*). This marked the beginning of extensive regulatory supervision by the FCC that was to last more than three decades.

By the late 1970s, business interests prevailed in government and were persuasive in moves to deregulate broadcasting. At a time when broadcast codes and self-regulation became increasingly more important, they were softened so that ethical decisions could be made by the licensees, rather than a national board at NAB.

In 1982, a television advertiser complained to the Justice Department that the constraints of advertising time made it difficult to get access to commercial time slots on the TV networks. In the case of *U.S. v. NAB,* the Justice Department found this to be a violation of antitrust (attempts to limit competition in an open marketplace) and challenged the NAB Code on that basis. The government prevailed, and the NAB did away with the codes, both for radio and television, and not only for advertising but for programming and other ethical considerations.

Studies on the effect found that half the station managers surveyed felt that codes or standards relating to practices of news, programming, and advertising ought to be retained in a new national code of ethical standards. Many stations did not have their own corporate or business practices of ethics.

In 1990, the NAB announced a new "Statement of Principles of Radio and Television Broadcasting" but made it clear that these were general advisory guidelines with "no interpretation or enforcement of these principles by NAB or others." While general in nature, the statement identified that there be caution in dealing with violence, drugs and substance abuse, and sexually oriented material. Also, the special responsibility of exercising artistic freedom and responsibility in children's programming were specifically described.

Today, the once important nationally visible NAB broadcasting code is all but gone but, in many cases, replaced by those of individual licensees. Some observers express concern about the unevenness with which some radio broadcasters exhibit ethical responsibility in the absence of any strong code.

Limburg, Val E. *Electronic Media Ethics.* Boston: Focal Press, 1994.

Val E. Limburg

COLLEGE AND UNIVERSITY STATIONS. More than a year before the historic commercial broadcast of KDKA in Pittsburgh, experimental radio station 9XM at the University of Wisconsin was broadcasting news and weather information to a handful of crystal sets in the Madison community. Hence, public radio enthuiasists point with pride to the origins of college and university stations that predate the development of a commercial radio system in the United States. Unfortunately, many of the early standard-broadcasting stations that were licensed to colleges and universities across the country were operated by the academic departments of electrical engineering. The primary instructional objectives of those responsible for station operations focused on the technical aspects of radio broadcasting rather than the public service potential. By 1925 there were 171 of these stations in operation, but by 1937 only 38 were still in operation. Most disappeared because of a general loss of faculty interest when fascination with the novelty of radio wave propagation disappeared. Some college and university stations that wanted to continue as AM broadcasters lost their licenses to commercial interests through comparative hearings before the Federal Communications Commission (FCC).

Early accounts of education by radio underscore the importance of college and university station representatives in the struggle to reserve a portion of the electro-magnetic spectrum exclusively for noncommercial educational use. Historian S. E. Frost, Jr., chronicles the accomplishments of these early stations in his classic work *Education's Own Stations* and helped set the stage for the preservation of so-called curricular channels by the FCC in 1938. Much of the lobbying efforts on behalf of these channels and the later reservation of 20 FM channels for educational use in 1945 was led by the Association of College and University Broadcasting Stations, which later became the National Association of Educational Broadcasters. During the 1960s, 1970s, and 1980s, the FM stations licensed to colleges and universities throughout the United States continued to provide leadership for the nation's public radio movement. By the mid-1990s, more than half of the 1,800 noncommercial educational "public" radio licenses were still held by institutions of higher learning.

Engelman, Ralph. *Public Radio and Television in America.* Thousand Oaks, Calif.: Sage Publications, 1996.
Frost, S. E., Jr. *Education's Own Stations.* Chicago: University of Chicago Press, 1937.
Witherspoon, John, and Roselle Kovitz. *The History of Public Broadcasting.* Washington, D.C.: Current Publishing, 1987.

Robert K. Avery

COLUMBIA BROADCASTING SYSTEM (CBS) came into being in the early days of radio broadcasting in the United States, as the second network to be formed (see also **CBS News**). The first was NBC, owned by the Radio Corporation of America (RCA).

In the spring of 1926 at one of the earliest meetings of the National Association of Broadcasters, a group of radio broadcasters attempted to solve some industry problems, namely, wave piracy. They met in the Aster Hotel in Manhattan, and an onlooker, George Coats (a promoter and paving machinery salesman), was deeply impressed with the enthusiasm of the radio men who filled the lobby. He sat in on some of the sessions and, after listening, decided radio was the business to get into. Coats, who did not have much money, arranged a meeting with Arthur Judson, who managed most of the leading concert stars of the time and was having a difficult time promoting them. Judson brought along Major Andrew J. White, onetime editor of RCA's *Wireless Age* who had been connected with General Electric's (GE's) WGY. Francis Marsh, a New York song booker, made a fourth at this meeting. Each had a reason to have a hand in broadcasting. Judson wanted an outlet for his talent; Coats wanted an entree into a coming industry; White itched to start a new network; and Marsh wanted an outlet for his songs.

A little later, the assistant manager of the New York Philharmonic Symphony Society was added and the quintet, without any real money to speak of, organized the United Independent Broadcasters, Inc. (UIB) in January 1927. With the company now a legal entity and Major White in the director's chair, UIB took a lease on WOR in Newark for four days a week. Coats set out to sign up radio stations in other cities. He returned some two months later, very pleased over signing up 16 stations, granting each station 10 hours a week of programming at $50 an hour. That meant an outlay of $8,000 a week by a network that didn't have any funds.

The incident that saved the day was the imminent collapse of the phonograph industry. Columbia Phonograph Company had heard that its biggest competitor, Victor, had signed an agreement to join RCA/NBC. At this moment, Major White approached Columbia Records with an offer to sell the operating rights of United Independent Broadcasters. Columbia grabbed the offer, organized the Columbia Phonograph Broadcasting Company to act as its sales agent and operating company for the network, and on September 18, 1927, the new network went on the air.

For its debut on air, Columbia presented Deems Taylor's American Opera, *The King's Henchmen.* Deems Taylor himself served as narrator, but as broadcast time approached, a storm took out some power lines, and the broadcast was delayed at least 15 minutes.

Initially, Columbia was losing $100,000 a month, and at the end of three months, it was ready to cash in and get out of the business. White's group bought the network back for $10,000 and 30 hours of free broadcasting for Columbia. But it kept the name Columbia Phonograph Broadcasting System (CPBS). Not having the $10,000, luck intervened. White had connections in Philadelphia who were interested in radio. Jerome H. Louchheim, a wealthy Philadelphian, owner of the Keystone State Construction Company, was the "angel" who rescued the company. White persuaded him to put $150,000 into the new network. With check in pocket, White started a trip to the other stations with the intent of getting them to accept a new and less profitable but more practical contract. When he returned to New York, all 16 stations had accepted the new terms.

Among the earliest accounts placed with CBS was the Congress Cigar Company, manufacturers of La Palina cigars. The competition from cigarettes had driven down the market for cigars, and the cigar company decided to try radio for 26 weeks in an effort to regain sales. At the end of the contract, La Palina sales had leaped to a million a day.

The sales manager of the cigar company was impressed with the success of the broadcast experiment. William S. Paley, 25, felt that maybe here was a business for him. He was wealthy, he looked at radio only as an avocation, and in direct contrast to Major White, he was driven by ambition.

By sheerest coincidence, Paley's brother-in-law, Dr. Leon Levy, was the friend who had introduced the company to Louchheim. Paley went to work on Louchheim, and by the summer of 1928 (just a year later), he had gotten Louchheim to sell his shares to him. Bill Paley became the president of United Broadcasters, while White remained the president of CPBS. After a year of dividing his time between cigars and radio, Paley decided he had to make a choice, and in January 1929, he merged Columbia Phonograph Broadcasting with United Broadcasters and called the new entity Columbia Broadcasting System. From the day he took over the new company,

Paley was driven to make CBS the country's leading network. His chief rival was NBC, headed by David Sarnoff.

His first mission was to change the contracts for his network's 22 affiliates. He proposed the concept of a free-sustaining service, guaranteeing not 10, but 20 hours of programming per week, paying $50 an hour for commercial hours used—but with a new proviso: The network would not pay the stations for the first 5 hours of commercial broadcast time. And to allow for more business to come, the network would receive an option on additional time. Also, networks for the first time would have exclusive rights for network broadcasting through the affiliate. It was a contract that was to become standard fare for networks.

A New York outlet was added, the flagship station now WCBS. Paley set about recruiting the best programs and personalities in radio. He also added other divisions to the network besides broadcasting. It eventually became a conglomerate, with publishing firms, a sports acquisition (the New York Yankees), children's educational toys, and CBS Laboratories (the research and development arm of the company). Since it was no longer just in broadcasting, the formal title of the company was changed to CBS, Inc.

Paley encouraged quality radio, and the industry developed its own playwrights, including Norman Corwin and Arch Oboler. Part of Paley's success was assembling an outstanding news staff. CBS established the standard for radio news reporting during World War II, headlined in the early days by Edward R. Murrow. It was Murrow who pulled together the great team to cover the European theater of the war, with Murrow giving his never-to-be-forgotten reports from bomb-ravaged London.

CBS made a bold stroke by committing to a half-hour foreign news report on the Nazi's occupation of Austria. London, Paris, Berlin, and Rome were all connected, with Edward R. Murrow the anchor in London, Robert Trout in New York, and William L. Shirer in Berlin. Radio came into its own as a full-fledged news medium.

Television began programming on CBS in 1948. Many of radio's outstanding stars and programs were lured to the visual medium, leaving radio to seek a new format. Radio changed dramatically, broadcasting early talk programs such as *Arthur Godfrey Time* and the *Gary Moore Show.* News became its mainstay, along with music.

In its later history, with the takeovers that became common in the 1980s, CBS fended off a takeover by Ted Turner and his Turner Enterprises but weakened itself financially in so doing. Larry Tisch became the "money man" that helped save CBS. Tisch took over the operation of CBS, Inc. when Paley died. With Paley's death, in 1990, an era of broadcasting came to its conclusion. Cable and direct-satellite broadcasting now threaten network broadcasting.

ElDean Bennett

COLUMBIA PHONOGRAPH. *See* **Coates, George A.; Columbia Broadcasting System (CBS).**

COLUMBIA WORKSHOP, first broadcast in July 1936, introduced many of radio's finest writers and actors. The series originated with Irving Reis, a studio engineer, who was interested in experimenting with sound and dramatic techniques. Radio, still a primitive medium, relied on other arts for production ideas.

The series was sustained by CBS without commercial sponsors. It became a showcase for young artists and a creative laboratory. Programs appeared ranging from simple sound demonstrations, the first play about radio, classic verses by Keats and Coleridge, and Oscar Wilde fantasy *The Happy Prince.*

The first popular name to appear was Archibald MacLeish. His terse play *Fall of the City,* aired on April 11, 1937, establishing the *Workshop*'s reputation with other well-known writers. Starring Orson Welles, MacLeish's play had a historic impact, demonstrating that radio could restore great literature to mass audiences. Many short-story writers, novelists, poets, and playwrights became interested. Plays began to arrive from artists like Alfred Kreymborg, Stephen Vincent Benet, Pare Lorentz, Dorothy Parker, Arch Oboler, and Norman Corwin.

Performances, such as Benet's adaption of his *John Brown's Body* and the *Devil & Daniel Webster* became classics. Others were Crane's *The Red Badge of Courage,* T. S. Eliot's drama of Becket, *Murder in the Cathedral,* and Mark Twain's satire *Journalism in Tennessee.*

Not until the *Workshop* did plays devised for radio appear in significant numbers. The productions also pioneered sound techniques such as filters, echo chambers, and parabolic microphones. The series ended in 1941, was revived in 1946–1947, and again in 1956 as the *CBS Radio Workshop.*

Dunning, John. *Tune in Yesterday: The Ultimate Encyclopedia of Old-time Radio 1925–1976.* Englewood Cliffs, N.J.: Prentice-Hall, 1978.

Riley, Donald W. "The History of American Radio Drama." Ph.D. dissertation, Ohio State University, 1945.

Frank Chorba

COMMENTATORS. *See* individual personalities' names; **news programming criticism; politics and media.**

COMMERCE AND LABOR, U.S. DEPARTMENT OF, was given preliminary jurisdiction over radio with the *Wireless Ship Act of 1910,* the earliest federal regulation. The act specified that ships carrying 50 or more passengers be equipped with wireless. Following the sinking of the *Titanic,* which claimed the lives of more than 1,500 people, some of whom might have been saved if the wireless operator on a nearby ship had been receiving, Congress passed the *Radio Act of 1912,* requiring two radio operators for ships so that distress messages could be sent and received 24 hours a day. The act also required the Commerce Department to license stations and operators but provided minimal power for the department to regulate radio effectively. This offered little government authority but remained the basis for regulation until 1927. The department was divided into two separate departments in 1913, and under Commerce, the Bureau of Navigation attempted to settle differences among radio operators and stations. In April of 1917, radio operation was taken over by the U.S. Navy as America entered World War I. Efforts were made to place radio under government control permanently, but when these failed, regulation was again placed with the Commerce Department, which continued postwar attempts at overseeing the expanding growth of radio.

As more stations went on the air and consequent interference reduced the clarity and reception of radio signals, President Harding's secretary of commerce, Herbert Hoover, called a meeting of concerned government and private representatives in 1922 to develop guidelines for what was becoming a rapidly expanding enterprise. There was considerable lack of agreement as to what should be done to reduce interference. Amateur operators were defensive about their rights, and debates took place among private and government delegates on the fundamental question of who should control radio. Most commercial representatives supported continued regulation by the Commerce Department, but spokesmen for the Navy, War, Agriculture, and Post Office Departments sought greater control by their units. Secretary Hoover viewed the necessity for reducing interference as parallel to the conservation of natural resources and vowed to protect the interests of amateurs. Three later conferences were called by Hoover in 1923, 1924, and 1925. Continuing growth in the numbers of both stations and receivers furthered problems of signal interference. Delegates called for limitations on the number of new licenses and stations and a greater number of frequencies for broadcasting. Hoover advocated voluntary rules, a minimum of government regulation, and a preference for public service broadcast content. The recommendations resulting from these conferences were the basis of a bill leading to the *Radio Act of 1927,* which created the Federal Radio Commission (FRC), originally set up as a temporary body to address technical problems, reflecting the government's intent to leave broader matters of regulation with the Commerce Department. After several years of renewal, the FRC was replaced by the Federal Communications Commission, which was given primary jurisdiction over electronic media when the *Communications Act of 1934* was passed.

Bensman, Marvin. "Regulation of Broadcasting by the Department of Commerce, 1921–1927." In *American Broadcasting: A Source Book on the History of Radio and Television,* edited by Lawrence Lichty and Malachi Topping. New York: Hastings House, 1975.

Hoover, Herbert. *The Memoirs of Herbert Hoover: The Cabinet and the Presidency, 1920–1933.* New York: Macmillan, 1951.

Sarno, Edward. "The National Radio Conferences." *Journal of Broadcasting* 13 (1969): 189–202.

                                                                                    B. R. Smith

COMMITTEE ON INTERSTATE AND FOREIGN COMMERCE. *See* **House of Representatives: Committee on Interstate and Foreign Commerce.**

COMMON CARRIERS are service providers in communication, such as telephone companies and postal services, that make available for public use wired or wireless transmission, or other methods, for sending and receiving messages and information and can charge users for their services. In general, they must allow access by the public with no right to censor or edit the messages. They do not originate messages, programming, or information. The *Communications Act of 1934* brought wired and wireless common carriers under centralized federal regulation. According to the act, common carriers are "for hire." Broadcasters are not considered common carriers.

Communications Act of 1934. Title II Common Carriers (47 U.S.C. 201–228).

Steven C. Runyon

COMMUNICATIONS ACT. See **Telecommunications Act of 1996.**

COMMUNICATIONS ACT OF 1934, the body of law that provides the basic structure for the regulation of the electronic communications media. The act established the Federal Communications Commission (FCC) as the agency responsible for enforcement and has been amended several times over 70 years, but portions remain virtually unchanged.

Prior to 1934, Congress had passed other legislation to regulate broadcast signals. The *Wireless Ship Act of 1910* required any seagoing vessels with 50 or more passengers to have radio communications and a skilled operator on board. The *Radio Act of 1912* required that any radio station must obtain a license from the secretary of commerce before beginning its operations. The *Radio Act of 1927,* the precursor of the *Communications Act of 1934,* actually contained much of the latter's framework with regard to broadcast regulation.

The 1927 act, however, dealt only with broadcast communication. The significant difference between the *Radio Act of 1927* and the *Communications Act of 1934* was that the latter regulated not only broadcasting but also interstate telephone and telegraph. Congress intended that one federal agency be responsible for regulating all electronic communication. While president, Herbert Hoover had blocked amendment of the *Radio Act of 1927,* but under Franklin Roosevelt, reform came quickly. The new FCC was established with seven members, two more than the Federal Radio Commission had. One of the amendments passed in 1983 was a reduction in the commission's size from seven to five commissioners.

The act is divided into sections, called Titles, which govern different types of communication. Title I contains the purposes of the act, general definitions, and an explanation of FCC structure and duties. Title II explains FCC jurisdiction over common carriers (such as telephone companies). Of primary importance to broadcasters is Title III. This section outlines licensing requirements, equal opportunity requirements for political candidates, and a plethora of other technical requirements for over-the-air broadcasters. Title IV explains the enforcement of the act, and the appeal process for FCC decisions. Title V lists the penalties for rules violations. Title VI covers several miscellaneous categories, including the power of the president to suspend all rules in a war emergency. In 1984, Title VII was added, dealing with the regulation of cable television.

The *Communications Act of 1934* has "public interest, convenience, and necessity" as a recurring theme. It is given as the justification for granting or denying licenses to stations, empowering the FCC to make reasonable regulations, and even assigning station call letters. A number of sections of Title III have been challenged over the years. One of the most contentious is Section 315, the Equal Opportunities Requirement (often referred to inaccurately as the Equal Time Rule), which requires stations to provide equal opportunities for airtime for candidates for public office.

Dom Caristi

COMPACT DISC RECORDING, a system that samples audio waveforms and stores digital codes on a compact disc (CD). When the CD is rotated on a playback machine, the digital code is read by a laser beam and transduced into a near-perfect replica of the original sound. CDs are virtually noise-free and do not deteriorate in quality due to friction or wear as phonograph records do. Although some "purists" still collect only "vinyl" record albums, the CD has essentially replaced the record album in radio station and consumer music collections.

Alten, Stanley L. *Audio in Media.* 2nd ed. Belmont, Calif.: Wadsworth, 1986.

Frederic A. Leigh

COMPETITION, the rivalry among radio stations or networks for the same consumers and sponsors, is a contest striving for profit, ratings, talent, and listeners. As with any potential profit-making venture, the radio industry's historical development is fraught with corporate competition. Inventors tried to get patents before their competitors could do so. Phantom stations were set up to jam competitors off the air. Networks rivaled each other for control of the airways. They challenged each other in the courts. The federal government tried to restore some order out of the chaos by instituting rules and regulations. Moreover, the radio industry even tried to regulate itself to stem the tide of federal overseers.

During the 1920s, radio stations began actively to compete for listeners in a systematic fashion. In 1929, one of Archibald M. Crossley's interviewers picked up a telephone and asked a randomly selected person, "What radio stations did you listen to yesterday?"

The depression era gave radio a competitive edge. It was cheap entertainment for an audience with limited economic resources. After the initial cost for a set, radio programs were free. "Listening in" became a national pastime. Radio was a means of keeping up with the news, being entertained, or keeping loneliness at bay. Since radio could give the listener instant news and the latest top musical performers, the medium attracted all segments of society from the "haves" to the "have-nots." Newspapers, movies, and magazines could not compete with it. And it paved the way for "radio with pictures" television.

As radio audiences increased, stations vying with each other for listeners and advertisers started having special promotions for their listeners. Prizes and monetary compensation attracted listeners' attention. The National Association of Broadcasters established self-regulatory rules for commercial announcements. Networks also began to seek gifted celebrities to attract a broader audience. The Golden Age of Radio (1934–1941) established radio's effectiveness in the competition for consumers. By the 1950s, most automobiles included radios as standard equipment. Eventually, the advent of television cut into radio's competitive edge. However, radio's mobility remains an important advantage in the competition.

Archer, Gleason L. *History of Radio to 1926.* New York: American Historical Society, Inc., 1938. Reprint New York: Arno Press, 1971.

Mary Kay Switzer

CONGRESS CIGAR COMPANY. In 1926, William S. Paley's Congress Cigar Co. sponsored the *La Palina Hour* on Philadelphia radio station WCAU. ("Palina" was a play on "Paley.") Within six months, La Palina cigar sales jumped from 400,000 to over a million a day. Paley then invested Congress Cigar money in United Independent Broadcasters, a patchwork chain of 16 radio stations anchored by WCAU and known on air as the Columbia Phonograph Broadcasting System. Paley was elected president of the money-losing little network. WCAU's *La Palina Hour* was recast as *The La Palina Smoker,* and Congress Cigar became one of the new CBS's principal sponsors. CBS has been called "a network saved by a smoke ring" (DeLong, p. 46) (see **Columbia Broadcasting System [CBS]**).

DeLong, Thomas A. *The Golden Age of Musical Radio: The Mighty Music Box.* Los Angeles: Amber Crest Books, 1980.
Paley, William S. *As It Happened: A Memoir.* Garden City, N.Y.: Doubleday, 1979.

Michael Woal

CONGRESSIONAL INVESTIGATIONS. The power to seek information in order to make laws has long been a protected power of Congress. In theory, Congress, through its constitutional mandate to legislate, oversee federal regulatory agencies, and appropriate funds, must have informed knowledge upon which to base important decisions. Conducting investigations and fact-finding hearings are two methods used by Congress to obtain this knowledge.

Congress has been investigating the electronic communications industry virtually from its beginning. The first known congressional investigation was an 1870 proceeding conducted by the House Select Committee on Postal Telegraph Lines. Early investigations of radio began in 1909 when the House Committee on Merchant Marine and Fisheries studied the use of ship-to-shore radio communications, and subsequent inquiries tended to concentrate on the technical aspects of the medium. As radio developed into a mass medium, Congress's interest in the programming content and business practices became more pronounced. Alcohol advertising on radio was the focus of a 1939 investigation by the Senate Committee on Interstate Commerce, while another investigation studied the monopolistic business practices of NBC and CBS.

During WWII, Congress often investigated the use of radio in the dissemination of propaganda and moved to tighten security on ships to prevent subversive individuals from commandeering radio operations and revealing strategic convoy locations. The Federal Communications Commission (FCC) itself became the subject of a 1943 congressional investigation as charges of misconduct and interference in radio intelligence activities were leveled against the chairman and several commissioners.

Through the years, Congress has revisited many of these early concerns, only updating these investigations to reflect modern changes in the industry. Alcohol advertising on radio was investigated in both the 1950s and 1980s, as was the potential harm caused by broadcasting sexually explicit song lyrics. Other congressional investigations studied the impact of radio editorials, political broadcasts, and sportscasts, as well as the glamorization of drug use in modern popular music.

Recent inquiries focused on the explicit lyrics in music played on heavy metal, rap, and alternative radio stations. Fearing that lyrics that promoted drug usage and violence against women and police would encourage violence in society, members of Congress joined with citizen advocates to encourage self-regulation by the music and broadcast industries.

Brightbill, George D. *Communications and the United States Congress, a Selectively Annotated Bibliography of Committee Hearings, 1870–1976.* Washington, D.C.: Broadcast Education Association, 1978.

CIS/Index and *CIS/Annual.* Washington, D.C.: Congressional Information Service.

Cynthia A. Cooper

CONNER, G. C., was a pioneer broadcaster. In 1916, along with C. V. Logwood, he established 2ZK in New Rochelle, New York, and broadcast music over it.

Barbara Moore

CONRAD, DR. FRANK (1874–1941), Westinghouse engineer whose ground breaking experimentation is often credited for leading to the development of station KDKA and the initial popularization of the medium. Conrad began an experimental station 8XK from a workshop over his garage, near Pittsburgh. He tested amateur equipment, announcing his tests, including live band music and conversations with colleagues, well in advance, then tried to gauge the influence of his innovations.

As a Westinghouse employee, Conrad ran tests on the Signal Corps' transmitters and receivers and assisted his company in firming up equipment contracts on military items. A particular department store advertisement appearing in the *Pittsburgh Sun* in 1920 and citing a Conrad broadcast is frequently mentioned as being a central ingredient in the popular acceptance and buildup of radio. After the war, with support and encouragement from company vice president Harry P. Davis, Conrad also provided much of the technical know-how to help that company further compete in developing and marketing along with AT&T and RCA.

Conrad's broadcasts were also used to promote the idea that radio was becoming mainstream and more of a common convenience, which also further enhanced the sale of his companies' "wireless sets." He received letters responding to his experiments with recorded music, attesting to the fact that he had gained listeners beyond eccentrics and other amateur broadcasters. The assignment to build the then-powerful, 100-watt transmitter atop the Westinghouse plant in East Pittsburgh gave Conrad an incentive to complete the project and gain a tremendous publicity coup for radio's potential to report breaking news. The success of that station— KDKA's historic, November 2, 1920, coverage of the Harding-Cox election returns and a good many radio innovations—is frequently attributed to Conrad's foresight and vision, his ingenuity, and dedication. The early challenges he faced—lack of interest and understanding, not to mention physical challenges such as acoustical and weather-related problems, for example—set the stage for others and established Dr. Frank Conrad's status as a forerunner in the field.

Archer, Gleason L. *History of Radio to 1926.* New York: American Historical Society, Inc., 1938.

"Dr. Conrad and His Work." Unauthored Westinghouse Press Release. Mass Communication History Center, Wisconsin Historical Society, Madison, 1942.

Mason, Elizabeth B., and Louis M. Starr, eds. *The Oral History Collection of Columbia University.* New York: Columbia University, Oral History Research Office, 1979.

                                                                                                    Michael D. Murray

CONSULTANTS, RADIO, also known as "radio doctors" or "hired guns," advise station managers on how best to bring success to a given station, either by increased ratings, a change in format, or higher quality of presentation. According to Herbert Howard, Michael Kievman, and Barbara Moore, in *Radio, TV, and Cable Programming,* consultants base their advice on market research and their own expertise. Radio consultancy began in the late 1950s after radio programming became segmented according to listener interest. Michael Keith, in *Radio Programming: Consultancy and Formatics,* traces the radio consultancy business to Mike Joseph, a station programmer who decided to go into business for himself by guiding programming for his first client, WMAX-AM in Grand Rapids, Michigan. After quickly achieving ratings success for that station, Joseph went on to do the same for stations in Illinois, Michigan, Minnesota, and New York. As the number of radio stations increased during the 1960s, the market for consultants grew as well. Stations' need for consultants was especially high in major markets, where competition among the growing number of new stations was fierce. As the commercial radio field continued to grow with the rise of FM during the 1960s and 1970s, so, too, did the demand for consultants, who were frequently called in when a station's ratings began to drop. By the late 1980s, about one third of radio stations were using consultants. Future demand for consultants is expected, as radio formats and audiences become more fragmented and specialized.

Consultants' functions center on improving a station's standing in a market and include such analysis as determining successful formats and call letter combinations, examining a station's physical facilities and comparing them to the competition's, conducting market research in the form of focus groups, surveys, and music testing, and critiquing on-air quality, from the content of advertisements to the performance of announcers. The consultant usually monitors a station, either by listening to live broadcasts on location or by air checks. As Keith notes, many consultants work primarily in programming, but some offer a variety of other services including staff training and motivation and negotiating with syndication and music companies. Phyllis Stark, in *Billboard,* contends job consolidation at the station level in recent years has increased the duties of consultants. As a result, consultant/research firm and consultant/consultant alliances, especially during the 1990s, began to gain popularity. Regarding the demographics of consultants themselves, during the mid-1990s, few were women, according to an article by Carrie Borzillo in *Billboard* in early 1993. This reflects a general, and traditional, industry shortage of women in the programming field. However, some industry insiders predict more women will become consultants, provided that more of them are hired as program directors.

Borzillo, Carrie. "Women Consultants Hard to Find." *Billboard* (January 23, 1993): 75–76.

Howard, Herbert H., Michael S. Kievan, and Barbara Moore. *Radio, TV, and Cable Programming.* 2nd ed. Ames: Iowa State University Press, 1994.

Keith, Michael C. *Radio Programming: Consultancy and Formatics.* Boston: Focal Press, 1987.

Stark, Phyllis. "Consultancy Alliances Prosper." *Billboard* (June 10, 1995): 75–76.

Erika Engstrom

CONTEMPORARY HITS RADIO (CHR) format grew out of top-40 radio. *Radio & Records (R&R)* began using the term *contemporary hits radio* to describe the major radio markets in 1980. The term describes what was happening in the major markets better than the term *top 40,* according to Hurricane Heeran of *R&R.*

Contemporary hits radio stations play the records that are selling best in America's record stores, according to Michael C. Keith, author of *Radio Production: Art and Science.* Keith reports that CHR in 1990 had almost 20 percent of the radio listeners. This consisted of almost half of all rock listeners (p. 174).

Announcers on CHR stations are very dynamic in their delivery and "this is a production-intensive format" so the commercials are as upbeat as the music, says Keith, and there are a number of "contests and promotions" (p. 174).

To get an idea of the music, the CHR/pop top 50 the week of July 5, 1996, showed Alanis Morissette, Tracy Chapman, Natalie Merchant, and Mariah Carey in the top 10. Others on the charts included Eric Clapton, Toni Braxton, Hootie & The Blowfish, Tony Rich Project, Gin Blossoms, Lisa Loeb & Nine Stories, and Dishwalla. Songs with the most increased plays in the same week were recorded by Hootie & The Blowfish, Donna Lewis, Maxi Priest, Shaggy, Jewel, Mariah Carey, Tony Rich Project, Cranberries, and Natalie Merchant (*R&R,* p. 35).

R&R also lists a CHR/rhythmic top 50, and the top 5 in the same week, July 5, 1996, listed Bone Thugs number one with Toni Braxton, R. Kelly, Keith Sweat, and the Fugees (*R&R,* p. 41).

Carl Hausman, Philip Benoit, and Lewis B. O'Donnell, in *Modern Radio Production,* suggest that CHR stations adjust music depending on the daypart to entice a larger audience. CHR-formatted stations program to an age demographic that is approximately from 12 to 34.

"Contemporary Hits Radio." *Radio & Records* (July 5, 1996): 35–41.

Hausman, Carl, Philip Benoit, and Lewis B. O'Donnell. *Modern Radio Production.* Belmont, Calif.: Wadsworth, 1996.

Keith, Michael C. *Radio Production: Art and Science.* Boston: Focal Press, 1990.

Arthur Thomas Challis, Jr.

CONTESTS offer radio listeners a chance at prizes and fame; give advertisers the added value of a prominent, on-air position; and provide broadcasters with an element of excitement and opportunities for additional revenue. Primarily a promotional device, contests have evolved from the long-form quiz show formats of early radio to become an effective marketing tool and ratings builder.

Perhaps best typified by the "free-money" giveaways of contemporary hits radio (CHR) formats, contests have kept listeners vying for cash and merchandise as far back as 1933 when the CBS quiz show *True or False* pitted men against women for $30 in prize money. Countless other contest-driven shows followed, such as *Walk a Mile,* in which contestants won cartons of Camels. In 1944, the NBC Blue Network paired down the 30-minute quiz show format to a 5-minute short form with *Coronet Quick Quiz.* Short-form contests, still a radio mainstay, include "name it and claim it," a record or ticket giveaway (inspired by NBC's popular 1952 radio and television game show *Name That Tune,* itself a knock-off of Mutual's 1944 radio show, *What's the Name of That Song?);* and "the phrase that pays" (taken from the 1953 NBC game show of the same name), a call-out contest that encourages listeners to answer their telephone with a station's slogan.

Contests not requiring skill or talent to win are often referred to as sweepstakes, won by chance, and often include prizes contributed by cosponsors interested in generating awareness, retail traffic, and/or product sales; however, lottery laws are strict in requiring alternate methods of entry where no purchase is necessary.

In the past, the Federal Communications Commission (FCC) looked askance at contest hype during ratings periods, but since the mid-1970s when this authority was deregulated, the contest tease has been used effectively to force tune-in at specific times. High-value prizing, unique-sponsor visibility, and station image enhancement represent key components of contests.

Joseph R. Piasek

COOLIDGE, CALVIN (1872–1933), American President, 1923–1929, was born in Plymouth Notch, Vermont, on July 4, 1872. He graduated cum laude from Amherst in 1895 and established a law practice in Northampton, Massachusetts. Coolidge's political career began in 1898 when he was elected to the Northampton City Council. He rose steadily through the Massachusetts Republican Party and was elected governor in 1918. In 1920 Coolidge was Warren Harding's running mate and was elected vice president. Harding died suddenly on August 2, 1923, and Calvin Coolidge became president. In 1924, Coolidge was elected to a full term.

Coolidge was the first president whose speeches were carried over radio networks. His first message to Congress on December 4, 1923, was carried by stations as far away as Missouri and Texas. On October 24, 1924, 22 stations carried his address to the U.S. Chamber of Commerce in Washington. His inaugural ceremony in March 1925 was carried by 24 stations and reached an estimated 15 million listeners.

During Coolidge's second term, his secretary of commerce, Herbert Hoover, held the last of his four unsuccessful radio conferences in 1925. After the failure of these attempts at self-regulation, Coolidge gave his support to the *Radio Act of 1927,* which established the Federal Radio Commission. Coolidge signed the act into law on February 23, 1927. Coolidge declined to run for reelection in 1928. He retired to Northampton, where he suffered a coronary thrombosis and died on January 5, 1933.

Lindsey E. Pack

COON-SANDERS NIGHTHAWKS ORCHESTRA, the "Orchestra that Made Radio Famous," pioneered the programming concept that lured popular dance bands to radio in the mid-1920s through World War II, the progenitor of modern pop music formats. Although not the first hotel radio orchestra, the Nighthawks were the first to broadcast nightly nationwide, developing an audience habit of listening *regularly* to the same show. They are believed also to have been the first to play fan requests and the first with a national fan club.

WDAF first broadcast them from Kansas City's Muehlebach Hotel on December 3, 1922. Heard from Hawaii to England, Mexico to Canada, the band was co-led by pianist-vocalist-arranger Joe L. Sanders (1896–1965) and drummer-vocalist Carleton A. Coon (1894–1931). Witty announcer Leo Fitzpatrick created the *Nighthawk Frolic* to get away from WDAF's sound-dead studio. On air he read telegraphed tune requests and issued fan club charters for towns throughout the continent.

The Nighthawks recorded for Columbia and Victor and were popular on summer tours and college campuses. In 1924, they moved to Chicago and eventually performed on KYW, WBBM, and WGN. At the Blackhawk Hotel they were among Jules Stein's first bookings for MCA. They broadcast on CBS from Chicago and on NBC over New York's WEAF. Fame faded after Coon's untimely death. Sanders organized his own band, but the once-renowned Nighthawks were superseded by other big bands.

Eberly, Philip K. *Music in the Air.* New York: Hastings House, 1982.

William James Ryan

COOPER, JACK LEROY (1888–1970), was a "black-appeal" radio pioneer, and the first African American with a commercially sustained broadcast. Cooper built a broadcast dynasty in Chicago that made him a millionaire and influenced African-American radio programming throughout the country. Before entering broadcasting, Cooper worked in a variety of fields. He was a newsboy, a porter, and even an entertainer acting, singing, and dancing with his own vaudeville group during the early 1920s. As a performer on the black theater circuit, he learned how to entertain black audiences, and as a troupe owner he gained valuable experience in business management. In addition, Jack Cooper wrote for several black newspapers and clearly saw himself as a "Race Man," a man dedicated to the improvement of the "Negro race." In 1925, Cooper decided to try his hand at announcing on Washington, D.C. station WCAP. Because of racial discrimination, blacks were not allowed in that station. But the ever-resourceful Cooper dressed like a delivery man, entered the station, and presented his case. He was successful and thus began Cooper's illustrious radio career.

He moved to Chicago in 1926 and approached "ethnic" radio station WSBC about doing a show for African Americans. WSBC aired a mixture of foreign language programs for Chicago's numerous ethnic communities. So Cooper's proposal fit right into WSBC's "ethnic" concept, and he began programming for Chicago's African-American community. During radio's early days, announcers would buy or "broker" time from stations. The announcers could earn money by selling portions of their airtime to sponsors/advertisers. The consummate business-man, Cooper's WSBC radio program became a successful moneymaker, and by 1929, Cooper's *All-Negro Hour* was a fast-paced mix of live music and comedy sketches. It was so popular and financially lucrative that Cooper began to buy more time from the station and fill it with "black-appeal" programming.

During the early 1930s, Cooper began playing the latest recordings of the top black bands and artists of the day. His popularity continued to soar, and by the mid-1930s, Cooper controlled 9.5 hours of WSBC's 56 hours of weekly airtime. He even brokered and programmed time with his wife Gertrude on another Chicago station WHFC. In 1947, Jack L. Cooper Presentations, supported by nearly 50 sponsors, owned about 40 hours of weekly airtime on four different stations, a truly unprecedented feat for an African American.

Cooper employed African Americans as announcers or salespersons and pro-vided broadcast services that could be found no where else on the radio. He was a leader in broadcasting black gospel music in Chicago, and his *Missing Persons* program helped more than 20,000 African Americans, who had moved to this sprawling northern city from the South, find missing relatives and loved ones. Using African-American newspaper articles, Cooper was the first to regularly broadcast black-oriented newscasts, and he broadcast Negro baseball league games. Voted Chicago's top radio man in 1951, Jack L. Cooper was the model. He paved the way for what would become black-formatted radio and proved that radio programming for and by African Americans could be relevant, entertaining, and extremely profitable.

Black Radio: Telling It Like It Was. A 13-part radio documentary series with Lou Rawls. Washington, D.C.: Radio Smithsonian, Smithsonian Productions, 1996. (Series tapes are available for research at the Archives of African American Music and Culture, Indiana University, Bloomington and the Museums of Radio and Television in Los Angeles and New York.)

Dates, Janette L., and William Barlow, eds. *Split Image: African Americans in the Mass Media.* 2nd ed. Washington, D.C.: Howard University Press, 1993.

Newman, Mark. *Entrepreneurs of Profit and Pride: From Black-Appeal to Radio Soul.* New York: Praeger Publishers, 1988.

Sonja Williams

COPYRIGHT provides protection for "original works of authorship such as works of literature, musical compositions, works of art, drama, and other tangible expres-sions of ideas." Copyright also protects computer software, video and audio works, and material transmitted through cyberspace on the Internet. Copyright protection is available to published and unpublished works. United States copyright law is found in Title 17 of the U.S. Code.

The owner of a copyright retains the right to (1) reproduce the copyrighted work, (2) prepare derivatives of the copyrighted work, (3) distribute copies of the work to the public, (4) perform the work in public, or (5) display the work in public. The copyright owner may grant these rights to someone else either by sale, lease, or other arrangement. Anyone exercising the above rights without the permission of the copyright holder is subject to legal action.

Copyright protection is not unlimited. The doctrine of "fair use" allows limited use of copyrighted material for educational and certain other purposes. Copyright protection exists from the moment that a work is created and immediately becomes the property of the person who created it.

No registration or other action is required to secure copyright protection; however, registration of a work with the U.S. Copyright Office has several advantages. Registration establishes a public record of an author's claim of copyright protection. It also provides evidence that can be used in court in the event an infringement suit is filed. Registration also allows the copyright holder to recover statutory damages and attorney's fees in court actions. If a work is not registered, the copyright owner may only recover actual damages. Registration may be done at any time within the life of the copyright. Information on registering a work may be obtained by writing to the Register of Copyrights, Copyright Office, Library of Congress, Washington, D.C. 20559.

Length of Copyright Protection. Any work created on or after January 1, 1978, and in a fixed, tangible form is protected for the life of the author, plus an additional 50 years after the author's death. During that time the copyright may be willed to heirs, sold, or otherwise assigned by the copyright holder. In the case of joint works, the protection lasts for 50 years after the last surviving author's death. In the case of a "work-for-hire," copyright protection is 75 years from publication or 100 years from the work's creation, whichever is shorter. A work-for-hire is prepared by an employee within the scope of employment or is commissioned for use as a contribution to a collective work.

A work created before January 1, 1978, was protected for a maximum of 56 years, by two 28-year renewable terms. Copyright law now in effect extends the renewal term from 28 to 47 years, protecting these works for a total of 75 years.

Notice of Copyright. The notice of copyright contains three elements:

1. the © symbol, or the word "Copyright," or the abbreviation "Copr.";
2. the year of first publication of the work; and
3. the name of the owner of the copyright.

Copyright notice is optional on all works first published on and after March 1, 1989. Before that date the notice was mandatory. The Copyright Office recommends using the notice because doing so informs the public that the work is protected. Use of the notice will not allow a claim of "innocent infringement" to be successful.

Barrett, Margreth. *Intellectual Property: Cases and Materials*. St. Paul: West Publishing Co., 1995.

Miller, Arthur R., and Michael H. Davis. *Intellectual Property: Patents, Trademarks and Copyright in a Nutshell*. 2nd ed. St. Paul: West Publishing, 1990.

Copyright Basics Circular 1. http://lcweb.loc.gov/pub/copyright/circs/circ01.html (October 21, 1997).

Kenneth C. Creech

CORRECTIVE ADVERTISING was established by the Federal Trade Commission (FTC) in the early 1950s. This function requires an advertiser to correct the false impression left by deceptive advertising.

The FTC first required corrective advertising in 1971 when it required the ITT Continental Bread Company to correct false impressions of its Profile bread, according to Kent Middleton and Bill Chamberlin's *The Law of Public Communication*. The FTC also required Listerine to correct its advertisements, removing references to Listerine as a cold-prevention remedy.

When first used, advertisers were forced to set aside 25 percent of their advertising budget and time to make up for false impressions. Corrective advertising was popular in the 1960s and 1970s, according to Don Pember's *Mass Media Law*. There is a more probusiness attitude in the FTC, and for that reason, the FTC has backed down on these cases.

Middleton, Kent, and Bill Chamberlain. *The Law of Public Communication*. New York: Longman, 1994.
Pember, Don R. *Mass Media Law*. Dubuque, Iowa: Brown & Benchmark, 1996.

Ginger Rudeseal Carter

CORRELL, CHARLES AND FREEMAN GOSDEN were the famous team that wrote and performed *Amos 'n' Andy,*, one of radio's most popular shows. They are given credit for devising the comedy-serial format.

Charles Correll (1890–1972) was born in Peoria, Illinois. His relatives moved there from the South after the Civil War and were related to Jefferson Davis. He was musically gifted, but in high school, he learned shorthand and after graduation worked in the office of the state superintendent of construction. He returned to Peoria to learn to be a stone mason with his father but was employed to play background music at a silent movie theater. He also sang quartets in minstrel shows and danced. Correll took bit parts in any local production, and a Joe Bren producer (the Joe Bren Company produced shows for charitable organizations throughout the country) saw him and offered him a job managing rehearsals in another town.

Freeman Gosden (1899–1982) was born in Richmond, Virginia. His father was a member of the Confederate army. After high school he sold tobacco and cars and served in the navy during World War I. His real interest in life was the theater, and by age 10, he had appeared in carnival acts.

Correll met Gosden in 1919 when they both worked on a Joe Bren production in Durham, North Carolina. Afterwards, each man traveled around the country, supervising local shows. In 1924, both men were promoted to division managers, moved to Chicago, and became roommates. In 1925, they wrote a hit song in black dialect, "The Kinky Kids Parade." They developed a blackface song-and-patter act, which they tried over WEBH in 1925 in exchange for free meals. Later, WGN offered them a salary to remain in radio. They sang, told jokes, announced, and developed a radio serial, *Sam and Henry,* using black dialect. The show premiered in 1926 with Gosden (Sam) and Correll (Henry) acting all the parts in the 10-minute nightly show. They wanted to have a chain of stations around the country carry their show, but they were prevented from doing so by their WGN contract. They left the station after two years, and WGN claimed ownership of the characters.

In March of 1928, *Amos 'n' Andy* was first heard on WMAQ, Chicago. Again using black dialect, Gosden played Amos Jones, a simple, hardworking, trusting soul, and Correll played Andy Brown, the perfect fool, who never worked and always got taken in. During the early years, they played over 100 separate voice characterizations. They made recordings of the programs and sold them to 45 other stations. They also did two films, a comic strip, a book, dialogue, and song records.

In 1929, NBC Red approached them for a national show. They decided to do two live shows a night because of the time difference on the East and West Coasts. Richard Correll (Charles' son) said, "Freeman was the brains behind the team. My father was more laid back. While Freeman paced back and forth in the office verbalizing much of the black dialect, my father would be taking it down in shorthand. His background as a stenographer came in handy. He also typed every script, making an original and one carbon copy" (Andrews and Juilliard, p. 26).

Amos 'n' Andy was performed in a room that looked like a typical living room and even had a fireplace. They used one microphone and sat opposite each other. Correll played Andy in a very low voice close to the mike. Gosden spoke about two feet back from the microphone to play Amos and used a high-pitched voice. Described as "the more talented dialectician," he also played Lightin', Kingfish, and Calhoon.

In late 1938, with ratings slipping, they moved to CBS for a better deal. By 1943, the ratings had fallen, and they decided to take a break to devise a once-a-week half-hour situation comedy. They hired a team of writers and actors and rented an entire floor of a building on Wilshire Boulevard. In 1948, they returned to CBS and immediately began to think about television. Gosden helped in the search for television actors, although there was a question of whether to use black or white talent. One role that gave them great difficulty was that of Kingfish. They sought the aid of many friends; even President Harry Truman and General Dwight Eisenhower (both fans) had suggestions.

The television program debuted on CBS on June 28, 1951, and finished the first season in thirteenth place. The second season began with low ratings and constant pressure from the National Association for the Advancement of Colored People (NAACP). After 78 episodes, CBS canceled the series. The last date of broadcast was June 11, 1953.

In 1972, the year of his death, Correll explained the show: "We weren't kidding race. We were kidding people human nature things that happened to anybody and everybody. The show was clean. It had no violence. Our characters tried to depict cross sections of life. Everybody knew a wheeler-dealer like Kingfish, living off his wits; a blustering Andy, who never learned from experience. I knew a lot of people like that they were relatives of mine" (Andrews and Juilliard, p. 103). Correll also suggested the reason for their success was that the characters were likable.

August 19, 1981, was declared "Freeman Fisher Gosden Day" in Richmond, Virginia, the anniversary of the day *Amos 'n' Andy* debuted on NBC. Eighty-two-year-old Gosden spoke by phone and did some of his routines. He was still in good voice. Gosden died in 1982 at age 83. He always refused to talk publicly about the show, but it was reported that it bothered him his whole life that *Amos 'n' Andy* fell from public esteem. Gosden once said about the show: "Both Charlie [Correll] and

I have deep respect for black men. We felt our show helped characterize Negroes as interesting and dignified human beings" (Andrews and Juilliard, p. 103).

Andrews, Bart, and Ahrgus Juilliard. *Holy MacKeral!: The Amos 'n' Andy Story.* New York: E. P. Dutton, 1986.

Correll, Charles, and Freeman Gosden. *All About Amos 'n' Andy.* New York: Rand McNally, 1929.

Ely, Melvin Patrick. *The Adventures of Amos 'n' Andy: A Social History of an American Phenomenon.* New York: Free Press, 1991.

Mary E. Beadle

CORWIN, NORMAN (1910–), since his first programs in 1938, has been respected as the finest writer and producer of radio drama and documentary programs. Corwin was born on May, 3, 1910, in Boston. He worked for 10 years as a newspaperman before entering radio. Most of his programs were produced at CBS, and the most important were: Series—*So This Is Radio* (1939), *26 by Corwin* (1941), *An American in England* (series 1942), *Columbia Presents Corwin* (series 1944), *One World Flight* (1947); Episodes—"We Hold These Truths" (1941), "Election Eve Special" (1944), "On a Note of Triumph" (1945), "14 August" (1945). He has also written a score of books, plays, and movie scripts. He is a professor in the Annenberg School of Communication, University of Southern California. Charles Kuralt said Corwin was "the greatest of the writers for broadcast" and the "poet laureate of radio's age."

Bannerman, R. Leroy. *Norman Corwin and Radio: The Golden Years.* Tuscaloosa: University of Alabama Press, 1986.

Barnouw, Erik, *Radio Drama in Action: Twenty-five Plays of a Changing World.* New York: Rinehart & Company, 1945.

Bell, Douglas. *Years of the Electric Ear: Norman Corwin (an interview).* Metuchen, N.J.: Scarecrow Press, Inc., 1994.

Corwin, Norman. *Thirteen by Corwin.* New York: Henry Holt and Company, 1942.

Corwin, Norman. Several audio tape, or CD, collections of Norman Corwin's dramatized documentary and other drama programs are available from LodesTone, 611 Empire Mill Road, Bloomington, Ind. 47401; and Radio Yesteryear, Box C, Sandy Hook, Conn. 06482.

Langguth, A. J. *Norman Corwin's Letters.* New York: Barricade Books, 1994.

Lawrence W. Lichty

COST PER THOUSAND (CPM) is a means by which advertisers figure advertising costs in different media. The "M" represents the Roman numeral for 1,000. The CPM of any advertisement in any medium is calculated by dividing the cost of an advertisement by the number of thousand homes it reaches, represented as CPM ad cost × 1,000/circulation. According to Kleppner's Advertising Procedure, advertisers also use a weighted or demographic CPM that addresses that portion of a medium's audience falling into a prime-prospect category.

In radio, the CPM calculation allows an advertiser to compare the cost of advertising on radio compared with television, the cost from one station to another, even the difference from one program to another. The comparison permits the advertiser to get the most for his or her money.

Ginger Rudeseal Carter

COUGHLIN, CHARLES E. (1891–1979), known as "the radio priest." The Reverend Coughlin (pronounced *COG lin*) was a demagogue followed by millions of working-class Irish and Germans in the East and Midwest during the Great Depression.

In 1926, soon after he became pastor of the Shrine of the Little Flower, a parish in Royal Oak, Michigan, the Canadian-born Coughlin began broadcasting a show mostly for children called the *Golden Hour of the Little Flower* over WJR in Detroit. Gradually, Coughlin changed the show to promote social reforms advanced in papal encyclicals. Gradually, too, Coughlin's reach expanded. By 1929, Coughlin was heard in Chicago and Cincinnati. By 1930, he was heard nationally on CBS stations and internationally via shortwave from WCAU in Philadelphia. By 1932, Coughlin employed 106 clerks and four personal secretaries to handle the 80,000 letters that he received every week.

Coughlin's public involvement in politics began in earnest in 1930, when he castigated the Hoover administration for its anemic response to the country's economic crisis. Soon Coughlin's trademark themes emerged: He promoted the nationalization of currency as a panacea for economic recovery, and he railed against communism, international bankers, and unregulated capitalism. These themes reflected Coughlin's belief that greedy international bankers deliberately caused the Great Depression by creating an artificial scarcity of money to enrich themselves.

In 1932, Coughlin backed Franklin Roosevelt with his motto "Roosevelt or ruin." But the president's middle-of-the-road programs disappointed Coughlin, who called Roosevelt a "liar" and "a great betrayer" and accused his administration of being simultaneously communistic and plutocratic. In 1934, Coughlin organized the National Union for Social Justice to pressure the federal government, and in 1936 he formed the Union Party, which ran William Lemke and Thomas O'Brien for president and vice president. The hapless Union Party received fewer than 1 million votes and no electoral votes at all.

As the depression wore on, Coughlin's anti-Semitism became more and more pronounced. Coughlin supported Mussolini and Hitler. He blamed Jews for the depression. He advocated isolation even after Germany invaded Czechoslovakia. His weekly newspaper even published *The Protocols of Zion,* a bogus account of a Jewish conspiracy to control the world.

Despite Coughlin's bigotry and inflammatory rhetoric, his bishop, Michael James Gallagher of Detroit, supported him fully, so none of the mounting criticism inside or outside the Roman Catholic Church impeded Coughlin's public career. But Bishop Gallagher died in 1937. The following year, no radio networks would broadcast Coughlin's program, nor would any stations west of Kansas or south of Maryland. After the National Association of Broadcasters revised its code of standards in 1939 to prohibit controversial programs, few stations would sell time to Coughlin, and he canceled his program in 1940. Coughlin's public pronouncements ceased in 1942 at the order of Coughlin's new bishop, Edward Mooney. He spent the rest of his life quietly presiding over his parish.

Tull, Charles J. *Father Coughlin and the New Deal.* Syracuse: Syracuse University Press, 1965.

Warren, Donald. *Radio Priest: Charles Coughlin, the Father of Hate Radio.* New York: Free Press, 1996.

John P. Ferré

COUNTERPROGRAMMING is the tactic of engaging a successful competitor by providing distinctly different programming targeted at the same audience. Instead of trying to compete directly by offering a similar program, a counterprogramming strategy offers a program with different characteristics and appeals. For example, if one country music station has a very popular morning personality, another country station may deemphasize the presence of its own morning announcer by promoting the fact it plays more music. Counterprogramming may encompass such minute details as ensuring that when a competitor is playing commercials, one's own station is playing music.

Kenneth D. Loomis

COUNTRY AND WESTERN MUSIC. This important genre of American popular music originated as folk songs from England, Scotland, and Ireland but in time has produced such internationally famous stars as Patsy Cline and Garth Brooks. Originally sung with acoustic instruments including guitars, fiddles, and banjos, country music of the late twentieth century has dropped the "western" moniker and included electric amplified instruments and drums. The core audience for country music has always been poor white plain folks who settled the South and West in the United States. As an industry, it began in the 1920s when record executives recorded and distributed hillbilly performers, most notably first Jimmie Rogers and the Carter family. A western side was popularized by cowboy films in the 1930s, from such stars as Roy Rogers and Gene Autry. By the 1940s, radio barn dances, epitomized by the *Grand Ole Opry* and *Town and Country Time,* were winning new fans. During the post–World War II era, Hank Williams made his country songs big hits on the pop music charts. As top 40 took over radio airplay, country music emerged as a significant alternative genre. From Nashville, stars such as Johnny Cash, Loretta Lynn, and Dolly Parton pioneered a popularity that by the 1980s found country the most popular of radio's multiple formats.

Lewis, George H., ed. *All That Glitters: Country Music in America.* Bowling Green, Ohio: Bowling Green Popular University Press, 1993.

Malone, Bill C. *Country Music U.S.A.* Austin: University of Texas Press, 1985.

Douglas Gomery

COURT OF APPEALS, UNITED STATES, the court in the federal court system that hears appeals from federal district courts (the trial court in the federal system) and appeals of final orders of federal administrative agencies such as the Federal Communications Commission (FCC).

Sometimes called *circuit courts* because judges used to ride a particular "circuit" to hear cases, there are currently 13 courts of appeal, 12 of which serve a specific geographic area, and the thirteenth, the federal circuit, which hears certain federal contract, customs, and patent appeals. By law, all appeals of FCC-licensing decisions must be heard by the D.C. Court of Appeals. In practice, most other final decisions of the FCC that are appealed are taken to the D.C. Court of Appeals because the judges in that court have expertise in communication law matters and because most of the communications bar practice in the D.C. area.

In reviewing FCC decisions, the court of appeals must accept the factual record that was accumulated at the commission. No additional evidence is collected by the court. The court generally will review FCC decisions by looking for substantive errors of law and considering procedural issues. In the first situation, the court determines whether the commission in making its decision applied the pertinent law appropriately. If the court finds that the commission's action violates existing law, the court can overturn the commission's decision. In looking at procedural issues, the court tries to determine whether all the parties to the proceeding were treated fairly—whether due process was afforded to all participants.

Although the court of appeals is not supposed to substitute its policy judgments for those of the commission, at times the court has taken an active part in opening up the commission's processes. For example, the court forced the commission to allow radio listeners to participate in station-licensing decisions. In one famous case of judicial activism, the court ordered the FCC to consider the loss of specific radio formats when deciding whether to permit a station transfer. The commission refused, stating that the marketplace was the best determiner of entertainment formats. Ultimately, the dispute was appealed to the United States Supreme Court, which sided with the commission.

Krasnow, Erwin G., Lawrence D. Longley, and Herbert A. Terry. *The Politics of Broadcast Regulation.* 3rd ed. New York: St. Martin's Press, 1982.

Michael A. McGregor

COURTROOM, RADIO IN THE, shorthand phrase referring to several issues inhering in the use of radio in courtrooms in the United States. Such issues include courtroom decorum, conflicts with the Sixth Amendment right of criminal defendants to a fair trial, and liability for defamatory statements made during the trial.

One of the first documented cases of broadcasting courtroom proceedings occurred in 1934 in Chicago. The purpose of the broadcasts was to alert the public to penalties being imposed on traffic offenders. The next year the Bruno Hauptman trial received tremendous publicity, and the trial itself was broadcast. Using broadcasting equipment in a courtroom quickly became a source of confrontation between the bar and the media. The bar argued that broadcasting equipment damaged the decorum of the courtroom and could possibly affect a defendant's right to a fair trial by distracting the jury or making witnesses and other trial participants nervous. Trial lawyers also were concerned that excessive publicity via radio might prejudice a jury. The radio industry retorted that they were merely standing in for the public and that radio should have the same rights of access to trials as the print media. As early as 1936, an American Bar Association (ABA) report recommended that radio coverage of trials be severely curtailed. The ABA later adopted a canon of ethics specifically forbidding courtroom broadcasts. Whether to allow radio in the courtroom, however, was a state-by-state determination, with most states choosing restrictive policies.

The issues raised by radio in the courtroom became increasingly salient when courts began experimenting with allowing cameras in the courtroom. Ultimately, the Supreme Court ruled that cameras in a criminal trial did not necessarily violate the criminal defendant's Sixth Amendment right to a fair trial. Most states now permit to varying degrees the use of electronic media equipment in the courtroom.

With respect to issues of liability for the broadcast of defamatory material presented during a trial, the courts ruled that broadcasters had a qualified privilege to transmit a fair and accurate account of the proceedings. Thus, broadcasters were not liable for any defamatory material that they broadcast from an open court proceeding. See also **Canon 35**.

Charnley, Mitchell V. "Should Courtroom Proceedings Be Broadcast?" *Journal of the Federal Bar Association* 11 (1950): 64.
"Controlling Press and Radio Influence on Trials." *Harvard Law Review* 63 (1950): 840.

Michael A. McGregor

CRAVENS, KATHRYN (1899–1991). With her show *News through a Woman's Eyes* starting in 1934, Kathryn Cravens became the first woman radio commentator. She was born Kathryn Cochran in Burkett, Texas, about 1900. She began her career in 1919 as an actress in Hollywood and worked for Fox Films before marrying Rutherford Cravens in 1922. (Her marriage ended in 1937.) She moved to St. Louis where she acted in a few radio plays and became KMOX's expert on the woman's angle in 1933 with *Let's Compare Notes*. The show included household hints, fashion, beauty, and style.

Although Cravens saw no other women reporting the news, she listened to Boake Carter and Edwin C. Hill giving news commentary and thought she would try it, adding humor, sympathy, and drama behind the news. Her manager had at first told her to keep to her acting, but she was able to sell him a sample program. Her first news program started on February 11, 1934, and ran Monday through Saturday from 10:15 to 10:30 A.M., sponsored by a wholesale grocery business. She learned her reporting techniques from a *Kansas City Star* reporter, and instead of asking the who, what, where, and when questions, she made it her specialty to ask the how-does-it-feel questions.

She began editorializing. She advocated travel by air long before it became popular, and as a result, the airlines offered her free travel, a welcome benefit to her $85 a week salary. She became known as the flying reporter. When CBS bought her show in October 1936, they offered her $1,000 a week and travel expenses.

Her low, warm voice helped make her an instant celebrity in New York City. She awoke at 5:30 A.M. to write her script for that evening's 5:30 P.M. program and filled the time in between with interviews, lunches, teas, and the production of advertising spots for her sponsors. When Pontiac had her offer a free polishing cloth, nearly 250,000 people sent in for one, doubling the previous record for free merchandise offered on a daytime network program. Her popularity demanded four stenographers full-time to answer her mail.

In 1937 and 1938 Kathryn Cravens spoke on behalf of pacifism. In February 1938, CBS censored her comments against Hitler and warned her to stop her "pacifist propaganda." Her popularity had started to decline, and her program was dropped on April 8, 1938.

Cravens became a freelancer and returned to radio in the 1940s on WNEW, covering stories from the woman's viewpoint—stories on war relief, aid to war orphans, better schools for Harlem—and joined a radio committee to fight race hatred. When WNEW dropped her contract in 1945, she became an accredited war correspondent listed with Mutual Broadcasting System and entered Germany after the surrender. She was a commentator on WOL, Washington, D.C. and freelancer for WNEW. After the war, she wrote a fictional account of her adventures, *In Pursuit of Gentlemen*. She was a vice president of the Overseas Press Club in 1954.

Hosley, David H., and Gayle K. Yamada. *Hard News: Women in Broadcast Journalism*. New York: Greenwood, 1987.

Marzolf, Marion. *Up from the Footnote: A History of Women Journalists*. New York: Hastings House, 1977.

Margot Hardenbergh

CRONKITE, WALTER LELAND, JR. (1916–), voted in 1973 "The Most Trusted Man in America" and dean of broadcast journalists, got his start in journalism as a student at San Jacinto High School in Houston, Texas. Cronkite told *American Heritage* magazine that he has been in the business full-time since 1936, working for newspapers, wire services, radio, television, and in documentary film.

Cronkite, the only son of Dr. Walter L. Cronkite and Helen Lena Cronkite, was born in St. Joseph, Missouri, on November 4, 1916. An article in *American Boy* magazine about a foreign correspondent drew Cronkite into the study of journalism, and he began writing as a high school student. Cronkite became the campus correspondent for the *Houston Post* while a student at the University of Texas in Austin. He also worked part-time for a Houston radio station, KNOW, but eventually Cronkite left that job and college for a full-time job with the *Post*, a position he held for one year. In his television documentary *Cronkite Remembers*, he recalled applying for a position as a staff announcer at KNOW, but was not hired because the station manager said he would "never make it as a radio announcer."

According to his official CBS biography, Cronkite worked in radio as a sports announcer at Kansas City's KCMO radio after he left the *Post*. According to *Contemporary Heroes and Heroines*, Cronkite became a local celebrity because of his "faked" football broadcasts, where he would announce the scores while playing tapes of high school bands and describing the attire of local residents who had attended the game. It was at KCMO that Cronkite met Betsy Maxwell, whom he said was "the most gorgeous creature I'd ever seen." The two married in 1940.

In 1937, Cronkite left radio to join United Press (UP), becoming a World War II correspondent and covering battles including the invasion of Normandy in June

1944 and the Battle of the Bulge. After the war, he was the chief UP correspondent at the war crime trials in Nuremberg, then the UP's Moscow Bureau Chief.

Cronkite stayed with United Press until 1948, briefly returning to radio after the war's end. For the next two years, Cronkite was the Washington correspondent for a group of 10 midwestern radio stations. Cronkite told Richard F. Snow of *American Heritage* that he went into radio for the money, adding, "I had tried a little radio before the war and hadn't been terribly impressed with it. I thought it was pretty schlock. It didn't have the same principles that print did."

Cronkite added that the switch came after UP failed to give him a raise, adding that about that time, he ran into an old friend "who ran a radio station in Kansas City. [He] became convinced by what I was telling him about what I thought they needed to make their radio news really important to the community. I had no intention of doing it myself, but he decided he should have a Washington correspondent, and he asked what it would cost to send me there. I tripled my UPI salary and he said, 'That's fine.'"

Cronkite joined CBS News in 1950 following a call from Edward R. Murrow. CBS had acquired a television station in D.C., and Cronkite was assigned to the bureau to do a television show. It was his first foray into television. Cronkite said the early days of television were "pictorial radio news" and said he tried to make the newscasts newsy and legitimate.

He rose to fame through the 1950s, covering politics and anchoring political conventions for the network. In the late 1950s, with the launch of *Sputnik* and the beginning of the space race, Cronkite became CBS's lead space reporter through Projects Mercury, Gemini, and Apollo. *Newsweek* magazine called him "Dean of the Space Reporters" and dubbed him one of the "Golden Throats."

On April 16, 1962, Cronkite was named anchor of the *CBS Evening News,* then a 15-minute telecast. The show was lengthened to a half hour, the first show of that length, on September 2, 1963. Only two months later, Cronkite led Americans through the assassination and funeral of President John F. Kennedy. Cronkite's reporting also took him to the site of his third war, Vietnam.

Cronkite retired as anchor of the *CBS Evening News* on March 6, 1981, becoming a special correspondent for the network. His production company, Cronkite/Ward, continues to produce specials for CBS, the Discovery Channel, and the Learning Channel.

Cronkite, Walter L. *A Reporter's Life.* New York: Alfred A. Knopf, 1996.

Ginger Rudeseal Carter

CROSBY, HARRY LILLIS (1904–1977), known as Bing Crosby, was born in Tacoma, Washington, May 2, 1904. As a young man, he began studying law but gave it up to become a part of vaudeville. In 1925, he formed a band with a friend, Al Rinker, from Gonzaga University, Spokane, Washington, and they played throughout Washington state and along the West Coast. They began to gain a national reputation as the "Rhythm Boys." In 1930, while singing in Los Angeles, he met his wife-to-be—Ilma Winifred Wyatt. She was a young Hollywood star better known as Dixie Lee. Crosby's famous hit "I Surrender Dear" won him national recognition as well as her heart.

In 1931 he joined the CBS Network, appearing on the network with *Fifteen Minutes with Bing Crosby* and *The Bing Broadcast of 1932* and doing several films each year. He moved to NBC in 1935, where he hosted the *Kraft Music Hall,* a position he held for the next 10 years. In 1946, Crosby moved to ABC to host the *Philco Radio Time.* Under Philco he was able to become one of the first who would be allowed to "record and edit" the program, as opposed to doing it live each week.

Crosby's *Chesterfield* program began in 1949 and ran through 1952 on the CBS Network. Crosby appeared in films and on radio. He recorded on Decca Records, but he resisted television. He was at his best on radio and just being "Bing Crosby."

Crosby, Bing. *Call Me Lucky.* New York: Simon & Schuster, 1953.

ElDean Bennett

CROSLEY, POWEL, JR. (1886–1961), was the "The Henry Ford of Radio." He pioneered the development and manufacture of inexpensive sets. This gave a big boost to the popularity of radio, but it also required stations of greater power for reception on less sophisticated receivers. He promoted increased power for all stations and was the owner of the most powerful AM radio station ever to operate in the United States.

Crosley was born in Cincinnati, Ohio, on September 18, 1886. As a young man, his consuming interest was automobiles. Frustrated all of his life by his inability to build a financially successful car, he became a major American entrepreneur, and he had his greatest impact on the radio industry. After two years in law school, he quit to be a chauffeur and around cars, later working for a number of automobile manufacturers. He found success in selling many auto accessories and gadgets—a radiator cap to hold an American flag during World War I, for example—and with a small manufacturing plant making a number of wood products including phonograph cabinets.

In February 1921 his nine-year-old son asked for a "radio toy" as a birthday present. The least expensive retail set cost about $130, so he left the shop with a 25¢ instruction book and the parts. The father, not the son, caught the radio bug. Noting that a homemade set could be assembled for about $20 to $25, he hired two young engineering students from the University of Cincinnati—one was Dorman Israel, later chairman of Emerson Radio and Phonograph. Crosley and the students designed a set they could manufacture on an assembly line called the "Harko." It sold for $20, but later the price was reduced to only $9. He was the pioneer in making inexpensive sets, which he liked to call the "Model T of radio."

The first large sales campaign for the inexpensive sets was during Christmas shopping in December 1921: "It will tune from 200 to 600 meters, bringing in spark, voice and music, with an average amateur aerial." By July 1922, only a little more than a year after its beginning, Crosley was the largest manufacturer of radio sets and parts in the world—producing 500 sets a day. He purchased some smaller companies, and the Crosley Radio Corporation—later dropping "Radio" as other appliances were added—was a major corporation for 30 years. It was the first company to make refrigerators with shelves in the doors—the Shelvador—controlling a patent that made millions. He purchased the Reds baseball team and founded a professional football team in the city in the 1930s.

As a hobbyist, and to provide programming for purchasers of his sets, he started a radio station (see **WLW**). In 1934 the Reds were the first major league team to play a night game under lights, arranged by Crosley so the play-by-play could be carried on his radio station during more popular listening hours. WLW was also a founding station of MBS (see **Mutual Broadcasting System [MBS]**). Crosley was also a founder of the National Association of Broadcasters (NAB) (see **ASCAP [American Society of Composers Authors and Publishers]**).

The Crosley Corporation was an early TV set manufacturer and station owner. The company was purchased by the Aviation Corporation, later Avco, in 1945 and in 1954 was still the fifth largest manufacturer of radio and TV sets. The Crosley line of household appliances, including broadcast receivers, was discontinued in 1956. During the 1930s, the Crosley sets were extremely popular, especially the smaller kitchen art deco plastic (Bakelite) models, many of which looked like the front grille of a car.

Powel Crosley, Jr., introduced a small car intended to sell for about $300 and get 50 miles on a gallon of gas in 1939. Opposition from Detroit and World War II delayed manufacturing until 1946. In 1947 about 17,000 Crosley sedans, station wagons, delivery vans, and roadsters were sold; the next year nearly 47,000. But that was the peak: Americans wanted larger cars, and as they became available, the popularity of these smaller models declined. The auto plant shut down in July 1952. Crosley died in 1961—his impressive legacy including pioneer radio and televisions, leadership in the fledgling broadcasting industry, the small automobile, and night baseball.

Lichty, Lawrence W. "'The Nation's Station': A History of Radio Station WLW." Ph.D. dissertation, Ohio State University, 1964.

Lawrence W. Lichty

CROSSLEY, ARCHIBALD MADDOCK (1896–1985), audience and marketing researcher, was born December 7, 1896, in Fieldsboro, New Jersey, and graduated from Princeton University in 1917. A pioneer in the advertising research field, he studied public reaction to consumer products and researched radio listening habits, programs, and entertainers. He coined the term "rating."

In 1918, Crossley created Crossley Inc. to conduct political polling. In 1922, he moved into advertising, as a researcher, and later, research director, for *Literary Digest*. In 1927, the Association of National Advertising hired him to conduct research in the field of broadcasting. The goal was to discover more information from radio listening audiences than fan mail could provide and to determine to what extent listeners purchased products advertised over the air.

In 1929, Crossley developed the idea of estimating radio program audience sizes by telephoning radio owners and questioning them about what they listened to the previous night. In March of 1930, he helped establish the first radio audience measurement service, Cooperative Analysis of Broadcasting

(CAB), which routinely surveyed 33 cities where radio networks NBC and CBS had stations. The information gathered was relayed to advertising agencies and program sponsors, which used the information to pick shows and actors more closely linked to their products.

In 1934, a competing company, Clark-Hooper Inc., was established, which also used the telephone to survey radio audiences. However, unlike the CAB, Hooper phoned homes and asked those surveyed to identify programs they were listening to at the time of the call. This survey method became known as the "telephone coincidental."

Advertisers and sponsors soon preferred the Hooper ratings system because they felt it produced more accurate information about audiences. While Crossley's recall method required those surveyed to be at home at the time of the phone call, and remember the program listened to, Hooper's method measured the actual listening audience only as a percentage of the sample group potentially available to listen. Crossley also relied on subclass quotas, based on age, sex, and income, for his samples. Hooper, instead, used random samples.

A ratings battle ensued. By 1940, as a concession to advertisers who were switching to Hooper, CAB adopted a method whereby listeners were called two hours after the program had ended. In 1945, CAB dropped the recall ratings system in favor of the telephone coincidental. The changes came too late, however. By the mid-1940s, Hooper dominated the radio audience measurement business, and in 1946, CAB ended its 16-year-old research service.

Crossley himself opted out of the radio audience measurement business in 1938 to study magazine audiences. In 1947, Crossley began market surveys, in which he researched cost-effective ways for advertisers to promote products and how consumers responded to that advertising. In 1954, Crossley Inc. merged with S-D Surveys Inc., one of the oldest marketing consultant firms in the nation. Crossley died on May 1, 1985, in Princeton, New Jersey.

Buzzard, Karen S. *Chains of Gold: Marketing the Ratings and Rating the Markets.* Metuchen, N.J.: Scarecrow Press, 1990.

Robert C. Fordan

CROSSOVER is a song intended for a specialized audience that proves a hit in the broad pop music market. For example, Patsy Cline's "Crazy" was aimed at country record buyers but also appeared on the pop charts. Crossovers began in the late 1920s with hillbilly music being purchased by popular music buyers; by the late 1940s and early 1950s, country and rhythm and blues records were regularly crossing over and gave birth to rock 'n' roll. Crossovers sometimes happen by accident but most often are the results of a deliberative corporate attempt to increase sales.

Douglas Gomery

CROSS OWNERSHIP is the situation that arises when a daily newspaper and a radio station, or a television station and a radio station in certain circumstances, in the same market are owned by the same person or entity. Cross ownership has been prohibited by Federal Communications Commission (FCC) rules since 1975 (47 C.F.R. –73.3555). In the face of First Amendment attacks by the media, the United States Supreme Court upheld the cross-ownership ban in 1978 in *FCC v. National Citizens Committee for Broadcasting*, 436 U.S. 775 (1978). The cross-ownership ban is intended to prevent monopolization of local media by a single person or entity and thus ensure diversity of viewpoints in the marketplace of ideas.

The cross-ownership ban may be waived in particular circumstances, should the commission find that the waiver is required by the public interest. The FCC has consistently issued waivers of the cross-ownership rules since they were first put in place, and at least one attempt by Congress to end the issuance of such waivers was rejected by the courts. See *News Am. Publishing v. FCC*, 844 F.2d 800 (D.C. Cir. 1988).

Compaine, Benjamin M. "The Impact of Ownership on Content: Does It Matter?" *Cardozo Arts & Entertainment Law Journal* 13 (1995): 755.
Hamburg, Morton I., and Stuart N. Brotman, *Communications Law and Practice.* New York: Law Journal Seminars Press, 1995.
Wienberg, Jonathan. "Broadcasting and Speech." *California Law Review* 81 (1993): 1,103.

Robert A. Heverly

CRYSTAL SET is an inexpensive form of basic radio receiver that enabled listeners to pick up signals with sets simple enough to be made at home. In 1906, G. W. Pickard patented a receiving set based on a silicon crystal connected to a wire coil, antenna, and headset. The same year a slightly different version, featuring a carborundum detector, was developed by H. H. C. Dunwoody. Other forms of the crystal set were made with such components as lead ore and iron pyrite. These mineral detectors became very popular in the early days of wireless telegraphy and radio, and a potential audience existed even before broadcasting took hold in the 1920s. Although the homemade sets gradually became more elaborate, their construction remained within both the technical and financial means of many hobbyists and amateurs, who were able to listen to communications in the form of voice and music, as well as Morse code. Marine radio exchanges, disaster calls for assistance, and experimental broadcasts were generating increasing numbers of listeners, thanks to the affordable and increasingly popular crystal sets. Maintenance of a clear signal, however, generally required periodic, if not constant, attention to the "sweet spot," where the coil wire or "cat whisker" and crystal converged, and the quality of signal was seldom dependable. The superior sound of vacuum-tube radios and their consequent greater desirability eventually resulted in relegation of the crystal set to applications such as child-craft projects and novelty or technical antique collections.

Douglas, George. *The Early Days of Radio Broadcasting.* Jefferson, N.C.: McFarland, 1987.
Dunlap, Orrin E., Jr., ed. *Radio's 100 Men of Science.* New York: Harper, 1944.
MacLaurin, W. Rupert. *Invention and Innovation in the Radio Industry.* New York: Arno Press and *The New York Times,* 1971.

B. R. Smith

CUME, short for cumulative audience, is the estimated number of different people who listen to a radio station for a minimum of five minutes within a quarter hour in a given daypart. Cume is often referred to as the net or unduplicated audience and is a measure of how wide an audience a station reaches. Cume can be reported as cume persons or as a cume rating (a percentage of the total number of persons listening to radio during that daypart).

Fletcher, James E., ed. *Broadcast Research Definitions.* Washington, D.C.: National Association of Broadcasters, 1988.

Ronald Razovsky

D

DAB. *See* **digital audio broadcasting (DAB).**

DAVIS, ELMER (1890–1958), respected *New York Times* newspaperman who became a noted CBS commentator and head of the Office of War Information (OWI). The OWI, established by Franklin D. Roosevelt in June 1942, first included radio, when that medium was transferred from Archibald McLeish's Office of Facts and Figures to the newly established unit under Davis. Four departments were consolidated in this effort, with the OWI serving effectively as a censor and information clearinghouse at home with propaganda oversight abroad during the war years.

An Indiana native, Davis became a Rhodes Scholar in Great Britain and did some magazine editing before joining the staff of the *New York Times.* He served as a foreign correspondent and as an editorialwriter and also penned a corporate history of that leading newspaper. A series of freelance magazine articles for *Harpers* describing the worsening political situation in Europe so impressed Paul White of CBS News that Davis was asked to replace H. V. Kaltenborn as political commentator for that network. He achieved considerable success in this role until he was called to service as head of the OWI.

Under Davis's direction, the OWI issued guidelines and also established some shortwave broadcasts that helped to clarify U.S. government policy on war-related events. His approach was to coordinate government efforts in information dissemination carefully and attempt to seek voluntary compliance on issues involving the public and the press. This seemed to work well. Under Davis's direction, for example, radio broadcasters were asked to integrate prowar messages and talent into their regular popular programs, rather than force-feed information or try to create specialized programming. This also helped control costs and the overwhelming amount of information being offered to the public. Davis also effectively orchestrated news offerings and managed propaganda efforts outside the United States. His coordinated effort in controlling information flow won him supporters in newsrooms throughout the nation and the military.

When the war ended, Davis returned to radio as a commentator for ABC News, winning special praise and a Peabody Award in 1951 for his broadcasts addressing civil liberties issues raised in the era of the House Un-American Activities Committee. He made a brief transition to television in 1954 and died just four years later in Washington, D.C.

Bliss, Edward, Jr. *Now the News: The Story of Broadcast Journalism.* New York: Columbia University Press, 1991.

Fang, Irving E. *Those Radio Commentators!* Ames: Iowa State University Press, 1977.

                                                                    Michael D. Murray

DAVIS AMENDMENT was a rider attached to the House's bill authorizing the extension of the Federal Radio Commission (FRC) under the provisions of the *Radio Act of 1927.* The amendment, introduced in 1928, called for the Federal Radio Commission to develop an allocation scheme that would provide "equality of radio broadcasting service, both of transmission and reception" to all zones of the United States. The division of the standard broadcast band (AM) into local, regional, and clear channel assignments was an outgrowth of the FRC's attempt to implement the Davis Amendment.

Interference among radio stations became a great problem as radio stations proliferated during the 1920s. The standard broadcast band (AM) was subject to long-distance skipping at night, and early radio receivers were prone to producing an annoying whistling interference from stations on the same channel thousands of miles away. The Federal Radio Commission, originally established as a temporary one-year panel, was charged with the responsibility of eliminating interference and developing an allocation scheme for radio service in the United States. Unable to complete its charge for technical and political reasons within the first year, the continuation of the FRC required reauthorization. Some members of Congress felt that the FRC had not carried out mandates in the 1927 act that called for equitable service to all regions of the country.

During hearings about the commission's reauthorization, Edwin L. Davis (R–Tenn.), proposed substitute wording for the Watson Bill that would modify Section 9 of the *Radio Act of 1927.* The amendment called for equality of radio service among the regions of the country to correct what many perceived as a geographic imbalance of broadcasting stations favoring the large cities of the East and Midwest. The "Equal Division" clause suggested by Davis included language that specifically guaranteed an equal allocation of licenses, frequency bands, hours of operation, and station power among the five zones comprising the different regions of the United States. The Davis Amendment sparked a rancorous debate among politicians, broadcasters, engineers, listeners, and members of the commission itself. Representative Davis charged that a powerful radio trust was dominating every aspect of radio in the United States. Congress felt that its constituents wanted quick action to resolve the interference problems that plagued the country and supported the change in the *Radio Act of 1927.* Broadcast stations, particularly in the East, were concerned that their licenses and power allocations could change dramatically. Claims were made by both broadcasters and FRC members that the Davis Amendment would make it impossible to eliminate the interference problem.

Passed by Congress and approved by the president on March 28, 1928, the Davis Amendment required the FRC to survey the five geographical zones and create a plan that would redistribute broadcasting facilities equally among them. At the same time, Congress directed the FRC to eliminate some stations to reduce congestion in cities like New York and Chicago. Different interest groups including the National Association of Broadcasters, Radio Manufacturers Association, Institute of Electrical Engineers, and the Bureau of Standards proposed solutions to the interference and overcrowding problem for the AM broadcast band.

A plan to implement the equal-division clause of the Davis Amendment emerged from the Federal Radio Commission on August 30, 1928. Included in General Orders 40 and 42 was the idea of assigning "clear channel" stations, regional, and local assignments to each region of the country as a means of creating equality. Clear channel stations would be allowed to use higher power than stations on regional or local assignments. Clear channel frequencies would not be able to be reused in other regions of the country, thus reducing the problematic interference many rural listeners suffered before the creation of the FRC. Regional channels would be used by two or three zones, and low-power channels could be used in all five zones of the country. Under the plan described in General Order 40, 8 clear channels, 35 regional channels, and 6 channels for local use would be allocated to each of the zones. The FRC presumed that clear channels would provide dependable long-distance reception to rural and suburban areas. Regional stations would provide service to urban and suburban centers, while the 6 local channels would be able to be licensed in several locales within each region. The plan did not purport to give an equal number of licenses between the geographical regions of the country.

Anticipating a mixed reaction from the public, the Federal Radio Commission embarked on a high-visibility public relations campaign to educate the public about the unfamiliar aspects of the plan. Some experts claim that the plan closely followed the recommendations of earlier radio conferences held by broadcasters and the secretary of commerce; others contend that the commissioners manipulated the situation by packing small broadcasters closely together and severely limiting their operations in hopes of reclaiming the broadcast frequencies of those marginal broadcasters at a later date. As the FRC began implementing the reallocation of assignments, it also worked with large manufacturers and the Institute of Radio Engineers to develop more stringent standards of engineering. By implementing the allocation changes and forcing broadcasters to maintain modern equipment, the Federal Radio Commission hoped to eliminate or reduce interference for the listening public.

Federal Radio Commission. *Annual Report of the Federal Radio Commission to the Congress of the United States.* Washington, D.C.: U.S. Government Printing Office, 1927.

"The Problems of Radio Reallocation." *Congressional Digest* 7 (10) (October 1928): 255–286.

Rosen, Philip T. *The Modern Stentors: Radio Broadcasters and the Federal Government, 1920–1934.* Westport, Conn.: Greenwood Press, 1980.

Fritz Messere

DAYPART. *See* **dayparting;** *also see* different format descriptions.

DAYPARTING is the practice of segmenting the broadcast schedule into blocks for purposes of targeting listenership at a given time. *Morning-drive, midday, afternoon-drive, evening, late-night, and overnight* are discrete dayparts, each programmed for unique audience demographics and listeners' daily habits. The frequency of commercials and promos, the content of news stories and talk shows, and the rotation of music are all considered when dayparting.

Joseph R. Piasek

DEAD AIR, without sound, is different from dead rolling (or potting) when a record or tape is started with the fader turned down all the way. In the early days of radio, interruptions were commonplace, since equipment was often susceptible to weather and other interference. Stations were often going off the air. With techno-logical improvements, such interference is less and less frequent. Disc jockeys and operations people can create dead air by failing to roll a commercial, CD, or other program unit. With web site audio transmission, the dead air experienced comes when the computer goes down or the workstation user's system experiences "technical difficulties."

Mary Kay Switzer

DEES, RICK (1951–), is a broadcast personality and comedy performer, known for his zany sense of humor. Born in North Carolina and raised in Greensboro, Rick Dees graduated from the University of North Carolina and worked as a DJ on stations throughout the South. While morning announcer at WHBQ in Memphis in 1976, he recorded a novelty song, "Disco Duck," which parodied the disco craze and became an unexpected hit, selling 2 million copies.

With his "Cast of Idiots," a myriad of self-created voices, he moved to LA's KHJ-AM in 1979. Largely unsuccessful, Dees moved to LA's KIIS-FM in 1981 where he won *Billboard*'s "Radio Personality of the Year" award 13 times and is under contract through 2000. Since 1982, he has hosted radio's internationally syndicated show *The Rick Dees Weekly Top 40.* In TV, Dees hosted *Solid Gold* (1983–1984) and *Into the Night with Rick Dees* (1991). His film credits include parts in *La Bamba* and *Blind Date.*

Dees, Rick. http://www.rick.com

Robert C. Fordan and W. A. Kelly Huff

DE FOREST, LEE (1873–1961), was one of several critical inventors of radio apparatus. His most famous invention was a vacuum-tube detector called the audion. The audion was the prototype for all subsequent radio tubes whether they were used for detection, amplification, or transmission.

De Forest was born in Council Bluffs, Iowa, in 1873, but in 1879 his family moved to Talladega, Alabama, where his father was appointed president of Tal-ladega College, a Congregationalist institution established to educate the children of black freedmen. Shunned by both black and white society in the South, de Forest and his siblings spent a lonely and isolated childhood under the strict tutelage of their minister father.

In 1893, de Forest entered Yale's Sheffield Scientific School to study engineering. He had determined from an early age to become an inventor and made many attempts at such while at Yale. De Forest concentrated on electrical science during his doctoral studies at Yale and wrote a dissertation on high-frequency oscillation effects in parallel wires. De Forest's dissertation is sometimes credited for being the first American doctoral dissertation to deal with the field of wireless because he used Hertzian waves in his experiments.

After graduating from Yale in 1899, de Forest began to work in earnest in wireless telegraphy. His primary concern was developing a more sensitive replacement for Marconi's crude detection device, the coherer. Eventually, de Forest would abandon wireless telegraphy in favor of wireless telephony, which he saw as the future of radio. Within several years, de Forest established his own company, the de Forest Wireless Telegraph Company, for the purpose of raising research funds through the sale of stock. This and other similar de Forest ventures ended in misfortune for de Forest, as he often found himself maneuvered out of his assets by unscrupulous partners.

In 1906, de Forest produced a new detector that would represent a major shift in radio technology. Having worked on the detection of Hertzian waves using ionized gas, de Forest was led to the use of a glass envelope with a filament and plate. De Forest believed that as the gas inside the tube was heated by the filament, the current would be transferred to the plate circuit. Hertzian waves would disrupt the flow; thus, the plate *detected* the presence of waves as reflected in fluctuations in the plate-circuit current. John Ambrose Fleming had already achieved the same result while working for Marconi in England, albeit from a different starting point, that of the Edison Effect in incandescent light bulbs. De Forest's innovation was to add a third element into the glass tube. The audion had a zigzag piece of nickel wire inserted between the filament and plate. When the wire grid is positively charged, it attracts and accelerates the stream of electrons from the iron filament before they hit the nickel plate. As the charge on the grid is increased, so is the charge on the plate circuit. In this way, the third element serves as a controller of the current and can also amplify a weak signal. It was eventually realized that the audion could also serve as an oscillator since the juxtaposition of the input and output circuits created continuous waves of its own.

Patent disputes emerged between de Forest and Fleming that were not fully resolved until after the audion patent was sold to AT&T, the American rights to the Fleming valve were acquired by RCA, and these two companies entered into a cross-licensing agreement in 1920. De Forest never regained the prominence of his early life and, after three failed marriages and a number of failed business ventures, settled with his fourth wife in Los Angeles where he tinkered in a lab subsidized by Bell Telephone. Lee de Forest died of heart failure at the age of 87 with only $1,250 left in savings.

Aitken, Hugh, G. J. *The Continuous Wave: Technology and American Radio, 1900–1932.* Princeton, N.J.: Princeton University Press, 1985.

Lewis, Thomas S. W. *Empire of the Air: The Men Who Made Radio.* New York: HarperCollins
    Publishers, 1991.

Christina S. Drale

DEMOGRAPHIC APPEALS. Demographic segments identify an audience by
age, sex, and characteristics. In selecting on which station to purchase airtime,
advertisers are not interested in simply reaching the greatest number of people; they
are interested in reaching the greatest number of the right kinds of people. Specifically, advertisers seek to reach people who are of a certain age, have some
discretionary income, have the desire to spend that money on certain products, and
who respond to advertisements by purchasing those products. Because advertisers
have this focused need, radio stations seek to portray themselves as vehicles to reach
these attractive consumers. In so doing, stations create formats designed to target
listeners with the characteristics (demographic appeals) attractive to advertisers.
One audience "target" might be a particular age group such as young adults between
18 and 24 years old. Or, a station might target listeners of a specific ethnic group,
or gender, or education level. Each of these audience demographic characteristics
describe a consumer group of interest to advertisers. Each station's goal is to focus
its programming so that when ratings are taken, the demographic characteristics of
its audience appear to be more attractive to advertisers than the demographic
characteristics of the audiences of other radio stations and media.

Kenneth D. Loomis

DEPARTMENT OF JUSTICE (DOJ), UNITED STATES, headed by the attorney general, is the legal arm of the executive branch, charged with enforcing federal
law. DOJ decides which federal court and administrative decisions to appeal to
higher courts. The Antitrust Division of DOJ has primary enforcement power of
U.S. antitrust laws.

Early in the history of the broadcast industry, DOJ filed suit against General
Electric (GE), Westinghouse, and AT&T, alleging that agreements those companies,
and RCA, made regarding how to divide up the radio business violated the *Sherman
Act.* The agreements, reached in 1926, stipulated that AT&T would leave radio
broadcasting and receiver sales to RCA, while AT&T retained wireline transmission
rights. Further, RCA agreed to use AT&T lines for program transmission service.
Finally, RCA retained exclusive rights to deliver video over the air, and AT&T took
exclusive rights to deliver video over wire. A settlement to the lawsuit was reached
in 1932, when RCA and AT&T relinquished their exclusive rights. GE and Westinghouse also agreed to dispose of their RCA stock.

During the 1960s and 1970s, the Department of Justice took an active role in
formulating Federal Communications Commission (FCC) policies concerning
media ownership. DOJ participated in FCC rule-making proceedings dealing with
multiple- and cross-ownership rules.

Following passage of the *Telecommunications Act of 1996,* DOJ became very
active in reviewing radio acquisitions in local markets. Even though the new law
permits common ownership of up to eight radio stations in the same market, the

DOJ has indicated in several cases that it will oppose mergers that result in one owner controlling over 40 percent of the market's radio advertising revenue.

Michael A. McGregor

DEPRESSION, THE GREAT, made radio an American mainstay. With more than a third of the working population out of work, Bob Hope, Fibber McGee and Molly, and Arthur Godfrey, among others, helped to cheer the nation. In 1930, an estimated 12 million American homes had radio sets, and by the end of the decade, 30 million American households were tuning in radios. Families would forsake essential household items rather than give up listening to shows like *Amos 'n' Andy, Jack Benny, Ed Wynn, George Burns and Gracie Allen,* and *Edgar Bergen and Charlie McCarthy.*

Music and comedy were popular fare during the 1930s. *Rudy Vallee's Variety Hour, Kate Smith, Eddie Cantor, Your Hit Parade, Kay Kyser's College of Musical Knowledge,* and others filled half of the network schedule with music. The Metropolitan Opera began its regular broadcasts on NBC in 1931. Almost as popular as music programs were serials and mystery dramas, such as *Ma Perkins, The Shadow, Charlie Chan,* and *Lux Radio Theater. The Lone Ranger* was the cornerstone of a fourth network, the Mutual Broadcasting System, which began as a consortium of stations in Detroit, Chicago, Cincinnati, and New York City. Competition between NBC and CBS for hit programs was won by NBC since the older network could hire a show's stars away from CBS once they were successful.

Advertising revenues increased almost fourfold during the 1930s to $155 million; advertising agencies controlled most of the programs. George Washington Hill, president of the American Tobacco Company, fathered the radio spot using gimmicks like the auctioneer's chant and repeated slogans—"L.S.M.F.T." (Lucky Strike Means Fine Tobacco)—to make his point to the audience.

The first national rating service was organized in 1930 by Archibald Crossley for the Association of National Advertisers. The Crossley ratings were based on telephone interviews of a population sample. Crossley soon had competition from Hooper ratings introduced in 1935.

Americans looked to radio not just for music and entertainment but for news as well. President Franklin D. Roosevelt's *Fireside Chats* began on March 12, 1933, with his remedy for the banking crisis. Over the next 11 years, FDR reassured the nation by fireside 28 times in a format well suited to his informality and charm.

Ex-newspapermen were on the air during the 1930s reporting the tumult in Europe and the depression at home. When the *Brooklyn Eagle* laid off employees, CBS hired an editor, H. V. Kaltenborn, for $100 a week to become a radio commentator. Abel Schechter was at *The New York World* before becoming NBC's one-man news bureau, collecting stories by telling sources he was calling from the office of Lowell Thomas. Thomas introduced *Headline Hunters* in 1929 and reported on the NBC Blue Network until it became ABC in 1943. Radio's round-the-clock coverage of the Lindbergh baby kidnapping promoted the career of Boake Carter at CBS. Edwin C. Hill broadcast nightly on CBS *The Human Side of the News. The March of Time* combined news and drama beginning in 1928 as a program entitled *NewsCasting*. The rivalry between newspapers and broadcasters culminated in the Biltmore Agreement of 1933. Publishers, fearing radio competition, persuaded the networks to close their bureaus and limit newscasts to two short summaries a day. The agreement unraveled when wire services bowed to the demand from advertisers and audience for more radio news during the Great Depression.

William R. Davie

DEREGULATION. Radio broadcasting was at first regulated because it used the resources of the frequencies. Congress mandated that it serve in "the public interest, convenience and necessity." As it became part of the way of life for many people during the 1930s and 1940s, the Federal Communications Commission (FCC) imposed increased regulation, both technical and programming. By the 1970s, the FCC had built up more regulation than could be readily handled by radio's many small entrepreneurs. The promise to reduce government regulations was part of the Reagan and Bush administrations of the 1980s. This era, which was marked by a friendliness to business, eradicated many government rules and regulations. It was an era known as "DEREGULATION."

Among the primary broadcast regulations that were dismantled by the FCC were:

Station license renewal. Every three years, both radio and TV stations were required to submit lengthy forms through communications attorneys with access to the FCC. The renewal period was expanded to five years for television and to seven years for radio. The *Telecommunications Act of 1996* further expanded that to eight years and gave assurance that licenses would be renewed barring "serious" violation or "patterns of abuse" of FCC rules. Furthermore, the process was changed from complicated forms to a simple "postcard" renewal.

News (nonentertainment) programs. News and public affairs programs, once required of all stations, were no longer required.

Ascertainment of public needs. Once station managers were required to go into the community and talk to leaders of business, civic groups, churches, and so on, and determine the most pressing needs of the community that that station served. Presumably, then, those needs were addressed in the news and public affairs programming of the station. But with no news and public affairs required, there was no need for stations to go out and ascertain such needs. The rule was dropped. And with this requirement dropped, there was concurrent elimination of a list of community problems/issues that the station was required to keep in its files.

Paperwork reduction. Stations were once required to have logs kept of programming and technical information, and FCC financial reports. Now that was all gone—"deregulated."

Fairness Doctrine. It was once thought that broadcasting was such a powerful influence that there must be built-in measures of balance. Thus, if a station was used to advocate one side of a controversial issue, it must allow airtime for all other viewpoints on that issue. This FCC policy was even upheld by the U.S. Supreme Court (in *Red Lion Broadcasting Co. v. FCC,* 1969). But in 1987, the Fairness Doctrine was abolished by the agency that created it, the FCC.

Ownership limitations. Once the FCC would not allow one licensee to operate any more than 7 AM, 7 FM, and 7 TV stations. That was changed first to 12, then any number, so long as it did not exceed 25 percent of the national market. Then, with the *Telecommunications Act of 1996,* that percentage was increased to 35 percent. Duopoly, an owner with multiple stations in the same service in the same market, once taboo, was relaxed.

Antitrafficking. Once station licensees were not allowed to sell over a station license within three years after acquiring it. Such a turnaround was considered "trafficking," and the FCC had an "antitrafficking" rule. But the FCC dropped that rule, allowing the free selling of stations in whatever time period the market would allow.

Limitations on commercial time. Once a part of both a professional Code of Good Practice and the FCC, commercial limitations kept stations from running more than 18 minutes per hour and not running ads for certain products or advertising in abusive manners. Now all of that is gone.

Technical regulations. They were deregulated, leaving the station with the responsibility to keep the station running properly but subject to surprise FCC inspections.

Minor regulations. There were also a number of "underbrush" (minor) regulations, most of which have been deregulated by the FCC.

Some consumer groups have challenged the FCC's authority to reduce or eliminate these regulations, but in most cases, the courts have indicated that as long as there is a policy in place to allow valid public protests and file against the station's license, such deregulation was perfectly proper. The marketplace, both of ideas and of economics, could determine outcomes, not the government.

Smith, F. Leslie, Milan Meeske, and John W. Wright II. *Electronic Media and Government: The Regulation of Wireless and Wired Mass Communication in the United States.* White Plains, N.Y.: Longman, 1995.

Val E. Limburg

DETECTOR, a device to indicate the presence of radio frequency signals, contains an element such as metal that reacts to electromagnetic exposure. The first detector used for radio reception was the coherer developed by Edouard Branly of France. In its simplest form, the coherer consists of iron filings encased in a glass tube. When radio waves pass through the tube, the filings cling together or cohere and become a conductor of electromagnetic energy. Other early detectors include the microphone detector, electrolytic detector (liquid barretter), magnetic detector, crystal detector, tikker, and audion. More sophisticated detectors were eventually combined with tuning devices, amplifiers, and other components in the radio receiver.

Douglas, Susan J. *Inventing American Broadcasting 1899–1922.* Baltimore: Johns Hopkins University Press, 1987.

Mayes, Thorn L. *Wireless Communication in the United States: The Early Development of American Radio Operating Companies.* East Greenwich, R.I.: New England Wireless and Steam Museum, Inc., 1989.

Christina S. Drale

DEWEY, THOMAS EDMUND (1902–1971), lawyer, governor, and political leader born in Owosso, Michigan, on March 24, 1902. He graduated from the University of Michigan in 1923 and from Columbia University Law School in 1925.

In the early 1930s, Thomas Dewey prosecuted organized crime in New York. In 1937 he was elected district attorney of New York County, in part because of popularity after a series of radio talks on racketeering and political corruption. In 1938, Dewey ran for governor of New York. He replaced traditional automobile caravan tours of rural upstate New York with weekly radio addresses. He lost the election but won in 1942 and was reelected in 1946 and 1950.

In 1944, Dewey received the Republican nomination for president but lost the election to Franklin Roosevelt. In 1948, he defeated former Minnesota governor Harold Stassen in the Oregon primary to help win the nomination again. Key to his victory was a debate broadcast nationally from Portland's KEX. Dewey lost the general election to Harry Truman.

In his 1950 gubernatorial reelection campaign, Dewey was one of the first candidates to use television effectively. He took live questions from voters at remote locations in New York City. He appeared on an 18-hour marathon election-eve radio and television show.

In 1952, Dewey worked to get the Republican nomination for Dwight Eisenhower. In 1969, Dewey declined an offer by President Richard Nixon to appoint him to the U.S. Supreme Court. He died in Bal Harbour, Florida, on March 16, 1971.

Smith, Richard N. *Thomas E. Dewey and His Times.* New York: Simon and Schuster, 1982.
Walker, Stanley. *Dewey: An American of This Century.* New York: Whitlesey House, a division of the McGraw-Hill Book Company, 1944.

Robert C. Fordan

DIARY, a paper booklet, distributed by ratings companies, in which respondents record their TV viewing or radio listening, usually for one week. The first systematic research of radio using a "diary" to record listening was developed by Garnet Garrison when he was a professor at Wayne State University in 1937 (see **documentary programs**). CBS experimented with the method in the 1940s, and the Hooper rating measurement service added diaries to its sample for "areas that could not be practicably reached by telephone."

In the late 1940s, James Seiler, director of research for the NBC-owned radio station in Washington, D.C., proposed a diary method. Reluctantly management agreed to try it for its new TV outlet. Seiler called his company the "American Research Bureau" because he thought the official-sounding name would aid in getting better cooperation from the sample. The first report measured viewing for a week in May 1949. By the fall, the company was conducting surveys in Baltimore, Philadelphia, and New York. In 1951 the company merged with one called Tele-Que that had been doing diary-based ratings in Los Angeles since 1947. The company later became just ARB, then Arbitron, after electronic devices were installed for "instant" TV ratings in 1957, but still issued ratings and TV measurements based on returned diaries. In the 1990s Arbitron ceased providing TV measurements but is the major company issuing ratings for about 200 radio markets.

Webster, James G., and Lawrence W. Lichty. *Ratings Analysis: Theory and Practice.* Hillsdale, N.J.: Lawrence Erlbaum Associates, 1991.

Lawrence W. Lichty

DIGITAL AUDIO BROADCASTING (DAB), also known as digital audio radio service (DARS), is expected to change or replace traditional radio. DAB is an audio signal offering compact disc (CD) sound quality and can be transmitted to consumers in-band over existing AM or FM frequencies and/or by satellite. August 1, 1990, the Federal Communications Commission (FCC) initiated a Notice of Inquiry, and broadcast industry emotions have ranged from fear to excitement. Some traditional broadcasters see DAB as a threat to their existence, and others see it as a way to help radio prosper.

DAB offers improved stereo and reduction of signal interference and fading. DAB challenges the FCC unlike other advancements such as stereo. There has been little progress in choosing a standard system or delivery mode. Stations may be moved to another band, but should DAB be implemented via satellite, local radio stations will be forced to compete with national and regional stations. Proposals for DAB satellites, superstations, and other nontraditional delivery systems have clearly disturbed radio broadcasters. There is the possibility that AM may become obsolete. FM may be spared, if the National Association of Broadcasters (NAB) has its way through persistent lobbying against satellite DAB.

Overall, the broadcast industry appears excited about DAB but shares the NAB's concerns for existing AM and FM stations and the potential threat of satellite delivery. Some factions favor direct-satellite DAB delivery. Although conceding that many listeners will desire some local and regional radio programming, many travelers grow weary from constant station seeking. DAB satellite delivery would be a solution. Signals would be received by small omnidirectional antennas mounted atop automobiles.

The NAB and much of the radio industry, however, believe that DAB's future is probably in-band. In-band means implementing DAB through existing AM and/or FM frequencies. For example, about 10 DAB channels can be employed using the same space now taken up by one FM frequency. But which system will emerge as the standard? Other than technological impact, the real opportunity offered by DAB is that it puts the United States squarely in a position to regain its world leadership role in setting technological communications standards—a position the United States lost in the 1980s era of deregulation and exemplified by AM stereo.

Setting standards had always been a major concern of the FCC when implementing new and innovative technology, until AM stereo in 1982; since then, the FCC's trend has been to let the marketplace decide, and the result has been some havoc and chaos. The good news about DAB is that it offers great promise for an ailing radio industry, particularly for AM radio. Even if AM radio becomes extinct, with the FCC's assistance the stations can relocate their operations to one of the many new spaces opened up by DAB on the FM frequencies. In the end, both the industry and consumers may benefit from the much-improved sound quality offered by DAB.

Mirabito, Michael M. A. *The New Communications Technologies.* 2nd ed. Boston: Focal Press, 1994.
Rumsey, Francis. *Digital Audio Operations.* Boston: Focal Press, 1991.

W. A. Kelly Huff

DIGITAL AUDIO TAPE (DAT) is a magnetic-recording medium that stores audio information in digital form. While analog audio recordings use varying magnetic signals to represent the strength and frequency of an input audio signal, the DAT format uses a series of pulse codes to represent the sound as digitally sampled information. Digital audio recordings do not degenerate in quality when copied. Digital audio tape is a linear storage format, and information cannot be randomly accessed. Digital audio tape comes in many sizes, most commonly the DAT cassette, but also appears in reel-to-reel tape formats with widths of ¼, ½, and 1 inch.

Watkinson, John. *An Introduction to Digital Audio.* Oxford: Focal Press, 1994.

Donald Diefenbach

DIGITAL TECHNOLOGY relies on a series of coded pulses. Telegraphy illustrates the theory of digital technology. Telegraph signals consist of making and breaking an electrical circuit. In order to develop a means to transmit the alphabet, Samuel F. B. Morse came up with the idea of making those electrical contacts short (dots) or long (dashes) and assigning combinations of the dots and dashes to represent letters or numbers. Digital technology uses the same theory, turning electrical voltages into discrete numerical units, illustrated as zeros (0) or ones (1). Information can be transmitted by electrical energy through a wire or by switching on and off beams of light in optical-fiber strands. The switching on and off takes place at extremely high speeds.

Computers represent the most visible digital technology. It has two advantages. First, many streams of information can pass through a medium (such as a fiber-optic cable) that would only carry one analog signal. The result is higher capacity and lower cost when moving information from point A to point B, whether it is by cable or through the air. The second advantage is that a digital signal is less subject to degradation than an analog signal as it travels from point A to point B.

Digital technology has impacted broadcasting in many ways. The compact disc (CD) is a digital medium that is now the source of choice for music playout. It can store a great deal of information in a much smaller area than a comparable long-playing record. The CD also lacks the "noise" inherent in record or tape reproduction. A digital signal can be fed to a computer and then translated to a screen image, making it possible to edit text or sound.

The next leap for digital technology will be the conversion of transmission from analog to digital. Entrepreneurs foresee transmission of digital streams from satellites to receivers in automobiles (see **digital audio broadcasting [DAB]**). The digital signals from satellites would not have to pass through a terrestrial transmitter. The programming infrastructure is in place in the form of audio services that supply programming to broadcast stations and other consumers.

In the early 1990s, U.S. broadcasters began an accelerated effort to develop means of transmitting digital signals. After some debate over the question of making a phased transition, operating parallel transmitters, broadcasters generally decided to seek an "in-band" solution. This would require imbedding a digital signal in the analog transmission of either an AM or an FM radio station. This approach, if successful, would take up less of the spectrum and would encourage the replacement of consumer receivers. It would help ensure the survival of terrestrial radio broadcasting, which would still have to contend with direct broadcasts from satellites but could at least compete by offering localized programming and information.

While the issue of digital transmission was being worked out in laboratories and hearing rooms, the radio industry continued to replace analog technology with digital equipment inside its facilities.

Inglis, Andrew F. *Behind the Tube: A History of Broadcasting Technology and Business.* Boston: Focal Press, 1990.
The National Association of Broadcasters regularly publishes updated publications dealing with all aspects of digital technology.

Phillip O. Keirstead

DILL, CLARENCE CLEVELAND (1884–1978), was born of Scotch-Irish ancestry in Fredericktown, Ohio. He graduated from Ohio Wesleyan University in 1907 and shortly thereafter moved to Spokane, Washington, where he first became involved in politics. Politically, he has been described as a radical, independent, impartial La Follette Democrat. He was a product of the 1920s era. Dill's role in the history of broadcasting was limited because of his late entry into the legislative arena. (Secretary of Commerce Herbert Hoover and Representative Wallace H. White had been working on a radio law since the early 1920s.) Despite his late entry, his contributions to the *Radio Act of 1927* were significant. He spearheaded the act in the Senate. In fact, he was the only radio authority in the Senate and is credited with providing the leadership necessary for meaningful debate and successful passage. He adopted the language of White but shifted the major direction of the legislation toward establishing a commission to provide control over broadcast regulation.

During Dill's terms in Congress, he worked primarily on radio, the Grand Coulee Dam, and hydropower legislation. During his post-Senate career, he remained active in politics and ran his law office in Spokane, Washington.

Dill, Clarence C. *Where Water Falls.* Spokane, Wash.: C. W. Printing, 1970.
Godfrey, Donald G. "Senator Dill and the *1927 Radio Act.*" *Journal of Broadcasting* 23 (4) (fall 1979): 477–489.

Donald G. Godfrey

DILL-WHITE RADIO BILLS. Twenty bills were placed before the 67th Congress (1921–1923); 13 proposed laws submitted to the 68th Congress (1923–1925); and 18 bills introduced to the 69th Congress (1925–1927) all to regulate radio communication. Of these 51 bills, only 1 was to pass both houses of Congress—the *Radio Act of 1927.*

Congressman Wallace H. White's long-proposed bill was an administration bill. Senator Clarence C. Dill prepared a bill designed to take away radio control from the secretary of commerce. The Dill bill passed the Senate on July 2, 1926, but a conference committee failed to agree, and an attempt to pass an emergency resolution failed as Congress went into recess.

Secretary Hoover asked the attorney general for an opinion, which stated that the secretary had no power, based on the Intercity and Zenith cases. This served notice that the administration could not be held responsible for the breakdown in radio regulation, and the issue had to be faced by Congress.

In the second session of the 69th Congress in December 1926, Senator Dill and Representative White's subcommittee wrote a compromise bill. On January 25, 1927, the Senate and House conferees officially accepted the subcommittee report. Three days later, Representative White submitted the Dill-White Bill to the House, where it passed. The Dill-White Bill was then sent to the Senate, where it passed on February 18, 1927. On February 24, 1927, President Coolidge signed the bill, making the *Radio Act of 1927* the official radio law.

Bensman, Marvin. "The Zenith-WJAZ Case and the Chaos of 1926–27." *Journal of Broadcasting* 14 (4) (fall 1970): 423–440.
Godfrey, Donald G. "Senator Dill and the *1927 Radio Act.*" *Journal of Broadcasting* 23 (4) (fall 1979): 477–489.

Marvin R. Bensman

DIRECTIONAL ANTENNA radiates or receives radio frequency energy more effectively in certain directions than from all directions equally. All practical antennas exhibit some directionality. However, the term typically refers to antennas purposely designed to favor transmission or reception in one or more desired directions. Directional transmitting antennas often are used to "focus" the transmitter's energy into one or more narrow beams, increasing coverage in the favored direction(s). Directional receiving antennas favor energy arriving from some directions and discriminate against that arriving from all other directions, thus reducing interference from unwanted signals.

American Radio Relay League, Inc. *The ARRL Antenna Book.* Newington, Conn.: American Radio Relay League, 1974.
Graf, Rudolf F. *Modern Dictionary of Electronics.* Indianapolis, Ind.: Howard W. Sams & Co., Inc., 1984.

Tom Spann

DISC JOCKEY, presents the components of a radio station format, introducing music, reading announcements, and providing other ad-lib comments. Also known as a jock or deejay (DJ), the disc jockey term came about because the announcer plays record discs and rides the gain or controls the volume. The basic style originated in the 1930s when announcers like Martin Block (*Make Believe Ballroom*) introduced Big Band music played off phonograph records. During the 1950s development of format radio, early rock 'n' roll disc jockeys like Alan Freed (*Moondog's Rock and Roll Party*) and Wolfman Jack gained a great deal of prominence as DJs became personalities. More contemporary disc jockeys like Cousin Brucie (Morrow), Jim Ladd, "The Lonesome L.A. Cowboy," Larry Lujack, Charlie Tuna, and shock jock Howard Stern have attained celebrity status. Today's DJ is often a significant factor in defining a radio station's image and appeal. Over the years, the function of the disc jockey has moved from simply cuing and introducing records to chatting with the audience as an intimate friend or companion. There are numerous DJ styles ranging from the low-key soft speaker to the frenetic screamer, and everything in between.

Ladd, Jim. *Radio Waves: Life and Revolution on the FM Dial.* New York: St. Martin's Press, 1991.

Morrow, Bruce, and Laura Baudo. *Cousin Brucie! My Life in Rock 'n' Roll Radio.* New York: Beech Tree Books, 1987.

Poindexter, Ray. *Golden Throats and Silver Tongues: The Radio Announcers.* Conway, Ark.: River Road Press, 1978.

David E. Reese

DOCUMENTARY PROGRAMS. The best radio/audio ones are wonderful, but there are not many by comparison with the enormous material available on, and being produced each year for, film/video. Dramatized documentaries by Norman Corwin are among the best writing for any medium at anytime. In their very first seasons, radio networks tried "informative dramas"—*Biblical Dramas* and *Great Moments in History* in 1927–1928. *The March of Time,* which dramatized several of the most important news stories of the week with actors imitating known people, began on CBS on March 6, 1931 (see *The March of Time*). There were a large number of dramatized news and historical dramas (many produced by or in cooperation with the government for propaganda purposes) on the radio networks during World War II.

The documentary form, based on archives and compilation as with film, did not develop on radio prior to this primarily because the networks would not permit recordings on programs. This prohibition was not so strict on the Mutual Broadcasting System (MBS), which apparently was replaying recorded events in year-end programs as early as 1935. But, for the most part, important events were presented as live news or dramatized—like *The March of Time* reenactments.

Coverage of the D-Day landings at Normandy on June 6, 1944, was the single event most responsible for beginning a trend in the use of recorded material. A number of correspondents made disc recordings that day, the most famous being Charles Collingwood (CBS), but for the pool, of course, using a navy recorder on a troop ship and George Hicks, also on a ship in the channel crossing.

After that, recordings began to be used for many news and documentary programs, especially on local stations, but some carried to the networks. One was *Brave Men Are Afraid* on February 10, 1945, from WOR, New York, and carried on MBS. The show consisted of transcriptions made by GIs in the Pacific—"The voices of Purple Heart marines of the fighting 4th Division"—and included Lt. Bob Crosby, the band leader, talking with a fellow soldier who was a high school friend from Spokane, Washington. Although it was not very exciting and the microphone was seldom really near the front, these were the "actual voices."

The most important pioneer network documentary using recordings was produced at NBC on V-E day. It used the actual voices of speakers for many events, rather than having them reenacted by actors. This program was produced by Garnet Garrison, later a longtime professor of radio-television at the University of Michigan. It was on the same night as *On a Note of Triumph,* produced by Norman Corwin for CBS, which many think is one of the finest radio dramas ever produced. Ironically, Corwin himself soon switched to using recordings. After an around-the-world trip, he produced *One World Flight,* broadcast weekly from January 14, 1947, to April 1, 1947, which included interviews and sounds from more than 15 different countries.

There was one more series of dramatized news events before recording would really take over. *You Are There,* which used real CBS news correspondents but actors to portray historical figures, began on radio in 1947 and moved to TV in 1953. Just after the 1950 general elections, Edward R. Murrow, who had gained fame as a war correspondent during the war, and Fred W. Friendly produced *A Report to the Nation* with many campaign speeches, candidate appearances, interviews, music, and rallies all recorded on tape and produced as "a document for ear." The idea, partly based on an earlier phonograph documentary series (*I Can Hear It Now,* 1949), was a good one whose time had come. Within a month, it was a regular CBS series on Friday night called *Hear It Now,* using many tape-recorded segments in each weekly program—the most important usually being from the Korean War. The next season Hearst newsreel cameramen were substituted for audiotape recorders; *See It Now* was born. Hereafter, documentaries on film and presented on television would get most of the attention.

In the 1950s, NBC produced a fine series called *Biography in Sounds,* and there were some interesting phonograph documentaries during the 1960s—especially those recording the civil rights movement and others protesting the Vietnam War. With the beginning of National Public Radio in 1970 and on a few stations—commercial and educational—there are still some fine radio documentaries to be heard.

Bannerman, R. Leroy. *Norman Corwin and Radio: The Golden Years.* Tuscaloosa: University of Alabama Press, 1986.

Barnouw, Erik. *Radio Drama in Action: Twenty-five Plays of a Changing World.* New York: Rinehart & Company, 1945.

Several audiotape, or CD, collections of Norman Corwin dramatized documentaries and other drama programs are available from LodesTone, 611 Empire Mill Road, Bloomington, Ind. 47401; and Radio Yesteryear, Box C, Sandy Hook, Conn. 06482. A CD of the Murrow-Friendly three-LP record set of *I Can Hear It Now* is also available. Check several guides for available documentary phonograpy/CDs.

Lawrence W. Lichty

DRAGNET, one of the most successful police programs in the history of television, began on network radio in 1949. The series was premiered as a television program on *Chesterfield Sound Off Time* on NBC in 1951. It began as a regular series on NBC in 1952. The program starred Jack Webb as Sergeant Joe Friday and his partner, who was first played by Barton Yarborough from the original radio series. *Dragnet* featured a documentary style with narration provided by Sergeant Friday. The TV series aired on NBC from 1952 to 1959 and then was revived on the network in 1967 until 1970. The reruns can still be seen on television stations today.

Brooks, Tim, and Earle Marsh. *The Complete Directory to Prime Time Network TV Shows, 1946–Present.* New York: Ballantine Books, 1979.

Frederic A. Leigh

DRAKE, BILL (1937–), programming consultancy and syndication pioneer. Born Philip Yarbrough, the Waycross, Georgia, native began his career as a pop music disc jockey (DJ) on WMGR in nearby Bainbridge. Yarbrough attended Georgia Southern College on a basketball scholarship but abandoned the program after his first year to pursue a radio career at WAKE in Atlanta. There, Yarbrough adopted the airname "Bill Drake" because it rhymed with the station's call letters.

At age 23, Drake refined his philosophy toward a "much more music" approach to programming while serving as program director at San Francisco's KYA. Drake's ratings successes attracted the attention of California station owner Gene Chenault, and the pair formed Drake-Chenault Enterprises in 1963. Two years later, Drake-Chenault forged a consultancy relationship with RKO (Radio-Keith-Orpheum) General's Los Angeles outlet KHJ. By 1967, the remaining RKO outlets in New York, San Francisco, Boston, Memphis, and Windsor, Ontario (Detroit) signed with the company.

Drake succeeded in making each station a market leader by refining the content and presentation of the programming. Music playlists that ran 60 titles deep were pared to 30. DJ chatter was minimized to make room for more music, contests, and promotion. Drake's influence in elevating new records to hit status became widely regarded within the industry.

Drake-Chenault subsidiary American Independent Radio capitalized on the burgeoning FM medium with the introduction of *Hit Parade '68,* an adult-appeal pop music format designed for fully automated execution. The company expanded into other formats, eventually servicing more than 300 stations. Drake retired and returned to Georgia following the company's 1983 sale. During the period from 1988 to 1996, Drake consulted oldies-formatted KRTH in Los Angeles.

"Adviser Becomes Boss: Drake Signs with RKO." *Broadcasting* (October 16, 1972): 61–62.
"Programming: The Executioner." *Time* (August 23, 1968): 48.
"'Rock and Roll Muzak.'" *Newsweek* (March 9, 1970): 85.

Bruce Mims

DRAMA PROGRAMS. *See* **black drama; Depression, the Great;** specific program titles.

DRIVE TIME is a segment of the broadcast day characterized by unique programming strategies and elements such as announcing styles, music selections, and promotion spots. There are two drive times, and both are related to the commutes to work and school (morning) and back home (afternoon). These two dayparts are often the peak listening for a radio station, as measured by audience measurement services.

The morning-drive time may begin as early as 5:30 A.M. and end at 10:00 A.M., depending on the city or radio market area. As far as announcing is concerned, morning-drive time often features high-energy and friendly disc jockeys, whose lively banter keeps listeners alert and informed. Drive-time announcers also encourage their listeners to get to work on time and on other matters related to their lives. The station's top disc jockey fills the morning-drive time slot. In recent years, radio stations have used more than one announcer, sometimes a male and female, who bring listeners news, sports, weather, traffic, and time reports.

By contrast, the afternoon-drive time usually begins around 3:00 P.M. and ends at 7:00 P.M. It is more businesslike in tone, and the audience is about a third less. Radio stations use upbeat, lively announcers for the afternoon-drive time. The afternoon disc jockeys, however, are not as energetic as their morning counterparts. In addition, traffic, sports, and weather reports are common program elements in the afternoon-drive time. Weather and time updates are not as crucial, however. In addition, the afternoon-drive time often presents stock market reports and information about upcoming events.

Finally, commercials and "jingles"—musical or sounder signatures of a particular radio station—are played more often during a radio station's drive times. For instance, commercials are placed at specific times during the two drive-time dayparts. Generally, radio station programmers schedule commercials at 12, 22, 41, and 51 minutes after the hour during drive time. On the other hand, commercial "stop sets" in other dayparts, such as midday, evening or overnight, are played closer to the top of the hour and less often. The radio station's format may also play a role in deciding commercial placement as well.

Dominick, Joseph R., Barry L. Sherman, and Gary A. Copeland. *Broadcasting/Cable and Beyond: An Introduction to Modern Electronic Media.* 3rd ed. New York: McGraw-Hill, 1996.
Keith, Michael C., and Joseph M. Krause. *The Radio Station.* 3rd ed. Boston: Focal Press, 1993.
Drive Time. http://www.broadcast.net

Gilbert A. Williams

DRUG LYRICS. *See* **citizen groups and broadcasting;** *also* **lyrics and morality.**

DUNWOODY, H. H. C. (1842–1933), invented the carborundum crystal detector in 1906, first of a series of crystal detectors that became popular with amateur wireless enthusiasts. Carborundum is a compound of carbon and silicon and was typically found as an electrical furnace by-product. The carborundum crystal was placed between two copper contacts, and a thin wire or "cat's-whisker" was drawn across the crystal to pick up the radio signals. Later, crystal detectors developed by G. W. Pickard would use pure silicon, galena, and iron pyrites to act as the rectifier for electromagnetic waves. Dunwoody, a general of the U.S. Army, became vice president of the American de Forest Company and later of the United Wireless Company. Dunwoody's carborundum detector played an important role in the survival of United Wireless after Fessenden successfully prevented United from using his liquid barretter detector. The carborundum detector was patented by Dunwoody in time for United Wireless to exploit its use in its unscrupulous stock sales campaign.

Douglas, Susan J. *Inventing American Broadcasting 1899–1922.* Baltimore: Johns Hopkins University Press, 1987.

Christina S. Drale

DUOPOLY refers to the common ownership of more than one broadcast station in the same service in a particular community—service referring to AM, FM, and television. As early as 1938, the Federal Communications Commission (FCC) adopted a strong presumption against granting licenses that would create these combinations. In 1970, the FCC further restricted within-market ownership by prohibiting the licensee of a television station from also holding radio stations in the same community. However, the commission began to relax that rule in 1975 and has since permitted AM/FM/TV combinations in the top 25 markets as long as there are at least 30 separately owned stations in the market. It wasn't until 1989 that the commission began to relax the restriction on radio duopolies by permitting a single entity to own up to two AM and two FM stations in the same market. The *Telecommunications Act of 1996* further relaxed the radio duopoly restriction. In large markets, those with 45 or more commercial stations, a single owner can hold up to 8 stations, no more than 5 of which can be on the same band. In small markets, those with 14 or fewer commercial stations, the limit is set at 5 stations, no more than 3 of which can be on the same band. The act retains the prohibition on television duopolies, but it is anticipated that the FCC will conduct a rulemaking and permit VHF/UHF within-market combinations.

In the Matter of Amendment of Section 73.3555 [formerly Sections 73.35, 73.240, and 73.636] of the Commission's Rules Relating to Multiple Ownership of AM, FM and Television Broadcast Stations, 56 RR 2d, 859 (1984).
Duopoly. http://www.commlaw.com/

Marianne Barrett

DUPLICATED PROGRAMMING, AM/FM REDUCTION OF, is the curtailment of FM simulcasts by co-owned AM stations in response to a 1964 Federal Communications Commission (FCC) regulatory order. Several factors contributed to stagnancy in FM development during the 1950s, including opposition to the medium by a strong network/AM station alliance, a scarcity of FM-capable receivers, and the introduction of television broadcasting.

The failure to generate meaningful FM advertising revenues led numerous duopoly station owners to economize by duplicating AM programming over FM channels. Audience interest in FM languished in the absence of original programming. Citing a desire to foster FM development and criticizing duplication as a wasteful, inefficient use of scarce broadcasting channels, the FCC imposed the Program Nonduplication Rule.

Effective August 1, 1965, FM stations in cities of 100,000 population or greater were prohibited from duplicating more than 50 percent of the programming offered by companion AM stations during any given week. As a result, increasingly diverse and eclectic program formats were developed for FM by the end of the decade, attracting new audiences and advertisers. Automated broadcasting equipment, criticized harshly for creating sanitized, impersonal presentations, nonetheless helped accelerate FM growth by affording station operators an economical alternative to the employment of live announcers.

A 1976 rule revision placed virtually all duopolies under some degree of duplication restriction. In 1986, the FCC reasoned that its decision had served its intended purpose of establishing parity between the AM and FM services and deleted the rule.

Federal Communications Commission. *Report and Order in the Matter of Amendment of Part 73 of the Commission's Rules, Regarding AM Station Assignment and the Relationship between the AM and FM Services.* Washington, D.C.: 45 FCC Reports 1515, 1964.

"FM's Drag Feet on Program Split." *Broadcasting* 88 (June 21, 1965): 40–42, 44.

Sterling, Christopher. "Decade of Development: FM Radio in the 1960s." *Journalism Quarterly* 48 (1971): 222–230.

Bruce Mims

E

EASY-LISTENING FORMAT is a station's program design that is instrumental based, often referred to as beautiful music. Easy listening emphasizes low-key, mellow, popular music, generally with extensive orchestration and many classic popular songs (not rock or jazz). It was one of the first all-music formats that was very popular for radio stations, particularly FM, starting in the 1960s. It was a rigidly designed format that cut down on the number of commercial interruptions and spurred the hire of composers to write more music. At the height of its popularity, easy listening saturated waiting rooms, elevators, department stores, and other public spaces. Several syndicated easy-listening music services without commercials, such as Muzak, went out on FM subcarriers that required special adaptors for reception. The format was advertised to businesses as a means of relieving stress in the workplace, increasing sales, and combating fatigue.

Easy listening's popularity was fading out by the late 1980s as its audience aged and advertiser support for the age 55-plus market dropped, particularly on the national and regional levels. By 1988, less than 5 percent of all AM and FM stations carried this format, but it has continued with 2 percent of the stations in 1992 and about 1 percent of the listening audience nationwide in 1995.

Eastman, Susan Tyler, and Douglas A. Ferguson. *Broadcast/Cable Programming: Strategies and Practices.* 5th ed. Belmont, Calif.: Wadsworth, 1996.

Lanza, Joseph. *Elevator Music: A Surreal History of Muzak, Easy-Listening and Other Moodsong.* New York: St. Martin's Press, 1994.

Margot Hardenbergh

EBS/EAS. The EBS (Emergency Broadcast System) was a method the president could use to communicate directly with the public through radio and television stations in the event of a national emergency. It could also disseminate emergency information at the state and local levels. During its time, its main use was for weather-related emergencies. The Federal Communications Commission (FCC) established EBS in 1963 to replace the somewhat similar CONELRAD system that had been in place since 1953. In 1994 the FCC announced that EBS would be replaced by the EAS (Emergency Alert System), which was to be phased in between June 1995 and January 1998, with the official name change taking place on January 1, 1997.

Burkum, Larry G. "'This Is a Test': The Evolution of the Emergency Broadcast System." *Journal of Radio Studies* 2 (1993–1994): 141–150.

EAS Primer. Indianapolis, Ind.: Society of Broadcast Engineers, 1997.

"Emergency Alert System (EAS)." 47 CFR 0.1 [Code of Federal Regulations]. Published by the Office of the Federal Register, National Archives and Records Administration as a special edition of the Federal Register. Washington, D.C.: U.S. Government Printing Office, 1996.

Steven C. Runyon

EDISON, THOMAS ALVA (1847–1931), inventor, electrician, entrepreneur, and America's foremost wizard of invention, Thomas Edison became a celebrity and folk hero for his contributions to incandescent lighting, generating and distributing electric power, recording sound, and motion pictures. At his laboratories in New Jersey and New York, he also established the corporate model of invention prevalent in contemporary enterprise.

Edison was interested in wireless as early as 1875 when he described an unknown "etheric force" set off by sparks in his lab, and even had a brief foray into wireless telegraphy in the 1880s. He and Ezra Gilliland developed the "grasshopper telegraph," an induction wireless system to communicate with moving trains. After patent interference disputes, Edison merged his interests with Lucius Phelps to form the Consolidated Railroad Telegraph Company. Although there were several successful demonstrations, the technology proved not to be commercially viable. Edison reworked his ideas into a fantastic design with aerial conductors atop tethered balloons to transmit and receive signals around the world, obtained a patent in 1891, and eventually sold the rights to Marconi in 1904.

Edison's most important contribution to radio came almost by accident. While working on the incandescent light, he discovered that a hot filament in a vacuum gives off electricity. By adding a positively charged electrode, Edison could make this electric charge jump from the filament to the electrode. Dubbed the "Edison Effect" by Sir William Preece, this principle was the basis for the rectifier, the vacuum tube, and de Forest's audion.

Conot, Robert. *A Streak of Luck.* New York: Seaview Books, 1979.
Josephson, Matthew. *Edison.* New York: McGraw-Hill, 1959.

Robert H. Lochte

EDITORIALIZING is the act of presenting a commentary expressing the station's or network's opinion. In one form or another, editorializing by broadcast licensees has been controlled from the 1927 inception of radio regulation to the Federal Communications Commission's (FCC's) deregulation of radio in the 1980s.

The power to regulate a station's editorializing arises out of the commission's licensing procedures and its interpretation of the public interest. Historically, the commission used its editorial policy to muzzle broadcasters who were perceived to be mouthpieces for labor or socialist causes, attacked public officials, or engaged in partisan politics. In the late 1920s, the commission denied renewal of the license of KGEF in Los Angeles for its program *Bob Schuler's Civic Talk* on the ground that the station's regular broadcasts of pointed attacks on city officials and others were outside the scope of the public interest.

By 1941, the commission's Mayflower Doctrine banned editorial commentary by licensees. However, in 1949, the commission modified its position and ruled that broadcasters could editorialize subject to the general requirements of balance and fairness, a line of thinking that would lead to the much-debated Fairness Doctrine, upheld by the U.S. Supreme Court's *Red Lion* decision in 1969. Following the deregulation of radio in the 1980s and the commission's abandonment of its enforcement of the Fairness Doctrine, there has been a sharp rise in the influence and popularity of editorializing via the genre of talk radio.

Edward M. Lenert

EDUCATIONAL RADIO in the United States generally refers to that class of stations that, licensed as noncommercial educational radio stations, are authorized to broadcast between 88 and 92 megacycles in the FM band. This class was created in 1945 when the Federal Communications Commission (FCC) reauthorized FM broadcasting. The majority of the early educational radio stations were operated by colleges and universities, but following the passage of the *Public Broadcasting Act of 1967* and the more popular designation of "public radio," more nonprofit community corporations became actively involved in noncommercial educational radio.

Begun as a distinct counterpart to entertainment-driven commercial radio, which needed to attract the large audience numbers desired by advertisers, educational radio was envisioned as an electronic extension of the high school and college classroom. Listeners could often register for course credit with local educational institutions. By the mid-1970s, most of these formal radio courses had disappeared. The principal staples of educational public radio had become public affairs programs and classical and jazz music. Stations continue to do remote broadcasts of important lectures and other special broadcasts that fit within the original definition of educational programming, but the more elitist notions about the purpose of educational radio has broadened considerably to include a wide variety of program venues that are highly entertaining as well as informative.

Hill, Frank E. *Listen and Learn*. New York: American Association for Adult Education, 1937.
Muller, Helen M. *Education by Radio*. New York: H. W. Wilson Company, 1932.
Tyler, Tracy F., ed. *Radio as a Cultural Agency: Proceedings of a National Conference on the Use of Radio as a Cultural Agency*. Washington, D.C.: National Committee on Education by Radio, 1934.

Robert K. Avery

EDWARDS, DOUGLAS (1917–1990), a pioneer among broadcast journalists, began his broadcasting career in Alabama at the age of 15 announcing for a Dothan radio station. Edwards attended the University of Alabama for two years, then returned to Dothan to work in radio. In 1935, Edwards moved to Atlanta to work in news for WSB, and he wrote the occasional column for the co-owned *Atlanta Journal.*

At 21, Edwards moved to Detroit where he announced news and special events broadcasts and hosted dance band remotes. He shared some of his news-announcing duties with Mike Wallace, with whom Edwards reunited later at CBS News. Edwards told a biographer that WSB tried to lure him back to Atlanta as assistant news editor in 1940, but by then, he wanted to work for CBS News in New York.

Edwards joined the Columbia Broadcasting System (CBS) as an announcer in 1942 with the hope that he could join Paul White's news department. In 1943, Edwards was assigned to anchor *The World Today,* a prime early-evening broadcast. Edwards finally got his desired overseas assignment in 1945, when he reported to Edward R. Murrow and covered the war from London and Paris before returning to New York in 1946.

In 1947, Edwards, a junior correspondent, was assigned to something new, a television news program that CBS aired on Thursday and Saturday nights. In August 1948, Edwards began anchoring *The CBS-TV News* weekday evenings. The program ran for 15 minutes, putting it ahead of NBC's 10-minute *Camel Newsreel Theater* with John Cameron Swayze. After coping with a rotation of four directors, Edwards managed to get Don Hewitt named full-time director for the nightly broadcast. Hewitt later became executive producer of *60 Minutes.*

It took several years, but by the early 1950s, Edwards's news program was getting better ratings than John Cameron Swayze's on NBC. *Variety* magazine estimated that in December 1957 Douglas Edwards was viewed by over 14 million people per day and almost 34 million people per week.

Eventually, the broadcast, renamed *Douglas Edwards with the News,* ran until Walter Cronkite took over in 1962. Edwards continued to anchor radio news broadcasts, radio documentaries, and *For Our Times,* a production of the CBS News television religion unit. Although best known as an anchorperson, he was honored for covering the 1956 sinking of the ocean liner *Andrea Doria* off Nantucket Island, receiving one of broadcast journalism's highest recognitions, the George Foster Peabody Award for distinguished achievement in television journalism.

Edwards became the regular anchor of the weeknight *World News Tonight* broadcast on the CBS Radio Network. Douglas Edwards was well liked in the CBS News newsroom in New York, where his sonorous voice could be heard prereading his evening scripts. Edwards retired from CBS News in 1988 and died in Sarasota, Florida, on October 13, 1990.

Bliss, Edward, Jr. *Now the News: The Story of Broadcast Journalism.* New York: Columbia University Press, 1991.
Goldberg, Robert, and Gerald Jay Goldberg. *Anchors: Brokaw, Jennings, Rather and the Evening News.* New York: Birch Lane Press, 1990.

Phillip O. Keirstead

EEO (EQUAL EMPLOYMENT OPPORTUNITY) REQUIREMENT means that radio station licensees must develop and implement a written program intended to promote hiring and advancement of women and minorities in radio. The station's program must address dissemination of its existence and elements to job applicants and employees, the use of minority and women's organizations in recruiting, the station's employment profile and job turnover rate in light of the demographics of the station's recruitment area, promotion of women and minorities in a nondiscriminatory fashion, and review and evaluation of its program on an annual basis.

In addition, radio station operators are required to maintain records, relating to the program and how it has been implemented, utilized by the Federal Communications Commission (FCC) when the station is seeking to renew its broadcast license. Specifically, stations must file an annual employment report and maintain the required records on site. Failure to maintain the records, or file the appropriate forms, is the basis for the FCC's finding an EEO violation, which may lead to a fine or other penalty. When a station seeks license renewal, the FCC reviews the station's EEO performance, and if a violation is suspected, it will hold a hearing regarding the potential infraction. If a violation is ultimately found, the FCC may fine the station (known as a forfeiture), allow renewal for other than the full-license period (short-term renewal), or refuse to renew the license (nonrenewal).

Hamburg, Morton I., and Stuart N. Brotman. *Communications Law and Practice.* New York: Law Journal Seminars Press, 1995.

Kirby, Kathleen Ann. "Shouldn't the Constitution Be Color Blind? *Metro Broadcasting, Inc. v. FCC* Transmits a Surprising Message on Racial Preferences." *Catholic University Law Review* 40 (1991): 403.

Trigg, S. Jenell. "The Federal Communications Commission's Equal Opportunity Employment Program and the Effect of *Adarand Constructors, Inc. v. Pena.*" *Community Law Conspectus* 4 (1996): 237.

Robert A. Heverly

EFFECTIVE RADIATED POWER (ERP), a technical term for power output used by the Federal Communications Commission (FCC) in spectrum assignment. The *Geneva Radio Regulations* (1982) definition is "the product of the power supplied to the antenna and its gain relative to a half-wave dipole in a given direction." According to federal regulations, ERP should be expressed in kilowatts (kW) and in decibels above 1 kW (dBk). The term *ERP* is applied separately to the horizontally and vertically polarized components of radiation when circular or elliptical polarization is employed. Only the ERP authorized for the horizontally polarized component is considered for assignment purposes.

Code of Federal Regulations. Title 47, Part 2, Section 1 and Part 73, Section 681. Washington, D.C.: U.S. Government Printing Office, 1996. Published by the Office of the Federal Register, National Archives and Records Administration as a special edition of the Federal Register.

Mark J. Braun

8MK (WWJ). The *Detroit News* (Michigan) was the first newspaper to use radio to communicate late-breaking news to the public, and it did so more than two months before KDKA, known as 8XK, broadcast election returns on November 2, 1920. The *News* station, 8MK, operated from a corner of the newspaper's building in downtown Detroit and broadcast the election results from local, state, and congressional primaries on August 31, 1920.

8MK developed rapidly, changing its call letters to WBL and, later, to WWJ. It was not long before the station occupied an entire floor of the *News* building. Within two and a half years, the *News* installed a new transmitter and related equipment from Westinghouse Electric Company, the first of its type. With this new broadcast equipment, the station had an expected broadcast range of 1,500 miles, but listeners from as far away as 2,300 miles (i.e., Honduras, Alaska, Cuba) heard the broadcasts and wrote to the station.

While the argument about which broadcast station is the oldest may have been settled in favor of KDKA, Pittsburgh, in the minds of most people, some continue to champion 8MK. The Internet home page of WWJ, the successor to 8MK, declares WWJ the first commercial radio station in the United States. For many decades, the *Detroit News* owned and operated WWJ. In the 1980s, the newspaper and its parent, the Evening News Association, were acquired by Gannett. CBS now owns WWJ.

The most significant contribution may have resulted from its link to the newspaper and its programming to meet community needs. The focus seemed to be on programming rather than on the sale of radio receivers. The station broadcast live music as well as programs featuring public figures, celebrities, and clergymen. In addition to its firsts as a broadcaster of news and election returns on August 31, 1920, WWJ (8MK) claims the first sports broadcast (September 1, 1920) and the first sports play-by-play from the scene (October 25, 1924). According to WWJ, Ty Tyson described the University of Michigan–University of Wisconsin football game. WWJ was where both Fanny Brice and Will Rogers made their first radio appearances in the early 1920s. The station, claiming the first complete symphony broadcast on radio, aired the Detroit Symphony concert on February 10, 1922, and the symphony received contributions from listeners in many states. The station began its tradition of broadcasting special Christmas programs within its first few months of operation.

With sports, news, public affairs, celebrity guests, cultural events, and music, 8MK is the forerunner of modern radio and television programming. The *Radio Act of 1927* and the *Communication Act of 1934* required stations to broadcast in the public interest, convenience, and necessity. 8MK had set the standard years before.

Baudino, Joseph E., and John M. Kittross. "Broadcasting's Oldest Stations: An Examination of Four Claimants." *Journal of Broadcasting* 21 (1) (winter 1977): 61–83.
Douglas, Susan J. *Inventing American Broadcasting 1899–1922.* Baltimore: Johns Hopkins University Press, 1987.

Larry L. Jurney

8XK, the amateur radio station that served as the basis for Westinghouse's KDKA, is credited with transforming the radio industry in the early 1920s. 8XK was licensed to Frank Conrad, a Westinghouse engineer, in August 1916 in Wilkinsburg, Pennsylvania. Along with many other amateur radio enthusiasts, Conrad used his station to communicate with other amateurs as a hobby.

As the United States prepared to enter the European war, the Department of Commerce suspended all amateur licenses, including Conrad's, on April 6, 1917, as a means of preserving national security. Amateur interference with military transmissions could jeopardize the safety of the armed forces. During the war, Conrad supervised Westinghouse's manufacture and testing of lightweight transmitters and receivers for the Signal Corps. This allowed him to continue testing signals on radio apparatus in his home workshop and also gave him access to the most sophisticated radio technology to date, namely, the vacuum tube.

In 1919, after the armistice had been signed, the government lifted its ban on amateur radio activity. Conrad unpacked his transmitter and resumed his amateur broadcasts shortly thereafter. Using the new transmitting tubes to which he now had access, Conrad was able to rebuild his apparatus to produce high-quality sound transmissions of voice and phonographic music. Other amateurs were impressed and sent letters of praise. Along with his friend and fellow Westinghouse engineer Donald Little and a variety of family members and neighbors, Conrad continued to broadcast musical concerts, news, and talks, with the Hamilton Music Store providing phonographs in return for on-air identification.

In September 1920, a turning point came for 8XK and the whole radio industry when the Joseph Horne department store ran an advertisement in the Pittsburgh *Sun* encouraging readers to buy wireless sets at Joseph Horne's in order to listen to Frank Conrad's programs. The ad was noticed by Westinghouse vice president Harry P. Davis, who suddenly saw a solution to the postwar doldrums in radio manufacturing. With government contracts dropping off dramatically, Westinghouse could perhaps create a new market of ordinary consumers if it supported a well-publicized, regularly scheduled broadcast of news and entertainment.

Conrad was asked to build a new transmitter at the Westinghouse plant in Pittsburgh and have it ready for election returns in early November. The new transmitter, assigned commercial shore-station call letters KDKA, broadcast the results of the Harding-Cox presidential race on November 2, 1920, and continued to broadcast variety programming on a regularly scheduled basis. KDKA was largely responsible for initiating the transition of the radio industry from a purely manufacturing and point-to-point service industry to a broadcasting industry in its own right. Conrad continued to use 8XK for amateur transmissions until 1924 when he transferred his station to Westinghouse (see also **Conrad, Dr. Frank**).

Baudino, Joseph E., and John M. Kittross. "Broadcasting's Oldest Stations: An Examination of Four Claimants." *Journal of Broadcasting* 21 (1) (winter 1977): 61–83.

Christina S. Drale

EISENHOWER, DWIGHT DAVID (1895–1969), was the thirty-fourth president and served in that office between 1953 and 1961. Although the Eisenhower years coincided with the Golden Age of television, Eisenhower made many contributions to the radio medium. His most notable came in 1953, when he permitted his presidential news conferences to appear on radio for the first time.

Eisenhower, born and raised in Abilene, Kansas, was an obscure army officer for nearly 20 years following his graduation from West Point. He rose rapidly at the onset of World War II and as a master organizer caught the attention of General George Marshall, Franklin Roosevelt's military chief of staff. In 1942, Eisenhower was named Supreme Allied Military Commander in Europe. Eisenhower's reputation for having won World War II carried him into politics. He was elected president in a landslide victory in 1952 and reelected in an even bigger landslide in 1956, his two political campaigns the most media-intensive up to that time. Several million dollars had been raised and spent on radio advertising alone.

Eisenhower's closest friends included William Paley and David Sarnoff, the heads of CBS and NBC, who encouraged Eisenhower to use both radio and television in his political campaigns. Mostly on television, Eisenhower perfected an informal approach, and his TV broadcasts were considered the equivalent of Franklin Roosevelt's radio *Fireside Chats*. A spin-off of this effort was Eisenhower's decision to open his news conferences to radio coverage in 1953, a tactic Eisenhower employed to indirectly respond to charges of Wisconsin Senator Joseph McCarthy, who had alleged the widespread presence of communists in government. The radio news conferences represented a major victory for the broadcast media in their ongoing battle with the print media for legitimacy. The news conferences were recorded on audiotape and released to the wire services. Radio outlets could replay the entire news conference, or they could use audio clips from Eisenhower's remarks in the same manner print reporters had quoted the president. The radio news conferences also cleared the way for the first televised news conferences in 1955.

Through his administration and his career, Eisenhower frequently used radio as a means of drawing public support to his political endeavors and for offering his opinions about the state of American society. His single most famous radio broadcast was the short message he delivered to European listeners hours after the D-Day landing on the north coast of France in June 1944. In October 1957, Eisenhower appeared on radio to calm public fears in the United States following the launch of *Sputnik* by the Soviet Union. Just before leaving office in 1961, Eisenhower, in one of his most-quoted speeches, appeared on radio and television to express concern over what he called a "military-industrial complex." In the late 1960s, just before his death in 1969, Eisenhower used radio commentaries to attack opponents of the Vietnam War.

Allen, Craig. *Eisenhower and the Mass Media.* Chapel Hill: University of North Carolina Press, 1993.
Ambrose, Stephen. *Eisenhower.* 2 vols. New York: Simon and Schuster, 1983, 1984.
Hughes, Emmet. *The Ordeal of Power.* New York: Atheneum, 1963.

Craig M. Allen

ELECTION COVERAGE. *See* **polling, public opinion;** *also see* **politics and media.**

ELECTRIC AND MUSICAL INDUSTRIES, LTD. (EMI), a British company formed in April 1931 by merging H.M.V. (His Master's Voice) Gramophone Company and Columbia Gramophone. The Radio Corporation of America (RCA) was also involved, owning 27 percent of EMI's stock. In March 1934, the Marconi

Company and EMI formed the Marconi-EMI Television Company, Ltd. EMI's close ties with RCA provided access to proprietary information related to Vladimir Zworykin's revolutionary TV camera tube, the "iconoscope." Marconi-EMI developed an advanced version of the iconosope called the "Emitron." In February 1937, Marconi-EMI's all-electronic system (405 lines per frame/25 frames per second) was selected over John L. Baird's mechanical system as the national standard for TV broadcasting in Great Britain.

Abramson, Albert. *Zworykin: Pioneer of Television.* Chicago: University of Illinois Press, 1995.

Baker, W. J. *A History of the Marconi Company.* London: Methuen & Co. Ltd., 1970.

Shiers, George, ed. *Technical Development of Television.* New York: Arno Press, 1977. (Reprint of articles published between 1911 and 1970 by various publishers.)

Tom Spann

ELECTRONIC-AUDIENCE MEASUREMENT, the collection of media audience behavioral data by a metering device. Compared to other common methods of data collection, a principal advantage is the accuracy of data collected; cost and complexity are major disadvantages. Arthur C. Nielsen pioneered electronic-audience measurement with the introduction of the radio Audimeter in the 1930s. Modern TV "peoplemeters" record which channel is watched, for how long, and if used properly, by whom. Viewers must remember to "punch in and out" for the peoplemeter to log individual viewing behaviors. Efforts to develop a purely passive device providing such detailed individualized data continue.

Beville, Hugh Malcolm, Jr. *Audience Ratings: Radio, Television, and Cable.* Rev. ed. Hillsdale, N.J.: Lawrence Erlbaum Associates, 1987.

Webster, James G., and Lawrence W. Lichty, eds. *Ratings Analysis: Theory and Practice.* Hillsdale, N.J.: Lawrence Erlbaum Associates, 1991.

Tom Spann

ELVIS FORMAT is a radio programming approach that plays music by Elvis Presley exclusively. The dominance of FM caused many struggling AM stations to broadcast narrow, specialized programming to attract a niche audience. This strategy uses a format-radio approach. Examples of format-radio themes include all-sports, all-weather, and even all-motivational programming. The all-Elvis format was tested in many markets and was usually a short-lived novelty (see **niche**).

Howard, Herbert H., Michael S. Kievman, and Barbara Moore. *Radio, TV, and Cable Programming.* 2nd ed. Ames: Iowa State University Press, 1994.

Donald Diefenbach

ELWELL, CYRIL F. (1884–1963), founded, in 1909, the first "garage" electronics company in what is now called the Silicon Valley area of northern California. After receiving a degree in electrical engineering from Stanford in 1907, Elwell was hired by a San Francisco company to evaluate a new wireless telephone technology. That spark gap–based device invented by Francis McCarty proved to be unsatisfactory for voice transmission, but Elwell noticed that when he moved the spark elements close together, they behaved like a singing arc, thought to be a smoother carrier of voice. Elwell had read about a similar system patented by Danish inventor Valdemar Poulsen. Poulsen had taken the arc discovered by William Duddell and caused it to oscillate in the radio frequency spectrum. Elwell traveled to Denmark in 1908 and obtained the American rights to develop the device for two-way wireless telephone communication. In 1909, he formed in Palo Alto the Poulsen Wireless Telephone and Telegraph Company, later named Federal Telephone and Telegraph, and for the next 10 years manufactured arc transmitters for transcontinental communications. Ironically, the purpose for which Elwell obtained the rights to the Poulsen arc, the radiotelephone, was quickly discarded as unsuitable, and the arc became a telegraph-only device. In 1915, Lee de Forest, working in Elwell's Stanford garage, perfected his audion as an amplifier and sold it to the telephone company for transcontinental wired telephone conversations.

Adams, Mike. "The Race for Radiotelephone." *AWA Review* 10 (1996): 79–149.
Elwell, Cyril. "[Unpublished] Autobiography." Clark Radiana Collection, Clark Papers, Smithsonian, 1943.
Elwell, Cyril F. http://www.sfmuseum.org/hist/elwell.html

Mike Adams

EMERGENCY ALERT SYSTEM. *See* **EBS/EAS.**

EMERGENCY BROADCAST SYSTEM. *See* **EBS/EAS.**

EMERSON RADIOS were produced by the Emerson Radio & Phonograph Corporation, founded in 1923. During the 1920s Emerson bought and sold surplus radios produced by other manufacturers. The company began producing its own product line during the 1930s at a time when other businesses and industries were floundering as a result of the Great Depression.

Emerson responded to the economy of the times by reducing its radio prices. In 1932, in an effort to keep costs down, Emerson manufactured one of the first "midget" radios, Model 25–A. Compared to the large console models available, the six-pound, wooden, table-top radio seemed quite small. Until this time, the smallest radio had weighed 25 pounds. Initially, competitors were reluctant to produce the smaller radios, allowing Emerson an opportunity to dominate the market with its smaller, lower-price radios.

Despite the depression, Emerson sold its millionth radio in 1937. Production increased to a million receivers a year until the company converted its manufacturing facilities to wartime status for World War II. By 1950, Emerson was one of the world's largest producers of small radios. Following the war, Emerson had established its marketing strategy of providing many choices to buyers by continually introducing new models (an average of 60 a year in the early 1950s). Midget sets became smaller and smaller, culminating in the popular transistor radios of the 1960s.

Bunis, Marty, and Sue Bunis. *The Collector's Guide to Antique Radios.* Paducah, Ky.: Collector Books, 1996.
Library of American Broadcasting. http://www.itd.umd.edu/UMS/UMCP/BPL/bplintro.html
The Radio History Society. http://www.radiohistory.org/links.htm

Sandra L. Ellis

ENGINEERING/TECHNICAL DEPARTMENT. There are four basic functions performed within radio stations: administrative, programming, fiscal, and technical. The technical functions are typically carried out by the engineering or technical department. Usually supervised by the station's chief engineer, the engineering department keeps the station on the air, maintains equipment, and ensures that the station complies with Federal Communications Commission (FCC) technical requirements. With the exception of extremely small facilities, there is always an area set aside to house a station's engineering equipment, tools, and personnel. Some employees in a large engineering or technical department may specialize in studio work; others may specialize in transmitter operation and maintenance. The chief engineer in a larger station supervises a staff of technical maintenance and operational employees. In fact, at a very large station, the chief engineer would perform primarily administrative, purchasing, and planning duties. In a small radio station, the chief engineer may be the only technical employee; some small radio stations even share an engineer or contract for the services of an outside engineer. In any case, radio engineers must stay up-to-date with constantly changing FCC rules, engineering techniques, and broadcast technology.

Interestingly, while rules for FCC licensing of engineers have been relaxed since the mid-1980s, the demands on engineer departments in terms of signal quality have risen dramatically, as a better signal can translate to larger ratings. In addition, there is a trend toward self-regulation in engineering departments; the Society of Broadcast Engineers (SBE) certifies engineers who pass a written test widely considered to be superior in its ability to measure job-related qualifications to FCC tests of the past and present.

O'Donnell, Lewis B., Carl Hausman, and Philip Benoit. *Radio Station Operations: Management and Employee Perspectives.* Belmont, Calif.: Wadsworth, 1989.

Mark J. Braun

EQUAL TIME REQUIREMENTS. Section 315 of the *Communications Act of 1934* requires broadcasters provide "equal opportunities" to candidates running for public office when an opponent appears on the air. Often inaccurately referred to as the "equal time law," Section 315 requires only that the opportunity be afforded to candidates. Candidates who cannot afford to purchase the time or who do not request it from stations are not given the time. There is no affirmative obligation on the station to seek out candidates to achieve balance. Candidates wanting equal opportunity must request it within one week of the airing of an opponent. The requirement is in effect only 45 days before a primary election and 60 days before a general election. Most troublesome to broadcasters is the requirement that candidates be charged the station's lowest unit charge for any advertising sold.

Not all programming is subject to the equal opportunity requirement. Specifically, Section 315 exempts newscasts, news interviews, news documentaries, and on-the-spot coverage of news events. The rule is not intended to require a balanced journalistic approach to news but to ensure that stations do not sell (or give) more advertising time to one candidate than to another. In the 1990s, the law was modified so that candidate appearances that are not controlled by the candidate or the candidate's campaign committee are also exempted. In the 1976, 1980, and 1984 elections, stations airing old Ronald Reagan movies would trigger a Section 315 obligation, but that is no longer the case. Broadcasters are prohibited from censoring any material that falls under Section 315, regardless of how abhorrent. In 1972, a candidate for the Georgia Senate had his ads aired unaltered despite the fact that they contained racist statements.

Presidential debates have been viewed differently over time. In 1960, Congress voted to suspend Section 315 to allow the Kennedy-Nixon debates without forcing stations to provide equal opportunities to other candidates. In 1976, the Carter-Ford debates were televised after a Federal Communications Commission (FCC) decision that debates would be considered news events (and therefore exempt) if sponsored by someone other than the broadcaster or a political party. In 1984, the FCC interpreted the rule more broadly and decided that debates between major candidates are news events regardless of sponsor.

Section 315 in no way empowers candidates to determine how much time must be provided to them, or when that time must be provided. Equal opportunity does not have to be satisfied by providing exactly the same length of time in exactly the same time slot. Stations may meet an equal opportunity obligation by providing a candidate 10, 60-second slots instead of 20, 30-second slots. A station could not, however, meet its requirement by scheduling one candidate's ads during drive time, while another candidate's ads air overnight. The law also specifically states that licensees are under no obligation to allow candidates the use of their stations. It should be recognized, however, that stations still have an obligation to provide "reasonable access" to candidates for federal office under Section 312 of the *Communications Act of 1934.* There is also the general requirement that stations operate in the public interest, which implies that they cannot completely ignore elections.

Dom Caristi

ESPN, SPORTS RADIO. The ESPN Radio Network was created on January 4, 1992. The radio network was added to the ESPN Network by John Walsh, the executive editor of the ESPN Sports Network headquartered in Bristol, Connecticut (McLaughlin, p. 22). The network features sports talk and call-in programming.

ESPN Radio currently features the *Fabulous Sports Babe* radio show as well as *Sportsbeat,* a program with Brent Mussberger and Ben Davis. The *Fabulous Sports Babe* airs Monday through Friday, and *Sportsbeat* covers important sports stories from collegiate and professional ranks throughout the week. ESPN Radio also provides game-day reports from various sites during the collegiate major sports seasons and from professional sporting events. The network offers interviews with sports figures and sports analysts, and the personalities field questions from the listening public.

William F. Rasmussen began plans to start the sports network in 1978 and persuaded Getty Oil to buy 85 percent of the company in 1979. The Entertainment and Sports Programming Network started broadcasting on cable on September 7, 1979. Writing in *Sky* magazine, John McLaughlin sums up the importance of ESPN.

"In a meteoric 17-year rise, the cable network from unfashionable Bristol, Connecticut, has overcome the initial bemusement of sports fans and the open derision of the major networks to establish itself as the name in television sports" (p. 22).

ESPN is now owned by the Walt Disney Company after a $19 billion takeover in August 1995 of Capital Cities/ABC. ABC had purchased ESPN in 1984 for $227 million. The sports network, in addition to ESPN and ESPN radio, now has ESPN2 and the new ESPNEWS, a cable TV sports news channel that began broadcasting in November 1996.

McLaughlin, John. "The Wider World of Sport." *Sky: The Magazine of International Culture* (November 1996): 21–26.

Arthur Thomas Challis, Jr.

ETHER, the region of space beyond the earth's atmosphere, the clear sky, the heavens; physics' all-pervading, infinitely elastic, massless medium formerly postulated as the medium of propagation of electronic waves (radio waves). Simply put, it is the region in which radio waves, which disseminate broadcast signals, operate. The upper or bright air.

Morris, William, ed. *American Heritage Dictionary of the English Language.* Boston: Houghton Mifflin Company, 1981.

ElDean Bennett

ETHICAL ISSUES. *See* **codes of ethics.**

ETHNIC ISSUES, ETHNIC MUSIC, matters or points influencing a population subgroup characterized by a common cultural heritage, customs, music, and language. U.S. Census data projections indicate that the population of African Americans, Asians, and Hispanics will increase significantly over the next 60 years. As the proportion of these groups increases because of higher fertility rates and net immigration levels, it is expected that the Caucasian population will decrease due to a drop in the birthrate and the deaths of older age groups. By 2050, this shift in population distribution would reflect a Hispanic-origin population of 23 percent, followed by 16 percent black and 10 percent Asian and Pacific Islander.

The major issues that affect both the foreign- and native-born populations in the United States are immigration (both legal and illegal), assimilation, and language. According to the Strategy Research Corporation, 70 percent of Americans, including 63 percent of Hispanic Americans, believe that the United States cannot control its international borders. As a result, Hispanics and non-Hispanics alike feel threatened by the steady increase of immigrants. Interestingly, a majority of Hispanics and non-Hispanics believe that illegal and legal immigration should be stemmed and that deportation of illegals should increase.

Economic pressures from the immigrant arrivals has caused many non-Hispanic Americans to evaluate the future ethnic mix of their communities. This assessment, mixed with apprehension, has resulted in an upswing of legislation aimed at immigrants. Examples are the increase in the number of U.S. border patrol agents,

English-only propositions, and state laws denying schooling or social and health services to illegal immigrants except in emergencies.

Unlike the European immigrant populations of the early 1900s, Hispanics have maintained a strong ethnic identity and have not assimilated into the American "melting pot." This may be due to the relative proximity of their homelands (Mexico, Cuba, El Salvador, Dominican Republic, Colombia, Guatemala, Nicaragua, Peru, Ecuador, Honduras, and other Latin American nations), modern technology, mass media, and the flow of new arrivals into the United States. Today's Hispanic immigrant has a complete Spanish-language infrastructure available via media, education, goods, and services. In any of the major Hispanic markets in the United States, it is not necessary for the Hispanic immigrant to assimilate to the new culture. Some research indicates that although new arrivals may grow toward their new culture, after 10 to 12 years, they return to their cultural roots.

One of the ties to a common culture is music. *Broadcasting-Cable Yearbook 1996* designates 21 different radio programming formats in the United States and Canada focusing on ethnic audiences. They include American Indian, Arabic, black, Chinese, Eskimo, ethnic, Filipino, French, Greek, Italian, Japanese, Korean, Polish, Portuguese, Reggae (Jamaican), Russian, Serbian, Spanish, Tejano, and Vietnamese. The overwhelming number of stations are Spanish (447), followed by black (172). Tejano, bicultural programming including Spanish, is offered by 21 stations in a category separate from the Spanish format. Even though they are not formally designated formats, many Spanish-language stations in the top 10 Cupric markets in the United States also describe the music aired as Tex/Mex, Mexican contemporary, Tropical, Rancheras, Nortenas, and Banda.

Day, Jennifer Cheeseman. *Population Projections of the United States, by Age, Sex and Hispanic Origin: 1993–2050.* Washington, D.C.: U.S. Department of Commerce, Economics and Statistics, Bureau of the Census, 1993.
The Latin American Market Planning Report. Miami: Strategy Research Corporation, 1996.
The U.S. Hispanic Market. Miami: Strategy Research Corporation, 1996.

Fran R. Matera

EVANS, DALE. *See* **Rogers, Roy (King of the Cowboys), and Evans, Dale.**

EXCLUSIVE LISTENERS. Access limited to a certain audience. Radio programming geared to specific demographics. Wired-wireless or closed-circuit radio is transmitted to a specific area. For example, low-power radio has a limited pickup range, or Internet users can select specific audio programming. Arbitron defines the exclusive cume audience as people who listen to only one station within a reported daypart.

Mary Kay Switzer

EXECUTION, FORMAT. A graphic device called a "clock" guides the execution of a radio station's format. On this clock are times indicating the airing of each element of the format. For example, from the start of each hour until :20, the disc jockey airs a "music sweep" (nonstop music), followed by a "stop set" (commercials and talk), repeated three times every hour. A news clock could have network news at the top of each hour, traffic reports at :08, :18, :28, :38, :48, and :58 and sports at :15 and :45. This concept has been successfully copied by *CNN Headline News,* which periodically shows its "clock" to viewers (see **hot clock**).

Adams, Michael, and Kimberly Massey. *Introduction to Radio: Programming and Production.* Dubuque: Wm. C. Brown Communications, Inc., 1994.

Mike Adams

F

FAIRNESS DOCTRINE, requirement, now defunct, that broadcasters provide contrasting views on personal attack, political editorializing, or controversial issues. The requirement was first enunciated by the Federal Communications Commission (FCC) in 1949, and since 1972, the doctrine also applied to cable systems that originated programming. In 1964, 1974, and 1976, the FCC reexamined the doctrine and continued it. The FCC voted to repeal the doctrine in 1987. In 1989, a federal appellate court upheld the FCC's authority to eliminate it. Since 1987, Congress has discussed amending the *Communications Act* to include the Fairness Doctrine (making it impossible for the FCC to change the law) but has been unsuccessful, including a veto by President Ronald Reagan in 1987.

In its first decade, the FCC struggled with the issue of whether to allow radio to act as an advocate for the positions of station operators. In 1941, the FCC issued the "Mayflower Decision," prohibiting radio stations from editorializing on the premise that it was unfair, since the government decided who was given licenses. It was reasoned that if everyone could not own a radio station, it was a government-provided unfair advantage to have one's own station to influence public opinion. After eight years, the FCC reversed its position. Rather than expecting stations to ignore controversy, the Fairness Doctrine required stations to "devote a reasonable percentage of their broadcasting time to the discussion of public issues of interest in the community." It further required stations to provide a "reasonably balanced presentation of all responsible viewpoints." The Fairness Doctrine never required equal treatment or equal time for individuals or causes but instead required broadcasters to provide viewers and listeners with a diversity of viewpoints on controversies.

The decision as to how these issues were covered was always left to the discretion of the broadcaster. Newscasts, public service announcements, documentaries, and even entertainment programs were all seen as acceptable ways of dealing with controversial issues of public importance. Broadcasters were also given latitude in determining how to balance the issues. If one side of an issue was presented through a news story, the FCC would find it acceptable to have an opposing view expressed through public service announcements.

Although broadcasters could satisfy their obligation to provide opposing viewpoints by allowing spokespeople representing varying perspectives to appear on the air, the Fairness Doctrine never required that broadcasters provide access to anyone to present his or her views. Despite tag lines on most editorials that invited replies, broadcasters retained the authority to decide how those opposing views would be presented and by whom. The Fairness Doctrine did not provide any right of access, except in the clearly defined areas of personal attacks and editorial endorsements of a candidate.

Commercials presented an unusual dilemma for the FCC. In 1967, the Commission adopted the position that cigarette smoking was a controversial issue of public importance. As such, cigarette ads needed to be balanced by content discouraging people from smoking. In 1970, when Congress voted to ban cigarette advertising on radio and television, the FCC presumed the matter settled, and the Fairness Doctrine would no longer be applied to product advertising. Several groups saw the FCC's position on cigarette advertising as a chance to promote their causes through the Fairness Doctrine, however, and attempted to challenge the FCC's change of position. In 1971, Friends of the Earth successfully argued to a federal appeals court that advertisements promoting the sale of big, fuel-inefficient automobiles triggered a fairness requirement. In order to prevent what it saw as a possible fairness challenge to most commercials, the FCC issued a Fairness Report in 1974 explicitly stating that the Fairness Doctrine did not apply to ordinary product commercials, preempting any similar claims in the future. A federal court upheld the FCC's new position in a 1975 decision.

On the other hand, if a controversial issue were discussed in a sponsored program, the FCC ruled that a station must provide for opposing viewpoints, even if no one wished to pay for such sponsorship. This led many stations to refuse to accept any paid programming that raised controversial issues. An unsuccessful legal challenge was launched by the Business Executives' Move for Vietnam Peace and by the Democratic National Committee to try to require stations to accept editorial advertising. In each case, the challengers wanted to purchase advertising time from stations to state their positions on controversial issues. The stations refused to sell them time, claiming a First Amendment right to choose what material to air. In 1973, the Supreme Court ruled that stations could decide for themselves whether to air editorial advertisements. The Court stated that requiring stations to air such ads would result in an advantage to the wealthy. If the Fairness Doctrine were applied to these ads and broadcasters were required to provide opposing viewpoints, it would create a financial hardship on those stations while interfering with a station's right to decide what to air.

Although rarely enforced, the personal attack rule of the Fairness Doctrine has not been eliminated. This rule stipulates that stations are required to provide reply time to any individual whose honesty, character, or integrity is attacked during the broadcast of a controversial issue of public importance. While mere criticism of a public official is not considered the sort of broadcast to require a reply, allegations of criminal activity or vile behavior would be. In addition, the broadcaster is required to provide the individual attacked with either a transcript or tape of the personal attack. This requirement has been upheld by the Supreme Court (see *Red Lion Broadcasting Co., v. Federal Communications Commission* decision). Personal attacks made on foreigners, attacks made by political candidates or their campaigns, and attacks that occur during news coverage are exempted from the personal attack rule requirements.

As with personal attacks, the FCC requires stations to provide a transcript or tape to candidates whenever those stations air an editorial opposing a candidate or endorsing an opponent. The requirement applies only if the editorial is interpreted as the station's position rather than just the position of an individual commentator or political pundit.

Dom Caristi

FARM BROADCASTING. Radio has served farmers since U.S. Agricultural Department (USDA) wireless weather reports began in 1900. By 1914, amateurs relayed University of North Dakota wireless telegraph Weather Bureau forecasts. University of Wisconsin's pioneer 9XM sent regular weather reports to farmers. The USDA's W. A. Wheeler broadcast the first market reports on December 15, 1920. When commercial broadcasting began, broadcasters asked the USDA for permission to carry market reports. Some had speakers on farm topics; in 1922, KYW, Chicago, began a nightly farm program with speakers from the American Farm Bureau Federation and other groups. By 1923, 140 commercial stations carried both weather and market reports.

The first full-time farm broadcaster, KDKA's Frank E. Mullen, began in 1923. At NBC, Mullen started *National Farm & Home Hour* (1928–1944) with programming on modern farming techniques, consumer news, live music, and news commentators. State colleges broadcast similar programs. New England Radio Service (1928–1951) and Mississippi Valley Network were regional farm programmers. National programming came from CBS, Mutual, ABC, Commodity News Service Network, Judy Massabny's syndicated National Grange program, and other sources.

The National Association of Farm Radio Directors (NAFRD) was founded by Larry Haeg on May 5, 1944. NAFRD's 1946 code urged members "to gain a thorough understanding of farm conditions and problems and, thus, through radio, promote better agriculture and better family living." Many stations had farm directors into the 1960s. Kansas City's KMBC even operated an experimental farm. Farm radio's diminution coincided with the rise of format programming and deregulation. Still, in the 1990s, farm reports continued on approximately 1,230 stations.

Baker, John C. *Farm Broadcasting: The First Sixty Years.* Ames: Iowa State University Press, 1981.
Shurick, E. P. J. *The First Quarter-Century of American Broadcasting.* Kansas City: Midland Publishing Co., 1946.

William James Ryan

FARNSWORTH, PHILO T. (1906–1971), the inventor of the electronic system of television, has a curious relationship to the history of radio in the United States. Although best known as an inventor, Farnsworth's radio work was as a manufacturer and a broadcaster, although each of those roles was indirect through his Farnsworth Radio and Television Company. In 1938, the company bought the Capehart Company in Fort Wayne, Indiana. Capehart had been a manufacturer of phonographs and jukeboxes that had fallen on hard times. Farnsworth moved his Philadelphia laboratory to Indiana and entered the field of manufacturing radio and television sets. In 1945, Farnsworth Radio and Television purchased WGL-AM (1,250 kilohertz), which had been the first radio station in Fort Wayne going on the air in 1924. Farnsworth Radio and Television was sold in 1949 to ITT, and as part of that arrangement, WGL-AM was sold to the Fort Wayne *News-Sentinel* newspaper. Thus ended the radio career of the inventor of television.

Everson, George. *The Story of Television: The Life of Philo T. Farnsworth.* New York: W. W. Norton, 1949.

Farnsworth, Elma G. *Distant Vision: Romance and Discovery on an Invisible Frontier.* Salt Lake City: Pemberly-Kent Publishers, 1989.

Farnsworth Chronicles. http://songs.com/noma/philo/index.html

Jonathan David Tankel

FEDERAL COMMUNICATIONS COMMISSION (FCC), independent federal agency established by the *Communications Act of 1934* to regulate interstate and international electronic communication, wired and wireless. The FCC has five members (reduced from seven in 1983), one of whom serves as the chair. Members are appointed by the president and approved by the Senate. Term of office for commissioners is five years, and they may serve multiple terms. No more than three commissioners from one political party may serve simultaneously.

The FCC was preceded by the Federal Radio Commission (FRC), which was established in 1927. When the *Communications Act of 1934* was passed, it replaced the FRC with the FCC. Despite opposition from broadcasters who did not want the government to play a role in broadcasting, President Roosevelt signed the bill creating the FCC on July 1, 1934. One significant difference between the FCC and its predecessor the FRC is that the radio commission was established as a temporary agency, intended to distribute licenses, then cease to exist, turning over its remaining duties to the Commerce Department. When Congress established the FCC, it recognized that the agency would play a role long after the initial licenses were distributed. The FCC does not regulate government use of the spectrum, although its policies may impact government electronic communications.

As an independent agency, the "checks and balances" on the FCC are not the same as they would be for administrative agencies (such as the Food and Drug Administration), which answer directly to the president. While the president selects the chair and the commissioners (who must be approved by the Senate), he does not have the authority to remove commissioners during their terms. The FCC is much more beholden to Congress, which controls not only appropriations but also its very existence. Since 1981, the FCC is no longer a permanent agency but instead must be reauthorized by Congress every two years. Congress also has the authority to amend the *Communications Act of 1934*. Such amendment could result in changes in the FCC's duties or structure. The passage of the *Telecommunications Act of 1996* included a number of tasks that Congress required the FCC to accomplish along with the dates by which the FCC had to act.

Although the FCC has only five commissioners, there are hundreds of staff members in dozens of different departments, including offices across the country. The FCC is divided administratively into a number of offices and bureaus. Of greatest interest to broadcasters is the Mass Media Bureau (previously called the Broadcast Bureau), which processes license applications and renewals, among other duties. Each of these offices and bureaus is further subdivided into divisions. In the case of the Mass Media Bureau, the four divisions are for Audio Services, Video Services, Policy and Rules, and Enforcement.

In its attempt to carry out the wishes of Congress as expressed in the *Communications Act of 1934,* the FCC creates rules. Proposals for new rules come from a variety of sources, both within and outside the commission. If the FCC plans a new rule, it first issues a Notice of Proposed Rule Making (NPRM). The NPRM is formal notice that the FCC is considering a rule and provides for a required length of time that the commission must allow public comments. After sufficient comment and discussion, new rules are adopted in FCC Reports and Orders and are published in the *Federal Register.*

The FCC does not actively monitor the broadcasts of radio and television stations. It relies on information provided to it by the broadcasters themselves and their audiences. Determinations about whether a station deserves to have its license renewed are based on documents filed by the station, any public comments the commission receives about that station, or challenges to the renewal by interested parties.

The commission is able to enforce regulations primarily through the threat of action. The majority of license renewals are granted with no disciplinary action by the FCC. Should the commission find rules violations by a licensee, however, its actions can range from a letter admonishing a station to fines of up to $250,000, a short-term renewal of the license, or even the revocation of a license. It is the threat of this action that keeps broadcasters in compliance.

The FCC has the ultimate authority to revoke a station's license or deny its renewal, although that action has rarely been taken. In more than 50 years, the FCC has taken such action only 147 times: fewer than an average of three per year out of thousands of license renewals. More than one third of those revocations/ nonrenewals were due to misrepresentations to the commission. Although it has been infrequent, the FCC has acted severely in cases where licensees have lied intentionally.

Of all the powers given to the FCC, the *Communications Act of 1934* specifically states that the commission may not censor the content of broadcasts. According to Section 326, "Nothing in this Act shall be understood or construed to give this Commission the power of censorship over the radio communications or signals transmitted by any radio station." In spite of this, FCC reprimands and fines of stations for broadcasting indecent material at inappropriate times have been upheld by the Supreme Court. The FCC acknowledges its obligation to stay out of content decisions in most areas. The commission has declined to base license decisions on the proposed format of a radio station and does not stipulate the amount of time stations should devote to public service announcements.

The FCC has a dual role: While it makes the rules and regulations to carry out the *Communications Act of 1934,* it also serves as a judicial body, hearing appeals of its decisions. In this role, the FCC serves as the equivalent of a federal district court. FCC decisions that are upheld in appeal can then be challenged by appealing directly to the Federal Court of Appeals for the D.C. Circuit. The majority of commissioners over the years have been lawyers rather than engineers. Fewer than half the commissioners have served their full terms.

Dom Caristi

FEDERAL RADIO COMMISSION. *See* **Federal Communications Commission (FCC).**

FEDERAL TELEGRAPH COMPANY was established in 1909 as the Poulsen Wireless Telephone and Telegraph Company whose purpose was to develop and market the Poulsen arc transmitter in the United States. The company was established by engineer Cyril F. Elwell upon securing patent rights from Danish scientist and inventor Valdemar Poulsen. Elwell recognized the potential of the Poulsen arc to generate continuous waves for radio transmission and thus a clearer, stronger signal for long-distance radiotelegraphy and telephony.

After making several improvements, Elwell was able to start the first commercial radio service in the United States with continuous wave technology. The high-speed alternator would not be ready to compete with the arc for another decade, which left the field wide open for the Federal Telegraph Company to gain a foothold in continuous wave radio. Also to its advantage was the fact that Federal was established on the West Coast where competition from the powerful American Marconi Company was limited. By 1912, Federal had 13 stations in operation, with 8 on the coast and 1 in Heeia, Hawaii.

That same year, Elwell convinced the U.S. Navy to test the arc transmitter against NESCO's high-speed, rotary-spark transmitter at its Arlington, Virginia, installation. The arc performed so well that the navy subsequently adopted its use in a network of high-powered stations around the world, making possible reliable communications between all of its naval bases and ships.

After World War I, Federal was involved in several controversial patent deals with the U.S. Navy designed to squelch foreign competition. A 1921 contract with China for high-powered stations drew in both the navy and the newly formed RCA. Federal continued to operate its stations until 1927, when it agreed to be absorbed by the International Telephone and Telegraph Corporation.

Aitken, Hugh G., ed. *The Continuous Wave: Technology and American Radio, 1900–1932.* Princeton, N.J.: Princeton University Press, 1985.

Christina S. Drale

FEDERAL THEATER PROJECT (FTP) was developed as a program of the Works Progress Administration and was based on the idea that the unemployed deserved socially useful jobs. The FTP lasted from 1935 to 1939 and at its height employed over 13,000 people in 31 states. The FTP offered programs ranging from vaudeville and traveling circuses to group theater, drama, and radio programs. The Theater of the Air division of the FTP, in cooperation with independent commercial stations, CBS, NBC, and MBS (Mutual Broadcasting System), employed writers, actors, directors, and technicians. On March 15, 1936, the Theater of the Air broadcast its first weekly program and over the next three years presented over 3,000 programs a year to an estimated 10 million listeners a week.

Federal Theater Project Records. National Archives, Record Group 69: Records of the WPA.
Flannigan, Hallie. *Arena.* New York: Duell, Sloan and Pearce, 1940.

Mark A. Tolstedt

FEDERAL TRADE COMMISSION (FTC). In 1914, Congress passed the *Federal Trade Commission Act,* creating a government agency to regulate deceptive business practices and unfair commercial competition. Although the Federal Communications Commission (FCC) remains the main regulatory agency over radio, the FTC's Bureau of Consumer Protection is charged with regulating advertising, and its rulings may be applied to all mass media including radio.

Early concerns in Congress focused on unfair commercial competition, although the FTC investigated deceptive practices such as industrial espionage and secret concessions to suppliers and customers. As the advertising medium continued to grow, the commission's authority was expanded to include the regulation of exaggerated advertising claims. In 1938, Congress passed the Wheeler-Lea Amendment to the FTC act, which added the regulation of false and deceptive advertising to the commission's authority. The amendment also expanded the commission's area of concern to include protection of consumers; prior to this the commission's main concern was with business competitors only.

In general, the FTC has three main enforcement powers when dealing with false, deceptive, and exaggerated advertising consent decrees, cease-and-desist orders, and corrective advertising. It is important to note, however, that these punitive measures are applied to the advertiser (usually the manufacturer or distributor of a product) and not the radio station that broadcasts the deceptive commercial. The first step in dealing with a deceptive advertisement is the issuance of a consent decree. The advertiser admits no guilt but signs the consent decree and agrees to stop using the deceptive advertisement.

If the advertiser refuses to sign the consent decree the FTC may fine the advertiser and/or issue a cease-and-desist order, barring further use of the deceptive advertisement. An advertiser has the right to appeal a cease-and-desist order. A final enforcement power available to the FTC is a requirement to run a corrective advertisement. When the commission rules that an advertisement has misled consumers or misrepresented a product's qualities, it may require the company to run another advertisement that corrects that misconception. Perhaps the most famous example of this involved a Warner-Lambert advertisement for Listerine and its claim to prevent the common cold. The FTC required Warner-Lambert to run a corrective advertisement for roughly the same amount of time that the original deceptive commercial had been broadcast.

A more recent FTC action affecting radio stations involved its investigation of advertising sales and marketing practices. Responding to a soft advertising market, many radio stations formed local marketing agreements (also called joint sales agreements) to pool sales staffs and sell advertising more efficiently. Although stations, and many advertisers, claimed that such agreements actually led to increased audience reach for advertisers, the FTC investigated claims of price fixing caused by reduced competition.

Creech, Kenneth C. *Electronic Media Law and Regulation.* 2nd ed. Boston: Focal Press, 1995.

Stone, Alan. *Economic Regulation and the Public Interest: The Federal Trade Commission in Theory and Practice.* Ithaca, N.Y.: Cornell University Press, 1977.

Cynthia A. Cooper

FELDMAN, MICHAEL (1949–), radio personality born and raised in Milwaukee, Wisconsin. Feldman continues to live and work in the upper Midwest but has attracted a national audience. He began his radio career in 1977 with *Thanks for Calling,* a Madison (Wisconsin) call-in show. In 1978, Feldman created *The Breakfast Special,* a live show that broadcast from a Madison diner. Its unique, spontaneous format served him well and would be the impetus for his later work.

In 1981, Feldman joined with Madison Public Radio and hosted *A.M. Saturday,* a mix of live comedy and music. He briefly went with Chicago's WGN in 1984, but in the following year, he returned to Wisconsin Public Radio with plans for an audience participation show. In June 1985, *Whad'Ya Know? with Michael Feldman* made its debut on WHA, Madison. Through the National Public Radio (NPR) network, the weekly show got national distribution and, by the mid-1990s, was carried by over 200 NPR affiliates with an audience of close to 1 million listeners, making it one of public radio's most successful offerings.

In addition to Feldman's presence as host, *Whad'Ya Know?* has, over the years, maintained an unusually stable cast of supporting personalities, which gives it a continuity unusual in radio. Announcer Jim Packard has been with the show since its inception and participates in its production. The house band of John Thulin (piano) and Jeff Eckels (bass) provides live jazz and also trades quips with Feldman. Ostensibly a quiz show, *Whad'Ya Know?* serves as a vehicle for Feldman's rapid-fire humor. Performed before a live audience, Feldman establishes a quick rapport with both participants and onlookers. Even the listening audience has a sense of involvement, since the show uses an open-line telephone system that allows everyone to overhear all conversations.

Participants are asked humorous, trivia-based questions and compete for silly prizes donated by regional businesses. An occasional celebrity or expert in some offbeat area of knowledge may appear as a guest. For the most part, however, *Whad'Ya Know?* revolves around Michael Feldman. The quiz, the music, the interviews, and the interplay with the audience serve merely as backdrops for his running humorous observations.

Inevitably, comparisons between *Whad'Ya Know?* and the earlier quiz show *You Bet Your Life* (ABC Radio, 1947–1950; television, 1950–1960s) arise. Comedian Groucho Mark hosted the latter show and had the unflappable George Fenneman as his straight man. Feldman's quick wit and humorous patter are reminiscent of Marx, just as Packard's imperturbable announcing might remind listeners of Fenneman.

Whad'Ya Know? regularly goes on the road, allowing listeners in distant areas served by NPR to attend a live performance and participate as audience members. Its home base, however, remains Madison and WHA, a key factor in the production's folksy midwestern flavor and certainly a major element in the show's nationwide popularity.

William H. Young

FESSENDEN, REGINALD AUBREY (1866–1932), a Canadian, was a radiotelephony pioneer who developed a continuous wave generator to superimpose voice and music information on a high-frequency carrier. Fessenden developed the heterodyne receiver to detect and decode continuous wave signals. He also introduced a wireless telephone receiver that was a forerunner of today's wireless and cellular telephone systems. Fessenden is probably best remembered for transmitting what most consider the first publicly announced broadcast of radiotelephony.

Fessenden was an engineer and chemist for Thomas Edison and an electrician at the Westinghouse Company. He taught electrical engineering at Purdue University and the University of Pittsburgh. He brought wireless telegraphy and meteorology together for the first time when the Weather Bureau of the U.S. Department of Agriculture hired him to test ways to provide weather information via wireless.

In 1902, Fessenden patented the electrolytic detector, 1 of 500 patents he secured. His detector was used extensively in Germany and the United States until about 1913, when crystal detection became popular. In 1906, Ernst F. W. Alexandersen constructed the high speed alternating-current generator Fessenden had ordered from General Electric. In November, speech sounds were transmitted successfully 11 miles from Fessenden's laboratory in Brant Rock to a receiver at Plymouth, Massachusetts. Fessenden also successfully demonstrated the possibility of connecting a land telephone line to a wireless telephone station.

On Christmas Eve in 1906, wireless operators along the eastern seaboard heard "CQ, CQ" in Morse code, then Fessenden's faint voice break through the cold night air. He read a poem, played the violin, and then promised to broadcast again on New Year's Eve, which he did. United Fruit Company had alerted its operators to the transmissions, which they heard as far away as the West Indies.

Two Pittsburgh financiers joined Fessenden to form the National Electric Signaling Company (NESCO) to conduct further wireless research and development. In 1912 NESCO went into receivership when it faced financial and administrative difficulties. Fessenden did not cope well with the stresses of the marketplace. Westinghouse purchased NESCO in 1921.

Fessenden and other early experimenters were amateur radio operators. The program service they provided was incidental to promoting their wireless experiments. Their pioneer work caused interest in radio to spread rapidly throughout the United States. Fessenden was probably the first to apply alternator technology to radio communication. His 1902 detector patent is the earliest registered invention in the United States for a radiotelephone system using Hertzian waves. His beat or heterodyne system is one of the few early basic inventions that survives today. Fessenden was the first to produce both a practical transmitter and receiver of continuous waves.

Fessenden, Helen M. *Fessenden: Builder of Tomorrows.* New York: Coward-McCann, 1940. Reprint, with a new index, New York: Arno Press, 1974.

Fessenden, Reginald. Papers are in the State Archives of North Carolina in Raleigh.

Fessenden, Reginald A. "Wireless Telephony." In *The Development of Wireless to 1920,* edited by George Shiers. New York: Arno Press, 1977.

Peter E. Mayeux

FIBBER MCGEE & MOLLY, one of radio's most popular, longest-running comedy series, aired from 1935 to 1961 on the NBC Network. It starred, and was the creation of, Jim and Marian Jordan. Natives of Peoria, Illinois, the Jordans were high school sweethearts who married and eventually toured in vaudeville. Vaudeville eventually led to Chicago, where they augmented their income with radio appearances. Through these appearances, they met a failed cartoonist and budding writer Don Quinn.

With Quinn, the Jordans created a radio series set in a small-town general store titled *Smack Out* (where the store was "smack out" of everything but long-winded stories by its owner). It aired in Chicago from 1931 to 1935 and was national on NBC Blue from 1931 to 1933. An executive for Johnson's Wax saw potential in *Smack Out* and sold the Blue Network on a second Jordan/Quinn series.

Set at 79 Wistful Vista, *Fibber McGee & Molly* premiered on April 16, 1935. Folksy and character-driven, the series was usually without plot: simply the lives of frequently blundering Fibber and wife Molly and the neighbors who would stop by. Marian Jordan voiced many characters on the show, whose extensive cast included little girl Teeny, Mayor La Trivia, and Throckmorton P. Gildersleeve (a.k.a. The Great Gildersleeve, eventually spun off into his own series).

By 1941, the series was the number-one program on the air. It launched several national catch phrases including "T'aint funny, McGee," always stated by an exasperated Molly. The series was also famous for its running gag of Fibber's overstuffed closet, which was opened over 100 times on radio, always to crashing, banging sound effects. Marian Jordan died in 1961; Jim Jordan, in 1988.

"Fibber & Co." *Time* (April 20, 1940): 41.

Schaden, Chuck. "Speaking of Radio: Chuck Schaden's Conversation with Jim Jordan." *Nostalgia Digest* (December–January 1985): 33–40.

Stumf, Charles, and Tom Price. *Heavenly Days! The Story of Fibber McGee & Molly.* Wayneville, N.C.: World of Yesterday Press, 1987.

Cary O'Dell

FINANCING involves obtaining the funds necessary to construct, operate, and maintain a broadcast radio station. Initially, radio broadcasts were funded by the manufacturers of the radio broadcast and reception equipment in an attempt to provide content for the purchasers of their products.

Today, there are two main financing schemes for radio: commercial/private and noncommercial/public. Commercials advertisements, paid for according to the length of broadcast, were developed early on in radio's history and are the primary source of revenue for commercial radio stations. Noncommercial radio, on the other hand, grew mainly out of the Federal Communications Commission's (FCC's) reservation of certain frequencies for nonprofit and then noncommercial use. In 1967, the Corporation for Public Broadcasting was created to help support non-commercial stations. Early FCC regulations permitted noncommercial stations to utilize only underwriting to support the development of programming and the administration of the radio station. *Underwriting* is the announcement of the identity of a corporate or business sponsor, with no mention of the products or services the company sells or provides. As competition with commercial stations grew, the FCC allowed noncommercial stations to engage in enhanced underwriting, a more liberal version of underwriting that allows the mention of representative products and services but not prices.

There has been much discussion at the national level concerning the possibility of ending federal funding assistance to noncommercial stations. Whether public stations will continue to be supported by the United States government is in question, but corporate underwriting appears to be the most secure means of continuing to finance noncommercial broadcasting in the future. Commercial radio stations will most likely continue to rely on commercials for funding.

Of key importance to the development of radio has been, and will continue to be, the funding of technological innovations. Often funded, as radio broadcasts were initially, by the manufacturers of the equipment, government financing for the development of new technologies is also an important element of technological development.

Streeter, Thomas. *Selling the Air.* Chicago: University of Chicago Press, 1996.
White, Llewellyn. *History of Broadcasting: Radio to Television.* New York: Arno Press, 1971.
Robert A. Heverly

FINE ARTS/CLASSICAL FORMATS feature concert and operatic music. The term may be confusing because *classical* also describes a period in music history, roughly the last half of the eighteenth century, and features music by artists such as Beethoven, Mozart, and Haydn. For radio station formats, *classical* refers to the higher-order or best music.

The sound of the station is very important, and often the announcers' names are not known to the audience—the music is the star. The length of the music pieces is much longer than popular music, and the audience dislikes interruptions of the music. Therefore, fewer commercial breaks are heard. Typically, the audience is better educated and from a higher income bracket than other stations. Classical music formats compose about 3 percent of all stations; 17 AM, 456 FM; 53 commercial, 420 noncommercial (*Broadcasting and Cable Yearbook,* p. B604).

Fine arts format is often used to describe a classical music format but usually is a more inclusive term. Programming may include classical, jazz, folk, radio drama, in-depth news, and interviews. Stations affiliated with the Public Broadcasting Service (PBS) often refer to their format as fine arts. Like a classical format, the audience tends to be better educated and from a higher income bracket. Commercials may be fewer in number and produced with a more subdued sound.

Greenfield, Thomas A. *Radio: A Reference Guide.* Westport, Conn.: Greenwood, 1989.
Keith, Michael C. *The Radio Station.* 4th ed. Boston: Focal Press, 1997.

Mary E. Beadle

FIRESIDE CHATS. *See* **Roosevelt, Franklin D. (FDR).**

FIRST AMENDMENT RIGHTS. "Congress shall make no law respecting an establishment of religion, or prohibiting the free exercise thereof; or abridging the freedom of speech, or of the press; or the right of the people peaceably to assemble, and to petition the Government for redress of grievances" (United States Constitution, Amendment I [1791]).

The First Amendment specifically forbids Congress from making laws that abridge freedom of speech, press, peaceable assembly, and religion. Although written in absolute terms, the First Amendment has never been interpreted by the Supreme Court to mean that individuals or corporations have unlimited rights in these areas. As early as 1798, Congress passed the *Alien and Sedition Acts,* which limited criticism of the government and allowed for deportation of anyone deemed dangerous to the security of the United States. Although these acts were allowed to expire in 1801, numerous court cases have served to define and limit the First Amendment rights of Americans.

The first major cases dealing with freedom of speech and of the press did not occur until the early part of the twentieth century. The urbanization of society, America's involvement in World War I, and the development of more efficient and newer forms of communication technology may have served to bring First Amendment issues to the forefront.

When America entered World War I, Congress passed the *Espionage Act of 1917.* The act was designed to protect against spying by foreign countries and to protect military secrets. It was amended in 1918 to include what is commonly called the *Sedition Act* (not to be confused with the *Sedition Act of 1798*). This amendment dealt more with advocacy, speaking, teaching, printing, and inciting than did the original act. Although the *Sedition Act* was repealed in 1921, the *Espionage Act* remained in force into the 1940s.

The Clear-and-Present Danger Doctrine. It was during this time that the first serious interpretations of the First Amendment were attempted by the Supreme Court. In *Schenck v. United States,* 249 U.S. 47 (1919), Justice Oliver Wendell Holmes formulated the first guideline for determining the bounds of American's First Amendment rights, the Clear-and-Present Danger Doctrine. Schenck was found guilty of violating the *Espionage Act*, and the Clear-and-Present Danger Doctrine allowed punishment for speech that might bring about "evils which Congress has a right to prevent." It is in *Schenck* that Holmes writes that "the most stringent protection of free speech would not protect a man in falsely shouting fire in a Theatre and causing panic."

In spite of Holmes's articulation of the Clear-and-Present Danger Doctrine, its application was not entirely clear. In fact, Justice Holmes disagreed with a majority of the Supreme Court in the application of the doctrine shortly after *Schenck*. In *Abrams v. United States*, 250 U.S. 616 (1919), Justice Holmes borrowed from seventeenth-century British author John Milton's *Areopatgitica* and nineteenth-century philosopher John Stuart Mill's essay *On Liberty* to formulate the Marketplace of Ideas concept of the First Amendment. Holmes argued that all ideas should be heard, no matter how offensive they may be. He notes that government should only censor these ideas when they imminently threaten the security of the country.

The Clear-and-Present Danger Doctrine represents one method of adjudicating First Amendment disputes. Naturally, it cannot be applied to all First Amendment cases, and over the years other means of resolving issues have developed.

The Balancing Test. Sometimes the courts have worked to balance First Amendment rights against other rights guaranteed by the Constitution or laws. For example, the First Amendment right of the press to report on the proceedings of a trial has often been balanced against the Sixth Amendment right of a defendant to receive a fair and impartial trial by a jury of his or her peers. Sometimes this balancing has resulted in restricted press coverage when a court determines that the coverage might interfere with the trial proceedings.

Speech and Action. Throughout the years the courts have had difficulty in cases involving both verbal and nonverbal elements. In these cases, the courts have viewed actions as expression of opinion and thereby treated these actions as "speech." In determining whether actions are protected by the First Amendment, they must be balanced against laws prohibiting certain behavior. In *United States v. O'Brien*, 391 U.S. 367 (1968), the Supreme Court ruled that burning a draft card in protest of conscription during the Vietnam era was not protected speech because the draft card was government property. Had O'Brien burned a "symbolic" draft card, it would have been protected as speech. In *Texas v. Johnson* (1989) the Supreme Court ruled that burning an American flag is protected under the First Amendment as symbolic speech.

The First Amendment and Broadcasting. Material transmitted over the air on radio and television stations is not afforded the same First Amendment protection as printed matter or material transmitted on cable television. This rationale is based on the premise that broadcasters utilize the electromagnetic spectrum, which is a public resource. Therefore, broadcasters are granted use of the spectrum as public trustees. In *Red Lion Broadcasting Co. v. Federal Communications Commission*, 395 U.S. 367 (1969), the Supreme Court asserted that the people as a whole retain their interest in free speech by radio, and it is their collective right to have the medium provide free-speech opportunities for all. The Court notes that the right of the viewers and listeners is paramount, not the right of broadcasters.

Although the *Communications Act of 1934* prohibits the Federal Communications Commission (FCC) from censoring program content, the pervasive nature of the broadcast medium subjects radio and television to stricter standards than the print media or cable television. In *FCC v. Pacifica Foundation,* 438 U.S. 726 (1978), the Supreme Court held that broadcasters must consider the makeup of their potential audience when considering whether to broadcast "indecent" material. The FCC has also established time periods when indecent material may not be broadcast.

Unlike the print media, broadcasters and cablecasters must make equal time available to political candidates, and the rate at which this time is sold is governed by the *Communications Act of 1934.* In *Miami Herald v. Tornillo,* 418 U.S. 241 (1974), the Supreme Court rejected similar restrictions on newspapers as violative of the First Amendment. In *Turner Broadcasting System v. FCC* (1994), the Supreme Court reaffirmed the importance of the *Red Lion* decision and upheld the policy of reduced First Amendment protection for broadcasters based on the concept of the use of the public airwaves.

Barron, Jerome A., and C. Thomas Dienes. *First Amendment Law in a Nutshell.* St. Paul: West Publishing Co., 1993.

Creech, Kenneth C. *Electronic Media Law and Regulation.* 2nd ed. Boston: Focal Press, 1995.

Kenneth C. Creech

FLEMING, SIR JOHN AMBROSE (1849–1945), professor of electrical engineering at the University College in London, England, was the first to hold that title. His fame rests on his invention, the two-electrode, radio-rectifier vacuum tube called the Fleming valve. This provided a major step forward in radio and telephone communication technology.

In addition to being a successful academic, he was a consultant to Edison Electric Light Company in London and Marconi Wireless Telegraph Company and author of numerous scientific papers and books. He also worked in the areas of photometry and high-voltage alternating current and designed electric lighting for ships. Knighthood was bestowed upon him in 1929.

Fleming, Sir John Ambrose. http://www.antique-radio.org/bios/flm/html

William F. Lyon

FLEMING VALVE (1904) was the first electronic vacuum tube (radio rectifier) that enabled the development of radio communication as we know it. Also called the *thermionic valve,* or *vacuum diode,* it converted alternating-current radio signals into weak direct-current signals that could be heard with a telephone receiver. This two-electrode tube was improved upon by Lee de Forest the following year when he added an amplifier grid that allowed signals to be controlled and amplified. The vacuum tube was the foundation of electronics until the 1960s when solid-state technology was developed, replacing vacuum tubes in most electronic devices.

de Forest, Lee. http://www.antique-radio.org.bios/deforest.html

Diode. http://www.antique-radio.org/terms/diode.html

History of Radio Transmission. http://www.penstock.avnet.com/history.html

William F. Lyon

FLOW AND MIX pacing, texture, and mood result from techniques of production and execution of formatics that create a sound more than the sum of its parts. Flow affects the feel of a format, binding one daypart to the next, one program to the next, one song to the next, or one news story to the next, defining the relationship between often disparate programming elements such as music and commercials, or play-by-play sports and back-to-back polka favorites. Flow can be imperceptible and transparent, abrupt and definitive, or dynamically shifting between the two throughout the broadcast day.

Mix refers to the actual sound of programming elements, music rotation and segue, talk-ups and back announces, voiceovers in a commercial donut, news headlines over a sounder, or the content and order of stories in a newscast. Together, flow and mix represent the degree of fluidity and rhythm of a radio station.

Joseph R. Piasek

FM ALLOCATIONS AND CLASSES. In 1940 the Federal Communications Commission (FCC) approved FM broadcasting within the frequency band between 42 megahertz (MHz) and 50 MHz to begin January 1, 1941. Within this band the commission allocated 35 commercial channels and 5 educational channels. In 1945 the FCC moved the FM broadcast band to its current position within the radio frequency spectrum. This was done to make room for television channels. Unfortunately, this decision by the FCC made FM receivers then in existence useless and significantly slowed the growth and potential success of FM broadcasting. The FM broadcast band now includes the frequencies from 88 MHz to 108 MHz. This band is divided into 100 channels. Each channel has a bandwidth of 200 kilohertz (kHz) and is assigned a channel number between 201 and 300. As an example, channel 201 has a center frequency of 88.1 MHz and includes the bandwidth between 88.0 and 88.2 MHz. Channels 201 through 220, located between 88 MHz and 92 MHz, are reserved for noncommercial educational FM broadcast stations. Within the commercial portion of the FM band, the FCC has allotted specific channels to communities. These allotments, along with designated *classes* of stations and defined geographic *zones,* are intended to eliminate potential interference between stations. The FCC has divided the United States into three zones. Zone I includes the northeastern portion of the U.S. mainland. Zone I-A includes Puerto Rico, the Virgin Islands, and that portion of the state of California that is located south of the 40th parallel. Zone II includes Alaska, Hawaii, and all of the U.S. mainland not included in Zones I and I-A. There are eight classes of stations: A, B, B1, C, C1, C2, C3, and D. These classes of stations are generally defined by their transmitting power parameters, antenna height above average terrain, and the zone in which their transmitters are located. FM station coverage area is determined by transmitter power, antenna design, and the antenna's height above average terrain. Class A, B, and B1 stations may be authorized by the FCC in Zones I and I-A. Class A, C, C1, C2, and C3 stations may be authorized in Zone II. Class D stations are noncommercial educational FM stations that operate with no more than 10 watts of power.

The specific power and antenna height requirements for each class of station are relatively complex and beyond the scope of this dictionary. However, it should be noted that within Zones I and I-A, Class B stations are more powerful than Class B1 stations, which are more powerful than Class A stations. In Zone II, Class C stations are the most powerful, followed in descending order by Class C1, Class C2, Class C3, and Class A.

FM Allocations. Code of Federal Regulations. Title 47, Part 73, Sections 201–211 (FM Broadcast Stations) and 501–513 (Noncommercial Educational FM Broadcast Stations). Washington, D.C.: U.S. Government Printing Office, 1996. Published by the Office of the Federal Register, National Archives and Records Administration as a special edition of the Federal Register.

Steven C. Runyon

FM RADIO (FREQUENCY MODULATION) provides static-free, full-frequency range reception using a carrier wave modulated to reflect an input signal by varying the frequency of the wave, while the amplitude of the carrier wave remains constant. In the United States, the band of frequencies designated for FM radio is located in the very high frequency range, from 88 to 108 megakertz (MHz), with stations identifying themselves by center frequency. This band is divided into 100 channels, each 200 kilohertz (kHz) wide (20 times the bandwidth of AM radio). This wide band enables FM to reproduce high-fidelity sound covering most of the range of frequencies audible to humans, from 50 hertz (Hz) to 15,000 Hz.

Unlike most radio innovations, FM was largely the invention of one person (see **Armstrong, Edwin**) who proved in 1915 that static and radio waves have the same electrical characteristics. Armstrong engaged in a bitter 20-year legal battle with Lee de Forest over the patent for the regenerative or feedback circuit and achieved fame by inventing the superheterodyne receiver while serving in the U.S. Army Signal Corps in 1917. Eventually, he became the largest individual stockholder in RCA. By the late 1920s, Armstrong was convinced that it would be impossible to eliminate radio static without a radically new transmission system, and after two years he achieved excellent frequency response without static using a system based on frequency modulation, a wide 200 kHz band, and relatively low power. Armstrong was granted the first four FM patents in late 1933, and the following year he was allowed to install experimental equipment using RCA space at the top of the Empire State Building. By spring of 1935, RCA's David Sarnoff decided to devote that company's resources to television, and Armstrong was forced to remove his FM equipment to make room for RCA's experimental TV transmitters.

In the fall of 1935, the Federal Communications Commission (FCC) authorized spectrum space for 13 experimental FM channels (only 5 of them compatible with existing technology). Armstrong used his own fortune and attracted financial backers to build an experimental FM station on the Hudson River Palisades, just outside of New York City. By 1940, when FCC hearings on FM were held, more than 20 experimental stations were on the air, and FM service was authorized on 40 channels in the 42–50 MHz band. Although FM radio receivers went on sale for the first time in 1939, a number of factors prevented widespread adoption of FM radio, most notably the U.S. entrance into World War II.

When spectrum became increasingly scarce due to military necessities, a clash developed between FM and TV proponents for allocation of additional VHF channels. Hearings were held, and though Armstrong asked for more FM frequencies in 1943, by 1944 he was struggling to retain what little space FM already had been allocated. To its credit, the FCC utilized a planned approach to FM assignments, in order to avoid the more haphazard approach that characterized AM allocations two decades earlier. As FM and TV proponents fought over the 42–50 MHz band already used by 55 pioneer FM stations, Armstrong was pitted in a quixotic battle against RCA, which used its presence as a large industrial corporation to lobby hard for television. In 1945, FM was moved to 88–108 MHz. While this new allocation provided enough spectrum for 100 FM channels, a gain of 60 (including an educational service allocation in the 88–92 MHz band), it also rendered as many as 400,000 existing FM receivers obsolete when low-band FM transmission was canceled in 1948. Despite two congressional investigations propelled by Armstrong's persistence, the FCC held fast, causing reluctance for further investment in FM radio.

In order to simulate the growth of FM, the commission began calling it the "preferred" radio service and hinted that the new system would eventually replace AM. More than 600 FM station applications had piled up during the war, and existing AM broadcasters received most of those new licenses. By 1949, 85 percent of the FM stations were co-owned by AM licensees—usually to provide insurance for the unlikely demise of AM or to stave off additional outside competition for advertising dollars. Because AM broadcasters had convinced the FCC that FM would grow faster if the new FM stations could duplicate the programming of their existing co-owned AM stations, much of the FM programming was either duplicative or consisted of inexpensive classical and other "fine" music formats, which attracted loyal but small audiences. For these and a variety of other reasons, FM still failed to catch on, and eventually hundreds of FM stations began to go dark, even as the number of TV and AM stations kept growing. By the mid-1950s, FM was reduced from a potential mass medium to a high-class niche service that attracted only small numbers of hi-fi aficionados, and the exhausted and beaten Edwin Armstrong committed suicide.

FM's fortunes were aided when the FCC authorized multiplexing—carrying more than one signal simultaneously on the wide band—in 1953. Multiplexing allowed for FM broadcasters to make additional money by carrying specially encoded data, voice, and music signals, called Subsidiary Communications Services (SCS), in the FM sidebands. Additionally, FM got a shot in the arm when the FCC selected an FM stereophonic technical standard in 1961, while at the same time rejecting AM stereo. The FCC created three classes of FM stations in 1962, passed a rule leading to partial nonduplication of AM/FM programming in all but the smallest radio markets in 1963, and placed a freeze on AM station license awards between 1962 and 1964 and again from mid-1968 to 1973. The well-planned nature of the FM channel assignments kept FM signals strong and clear, and the nonduplication rule encouraged more innovative music programming. Although conversion to stereo was costly, many broadcasters made the investment, and FM stereo stations grew from about 25 percent in 1965 to 40 percent in 1971. As listenership began to increase, advertising revenue made further investment possible, and a large majority of FM stations were stereo by 1975. Demand continued to grow for FM licenses, and many former "classical" stations were sold to broadcasters intending to compete more aggressively with popular music formats, causing outrage in some markets among loyal "fine-music" audiences and a sticky regulatory situation as the FCC attempted to use programming as a licensing criterion in comparative renewal hearings. FM receivers became available in a wide variety of price ranges and styles, and FM surpassed AM radio in terms of U.S. audience size by the late 1970s. As the 1980s came to a close, about 75 percent of the U.S. listening audience was tuned to FM. In the future, digital audio broadcasting (DAB) will likely replace today's FM and AM analog radio broadcasting. For the time being, FM is the most popular form of radio transmission in the United States.

The technical definition of *FM* is "a system of modulation where the instantaneous radio frequency varies in proportion to the instantaneous amplitude of the modulating signal (amplitude of modulating signal to be measured after pre-emphasis, if used) and the instantaneous radio frequency is independent of the frequency of the modulating signal" (47 CFR Sec. 73.681).

Mark J. Braun

FM RADIO, OWNERSHIP OF. Licenses were first issued by the Federal Communications Commission (FCC) almost 20 years after the first AM license was issued. The first owners of FM radio stations were AM radio station owners. These FM licenses were obtained in case FM radio became popular. Newspapers, group owners, and networks joined individual station owners as FM buyers. A different type of FM owner emerged in the noncommercial portion of the FM band (88.1–91.9 megahertz [MHz]). These owners included nonprofit community associations, local or state governments, and educational institutions from high schools to universities. Religious organizations also proliferated these frequencies.

Linwood A. Hagin

FM RADIO ADVERTISING REVENUE comes from either agency business or retail development. Agencies represent large retailers, like chain stores, or businesses with a national market, like car manufacturers. Retailers include local businesses like restaurants, grocery stores, or appliance outlets. Nontraditional business development provides revenue from outlets like corporations, hospitals, factories, and governments. Additional revenue sources include concerts, marketing promotional items, barter, and contests. Compiling listener information in computer databases has allowed stations to develop additional revenue through offering the database to clients or by targeting clients' advertising buys to specific markets. Duopolies have allowed radio stations to structure advertising packages by combining several FM stations into one advertising package for a client.

Warner, Charles, and Joseph Buchman. *Broadcast and Cable Selling*. 2nd ed. Belmont, Calif.: Wadsworth Publishing Company, 1993.

Linwood A. Hagin

FM RADIO STATION GROWTH. Full-scale FM operations were authorized to begin on January 1, 1941, in the 42–50 megacycle (mc) frequency range. The Federal Communications Commission (FCC) issued the first 15 FM construction permits on October 31, 1940. By the start of World War II, there were more than 40 operating FM stations and over 400,000 receivers. World War II halted any further expansion of FM broadcasting. Simulcasting stunted the growth of FM and its acceptance as a viable medium by radio listeners and broadcasters. Another hindrance to FM's establishment among the public was the controversy over changing the medium's frequency location. After months of hearings, the FCC, on August 24, 1945, moved the FM band and expanded it to include the frequencies of 88–108 mc (39 FCC 0029). The main reason the FCC used for moving the FM band was that the FCC expected there would soon be 1,000 to 3,000 FM radio stations serving 50 million to 100 million receivers.

FM radio struggled with its "step-sister" image to AM for the next 15 years until broadcasters were authorized to use FM stereo, beginning June 1, 1961. Another growth enhancing effort for FM was the FCC's 5-year freeze on AM applications effective July 1968. At this time there were more than twice as many AM stations as there were FM stations on the air. FM listening continued to make a gradual climb toward superiority over AM. In 1979, FM had reached parity with AM. In the country's top-50 markets, FM had captured over half of the top 10 spots ("Putting FM in its Place"). Every top-50 market had at least four FM stations in the top 10. FM radio added another dimension of dominance over AM radio in February 1994 when the number of licensed commercial FM radio stations surpassed the number of licensed commercial AM radio stations in the United States.

"Putting FM in Its Place in the Top 50." *Broadcasting* (January 22, 1979): 40, 42, 45, 48–49.

Linwood A. Hagin

FORD FOUNDATION. During the early years (1951–1963) in developing educational broadcasting, the Ford Foundation used grants to help establish stations and provide workshops, seminars, and technical consultation. Grants for radio programming included the production of several series: *The Jefferson Heritage,* on the life and philosophy of Thomas Jefferson; and *The Ways of Mankind,* dramatic presentations in social anthropology. Experimental adult education programming was also supported in different media. *The Whole Town's Talking* was a television-newspaper citizen-access program that combined media presentations with discussion groups (Lashner, pp. 242–243).

The first major activity the foundation supported in educational broadcasting was the Radio-Television Workshop, begun in 1951 to explore the possibility of using the commercial system to provide educational programming (p. 241).

Lashner, Marilyn A. "The Role of Foundations in Public Broadcasting, II: The Ford Foundation." *Journal of Broadcasting* 21 (2) (spring 1977): 235–254.

Mary E. Beadle

FORMAT RADIO is the most popular and commercially successful method of building a radio station's program schedule to target a specific audience effectively, such as women ages 19 to 34 or adults ages 34 to 54. It ensures consistency in a station's programming and establishes a unique "sound" or "image" for each individual station. Following in-depth analysis of the characteristics of a particular radio market, including competing stations and other competing media, a station's management selects a specific format such as all-news, all-talk, or a particular music genre. The final selection is usually determined by which format is likely to attract the largest target audience, thereby ensuring top dollar for commercial time sold, which ultimately turns into higher profits. Most commercial radio stations adopt popular music formats: country, adult contemporary, CHR (contemporary hit radio/top 40), AOR (album-oriented rock), gold/classic rock, big band/nostalgia, progressive, R&B (rhythm and blues/ethnic). The most popular music formats on American commercial radio currently are country and adult contemporary. Many noncommercial and public radio stations also adopt music formats, albeit less popular genres like classical or jazz. Programmers build the schedule horizontally (weekly) by scheduling station breaks, news, commercials, and songs at the same time, Monday through Sunday. They build it vertically (daily) by scheduling the program elements consistently throughout the day, and with a hot clock (hourly), which places different program elements, minute by minute, within each hour in the same consistent pattern with the hours that precede and follow it.

Carroll, Raymond L., and Donald M. Davis. *Electronic Media Programming: Strategies and Decision Making.* New York: McGraw-Hill, 1993.
Eastman, Susan Tyler, and Douglas A. Ferguson. *Broadcast/Cable Programming: Strategies and Practices.* 5th ed. Belmont, Calif.: Wadsworth, 1996.

Robert G. Finney

45 RPM RECORDS. Records spinning at 45 revolutions per minute (RPM) were the 1948 RCA invention designed to supplant the 78 RPM record. The 45s, as they came to be known, did provide a lighter weight, more durable, plastic alternative to their forerunner, 78s. The 45 was introduced one year after the Columbia alternative, the 33⅓, the LP (long-playing), which was also lighter weight, more durable, and plastic and could hold more than 20 minutes of high-quality music, a far cry from the under-4-minute time limit of both 45s and 78s. RCA had developed a 33⅓ record as far back as the early 1930s, but it wore out after just a few plays. Because RCA made record players as well as records, they decided to market the small, donut-shaped records and the changer it took to play them. Sometimes referred to as the "Battle of the Speeds," RCA and Columbia waged full-scale promotion and marketing campaigns in an effort to convince consumers to buy their new product. With three speeds to choose from, the public chose none. Record sales dropped dramatically in 1949. The two sides called a truce in 1950 and agreed to begin using each other's formats. RCA would use the LP for its great artists and classical music, while Columbia would adopt the 45 as its format for popular music. The 45s also became the most popular format for jukeboxes.

Max Utsler

FOSDICK, REVEREND DR. HARRY EMERSON (1878–1969), was a prominent Protestant preacher in the first half of the twentieth century partly because of

National Vespers, his network radio program from 1927 to 1946. In 1939, *Time* called Fosdick "the nation's most famed Protestant preacher." Much of Fosdick's influence came through his pastorates. In 1919, Fosdick, a liberal Baptist, became associate pastor of the First Presbyterian Church of New York City. After battling fundamentalism there, he resigned in 1925. The following year, he became pastor of Park Avenue Baptist Church. In 1930, that congregation became interdenominational and moved to the neo-Gothic Riverside Church that John D. Rockefeller built.

In his sermons, Fosdick typically dealt with living the spiritual life, but two issues were especially important to him: pacifism and opposition to fundamentalism. Indeed, Fosdick's fame came after publicist Ivy Lee distributed his 1922 sermon "Shall the Fundamentalists Win?" which advocated reading the Bible for spiritual insights rather than for inherent rules and creeds, a theme Fosdick would reiterate throughout his career. Fosdick's predominance on radio galled fundamentalists, a generation of whom were largely excluded from broadcasting.

Fosdick became an ardent pacifist after he reexamined his support of the military during World War I. His two most notable sermons against war were "A Christian Conscience About War," which he preached from John Calvin's pulpit in Geneva in 1925; and "My Account with the Unknown Soldier," which he preached in Riverside Church in 1933.

He preached his first radio sermon over New York's WJZ in 1924. In 1926, WJZ broadcast Fosdick's morning service, and in 1927, Fosdick took over *National Vespers,* one of NBC's new public service programs. *National Vespers* began as a one-hour program broadcast at 5:30 P.M. from October through May. It went to a half-hour format in 1931, eventually beginning at 2:30 P.M. *National Vespers* continued as a sustaining program on ABC when NBC sold its Blue Network in 1943.

By all measures, *National Vespers* was a popular program. Between 1936 and 1946, more than 1 million mimeographed copies of Fosdick's sermons were mailed to listeners on request. After preaching "A Time to Stress Unity" in 1944, Fosdick received 8,248 letters. And between October 1944 and May 1945, *National Vespers* received 134,827 letters. The *New York Times* estimated that Fosdick eventually reached between 2.5 and 3 million listeners per week.

Because NBC donated the facilities and Fosdick donated his services, *National Vespers* required funds only for secretaries, the male quartet, and the cost of answering letters and distributing sermons. These costs were met at first by some of Fosdick's affluent friends, but within a few years, donations from appreciative listeners carried the budget.

Fosdick preached more than 500 sermons on the radio and also preached one of the first sermons on television, delivering "The Decisive Babies of the World" in 1941. After retiring from Riverside in 1946, Fosdick returned occasionally to its pulpit, but he delivered no more sermons over *National Vespers.*

Miller, Robert M. *Harry Emerson Fosdick: Preacher, Pastor, Prophet.* New York: Oxford University Press, 1985.

Ryan, Halford R. *Harry Emerson Fosdick: Persuasive Preacher.* Westport, Conn.: Greenwood Press, 1989.

John P. Ferré

FREDERICK, PAULINE (1980–1990). Often cited as the first woman network news analyst and diplomatic correspondent in American radio, Pauline Frederick was born February 13, 1908, in Gallitzin, Pennsylvania. She began her reporting career covering society news for the *Harrisburg Telegraph* while still in high school. She received a B.A. in political science and an M.A. in 1931 in international law from American University in Washington, D.C. During the 1930s, she covered politics and foreign diplomacy for a number of publications and had her radio debut in 1939 on NBC, interviewing the wife of the Czechoslovakian minister just after Hitler invaded that country. She worked part-time for NBC, providing occasional interviews, and continued her newspaper work for the next seven years. In 1945, she became a war correspondent for the North American Newspaper Alliance and toured 19 countries in North Africa and Asia within two months. She then worked freelance for the Western Newspaper Alliance and ABC Radio, covering the Nuremberg trials, but only went on air once when Hermann Göring took the stand, because the first-string male reporter wasn't there.

In June 1946, Frederick joined the news staff of the American Broadcasting Company, and became the first woman to cover political events for them. Starting in September 1947, she shared the United Nations beat with Gordon Fraser and covered the 1948 Republican and Democratic conventions, the presidential campaign and inauguration, and the perjury trial of Alger Hiss. She covered the lifting of the Berlin blockade by joining the airlift and rode on the first train into Berlin, then flew to Warsaw to observe the Polish reaction. She covered the opening meeting of the Council of Foreign Ministers, but the United Nations was the beat she developed as hers. She was the only American woman commentator to cover the Korean crisis in the United Nations. She was on radio five days a week and television at least three times a week and also wrote and presented a weekly Saturday evening program on ABC-TV, *Pauline Frederick's Guest Books*. She preferred radio, however, as it permitted more time for background and analysis.

Frederick returned to NBC in June 1953 and had a daily 15-minute program of national and world events, *Pauline Frederick Reporting*. She retired from NBC in 1974 and then commented on foreign affairs for National Public Radio. In 1976, she was the first woman to moderate a presidential debate, between Gerald R. Ford and Jimmy Carter. She was the first woman winner of many awards including the Alfred I. Dupont Awards' Commentator Award, the Paul White Award from the Radio-Television News Directors' Association in 1980, and the George Foster Peabody Award in 1954 for her coverage of the United Nations. In 1975, she was named to the Hall of Fame of Sigma Delta Chi, the journalists' society and received honorary doctorate degrees in journalism, law, and the humanities from 23 colleges and universities.

On March 31, 1969, she married Charles Robbins, former managing editor of the *Wall Street Journal* and former president of the Atomic Industrial Forum. He predeceased her by 10 months. Pauline Frederick died of a heart attack on May 9, 1990.

Beasley, Maurine H., and Sheila Gibbons. *Taking Their Place: A Documentary History of Women and Journalism.* Washington, D.C.: American University Press in cooperation with the Women's Institute for Freedom of the Press, 1993.
Blau, Eleanor. "Pauline Frederick, 84, Network News Pioneer, Dies." *New York Times,* May 11, 1990, p. D18.

Margot Hardenbergh

FREED, ALAN (1894–1965), a Cleveland disc jockey credited with coining the term *rock 'n' roll.* Freed worked at stations in New Castle and Akron before moving to WJW in Cleveland. He liked primarily rhythm and blues or "black music" at the time. To avoid any kind of racial problem with his predominantly white audience, he gave the music another name. In 1951, he began hosting *Moondog's Rock and Roll Party.* He promoted what may have been the first rock concert, "The Moondog Coronation Ball." Some 25,000 fans turned out and caused a near riot.

Two years later, Freed took a job with WINS in New York. His delivery and choice of songs appealed to the young audience. In 1956 and 1957, he appeared in several films: *Don't Knock the Rock, Rock around the Clock, Mr. Rock and Roll,* and *Rock, Rock, Rock.*

After moving to WABC in New York, Freed became involved in the famous payola scandal. The station asked him to sign a statement confirming he had never accepted payola. He refused and was fired. He was charged with 26 counts of commercial bribery and received a suspended sentence and a fine. His career was over. He left New York and died penniless in 1965. The 1978 film *American Hot Wax,* while short on historical accuracy, captures the mood of those early days of rock 'n' roll. He was in the first group of inductees into the Rock and Roll Hall of Fame.

Rock and Roll Hall of Fame, Cleveland. http://www.rockhall.com

Max Utsler

FREEDOM OF INFORMATION ACT OF 1966 (FOIA) was the first congressional effort to provide the kind of access to government records that Americans needed in becoming an informed citizenry to democratic governance. The overriding purpose of the *FOIA* was to ensure the fullest possible disclosure of government-held records to the public and to withhold only when necessary.

Under the 1974 amendment to the *FOIA,* federal executive and administrative agencies are required to publish in the Federal Register the procedures and policies relating to the public availability of their records. Once a federal agency receives an *FOIA* request, the agency is supposed to respond by providing the requested record or denying the request with an explanation within 10 working days. If the *FOIA* request is denied, the requester has a right to appeal the denial first to the agency and then to the federal courts. The federal courts are authorized by the 1974 and 1976 amendments to the *FOIA* to review the requested documents in private and to rule on the agency's denial of the request.

If the requested information falls within one of the nine *FOIA* exemptions, it can be withheld. Among the documents exempted from disclosure under the *FOIA* are those relating to national security, "internal personnel rules and practices" of agencies, material exempted by other statutes, trade secrets, working papers, personnel and media files, and law enforcement records. Especially noteworthy is that the *FOIA* exemptions are not mandatory but discretionary. That is, federal agencies are not required to withhold information from disclosure merely because they are exempted under the law. Federal agencies may release the requested records to the public even though they may arguably fall within one or more exemptions.

Archibald, Sam. "The Revised F.O.I. Law and How to Use It." *Columbia Journalism Review* (July–August 1977): 54.
How to Use the Federal FOI Act. 6th ed. Washington, D.C.: FOI Service Center, 1987.

Kyu Ho Youm

FREEFORM RADIO, an approach to radio programming in which a station's management gives the disc jockey (DJ) complete control over program content. Freeform shows are as different as the personalities of DJs, but they share a feeling of spontaneity, a tendency to play music that is not usually heard. Their ideology tends to be liberal or radical, though their program content is not usually overtly political. Many DJs mix diverse musical styles, engage in monologues between music sets, or accept callers on the air. The only rules that freeform DJs are bound by are the Federal Communications Commission (FCC) regulations such as station identification and restrictions on foul language.

The first stations to try freeform programming were a few FM community and college stations around the country in the late 1950s and early 1960s. The first freeform show was John Leonard's *NightSounds* on the Pacifica Foundation's KPFA-FM in Berkeley, soon followed by Bob Fass's *Radio Unnameable* on Pacifica's WBAI-FM in New York. Lorenzo Milam, who founded Seattle's KRAB-FM in 1962, was an influential freeform pioneer. Milam went on to help build several similar, freeform-oriented community stations around the country during the 1960s.

Freeform radio had its heyday in the late 1960s and early 1970s. Its implied individualist ethic and its minimal rules resonated with the massive youth counter-culture of the time. Some stations, such as Upsala College station WFMU-FM in New Jersey, went completely freeform around this time. Freeform radio has always been more readily accepted in the reserved noncommercial FM band than by commercial stations; its proponents and its detractors agree that it is not appealing to most commercial sponsors because of its iconoclastic reputation. However, in 1967, when the FCC's "FM Nonduplication Rule" forced many commercial FM stations to change their formats, some decided to try freeform programming because the noncommercial stations proved its popularity with teenagers and young adults. Commercial freeform stations such as WPLJ and WNEW in New York, KMPX in San Francisco, and WHFS in Baltimore flourished for a few years, but their management gradually reinstated playlists or other controls on the DJs. Many of the changes were a voluntary reaction to a 1971 FCC ruling on a Des Moines freeform station involving "questionable practices," which implied that stations needed to exercise stricter control over programming.

A few stations around the country continue to air freeform programming. One of very few surviving commercial freeform DJs is Vin Scelsa, whose popularity has enabled him to retain control over his shows; he is now on WNEW-FM in New York. Bob Fass's *Radio Unnameable* currently broadcasts on WBAI after a few absences over the years. A few college stations are completely freeform, such as WZRD near Chicago and KDVS in Davis, California. WFMU, which became an independent community station in 1994, is still exclusively freeform.

Milam, Lorenzo W. *The Radio Papers: From KRAB to KCHU.* San Diego: MHO & MHO Works, 1986.

Post, Steve. *Playing in the FM Band: A Personal Account of Free Radio.* New York: Viking Press, 1974.

Freeform Radio. http://www.wfmu.org

Kathleen M. O'Malley

FREEZE ON LICENSING. *See* **Sixth Report and Order.**

FREQUENCY. *See* **reach/frequency.**

FREQUENCY ASSIGNMENT, authorization given by the government for a radio station to use a frequency under specific conditions. International agreements establish which frequencies are designated for particular purposes. Some agreements apply worldwide, whereas others apply to one of the regions designated by the International Telecommunications Union (the United States is a part of Region II). Countries make individual frequency assignments consistent with international agreements. In the United States, nongovernmental use of frequencies is governed by the Federal Communications Commission (FCC). Government use of frequencies (such as by the military and national parks) is coordinated by the National Telecommunications and Information Administration (NTIA).

Title 47 of the Code of Federal Regulations contains a Table of Frequency Allocations that lists frequencies from 9 kilohertz to 400 megahertz and their allocation, both internationally and within the United States. Any frequency assignment must be consistent with the Table of Allocations, although there is a provision for temporary authorization of frequency use not consistent with the table. All frequency uses are governed by the table, including the use of radio waves for garage door openers, cordless telephones, or satellite transmission.

The FCC or NTIA assigns frequencies to users based on stated criteria. In the case of broadcasters, the FCC has an extensive set of rules and guidelines for station licensing. Applicants for AM radio stations must propose the use of a specific frequency and present engineering data to show that such a station will not cause unacceptable interference with existing transmitters. Applicants for FM radio or television stations must find an assigned frequency from the respective Table of Allotments, also found in the Code.

Dom Caristi

FREQUENCY SHARING occurs when two or more radio stations divide broadcast time on the same assigned frequency in the same community. Though many early broadcasting pioneers had envisioned geographically exclusive use of radio frequencies, the idea of frequency sharing was accepted by the Second National Radio Conference called by Secretary of Commerce Herbert Hoover in March of 1923 and adopted as official policy by Hoover that same year. At the time, only three frequencies (618.6 kilocycles [kc], 750 kc, and 833.3 kc) were available for broadcasting, while many more than three stations were licensed in many communities. Even as the number of frequencies for broadcasting expanded, forced frequency sharing became one of Hoover's most powerful tools in the attempt to reduce the chaos that plagued radio during much of the 1920s. The *Radio Act of 1927* gave power to allocate broadcast hours, including forced frequency sharing, to the new Federal Radio Commission (FRC). Stations sharing a frequency were to arrange among themselves for the division of broadcasting hours. In cases where stations were unable to agree, the FRC would divide the time.

Nearly 30 percent of the 677 stations licensed in 1928 were in frequency-sharing situations. In 15 communities, 4 stations were dividing time on the same frequency; in 24 communities, 3 stations were dividing time; and in 164 communities, 2 stations were dividing time. At least 1 shared frequency remains. Commercial station KDEC and Luther College noncommercial station KWLC divide time on the 1240 kc frequency in Decorah, Iowa.

Federal Radio Commission. *Second Annual Report of the Federal Radio Commission to the Congress of the United States, 1928.* Washington, D.C.: U.S. Government Printing Office, 1928.

Schmeckbeier, Laurence F. *The Federal Radio Commission: Its History, Activities and Organization.* Washington, D.C.: Brookings Institution, 1932.

Mark J. Heistad

FREQUENCY WAVE, RADIO. Building on more than a century of experiments involving electricity and magnetism, James Clerk Maxwell published essays in 1865 and 1873 predicting the existence of electromagnetic waves. That theory was demonstrated in 1888 by German physicist Heinrich Hertz, who produced and detected waves similar to those suggested by Maxwell. Although the transmission of electricity by wire was well known and was the basis for the telegraph and telephone, researchers were slow to see the significance of Hertzian waves. It was Guglielmo Marconi who took the theory out of the laboratory and demonstrated the practical use of radio waves to transmit information and generate revenue.

Electromagnetic energy travels through space in much the same way that waves travel through water. If a large object is dropped on a smooth body of water, the surface of the water is disturbed by waves spreading or propagating in a circular form from the focal point. But electromagnetic energy is not dependent on air or any other medium to propagate, allowing it to travel through a vacuum. Another difference is that electromagnetic propagation is spherical, or three dimensional, as opposed to waves on a body of water traveling in a two-dimensional plane.

A sine wave represents energy as a wave. The height of that wave is designated as *amplitude* and measures the relative strength of the energy. The number of waves or cycles in a given period of time is known as the *frequency.* The distance between each crest of the wave is called the *wavelength.*

In order for radio waves to be useful, a broadcast transmitter emits an electromagnetic wave or carrier. The characteristics of the carrier are changed (modulated) to match the characteristics of the sound waves, also represented as a sine wave. The frequency of radio waves makes it possible for receivers to distinguish differing radio waves. The receiver detects the radio waves, and they are changed into sound waves. Wavelengths useful for broadcasting vary in length from 200 to 600 meters.

Gernsback, Hugo. *Radio for the Beginner.* New York: Radio Publications, 1938.

Marcus, Abraham, and William Marcus. *Elements of Radio.* 5th ed. Englewood Cliffs, N.J.: Prentice-Hall, 1965.

McNicol, Donald. *Radio's Conquest of Space.* New York: Murray Hill Books, 1946. Reprint, New York: Arno Press, 1974.

David Spiceland

FULL-SERVICE ADULT RADIO, a radio format consisting of personalities, news, weather, sports, and music. Also known as middle-of-the-road (MOR), the format is commonly found on the AM dial, with information segments dominating music cuts.

Carroll, Raymond L., and Donald Davis. *Electronic Media Programming: Strategies and Decision Making.* New York: McGraw-Hill, 1993.

Frederic A. Leigh

G

THE GAVIN REPORT, a trade publication or "tip sheet" used by radio professionals for information on new music releases and airplay by stations in various markets.
Radio program directors and music directors report station playlists regularly to
Gavin and other trade publications to maintain station visibility and relationships
with record distributors.

Carroll, Raymond L., and Donald M. Davis. *Electronic Media Programming: Strategies and
Decision Making.* New York: McGraw-Hill, 1993.

Frederic A. Leigh

GENERAL ELECTRIC (GE) COMPANY, one of several electrical manufacturing companies important in the early days of radio development, held many
important radio patents and was instrumental in the formation of the Radio
Corporation of America (RCA).

GE was incorporated on April 15, 1892, through the merger of the Edison
General Electric Company and the Thomson-Houston Electrical Company. The
merger was motivated by a desire to resolve patent infringement conflicts and to
develop and market a single, efficient American electrical system.

GE became involved in radio in 1900 when wireless pioneer Reginald Fessenden asked GE to build him a high-speed alternator for the purpose of creating a
continuous wave wireless transmission. Fessenden initially requested bids from
both Westinghouse and GE; however, Westinghouse declined to bid. GE had the
advantage of having a newly created research laboratory that was directed by
Charles Proteus Steinmetz, a brilliant mathematician and engineer with an established reputation in alternating-current research. Steinmetz agreed to take on the
project, building a 10,000-cycle alternator by 1901. The Steinmetz alternator was
faster than any previous machine of this type but still was not fast enough to radiate
radio frequency waves. The development work continued and was eventually
assigned to a young Swedish engineer named Ernst Alexanderson.

Alexanderson developed the high-speed radio frequency alternator that Fessenden wanted and that would become a key element in later corporate wrangling. The

first 100,000-cycle alternator was installed in Fessenden's Brant Rock experimental radio station in 1906, which made possible his famous Christmas Eve sound broadcast that same year. GE continued to support work on the alternator even after Fessenden's company went into receivership in 1912.

In 1909, Irving Langmuir joined the research team and was initially assigned to work on improving the incandescent light bulb. In 1913, at the suggestion of Alexanderson, Langmuir turned his attention to improving de Forest's audion. Langmuir's experiments with incandescent lamps convinced him that a high vacuum was a more efficient environment for electron emission. Langmuir was able to develop a radio tube that could use far higher voltages than the audion with less distortion. Subsequently, GE supported a major research and development effort in the area of vacuum radio tubes.

As war broke out in Europe in 1914, the United States began to gear up for possible involvement by issuing contracts for supplies. GE, which was already equipped to manufacture incandescent lamps, could easily retool to mass-produce radio tubes for the military. Patent infringement concerns were temporarily set aside in the interest of producing standardized parts for military use in the field. GE, along with Westinghouse, became an important defense contractor for electronic equipment.

By 1915, Guglielmo Marconi had finally become convinced that continuous wave technology would replace the spark-gap method of transmission. Marconi proposed a deal with GE whereby the Marconi companies would be afforded exclusive use of the Alexanderson alternator in return for a promise of a large number of orders. This arrangement was initially attractive to GE because the future market for radio apparatus was uncertain at this time, and Marconi was the largest radio service interest in the world. Negotiations were interrupted by the war but resumed shortly thereafter. GE general counsel Owen D. Young decided to bring the government in on the discussion. There was concern that, if the deal went through, it would give a foreign company nearly complete control over American radio service. Navy officials suggested that if radio could not be controlled by the military, then it should be in the hands of an American radio monopoly, thereby urging GE to pursue such a course of action. American Marconi interests were quietly bought up by GE, and Marconi was given the option of buying alternators for overseas installations.

In 1919, the assets of the American Marconi company, including the U.S. patents for the Fleming valve and other key Marconi inventions, were transferred to a new company called the Radio Corporation of America, in which GE held a controlling interest. Having established cross-licensing agreements between GE and RCA, Young then set out to negotiate similar agreements with three other important patent holders: AT&T's subsidiary Western Electric, which owned de Forest's audion patent; Westinghouse; and the United Fruit Company. With this five-way alliance in place and patent disputes largely out of the way, RCA became a world force in international communication.

With RCA established to handle the radio service end of the business, GE continued to concentrate on research and manufacturing. In 1922, however, GE started a commercial broadcasting station, WGY, to compete with Westinghouse's KDKA. Because of the shortage of singers and musicians in Schenectady, the program manager, Kolin Hager, decided to concentrate on drama, eventually assembling the WGY players. WGY was one of the few stations attempting regularly scheduled dramatic programming at this early date.

In 1924, the Federal Trade Commission (FTC) charged the patent allies with effectively maintaining a monopoly on radio manufacturing and broadcasting. In 1930, the U.S. Department of Justice filed an antitrust suit against RCA, GE, Westinghouse, and AT&T based in large part on the FTC report. AT&T had already been distancing itself from the radio group and at this point agreed to withdraw completely. The others, including GE, attempted to negotiate a favorable settlement. The Justice Department stood firm, and by 1932, a consent decree was issued requiring GE and Westinghouse to divest themselves of ownership of RCA and its newly formed subsidiary, the National Broadcasting Company. They were allowed to keep their broadcast stations, but NBC would manage them.

GE continued as a major manufacturer of consumer electronics and was well known for its sophisticated research facilities. In the 1920s and 1930s, Ernst Alexanderson experimented with mechanical television and by 1928 was broadcasting pictures over W2XAD. The first dramatic production broadcast with this system was *The Queen's Messenger,* broadcast on September 11, 1928.

GE reacquired RCA and NBC in 1985 by means of a takeover. In 1987, GE sold its combined RCA and GE consumer electronics business to the French company Thompson S.A. and in the same year sold the NBC Radio Network to Westwood One. GE has diversified its operations over the years to include financial services, plastics, satellites, and various defense technologies to become one of the most highly valued companies in the world.

Hammond, John Winthrop. *Men and Volts: The Story of General Electric.* New York: J. B.
    Lippincott Company, 1941.

Christina S. Drale

GENERAL ORDER 40 (August 1928) established the radio service's AM classes, the most important of a number of commission actions implementing the *Radio Act of 1927*'s Davis Amendment, which required equalization of radio service among five regional zones. The order divided the 90 AM channels equally among the zones, with each channel designated for local, regional, or national service based on limitations on broadcast power. Forty "clear channel" stations were established and given the exclusive nighttime use of their frequencies. Another 44 channels were each to be shared by two or three regional stations. The final 6 channels would be shared by the hundreds of remaining low-power local stations.

General Order 40 effectively divided AM broadcasters into "haves," particularly the 40 clear channel stations, and "have-nots," the local stations limited to low power. Stations owned by or affiliated with the national networks occupied the clear channel assignments, while college, labor, church, and other noncommercial stations were relegated to local assignments.

Federal Radio Commission. *Second Annual Report of the Federal Radio Commission to the Congress of the United States, 1928.* Washington, D.C.: U.S. Government Printing Office, 1928.

Schmeckbeier, Laurence F. *The Federal Radio Commission: Its History, Activities and Organization.* Washington, D.C.: Brookings Institution, 1932.

Mark J. Heistad

GIBBONS, [RAPHAEL] FLOYD [PHILLIPS] (1887–1939), early radio foreign correspondent and first network daily newscaster, was born in Washington, D.C., the oldest of five children, and expelled from Georgetown University for excessive pranks. His journalism career began with several night posts at North Dakota newspapers, followed by press positions in Milwaukee, Minneapolis, and in the years before and during World War I, Chicago papers. He covered the American incursion into Mexico to find Pancho Villa, and his ship was torpedoed on the way to cover battles in Europe. He lost his left eye at Belleau Wood in 1918 and always wore a white-linen eye patch thereafter. By the end of the war, Gibbons had developed a reputation for reportorial derring-do and getting the scoop no matter what. He reported the 1920 war between Poland and Russia and events throughout Africa for a year.

His first broadcast experience came in January 1925 in the Philippines. At the end of the year, he returned to the air on the *Chicago Tribune*'s station WGN in what became a month-long series on his past adventures. In 1929, NBC signed Gibbons for a weekly sustaining program, *The Headline Hunter,* which GE began sponsoring a month later. Most of the rapid-fire programs concerned his own exploits, but a few featured remote-location reports. The emphasis, however, was on entertainment value, not hard news. As he continued writing and lecturing, many of his broadcasts had to be fed to the network from local stations near where he was appearing. He became the first daily network, nationwide newscaster in early 1930 when *The Literary Digest* sponsored a six-nights-a-week program over NBC Blue for six months. He began a professional school of broadcasting in Washington, D.C. and appeared regularly on a series of programs into the 1930s. He covered the Italian invasion of Ethiopia and the Spanish Civil War, often from the front lines. But the frenetic pace of his multifaceted life felled him with a series of heart attacks, the first at age 46 and the fatal one when he was but 52.

Fang, Irving E. "Floyd Gibbons." In *Those Radio Commentators!* (pp. 45–63). Ames: Iowa State University Press, 1977.

Gibbons, Edward. *Floyd Gibbons: Your Headline Hunter.* New York: Exposition, 1953.

Gilbert, Douglas. *Floyd Gibbons: Knight of the Air.* New York: Robert McBride, 1930.

Christopher H. Sterling

GODFREY, ARTHUR (1903–1983), red-haired folksy announcer/ukelele player, proved a radio and television favorite on CBS throughout the post–World War II era. He started his radio career in 1929 at WFBR-AM in Baltimore, then later moved to Washington, D.C., first to WMAL-AM and then to WJSV-AM. The latter, a CBS affiliate, led to his network career. In 1941, he moved to CBS's New York flagship WABC-AM. In 1945, Godfrey began his network morning show; a year later he added *Arthur Godfrey's Talent Scouts.* By 1949, both *Talent Scouts* and a variety show, *Arthur Godfrey and Friends,* were being simulcast by CBS nationally on both radio and television. *Talent Scouts* was a particular Monday-night favorite through the 1950s. Often a top-10 show, "scouts" brought on their discoveries to perform live before a national audience. Most were in fact struggling professionals looking for a break. So, for example, on January 21, 1957, Patsy Cline was presented by her mother and sang her most recent recording of "Walkin' After Midnight." To industry insiders, all Godfrey's shows were simply efficient showcases for a great pitchman who blended a southern folksiness with enough sophistication to charm audiences measured in the millions and generate record CBS advertising billings. Godfrey frequently kidded sponsors but always "sold from the heart"; no fan doubted that Godfrey truly did love Lipton Tea and drank it every day as he told his audiences: "Aw, who wrote this stuff? Everybody knows Lipton's is the best tea you can buy."

Douglas Gomery

GOLDEN AGE OF RADIO, the period marking broadcasting's initial popularization in the United States—the mid-1930s up to the introduction of television in the early to mid-1940s. Changes in American culture and improvements in the economy and the workplace, enhanced radio's role as a popular entertainment and news/information source. Aggressive network entrepreneurs transmitted high-quality entertainment directly to listeners in the comfort of their homes. Commercial products could be marketed coast to coast with very short turnaround for the first time. In addition, using radio to provide social context and cover key events helped to further establish its influence with the public.

Three key developments show radio's evolution and growing influence in the information arena: President Franklin D. Roosevelt usage, particularly his *Fireside Chats* going directly to the American people with his message of change; coverage of the Lindbergh baby kidnapping and trial of the alleged kidnapper; and announcement of the British monarch's marriage to an American (thereby giving up the throne).

By the early 1940s, key figures both in front of and behind the microphone emerged at the four major national radio networks: NBC Red and Blue, CBS, and Mutual. Innovative managers such as David Sarnoff and William S. Paley provided impetus for movement, evolution, and change. As a result, competitive pressures and direct involvement by advertising agencies improved program quality and increased popularity, which directly challenged newspapers and motion pictures.

Programming genres evolved in part from consumer special interests in specific products. The so-called radio soap opera satisfied needs and established a niche. Serials in which heroines, such as Helen Trent and Stella Dallas, succeeded week after week against incredible odds provided housewives with escapist fare. Children's western and adventure programs, such as *The Lone Ranger* and *Jack Armstrong, the All-American Boy,* succeeded and often produced clubs tied to sponsor products. Older listeners tuned to suspense offerings such as *The Shadow* and *Inner Sanctum.* Variety programs and those produced before "live" studio audiences highlighted the popularity of comedy and musical fare. A handful of vaudeville comedians, such as Jack Benny and Bob Hope, made the successful transition to radio.

At the beginning of the medium's "Golden Age," comedy programs such as *Amos 'n' Andy* attracted large numbers of listeners and had earned a special status. The period of "Big Band" music, with groups like Tommy Dorsey's and Benny Goodman's, produced a groundswell of opportunity for musical artists. Popular singers including Rudy Vallee, Kate Smith, and Frank Sinatra emerged, and eventually radio faced the thorny issue of recorded music license fees (associations were formed to represent interests on both sides of that question).

The major networks also developed symphony programming; NBC took the lead with Arturo Tuscanini conducting the NBC Symphony Orchestra. Quiz and variety shows, often including studio audience participation, reinforced direct contact with the public and let amateurs exhibit their raw talents. In fact, a couple of programs with "Amateur Hour" themes, including national programs led by Major Bowes and later Ted Mack, developed tremendous followings. Capitalizing exclusively on this specialty, some program alumni became major figures on radio and in the movies.

Regional and statewide networks developed around American population centers. Some religious programs, such as *The Lutheran Hour*, are still broadcast today. Educational programming including the *University of Chicago Roundtable* lasted for close to a quarter of a century. Some news and information programming standards still with us today began with the work of Paul White. Aggressive information gathering by radio broadcasters began at the local level. After an initial period of scepticism, uncertainty, and downright hostility, major newspapers (which owned broadcast stations) supplemented and bolstered these efforts financially, encouraging their staff to consider radio assignments. Such national newspaper figures as H. V. Kaltenborn and Elmer Davis emerged to stake a claim for information coverage. Edward R. Murrow and his CBS European recruits covered the war years and, like many entertainment counterparts, earned unique credentials for later work in television.

Efforts to measure listenership and influence began during this era, as did government attempts to regulate transmission and content. The Federal Radio Commission (FRC), created early in this period, addressed basic challenges including the excesses of some early stations and activity of some individual broadcasters. When the FRC became the Federal Communications Commission in 1934, the regulatory body continued to examine issues including patterns of physical interference—some stations operated well beyond the frequency bounds or channel assignments, with some advertising abuses. These issues were addressed in the Blue Book, designed specifically to outline emerging problem areas and government concerns with them. It discussed specific stations and clarified views on their performance. Other early concerns included independent station owners, such as John R. Brinkley of Kansas, offering claims of medical cures over the airwaves. This produced attempts at self-regulation led by the National Association of Broadcasters (NAB), which created a code authority specifically to address abuses.

Rating services, including Hooper and Crossley, were developing for both advertising agency and network use. The major network organizations themselves began taking special interest in audience response, with concerns extending to psychological impact. Hadley Cantril studied the effects of Orson Welles's *Mercury Theatre of the Air*'s "War of the Worlds" program and set a formal standard for investigating effects on listeners. Dr. Frank Stanton continued extensive audience measurement efforts at CBS, which marked the increased sophistication of radio.

Cantril, Hadley. *The Invasion from Mars: A Study in the Psychology of Panic.* Princeton, N.J.: Princeton University Press, 1940.

Dunning, John. *Tune in Yesterday: The Ultimate Encyclopedia of Old-time Radio, 1925–1976.* Englewood Cliffs, N.J.: Prentice-Hall, 1976.

MacDonald, J. Fred. *Don't Touch That Dial: Radio Programming in American Life, 1920–1960.* Chicago: Nelson-Hall, 1979.

Michael D. Murray

GOLDEN OLDIES FORMAT generally refers to rock 'n' roll–era music from 1954 through 1967. However, the term has been used, at one time or another, to describe any music not written in the previous six months. No one can actually pinpoint a time or place when the term *golden oldies* came into play. Many music historians say "oldies" wasn't invented—it just evolved. Also, many "nonoldies stations" had "oldies programs."

Program director Paul Sidney began playing "Sidney's Souvenirs" in 1961 at WLIS in Old Saybrook, Connecticut. He also used the term *oldies* and was criticized for living in the past. He moved his oldies format to WLNG, Sag Harbor, New York, in 1964, which has programmed oldies ever since.

"Cousin Brucie" (Bruce Morrow) played music he called the "Hall of Fame" starting in 1961, attaining national prominence in the late 1960s at WCBS, New York. WCBS celebrated its twenty-fifth anniversary of playing oldies in 1996. Bill Drake and Chuck Blore are two other names commonly mentioned in the development of oldies music.

Max Utsler

GOLDEN WEST BROADCASTERS, a West Coast broadcasting group, is owned by Gene Autry, former movie star and singing cowboy. Autry has been in business since the 1950s and owns other properties outside the broadcast business. Near the end of World War II, he and his partner Tom Chauncey purchased radio station KPHO in Phoenix, Arizona, while Autry was stationed at Luke Field. When he was shipped to Detroit, Chauncey managed the property. After the war ended, they applied for a new radio station in Tucson and for a television franchise in Phoenix, which became KOOL-TV, Channel 10.

Formed in 1952, Golden West's KMPC in Los Angeles (purchased for $800,000) was the flagship. It was organized and paid for with capital stock of $300,000, the down payment on KMPC. No other cash was ever put into the station, as the remainder of the purchase price came from cash flow. Other stations were added quickly in San Francisco, Seattle, and Portland. The San Francisco and Portland stations were bought for about a million dollars each; Seattle's KVI, for a little less. KVI at the time was losing money broadcasting religious music and gospel programs. All contracts were canceled, and new programming was put in place. All the stations have been profitable.

Golden West made its biggest move in 1964 when it paid Paramount Pictures $12 million for KTLA, Channel 5, Los Angeles. Three years later it purchased the land it had been leasing for the KTLA-TV studios. When Golden West celebrated its sixteenth year in June 1968, the staffs of KMPC radio and KTLA-TV were on the same property. Shortly after, Signal Companies, a Los Angeles conglomerate, offered to buy out the minority stockholders. Signal got 49.9 percent for $25 million, paying off the other shareholders in cash. When Autry died, Signal bought the remaining shares for $20 million.

Autry's personal investments included hotels in Palm Springs, Los Angeles, and eventually Las Vegas. He also purchased the California Angel baseball franchise in 1958 and vested it in Golden West along with the broadcast properties. Autry was the chairman of the board, and his wife was chief stockholder.

Autry, Gene, with Mickey Herskowitz. *Back in the Saddle Again.* Garden City, N.Y.: Doubleday & Company, Inc., 1978.

ElDean Bennett

GOLDSMITH, ALFRED NORTON (1888–1974), radio and motion picture engineer, inventor, author, and teacher. Born in New York City, he graduated from City College of New York (CCNY) in 1907 and received a Ph.D. from Columbia University in 1911. He served on the CCNY electrical engineering faculty from 1907 to 1919 while also serving as consulting engineer with General Electric (GE) (1915–1917) and director of research for American Marconi (1917–1919). Goldsmith authored *Radio Telephony* (Wireless Press, 1918), one of the first books devoted to the use of wireless for voice and music, and hundreds of technical papers, many published in the *Journal of the Society of Motion Picture Engineers* (he joined the group in 1922 and had special interest in problems of movie projection).

Goldsmith joined RCA on its formation in 1919 as director of research and later became a vice president and general engineer. He worked with the conglomerate for a decade, resigning to become an independent consulting engineer in 1931, doing work for RCA, its NBC subsidiary, and Eastman Kodak among others. He served as a member of the National Television Systems Committee (NTSC) in 1940–1941 that developed technical standards for black-and-white television.

Goldsmith held some 200 patents in motion pictures, radio, television, and air conditioning, granted from 1919 to 1972; 134 were devoted to radio or television. Among his patented work were efforts in radiotelephony, phonograph recorders and reproducers, television systems (the first in 1930), sound motion picture apparatus, various transmission systems, and both stereo and 3-D television. He was one of three cofounders of the Institute of Radio Engineers (IRE) in 1912 and edited its *Proceedings* for more than 40 years (1912–1954).

"Alfred Norton Goldsmith, Engineer, Inventor and Teacher." In *Radio's 100 Men of Science,* edited by Orrin E. Dunlap, Jr. (pp. 224–226). New York: Harper, 1944.

"Biographical Notes: Alfred N. Goldsmith." *Journal of the SMPTE* (November 1972): 869–870.

Dreher, Carl. "His Colleagues Remember 'The Doctor.'" *IEEE Spectrum* (August 1974): 32–36; same issue, obituary, pp. 114–115.

Kraueter, David W., ed. "Alfred N. Goldsmith (1888–1974)." In *Radio and Television Pioneers: A Patent Bibliography* (pp. 158–170). Metuchen, N.J.: Scarecrow Press, 1992.

Christopher H. Sterling

GOOD-MUSIC FORMAT features conservative instrumental and vocal music; also called *easy-listening, beautiful,* or *soft music.* KABL-FM (San Francisco) experimented with a beautiful or easy-listening format in 1959. Dozens of stations tried the format in the 1960s, often using an automated music delivery system and stereo sound. The genre still favors the original mix of 75 percent instrumental and 25 percent vocal selections.

Easy-listening stations pioneered continuous music sweeps and clustering of commercials to keep a loyal audience in the 34 to 50 age bracket. Stations program 8 to 10 minutes of music between three to four clusters of 2-minute spot sets. Announcers have polished voices, read their music notes, and rarely engage in the chatty style of "morning-zoo" personalities. News is secondary to music.

In 1995, 240 stations (90 percent of them being FM stations) identified themselves as good-music or easy-listening stations. Their main competitors are lite rock/adult contemporary (AC) stations. In fact, easy-listening stations study the competition's playlists to keep abreast of music that might be suitable for their younger listeners. The biggest challenge for easy-listening programmers is to maintain soft, easy music while keeping a fresh, vibrant sound.

In the 1970s, easy-listening stations lost share to rapidly growing AC, middle-of-the-road (MOR), and country stations. During the 1980s, they won back listeners with a playlist appealing both to younger listeners and to older ones. Typical fans are college educated, loyal, and tuned in for the emphasis on relaxing, good music without a lot of talk.

Hilliard, Robert L. *Radio Broadcasting: An Introduction to the Sound Medium.* 3rd ed. New York: Longman, 1985.

Keith, Michael C. *Radio Programming: Consultancy and Formatics.* Boston: Focal Press, 1987.

Lull, J. T., L. M. Johnson, and C. E. Sweeney. "Audiences for Contemporary Radio Formats." *Journal of Broadcasting* 22 (4) (fall 1978): 439.

J. R. Rush

GORE, TIPPER. *See* **citizens groups and broadcasting.**

GOSDEN, FREEMAN. *See* **Correll, Charles, and Freeman Gosden.**

GOSPEL MUSIC FORMAT includes several variations of religious programming based on Christian music; the more widely known derivatives are black gospel, country or southern gospel, contemporary gospel, and Christian rock. All offer songs with religious lyrics. Religious programming, including gospel, has been featured on radio stations since the beginning of commercial broadcasting, often as a public service on Sunday mornings. Many of the radio stations that program gospel music exclusively are nonprofit, noncommercial entities on the FM band and are supported by the religious groups that own them.

Dupree, Sherry Sherod, and Herbert Clarence Dupree. *From Natural Music to Contemporary Gospel: Field Songs, Rock 'n' Roll, Rap, and Film.* Institute of Black Culture. Found online at http://www.ufsa.ufl.edu/oss/IBC/choirlinenotes.html

Montell, William Lynwood. *Singing the Glory Down: Amateur Gospel Music in South Central Kentucky 1900–1990.* Lexington: University Press of Kentucky, 1991.

Routt, Edd, James B. McGrath, and Fredric A. Weiss. *The Radio Format Conundrum.* New York: Hastings House, 1978.

Tim England

GRAND OLE OPRY, the country music program that is still broadcast live from WSM, Nashville, has been on radio almost from the medium's beginning. From it, and a number of other similar programs, grew a country music industry, the most numerous radio format, a cable network, and a theme park. In the 1920s, phonograph-recording companies began to do more field recordings and rural music slowly grew in popularity. Two of the first artists to be widely distributed were "Fiddling" John Carson, who recorded in Atlanta in June 1923, and Ernest "Pop" Stoneman from Galax, Virginia. Stoneman's neighbors, seeing his success, went to New York and recorded six sides for Okek records. As they left the studio, they were asked the name of their group. They did not have one and said, "We're nothing but a bunch of hillbillies from North Carolina and Virginia—call us anything." The ledger sheets listed "The Hill Billies."

C. A. Craig, one of the founders of the National Accident Insurance Company, Nashville, like so many men in the 1920s, was also interested in radio. He ask the company to build a radio station, which began operation on October 5, 1925, having received the call letters WSM—We Shield Millions, the company slogan—from a ship's station after a request to the Department of Commerce. One guest at the station opening was George D. Hay. He was from Indiana, but as newspaper reporter in Memphis covering a story in Arkansas, he had been invited to a hoedown— fiddling till the crack of dawn in someone's cabin. His paper, *The Commercial Appeal,* had a radio station and Hay became an announcer. In 1924, having made a name for himself, he became chief announcer at WLS, Chicago—owned by Sears Roebuck and appealing to a largely rural audience. WLS had a Saturday night "barndance" program, later called *The National Barndance,* which had been started by George C. Biggar, who had come as station manager from the radio service of the Agriculture Department. The flamboyant Hay, as announcer on the program, blew a steam whistle, like those on river showboats, and called himself "The Solemn Old Judge."

Hay probably moved to WSM in early November 1925. A country music show may have actually been on the station a week or two before he arrived, but Hay would always say he started the program on November 28, 1925. Newspaper listings for that date show "string quartet of old-time musicians." Starting on December 26, 1925, the program became two hours each Saturday night. Uncle Dave Macon was the first professional musician signed by the station, and by early 1926, there were 25 acts.

By 1927, WSM, now using 5,000 watts, was an NBC affiliate. The local barndance show, which still did not have a title, followed the *National Symphony Orchestra* with Walter Damrosch, from 8 P.M. to 9 P.M. One night, probably December 8, 1928, conductor Damrosch commented that in the classics there was no place for realism. When Hay started the barndance program a couple of minutes later, he said that for the next few hours he would present nothing but realism, down to earth for the earthy. Then, he is reported to have said: "For the past hour you have heard music taken largely from Grand Opera; now we will present the Grand Ole Opry." That's the story. The title stuck.

By 1932, WSM was broadcasting with 50,000 watts, on a clear channel, and had a new state-of-the-art vertical tower (radiator). From its central location, it was readily heard all over the heart of country music—north to Louisville and Cincinnati, east to Knoxville and Bristol straddling the Virginia border, south to Atlanta and west to Memphis and beyond deep into Arkansas. On Saturday, especially cold winter nights, it could be tuned in from the Atlantic seaboard to the Rocky Mountains and was especially welcome in rural areas with few stations and little man-made interference. Many other country shows were started on radio stations in Cincinnati, Wheeling, Richmond, Dallas, Shreveport, Yankton, and even Los Angeles—where it soon spread to "B" westerns.

The National Barndance, from WLS, was already on NBC when a half hour of the *Grand Ole Opry* was added in October 1939. Prior to that the *Opry* was only on a regional web of about 26 stations in the South. The program had been adding full-time performers—Pee Wee King (1937), Roy Acuff (1938), and Bill Monroe (1939). And there was a 1940 Republic movie. In 1939–1940, *The National Barndance* had been on NBC for seven seasons and *Plantation Party* from WLW, two. But gradually *Opry* would grow to be the biggest. GIs from the South helped spread country music during the war.

The biggest boost for the *Opry* came in the late 1940s. Red Foley, moving from WLS, became the network-portion star. Many stars from other shows were also attracted, including "Little" Jimmy Dickens and Ernest Tubb. Lester Flatt and Earl Scruggs joined Monroe, and most important, Hank Williams, who had appeared on *Louisiana Hayride,* made a guest appearance on July 11, 1949—the next week he was a regular. The *Opry* is still on WSM every Saturday from 6:30 to midnight, and since April 20, 1985, a half hour is carried on the Nashville Network.

Hagan, Chet. *Grand Ole Opry.* New York: Henry Holt, 1989.

Also see a number of different books by Charles Wolfe. There are a growing number of documentaries on the history of country and bluegrass music and many including some information on the *Opry.* See, for example: *The Life and Times of Hank Williams* (Greystone, 1997); *American's Music: The Roots of Country,* six hours (Turner, 1996); *Bill Monroe, Father of Bluegrass Music* (1993); *Cradle of the Stars: Story of the Louisiana Hayride* (1985); and *The High and Lonesome Sound* (1963). There is much historical information on the Nashville Network. There are also many CD collections of, or that include, *Opry* performances.

Lawrence W. Lichty

GREASEMAN (1950–), Doug Tracht (born and raised in the Bronx) was tall and skinny, but he wanted to be macho. Tracht attended Ithaca College, where he worked at the student station and vomited his first time on the radio. After graduating in 1972 with a radio and television degree, he was hired by Washington, D.C.'s WRC to work evenings. He moved to WAPE-AM 690, Jacksonville, Florida, in 1975. In August 1982, he replaced Howard Stern on WWDC-FM. His show commanded over 10 percent of the city's morning-drive listeners. In 1993, he turned down a $6.5 million renewal offer from WWDC to move to Los Angeles, where Infinity Broadcasting nationally syndicated his show.

Early in his career, Tracht perfected a boss-jock routine based on the prevalent, music-driven radio style of the late 1960s. Once obsessed with anonymity, Tracht hid for many years behind his microphone, but after becoming a bodybuilder, he became comfortable with his true identity. He created words (to replace those forbidden by the Federal Communications Commission [FCC]), running gags, and ad-libs and played off callers. Tracht did no advance preparation and got his ideas from callers or newspapers while on the air. Tracht used several running characters—one is the "lawman" sketch. He believed that he would have been a lawman if he had not found radio, and he actually did some volunteer police training and work during his Jacksonville years.

W. A. Kelly Huff

GROUP OWNERSHIP, single ownership of a number of stations, has flourished since the Federal Communications Commission (FCC) began deregulating the industry in the 1980s. The first restriction of radio station ownership on the national level was formalized at 7 AM stations and 7 FM stations in 1954. This national limit on radio stations was raised to 12 AM and 12 FM in 1985; to 18 AM and 18 FM stations in 1992; to 20 AM and 20 FM stations in 1994; then altogether eliminated in 1996 with the passage of the *Telecommunications Reform Act.* In local markets, group ownership restrictions have focused on the number of like service stations owned and whether those stations are owned by a newspaper or television stations. Owners were limited to 1 AM and 1 FM until 1992. The limit increased to 2 AM and 2 FM stations in the larger markets and in 1996 increased to a maximum of 8 stations, 5 of any one service, in markets with 45 or more signals. Deregulation of station counts and other deregulatory efforts introduced conglomerates to radio group ownership. Companies with interests other than broadcasting began purchasing radio stations to increase their profit margin. After 1992, group owners began to swap stations between markets. The largest group owners began to merge with smaller group owners, forming even larger companies and fewer owners in radio.

Alexander, Alison, James Owers, and Rod Carveth. *Media Economics: Theory and Practice.* Hillsdale, N.J.: Lawrence Erlbaum Associates, 1993.

Linwood A. Hagin

GROUP W. *See* **KDKA; Westinghouse.**

GUNSMOKE, the radio western, was broadcast from 1952 to 1961 and spawned a TV version that is the longest-running drama series. It was born of a collaboration of several writers and producers—including John Meston, William N. Robeson, and John Macdonnell—who worked together at CBS from 1947 on *Escape* and other radio dramas. Two pilots of what they conceived of as an "adult western" were produced in 1949.

When another program was abruptly canceled and with apparently only a week's warning. Macdonnell, with writer Walter Brown Newman, fashioned the first program, in part on several earlier western stories Macdonnell had done on other series. The first episode, "Billy the Kid," ran on April 26, 1952. There were 412 more stories, and repeats, until June 18, 1961. The cast of William Conrad as Marshall Matt Dillon, Georgia Ellis as Kitty Russell, Howard McNear as Doctor Charles Adams, and Parley Baer as Chester Wesley Proudfoot never varied.

Among fans of radio drama, it is considered the best western ever. The series was marked by high-caliber writing—only a score of authors during the entire run (Meston wrote 183, more than 45 in each of three years). Veteran radio actors appeared in episode after episode, and innovative sound patterns and evocative music made the program a favorite of radio devotees as the audience for radio moved to TV—which produced 233 half-hour and 402 one-hour episodes, beginning on September 10, 1955. There were also four movies.

Barabas, SuzAnne, and Gabor Barabas. *Gunsmoke: The Complete History and Analysis of the Legendary Broadcast Series with a Comprehensive Episode-by-Episode Guide to Both the Radio and Television Programs.* Jefferson, N.C.: McFarland & Company, 1990.
The Story of Gunsmoke. Produced by John Hickman. Washington, D.C.: WAMU, 1976. An audio history with interviews and excerpts. 5 hours.

Lawrence W. Lichty

H

HALL, JOSEF WASHINGTON. *See* **Close, Upton.**

HAM RADIO, popular term for the hobby that the Federal Communications Commission (FCC) regulations call "amateur radio" or the "amateur-radio service." Ham-radio operators, or "hams," are licensed by the FCC to communicate via radio with each other, one to one. Hams are not allowed to broadcast, play music, communicate on bands other than those set aside for them except in emergencies, or transmit for commercial purposes. The FCC expects hams to use their unique skills to serve the community in emergencies and to promote international goodwill, to improve their skills, and through doing all of these things, to advance both the communication and technical aspects of the radio art. A ham's transceiver, whether it is a walkie-talkie or an elaborate setup, constitutes a "station."

There have been ham-radio operators in the United States since the earliest radio equipment was available. The federal government began licensing hams in 1912, and by 1914, there were thousands of them. The Amateur Radio Relay League (ARRL) was founded in 1914 to promote the hobby and help maintain standards of operation and knowledge among hams. The ARRL is the largest organization of hams today, with over 170,000 members. This group, and hams in general, defy demographic classification; they represent a wide range of socioeconomic, ethnic, age, and national groups.

The most popular activity among hams is conversation with other hams by radio, or "ragchewing." They usually just talk, but some also use Morse code, printed text, or video. Recently, some have started using a computer-to-computer method called "packet radio." Hams can reach each other around the world, depending on the sophistication of their equipment and with the help of satellites, so international ragchewing is common. The greatest appeal of ragchewing seems to be the opportunity to be part of a diverse group of people linked by a common interest in radio. "DXing," or trying to contact hams beyond the normal communication range in a given frequency band, is related to ragchewing, but since the main goal on both ends is to contact as many hard-to-reach hams as possible, conversation is minimal. DXers confirm these contacts by exchanging identification cards through the mail.

Hams often provide important emergency communication and are sometimes the only source of radio communication in the aftermath of a major disaster such as an earthquake or storm. Some hams have created volunteer early-warning systems to help track tornadoes or other violent weather using mobile equipment.

Most hams are eager to improve their equipment and technical knowledge because of interest in the technology and/or a desire to improve the quality of their ragchewing, DXing, and emergency communication ability. A variety of books and magazines, as well as training programs offered by the ARRL and other groups, are available to help them.

American Radio Relay League, Inc. *The ARRL Handbook for the Radio Amateur.* Newington, Conn.: American Radio Relay League. Annual.

Helms, Harry L. *All about Ham Radio: How to Get a License and Talk to the World.* Solana Beach, Calif.: HighText Publications, 1992.

Kathleen M. O'Malley

HARDING, WARREN G. *See* **Commerce and Labor, U.S. Department of; Coolidge, Calvin; Hoover, Herbert Clark; politics and media.**

HARVEY, PAUL (1918–) is a pioneer radio news commentator and one of the most popular radio news figures ever to appear on the medium. His career at ABC spanned more than 50 years. Raised in Tulsa, Harvey began at KVOO radio there in 1941. After service at stations in Salina, Kansas, and Kalamazoo, Michigan, Harvey joined ABC in 1944, where he became an institution. Harvey is known for a staccato delivery and for the highly informal tone of his writing. His two daily radio programs, *Paul Harvey Comments* and *The Rest of the Story,* are among the highest-rated radio news broadcasts ever aired. Harvey received a Peabody Award for his commentaries in 1993. He was named to the Radio Hall of Fame three years earlier.

Craig M. Allen

HAWAII CALLS, musical program from the shores of Hawaii to the United States, created by Webley Edwards in 1934; he also produced and directed the show as well as acted as emcee.

The show featured islander music broadcast each Saturday from the shores of Waikiki Beach before a live audience of about 2,000 persons. It featured Hawaii's best singers and musicians. Sound effects were the swish of wahine skirts and the roar of the Pacific (one sound man was assigned to the beachfront with a microphone to add to the mood).

Performers included Al Kealoha Perry, Harry Owens, Hilo Hattie, and Alfred Anaka. The announcer was Jim Wahl. The group used only drums, guitars, and ukeleles. They performed 10 songs a week, 3 purely Hawaiian and the rest in English or novelty form. Edwards made use of a "campfire" atmosphere, always talking about the show being produced under the banyan tree with famous Diamond Head in the background. The show was picked up by the Mutual network for distribution in 1945. It lasted many years and could still be heard into the 1970s.

Dunning, John. *Tune in Yesterday: The Ultimate Encyclopedia of Old-time Radio 1925–1976.* Englewood Cliffs, N.J.: Prentice-Hall, 1976.
Terrace, Vincent. *Radio's Golden Years: Encyclopedia of Radio Programs: 1930–1960.* San Diego: A. S. Barnes and Company, Inc., 1981.

ElDean Bennett

HEATTER, GABRIEL (1890–1972), was the voice of nightly radio commentaries on the Mutual Broadcasting System (MBS) for over 30 years spanning the Great Depression, World War II, and the Korean War. He told tales of heroism and faith, which usually ended with an upbeat message of hope.

Born on the lower East Side of immigrant parents, Heatter worked on a variety of New York City newspapers from the age of 15. After a trip to Europe, he wrote inspirational pieces for an outdoor magazine and later a house organ of the steel industry.

His radio career as a commentator began on WMCA in 1932. He quickly moved to the MBS network and WOR in New York. His coverage of the trial of Bruno Hauptmann, the man convicted of killing the Lindbergh baby, brought Heatter fame. The execution was delayed, and Heatter had to ad-lib to a nationwide audience for 50 minutes.

From late 1937 to 1944, he was also host of *We the People* on CBS. Ordinary citizens, as well as celebrities, told tales of interesting events in their lives. Other programs he hosted were *Behind the Front Page, A Brighter Tomorrow,* and *Cavalcade of America,* all dramatizations of real events.

His commentaries began with the reassuring phrase "Ah, there's good news tonight" and reflected no political ideology. They were meant to encourage, not to analyze. Many journalists criticized his choice to deliver his own commercials and weave them into his narrative.

In 1951, Heatter moved to Miami Beach and continued his daily radio news show for MBS and a TV program until 1965. He was married to Saidie Heatter for 51 years, and they had two children, Nada and Basil. In 1967, he suffered a stroke, then died of pneumonia in 1972.

Fang, Irving E. *Those Radio Commentators!* Ames: Iowa State University Press, 1977.
Poindexter, Ray. *Golden Throats and Silver Tongues: The Radio Announcers.* Conway, Ark.: River Road Press, 1978.

Barbara Moore

HEAVY METAL, music style characterized by electrified guitars and heavy percussion played at high volume with an "aggressive edge." Heavy metal is also known as "loud rock." Musical groups generally included in the heavy metal category are Metallica, White Zombie, and Pantera. Heavy metal radio format is a fragmentation of the album-oriented rock format.

Carroll, Raymond L., and Donald M. Davis. *Electronic Media Programming: Strategies and Decision Making.* New York: McGraw-Hill, 1993.

Frederic A. Leigh

HERROLD, CHARLES DAVID (1875–1948), West Coast radio inventor and first regular radio broadcaster, Herrold was born in Fulton, Illinois, oldest of three brothers. His father was a businessman and part-time inventor. The family moved to San Jose in 1889 and took up farming. Herrold entered Stanford as an astronomy major in 1895 but did not complete a degree. From 1900 to 1906 he went through a period of both invention and manufacturing in San Francisco. After losing everything in the 1906 earthquake, he became head of the technical department of a trade school, Heald's College, in Stockton, where he stayed until 1908.

Returning to his hometown, he opened a vocational school, the Herrold College of Wireless and Engineering, on the fifth floor of a new bank building in downtown San Jose in early 1909. He was soon called "Doc" Herrold by his students and "Dr." in advertising for the school. With the help of students and his family, he began occasional broadcasts that year, eventually using informal call letters of FN, and later 6XE and 6XF, with a regular schedule (each Wednesday evening) a year later. Some sources suggest regular broadcasts on a weekly basis did not begin until 1912. Daily broadcasts were offered during the Panama-Pacific Exposition in San Francisco in 1915.

The intermittent broadcast operation began with spark-gap technology and moved steadily toward use of Poulsen's arc. At the same time, Herrold was trying to perfect his "arc-fone" transmitter system, with many patents applied for and five actually granted from 1914 to 1917. There was considerable concern over possible patent interference litigation over the Poulsen arc and Marconi's patents, but World War I interfered, and after 1918, arcs were no longer commercially important in radio transmission.

Herrold had to close down his station in 1917 as the U.S. Navy took over control of radio for the duration of World War I. This marked the effective end of his radio work, as his crude technology did not work in the frequencies assigned to fledgling broadcasting after the war. Some experimental licenses appear under his name in 1920–1921, but there is little evidence he was actually on the air, let alone regularly so. A commercial station, KQW in San Jose, was assigned to Herrold at the end of 1921 and continued operation into the middle of the decade, offering programs two evenings a week. It was eventually taken over by the First Baptist Church in the area (and still later sold to CBS and moved to San Francisco as the present KCBS).

Herrold's trade school closed in the early 1920s as other operations, better and more currently equipped, took over the market. Herrold moved through a series of odd jobs at public schools and elsewhere but was virtually forgotten at his death.

Adams, Michael. *Broadcasting's Forgotten Father: The Charles Herrold Story.* San Jose: Perham Foundation, 1994. 60 min. VHS videotape.

Baudino, Joseph E., and John M. Kittross. "Broadcasting's Oldest Stations: An Examination of Four Claimants." *Journal of Broadcasting* 21 (1) (winter 1977): 61–83.

Greb, Gordon L. "The Golden Anniversary of Broadcasting." *Journal of Broadcasting* 3 (1) (winter 1958–1959): 3–13.

Christopher H. Sterling

HERTZ, HEINRICH (1857–1894), German physicist who first demonstrated electromagnetic or "Hertzian" waves. Son of an attorney, Hertz was born in

Hamburg and went to Munich to study engineering. At the last minute, he changed to natural science with an emphasis in mathematics and magnetics and studied under Hermann Helmholtz. Hertz began serious wireless research in 1879 to seek a prize initiated by Helmholtz designed to solve a problem in the theories proposed by James Clerk Maxwell some years earlier. Hertz was appointed to the faculty of Technische Hochschule (Technical High School) of Karlsruhe in 1885 and began active experimentation a year later.

Hertz earned his Ph.D. in 1888 and became an assistant to Helmholtz while doing lecturing at the University of Kiel. He became a professor of physics at the University of Bonn in 1890, in time to publish his final papers. His central 1886–1888 experiments that proved Clerk Maxwell's theories correct were first described in a May 1888 paper, "Electromagnetic Waves in Air and Their Reflection." As often happens early in any technical development, Hertz stumbled across his key finding while doing something else—in this case, conducting a class demonstration in electricity. He proved that electricity could be transmitted in the form of electromagnetic (or, as they later became known in honor of his work, "Hertzian") waves acting similar to and as fast as light waves, just as Clerk Maxwell had postulated years before.

Hertz did not invent wireless (no one person did) but rather demonstrated that electromagnetic waves could be propagated through space (without wire connections, hence "wireless") and could be detected at a point remote from the transmitting source. He focused on proving Clerk Maxwell's theory rather than extending his work to potential applications, in part because his means of detecting signals (use of a spark gap) was so crude. Yet Hertz's work was both important and rapidly and widely understood, in part because of his active correspondence with a number of researchers in Britain and Ireland. Researchers in Germany and the United States also took up the quest for further knowledge and application of Hertzian waves.

While at the peak of his innovative power, Hertz tragically died at age 37 of chronic blood poisoning. His name is now used internationally to indicate a unit of frequency (what had been called a cycle, as in kilocycle, is now hertz or kilohertz).

Aitken, Hugh G. J., ed. "Hertz." In *Symphony and Spark: The Origins of Radio* (pp. 40–79). New York: Wiley, 1976.

de Tunselmann, G. W. "Hertz's Researches on Electrical Oscillations." In *Annual Report of the Board of Regents of the Smithsonian Institution* (pp. 145–203). Washington, D.C.: Government Printing Office, 1890.

Lodge, Oliver. *Signaling Through Space without Wires: The Work of Hertz and His Successors.* New York: Van Nostrand, 1894, 1898, 1900. (Latter edition reprinted by Arno Press, 1974).

O'Hara, J. G., and W. Pricha. *Hertz and the Maxwellians.* London: Peter Peregrinus, 1987.

Christopher H. Sterling

HETERODYNE RECEIVER is one that mixes a locally generated signal with an incoming broadcast signal using the heterodyne, or beat, principle. Two signals at different frequencies combined in a nonlinear component produce two new frequencies: one equal to their sum and one equal to their difference. For example, a broadcast signal at 600 kilohertz (kHz) mixed with a locally generated signal at

599 kHz creates new signals at 1,199 kHz and 1 kHz. The 600-kHz radio frequency signal becomes audible because the new 1-kHz signal created is within the range of human hearing. Devices using the heterodyne principle, in order of increasing complexity, include autodyne (regenerative), synchrodyne (direct conversion), and superheterodyne (single or multiple conversion) receivers.

DeMaw, Doug. *QRP Notebook.* Newington, Conn.: American Radio Relay League, 1989.
Graf, Rudolf F. *Modern Dictionary of Electronics.* Indianapolis, Ind.: Howard W. Sams & Co., Inc., 1984.

Tom Spann

HI-FI (HIGH-FIDELITY), ERA OF, the decades after World War II when radios and recording devices with capability of wide-frequency response became generally available consumer products. The term *high-fidelity* originated in 1926 with English electric engineer Harold Hartley and came into more general use in the early 1930s by some American radio stations, including New York's WQXR (see **Hogan, John Vincent Lawless**). E. H. Scott (and, for a brief time, McMurdo Silver) manufactured expensive custom-console radios in the 1930s that emphasized improved sound systems for their AM radio receivers and built-in phonographs. The first FM stations (1941) emphasized their improved (over AM) tonal quality or greater frequency response. By 1944, Decca introduced "full frequency-range recordings" (ffrrs) with frequency ranges exceeding 12,000 hertz (Hz) and sometimes reaching 20,000 Hz. Many postwar FM listeners depended on high-quality components tuner, amplifier, turntable, speakers by Scott, Fisher, and other manufacturers, to fully appreciate FM and record-sound quality. Imported high-quality components (then almost all from England and then Germany) helped to feed the still-limited demand.

Postwar long-playing (33⅓ rpm) records were first released by Columbia in 1947, followed by 45 rpm records from RCA. The first consumer magnetic-tape recorders were available by the mid-1950s. All emphasized high-fidelity sound. By late 1953, perhaps a million households had hi-fi gear, and interest was being aroused further by occasional binaural broadcasts that made use of separate AM and FM stations, one for each sound channel. In the 1950s, rising consumer demand for hi-fi was one cause of FM's rebound from seeming failure to what by the 1960s had become the fastest-growing electronic medium. Where consumer magazines tested only 4 hi-fi AM-FM receivers in 1953, the number had grown to 18 by 1957. Countless guides for developing home hi-fi units appeared. Development of stereo recordings (1958) and inception of regular FM stereo broadcasts (1961) pushed hi-fi into broader consumer acceptance.

Hi-fi audiocassette players (1966), made possible by use of integrated circuits, brought quality component prices down sharply. So did the growing number of imported components, now coming in largely from the Far East. Four-channel or "quadraphonic" stereo tapes and players became available in 1969, though the expense of the systems limited their appeal. Appearance of the consumer compact disc (CD) (1983) ushered in the digital era of hi-fi consumer products. Satellite-delivered audio services in the 1990s stress their CD-quality sound, and digital audio broadcasting (DAB) is on the near horizon.

Dearling, Robert, and Celia Dearling. *The Guinness Book of Recorded Sound.* Enfield, England: Guinness Books, 1984.

Jordan, Robert Oakes, and James Cunningham. *The Sound of High Fidelity.* Chicago: Windsor Press, 1958.

The U.S. Consumer Electronics Industry in Review. Arlington, Va.: Electronic Industries Association, 1958. Annual.

Christopher H. Sterling

HINDENBURG **CRASH COVERAGE** marked the first time the National Broadcasting Company knowingly allowed a recording of a news event to be broadcast over its networks. About 6:30 P.M. on May 6, 1937, Herbert Morrison, an announcer from WLS, Chicago, began: "How do you do everyone. We're greeting you now from the Naval Air Base at Lakehurst." His words were preserved on a disc recording by engineer Charles Nehlsen. He continued saying that the giant airship, which was due that morning, had arrived too late to dock during the calm dawn and had to wait till this evening. It was the first anniversary of the inauguration of the across-the-Atlantic service and the first flight of this year's season. Morrison had flown to New York on American Airlines, which provided connecting flights for passengers bound for many American cities. For about eight minutes, he described the ship and its crew, the trip, and the setting:

> The ship is riding majestically toward us like some great feather, riding as though it was mighty, mighty proud of the place it's playing in the world's aviation. The ship is no doubt bustling with activities, as we can see, orders are shouted to the crew, the passengers probably lining the windows looking down [at] the field ahead of them [voice in background as if over loud-speaker: "mooring now"], getting their glimpse of the mooring mast, and these giant flagships standing here, the American Airlines Flagships waiting to rush them to all points in the United States when they get the ship moored. There are a number of important persons on board and no doubt new commander Captain Max Pruitt is thrilled too, for this is his great moment, the first time he commanded the Hindenburg, for on previous flights he acted as the chief officer under Captain Leyman. It's practically standing still now, they lowered ropes out of the nose of the ship, and uh, it's been taken a hold of down on the field by a number of men. It's starting to rain again, the rain had slacked up a little bit. The back motors of the ship are just holding it uh, just enough to keep it from [a nearby shout is heard].
>
> It burst into flame [click, apparently the arm knocked off the machine, then replaced, and Morrison is heard again]. Get out of the way. Get out of the way. Get this, Charlie. Get this Charlie. And it's crashing, it's crashing, terrible. Oh my, get out of the way please. It's burning, bursting into flame and it's falling on the mooring mast, and all the folks between it. This is terrible. This is one of the worst catastrophes in the world. . . . It's a terrific

crash, ladies and gentlemen, the smoke and the flames now. And the frame is crashing to the ground, not quite to the mooring mast. Oh, the humanity and all the passengers screaming around here.

A bit later he told Nehlsen to stop the recording so he could catch his breath. In all, he recorded about 40 minutes on several discs, pausing several times to get more information and to help with the wounded. His reporting on the discs covered a span of about two hours. And while at first he said it was not possible for anyone to survive, he soon corrected himself. Sixty-one people did survive. Thirty-five— passengers, crew, and one ground handler—were killed in the fire that lasted just over half a minute.

The first news bulletin describing the tragedy was reported on both of NBC's networks about 7:45 P.M. EST. There were later bulletins and a live report from an NBC mobile unit about 2:50 A.M. The next day, NBC broke a long-standing rule prohibiting recordings on the networks and presented parts of Morrison's recording and interviewed him live from a studio in Chicago. WLS later made commemorative copies of the recordings. The most sensational part—"it burst into flame"—is contained in many documentaries.

Many historians have thought that the disc were recorded too slow, so when they were played back, they pitched Morrison's voice sound high and more hysterical. Sixty years later, another recording of Morrison at a band remote was found that could be used for reference. A carefully speed corrected and restored version of the original recordings, produced by the Museum of Broadcasting Communication, is now available.

Previous presentations of the slight-off-speech version and use of only small parts of the recordings have given the wrong impression. Morrison was under-standably shocked at the moment of the explosion, and he erroneously assumed that all aboard had died. Listening to the entire set of recordings shows that he was mostly calm. He did an excellent job, one that any reporter would admire.

"Hindenburg Air Disaster." Milo Ryan Phonoarchive, National Archives, Washington, D.C., tape #3986, cut 2.

Lawrence W. Lichty

HISPANIC FORMATS. *See* **ethnic issues; ethnic music; minority program-ming and employment; racial issues; urban contemporary format.**

HISPANIC LISTENERS AND RADIO MARKETS, population demographics, characteristics, radio usage of Spanish-speaking residents of the United States. The Hispanic audience is composed of immigrants from 22 Spanish-speaking countries. It is the fifth largest Spanish-speaking population in the world and is projected to be the largest Hispanic population by 2025. Ten states—California, Texas, New York, Florida, Illinois, Arizona, New Jersey, New Mexico, Colorado, and Massa-chusetts—account for 90 percent of the nation's Hispanic population. The Hispanic market is defined on a linguistic basis; however, Strategy Research Corporation reports that with relatively flat immigration since 1990, English is now used more in the work environment than Spanish by the Hispanic working population.

The Census Bureau estimates that as of January 1, 1997, the Hispanic population in the United States is 28,242,000 or slightly more than 11 percent of the total U.S. population of 266.4 million. Since 1950, the ranks of Hispanics living in the United States has swelled from 4 million to 28.24 million. Hispanics account for nearly 21 percent of our nation's total population growth and represent the largest segment. Mexicans represent the largest group of Hispanics living in the United States at about 64.2 percent of total Hispanics. Central and South Americans make up the second largest cohort at about 15 percent, followed by Puerto Ricans at 11 percent and Cubans at 5 percent. The mean age for the group is 28.6 years, with 0 to 11 years of age reflecting the largest percentage at 25 percent. Men 35 to 49 (10 percent) and 25 to 34 (9.9 percent) and women 35 to 49 (9.7 percent) and 25 to 34 years (8.7 percent) represent the second and third largest groups by age. The size of the average Hispanic household is larger at 3.41 than its non-Hispanic counterparts at 2.63. The largest household sizes are reported for Mexicans; the smallest, for Cubans. The mean household income is $37,500, with Cubans leading the group at $45,200.

According to Strategy Research Corporation, the top three markets are Los Angeles, New York, and Miami, with San Francisco, Chicago, Houston, San Antonio, McAllen/Brownsville, Dallas/Fort Worth, and El Paso rounding out the top 10. These markets total more than 17 million Hispanic residents, or 63 percent of the U.S. total Hispanic population. *Hispanic Business,* and its Internet site Hispanstar (www.hispanstar.com), varies in its top markets with the addition of Sacramento/Stockton/Modesto and San Diego based on U.S. Hispanic media expenditures. Its Hispandata research arm indicates that in 1996 the total U.S. Hispanic purchasing power represented $223.44 billion, with Hispanic radio media expenditures reaching $322 million.

According to Arbitron, 96 percent of all Hispanics listen to Spanish-language radio stations. Arbitron reports that it is more popular with women 55+ in terms of daily listening time, but men ages 18 to 34 show the greatest weekly reach at 96.6 percent. On a daily basis, adult Hispanics in the United States spend about three hours and 40 minutes listening to the radio. Sixty percent of the daily listening hours are spent with Spanish-language radio, which translates to approximately one hour and 53 minutes. Listenership is highest on Saturdays from 10 A.M. to 3 P.M., but they listen in all dayparts and use both AM and FM radio. Older Hispanics tend to rely on Spanish-language radio more than their younger counterparts. Strategy Research reports that 71.6 percent of those Hispanics surveyed listened to the radio in Spanish; however, 60.7 percent listen in English as well.

Broadcasting & Cable Yearbook reports that the majority of stations are AM (302) and are community oriented. Their public service programming tends to focus on helping recent immigrants and longtime residents find their way to social service agencies and the job market. Many have raised aid for victims of disasters and aided local charities. Formats differ from market to market, but musical programming dominates with the exception of Miami, with a preference for news/talk formats.

Newscasts are normally limited to drive times with hourly updates. Many stations use wire services for their information; others rely on the local newspaper. Stations with longer newscasts use their own news staff and employ on-air personalities to double as reporters. Few stations offer their own editorial opinions, preferring to air programs in which listeners are encouraged to call in and voice their concerns. The New Heftel Group is the largest Spanish-language radio network with 34 stations. It was created by the merger of Heftel Broadcasting Corporation and Tichenor Media Systems.

Day, Jennifer Cheeseman. *Population Projections of the United States, by Age, Sex and Hispanic Origin: 1993-2050.* Washington, D.C.: U.S. Department of Commerce, Economics and Statistics, Bureau of the Census, 1993.
Hispanic Business magazine.
The Latin American Market Planning Report. Miami: Strategy Research Corporation, 1996.
The U.S. Hispanic Market. Miami: Strategy Research Corporation, 1996.
The U.S. Hispanic Population Book. Miami: Strategy Research Corporation, 1997.
Veciana-Suarez, Ana. *Hispanic Media, USA.* Washington, D.C.: Media Institute, 1987.

Fran R. Matera

HOGAN, JOHN VINCENT LAWLESS (1890–1960), radio consulting engineer and author. Born in Bayonne, New Jersey, Hogan worked for several months with Lee de Forest in 1906–1907. He attended Yale's Sheffield Scientific School in 1908–1910 (as de Forest had done a decade earlier), focusing on physics and mathematics. Hogan then served as a telegraph engineer at National Electric Signaling Co. in Brant Rock, Massachusetts (working with Reginald Fessenden) and in Brooklyn. With Alfred N. Goldsmith and Robert H. Marriott, he cofounded the Institute of Radio Engineers in 1912.

Among 34 other patents earned from 1910 to 1952, he patented a single-dial tuning system for radio receivers. He was in charge of acceptance tests for the U.S. Navy's high-powered Arlington (Virginia) station in 1913. From 1914 to 1917 he worked on automatic high-speed recorders for long-distance wireless. After World War I, Hogan turned to consulting, with considerable writing including a widely popular introduction to the subject. In the 1930s, he was very active in attempts to make facsimile a commercially viable service.

Hogan and Elliott Sanger put New York City station WQXR on the air in late 1936 with a classical music format, based on Hogan's 250-watt W2XR experimental outlet that had broadcast intermittently for several years. From the beginning, they identified the station with "high-fidelity" (see **hi-fi [high-fidelity], era of**) sound, though it was on the AM band. They added an FM station (the first in New York City) in November 1939. They operated their outlets until selling them both to the *New York Times* early in 1944 (with Sanger staying on as general manager for another two decades).

Hogan, J. V. L. *The Outline of Radio.* Boston: Little, Brown, 1923, 1925, 1928.
"John Vincent Lawless Hogan: Invented a Uni-Control Tuner." In *Radio's 100 Men of Science,* edited by Orrin E. Dunlap, Jr. (pp. 245–247). New York: Harper, 1944.
Sanger, Elliott M. *Rebel in Radio: The Story of WQXR.* New York: Hastings House, 1973.

Christopher H. Sterling

HOOK, RECORD, novel segment of a popular recording that is most remembered by the audience. If there are no truly novel elements, then a short, melodic phrase (usually in the chorus) is what becomes identified with the song. However, the novel element could be a production special effect, a vocal inflection, a rhythmic change, a sound effect, or an unexpected timbre.

In typical call-out and auditorium music testing, it is usually the hook of the record that is played for the listener, since the hook is often the most recognizable part of the song. Truly innovative hooks do not stay novel for long, because other record producers imitate the hook in an attempt to emulate the success of the original.

David T. MacFarland

HOOPER (C. E. HOOPER COMPANY), research firm responsible for publishing the Hooperatings radio audience estimates. Beginning in 1934, C. E. Hooper used a coincidental telephone survey technique to gather information on network radio audiences. Respondents were asked if they were currently listening to a radio program and to identify the program and station. Samples were drawn for 36 cities that had radio stations carrying the four national networks operating at the time. Hooper used the information gathered to produce three audience estimates: program ratings, audience shares, and scts in use. Hooper continued to produce the Hooperatings until 1950 when competitor A. C. Nielsen took over the network ratings business.

Chester, Giraud, Garnet R. Garrison, and Edgar E.Willis. *Television and Radio.* 3rd ed. New York: Appleton-Century-Crofts, 1963.

Frederic A. Leigh

HOOPER, STANLEY C. (1864–1955), U.S. Navy officer; "father of naval radio." Born in California, Hooper graduated from the Naval Academy in 1905. Following seven years of sea duty, he returned to Annapolis as an instructor in electricity, radio, physics, and chemistry. He became fleet radio officer in 1912 and was a U.S. observer of radio applications in Europe early in World War I.

Hooper served two terms as head of the Navy Bureau of Engineering's Radio Division, first during World War I and again in 1923–1925. While in this role, he played a key part in the creation of RCA. While still a serving officer, he was appointed a technical adviser to the new Federal Radio Commission in 1927. From 1928 to 1934, he was director of naval communications and served as a member of the president's advisory radio board. Hooper directed the Radio Division and served as a technical assistant to the chief of Naval Operations during World War II. He retired in 1945 as a rear admiral.

Howeth, Captain L. S. *History of Communications—Electronics in the United States Navy.* Washington, D.C.: Government Printing Office, 1963.

Christopher H. Sterling

HOOVER, HERBERT CLARK (1874–1964), as secretary of commerce from 1921 through 1927, formulated the development of governmental regulation of

American broadcasting. Hoover was born in the village of West Branch, Iowa, on August 10, 1874. His father died of typhoid fever when Herbert was six years old; his mother died in 1884 when he was nine years old. The three Hoover children were separated, and Herbert went to live with relatives.

He worked his way through the newly formed Stanford University and organized a campus political party that developed Stanford's student government. The student government constitution he helped design served Stanford for more than 35 years. In the spring of 1895, Herbert Hoover was in the first 4-year class to graduate.

Hoover was employed by a British firm to introduce America mining methods to Australia. He was then hired by the Chinese government to develop mining properties. Before departing for China in 1899, he married Miss Lou Henry. Just as he and his wife were about to start on an inspection trip of the interior, Mrs. Hoover became ill and had to be taken to Tientsin where a European doctor was available. This enforced detour and delay saved their lives, for the Boxer Rebellion began shortly after they arrived in Tientsin.

Tientsin itself came under siege, and Hoover's engineering talents helped in defending and provisioning the inhabitants as well as thousands of refugees. Hoover had his initial experience with relief work and lost his position in China as a result of the Boxer Rebellion. In late 1901, Hoover became a junior partner in his engineering firm but did not like the constant travel; in 1908, he quit the firm to set up an office as a consulting engineer, which he managed until the outbreak of World War I in 1914.

He was in London at the beginning of the war and organized a committee of permanent American residents to provide temporary food and shelter, currency exchange, and emergency loans to Americans who were stranded. Later in September 1914, Hoover was asked to head a relief program to assist Belgium, which was under blockade by the Allies and Germany refused to feed the population. He organized a Commission for Relief of Belgium, which dispensed more than $927 million in food, clothes, and shelter and operated a fleet of 200 ships under its own flag. The recognition he received for this task caused President Woodrow Wilson, on April 6, 1917, the day the United States entered the war, to ask Hoover to take the position of food administrator.

After the armistice in November 1918, Hoover began a massive program to feed a starving Europe, and for a year, he had more power and influence than any other person in Europe. His work soon caused some whispers concerning his potential as a presidential candidate. In September 1919, Hoover left Europe and at the age of 44 intended to resume his engineering profession. But the government and various private agencies kept calling upon him. He organized a European Children's Relief Agency and spent time giving speeches, appearing before congressional hearings, and presiding over meetings.

In the presidential election of 1920, Harding, an admirer of Hoover from the Food Administration days, appointed Hoover as secretary of commerce on March 4, 1921. Though he served both the Harding and Coolidge administrations, Herbert Hoover was not of their political philosophies.

Because of the limited use made of radio prior to the advent of broadcasting, there was no pressing need for further legislation. With the advent of broadcasting, it became increasingly difficult to apply the law of 1912 to this new use of radio. At first, the Department of Commerce selected two frequencies (750 and 833 kilohertz [kHz]) and licensed all broadcast stations to operate on one or the other of these channels. This physical limitation was soon found to be such that all who sought to broadcast could not do so without interfering with others. Attempts had to be made at the federal level to change the situation.

Secretary Hoover sought to adapt the department's authority under the *Radio Act of 1912* to the new conditions that were developing. He called the various segments of the radio industry together for a series of conferences. These were to advise the Department of Commerce as to the application of its powers of regulation and to formulate recommendations to Congress on the legislation deemed necessary. However, the legislative suggestions of the Department of Commerce were not acted upon by Congress until the passage of the *Radio Act of 1927*.

Hoover became the thirty-first president of the United States and served one term of office, beginning in 1928. His successive triumphs came to an end with the Great Depression, as critics attacked his methods of dealing with the crisis. In 1932, he ran against Franklin D. Roosevelt, but by this time, bank failures, 14 million unemployed, and farm distress worked against him. Roosevelt won the election.

In his postpresidential years, Hoover continued to be active in public service, most significantly as the leader of the Commission on the Organization of the Executive Branch of Government. Known as the Hoover Commission, two reports were issued (1947–1949, 1953–1955). The commission made many recommendations concerning government structure, and most were subsequently adopted.

The Hoover Commission of 1955 reported that the FCC had taken corrective action, as suggested, to cut down the amount of paperwork required of broadcasters. In his later years, Hoover received numerous honors from various elements of the broadcast industry that recognized his role in the development of the American system of broadcasting. At the age of 90, Hoover, former secretary of commerce and president of the United States, died on October 20, 1964.

Hoover, Herbert. *Memoirs.* Vols. 1–2. New York: Macmillan Company, 1951–1952.
Wolfe, Harold. *Herbert Hoover: Public Servant and Leader of the Loyal Opposition.* New York: Exposition Press, 1956.
Straub, Duane G. "The Role of Secretary of Commerce Herbert Hoover in the Development of Early Radio Regulation." Master's thesis, Michigan State University, 1964.

Marvin R. Bensman

HOT CLOCK, a visual representation of the components of a radio format usually displaying hourly programming. The display, resembling a clock, shows musical selections, commercials, and other types of announcements in the order they will be broadcast by a radio station.

Frederic A. Leigh

HOUSE OF REPRESENTATIVES: COMMITTEE ON INTERSTATE AND FOREIGN COMMERCE. Congress plays an important role in the regulation of the broadcasting industry, through both direct legislation and its oversight of the Federal Communications Commission (FCC). These federal regulators are concerned with a variety of issues including technical requirements, ownership, and business aspects as well as programming practices. The House of Representative's Committee on Interstate and Foreign Commerce routinely investigates the business aspects of the broadcasting industry.

The first known inquiry by the House committee can be traced back to 1897 when Congress was debating the Pacific Cable Bill, an initiative to facilitate the construction and maintenance of telegraphic communications between the United States and the Hawaiian Islands, Guam, Japan, and China. This initiative was the subject of considerable investigation as the committee convened hearings on the initiative through 1902. Later, the Interstate and Foreign Commerce Committee was instrumental in developing and regulating wireless telegraphy, radio frequency modulation, and spectrum allocation. The committee also reviewed the federal control and operation of radio services during times of war.

The House committee played an important function in the creation of the FCC and continued in an advisory and supervisory role as the commission developed throughout the years. Sometimes this oversight focused not only on the regulatory actions of the FCC but also on the behavior and actions of the commissioners themselves. A 1958 committee hearing that included a routine review of the FCC (and other regulatory agencies) quickly cast an investigatory eye as several commissioners were exposed for accepting bribes, jobs for family members, and free travel from broadcasters in exchange for broadcast licenses.

The commission is still subject to annual reviews of its policy and regulatory actions, as well as rulings on specific broadcasting issues. If the committee believes that the FCC has acted inappropriately on a given issue, it may exert its pressure in an effort to coax additional agency action.

Although the business aspect of broadcasting has been a primary focus, the House Committee on Interstate and Foreign Commerce has occasionally investigated programming issues. Early concerns focused on government interference in educational radio programs and proposed bans on alcohol advertising and deceptive broadcasts. More recently, the committee was involved in developing the equal time provision for federal candidates and the controversial issue of continued funding for public radio and television.

Brightbill, George. *Communications and the United States Congress, a Selectively Annotated Bibliography of Committee Hearings, 1870–1976.* Washington, D.C.: Broadcast Education Association, 1978.
Ray, William. *FCC: The Ups and Downs of Radio-TV Regulation.* Ames: Iowa State University Press, 1990.

Cynthia A. Cooper

HUBBARD, GARDNER (1822–1897), was a nineteenth-century electronic media pioneer whose major contribution was in spearheading development of technology that eventually ushered in voice communication. He was raised in Boston and entered Dartmouth College in 1838. After graduating in 1842, Hubbard returned to Boston and entered the public utility business. He subsequently married an associate, Gertrude McCurdy, and their daughter, Mabel G. Hubbard, eventually married telephone inventor Alexander Graham Bell. Rising as the head of the Boston utility company in the late 1850s, Hubbard was credited with introducing its first gas lighting. An important career change materialized in the 1860s, when he became a leader in a movement that led to the formation of the Clarke Institution for Deaf Mutes. This initiative generated research and developmental funds eventually secured by Bell and used in perfecting telephone communication. In 1876, Hubbard helped found the Bell Telephone Company.

In addition to supporting Bell and developing the telephone as a profit-making enterprise, Hubbard instituted the system by which users rented rather than purchased telephone lines and equipment. This so-called federated system of telephone service remained until the breakup of the Bell System in 1982. While still engaged in a lifelong interest in helping the deaf, Hubbard began a series of expeditions to Alaska. He was named a regent of the Smithsonian Association in 1895. Prior to this, Hubbard's most enduring and best-known achievement, founding the National Geographic Society, occurred in 1888.

Craig M. Allen

HUMMERT, ANNE AND FRANK, husband and wife team, were the producers and lead writers of over 30 different daytime serials that accounted for over half of the advertising revenue generated by daytime radio in the 1930s and early 1940s. Their cooperative venture began in Chicago at the advertising agency of Blackett, Sample & Hummert. Frank Hummert, a former journalist from St. Louis, was a successful copywriter and partner in the advertising agency when Anne Ashenhurst joined him as his assistant in the late 1920s. Born Anne Schuacher, she graduated magna cum laude from Goucher College at age 20 in 1925 and worked as a reporter in Baltimore and then Paris, France, after graduation. In France, she married and divorced fellow reporter John Ashenhurst and returned to settle in Chicago with an infant son in 1926. After working together in the agency for six years, Anne married Frank, 20 years her senior, in 1934. They formed their own company, Hummert Productions, a sort of literary factory, and moved to New York in the mid-1930s.

One of their first successes, *Just Plain Bill,* started in daytime in 1933, having started in the evening in 1932. It became very popular, in spite of the generally held belief that women would be too distracted with their chores during the day to attend to their radios. They had as many as 18 different series on the air at the same time, including: *Arnold Grimm's Daughter, Backstage Wife, Betty and Bob, David Harum, John's Other Wife, Just Plain Bill, Lovernzo Jones, Our Gal Sunday, The Romance of Helen Trent, Stella Dallas,* and *Young Widder Brown.*

The plots for the serials would be outlined by the Hummerts, then the script writing farmed out to many writers who were given details about characters and plot development. Merchandising plans were incorporated into the story lines—but also propaganda: During World War II, the State Department asked the Hummerts to write their dramas to help overcome the white soldier's fear of the black soldier and to help the war effort in general.

When television replaced radio as the medium for soap operas, the Hummerts retired to travel. Frank died in 1966; Anne died 30 years later on July 5, 1996, at the age of 91.

Thomas, Robert McG. "Anne Hummert, 91, Dies: Creator of Soap Operas." *New York Times,* July 21, 1996, p. 27.

Margot Hardenbergh

HYDE, ROSEL H. (1900–1992), commissioner at the Federal Communications Commission (FCC) with the longest tenure (1946–1969) and the only one appointed by both Democrat and Republican presidents. Hyde was born on April 12, 1900, in a Mormon farming community, Downey, Idaho. In 1924, he married Mary Henderson, moved to Washington, D.C., and began law studies at George Washington University Law School, while working as a disbursement officer for the Civil Service Commission.

He passed the bar in 1928 and joined the newly formed Federal Radio Commission as an attorney examiner. Then he became an attorney examiner with the FCC when the *Communications Act of 1934* was passed. As radio/TV section chief, assistant general counsel, and then general counsel to the FCC (from 1939 to 1945), Hyde was a key player in formulating many agency policies, including international treaties, broadcast license and frequency allocation rules, and adoption of the *Sixth Report and Order* in 1952. This latter decision ended a four-year freeze on granting new TV station licenses.

U.S. President Harry S. Truman appointed Hyde to fill a partial term as a commissioner on April 17, 1946. He was reappointed by President Truman to a full seven-year term in 1952, an unprecedented move by a Democratic administration. Ironically, in 1953, when Dwight D. Eisenhower became the first Republican president, Hyde was retained as a commissioner and named chairman, but he was not entirely trusted owing to political views that his years under Democratic regimes might have compromised his loyalty. Eisenhower replaced Hyde as chairman after 18 months.

During the 1950s, when Congress challenged the politics and acts of several FCC commissioners, Hyde had to answer but was cleared of all charges about his loyalties and his actions. At a time when many commissioners and career FCC employees were leaving the FCC to take well-paying jobs in private industry, Hyde elected to stay with the commission.

In the 1960s, Hyde's contributions and long-standing communications expertise were recognized when he received the International Radio and Television Society's (IRTS's) highest honor, the Gold Medal. He had won many friends and the respect of both political camps for his service and expertise. The *New York Times* carried an editorial in 1965 lauding Hyde's integrity, modesty, and distinguished career. Then, in 1966, another Democratic president, Lyndon B. Johnson, appointed Hyde as chairman at age 65. This was the first such appointment of a Republican by a Democrat.

When his term ended in 1969, Hyde retired from the FCC but took a position with the Washington, D.C. communications law firm of Wilkinson, Cragun, and

Barker. He worked there until his official retirement in 1990. Rosel H. Hyde's government and law career spanned 62 years. He saw and participated in major policy making involving the development of radio, TV, cable TV, satellite systems, color TV standards, mergers of communications firms, and important telephone decisions. He helped shape electronic media from the maritime uses of radiotelegraphy to the heyday of commercial radio and the rise of TV to the development of new technologies. Hyde died at the age of 92 on December 19, 1992.

Baker, LeGrand, Kelly D. Christensen, Darren Bell, and Thomas E. Patterson, eds. *Register of the Rosel H. Hyde Collection*. Provo: Brigham Young University, 1992.

Flannery, Gerald, ed. *Commissioners of the FCC: 1927–1994*. Lanham, Md.: University Press of America, 1995.

J. R. Rush

I

IMUS, DON (1940–), has been the morning personality on WNBC, later WFAN, New York, since 1971. After the Don Martin Radio School, Hollywood, in 1968 he quickly moved from Palmdale, Stockton, and Sacramento in California to Cleveland and won the *Billboard* major market award. His comedy routines, and irreverent style, have kept his program near the top of the ratings. After 1991, his programming has featured more and more calls from political figures and celebrity journalists.

Imus has admitted to problems with alcohol and cocaine, which nearly ruined his career in the mid-1980s. He has feuded with Howard Stern (they were once on the same station and worked for the same group owner). He often calls his brother Fred, who lived in El Paso but now resides in Sante Fe, on the program. The program has occasionally been carried on C-SPAN during election campaigns, is syndicated to other stations, and since September 1996, has been part of the morning programming for the cable channel MSNBC. In April 1997, *Time* magazine listed Imus as one of the "25 most influential people in America."

Imus, Don. *God's Other Son: A Novel.* New York: Simon & Schuster, 1994.
Imus, Don. *Imus in the Morning: One Sacred Chicken to Go.* RCA Records, 1973. LSP-4819.
Imus, Don, and Fred Imus. *Two Guys Four Corners.* New York: Villard, 1997. Photographs.

Lawrence W. Lichty

INDECENCY. A prohibition on broadcasting obscene or indecent content by broadcast stations is incorporated in Section 1464 of the United State Code. This section gives the Federal Communications Commission (FCC) the power to revoke a broadcast license if the licensee transmits obscene or indecent material over the airwaves. The FCC may apply lesser penalties, such as fines or shortened license periods, in lieu of license revocation.

Neither term, *obscenity* nor *indecency,* has a legal definition that can be clearly understood by the average person. In 1973, the U.S. Supreme Court created a three-part analysis, called the "Miller Test," that is used in determining if material is obscene. An average person, who applies contemporary local community standards, must find that the work, taken as a whole, appeals to prurient interest. The work must depict in patently offensive ways sexual conduct that is specifically defined in state law. The work must lack serious literary, artistic, political, or scientific value.

The vague definition of *obscenity* gives broadcasters sufficient guidance to avoid broadcasting obscene material. The definition of indecency was developed by the FCC, and while the U.S. Supreme Court issued a restricted definition of indecency in 1978 (*Federal Communication Commission v. Pacifica Foundation,* 438 U.S. 726, July 3, 1978), the FCC has continued to use its own broad interpretation.

The commission defines indecency as: "exposure of children to language that describes in terms patently offensive as measured by contemporary standards for the broadcast media, sexual or excretory activities and organs." The Supreme Court, in its 1978 *Pacifica* ruling, forbade broadcasters from airing content that contains repeated use, for shock value, the specific words, or similar words, that the court listed in its decision, at a time when children might be in the audience. There was a presumption that children would not be part of the audience after 10 P.M.

FCC prosecution of radio stations for violating the indecency rule dates to 1962 when the commission refused to renew the license of WDKD because a disk jockey frequently told "off-color" or "indecent" jokes on the air (in re *Palmetto Broadcasting Co.,* 33 FCC 250 [1962]). Other offenses for which the FCC has levied fines include broadcast of "indecent" four-letter words by a college radio station and a discussion of oral sexual practices between an announcer and a listener in Illinois.

A listener-supported FM radio station in New York City triggered the Supreme Court's 1978 decision by playing at midafternoon, after warning listeners, a George Carlin monologue called "Seven Dirty Words." One complaint was received by the FCC, which then prosecuted Radio Station WBAI. The Supreme Court sustained the FCC ruling but issued its narrowed definition of indecency.

The deregulation of broadcasting in the 1980s and insertion of additional frequencies in the FM band led to fractionalization of the radio audience, causing some broadcasters to try "adult" programming in their efforts to maintain their audience. The use of frank, suggestive language by air personalities triggered another round of FCC prosecutions. In 1987, three radio stations were fined for carrying indecent programming.

One of the stations cited broadcast a morning-drive program hosted by Howard Stern, who specialized in using shocking language. The FCC began a long-running battle with Infinity Broadcasting, the company that syndicated Stern's program. In 1995, Infinity paid a fine of $1.7 million in response to multiple actions against Stern's broadcasts by the FCC. At the time, Stern was broadcasting over 35 stations.

In October 1996, the commission levied a $10,000 fine on the former owner of radio station WVGO (FM) in Richmond, Virginia. The station carried Stern's broadcast and was accused of permitting indecencies to be broadcast. In one instance, Stern described having sex with his wife, and in the other instance, he engaged in a discussion of vaginas (*Broadcasting & Cable* [October 21, 1996]: 23). The FCC said: "[T]he subject excerpts are indecent in that they contain language that describes sexual and excretory activities or organs in patently offensive terms."

The remarks, the FCC said, were made "when there was a reasonable risk that children might have been in the audience."

Following its flurry of station fines in 1987, the FCC announced it was narrowing the "safe harbor" when indecent material could be broadcast from midnight to 6 A.M. The lobbying organization Action for Children's Television filed suit challenging the new indecency standards. In 1988, a federal court upheld the FCC's definition of indecency, and the safe harbor, but questioned the assumption that there were no children listening or viewing between midnight and 6 A.M. The court said the FCC had no scientific evidence to support one time being more appropriate than another for indecent programming, which, the court reminded the commission, was protected by the First Amendment. (Obscenity is not protected by the First Amendment.)

Congress entered the debate. Senator Jesse Helms pushed through an amendment in mid-1988 calling for a total ban on indecent programming. The FCC capitulated and in December 1988 issued a total ban on broadcasting indecent programming. In 1989, the U.S. Court of Appeals for the District of Columbia blocked implementation of the FCC ban. The commission was ordered to conduct an inquiry into actual viewing habits of children. The court said, in the meantime, the safe harbor hours would be 8 P.M. to 6 A.M. In mid-1990, the commission said its inquiry had stirred up an outpouring of public concern, and it again ordered a 24-hour ban on indecent broadcasts.

The U.S. Court of Appeals tossed out the latest ban in May 1991, and in 1992 the U.S. Supreme Court declined to hear an appeal from the FCC. Congress intervened by passing the *Public Telecommunications Act of 1992,* which required the FCC to publish a rule banning indecent content between 6 A.M. and midnight. The court of appeals responded in 1993 by striking down the FCC rule, reiterating that indecency was still protected speech under the First Amendment. That ruling was vacated so a full panel of judges could reconsider, and in 1995, the appeals court upheld the FCC rule in a version that prohibits indecent content between 6 A.M. and 10 P.M. In January 1996 the Supreme Court declined to reconsider (see also **lyrics and morality**).

Pember, Don R. *Mass Media Law.* Dubuque, Iowa: Brown & Benchmark, 1996.

Phillip O. Keirstead

INDUCTION WIRELESS. When a current passes through a primary coil, it establishes a magnetic field; when a secondary coil is placed within this field, the primary will induce a variable current into the secondary.

In 1842, Joseph Henry used induction to transmit messages, but the heyday of this wireless technology was the 1880s. During this decade, Granville Woods, Thomas A. Edison, and Lucius Phelps developed wireless telegraph systems to communicate with trains, and Amos E. Dolbear patented a wireless telephone. In 1891, John Trowbridge demonstrated that induction wireless was limited to a distance of half a mile and had little practical value.

Fahie, John J. *A History of Wireless Telegraphy, Including Some Barewire Proposals for Subaqueous Telegraphs.* Edinburgh: Blackwood, 1899. Reprint, New York: Arno Press, 1971.

Hawks, Ellison. *Pioneers of Wireless.* London: Methuen and Co., 1927. Reprint New York: Arno Press, 1974.

Robert H. Lochte

INFORMATION FORMATS, where news and talk dominate the information formats; programming heard primarily on AM radio. However, information formats are also programmed on many FM public stations. Another genre of the information format is sports/talk.

News, weather, sports, time, traffic, editorials, and features are commonly offered as content on news stations. The content of talk radio relies heavily on listeners who call in to interact with on-air personalities and their guests. Many stations program a hybrid of the news and talk formats, combining the two to emphasize news during the morning and afternoon and talk during the midday and at night. The sports/talk format is commonly programmed at night and on weekends.

The on-air personalities who host radio talk shows play a key role in attracting audiences. Often controversial and outspoken, they can stimulate loyal listening among those interested in their views. Information formats are expensive to produce compared with music-oriented formats, because information gathering tends to be labor-intensive. However, stations have found that syndicated and network programming can provide a cost-efficient means of delivering quality news, talk, and sports. Among the better-known syndicated personalities are Rush Limbaugh, G. Gordon Liddy, Dr. Laura Schlesinger, and Bruce Williams.

Public radio stations also depend on syndicated and network programming for their information formats. The highly acclaimed news programs *Morning Edition* and *All Things Considered* are products of National Public Radio, based in Washington, which produces several hours of news and talk programming each week, along with a competing radio network, Public Radio International.

Eastman, Susan Tyler, and Douglas A. Ferguson. *Broadcast/Cable Programming: Strategies and Practices.* 5th ed. Belmont, Calif.: Wadsworth, 1996.

Laufer, Peter. *Inside Talk Radio: America's Voice or Just Hot Air?* Secaucus, N.J.: Carol Publishing Group, 1995.

Tim England

INTERCITY RADIO COMPANY **CASE** was the first test before the courts of the Department of Commerce's power to make regulations under the *Communications Act of 1912* where such power was found nonexistent. The Intercity Radio Company opened a wireless telegraphy station on December 1, 1920, in New York City. The *New York Times,* U.S. Navy, and others complained to the Department of Commerce that their stations were being interfered with by Intercity Radio. On May 12, 1921, the Department of Commerce revoked the Intercity license on the grounds that it was interfering with ship-to-shore traffic. Intercity sued, and the court held that any corporation that had applied to the Department of Commerce had to be given one.

On August 24, 1921, the license of Intercity expired and renewal was denied. The District of Columbia Supreme Court on November 18, 1921, ordered Secretary Herbert Hoover to issue a radio license to the Intercity Company. The court of appeals affirmed that the secretary had no authority to refuse to license any station that applied for a license.

New legislation would be needed. On August 25, 1924, Secretary Hoover was informed that Intercity was no longer operating a radio station in New York, and on September 15, 1924, the *Intercity Radio Company* case was declared moot by the Supreme Court and dismissed. Secretary Hoover went to the cabinet on February 7, 1922, to ask for permission for a national radio conference two days after the court of appeals decision against the department on the *Intercity* case.

Hoover v. Intercity Radio Company, 52 App. D.C. 339, 286 F. 1003, writ of error dismissed as moot, 266 U.S. 636 (1924).

Howeth, Captain L. S. *History of Communications—Electronics in the United States Navy.* Washington, D.C.: Government Printing Office, 1963.

Marvin R. Bensman

INTERNATIONAL BROTHERHOOD OF ELECTRICAL WORKERS (IBEW). *See* **unions.**

INTERNATIONAL RADIO. 1. Any radio programming heard around the world, normally on shortwave frequencies. Examples include the *BBC World Service* (aired by the British Broadcasting Corporation) with over 140 million worldwide listeners, *Deutsche Wella Radio, Radio France International, Radio Netherlands,* and the United States' *Voice of America.* These radio services are broadcast to serve citizens of current and/or former colonies/annexations; to provide commercial-free programming; and in some cases, to advocate a political or philosophical ideology.

2. An assessment of comparing national radio systems within different countries. The radio system in the United States can be characterized as a large market (approximately 11,000 radio stations) consisting mainly of privately owned, commercial radio stations, broadcasting local programming and using advertising as a profitable revenue source. In the U.S. model there also is a small sector of publicly owned public radio stations using listener donations and government funding as break-even revenue sources; community radio stations, using listener donations and commercial sponsorships as break-even revenue sources; and college radio stations, using student fees and/or commercial underwriting as funding sources. Programming in the U.S. model tends to have local origination, to be format driven, and to be designed to appeal to a niche demographic. The radio systems in European countries can be characterized by small markets consisting mainly of state-controlled station operations broadcasting national programming. In a typical European country, there are just three or four radio stations. One station (sometimes named "Radio 1") may program "high-culture" music, a second ("Radio 2") "pop" music, and a third ("Radio 3") talk and/or sports. Advertising is not as prevalent in European radio programming as it is in U.S. radio programming. European pop music stations tend to define the rock format more broadly than "contemporary hit

radio" (CHR) in the United States. Over the course of a given day, European pop stations may play oldies, rock, hits, dance, and rap. European pop music deejays adhere to "needle-drop" copyright requirements for every song, which require the deejay to talk over the beginning or ending of a song so the song does not play in its entirety and offer listeners the chance to record it. CHR deejays sometimes talk over the beginning or ending of songs, but not because of a legal copyright requirement.

Gebbels, Tim. "The BBC World Service." *Contemporary Review* 267 (1556) (September 1995): 139 (3).

International Radio. http://guide-p.infoseek.com/International_radio_stations?tid'2881

Robert McKenzie

INTERNET RADIO, audio programming delivered by way of the Internet (on the World Wide Web) in real time from one computer to other computers. The audio data is transmitted over the Internet from the station's server and arrives via modem to the user's computer. Key to the development of Internet radio was the 1995 arrival of "streaming." Previously, users had to wait for an entire audio file to download and then listen to the file off their own hard disk. A 10-minute audio file might take two hours to download. Streaming allows the user to listen to audio programming and music as it arrives in real time. The user simply clicks on a word or icon associated with the audio programming desired and the audio is brought directly to the user's computer where it can be played, rewound, or fast-forwarded. In other cases, the user can select a program source that is happening live.

Internet radio requires a relatively fast computer, a modem (preferably at least a 28.8 kilobytes per second [Kbps] baud modem), a sound card, and special software matching the software used by the station to encode and transmit the signal. Two companies have been most responsible for the development of Internet radio software, RealNetworks in Seattle, Washington and Xing (pronounced Zing) Technology in Arroyo Grande, California. RealNetwork's "RealAudio" and Xing Technology's "StreamWorks" can be downloaded by the user at no cost on the Internet.

Internet radio audio quality is usually far less than radio listeners are accustomed to hearing from traditional over-the-air radio broadcasting. Sound quality is sacrificed because of the need to compress the signal into the narrow bandwidth of modem-based telephone connections. (However, those with faster connections, such as 128 Kbps ISDN, will be able to approach CD-quality stereo sound.)

Most often, Internet radio is used by existing traditional radio stations to stream their over-the-air signals on the Internet with the potential of reaching a new and geographically broader audience, attracting more listeners and increasing revenues. Technology companies may be especially interested in advertising on the new medium. For "local" listeners who move out of an area, Internet radio expands their ability to access news, live sporting events, and even live talk shows where they can call in from across the country or around the world.

In some cases, Internet radio stations exist only on the Internet and often play lesser-known groups with independent labels. For music composers, recording artists, and publishing companies who find it difficult to get "play-time" on over-the-air stations, Internet radio provides a more easily accessible alternative.

The cost of starting up an Internet radio station is far less than the cost for setting up an over-the-air radio station. An Internet station can be started with as little as $10,000, as compared to about $250,000 for even a rural low-power AM station.

At this time, the Federal Communications Commission (FCC) does not regulate Internet radio, and therefore Internet radio stations do not need to go through the costly and time-consuming process of obtaining a license to operate. Anyone with access to a web server and the encoding software could create an Internet radio station and broadcast to a potential international audience.

Sullivan, R. Lee. "Radio Free Internet." *Forbes* (April 22, 1996): 44–45.
Wiener, Leonard. "Tinkering with Radio on the Web." *U.S. News & World Report* (April 1, 1996): 72.
"AudioNet: The Broadcast Network on the Internet." http://www.audionet.com (November 21, 1996).
"Real Audio WWW Site." http://www.realaudio.com/ (November 21, 1996).
Yahoo!: Internet Radio Sites. http://www.yahoo.com/Computers_and_Internet/Internet/Entertainment/Internet/Broadcasting/Radio/Stations/ (November 21, 1996).

Steven D. Anderson

INTERSTATE COMMERCE COMMISSION. In 1887, the United States Congress passed the *Act to Regulate Commerce* in an effort to provide remedy to the abusive practices of the railroads. The act created and established the Interstate Commerce Commission, the first federal regulatory agency. Ten years later, following a series of adverse court decisions, Congress increased the commission's powers to enable it to exercise its authority fully. Subsequently, the commission took a proactive approach to prohibiting the railroads from engaging in price discrimination and other illegal activities. The commission's powers were further expanded through the first two decades of the twentieth century, reaching a peak with the passage of the *Transportation Act of 1920*. This legislation gave the commission the complete and well-rounded control that it had previously lacked and made it possible to have comprehensive regulation, particularly of rates. Because telegraph lines were in large part constructed by the railroads, the commission's authority extended to those lines. Recognizing that telegraph lines were more a mode of communication than transportation, through its passage of the *Communications Act of 1934*, Congress transferred from the Interstate Commerce Commission to the Federal Communications Commission all duties, powers, and functions relating to the operation of telegraph lines. In the early 1980s, deregulation stripped away much of the Interstate Commerce Commission's vast powers. In December 1995, the commission was eliminated, with its powers over trucking, buses, and railroads assigned to the Surface Transportation Board, a semi-independent agency within the Department of Transportation.

Worsham, James. "End of the Line for the ICC." *Nation's Business* 84 (3) (March 1996): 32.

Marianne Barrett

IN THE MATTER OF EDITORIALIZING BY BROADCAST LICENSEES, the foundation of the Fairness Doctrine, is a report issued by the Federal Communications Commission (FCC) on June 1, 1949. Written to restate and clarify the FCC's position on news, commentary, and opinion aired by broadcast licensees, it effectively reversed the FCC's policy discouraging broadcast editorials as stated in its 1941 Mayflower Decision.

Because of the questions and disagreement by broadcasters and the public concerning the FCC's policies and statements on broadcast editorializing and commentaries during the 1940s, the FCC held public hearings in March and April 1948. As a result, according to the FCC, "we have deemed it advisable to set forth in detail and at some length our conclusions as to the basic considerations relevant to the expression of editorial opinion by broadcast licensees and the relationship of any such expression to the general obligations of broadcast licensees with respect to the presentation of programs involving controversial issues." This document, *In the Matter of Editorializing by Broadcast Licensees,* provided the commission with the opportunity to reexamine and reiterate its views.

The report points out that licensees have the responsibility for the selection and broadcast of specific programming and program elements in consonance with the interests and rights of the general public within the communities served. There should be an overall fairness in the presentation of news and opinion. Further, there is a mandate for licensees to provide a reasonable amount of time for the presentation of news and programs devoted to public issues including controversial issues of public importance. Fairness includes allowing expression of contrasting views on public and controversial issues. The licensee has an affirmative duty to "afford a reasonable opportunity for the presentation of all responsible positions on matters of sufficient importance." This includes encouraging and implementing the broadcast of all sides of controversial public issues. The licensee must actively bring about a balanced presentation of the opposing viewpoints. The licensee must decide on the best method for providing fair and balanced presentations of public issues as reflected in the overall programming of the station. Licensee editorialization ("the use of radio facilities by the licensees thereof for the expression of the opinions and ideas of the licensee on the various controversial and significant issues of interest to the members of the general public afforded radio [or television] service by the particular station") is one aspect of freedom of expression. Within the framework of fairness, balance, and reasonable limits, station editorial expression is not contrary to the public interest and is, therefore, not discouraged. "For the licensee is a trustee impressed with the duty of preserving for the public generally radio as a medium of free expression and fair presentation."

In the Matter of Editorializing by Broadcast Licensees. 13 FCC 1246, 1949.
Kahn, Frank J., ed. *Documents of American Broadcasting.* Rev. ed. New York: Appleton-Century-Crofts, 1972.

Steven C. Runyon

INVESTIGATIONS. *See* **congressional investigations.**

J

JACK ARMSTRONG, THE ALL-AMERICAN BOY, a juvenile adventure series in the *Little Orphan Annie* mold, ran on various networks from 1933 to 1951. Jack Armstrong was student and star athlete at Hudson High, where the school fight song (which doubled as the series theme) frequently cheered him on to end-of-the-ninth-inning saves.

But young Jack's real role was as a globe-trotting adventurer with his Uncle Jim and cousins Billy and Betty. From mountain climbing and airplane flying to undersea diving to chasing down evildoers and pirates, Armstrong's adventures ran daily in the late afternoon in 15-minute episodes. In true serial format, each story had a cliff-hanger ending that encouraged listeners to tune in tomorrow. Each script was scrutinized by child psychologist Martin Reymert and was always purposely devoid of excessive violence.

For its entire run, the show was sponsored by Wheaties. The program's ongoing celebration of athletics and basic American values worked well for the "breakfast of champions." In addition, for the right number of Wheaties box tops, youthful listeners could obtain secret decoders or "hike-o-meters." Girls listening could send away for a bracelet "just like Betty's."

The broadcast during its run went through many cast changes including five different Jacks (most notably Jim Ameche). Eventually, in its last years, it dropped Uncle Jim and Betty altogether, and Jack, who had become too old to be considered a "boy," became an adult agent for justice in the retitled series *Armstrong of the SBI*. The series was the creation of former journalist Robert Hardy Andrews and originated from Chicago.

Buxton, Frank, and Bill Owen. *The Big Broadcast 1920–50*. New York: Viking Press, 1972.
Dunning, John. *Tune in Yesterday: The Ultimate Encyclopedia of Old-time Radio 1925–1976*. Englewood Cliffs, N.J.: Prentice-Hall, 1976.
Terrace, Vincent. *Radio's Golden Years: The Encyclopedia of Radio Programs: 1930–1960*. San Diego: A. S. Barnes & Company, Inc., 1981.

Cary O'Dell

JAZZ FORMATS ON RADIO, over the years, have been at best rather uneven. Never as commercially popular as many other musical forms, jazz particularly in the 1920s and 1930s also suffered the onus of being "not quite respectable." Many people perceived jazz as raucous noise, as "race music" (i.e., black music), and as lacking in any serious intent. Thus jazz was frequently ignored or only occasionally featured in station playlists.

With the enormous popularity of swing, Big Band, and dance music in the 1930s, most serious jazz compositions went unnoticed. Although much of swing really grew out of the jazz tradition, its jazz roots usually were conveniently overlooked or ignored during the 1930s and 1940s.

In the meantime, jazz itself was going through significant evolutionary change. Early jazz (e.g., New Orleans, Dixieland, Chicago-style, the blues) became more complex, slowly developing into bop, modern, cool, and other more contemporary formats. Audiences familiar with the older styles frequently resisted any innovations, and many fans of the newer movements likewise rejected tradition. The result was a divided audience, difficult to identify with any precision. Thus radio continued, in the 1940s and 1950s, to exclude jazz from much general airplay. Instead, big bands and pop singers inundated the airwaves, and most of that music at best only tipped its hand to any jazz connections.

Nevertheless, occasional exceptions could be found. For several years in the early 1950s, jazz trumpeter Rex Stewart had his own show in upstate New York. Critic and composer Leonard Feather could also be found on the AM dial. A few disc jockeys would sneak an occasional side into their programming, and given its cultural associations, jazz might be found on some late-night shows.

In the late 1950s and into the 1960s, jazz enjoyed a momentary wave of public popularity. With that came a significant increase of jazz programming on radio. Also, those same years saw the extraordinary growth of FM and the perception that FM stations could play more "serious" (e.g., classical, opera, jazz) music. With the decline of network radio and the rise of narrowcasting, more and more stations, both AM and FM, searched for distinctive identities, with the result that jazz flourished as never before on radio. The rapid rise of small college-run stations during this period provided another receptive base and audience.

In the early 1970s, National Public Radio came to be a home for many jazz-oriented productions. Shows like *Jazz Revisited, Jazz Alive,* and *Piano Jazz with Marian McPartland* became fixtures on the new network. In addition, many locally produced jazz shows appeared, often hosted by afficionados using their own extensive collections of classic tracks.

Nevertheless, on a nationwide basis, jazz continues to occupy less than 1 percent of the total radio music spectrum, and there appears to be little chance of significant change.

William H. Young

JOHNSON, NICHOLAS (1934–), born in Iowa City, was appointed to the Federal Communications Commission (FCC) by President Lyndon Johnson on June 21, 1966, to a seven-year term, essentially replacing William Henry. Prior to his appointment, he was the U.S. Maritime administrator for two years where his zeal for reform agitated the shipping industry. The *New York Times* editorialized in favor of this appointment because of his "vigorous curiosity" (June 20, 1966). This zeal was applied to his term on the FCC. He regularly attacked FCC decisions that were not in the public interest, like the proposed ATT–ITT merger. He left the commission shortly before the end of his seven-year term in 1973 to become the director of the National Citizens Committee for Broadcasting. He ran for the House of Representatives in 1974, representing the Third District. He called for a ban on advertising of large-engine automobiles because of their inefficient energy use. In 1976, he organized 28 consumer and citizens' groups to ask television stations to devote one hour a week to public affairs programs. He wrote and spoke against the Bell-TCI merger in 1993.

He is a prolific author on several topics ranging from communications to oil and gas law. He has authored over 400 opinions in the FCC Reports. Among his other writings include two books, *How to Talk Back to Your Television Set* (1970) and *Test Pattern for Living* (1972). His most current writing is *Electronic Passages* (1995). Johnson has contributed to 51 books, written for many law review journals, delivered many speeches, won several awards, and visited many universities in the 30 years since his appointment. He is currently teaching at the University of Iowa College of Law and active in many public interest groups.

Johnson, Nicholas. *Broadcasting in America: The Performance of Network Affiliates in the Top 50 Markets*. 42 FCC 2nd 1, 1973.
Johnson, Nicholas. http://www.avalon.net/~mvasey/njohnson.html

Wenmouth Williams, Jr.

JOURNAL OF BROADCASTING AND ELECTRONIC MEDIA, a scholarly quarterly of the Broadcast Education Association, appeared in the winter of 1956–1957 as *Journal of Broadcasting*. Named the Association for Professional Broadcasting Education at that time, it is an alliance of universities and professors with the National Association of Broadcasters, broadcasting companies, and broadcasters for purposes of advancing the study of radio, television, and other electronic media of communication. Articles typically offer perspectives of humanities, social sciences, law, and engineering, with quantitative methods being represented more often in later years.

Early articles on radio treat philosophy of programming, Herbert Hoover's contributions to broadcasting, and the development of sound effects from 1921 to 1940. Some recent studies are of political values in top-of-the-hour radio news, audience research in public radio, and the changing conception of localism in public radio.

With annual volume number 29 in 1985 the name of the *Journal* changed to its present form, reflecting the rise of cable television, videocassettes, and computers. The first issue of volume 29 has articles and reviews on radio broadcasting, television broadcasting, videocassettes, interactive computing, communication satellites, filmmaking, mass communication, journalism, cable television, and advertising. Although television broadcasting in the United States remains the central subject, the new title serves wider media interests and somewhat more international interests than the old.

The *Journal,* through publishing reports of notable research and distributing results of studies worldwide, sustains academic recognition of a field of study. Articles are indexed or abstracted in *Arts and Humanities Citation Index; Communication Abstracts; Current Contents; Index to Journals in Education; Current Law Index; Humanities Index; Index to Journals in Communication Studies; Psychological Abstracts; Public Affairs Service Information Bulletin; Social Sciences Citation Index; Social Welfare, Social Planning-Policy and Social Development;* and *Sociological Abstracts.* University Microfilms International publishes the *Journal* in microform.

Harwood, Kenneth. "Competition and Content in Communication Research." *Journal of Broadcasting and Electronic Media* 35 (1) (winter 1991): 95–99.
Kittross, John M. "The *Journal* and Communication Scholarship." *Journal of Broadcasting and Electronic Media* 35 (1) (winter 1991): 101–104.
Sterling, Christopher H. "A Critique of the Changing Role of the *Journal.*" *Journal of Broadcasting and Electronic Media* 35 (1) (winter 1991): 105–107.

Kenneth Harwood

JOURNAL OF RADIO STUDIES (JRS). Founded in 1992 as an independent scholarly publication, the *JRS* represents the first international forum in the history of broadcasting dedicated exclusively to radio research. The journal strives to encourage interdisciplinary inquiries regarding radio's contemporary and historical subject matter. *JRS* was adopted by the Broadcast Education Association in 1997.

A wide range of topics and methodological approaches appear. Areas of study include radio history, personality studies, technology research pertaining to radio's past and future, international radio, rhetorical dimensions of radio, listening patterns, policy and regulation research, news and program content surveys, talk radio, and others demonstrating a great diversity of investigation.

JRS also sponsors symposia focusing on specific subject areas. Symposia have appeared on "Country Music Radio" (Vol. 1., 1992), "The Future of AM Radio" (Vol. 2, 1993–1994), "Radio Programming" (Vol. 3, 1995–1996), and "The Rhetoric of Radio" (Vol. 4, 1997). Each volume features book reviews, updates recent dissertations on radio studies, and provides a cumulative index. *JRS* is a refereed publication that appears on an annual basis. Its editorial review board includes many prominent names in media research. The acceptance rate of published articles is 20 percent.

Since its inception, *JRS*'s editor has been Frank J. Chorba, professor of media studies, Washburn University. Others who participated in the original planning of *JRS* are Martin P. LoMonaco (Nassau Community College), David T. MacFarland (Kansas State University), Steven O. Shields (University of Wisconsin at Whitewater), Robert M. Ogles (Purdue University), and Frank Tavares (Southern Connecticut State University).

Frank J. Chorba

JUKEBOX is a coin-operated phonograph that plays music of a customer's choice. Twelve years after Edison's invention of the "phonograph," 1889, Louis Glass fitted an Edison machine with a coin slot and installed it at the Palais Royale Saloon in San Francisco. That phonograph had four listening tubes. A nickel would buy two minutes of listening. John Gabel offered the first machine with multiple selections in 1906.

Jukeboxes grew into prominence around 1927 when the Automatic Music Instrument (AMI) Company of Grand Rapids invented the first electronically amplified, multiple-selection box. For the first time, large audiences could hear the same music. The actual term *jukebox* came into usage in the 1930s. Historians differ on the origin of the term. Some say it came from the African word *jook,* which means "to dance." Others suggest the term is a derivative of *jute,* referring to the workers in southern jute fields who frequented the roadhouses. *Jute joint* evolved into *juke joint; jutebox* evolved into *jukebox.*

In the 1930s and 1940s, jukeboxes, combined with radio, created widespread public awareness of artists and their songs. You could find a jukebox in most every bar, restaurant, and club. Early radio was a biased medium, and only a few blacks could afford radios, so the jukebox was the only way their music could be heard. Competition among Wurlitzer, Seeburg, and Rock-ola helped spur a tremendous growth in the business during the 1940s and 1950s. Today, only Rock-ola survives, as Wurlitzer left the jukebox business, the *Sherman Antitrust Act* doomed Seeburg, and AMI merged with Rowe (see also **Capehart, Homer E.**).

Hench, Bill, and Vincent Lynch. *The Golden Jukebox Age.* Berkeley: Lancaster-Miller, 1981.
Pearce, Christopher. *Jukebox Art.* London: H. C. Blossom, 1991.
Jukebox. http://www.discjockey.com/jukebox

Max Utsler

K

KALTENBORN, H. V. (1878–1965), pioneer news broadcaster and quintessential news commentator during radio's first 30 years, was born in Milwaukee, Wisconsin, on July 9, 1878. Self-motivated to become a journalist, as a teenager he learned the fundamentals at the hometown Merrill (Wis.) *Advocate.* In the army during the Spanish American War, he sent dispatches to the Milwaukee *Journal.* His journalism career matured at the Brooklyn *Eagle,* and he honed public-speaking skills on lecture tours.

At age 27, he entered Harvard on a special program for journalists. Continuing as a regular student, he ran cross country, helped organize the Dramatic Club, was elected to Phi Beta Kappa, and received a B.A. in political science, cum laude. After an experimental broadcast in 1921, he made the first U.S. radio commentary in a regular series on current events on April 4, 1922. As an *Eagle* editor and sponsored by the newspaper, he spoke on AT&T's WEAF, New York City, with a sense of editorial freedom. Soon, however, WEAF tried stifling his editorialization on controversial issues.

Leaving WEAF, Kaltenborn became the first radio commentator to tour the United States, giving radio talks in various cities. His first network talks were in 1929 on CBS, which hired him in 1930. He refused to avoid controversy. In the 1930s, Alabama's attorney general complained to the Federal Radio Commission when Kaltenborn advocated a fair trail for the Scottsboro boys. In the 1940s, Kaltenborn opposed CBS news director Paul White's objectivity campaign. And at NBC, in spite of his popularity, Kaltenborn was urged to tone down his opinions.

Fluent in English, German, and French, and expert on international politics, he was well-equipped for overseas reporting. During the Spanish Civil War, at age 58, he was the first U.S. radio war correspondent to report live from a battle for CBS. He eventually reported from most European capitals, interviewing major political leaders, including Hitler and Mussolini. He recalled making 120 CBS broadcasts during the 20-day Czechoslovakian crisis that led to the Munich Agreement of 1938, the first international crisis covered by radio.

Kaltenborn's keen insight into political developments was typified by his warning of Japanese aggression weeks before Pearl Harbor. During the war, he got close to events, experiencing bombing in London and interviewing soldiers about their experiences. He went from CBS to NBC in 1940.

He preferred speaking extemporaneously with few notes, relying on his vast knowledge and experience. He skillfully handled the wartime pressure of news flashes coming before and during broadcasts. The indefatigable Kaltenborn covered postwar events in Europe and Asia and reported the San Francisco opening of the United Nations. His worldwide travels included trips to the USSR and China. At 71, he with his wife Olga visited nations across Africa, from Tunisia to South Africa.

Known as the "Dean of Radio Commentators," he won the 1945 DuPont Foundation award and nine more awards in 1946. He ended regular radio commentaries in 1953, although he continued occasional radio and TV commentaries. He died on June 14, 1965.

Fang, Irving E. *Those Radio Commentators!* Ames: Iowa State University Press, 1977.
Kaltenborn, H. V. *Fifty Fabulous Years.* New York: G. P. Putnam's Sons, 1950.

William James Ryan

KASEM, CASEY (born Kemal Amin Kasim; 1932–), a radio personality, the son of Druze Lebanese parents, was raised in Detroit, Michigan. In high school Kasem was part of the Radio Club, working as a sports announcer. He served in Korea with the Armed Forces Network, returning to civilian life in 1954. Kasem then found acting jobs in national radio shows like *The Lone Ranger* and *Sergeant Preston of the Yukon.* Next he became a disc jockey, serving many different cities and stations. In 1963, while based in Los Angeles, Kasem first added some acting in television to his experiences and followed that with occasional film parts. Starting in 1968, he did frequent commercial and cartoon voice-overs.

From these varied endeavors, Kasem was determined to create a new and different kind of disc jockey show. In 1970, *American Top 40* made its radio debut and proved remarkably popular. What Kasem originated was a formula he called the "teaser-bio format." Instead of simply playing songs, he added a running commentary on the artists that was a mix of trivia and solid information. For instance, he would pose questions like: "How many times does 'love' form part of a title?" "Name the three Number One hits the Beatles had in 1968." He typically used 12 to 15 of these teasers in the space of his four-hour show. He also employed a "countdown" approach to the music (playing the songs in reverse order—40 first and 1, the top song of the week, being played last after generating suitable suspense) that was reminiscent of the old *Your Hit Parade* from the 1930s and 1940s.

The popularity of *American Top 40* led to a host of imitators, but none has ever duplicated Kasem's success. In 1989, *American Top 40* was replaced by *Casey's Top 40,* a virtually identical show. In the mid-1990s, *Casey's Top 40* was heard on more than 1,000 stations worldwide, which meant that it played to an average weekly audience of some 10 million listeners.

Because of his growing celebrity status ("the most listened-to voice in America"), the 1970s and 1980s saw more acting. Kasem frequently appeared as himself on various shows and began to serve as host for charity and award functions. Beginning in the 1980s, Kasem's productions have included at one time or another *Casey's Top 40, with Casey Kasem* (his flagship show), *Casey's Countdown, Casey's Hot Adult Contemporary, Casey's Adult Contemporary, Casey's Hot 20,* and *Casey Kasem's Biggest Hits.* Carried by the Westwood One Radio Network, his diverse efforts are syndicated to some 450 stations. Despite his close identification with his various shows, Kasem's role in them is actually somewhat limited. He seldom listens to the music he talks about; instead, he simply records the intros and outros to all his patter. In addition, he does not research or write his scripts, although he does rehearse and edit. Listeners assume a deeper connection with his material than is the case because he sounds so sincere and authoritative.

Popularity has allowed Kasem, outside his shows, to become something of a spokesperson for various causes. He has been involved in antinuclear movements, vegetarianism, and antismoking campaigns. He is best known for his efforts protesting discrimination, especially Arab stereotyping, and has served on the board of directors for FAIR (Fairness and Accuracy in Reporting). Despite his involvement in many crusades, his shows remain studiously neutral. Kasem will not proselytize over the air, saying he would lose his credibility.

His success and longevity have brought tangible rewards. The youngest member ever inducted into the Radio Hall of Fame, he also has his star on Hollywood Boulevard's Walk of Fame. His last contract called for $20 million over five years, which certainly makes this disc jockey one of the highest paid radio personalities of any era.

William H. Young

KDKA radio in Pittsburgh, Pennsylvania, began operation in 1920 as the first regular broadcast station in the United States. The station is still owned by the Westinghouse Corporation through its Group W broadcasting/cable subsidiary.

KDKA radio began as experimental radio station 8XK in the Wilkinsburg, Pennsylvania, garage of Dr. Frank Conrad, an electrical engineer employed by the Westinghouse Corporation's East Pittsburgh plant. Conrad's experimental station was established as a point-to-point operation to test radio equipment manufactured by Westinghouse for U.S. military use in World War I. In 1919, the U.S. government canceled Westinghouse's remaining military contracts, and the corporation was facing idle factories. Conrad was among the first to put his 8XK back on the air as an amateur radio-telephone station and in contact with ham (amateur) radio operators. Conrad's main concerns were with the quality of his signal and the distance it would travel. He would read from newspapers and then await reports from listening posts commenting on the quality of the reception.

The people who were operating the listening posts soon tired of hearing news they had already seen in the newspapers, and they grew weary of hearing Conrad's voice. One of them suggested that Conrad play a phonograph record. Conrad did so, and soon the Westinghouse headquarters received a flood of mail requesting newer music and specific song titles. Frank Conrad had become the world's first disc jockey.

The news of Conrad's airborne music reached a department manager of Pittsburgh's Joseph Horne Department Store, and he realized that people who wanted to listen to Conrad might want to purchase assembled radios. An ad was placed in the September 29, 1920, issue of the Pittsburgh *SUN* featuring wireless sets for $10.

That ad was seen by Conrad and H. P. Davis, a Westinghouse vice president, and both men realized that a vast potential market existed for home wireless sets (like the home music box idea proposed to American Marconi by David Sarnoff in 1916) and that Westinghouse already had the ideal product: the SCR-70, a radio receiver made for the U.S. military in the recently concluded world war.

The decision was made to move the station to the roof of the stronger transmitter and redesign the station for public entertainment. All was to be ready by November of 1920, a presidential election year. On November 2 the Harding-Cox election results were broadcast by KDKA, the newly assigned call letters, and the commercial license from the Department of Commerce arrived just in time. The success of KDKA was assured, and soon many newspapers across the country were publishing the station's program schedule (usually one hour of music and talk in the evening).

Since that historic broadcast, other stations have tried to claim the title of being first on the air. WWJ in Detroit, KCBS in San Francisco, and WHA Madison, Wisconsin, have contended for the prize of being first. KDKA's limited commercial license was dated October 27, 1920, and arrived just before the Harding-Cox election.

According to Baudino and Kittross, KDKA is the oldest U.S. station still in operation as illustrated by the following: (1) KDKA used radio waves (2) to send out noncoded signals (3) in a continuous, scheduled program service (4) intended for the general public and (5) was licensed by the government to provide such a service.

As the broadcasting industry grew, so did KDKA and Westinghouse. Westinghouse began to open and operate other stations such as WBZ Springfield, Massachusetts (later moved to Boston), WJZ Newark, KYW Chicago (later moved to Philadelphia), and repeater stations for KDKA in Hastings, Nebraska, and Cleveland, Ohio. KDKA radio carried local and NBC network programming (after NBC's formation in 1926) and became the keystone in Westinghouse's Group W broadcasting operations.

In the early 1950s, KDKA expanded into television with the acquisition of Pittsburgh's Dumont affiliate WDAM-TV. The call letters were changed to KDKA-TV. Currently, KDKA radio and television and Group W are important entities in American broadcasting.

Baudino, Joseph E., and John M. Kittross. "Broadcasting's Oldest Stations: An Examination of Four Claimants." *Journal of Broadcasting* 21 (1) (winter 1977): 61–83.
Mitchell, Curtis. *Cavalcade of Broadcasting.* Chicago: Follett Publishing Company, 1970.

Regis Tucci

KEILLOR, GARRISON (1942–), is an author and public radio personality who hosts the popular variety show *A Prairie Home Companion,* broadcast live nationwide on Saturday evenings. Born in Anoka, Minnesota, in 1942, Garrison Keillor began his radio career as a freshman at the University of Minnesota. While working for Minnesota Public Radio (MPR), he hosted a morning music program called *A Prairie Home Companion,* named after the Prairie Home cemetery in Moorhead, Minnesota. After visiting Nashville to write a magazine story about the Grand Ole Opry, Keillor got the idea for a live-radio variety show, which debuted on MPR in 1974 under the name *A Prairie Home Companion.* It featured an eclectic mix of music, comedy sketches, and Keillor's signature monologue "The News from Lake Wobegon," a fictional Minnesota community "where the women are strong, the men are good looking, and all of the children are above average." Though live-variety programs had virtually disappeared from the radio airwaves, *A Prairie Home Companion* caught on in Minnesota, and MPR sought to syndicate the program nationwide. After National Public Radio declined to distribute the program nationwide, believing its appeal was regional, Minnesota Public Radio chose to distribute the program itself to the public radio system via satellite in 1980.

Today, *A Prairie Home Companion* is broadcast by more than 350 public radio stations each Saturday night to an estimated 2 million listeners; many stations also rebroadcast the program on Sundays. Keillor also hosts a daily five-minute program, *The Writer's Almanac,* writes for several magazines, and has authored eight books of fiction.

Keillor, Garrison. *WLT: A Radio Romance.* New York: Penguin Books, 1991.
Scholl, Peter. *Garrison Keillor.* New York: Macmillan, 1993.
"Thoughts from Lake Wobegon on the Superhighway." *Broadcasting & Cable* (January 10, 1994): 56–58.

Alan G. Stavitsky

KENNELLY-HEAVISIDE LAYER is a portion of the ionosphere that reflects clear-channel AM signals back to earth at night. The reflective nature of this layer is thought to be related to lack of sunlight, which alters electromagnetic and temperature characteristics of the ionosphere.

Charles F. Aust

KING, LARRY (born Lawrence Harvey Zeiger; 1933–), became America's premier radio-talk show in the 1980s. His Mutual Radio program *The Larry King Show* pioneered the late-night radio genre. Although King would attain his widest fame as the host of a televised version of his Mutual Radio show, the greatest part of his career was based in the radio medium.

A native of New York, King was the son of Jewish immigrants who ran a bar and grill in Brooklyn. Having never attended college, but with a fascination for radio and television, King left New York and joined Miami radio station WAHR in 1957 and would move to competitor WIOD in 1961, where he remained for 10 years. Following an arrest on embezzlement charges, which later were dropped, King was fired by WIOD in 1971, to rejoin the station in 1975. In 1978, he left WIOD and joined Mutual Radio in Washington. *The Larry King Show,* which broadcast nationally from midnight until the early morning hours, began that year on January 30.

Heard in nearly every U.S. radio market by 1981, it rapidly became the most popular talk program on that medium. In 1983, the cable network C-SPAN began occasionally televising King's radio broadcast by merely placing cameras in Mutual's radio studios. These C-SPAN originations, while infrequent, were exceedingly popular. In 1985, King was hired by Cable News Network (CNN) for a regularly televised nightly interview program. What became known as *Larry King Live* became CNN's highest-rated program and was acclaimed for the spectrum of guests it featured. The pinnacle in King's career was a broadcast in 1992, in which billionaire Ross Perot announced what became a bellwether presidential campaign. Because of the public's positive reaction to this Perot broadcast, leading politicians would flock to be on King's CNN program. It was on this program in 1993 that Perot and Vice President Al Gore conducted a national debate on the North American Free Trade Agreement.

King was best known for his interviewing style. With easy going and innocuous lines of questions, King was able to draw revealing insights from many of the world's most famous people. King won two major accolades for his radio show, a Peabody Award in 1982 and a National Association of Broadcasters National Radio Award in 1986. His CNN television program won an ACE Award in 1987.

After helping to set a large part of the nation's political agenda in the early 1990s, the later half of the decade saw King in some decline. He abandoned his late-night Mutual Radio broadcast in 1993 and concentrated on television. Then in 1995, King's CNN broadcast each night was devoted to a single subject, such as the murder trial of former football star O. J. Simpson. Many felt that because of this single-subject coverage, King was overshadowed by the trial and had lost an edge he once had.

King, Larry. *Larry King.* New York: Simon and Schuster, 1982.
Occhiogrosso, Peter. *Tell It to the King.* New York: Putnam, 1988.

Craig M. Allen

KQW, a San Jose radio station, was the final attempt by broadcast pioneer Charles David Herrold (1875–1948) to own and operate a radio station. KQW first went on the air in December 1921, and while it wasn't the first licensed station, it evolved out of one of the earliest efforts to broadcast on a regular schedule. As the owner of a trade school, the Herrold College of Wireless and Engineering, and a Stanford-educated experimenter, Herrold spent the decade prior to the licensing of KQW training students and constructing a wireless radiotelephone.

In a notarized statement in the 1910 *Electro Importing* catalog, Herrold is quoted: "We have been giving wireless phonograph concerts to amateur men in the Santa Clara Valley." This early reference to broadcasting for an audience was reinforced in 1912 by a San Jose *Mercury Herald* newspaper story about a broadcast by Herrold's student Emil Portal: "For more than two hours they conducted a concert in Mr. Herrold's office in the Garden City Bank building, which was heard for many miles around. The music was played on a phonograph. Immediately after the first record was played numerous amateurs from various points in the valley notified Mr. Portal that they had heard the music distinctly. Mr. Portal gave the names of the records he had on hand and asked those listening to signify their choice. One asked for 'My Old Kentucky Home,' which was furnished." Between 1912 and 1917, Herrold and his students continued to send out similar programs of music and talk on a regular basis. The students built crystal receivers for friends and family, which helped to create their listening audience.

The April 1917 wartime ban on wireless activity ended the Herrold broadcasts. When the war ended, the preferred technology of the wireless transmitter had changed from an arc to the vacuum-tube oscillator developed by Lee de Forest and perfected by Frank Conrad and others in wartime experiments. And while Conrad was ready with a tube-based transmitter and received a license as KDKA in late 1920, Herrold's arc would not operate on the government-assigned frequency of 360 meters. By 1920, Herrold had abandoned his wireless school and opened a radio parts store and, by late 1921, had constructed a tube transmitter and received his license for KQW.

His income dwindling, Herrold in 1924 transferred KQW to the First Baptist Church with the proviso that they would retain him as chief engineer. After one year, he was removed. A local headline read: "Father of Broadcasting fired!" Herrold was finished as a station owner, but he spent the next 10 years freelancing at Bay Area radio stations, trying in vain to convince an uninterested public that he was the "Father of Radio Broadcasting." In 1927, KQW's license passed from the Baptist Church to the Farm Bureau, and in 1949, it was purchased by the Columbia Broadcasting System, moved to San Francisco, and renamed KCBS, now a 50,000-watt all-news station.

Adams, Mike. "The Race for Radiotelephone." *AWA Review* 10 (1996): 79–149.

Greb, Gordon. "The Golden Anniversary of Broadcasting" *Journal of Broadcasting* 3 (1) (winter 1958–1959): 3–13.

KQW. http://www.kteh.org/prod/docs/docherrold.html for Adams, Michael. *Broadcasting's Forgotten Father: The Charles Herrold Story.* San Jose: Perham Foundation, 1994. 60 min. VHS videotape.

Mike Adams

L

LATIN MUSIC FORMATS, defined by *Broadcasting & Cable Yearbook* as Spanish musical programming broadcast more than 20 hours on a weekly basis that tends to be tailored to the area's particular audience. In California and Texas, for example, listeners can expect to hear rancheras and nortenas. In New York and Miami, salsa dominates because the majority of listeners are from Cuba, the Dominican Republic, and Puerto Rico. However, as a greater array of Spanish-speaking people arrive in the United States, they bring with them a greater variety of musical styles popular in their own countries. Latin jazz, rock, merengue, pop, vallenata, cumbia, and bachata are all represented on the 447 Spanish-language stations across the United States. AM stations outnumber FM at 302 to 145, with 413 designated as commercial enterprises. Tejano is a designated format in itself and represents 4 AM and 17 FM stations, all of the commercial variety. This bicultural programming is popular in Texas and near the Mexican border. This type of music surged during the early 1990s but continues to gain listeners and attention, especially after the highly publicized death of recording star Selena. Latin music is reaching beyond the bounds of radio itself into the realm of the Internet, where several sites offer reviews, real-audio segments, and city-by-city/station-by-station rundowns of the music offered.

Latin Music Formats. http://www.lamusica.com; http://www.hurucaan.com

Fran R. Matera

LAUCK, CHESTER (1902–1980), was born on February 9, 1902, in Alleene, Arkansas, and later settled in Mena, Arkansas. With his partner, Norris Goff (1906–1978), they starred in the *Lum 'n' Abner* show on radio. Both played the proprietors of the "Jot 'Em Down Store" in Piney Ridge, Arkansas. Lauck was Lum Edwards, and Goff played Abner Peabody. They also starred together in six movies from 1940 to 1946. Although the radio show ended in 1952 due to Goff's illness, they went on to do one more movie together in 1956.

Lauck later worked for the Conoco Oil Company doing public relations until his retirement in the late 1960s. He died on February 21, 1980, and was buried in

Hot Springs, Arkansas. Although Lauck's papers were left with the University of Arkansas at Little Rock, additional papers are collected at the National Lum and Abner Society (81 Sharon Boulevard, Dora, Alabama, 35062; [205] 648-6110).

New York Times Biographical Service. *A Compilation of Current Biographical Information of General Interest* 11 (2) (February 1980, Chester Lauck). New York: Arno Press.

Stewart, V. A., ed. *"Lum & Abner* Episode Guide." http://www.old-time.com/logs.cgi (1995).

David Spiceland

LET'S PRETEND is considered to be one of "radio's outstanding children's theatre programs." It delighted young children for more than 23 years, with tales that involved princes and princesses, witches and goblins, and leprechauns and talking animals.

Let's Pretend began at CBS in 1939 and was already going strong when CBS hired young Nila Mack as writer and later director. She wrote the stories, adapting them from traditional children's favorites such as *Arabian Nights* and the works of Hans Christian Anderson, the Brothers Grimm, and Andrew Lang. Under her direction, *Let's Pretend* won almost 50 national awards. Nila Mack passed away on January 20, 1953, and her responsibilities on *Let's Pretend* passed to Johanna Johnston. The last show was heard on October 23, 1954.

Dunning, John. *Tune in Yesterday: The Ultimate Encyclopedia of Radio Programs: 1930–1970.* Englewood Cliffs, N.J.: Prentice-Hall, 1976.

ElDean Bennett

LEWIS, FULTON, JR. (1903–1966), was a conservative commentator on the Mutual Broadcasting System (MBS) for over 30 years. He was opposed to President Franklin Roosevelt's New Deal, America's entry into World War II, and President Harry Truman's Fair Deal. He was a supporter of Senator Joseph McCarthy and his attacks on communism.

Lewis was born in Washington, D.C. to a prosperous family with distinguished ancestors on both sides. His early ambition was to be a composer, and he wrote the music for the fight song at the University of Virginia while he was a student there.

He left school in 1924 without graduating to become the fishing columnist for the *Washington Herald.* He became city editor there and left in 1928 to become assistant bureau manager of Hearst's Universal News Service, which later merged with the International News Service (INS). He became chief of the Washington bureau for the wire service and from 1933 to 1936 wrote a syndicated column, *The Washington Sideshow,* which specialized in insider gossip about the political scene but also included some significant investigative reporting. Lewis was persistent in his efforts to reveal government irregularities in granting airmail contracts and evidence about a naval lieutenant later found guilty of espionage.

In 1937, he decided to try radio and became a substitute newscaster on MBS's affiliate WOL. Within a few months, his commentary was carried on the Mutual lineup of stations. He led a successful fight to get radio journalists the same access as print journalists in the press gallery of the Senate and the House and in White House press conferences. Perhaps the most controversial aspect of his career was his invitation to Charles Lindbergh to address the United States after World War II broke out in Europe in 1939. Both men were isolationists. In 1941, he did a series of programs sponsored by the National Association of Manufacturers that described the defense efforts of big business. Critics saw the shows as boring propaganda.

During the war, Lewis was not one of the most popular commentators and depended on local sponsors rather than national ones, a decision that he believed gave him more freedom to express his opinions. After the war, Lewis aligned himself with Senator McCarthy. When McCarthy was criticized by Edward R. Murrow on his TV program *See It Now,* the senator turned to Lewis's program to defend himself.

Lewis attacked those whom he opposed with a vigorous barrage of adjectives. His best-known description was: "piddle-paddle, double-talking, CIO-Communist-backed, left-wing crackpots." His fervent criticism of former New Dealers brought howls of protest from liberals, who called him "The Voice with the Snarl." An investigation of his accusation that Secretary of Commerce Harry Hopkins had given away A-bomb secrets to Russia was dropped because of a lack of credible evidence.

In the 1950s, he tried television, but his style of reporting was not suitable for a visual medium. By 1960, his pro-McCarthy stance was no longer popular, and MBS quit carrying his commentary. He was married to Alice Huston, and they had two children, Alice Elizabeth and Fulton Lewis III. He died of complications after surgery for pancreatitis, which had been caused by two heart attacks.

Culbert, David Holbrook. *News for Everyman: Radio and Foreign Affairs in Thirties America.* Westport, Conn.: Greenwood, 1976.
Fang. Irving E. *Those Radio Commentators!* Ames: Iowa State University Press, 1977.

Barbara Moore

LIBEL AND SLANDER. Defamation is classified into libel (written defamation) and slander (oral defamation). The traditional distinction between libel and slander is not as clear-cut as it was, as new modes of communication have developed in the twentieth century. Broadcast defamation is, more often than not, treated as libel. Nearly all libel cases in the United States are civil actions, in which plaintiffs claim monetary damages for their reputational harm from the defendants' publication of defamatory statements about the plaintiffs. While libel is still recognized as a crime in some jurisdictions, criminal libel is rarely a major issue to the news media.

To claim damages for defamation, a plaintiff must establish the following elements at minimum: (1) A false and defamatory statement of fact concerning the plaintiff was published to a third party; (2) the publication was unprivileged and made with the requisite degree of fault amounting at least to negligence on the part of the publisher; and (3) actual injury was caused to the plaintiff by the publication.

Identifying defamatory language is the first order of business in libel law. In considering whether a word is libelous or not, therefore, one cannot say with assurance that a word is or is not prohibited by law unless and until the word has been placed in time, in location, and in association so that its meaning can be determined. In other words, context is the key.

An important element of a cause of action for libel requires that the defamatory allegation should be a statement of *fact*. False statements of fact can be defamatory and thus actionable. On the other hand, statements of opinion cannot be actionable so long as they are properly based on verifiable facts.

In order to claim damages in defamation cases, a plaintiff must prove that the allegedly defamatory statement was "of and concerning" him or her. While a defamatory statement must be about the plaintiff, it does not necessarily mean that the plaintiff be mentioned by name. It meets the burden of proof if the plaintiff can be identified by other information in the statement or by the existence of extrinsic facts not included in the article.

Group defamation has raised a host of thorny problems in the identification of plaintiffs. As a general rule, courts have refused to allow any member of a large group to sue for defamation that refers to an entire group. Vicarious defamation is not allowed in libel law. That is, a news story that relates an individual to a criminal cannot constitute a cause of action.

In defamation law, *publication* is a term of art. It has little to do with the dictionary definition of publishing or printing to mass media. Publication occurs when defamatory communication is conveyed to someone other than the person defamed and the originator. With libel actions, the time limitation varies from state to state. The time period for defamation actions typically ranges from one to three years. Nearly half (25) of the 51 jurisdictions including the District of Columbia have one-year limitation periods. In considering libel actions against media organizations, the issue of whether defamatory statements are privileged is often crucial. Especially where the statements are covered by the "fair report privilege," they cannot be actionable.

U.S. libel law is often characterized by the First Amendment principle that requires that speech be overprotected rather than underprotected. The "actual malice" rule established in *The New York Times Co. v. Sullivan* (376 U.S. 254, 1964) is a case in point. Under the actual malice rule, a public official is prohibited from recovering damages for a defamatory falsehood relating to his official conduct unless he proves the knowledge of falsity or the reckless disregard for the truth on the part of the defendant (376 U.S. at 279–280).

As a result of the *Sullivan* rule, public officials are now required to establish actual malice on the part of the defendant in publishing the defamatory statement in question, in addition to proving the common law elements for liability for defamation. "Actual malice" does not mean hatred, ill-will or enmity or a wanton desire to injure in its common law sense.

In 1967 the *Sullivan* rule was expanded to include "public figures," not holding government office. The actual malice doctrine was extended in 1971 to apply to any defamatory story involving matters of "public or general interest." In 1974, however, the U.S. Supreme Court in *Gertz v. Robert Welch, Inc.* (418 U.S. 323, 1974) held that the actual malice rule does not apply to libel actions involving private persons. The *Gertz* Court held that "so long as they do not impose liability without fault, the states may define for themselves the appropriate standard of liability for a publisher or broadcaster of a defamatory falsehood injurious to a private individual" (418 U.S. at 347).

The Court also said that the states may not permit recovery of presumed or punitive damages against publishers or broadcasters at least when liability is not based on a showing of actual malice. Those who cannot prove actual malice may be compensated only for actual injury. The *Gertz* requirement that actual malice should be proved to support an award of presumed or punitive damages does not apply to speech on matters "of purely private concern."

In a libel action, four types of compensatory damages are recognized. Nominal damages are awarded to plaintiffs who have not suffered from provable injury to their reputations. Second, general damages include recovery for presumed injury and actual injury. Third, special damages are damages designed to compensate for actual loss of pecuniary value as a result of defamation. And finally, punitive or exemplary damages are used to punish the defendant for outrageous and willful defamation. They aim at deterring the defendant and others from repeating the defamation in the future. Actual malice must be proved for plaintiffs to recover punitive damage for publication of defamatory statements on matters of public interest.

Ashley, Paul. *Say It Safely.* Seattle: University of Washington Press, 1972.
Sack, Robert D., and Sandra S. Baron. *Libel, Slander, and Related Problems.* 2nd ed. New York: Practising Law Institute, 1994.
Sanford, Bruce W. *Libel and Privacy.* 2nd ed. Englewood Cliffs, N.J.: Prentice-Hall Law & Business, 1996.
Smolla, Rodney A. *Law of Defamation.* New York: Clark Boardman Callaghan, 1996.

Kyu Ho Youm

LIBERTY BROADCASTING SYSTEM (LBS) was the brainchild of Gordon McLendon, who later would gain fame for his innovative radio program formats. Liberty's operations spanned a period from 1948 through 1952. Prior to its demise, LBS counted 458 radio stations among its affiliates, making the network the second largest in America. Liberty's major attraction was its schedule of college and professional sports programs.

Liberty's birth came shortly after McLendon's KLIF began broadcasting in Dallas, Texas, in 1947. In order to compete with established stations, McLendon decided to provide listeners with coverage of major league baseball games, something that persons who lived outside the Northeast and Midwest were unaccustomed to hearing on a daily basis. KLIF's *Game-of-the-Day* was broadcast not from the ballpark but rather from the station's studio where Gordon McLendon recreated the game while following its progress via Western Union tickertape.

Radio station owners in Texas, then in surrounding states, then nationwide, asked to carry McLendon's KLIF baseball game recreations. The resulting network was formalized in 1948 as the Liberty Broadcasting System. McLendon's efforts to move from game recreations to live broadcasts from the ballparks met with an initial rebuff from major league baseball officials, who claimed territorial exclusivity for radio networks organized by individual ball clubs. Coverage rights finally were granted when McLendon threatened to sue the officials.

The Liberty Broadcasting System was built around sports, but the program schedule soon took on a more traditional network sound. Programs like *Liberty Minstrels,* a popular musical variety show, and *Musical Bingo* were joined by soap operas performed by Liberty's own repertory company. These programs, along with baseball and football game broadcasts, accounted for a program schedule that ran for nearly 16 hours per day by the end of 1950.

Money needed to keep Liberty in operation never had been in great supply. So when additional income was required to help finance the network's expanded program service, Gordon McLendon had little choice but to raise advertising rates. A financial crisis followed when several national advertisers responded to Liberty's rate increase by moving to other networks.

Financial woes, however, took a backseat to the blow struck by baseball officials who, claiming that the popularity of LBS broadcasts was lowering attendance at minor league ballparks, once more denied Liberty coverage rights to major league baseball games for the 1952 season. McLendon immediately filed a $12 million antitrust suit against major league baseball officials, but the loss of Liberty's most popular programming left McLendon with little choice but to declare LBS bankrupt.

The Liberty Broadcasting System's final day of broadcasting fell on May 15, 1952. Gordon McLendon used part of that time to inform network listeners that the decision to suspend Liberty's service resulted from a "conspiracy" perpetrated by the "monopolists" of major league baseball. Liberty was not legally laid to rest until February 1955 when McLendon agreed to drop his $12 million suit in exchange for a $200,000 out-of-court settlement offered by major league baseball officials.

Garay, Ronald. *Gordon McLendon: The Maverick of Radio.* New York: Greenwood, 1992.
Glick, Edwin L. "The Life and Death of the Liberty Broadcasting System." *Journal of Broadcasting* 23 (2) (spring 1979): 117–135.
Harper, Jim. "Gordon McLendon: Pioneer Baseball Broadcaster." *Baseball History* (spring 1986): 42–51.

Ronald Garay

LICENSES/LICENSING MUSIC. A license confers the right to use musical compositions as part of a performance, broadcast, recording, film or video, or other presentation. The appropriate music license is issued by an organization or agency that controls these rights. The agency acts on behalf of the author or copyright holder. Fees charged for the use of musical compositions are distributed back to the author or copyright holder in the form of royalties.

Licenses, Performance Rights. Writers and publishers affiliate with performing rights societies such as the American Society of Composers Authors and Publishers (ASCAP), Broadcast Music Incorporated (BMI), and the Society of European Stage Authors and Composers (SESAC). These organizations issue music licenses to radio and television stations, broadcast and cable networks, as well as any venue utilizing music on its premises including restaurants, taverns, arenas, and hotels. Fees for performing rights licenses are usually collected as part of a blanket-license arrangement. The blanket license allows the licensee to perform any song in the catalog of the performing rights society for the duration of the license. Cable television distant-signal transmissions are not covered under the blanket license. These cable transmissions are covered under the compulsory license of the *Copyright Act of 1976*. Under this provision, cable systems pay fees to the Copyright Office, which distributes royalties to copyright claimants. An alternative, popular for television and radio, is the per-program license that allows a licensee unlimited use of the catalog only in programs that actually use music. Broadcast stations pay the performing rights societies a fee based on the station's gross income. Networks pay a negotiated flat fee for a music license. Fees charged to other users vary widely and are usually based on factors such as income, seating capacity, and the amount of music used.

In determining how royalties are disbursed to writers and publishers, performing rights societies use two primary methods. They may conduct a census, which involves reviewing lists of all music performed on the television networks. They sample other broadcast licensees by reviewing cue sheets, tapes, and program listings. Some may request written documentation from stations, periodically verifying music used on the air. Television and radio performances serve as the basis for distributing royalties to writers and publishers, since it is not economically feasible to survey all other venues.

Licenses, Mechanical and Synchronization Rights. Mechanical rights licenses allow the reproduction of a copyrighted work in records, tapes, CDs, and other forms of electronic reproduction for distribution to the public. The right of reproduction for the purpose of synchronizing music with video and film is called a synchronization right license.

Publishers most often use the Harry Fox Agency to issue mechanical licenses to manufacturers of recordings. Mechanical rights are negotiated with the licensing agency, and royalties are collected and distributed to the publisher. Usually the licensing organization will receive a small commission on royalties collected. Upon receiving the royalty payment, the publisher shares the income with the songwriter.

The Harry Fox Agency also issues synchronization licenses to producers of films and video recordings. The cost of obtaining a synchronization license may vary greatly but is usually determined by how the music will be featured in the film or video and the current market value of the music.

Baskerville, David. *Music Business Handbook & Career Guide.* 6th ed. Thousand Oaks, Calif.: Sage, 1996.
Fink, Michael. *Inside the Music Industry.* 2nd ed. New York: Schirmer Books, 1996.
Sheml, Sidney, and M. William Krasilovsky. *This Business of Music.* 2nd ed. New York: Billboard Books, 1990.

Kenneth C. Creech

LICENSES/LICENSING STATIONS is the process of authorizing the operation of a broadcast station for a fixed length of time on a particular, prescribed frequency. The Federal Communications Commission (FCC) must grant a license to every radio and television station operating in the United States. Under the *Telecommunications Act of 1996,* radio and television stations are licensed for a period of up to eight years, at which point they may be renewed. Although renewal is not quite automatic, there is a certain renewal expectation by licensees, provided they have not seriously violated FCC rules.

Licenses are obtained in several ways. Applicants can apply for a new license for a station that has never before been licensed. Applicants for a new AM station must show that it will not cause interference to existing transmissions. Applicants for FM or TV stations must either find an assigned channel in the Table of Allotments or petition for a change to the table, if the channel they seek is not available. New station license applications can take as long as 5 to 10 years.

More often, licenses are obtained by transfer. This is when the current license holder decides to sell the station. Providing that the buyer meets all the legal requirements for licensees, the FCC will authorize the license transfer. On rare occasion, licenses are obtained by challenging the existing license holder. At license renewal time, a challenger may claim that the licensee has not cperated in the public interest and that the challenger would be a better public trustee. This action happens rarely for two reasons: The legal costs associated with such a challenge can be astronomical, and the challenger is unlikely to be successful unless the incumbent broadcaster has been extraordinarily irresponsible.

For 50 years, the FCC licensed broadcast stations for only three years, and the renewal process was almost as complicated as the original license application itself. As part of the deregulation process, in 1983 the license periods were extended to five years for television and seven years for radio. In 1991, the process was further simplified by reducing the amount of paperwork required in filing a license renewal to a form the size of a large postcard.

The FCC charges two types of fees associated with licenses: application processing fees and regulatory fees. Since passage of the *Omnibus Budget Recon-ciliation Act of 1989,* all commercial broadcasters pay processing fees when they apply for licenses, ranging from $3,080 for a new television station license to $125 for a station renewal (radio or television). If a hearing must be conducted because a license is challenged, the cost is $8,215 in addition to all other fees (1996 figures). The fees are directly related to the FCC's costs associated with processing each application.

With the passage of the *1993 Omnibus Budget Reconciliation Act,* the FCC was authorized to charge commercial broadcasters an annual fee to recover the costs of enforcement, policy and rule making, user information, and international activities. These fees range from $280 per year for the smallest AM stations to $32,000 annually for VHF television stations in the nation's largest markets.

Broadcast station licenses can only be held by U.S. citizens who have not been convicted of a felony nor previously misrepresented themselves before the commission. Applicants must demonstrate that they have the financial and technical expertise to operate a broadcast station. This does not necessarily mean that the individual must be an engineer but must have access to the services of a competent engineer. Licensees must also adhere to the commission's requirements for equal employment opportunities (EEOs).

In applying for a new license, an applicant must first obtain a Construction Permit (CP). This authorizes the applicant to construct and test the transmission equipment. As with renewals, the applicant must provide public notice and afford people an opportunity to comment on the application. Theoretically, an applicant could be granted a CP and subsequently have his/her license denied, but that rarely happens. Once a CP is granted, a licensee has up to two years to construct a TV station or 18 months to construct a radio station. Extensions can be granted if requested.

Prior to deregulation, the FCC was concerned about the "trafficking" of station licenses. Their fear was that competent candidates would apply for licenses with the sole intent of selling them to others who would not be as likely to succeed. Antitrafficking rules existed that prohibited an owner from transferring a license within the first three years (s)he held it unless the station was in a financial emergency. With deregulation, the FCC no longer has such a requirement, although it still must approve of the transfer of a license.

In 1965, the FCC issued a policy statement on comparative broadcast hearings. The statement provides a list of items that the FCC will consider when choosing between competing applicants for a license. In order to achieve the goals of maximum diffusion of control of mass media and provide the best possible public service, the FCC established preferences for applicants who provided: diversification of media ownership; full-time participation by station owners; commitment to local community programming; favorable past broadcasting records; efficient use of frequency, and acceptable character. In 1992, the FCC reexamined and refined the policy, assigning specific points for various preferences and enunciating "other factors" such as service continuity, minority and female ownership, and a "finder's preference" for applicants who take the initiative to request the allotment of new frequencies. All these preferences are still used by the FCC except participation by owners in station management. A 1993 U.S. Court of Appeals decision found that preference to be arbitrary.

A problem that surfaced in the 1980s was the challenge of license applications or renewals for the purposes of "greenmail." Because the costs associated with a license challenge can be so high (including legal fees) and the application can be delayed months, applicants for a license would often pay off challengers to get them to drop out of the competition. As a result, some entrepreneurs began challenging licenses specifically to be bought off. To address the problem, the FCC adopted rules in 1989 that limit the payment a competing applicant can pay to a challenger. No payments may be made to a challenger if the challenger withdraws before the initial decision in a comparative hearing. After the comparative hearing, a competing applicant can only pay "legitimate and prudent expenses" to a challenger who withdraws.

Dom Caristi

LIMBAUGH, RUSH HUDSON, III (1951–), is the host of the most popular syndicated call-in talk-radio program in the United States. In 1988, Limbaugh was hosting a call-in radio talk show in Sacramento, California. Ed McLaughlin was searching for someone to host an afternoon political talk show to be syndicated to AM radio stations nationwide. McLaughlin's vision of supplying programming to stations desperate for quality programming during the day combined with Limbaugh's talent as an on-air performer to provide the perfect niche programming.

Within three years of coming to New York to broadcast locally on WABC-AM, Limbaugh's program was carried on more than 600 radio stations. His success was based on his use of humor to convey a political message by using techniques identified with music formats, such as song parodies, sound effects, and set pieces (such as the infamous "caller abortion"). His conservativism has created a listening audience estimated at times to be in excess of 16 million. Many of those listeners refer to themselves as "dittoheads" in recognition of Limbaugh's timesaving device of asking his callers to dispense with the usual introductory remarks (such as "I love your show . . .") with a quick "ditto." Limbaugh's increasing partisanship in recent years has not seemed to diminish his audience greatly, since, with a Democrat in the White House, Limbaugh has been dubbed "The Leader of the Opposition" by *National Review*. In recognition of his perceived influence, he was named an honorary member of the Republican freshman class in Congress in 1995.

Colford, Paul. *The Rush Limbaugh Story: Talent on Loan from God: An Unauthorized Biography.* New York: St. Martin's Press, 1993.

Eastland, Terry. "Rush Limbaugh's Revolution." *American Spectator* (September 1992): 22–27.

Seib, Philip M. *Rush Hour: Talk Radio, Politics and the Rise of Rush Limbaugh.* Ft. Worth, Tex.: Summit Group, 1993.

Jonathan David Tankel

LINDBERG, CHARLES A. (1902–1974), American aviator who made the first nonstop New York–Paris flight in 1927. Lindbergh's flight in the *Spirit of St. Louis* won him the $25,000 Orteig prize and made him into a hero and celebrity. Press coverage included extensive newsreel footage of the takeoff, his reception in Paris and Europe, and his return to the United States; his arrival in Washington, D.C. was broadcast live on radio. He followed up his pioneering flight with a flying tour of North and South America, promoting commercial aviation as the transportation mode of the future.

The kidnapping and murder of Lindbergh's first son, Charles, Jr., pushed Lindbergh back into the media spotlight in 1932. Three years later, newsreel cameras recorded the trial of Bruno Richard Hauptmann in Flemington, New Jersey. The verdict and much of the trial were broadcast over radio. The circus atmosphere surrounding the trial was a contributing cause to the American Bar Association's ban of cameras and microphones from courtrooms.

Lindbergh and his family moved to England and France in the 1930s to avoid intrusion into their private lives, and he maintained an intense dislike of publicity and news reporters that began prior to his 1927 flight and continued through his many years as a celebrity.

In 1939, Lindbergh embarked on a political crusade opposing U.S. lend-lease aid to Great Britain and involvement in the early stages of World War II. On behalf of the America First Committee, an isolationist group, he made a series of speeches and radio broadcasts that argued for keeping the United States neutral. In the 1960s, Lindbergh returned to the public spotlight as a result of his work on behalf of the World Wildlife Fund and other environmental organizations.

Cole, Wayne S. *Charles A. Lindbergh and the Battle against American Intervention in World War II*. New York: Harcourt Brace Jovanovich, 1974.
Lindbergh, Charles A. *The Spirit of St. Louis*. New York: Charles Scribner's Sons, 1953.
Milton, Joyce. *Loss of Eden: A Biography of Charles and Anne Morrow Lindbergh*. New York: HarperCollins, 1993.

John R. Broholm

LINER is a radio programming component consisting of nonmusical material such as a comedy sketch or a promotional announcement. Some radio stations categorize news and sports segments as liners.

Frederic A. Leigh

LITE-ROCK FORMAT, features popular contemporary and "oldie" rock 'n' roll music; a variation of the adult contemporary (AC) format and a relative of middle-of-the-road (MOR) programming. The parent of lite rock, adult contemporary music programming, got started during the 1960s as the softer side of rock 'n' roll. Dubbed "chicken" rock because of the ultraconservative way it played the less harsh music of rock, a station would flirt with rock 'n' roll by playing the Beatle's "Yesterday" but not the harder "Yellow Submarine." In the 1970s, the format became "mellow rock" as an alternative to heavy rock.

AC music is called "America's radio format" because of its popularity and success; only country music (2,767 stations) had more stations than AC's 2,078 in 1995. Today lite-rock stations play softer rock music, often with a nostalgic tinge. "Hot rock," a cousin to lite rock, plays more fast-paced rock music.

WLTW-FM (New York) leads in lite rock, targeting aging baby-boomers with a mix of "sharp, with-it sounds" sprinkled with some oldies. Many stations are successful with the lite format using the concept to identify themselves, for example, 106.1 FM-Lite. Lite rock specifically uses continuous music sweeps and clusters of commercials to maintain a largely uninterrupted music flow. News and information is programmed during the day but mainly in drive-time dayparts. Lite rock's main competitors are contemporary hit radio with younger listeners and easy listening with an older audience.

Hilliard, Robert L. *Radio Broadcasting: An Introduction to the Sound Medium*. 3rd ed. New York: Longman, 1985.
Keith, Michael C. *Radio Programming: Consultancy and Formatics*. Boston: Focal Press, 1987.
Lull, J. T., L. M. Johnson, and C. E. Sweeney. "Audiences for Contemporary Radio Formats." *Journal of Broadcasting* 22 (4) (fall 1978): 439.

J. R. Rush

LOCALISM is a Federal Communications Commission (FCC) policy fostering local radio or TV station outlets in as many U.S. communities as feasible. The *Communications Act of 1934* directs the FCC to allocate radio frequencies and to assign station licenses among various communities "to provide a fair, efficient and equitable distribution of radio service" (47 USC 307[b]). The commission's policies provide local outlets of electronic expression in most cities and towns, including at least one radio service available to nearby rural small towns.

The doctrine of localism is rooted in the uniquely American democratic notion that popular self-government requires access to popular means of self-expression, here the powerful electronic means of radio. Today, over 12,000 local radio stations provide the majority of the United States with at least one local station. That many local stations require complicated rules to control antenna construction and signal radiation so that the local system will work. By comparison, West European countries have a few government-controlled radio stations broadcasting national or regional programming.

Critics argue that the FCC's policy of spatial, geographic localism ignores the reality: U.S. radio represents a diverse, national system. Concentration of ownership, national radio networks, and national music and news sources seem to support a view of nationalism. Another idea is that social communities of special interest, taste, and style in music, entertainment, and information have evolved. Elimination of multiple station ownership rules, in the *Telecommunications Act of 1996,* also seems to support a critical view of localism.

Collins, T. A. "The Local Service Concept in Broadcasting." *Iowa Law Review* 65 (1980): 553.
Josiah, W. J., Jr. "The Superstation and the Doctrine of Localism." *Communications and the Law* 3 (fall 1981): 3.
Stavitsky, Alan G. "The Changing Concept of Localism in U.S. Public Radio." *Journal of Broadcasting and Electronic Media* 38 (1) (winter 1994): 19.

J. R. Rush

LOCAL MARKETING AGREEMENTS (LMAs). A radio or television station entering into one of these agreements with another radio or television station merges a portion of its operations; however, both licensees retain responsibility for their licenses. The local marketing agreement generally affects the programming content and the sale of time at the brokered station. The brokered station is required to air its own station identifications and to maintain its own main studio within its principal community contour while remaining responsive to the needs of its community of license, or risk losing its license through the denial of a renewal expectancy (6 FCC Rcd 1869). Relaxation of the Federal Communications Commission's (FCC's) ownership regulations in 1992 allowed radio station owners to expand their LMAs into part of their ownership structure. Many LMAs are formed for the period between an announcement of a station transaction and the FCC approval of that assignment of license. TV LMAs are not currently regulated.

Anderson, J. T., and Tony Sanders. *LMA Handbook.* Alexandria, Va.: Radio Business Report, 1992.
Hagin, Linwood A. "U.S. Radio Consolidation: The Structures and Strategies of Selected Duopolies." Ph.D. dissertation, University of Tennessee, 1994.

Linwood A. Hagin

LOGS play a vital role in programming and maintaining a station's license. There are two kinds of station logs: programming and engineering. The programing log is the official transcript of the day-to-day over-the-air operations. It is a detailed form that includes programs, announcements (commercial, public service, and political), promotional messages, and contests. Each log will include source (live or taped), type of announcement, and time of broadcast. The engineering log is an official transcript of the daily technical operations of a radio station. This transcript includes, but is not limited to, operator sign-on and sign-off; hourly tower readings—final volts, final current, forward power; transmitter carrier; station sign-on and sign-off; and any Emergency Broadcast Service test.

Gloria G. Horning

LONE RANGER, THE, has become one of the most well-known fictional figures in American popular culture, featured in films, television, and comic books for children. His debut was on the radio in 1933, at WXYZ, Detroit. The series became an early staple of the Mutual Broadcasting System and was later carried on the NBC Blue Network, and eventually ABC, where it maintained a nationwide radio audience, broadcast live until 1954 and in rerun form until 1958. The show was originally created and produced by George W. Trendle and written by Fran Striker. Several people played the role of the Lone Ranger, perhaps the most memorable being Earle Graser (1935–1941) and Brace Beemer (1941–1954). The role of Tonto was played by John Todd during the entire radio series. The most popular story of the Lone Ranger's origin involves his being the sole survivor of an ambush on a group of Texas Rangers, all of whom were left for dead. However, one survived, leading to the name the Lone Ranger. He wore a black mask to protect his anonymity as he and his faithful companion, Tonto, successfully battled a variety of villains in the Old West. His silver bullets, his horse Silver, and his cry, "Hi-Yo, Silver Away," along with the famous musical theme Rossini's *William Tell Overture,* will always be associated with the "thrilling days of yesteryear" in the minds of radio fans who recall listening to this famous program, designed primarily for children but reaching many adults.

Boemer, Marilyn. *The Children's Hour: Radio Programs for Children, 1929–1956.* Metuchen, N.J.: Scarecrow Press, 1989.

Buxton, Frank, and Bill Owen. *Radio's Golden Age: The Programs and the Personalities.* New York: Easton Valley Press, 1966.

Harmon, Jim. *Radio Mystery and Adventure and Its Appearances in Film, Television and Other Media.* Jefferson, N.C.: McFarland, 1992.

B. R. Smith

LONG, HUEY (1893–1935), was elected governor of Louisiana in 1928. He moved quickly to dominate state government by assuming control of Louisiana's political patronage system. Huey Long's consolidation of power won him grassroots support, but his political enemies considered his methods those of a dictator.

When political opponents used the print media to criticize Long, the governor responded by using radio to speak directly to his constituents. He became a master of the medium, speaking for hours at a time without note or script. He opened his radio marathons by inviting listeners to phone their friends because they, too, needed to hear what Huey Long had to say. The otherwise educated and articulate Long then would deliberately mispronounce words and ignore rules of grammar in order to appeal more effectively to his audience.

Long moved to the U.S. Senate in 1932 and soon gained the attention of depression-weary Americans by promoting his plan to redistribute this country's wealth. He once more used radio to reach his audience. Taking advantage of the National Broadcasting Company's offer of free airtime, Huey Long delivered a total of nine network addresses from 1933 through 1935. Audience measurements indicated that a significant number of listeners heard Long's remarks.

Huey Long was said to have been the equal of President Franklin D. Roosevelt as a political radio personality. Many persons, in fact, assumed that Long would challenge Roosevelt for the presidency in 1936. But the challenge never materialized. Huey Long was gunned down by an assassin on September 7, 1935, and died three days later.

Bormann, Ernest. "This Is Huey P. Long Talking." *Journal of Broadcasting* 2 (2) (spring 1958): 111–122.

Brinkley, Alan. *Voices of Protest: Huey Long, Father Coughlin & The Great Depression.* New York: Vintage Books, 1982.

Williams, T. Harry. *Huey Long.* New York: Alfred A. Knopf, 1969.

Ronald Garay

LONG-PLAYING. *See* **LP.**

LOOMIS, MAHLON (1826–1886), is recognized as one of the first individuals to suggest messages could be relayed from tall antennas. A nineteenth-century inventor, Loomis theorized messages could be sent through the atmosphere from one elevated wire to another without the aid of an external power source. He based his assumption on the belief that the earth's upper atmosphere was already charged with electricity and that an electrical disturbance at one point could be detected at a different point at the same elevation.

Although no hard evidence remains, Loomis apparently was successful in proving his theory with experiments conducted in 1872 from two high mountain peaks in West Virginia. From one peak, Loomis elevated a kite grounded with wire rather than string. To this wire he attached a switch that, when engaged, caused a change in the electrical atmosphere at the tip of the kite. This change was recognized by a detector attached to a similar kite flown from another mountain peak 10 miles away. The experiment was later successfully repeated by Loomis himself from two ships two miles apart on Chesapeake Bay, and again in 1909 by an individual at the London Telegraph Training College.

As intriguing as Loomis's theory may have been, he was unable to receive government funding to further his work. Generally, the "aerial telegraph" was considered impractical due to the constantly changing conditions in the atmosphere and a lack at the time of adequate detection equipment. However, Loomis's work is relevant in broadcast history because it showed a sudden discharge of energy could be used to create electromagnetic waves.

Kenneth D. Loomis

LP is the shorthand term for long-playing record, the 33⅓-rpm standard introduced by CBS in the late 1940s. This new technology, used on a 12-inch disc, enabled far more music to be recorded and played than was possible with the same sized 78-rpm standard disc. With an LP a complete symphony could be recorded and played on a single record, while for the same in 78 rpm, one would need several discs.

Channan, Michael. *Repeated Takes: A Short History of Recording and Its Effects on Music.* London: Verso, 1995.

Douglas Gomery

LYRICS AND MORALITY. Since the advent of rock 'n' roll music, there has been a concern over the impact and influence of musical lyrics on the youth of America. Of particular concern are songs that discuss sexual activity, violence, and suicide. Some advocates have called for a complete ban on any explicit references to these activities, claiming that such lyrics encourage antisocial behavior. Still others see the issue as one of informed consumerism and encourage the music industry to provide information about a record's content so that parents can have more control over what their children listen to. At the core of this debate is the confrontation between a musician's creative and artistic freedom and the need to protect children from potentially harmful material.

One of the first advocacy groups to tackle the issue of music lyrics was the Parents' Music Resource Center. The center was cofounded by Tipper Gore (with Susan Baker, wife of former Secretary of State James Baker III) in 1985 after she heard lyrics describing masturbation on the album *Purple Rain* by Prince. Gore claimed that she did not believe in censoring musicians' lyrics but did believe that there should be some way for parents to know the content of an album before they bought it. Center representatives (including Gore) testified at a series of Senate hearings and met with music industry officials to encourage labeling music whose themes or lyrics related to sexuality, violence, drug usage, suicide, or the occult. In 1985, the Recording Industry Association of America (RIAA) agreed to introduce a uniform labeling system using the warning "Parental Advisory Explicit Lyrics." However, RIAA provided record companies with no guidelines for determining what music should be labeled, leading to a patchwork of standards and criteria throughout the industry.

More recent concern over music lyrics has focused on gangsta rap and alternative music. In 1995, a group of citizen advocates and congressional leaders teamed to level a number of charges against some of the music industry's most successful performers. Former Education Secretary William Bennett (representing Empower America), C. Dolores Tucker (chair of the National Political Congress of Black Women), Senator Joseph Lieberman (D–Conn.), and Senator Sam Nunn (D–Ga.) held a series of news conferences protesting pro-drug lyrics as well as songs that degrade women and advocate the killing of police. Their crusade was praised by Senator Bob Dole, who advocated an entire ban on gangsta rap.

The group sponsored a radio commercial calling for more corporate responsibility among the major record labels and later focused its attention on media conglomerate Time Warner in particular. At the heart of the group's concern with

Time Warner was its 50 percent ownership of Interscope Records, which distributed the music of Nine Inch Nails and rappers Snoop Doggy Dogg and Dr. Dre. Interscope was accused of supporting artists who promoted drug use and the rape, torture, and murder of women. Although Time Warner officials denied that they succumbed to the pressure by Bennett and Tucker, the conglomerate sold its ownership stake in Interscope in September 1995.

After the Parents' Music Resource Center lost the active participation of its two cofounders (Tipper Gore and Susan Baker), the organization became less involved in direct advocacy and remained largely a resource for parents. The center sponsors a 1-900 telephone service that provides information on controversial lyrics and reviews the content and language on specific albums. The center continues to lobby the record industry for better labeling of controversial music and joined in the call to establish a ratings system for music that would be similar to the one used by the motion picture and video game industries. Claiming that it would be impractical to rate the approximately 10,000 new songs released each year, the Recording Industry Association of America resisted the proposed ratings system. It did, however, agree to encourage better music labeling among its member record companies.

Although the protests of groups such as Empower America and the Parents' Music Resource Center often attract media attention, several organizations are working equally as hard to fight music censorship. Three national censorship watchdog groups—Parents for Rock and Rap, Rock Out Censorship, and Massachusetts Music Industry Coalition—joined forces in 1996 to sponsor a "Fight Music Censorship" petition. In an Internet press release explaining the petition drive, the organizers stress that music should no longer be used as a convenient scapegoat for "self-appointed moral guardians" such as Bennett and Tucker.

Arts Censorship Project. *Popular Music under Siege*. New York: American Civil Liberties Union, 1996.
Clark, Charles. "Sex Violence and the Media." *CQ Researcher* 17 (November 1995): 1019–1036.

Cynthia A. Cooper

M

MAGNETIC-TAPE RECORDING of information is utilized in several familiar technologies, including the audiotape recorder, the videocassette recorder, and the computer-disk drive, and it is the basis of a major international industry. Although this technology was invented in the 1880s, it was virtually undeveloped in the United States before World War II. Spurred by war-related research and the transfer of technology from Germany, a new magnetic-recording industry developed in the United States between 1940 and 1945. After 1945, the makers of magnetic-tape recorders enjoyed huge commercial successes, first in the field of broadcasting and then in studio recording, computers, and consumer audio applications.

"Creating the Craft of Tape Recording." *Hi Fidelity* (April 1976): x.

Mullin, John T. "The Birth of the Recording Industry." *Billboard* (November 18, 1972).

Marvin R. Bensman

MARCH OF TIME, THE, was the most important news dramatization program. The program lasted 11 seasons on network radio and led to the motion picture documentary series of the same name. It is best remembered by the very words of the title, for virtually all of its run spoken by the mellifluous Westbrook van Voorhis, who also narrated the newsreel version. In early 1922, Briton Hadden and Henry R. Luce quit their jobs at the Baltimore *News* to found a magazine called *Time*, first published on March 2, 1923, based on an idea they first discussed as college undergraduates. Also in 1922, Fred Smith began as the first station director at WLW, a Cincinnati radio station founded by Powel Crosley, Jr. (see **Crosley, Powel, Jr.; WLW**).

Smith introduced many program ideas at the station and in 1925 hit upon the novel idea of reading various items—taken without permission—from newspapers and magazines. After each story an "appropriate" musical number was played by the staff organist, who incidentally spoke only broken English. He called the program *Musical News*. In 1928, Smith got permission from *Time* to get an advanced ("makeready") copy of the magazine by airmail (then just begun) from Chicago so that he could rewrite items for a weekly news summary he started at WLW. Soon

Smith was hired by *Time* and traveling the Midwest, signing up stations for a new daily summary the magazine would syndicate to radio stations. Beginning on September 3, 1928, 10-minute scripts were airmailed to stations and read by local announcers on more than 60 stations. On WOR, New York, the program was carried from 5:50 P.M. to 6 P.M., Monday through Friday, and was called *NewsCasting*. Smith himself was the New York news reader for the first year.

This is apparently the first use of the word *newscast*. Smith had made up such words while at WLW; he coined *radarios* after radio and *scenario* for original radio plays he wrote and produced. *Time* was even more well known for coining *cinemaddict* and *newsmagazine,* among others. By the spring of 1929, the 10-minute summaries were being carried on as many as 90 stations—the first large-scale regular daily news broadcast carried in the United States—although it was never an interconnected network program. The first daily news program on the national networks, with Lowell Thomas, began on September 29, 1930, on Blue.

In September 1929, Smith made a five-minute "news drama," again in coop-eration with *Time,* and submitted his audition program to a number of stations with the title *NewsActing.* That word did not catch on, but the program idea did. By December 1929, Smith, with a crew of six to eight actors, was producing a weekly five-minute drama on electrical transcriptions. These were hardly full-scale dra-matic productions, but they did include sound effects and occasional music. Within a few months the *NewsActing* records were being broadcast over more than 100 stations.

Time wanted network exposure, and on February 6, 1931, an experimental program was sent via telephone wires to the home of a *Time* executive where a small group (including William S. Paley, CBS president) listened. Exactly a month later, on Friday March 6, 1931, *The March of Time* was fed from Columbia's New York studios and carried on 20 (of about 80) affiliates at 10:30 P.M. EST. The program's title was taken from a song of that name that was in a play on Broadway at the time. After a five-second fanfare, the announcer said:

> *The March of Time.* On a thousand fronts the events of the world move swiftly forward. Tonight the editors of *Time,* the weekly newsmagazine, attempt a new kind of reporting of the news, the re-enacting as clearly and dramatically as the medium of radio will permit some themes from the news of the week. (transcribed from program)

The first program dramatized the reelection of William "Big Bill" Thompson as mayor of Chicago, the sudden death of the *World* when it merged with the New York *Telegram,* and shorter segments on French prisoners sent to Devil's Island, revolution in Spain, prison reform in Rumania, a roundup of news of royalty, an auction of Czarist possessions in New York, and the closing of the 71st Congress.

During that first season the program ran 13 weeks. It returned on September 8, 1932, but as a sustaining feature. *Time* editors decided they could not afford advertising, which they said they no longer needed—"should a few (400,000 *Time* subscribers) pay for the entertainment of many (9,000,000 radio owners)?" The magazine also argued: "For all its blatant claims to being a medium of education, radio contributes little of its own beyond the considerable service of bringing good music to millions" (*Time* [February 29, 1932]: 32; see Lichty and Bohn).

But in November, the magazine resumed its sponsorship. During the 1933–1934 season it was sponsored by Remington-Rand and van Voorhis became "the voice" of the program. On February 1, 1935, *The March of Time* newsreel began as a monthly film series in theaters. Originally a newsreel with a number of items each issue, in January 1938 it covered only "Inside Nazi Germany." After October 1938, single subjects were being treated exclusively. The theatrical version ran until 1951, and the title was also used for a series of TV documentaries.

From 1935 there were a variety of sponsors, daily 15-minute versions were tried for one season, and the program was not on radio at all from 1939 to 1941. After seven years on CBS, it moved to Blue. In July 1942, the format was changed with only one or two dramatized segments and many more live on-the-spot news reports. The 1944–1945 season was the last; listeners were now hearing the actual voices of newsmakers on many network news programs.

There were dramatized news programs on other networks and at local stations. *The March of Time* was only a small part of growing news and documentary coverage on radio in the 1930s. Few who worked on later programs would even know their debt to *Musical News, NewsCasting, NewsActing,* and *The March of Time*—both the radio and film versions. But the number of docudramas on TV now attest to the interest in "dramatized news."

Bohn, Thomas W., and Lawrence W. Lichty. "*The March of Time:* News as Drama." *Journal of Popular Film* 2 (4) (fall 1973): 373–387.
Lichty, Lawrence W., and Thomas W. Bohn. "Radio's *March of Time:* Dramatized News." *Journalism Quarterly* 51 (3) (autumn 1974): 458–462.

Lawrence W. Lichty

MARCONI, GUGLIELMO (1874-1937), Nobel Prize winner for physics, pioneer of wireless communication, and founder of rich and powerful companies for the development of radio: the "Father of Radio." Guglielmo Marconi was the second child of an Italian father, Giuseppe Marconi, and his second wife, Annie Jameson of Ireland. He was born on April 25, 1874, in Bologna, Italy.

Early in his life, young Marconi became interested in the work of James Clerk Maxwell and Heinrich Hertz on the phenomenon of "electromagnetic waves," as Hertz labeled them. In 1887, when Marconi was just 13, Hertz had discovered that electrical energy could be radiated through space from one place to another. Neither Maxwell, who had posited the theory, nor Hertz, who had expanded the theory, was interested in going beyond the theoretic stage of study. It was Marconi, who had just been entered in the Leghorn Technical Institute where he began his formal study of physics, who was the more practical inventor and took the study further. He began his serious studies at the Bologna University under Professor Righi, a fine experimental physicist and brilliant lecturer in his subject. Righi was at the time one of the more eminent workers in the field of Hertzian waves.

Earlier in his life, Marconi had experimented with simple ideas. He had created a miniature still that actually produced crude spirits, he converted a cousin's sewing machine into a turnspit, and he rigged up some wires and a battery to create a doorbell for the family's home. Living in a well-to-do family, he had the means to pursue his interests. He began at the Bologna townhouse, then moved to a family country estate where his major experiments took place. His father, a penny-pincher, had to be convinced by Guglielmo's mother to let the boy have the necessary materials for his experiments.

In his early days at school in Florence, he had been shunned by other students as "stuck up." He loathed almost everything about the school period but did make one friend, Luigi Soleri, who became his closest friend, lieutenant, and confident. It was Soleri who assisted with experimenting and who later persuaded the king of Italy to lend Marconi a warship with which to conduct his experiments in wireless telegraphy.

Marconi began by building a simple transmitter and receiver going from one room to another in the country house, then he moved from the house onto the grounds. Each experiment strongly convinced Marconi that there was something to the concept and it could be a valuable asset.

One of the biggest problems with communication in the navies of the time was that once a ship was out of sight of land, it was also out of touch with land. Marconi was ready to give his new invention to the Italian navy but was met with rejection. His mother promptly took things in hand and hurried him off to Great Britain, where she had some influential friends. In July of 1896, they arrived in Britain where the British Post Office took great interest in the invention. They were already working on a wireless system of their own, but not one based on Hertzian waves. Someone thought to notify the British Ministry of Marine, and the Royal Navy took a strong interest in what Marconi was doing.

The navy made ships available for his experiments. He successfully demonstrated the ability of ship-to-shore communication, even when the ship was out of sight over the horizon. He registered his patent on a wireless telegraph in 1896. In 1897, he set up his own company, with financial help from his mother's family, to offer wireless telegraphic service to the public. He proved over the years to be a remarkable combination of inventor and business innovator.

In his experiments, he became obsessed with distance. He began to transmit between Ireland and England, then across the English channel to France. He also set up his own facilities in the Americas, both the United States and Canada. In 1899, he founded American Marconi, a company that was to have decisive influence on the development of radio. By 1913, American Marconi had begun to receive substantial profits as it achieved virtual monopoly on patents for U.S. wireless communication. The company owned 17 land stations and 400 shipboard stations. All used the wireless system invented by Marconi.

He had been trying for transoceanic capability and, in December 1901, succeeded in transmitting from Poldhu, in Cornwall, to St. Johns, Newfoundland. Over these years, Marconi was the leader in development of wireless, feeding an insatiable world hungry for new communication channels. He had the vision, the drive, and the courage to reduce the time between laboratory experimentation and the commercial exploitation of that experiment. His methods did not endear him to other scientific researchers or other businesspeople, and he spent much time in fending off lawsuits over patents.

In 1909, Marconi received the Nobel Prize for physics, sharing it with Germany's Ferdinand Braun, for achievements in wireless telegraphy. World War I saw the navy taking over all broadcast stations for war purposes. At the end of the war, the "borrowed" patents were returned. It proved to be an era of change. Whereas before the war, radio was the domain of the inventor-entrepreneurs, after the war, big business took over. AT&T secured the wireless rights to its original purchase of de Forest's audion, while General Electric (GE) owned the powerful alternator patents and the ability to mass-produce vacuum tubes. Westinghouse, another producer of vacuum tubes, sought new ways of capitalizing on wireless. In 1919, many of the U.S. companies formed a holding company to handle the patents for radio in the United States. They bought out American Marconi and created a company called Radio Corporation of America. Marconi was out of business in the United States.

Chase, Francis, Jr. *Sound and Fury. An Informal History of Broadcasting.* New York: Harper & Brothers Publishers, 1942.
Jolley, W. P. *Marconi.* New York: Stein and Day/Publishers, 1972.
Marconi, Degna. *My Father, Marconi.* New York: McGraw-Hill, 1962.

ElDean Bennett

MARKET is the geographic area within which a station operates, generally designated by city or metropolitan area. It is licensed to a market and broadcasts to the audience living within that designated market area. The market size that determines advertising potential, programming budgets, and prices paid for advertising and programming is generally ranked by population. Arbitron's area of dominant influence (ADI), developed in 1965, was until recently the most widely accepted system for defining markets; Nielson's version is the designated market area (DMA).

Gloria G. Horning

MARKET SHARE, an estimate of the percentage of persons or households tuned to a specific station or network within a market. An audience share is the percentage of the people using radios tuned to a specific station. It is determined by dividing the number of persons tuned to a station by the number of persons using their sets (see also **ratings systems; research**).

Gloria G. Horning

MAXWELL, JAMES CLERK (1831–1879), was a physicist and mathematician born near Edinburgh, Scotland. In 1888, Hertz proved Maxwell's theory that electromagnetic waves behave in the same way as light waves. Marconi used these results to develop a useful and commercially successful spark-coil transmitter in 1897.

In 1820, Hans Oersted demonstrated that an electric current had a magnetic effect on a compass needle. Michael Farraday later suggested that these "electro-magnetic" (electric and magnetic) forces spread out in "fields" from their sources. In 1855, Maxwell developed Farraday's ideas and gave a mathematical explanation for the transmission of electromagnetic forces. Maxwell showed that the magnetic field generated by an electric current spreads outward from its source at a constant speed, approximately the same as the speed of light (186,000 miles per second). Maxwell reasoned that light must therefore be some type of electromagnetic wave and that the light we can see may be only one of many types of electromagnetic radiation or emission of rays from a source.

In 1865, Maxwell published his *Dynamical Theory of the Electro-Magnetic Field* in which he argued that electromagnetic waves exist and could travel through space. Most scientists did not accept Maxwell's theory until 1873, when he expanded his original 1865 paper into his famous *Treatise on Electricity and Magnetism.* For Maxwell, implicit in his notion of similar properties of different types of waves was the belief in a single medium (the ether) that transmitted several forces: gravity, electricity, light, and magnetism.

Maxwell had a distinguished academic career. He was appointed professor of natural philosophy at Marischal College, Aberdeen, Scotland, in 1856. He held the same title from 1860 until 1865 at King's College, London. In 1871, he was appointed the first professor of experimental physics at Cambridge, a position he held until his death.

Maxwell investigated other scientific phenomena, including the theory of colors and their impact on color blindness (1855); Saturn's ring system (1857); and the kinetic theory of gases and the constitution of molecules (1860). Most important, Maxwell helped to establish the importance of electricity to the study of physics. He showed that not only were light and electric waves identical in nature but that they were actually different forms of electromagnetism.

His theories about electromagnetism led Hertz, Fessenden, de Forest, Lodge, Marconi, and others to eventually translate scientific discovery into practical reality and develop useful and potentially profitable devices. Maxwell did not live to see the vindication of his theories. He became ill while visiting "Glenair," his Scottish home, in 1879. He returned to Cambridge and died at the early age of 48.

Campbell, Lewis, and William Garnett. *The Life of James Clerk Maxwell.* London: Macmillan and Co., 1882. (Reprinted in 1969 by Johnson Reprint Corporation, New York and London, as No. 85 in *The Sources of Science* series.)

Goldman, Martin. *The Demon in the Aether: The Story of James Clerk Maxwell.* Edinburgh, Scotland: Paul Harris Publishers in association with Adam Hilger Ltd., 1983.

Tricker, R. A. R. *The Contributions of Farraday and Maxwell to Electrical Science.* New York: Pergamon Press, 1966.

Peter E. Mayeux

MAYFLOWER DECISION. In 1939 the Mayflower Broadcasting Corporation applied to the Federal Communications Commission (FCC) for a radio station construction permit on a frequency then in use by the Yankee Network, Inc. for its station WAAB in Boston, thereby effectively challenging the renewal of WAAB's license. Mayflower's major argument was that WAAB had broadcast editorials in defiance of federal law. On January 16, 1941, the FCC denied Mayflower's application based on misrepresentation and a lack of financial qualifications. However, the importance of this FCC decision rests upon the commission's interpretation of the law affecting the rights of broadcasters to editorialize. According to the commission, a station "cannot be used to advocate the causes of the licensee. It cannot be used to support the candidacies of his friends. It cannot be devoted to the support of principles he happens to regard most favorably. . . . As one licensed to operate in a public domain the licensee has assumed the obligation of presenting all sides of important public questions, fairly, objectively and without bias. The public interest not the private is paramount." This interpretation of the law discouraged broadcasters from editorializing and upheld the principle of unbiased programming in the public interest. In 1949 the FCC reversed its policy on broadcast editorials (see *In Matter of Editorializing by Broadcast Licenses*). Because the licensee of WAAB made assurances that editorials had been discontinued previous to the application for license renewal and would not in the future be broadcast, the FCC granted the renewal of license to the Yankee Network.

Mayflower Decision. 8 FCC 333, 338.

Kahn, J. Frank, ed. *Documents of American Broadcasting*. Rev. ed. New York: Appleton-Century-Crofts, 1972.

Steven C. Runyon

McBRIDE, MARY MARGARET

McBRIDE, MARY MARGARET (1899–1976), was the first radio talk-show host of significance. From 1934 to 1954, it is estimated that McBride conducted 30,000 interviews on more than 15,000 programs, having worked for every flagship station of the networks. There was hardly a famous political, literary, scientific, military, naval, or diplomatic figure living in or visiting New York who did not appear on Mary Margaret McBride's show. However, McBride said she usually preferred "the average man" for a guest. Eleanor Roosevelt appeared on her program more than a dozen times. McBride was the first radio personality to interview General Omar Bradley upon his return from World War II. Many of her interviews have been saved by the Sound Recording Section of the Library of Congress.

Her earliest broadcasts were in 1934, under the grandmotherly pseudonym of Martha Deane over WOR (then New Jersey). Martha Deane became a household word to listeners, many of them housewives. There were numerous Martha Deane imitators, and even Author Godfrey is said to have mimicked McBride's interviewing style. Ironically, at WOR, "Martha Deane" had been given the so-called dead time on the air, 2:30 to 3:30 P.M. She catered to the woman of the house, who was not as yet perceived as a consumer who could buy products. In the lucrative marriage of radio and advertising, McBride became an early matchmaker.

After only two years on the air, in 1936, Mary Margaret McBride was awarded a medal by the Women's National Exposition of the Arts and Industries for the year's "greatest contribution to radio." The award was based on her being the most listened-to woman on radio.

Later, when the many sponsors courted McBride, the increasingly popular program, now under her own name, moved to an earlier afternoon spot on network radio (usually heard 1 to 2 P.M., EST): 1937 to 1941, for CBS; 1941 to 1950, the flagship station of WEAF (superseded by the call letters WNBC) for NBC; and 1951 to 1954, WJZ, for ABC. She broadcast out of her own South Central Park apartment for ABC.

As to McBride's legendary salesmanship, she was once characterized by one of her advertisers as Mother Hubbard, "her hands still floury from the morning's baking, dropping in for some gossip over the kitchen table," according to Barbara Heggie of *The New Yorker.* McBride drew the line at liquor advertising and cigarette advertising, which were often heard on radio from the 1930s to the 1950s. Her reputation as a sales personality who could sell anything brought about unexpected announcements. A state senator from New York cautioned the public to beware of those door-to-door vendors who prey on housewives, falsely representing themselves as Mary Margaret McBride, Lowell Thomas, or Francis Cardinal Spellman.

McBride usually devoted the first 30 minutes of her programs to matters of the mind. Then she moved to matters of the stomach. When her first radio show on WOR (CBS flagship station/CBS network, 1934–1940) was three quarters of an hour long, McBride advertised 12 products, many of those food items; for an hour-long program, she added 4 more. Each radio sponsor paid $175 per week.

Later, on the flagship station of WEAF (later WNBC/NBC Network, 1940–1950), 12 advertisers paid $275 a week to the station for radio time and $150 a week (total $425) to McBride for mentioning their products during every weekday broadcast. There were two dozen or so sponsors on the waiting list. The fee continued to climb. By 1948, according to *Life,* McBride's WNBC sponsors paid $475 each.

A description of her day-to-day broadcasts at NBC is provided by one of McBride's contemporaries, Allen Churchill, a writer for *The American Mercury.* Apparently, after arriving in the flagship studio and greeting the live audience of 60 or so, McBride sat down behind a battered, antique table, winding her legs around the side rungs of her chair and hooking her feet, as if to anchor herself to one position. McBride then visibly braced up for the interview, facing her guest, who usually sat across the table. During the interview itself, McBride referred to a pile of notes she had drafted herself and drank water poured from a battered green thermos. As McBride hunched forward on her elbows, hands clenched into tight fists, she sat tensely, eyes fixed full on her guest's face.

Barbara Heggie said McBride came across as a corn-fed ingenue. The secret of the popularity of her programs was that McBride would rather ad-lib than be held to a prepared script. She told listeners that a person who really knows his or her subject doesn't need a script. Nor did McBride allow any of her guests to bring notes to her broadcast.

Jay Nelson Tuck of the *New York Evening Post* said McBride hated to listen to recordings of her own schoolgirlish midwestern voice. Radio critic Ben Gross said McBride's voice could only be described as "a high-pitched rural twang" in a time when radio speakers were judged for their diction. Manager Estella Karn told

McBride in her own blunt way that she, Fred Allen, and Jack Benny had the *worst* three voices on the air, according to McBride in her autobiography *Out of the Air.*

After years on radio, McBride would speak out favorably of her on-air style. In 1950, for an autobiographical article in *Good Housekeeping,* McBride revealed her on-air secrets. She could make the overwhelming majority of her guests forget about the radio audience because she had the ability to forget herself and focus wholly on her guest. *New York Herald Tribune* book reviewer John K. Hutchens said: "Not only did she draw out the most timid of them [authors], giving them briefly the illusion that they were speaking with the felicity of John Mason Brown, but she demonstrated that she actually had read and thought about what they had written" (*New York Herald Tribune,* December 2, 1960, p. 23).

In her retirement years, McBride broadcast out of her own home above Ashokan Reservoir, over WGHQ, Kingston, New York. At age 61, in July 1960, she launched a talk show called *Your Hudson Valley Neighbor.* The talk-show host broadcast three times weekly—Monday, Wednesday, and Friday. McBride continued to broadcast out of WGHQ until a few months before her death on April 7, 1976, at the age of 76.

McBride, Mary Margaret. *Out of the Air.* New York: Doubleday, 1960
McBride, Mary Margaret. "Secrets." *Good Housekeeping* 129 (March 1950): 41.
Stix, Harriet. "Sincerity Is 'Secret' Behind Her Success." *New York Herald Tribune* (November 28, 1960).

Beverly G. Merrick

McLENDON, GORDON BARTON (1921–1986), was born in Paris, Texas. He was educated at Yale University and served as a U.S. Navy intelligence officer during World War II. McLendon entered broadcasting in 1946 with the purchase of KNET in Palestine, Texas. He moved to Dallas in 1947 and established radio station KLIF. The station soon became the flagship of the Liberty Broadcasting System (LBS). Liberty's 458 affiliates made it for a time the nation's largest independent radio network. Much of the LBS success rested on McLendon's play-by-play re-creation of baseball and football games, a skill that earned McLendon, who called himself the "Old Scotchman," the 1951 *Sporting News* award as America's Outstanding Sports Broadcaster.

Gordon McLendon's programming genius helped popularize the top-40 radio format during the early 1950s. His trademark brand of top-40 radio with its rock 'n' roll music, disc jockey patter, promotional contests, and fast-paced news was copied by radio stations nationwide. McLendon eventually owned 12 radio stations and used them to experiment with innovative programming formats such as beautiful music, all news, and all want ads. But KLIF remained the station where most of McLendon's program and promotion ideas were tested. By the time Gordon McLendon sold KLIF in 1967, his creative skills had made it the single highest-rated radio station in America.

McLendon's career outside of broadcasting included two unsuccessful bids for political office, motion picture production, and co-ownership of a major chain of outdoor theaters. Gordon McLendon died on September 14, 1986 (see also **Liberty Broadcasting System [LBS]**).

Fornatale, Peter, and Joshua E. Mills. *Radio in the Television Age.* Woodstock, N.Y.: Overlook Press, 1980.

Garay, Ronald. *Gordon McLendon: The Maverick of Radio.* New York: Greenwood, 1992.

Patoski, Joe Nick. "Rock 'n' Roll's Wizard of Oz." *Texas Monthly* (February 1980): 101–104, 167–171.

Ronald Garay

McLUHAN, MARSHALL [HERBERT] (1911–1980), an intellectual celebrity of the 1960s, he was dubbed the "the oracle of the electric age." From 1963 to 1980, he directed the University of Toronto's Center for Culture and Technology. Its mission was to investigate the psychic and social consequences of all technologies. The principle behind McLuhan's theories is that the radical social changes of the twentieth century can be attributed to the influence of electronic technologies. More important than the content, it's the nature of radio, television, and computers that shapes civilization.

Versed in literature, rhetoric, and philosophy, McLuhan graduated with a Ph.D. from Cambridge in 1943. He served in the English Department at St. Louis University (1940–1944), where he directed Walter Ong's thesis on Renaissance theologian Peter Ramus. From 1946 until his death, he was associated with the University of Toronto. His early writings were critical literary pieces.

His fascination with popular culture led to his first book, *The Mechanical Bride* (1951), an analysis of the social pressures generated by radio, newspapers, and advertising.

McLuhan's holistic vision of media builds upon Harold Innis's *The Bias of Communication* (1951) and the Sapir-Whorf's hypothesis, which claims that language shapes thought. McLuhan extended the types of languages to include media. With anthropologist Edmund Carpenter, he conducted a Ford Foundation seminar on culture/communications. The seminar's research appeared in *Explorations* (1953–1959), the first major outlet for McLuhan's notions about communications.

McLuhan's next two books are his most influential. *The Guttenberg Galaxy* (1960) introduces McLuhan's insights regarding the impact of print technology. He demonstrated that the linear characteristics of print account for the linear, visual orientation of reality persisting in Western cultures until the electronic revolution.

Another catalyst for McLuhan's popularity was a project with the National Association of Educational Broadcasters (NAEB) to develop a media studies syllabus (1959–1960). *Understanding Media* (1964), the eventual result of the NAEB work, examined 26 media. McLuhan stated that each historical era is characterized by the prevailing media. "The media is the message." He classified media as "hot" or "cool." All media, he argued, are extensions of ourselves.

Regarding radio, McLuhan said it was the first medium to undermine the linear orientation of print. Radio retribalizes humankind by extending our acoustic world. It produces an intimate experience and a tribal bond with song and music.

Corporate groups sought McLuhan's advice. He informed IBM that they were selling information, not machines. He published a monthly consulting report, *The*

McLuhan Dew-line (1968–1970). In all, he authored 18 books. Some, like *War and Peace in the Global Village* (1968) and *Culture Is Our Business* (1970), are in popular formats consisting of reprints of photos accompanied by one-liners or aphorisms.

Casting him as a media determinist, NBC featured McLuhan in an hour documentary, *The Media is the Message,* in March 1967. A *Playboy* interview with him appeared in March 1969. His last article, "A Day in the Life: Marshall McLuhan," appeared in *Weekend* during June 1978. He died in December 1980.

Duffy, Dennis. *Marshall McLuhan.* Toronto: McClelland and Stewart, 1969.
Finkelstein, Sidney. *Sense and Nonsense of McLuhan.* New York: International Publishers, 1968.
Marchand, Philip. *Marshall McLuhan: The Medium and the Messenger.* New York: Ticknor & Fields, 1989.
Miller, Jonathon. *McLuhan.* London: William Collins, 1971.
Rosenthal, Raymond, ed. *McLuhan: Pro and Con.* Baltimore: Penguin, 1968.
Stearn, Gerald Emanuel, ed. *McLuhan: Hot and Cool.* New York: Dial, 1967.
Theall, Donald F. *The Media Is the Rear View Mirror: Understanding McLuhan.* Montreal: McGill-Queen's University Press, 1971.

Frank Chorba

MEDIA TREND, content analysis to determine the major trends in modern American life and media usage. A trend study is a longitudinal study in which the topic is restudied using different groups of respondents over a period of time.

Gloria G. Horning

METROPOLITAN OPERA BROADCASTS, after two decades of sporadic radio broadcasts on various stations such as WEAF-New York, began to have regular radio broadcasts in 1931. After a rapid succession of sponsors, the Texaco oil company began sponsoring the Metropolitan Opera broadcasts on December 7, 1940 considered the longest-running sponsorship in broadcast history. The Metropolitan Opera broadcasts were carried by three different networks: NBC from 1940 to 1943, ABC from 1943 to 1958, and then CBS from 1958 to 1960. As the program moved from network to network, the show's time slot also changed frequently, and the broadcast was often preempted for other programming. In 1960, the Texaco–Metropolitan Opera Radio Network was created. Member stations must carry the entire 20-week season, and each opera must be broadcast live and in its entirety. In 1990, this network expanded into the Texaco–Metropolitan Opera International Radio Network with affiliate stations in 22 European countries. For more than 40 years, Milton Cross was the announcer for the broadcasts until his death in 1975. Since then, Peter Allen has been the radio voice of the Met broadcasts, bringing listeners around the world popular features such as the *Texaco Opera Quiz, Opera News on the Air,* and interviews with various members of the Metropolitan Opera family.

Jackson, Paul. *Saturday Afternoons at the Old Met: The Metropolitan Opera Broadcasts, 1931–1950.* Portland, Oreg.: Amadeus-Timber, 1992.

MacDonald, J. Fred. *Don't Touch That Dial!: Radio Programming in American Life, 1920–1960.* Chicago: Nelson-Hall, 1979.

"Texaco–Metropolitan Opera." *Texaco Online.* http://www.texaco.com/met/methome.htm (October 22, 1996).

Carla E. Gesell

METROPOLITAN STATISTICAL AREA (MSA) is an urban and core-retail geographic area within a market for which ratings are gathered. MSAs are composed of one or more counties and are defined by the federal government's Office of Management and Budget. *Metro survey area* is the name ratings supplier Arbitron uses for the acronym MSA. Arbitron provides some audience listening figures only for the MSA, including cume ratings and time spent listening.

Fletcher, James E., ed. *Broadcast Research Definitions.* Washington, D.C.: National Association of Broadcasters, 1988.

Ronald Razovsky

MIDDLE-OF-THE-ROAD (MOR) FORMAT is one of the oldest and most enduring radio formats. During the 1950s, radio stations responded to the growing popularity of television by developing various music formats. At the time, MOR came to represent the array of popular songs between rock 'n' roll and classical music. Typically, the original MOR formats played hits by artists such as Frank Sinatra, Tony Bennett, Johnny Mathis, and Henry Mancini. However, as listeners loyal to this format aged in the 1980s, and as major music formats began to splinter into new, more specialized formats, a new type of MOR emerged. This fresh MOR (also known as soft-adult contemporary) featured hits by younger artists such as Barry Manilow, Michael Bolton, Air Supply, Kenny G, and Lionel Richie. Both MOR types still exist, although the original MOR format is now usually found only on AM stations. The original MOR customarily features deeper-voiced male announcers with a style familiar to the older audience. On some of these stations, the announcers might talk more often than their peers on other formats and may be valued by some listeners as much as the music. These stations often program more newscasts than are found on other music stations, while the commercials generally target people over the age of 50. Meanwhile, the newer MOR stations are usually found on the FM dial and are consistent with the more-music-less-talk philosophy of other music formats. Announcers are of both genders, talk less often and for shorter amounts of time, and are valued for their ability to communicate their personalities in concise, well-chosen phrases. The newer MOR stations typically target listeners slightly younger than the original MORs, usually between the ages of 35 and 50.

Kenneth D. Loomis

MINNESOTA PUBLIC RADIO (MPR), pioneer regional public radio network and producer of nationally distributed public radio programming, is widely considered to be the most successful public radio broadcaster in the United States. MPR began in 1967 as KSJR, a single noncommercial, educational FM station owned and operated by St. John's University in Collegeville, Minnesota. By the mid-1990s,

MPR was a St. Paul, Minnesota–based, independent, nonprofit corporation operating a total of 27 public radio stations and 18 low-power translators in Minnesota and surrounding states. The stations are divided into two networks—one providing 24-hour-a-day news and information and one providing 24-hour-a-day music, mostly classical. A few stations take programs from both of MPR's networks.

MPR programs have won numerous national and regional awards including four Peabody Awards. The network's premier program is *A Prairie Home Companion with Garrison Keillor,* distributed by Public Radio International to more than 225 public radio stations. Other high-profile programs include the personal finance program *Sound Money,* the chamber music program *Saint Paul Sunday* hosted by conductor Bill McGlaughlin, and broadcasts of the Minnesota Orchestra and St. Paul Chamber Orchestra. MPR is the largest station-based producer of nationally distributed public radio programs in the country.

Under the leadership of visionary and controversial president William H. Kling, MPR is one of the most entrepreneurial of U.S. nonprofits. It is seen by some observers as a model for public broadcasting not dependent on government funding. Through a for-profit subsidiary, the network publishes a glossy monthly magazine and operates a multimillion-dollar mail-order-catalog sales firm and a for-profit radio network that sells news, sports, and other programming to commercial stations. The for-profit ventures provide several million dollars each year to support MPR's public radio programming. One indication of the network's financial strength came in 1990 when MPR purchased the highly rated commercial station WLOL-FM in Minneapolis/St. Paul to provide an FM outlet for MPR's news service in its home market. It was a $12 million purchase few other public radio stations could have contemplated, let alone financed.

MPR receives financial support from more than 70,000 members, institutional sponsorship from eight colleges and universities, and substantial contributions from commercial underwriters including such corporate giants as Cargil, 3M, General Mills, International Dairy Queen, and Dayton Hudson Corporation. Its annual budget is by far the largest in public radio.

MPR critics include commercial competitors to its for-profit ventures, who say those profit-generating operations have an unfair advantage because they were begun with help from government funds and/or listener contributions. In part because of those criticisms, MPR spunoff its for-profit companies into a separate tax-paying corporation in the mid-1980s. Critics of MPR programming say the network broadcasts little in the way of minority-interest programs of the sort many other public radio outlets provide. Rather, the critics say, MPR offers only the most popular and financially successful programs, which are able to draw corporate support from commercial underwriters seeking to reach the network's largely up-scale audience.

Holder, Dennis. "Mixing Public Radio with Private Enterprise: Minnesota Public Radio Cashes In." *Washington Journalism Review* 6 (5) (June 1984): 42–47.

Mark J. Heistad

MINORITY PROGRAMMING AND EMPLOYMENT. Minority radio programming consists of news, public affairs (information), and entertainment (music, sports, etc.) shows created for African Americans, Asian Americans, Native Americans, and Hispanics. Employment trends document the numbers of minorities hired at local, network, and syndicated radio outlets.

The U.S. broadcasting industry developed as a system in which minorities had little power. These media institutions are large, capital-intensive conglomerates. Early attempts by minority groups to influence radio broadcasters failed, mainly because the industry focused on mass audiences and developed policies that ignored minority concerns. It was not until the Kerner Commission of 1967, which pointed out the broadcasting industry's role in perpetuating racism, that these institutions took seriously minority groups' concerns about programming and employment opportunities.

During the 1970s, minorities started to make progress in radio station ownership. Gains in this area occurred mainly as a consequence of the *Minority Ownership Policy of 1978*. In addition, the Equal Employment Opportunity Commission (EEOC) began to track employment trends systematically. The EEOC used its employment statistics as measures of compliance with Federal Communications Commission (FCC) policies and rules.

In 1993, minorities made up 14 percent of all full-time employees at commercial AM radio stations. Sixteen percent of commercial FM radio station employees are minorities. At public radio stations, 18 percent of full-time employees are minorities. Nevertheless, 85 percent of radio stations employ no minorities.

Programming for minority audiences is often found in cities with large populations of either African Americans, Asian Americans, Native Americans, or Hispanics. In the Los Angeles area, for example, Asian-American programming is a common feature on local radio stations. In Miami, parts of the Southwest, and southern California, Spanish-language radio programs are heard. Additionally, in urban areas with large African-American populations, radio stations schedule music and other program elements for this target audience.

Dates, Janette L., and William Barlow, eds. *Split Image: African Americans in the Mass Media.* 2nd ed. Washington, D.C.: Howard University Press, 1993.

Fife, Marilyn D. "Regulatory Processes in Broadcasting." Ph.D. dissertation, Stanford University, 1983.

McAdams, Katherine. "Minorities." In *The Handbook on Mass Media in the United States,* edited by Erwin K. Thomas and Brown H. Carpenter (pp. 191–206). Westport, Conn.: Greenwood, 1994.

Gilbert A. Williams

MINOW, NEWTON (1926–), former chairman of the Federal Communications Commission (FCC), was appointed by the Kennedy administration in 1961. Minow quickly gained prominence after a now-famous address to the National Association of Broadcasters in which he labeled television broadcasting of that time "a vast wasteland." He had been in office just two months when he addressed the convention in Washington, D.C. Minow challenged owners and managers to watch a full day of their own programming to see violence, formula comedies, too many commercials, and most of all, boredom. He also challenged them to do a better job of serving the public interest. Minow put the responsibility for content squarely on industry executives and dismissed notions that the audience basically determined programming by its willingness to view it. Minow cautioned broadcasters that license renewals were not guaranteed, saying, "There is nothing permanent or sacred about a broadcast license."

This was a key signal that Minow would run an activist FCC and move away from the informal controls the industry had grown accustomed to exerting on the commission. Many broadcasters felt the speech was overly antagonistic and expressed fear that the government was headed toward censorship. But most observers agree that television programmers did cut back on violent content in the several years immediately following.

Years later, Minow characterized the frequently quoted speech as a failure. He had not wanted the focus to be on the "vast wasteland" notion but rather on its references to having broadcasters serve the "public interest." He believed the "public interest" wording in the *Communications Act of 1934* was too vague and that broadcasters were not held to a high enough standard for public service. He had hoped the speech would focus more attention on defining broadcasters' roles in this area and promote a more sensible balance between broadcasters' profit-making motives and commitment to public service.

Minow's chairmanship at the FCC lasted less than three years. He returned to private law practice in 1963 and was involved in a number of communication-related efforts after leaving the FCC. He served for a time as chairman of the Public Broadcasting Service and directed a commercial broadcasting outlet and an advertising agency. He has also been a professor at Northwestern University. Regardless of his other accomplishments in the media world, he is remembered mostly for coining the "vast wasteland" concept.

Minow, Newton N. *How Vast the Wasteland Now?* New York: Gannett Foundation Media Center, Columbia University, May 9, 1991.
Minow, Newton N., and Craig Lamay. *Abandoned in the Wasteland.* New York: Hill and Wang, 1995.

Jeffrey M. McCall

MIX FORMAT, a variation of the adult contemporary (AC) format that is designed for the younger segment of the 25 to 54 demographic. The format contains a mix of carefully selected contemporary hits along with oldies. Generally, the music mix does not contain rap or heavy metal selections. "Mix" formats often include contests and lifestyle-oriented news.

Gloria G. Horning

MONOPOLY INVESTIGATIONS. In 1941, the Federal Communications Commission (FCC) adopted rules restricting "chain broadcasting" when it believed that networks were exercising too much control over their affiliated stations. The rules were upheld by the Supreme Court in a 1943 decision. As a result of increased competition and deregulation, the 1941 rules are no longer applied to radio.

Congress had expressed concerns about possible monopoly of radio as early as 1919 when Marconi held most of the equipment patents. Again in 1924, there were concerns that an RCA proposal to build a chain of superpowered radio stations would eliminate competition. In the late 1930s, Congress questioned the FCC about its apparent lack of concern over monopoly of radio by the national networks. As a result, the FCC began an investigation in 1938 that resulted in the *Report on Chain Broadcasting* in 1941. Since the FCC does not have the authority to regulate networks, the rules were worded to prevent licensed stations from entering into noncomplying agreements. The rules limited a network station affiliation contract to one year (later changed to two) and prohibited both exclusive network agreements and affiliation with any organization that maintained more than one network. The FCC had no authority to force NBC to divest itself of one of its two radio networks, but it could prohibit any of its licensees from affiliating with such a network.

NBC and CBS immediately filed suit in federal court to eliminate the chain-broadcasting rules. While the court decided it lacked jurisdiction in the suit, the Justice Department filed an antitrust suit against the networks. As a result, the Supreme Court agreed to review the chain-broadcasting rules. In 1943, the Court upheld the FCC's right to regulate the licensees in the public interest, including rules that would require NBC to divest itself of one of its networks (which became ABC). In 1967, ABC was granted a waiver from the chain-broadcasting rules when it began providing four radio networks to affiliates. By 1977, the FCC had ceased applying chain-broadcasting rules to any radio stations. Other rules exist to prevent monopolization of broadcasting by an individual or corporation.

Dom Caristi

MORMON TABERNACLE CHOIR, broadcasts the longest-running, continuous network radio program—*Music and the Spoken Word.* This long-enduring choir owes much of its fame to its weekly radio broadcasts on the CBS Radio Network. The choir began with English emigrants in the middle of the nineteenth century and on July 15, 1929, began broadcasting with Salt Lake City radio station KSL, then an NBC affiliate. Its broadcasts have been aired through war, depression, peace, and prosperity.

In 1933, when KSL became a CBS affiliate, the choir broadcasts switched to that network. Added to the choir's music in 1936 were "inspirational messages" from host Richard L. Evans. This became known as *Music and the Spoken Word,* a program that has been translated for radio distribution into several languages.

As each era of broadcast history came on the scene, the Mormon Tabernacle Choir became part of that history. In 1948, it was seen by those in Salt Lake City who had television sets. In 1961, it was part of the international shortwave radio transmission efforts of the Church of Jesus Christ of Latter-day Saints, commonly known as Mormons. About that same time, the choir was part of the first satellite transmission between the United States and Europe. Its performance in front of Mount Rushmore was seen only briefly, for the satellite transmission was orbital, and the common line-of-sight for both continents lasted only a few minutes. Later, when geosynchronous satellites came into use, the Church obtained transponder capacity and built uplink facilities, making transmission of the choir possible as well as for several other purposes.

The 300-voice choir has released more than 130 recordings and several films and videotapes. Five of its recordings have achieved a "gold-record" status. In 1959, it received a Grammy Award with its release of "The Battle Hymn of the Republic" with the Philadelphia Orchestra. More recently, its fame has been further enhanced by appearances on stages of historical renown throughout the world, attracting media attention on a much wider scale than its humble beginning on radio in 1929.

"Mormon Tabernacle Choir." In *Encyclopedia of Mormonism* (2: 950–952). New York: Macmillan Publishing Company, 1992.

Val E. Limburg

MORNING DRIVE is the prime-time daypart of radio, weekdays from 5:30 or 6:00 A.M. to 9:00 or 10:00 A.M., depending on the region. Morning drive traditionally generates the largest audience. A successful morning-drive show can demand the station's top commercial rate and provides a valuable lead-in to the rest of the broadcast day.

A potentially large listenership, rapid turnover in audience, reliance on repetition of basic information such as time and temperature, and the high volume of automobile radios in use (hence the *drive* in morning drive) are all unique to this daypart. To ensure its viability, morning drive is usually hosted by a radio station's most colorful, popular, and highest-paid talent.

Joseph R. Piasek

MORNING EDITION. *See All Things Considered*; **information formats; National Public Radio (NPR); public radio.**

MORRISON, HERBERT (1903–1989), was an early pioneer of both radio and television news and best known for his gripping microphone account of the 1937 crash of the German airship *Hindenburg*. A broadcast-news principal for almost 50 years, Morrison worked mostly at broadcast stations in the upper Midwest and achieved his greatest fame while working for WLS in Chicago.

Morrison was a native of Scottdale, Pennsylvania, and began his broadcast career in the 1920s in the Pittsburgh area. In the early 1930s, he was hired by WLS, initially a subsidiary of the Sears corporation and later a unit of ABC. In 1937, he persuaded the news director of WLS to allow him to travel to Lakehurst, New Jersey, for the *Hindenburg*'s first transatlantic arrival that May 6. Morrison was the only radio reporter present. Listeners all over the country heard Morrison say: "It's bursting into flames! Oh, the humanity! All the passengers! I don't believe it." The broadcast was not carried live on WLS, but the station had Morrison's account transcribed, which enabled its preservation.

Continuing his interest in aviation, Morrison suspended his radio news career by serving in the Army Air Force during World War II. After the war, he returned to WLS radio, although with an increasing interest in television. In the early 1950s, he moved back to Pittsburgh and became the first news director of the television station that became WTAE. In this capacity, Morrison helped bring TV news to western Pennsylvania.

After retiring from broadcast news in the late 1960s, Morrison wrote and lectured on his *Hindenburg* broadcast. He died in Morgantown, West Virginia, on January 10, 1989.

Craig M. Allen

MORROW, "COUSIN" BRUCIE (1935–), was the most popular disc jockey on WABC-AM, New York, during its heyday in the 1960s. He filled the 7–11 P.M. time slot from 1961 to 1974. During his tenure at WABC-AM, "Cousin Brucie" occupied a unique place in the New York radio market, as he created a listening audience of "cousins" from New York to Ohio and up and down the East Coast. While broadcasting the evening on clear channel rock 'n' roll stations, Morrow helped define teen music from many of his listeners at the peak of AM radio's influence on the record industry. Along with rival Murray (the K) Kaufmann from WINS-AM, Morrow contributed to Beatlemania as "the fifth Beatle." He was well known for his live music shows during the summers at Palisades Amusement Park (New Jersey). After leaving WABC-AM, he continued to play the music of the 1950s to 1970s on New York rival stations WNBC-AM and WCBS-FM into the 1980s and through national syndication into the 1990s with *Cruisin' America*. Morrow also became a broadcast station owner as a partner in the Sillerman Morrow Broadcast Group.

Fornatale, Peter, and Joshua Mills. *Radio in the Television Age*. Woodstock, N.Y.: Overlook Press, 1980.
Morrow, Bruce, and Laura Baudo. *Cousin Brucie! My Life in Rock 'n' Roll Radio*. New York: Beech Tree Books, 1987.
Sklar, Peter. *Rocking America: An Insider's Story*. New York: St. Martin's Press, 1984.

Jonathan David Tankel

MORSE, SAMUEL FINLEY BREESE (1791–1872), was an inventor, electrician, and artist. Considered one of the finest portrait painters of his day, Samuel F. B. Morse is best remembered, however, as the inventor of the telegraph—a claim that is not strictly true. On his second trip to Europe, Morse became interested in electrical experiments and was inspired by the prospect of using electricity to communicate intelligence. Aided by Joseph Henry's discoveries in electromagnetism, Morse and Alfred Vail perfected a telegraph system that they demonstrated for Congress in 1838. Although Morse was not the only electrician who devised a telegraph, he did create the simple code that bears his name. Telegraphers still use a version of Morse code to transmit messages today.

Inadvertently, Morse also invented the wireless telegraph. He and Vail had planned a demonstration of underwater telegraphy in June 1842 in New York harbor. They had strung a cable across the channel from the Battery to Governor's Island. Before the demonstration, however, a boat snagged the cable with its anchor, and the sailors on board pulled it up and cut it away. Not to be embarrassed again, Morse recalled the experiments of Professor Soemmerling in Munich using tubs of water to complete electrical circuits. Morse reasoned that he could do so with a body of water as well and, by December of that year, had transmitted and received a telegraph signal using an 80-foot-wide canal near Washington, D.C. as a natural conductor. Later Vail would demonstrate this wireless technology across the Susquehanna River at a distance of one mile. Morse never pursued these experiments for commercial purposes, and the establishment of transatlantic and other reliable cable services made this type of wireless telegraphy unnecessary.

Mabee, Carlton. *The American Leonardo: A Life of Samuel F. B. Morse.* New York: Alfred A. Knopf, 1944.

Morse, Edward Lind, ed. *Samuel F. B. Morse: His Letters and Journals.* Boston: Houghton Mifflin, 1914.

Robert H. Lochte

MORSE CODE. *See* **Branly, [Desiré] Edouard; crystal set; Fessenden, Reginald Aubrey; ham radio; World War I and radio.**

MOTOWN, the name of a black popular music genre that in the 1960s bridged African-American artists into mainstream pop radio airplay. Former Ford Motor Company assembly-line worker Berry Gordy, Jr., founded "the sound of young America" in Detroit or the "Motor City," which inspired his company name, Motown.

Gordy manufactured an entertainment empire by taking local soul artists and propelling them onto an international platform. The artist lineup rolls out like vintage milestones in the history of pop music—Diana Ross and the Supremes, Michael Jackson and the Jackson Five, Smokey Robinson and the Miracles, Lionel Richie and the Commodores, The Temptations, and a host of other groups and solo acts ranging from vocal stylist Marvin Gaye to the shrewd music texture of Stevie Wonder. Music historian Philip Ennis notes that, "although Motown's acts were all black-oriented, the tours and the venues in which they played stimulated rock and roll audiences' easy acceptance of black pop as part of their music" (p. 275).

Gordy marketed his artists on his own group of record labels including Motown, Tamala, and Gordy. He cross-pollinated his empire using music composition teams, like Holland-Dozier-Holland or Ashford and Simpson, to create one tune that could be multiply marketed, making money as different hits for different artists. For example, Gladys Knight and the Pips first chugged through "I Heard It Through the Grapevine" to hit status for Gordy's Soul label in 1967. A year later, the same words and music slowed to a sinister, melancholy love poem by Marvin Gaye, becoming a megahit for the Tamala label. By the mid-1970s the Motown record company joined with A&M, 20th Century, and United Artists as one of four major independents capturing sales away from the traditional corporate giants, ABC, CBS, EMI, Polygram, and Warner.

Motown began a western migration to Hollywood in 1969, shifting headquarters there by 1972. Television and movie productions launched company acts like Diana Ross onto the big screen in films like *Lady Sings the Blues* and *Mahogany.*

Ennis, Philip H. *The Seventh Stream: The Emergence of Rocknroll in American Popular Music.* Hanover, N.H.: University Press of New England, 1992.

Waller, Don. *The Motown Story.* New York: Charles Scribner's Sons, 1985.

Motown. http://www.Motown.com

B. William Silcock

MSA. *See* **metropolitan statistical area (MSA).**

MTV (MUSIC TELEVISION) was one of the earliest, and most successful, cable television networks to target the teenage audience by airing music video clips. MTV applied the radio music formula to television; it programmed a rotation of popular music and artists in the form of music videos. MTV contributed to increased record sales and a revival of top-40 radio in the 1980s by introducing new music and artists through videos.

Warner AMEX Satellite Entertainment Company (WASEC), a partnership of Warner Cable and American Express, debuted the 24-hour video music network on August 1, 1981. The station had a library of 250 clips from which to choose. In its early days, MTV played mostly album-oriented rock (AOR), supplemented with occasional videos by new-wave artists. As MTV became available in more homes throughout the 1980s, and record companies increased their music video output, the network expanded its playlist to include rap, heavy metal, and dance music.

Bob Pittman, who directed MTV programming from 1980 to 1986, adapted many techniques and practices from AOR and top-40 radio. The network employed a rigid playlist, based largely on audience research techniques that Pittman had relied on as a radio programmer before he joined MTV. Veejays, like radio deejays, introduced the clips and provided between-song banter. The network produced a variety of creative promotional announcements. It also devised contests with fantastic prizes, frequently flying winners to exotic locations, where rock stars waited to meet them.

Record labels recognized that MTV exposure boosted sales, and they provided the promotional clips for free. Artists like Duran Duran and Madonna were MTV staples before they appeared on most radio stations playlists. The network's influence extended beyond the music industry. Performers like Cyndi Lauper, Boy George, Madonna, and Nirvana started fashion trends based on their appearances in MTV videos. In addition, television programs, movies, and commercials incorporated the MTV style: quick-cut editing, slick, flashy imagery, and loud rock music.

In the wake of MTV's early success, Ted Turner established his Cable Music Channel, which lasted only a month before MTV bought its assets in 1984. Only *The Box,* which reached 20 million homes in 1994, has offered a sustained pop music alternative to MTV. Cable networks like Country Music Television, MOR Music, and Z Music have found niches outside of mainstream pop and rock. On January 1, 1985, MTV began its VH-1 service, featuring adult contemporary videos and classic clips from the 1960s and 1970s, for the 25- to 54-year-old audience.

In early 1986 MTV executives responded to dwindling ratings by adding several new shows and reducing the number of music videos. Viacom's purchase of MTV in March 1986 accelerated the network's move toward longer programs, with videos selected and aired according to more narrow pop music generic classifications. In early 1986, for example, the network premiered *120 Minutes,* two hours of alternative rock. *Yo! MTV Raps* began in 1988. Some new series included little or no music. MTV had success with a game show, *Remote Control* (1987 debut), a nonfictional soap opera, *The Real World* (1992 debut), and a cartoon, *Beavis and Butt-head* (1993 debut).

By 1991, MTV aired 27 hours a week of nonmusic programming, though the network maintained its youth-culture orientation. In 1992, MTV began to cover national politics. Reporter Tabitha Soren promoted voter registration and interviewed key figures at the political conventions. Bill Clinton tacitly acknowledged the network's influence among young voters by fielding questions at an MTV forum during the campaign and appearing at the MTV Inaugural Ball after his election.

MTV has attempted to tailor its products to different markets and regions around the world. International programming started with MTV Europe in October 1984. By 1995, MTV had built six different global services: MTV Asia, MTV Europe, MTV Brazil, MTV Japan, MTV Latino, and MTV Mandarin. International business generated 28 percent of the network's revenue in 1995.

Denisoff, R. Serge. *Inside MTV.* New Brunswick, N.J.: Transaction Publishers, 1988.
McGrath, Tom. *MTV: The Making of a Revolution.* Philadelphia: Running Press, 1996.
Polskin, Howard. "MTV at 10: The Beat Goes On." *TV Guide* 3 (August 1991): 4–8.
                                                                                      David Weinstein

MULLIN, JACK, introduced superior tape recorders in the 1940s that helped end the network ban on recorded entertainment programming. During a 1945 field trip to inspect captured Germany communications equipment, U.S. Army Signal Corpsman Jack Mullin discovered several very high-quality tape recorders in a radio station outside Frankfurt. Although the machines looked similar to other early German machines, Mullin found these recorders produced a livelike sound that was far superior to anything available in the United States.

At the end of the war, Mullin shipped two of the German tape recorders (called Magnetophons) back to the United States along with dozens of German tape recordings. Rebuilding the electronics with U.S. parts, he was able to extend the Magnetophon's already impressive 10 kilohertz (kHz) frequency response to nearly 15 kHz. The improved Magnetrack, as Mullin dubbed his machine, was first unveiled publicly at a meeting of recording engineers in 1946. In attendance were engineers representing Ampex Corporation and popular radio performer Bing Crosby, who had sat out the entire 1945–1946 season because of NBC's policy against recorded-entertainment programming. Crosby jumped to ABC when that network agreed to let him record his show and hired Mullin to record the next season's programs.

Largely because of Crosby's influence, ABC placed an order for 12 of the new Ampex model 200 recorders, which were based on Mullin's machine. NBC, CBS, record companies, and others soon followed ABC into the tape age. The Mullin Collection documenting the history of recorded sound, including an original

Magnetophon, is housed at the Pavek Museum of Broadcasting in St. Louis Park, Minnesota.

Hammer, Peter. "Jack Mullin: The Man and His Machines." *Journal of the Audio Engineering Society* 37 (6) (June 1989): 490–504.

Hammer, Peter, and Don Ososke. "The Birth of the German Magnetophon Tape Recorder 1928–1945." *db* 30 (March 1982): 47–52.

Mark J. Heistad

MULTIPLEXING. In radio, multiplexing is transmitting more than one signal simultaneously on a carrier wave within the bandwidth of the station. By multiplexing, FM radio stations are able to offer stereo programming (separate left and right channels) to an audience. This ability made FM radio more competitive with AM radio and helped FM's growth in audience beginning in the early 1960s. Through the use of multiplexing, FM stations are also able to transmit additional signals that can be received by special subcarrier receivers.

Both AM and FM broadcasters are permitted to multiplex services on the same carrier. These subcarrier transmissions are usually referred to as SCS (Subsidiary Communications Service), formerly known as SCA (Subsidiary Communication Authorization). In the early 1980s, the Federal Communications Commission relaxed the rules relating to subcarrier transmission and allowed data services as well as audio services. It also allowed noncommercial stations to offer services on their subcarrier for profit.

In addition to stereo, broadcast stations can use multiplexed services for background music for offices and stores, reading services for the blind, distribution of audio networks, data transmission, paging services, and regulation of appliances during periods of peak electrical demand.

Spiceland, David, ed. "Multiplexing." In *McGraw-Hill Encyclopedia of Science and Technology.* 7th ed. New York : McGraw-Hill, 1992.

Steven C. Runyon and David Spiceland

MURROW, EDWARD R. (1908–1965), was radio's first journalist of eminence. His insightful reporting from London during World War II gave the journalism of radio the same status as print journalism. Because of his integrity as a reporter and the high standards he set, Murrow has been accepted as the standard bearer for all reporters in broadcasting.

Edward R. Murrow was born on April 25, 1908, the third son of Roscoe and Ethel Murrow, on a farm in Guilford County, North Carolina. The 120-acre farm on Polecat Creek had been Murrow property since the 1750s. Because the mother regarded tobacco, the best cash crop, as sinful, the family faced financial difficulties and in 1914 moved west to the small town of Blanchard on Puget Sound, where cousins of Ethel were living. This was lumber country, and Roscoe Murrow, after working briefly as a brakeman, was promoted to engineer for a railroad, hauling Douglas fir and cedar down from the logging camps.

Murrow attended Washington State College, now Washington State University, where he excelled as president of student government, colonel in the ROTC, head of the Pacific Student Presidents Association, and star debater. During summer vacations he worked in logging camps, advancing from axman to surveyor's assistant. To avoid the scorn of fellow timbermen, he changed his given name, Egbert, to Edward.

Murrow chose speech as his major and was instructed by Ida Lou Anderson, a young professor crippled by polio to whom he paid lifelong tribute for her teaching. He also enrolled in a radio course and acted in student plays. He qualified for Phi Beta Kappa.

On graduation, Murrow moved to New York as president of the National Student Federation. Occasionally, he traveled to Europe, setting up debates between students attending American and European universities. In 1932, he became assistant director of the Institute of International Education and was instrumental in bringing to America noted German scholars threatened by Nazi persecution.

He joined CBS in 1935 as director of talks, lining up educators, scientists, and leaders in government as speakers on radio. Two years later, he was assigned to London, where as CBS European director, he performed a similar role. In 1938, he was arranging the broadcast of a boys' choir from Warsaw when Hitler seized Austria. Hearing the news, he flew to Vienna and, turning correspondent, broadcast radio's first eyewitness report of the coup. "Young storm troopers are riding about the streets, riding about in trucks and vehicles of all sorts, singing and tossing oranges out to the crowd."

Anticipating the outbreak of war, Murrow recruited a staff of correspondents that included William L. Shirer, Larry LeSueur, Eric Sevareid, Richard C. Hottelet, Charles Collingwood, and Howard K. Smith. He said he was hiring people who could write and knew what they were talking about. These capable young reporters came to be known as "Murrow's boys," an appellation regarded as an honor.

Murrow himself won fame during the Battle of Britain. His broadcasts starting "This is London" were delivered calmly but with compelling detail. The librarian of Congress, Archibald MacLeish, told Murrow, "You laid the dead of London at our door." Aside from those made during the Battle of Britain, Murrow's best-remembered broadcasts of that period are his graphic reports on a night bombing mission against Berlin—"Berlin was a kind of orchestrated hell, a terrible symphony of light and flame"—and on the liberation of the Buchenwald concentration camp, one of the largest in Germany.

Murrow shocked listeners on December 13, 1942, when he reported that in Germany "[m]illions of human beings, most of them Jews, are being gathered up with ruthless efficiency and murdered." Many Americans were hearing of the Holocaust for the first time.

In 1946, Murrow became head of CBS News. He set up a documentary unit and created innovative programs such as *As Others See Us,* a foreign opinion broadcast, and *CBS Views the Press,* which critiqued the performance of New York newspapers. Dissatisfied with the postwar work of William L. Shirer, he accepted his colleague's resignation, a rupture between two friends that never healed.

After 18 months, Murrow quit his executive position. He felt uncomfortable administrating and missed reporting and went back on the air with a prime-time program, *Edward R. Murrow and the News*. The 15-minute broadcast, consisting of hard news followed by commentary, premiered on September 29, 1947, and ran Monday through Friday for 12 years. It was the most prestigious newscast in radio.

In 1950, Murrow teamed up with Fred W. Friendly to produce a radio magazine called *Hear It Now,* which pioneered in making extensive use of audiotape. The one-hour weekly program also benefited from a musical score by Virgil Thompson and popular contributors like Red Barber and Abe Burrows. The program's significance is that, by means of audiotape, listeners now could hear what had happened, such as artillery fire in Korea and what had been said by some political candidate.

Although highly successful, the program was dropped after one season. The audience was turning to television, and the Murrow-Friendly team, adding sight to sound, gave up *Hear It Now* for *See It Now,* television's first major documentary series. It was on *See It Now* on March 9, 1954, that Murrow documented the unscrupulous methods of Senator Joseph McCarthy and helped bring his downfall. He also coproduced and reported for the TV series *CBS Reports.*

In 1960, Murrow did a Sunday program for CBS Radio titled *Background.* Although Murrow commentary was featured, most of the half hour was taken up with reports by CBS correspondents in Washington and overseas.

By this time CBS chairman William S. Paley had cooled toward Murrow. He was tired, he said, of controversial documentaries and the newsman's criticism of television programming, and Murrow left the network in January 1961 to become director of the United States Information Agency. He served until 1964 and for that service received from President Lyndon Johnson the Medal of Freedom, the nation's highest civilian award.

Murrow, a heavy smoker of cigarettes, died of lung cancer on April 27, 1965. He was 57. Surviving were his wife, Janet Huntington Brewster, and a son, Charles "Casey" Murrow.

Bliss, Edward, Jr., ed. *In Search of Light: The Broadcasts of Edward R. Murrow, 1938–1961.* New York: Alfred A. Knopf, 1967.

Cloud, Stanley, and Lynne Olson. *The Murrow Boys: Pioneers on the Front Lines of Broadcast Journalism.* New York: Houghton Mifflin, 1996.

Kendrick, Alexander. *Prime Time: The Life of Edward R. Murrow.* Boston: Little, Brown, 1969.

Persico, Joseph E. *Edward R. Murrow, an American Original.* New York: McGraw-Hill, 1988.

Sperber, A. M. *Murrow: His Life and Times.* New York: Freundlich Books, 1986.

Edward Bliss, Jr.

MUSICAL CLOCK. *See* **execution format; format radio; hot clock.**

MUSIC OF YOUR LIFE, one of the radio nostalgia formats, is delivered by satellite to subscribing stations across the United States. Under the theme, "music of the 1940s, 1950s, and 1960s," the music is mostly from the 1950s and some from the 1970s. It is directed at an audience that remembers the Big Band days, singers such as Frank Sinatra, and so on. *Music of Your Life* was created in 1982 and was initially under Trans Star but was acquired by Westwood One, located in Valencia,

California, a suburb of Los Angeles. It is one of eight such formats offered by Westwood, all in the nostalgia genre.

The service operates 24 hours a day, seven days a week, so it is available to any station in any time zone around the clock. Delivery by satellite allows the originating studio to trigger the commercials and call letters of the stations that subscribe to the service. A silent pulse is sent with the signal that triggers whatever is cued up. Local staff can put in local news or tie into one of the national news services, such as CNN Radio News or AP Radio news. At the present time, *Music of Your Life* is on 230 radio stations across the country.

ElDean Bennett

MUSICSCAN, computer software designed to schedule musical selections according to a particular radio format or formula. The software selects songs to fit a music rotation created by a program or music director (see **hot clock**).

Frederic A. Leigh

MUTUAL BROADCASTING SYSTEM (MBS), radio network that originated in 1934 when WGN, Chicago, and WOR, New York, joined with WXYZ, Detroit, and WLW, Cincinnati, to sell commercial time. At the time, WGN and WOR were the only clear channel radio stations in major markets not affiliated with CBS or NBC. The four-station group also exchanged programs, the most famous of which was *The Lone Ranger,* which originated on WXYZ in 1933. Unlike the big three networks, MBS never made the transition to television and is owned today by Westwood One.

Frederic A. Leigh

N

NAB. *See* **ASCAP (American Society of Composers Authors and Publishers).**

NARROWCASTING, the opposite of broadcasting, develops and delivers programming to a narrowly defined, target audience. Radio stations and magazine publishers have been "narrowcasting" for years, as they provide content to specialized audiences. Some radio stations serve further subdivisions within major radio formats (e.g., an "all-Beatles" oldie station).

Cable TV operators and cable networks presently narrowcast the majority of their offerings: 24-hour/all-news, science fiction, shopping, golf, gardening, old movies, all-sports, or specialized audio channels. The audiences for this programming are niche or targeted groups, unlike the mass-media audience targeted by major TV network programs.

Waterman, David. "Narrowcasting and Broadcasting on Non-broadcast Media." *Communication Research* 19 (February 1992): 3.

J. R. Rush

NASHVILLE, based on the success of clear channel WSM-AM's live barn dance show, the *Grand Ole Opry,* became country music's centralized home. Although Nashville itself has had many other radio stations, only WSM and the *Grand Ole Opry* have achieved the fame leading to an Opryland theme park and a "Music Row" of recording studios. WSM-AM, 650 in the AM dial (heard from Kansas to Virginia to Florida to Michigan), originated to sell National Life and Accident Insurance Company (*We Shield Millions*) policies throughout the South and Midwest. It pioneered the *Grand Ole Opry* shortly after it went on the air in 1925, and through the 1930s and 1940s, the *Grand Ole Opry* remained a regional favorite. During the 1950s, as radio stations switched to top-40 and other youth-oriented formats, WSM stuck with the *Grand Ole Opry,* and by 1960, Nashville had emerged as the center of country music. At first, the WSM radio studios served as recording centers, but by 1956 entrepreneurs like Owen Bradley had built their own studios and created "Music Row," which made artists like Patsy Cline and Hank Williams internationally famous. A decade later came the theme park and the Country Music Hall of Fame.

Hagen, Chet. *Grand Ole Opry.* New York: Henry Holt, 1989.
Kinsbury, Paul. *The Grand Ole Opry History of Country Music.* New York: Villard, 1995.

Douglas Gomery

NATIONAL ASSOCIATION OF BLACK OWNED BROADCASTERS

(NABOB) is a trade organization that represents the interests of African-American owners of radio and television broadcast facilities throughout the United States. Through its lobbying efforts, NABOB informs Congress, the Federal Communications Commission (FCC), and others about legislative and regulatory concerns of its members. Created in 1976, NABOB began its advocacy role at a time when there were only about 30 African-American–owned radio stations and no black-owned television stations. NABOB and other media advocacy groups, like the National Black Media Coalition, pressured the FCC to address and remedy such media-ownership inequalities. Thus, in the late 1970s, the FCC instituted the comparative hearings process for station applicants and the Tax Certificate and Distress Sale Policies that enabled African Americans, other people of color, and women to increase opportunities to own broadcast facilities. By 1980, NABOB's membership had grown to include about 140 black-owned radio stations and 7 black-owned television stations. In 1996, NABOB represented about 170 African-American–owned radio stations and 25 black-owned television stations. But by the mid-1990s, the FCC had curtailed many of the aforementioned policies, and the *Telecommunications Act of 1996* partially eliminated prior restrictions on multiple-station ownership by a single company. Today, NABOB continues its lobbying efforts to ensure that African-American broadcast owners are not forced to sell nor are they prevented from buying in a broadcast marketplace where small-station owners/buyers increasingly have to compete against media conglomerates with multiple-station holdings—sometimes in the same market.

Black Radio: Telling It Like It Was. A 13-part radio documentary series with Lou Rawls. Washington, D.C.: Radio Smithsonian, Smithsonian Productions, 1996. (Series tapes are available for research at the Archives of African American Music and Culture, Indiana University, Bloomington, and the Museums of Radio and Television in Los Angeles and New York.)
Smith, F. Leslie, Milan Meeske, and John W. Wright II. *Electronic Media and Government: The Regulation of Wireless and Wired Mass Communication in the United States.* White Plains, N.Y.: Longman, 1995.
Federal Communications Commission (FCC) Internet Homepage. http://www.fcc.gov/

Sonja Williams

NATIONAL ASSOCIATION OF BROADCAST EMPLOYEES AND TECHNICIANS (NABET),

the radio, TV, and cable workers sector of the Communication Workers of America (CWA), is affiliated with the AFL-CIO. While NABET today represents radio and TV station employees in many different job categories, it was the first union representing broadcast technicians exclusively and is one of three major technical and engineering trade unions in broadcasting; the other two are the International Brotherhood of Electrical Workers (IBEW) and the International Alliance of Theatrical and Stage Employees (IATSE) and Moving Picture Machine Operators of the United States and Canada. The National Association of Broadcast Engineers and Technicians was founded in 1953 at NBC, but later the word "Engineers" was changed to "Employees" in order to appeal to more workers (see **unions**).

Mark J. Braun

NATIONAL ASSOCIATION OF EDUCATIONAL BROADCASTERS (NAEB). Founded as the Association of College and University Broadcasting Stations on November 12, 1925, the NAEB served as the singularly most important professional organization during public radio's formative years. The association provided a unified voice supporting the use of radio for educational purposes. Ineffective lobbying efforts before the newly created Federal Radio Commission in the late 1920s prompted association members to push for the preservation of 25 percent of all standard radio frequencies when the *Radio Act of 1927* was being rewritten in 1933. The association played a major role in creating the Wagner–Hatfield Amendment to the *Communications Act of 1934,* which would have protected one fourth of all broadcast allocations for educational use. While the amendment failed to carry the needed majority, it did serve to unite the association membership and gave them a sense of mission that eventually reached fruition in the preservation of FM frequencies for noncommercial educational use in 1938.

The name of the association was changed in September of 1934 in response to a broadening base of support for educational broadcasting that extended beyond college and university campuses. The reconstituted NAEB provided a more effective voice for educational radio interests before the new Federal Communications Commission, and the association also served to secure equipment grants that enabled member stations to exchange programming. In 1950 the NAEB secured a major grant from the W. K. Kellogg Foundation to establish a permanent headquarters and mount an audiotape network. Headquarters for the NAEB were originally located on the University of Illinois campus, and the National Educational Radio Network was born. The decade of the 1950s witnessed a shifting emphasis on the struggle to preserve channels for educational television and to get these fledgling new television stations on the air. NAEB's expansion to meet these challenges resulted in both relocation and reorganization. In September of 1960, the national headquarters moved to Washington, D.C., and in January 1964, separate divisions for radio (National Educational Radio [NER]) and television (Educational Television Stations [ETS]) were formed. NER's executive director, Jerrold Sandler, played a vital role in getting radio included in the *Public Broadcasting Act of 1967,* but the creation of the Public Broadcasting Service and National Public Radio in the early 1970s forced the NAEB to change its mission again. With the demise of NER and ETS, the NAEB attempted to serve the public broadcasting profession and academic community as an individual member organization, providing an annual convention, educational seminars, and a scholarly publication program. But limited financial resources forced the association to declare bankruptcy, and it closed down its headquarters in November of 1981.

Alford, W. Wayne. *NAEB History, 1954–1965*. Washington, D.C.: National Association of Educational Broadcasters, 1966.

Avery, Robert K., Paul E. Burrows, and Clara J. Pincus. *Research Index for NAEB Journals*. Washington, D.C.: Public Telecommunications Press, 1980.

Hill, Harold E. *NAEB History, 1925–1954*. Washington, D.C.: National Association of Educational Broadcasters, 1954.

Robert K. Avery

NATIONAL BARN DANCE, THE. See **country and western music;** *Grand Ole Opry*; **Nashville.**

NATIONAL BROADCASTING COMPANY (NBC) arose from disputes during the 1920s among companies holding patents to radio, including the Radio Corporation of America (RCA), General Electric (GE), Westinghouse, and American Telegraph and Telephone (AT&T). From 1919 through 1921 these companies had signed cross-licensing agreements, which allowed all signatories to share their patents and inventions. But under these agreements, two adversarial groups evolved to claim sole control over broadcasting: the "Radio Group," comprised of Westinghouse, RCA, and GE; and the "Telephone Group," composed of AT&T and Western Electric. Each group believed it held rights to broadcasting under the agreements. From 1922 to 1924, they attempted to reconcile their differences but could not reach an agreement. The Radio Group was led by Owen Young and David Sarnoff, while various individuals represented the Telephone Group. Their negotiations were secret, because the Federal Trade Commission (FTC) was investigating the companies for restraint of trade, and any hint of the feud would have fueled the FTC's inquiry.

In 1925, both groups agreed to binding arbitration, but a stalemate soon resulted after the arbiter, Boyden Hull, found in favor of the Radio Group. The Telephone Group then asserted that the agreements must have given the Radio Group a monopoly and therefore were illegal. Not willing to make their dispute public, the companies reentered mediation that finally settled their concerns.

Under new agreements signed in 1926, each group received a portion of the growing broadcast business. AT&T became the provider of wire interconnections, or networks, for stations, sold its station WEAF to RCA for $1 million, and agreed not to reenter the broadcast field. The Radio Group was left with broadcasting and set manufacturing. The Radio Group, under Owen Young and David Sarnoff's leadership, formed a new company on September 9, 1926, the National Broadcasting Company.

Under AT&T, WEAF had been the flagship station of a network of more than 20 stations, while RCA operated a smaller network with station WJZ as its flagship. Under the new agreements, the two networks became separate networks of NBC. The old WEAF network became known as NBC Red, while WJZ's network became NBC Blue. A smaller NBC network, NBC Orange, operated on the West Coast from April 1927 until late 1928, when broadcasting became coast to coast.

In 1930, a Department of Justice investigation of RCA, GE, and Westinghouse for antitrust violations led to GE's divestiture of RCA and its broadcasting arm, NBC, in 1932. By then, the NBC networks dominated radio business and had affiliates in most large cities. By 1941, 25 percent of the country's radio stations were affiliated with the NBC networks, and many were dominant clear channel operations. The one-sided control NBC and the Columbia Broadcasting System (CBS) had over their affiliates and their programming became the reason the Federal Communications Commission (FCC) initiated an investigation of network power in March 1938. In May 1941, after months of hearings, the FCC issued its chain broadcasting report. Its new rules were designed to eliminate network abuses. Among the most controversial rules were those forbidding stations to affiliate themselves with entities owning more than one network and rules prohibiting duopoly, or owning two stations of the same type (e.g., AM or FM) in the same broadcast service area. NBC's networks and CBS challenged these rules in court. Fighting all the way to the Supreme Court, the companies contended the new rules went beyond the FCC's power, violated the First Amendment, and would destroy American broadcasting.

In the landmark 1943 case *NBC v. U.S.,* the Supreme Court upheld the FCC's right to regulate broadcasting, stating the rules did not deny the network's free speech rights. Reluctantly, NBC agreed to sell one of its networks, and it chose the weaker of the two, NBC Blue. Candy producer Edward Noble bought the network for $8 million, and in 1945, NBC Blue became the American Broadcasting Company (ABC).

In the decade following World War II, network radio declined as network television grew. Many popular radio shows moved to television, and advertisers soon followed. By 1960, radio network programming so popular in the 1930s and 1940s was dead.

NBC maintained its network-owned and -operated stations until the 1980s. In late 1986, GE bought NBC's parent company, RCA, bringing the company back to its original owner. In July 1987 the new owners sold off the NBC Radio Network for $50 million to Westwood One and then sold off its owned and operated stations separately so it could concentrate on television. The pioneering radio network was no more.

Sobel, Robert. *RCA.* New York: Stein and Day, 1986.

Louise Benjamin

NATIONAL COMMITTEE FOR EDUCATION BY RADIO (NCER), early educational broadcasting group that pushed for a set-aside of frequencies for noncommercial, educational radio stations in the 1930s. NCER and the National Advisory Council on Radio Education (NACRE) were two influential early educational broadcasting organizations. Though sometimes confused, the two were very different and often rival organizations.

NCER, subsidized by the Payne Fund, advocated a government set-aside of frequencies for noncommercial, educational radio stations. Under the leadership of fiery chairman Joy Elmer Morgan, the committee lobbied Congress on behalf of the unsuccessful 1931 Fess Bill, which would have set aside 15 percent of all radio frequencies for educational broadcasting, and led the set-aside forces during a 1934 Federal Communications Commission (FCC) hearing on noncommercial broadcasting. Following defeat of the 1934 Wagner-Hatfield Amendment, the NCER leadership passed to the more moderate University of Wyoming president Arthur Crane, and the committee began advocating cooperative production of educational programming with commercial broadcasters. The most successful result of this effort was the Rocky Mountain Radio Council. NCER disbanded in 1941.

NACRE, funded by the Carnegie Corporation and John D. Rockefeller, supported broadcasting educational programs on commercial stations and networks. NACRE has particularly close ties to NBC, which broadcast a number of its educational programs in the mid-1930s, including *Your Government and You, The Construction of the 20th Century,* and *Government in a Depression.* However, a 1937 NACRE report concluded that any systematic attempt at a national program of educational broadcasting was doomed to failure because the network distributed the programs in unsatisfactory time slots and because NBC affiliates were largely unwilling to run them. The organization disbanded later that same year.

Hill, Frank Ernest. *Tune in for Education.* New York: National Committee for Education by Radio, 1942.

Leach, Eugene. *Tuning Out Education: The Cooperation Doctrine in Radio, 1922–38.* Washington, D.C.: Current, 1983.

McChesney, Robert W. *Telecommunications, Mass Media and Democracy: The Battle for the Control of U.S. Broadcasting, 1928–1935.* New York: Oxford University Press, 1993.

Tyler, Tracy F., ed. *Radio as a Cultural Agency: Proceedings of a National Conference on the Use of Radio as a Cultural Agency.* Washington, D.C.: National Committee on Education by Radio, 1934.

Mark J. Heistad

NATIONAL PUBLIC RADIO (NPR), a network based in Washington, D.C., produces and distributes programming; manages the public radio system's satellite interconnection; and provides lobbying, training, and other services to its affiliated stations.

The creation of NPR flowed from the *Public Broadcasting Act of 1967,* which called for the new Corporation for Public Broadcasting (CPB), among its other charges, to foster development of a system of public radio stations.

CPB sponsored a series of meetings of educational radio station managers in 1969 and 1970 from which emerged the concept of a network owned by its member stations. Early in 1971 NPR distributed its first programming, taped concerts by the Los Angeles Philharmonic; that May the network launched an afternoon news offering called *All Things Considered,* originally broadcast to 104 stations in 34 states and Puerto Rico.

Although the network attracted a loyal following and added programming (including a morning news program *Morning Edition,* in 1979), NPR nearly folded in a 1983 fiscal crisis. With the Reagan administration seeking to reduce significantly, if not eliminate, funding for public broadcasting, NPR undertook an ambitious, entrepreneurial program intended to wean itself from federal support. Instead, the network almost went bankrupt, accumulating a deficit of more than $6 million. Loans from CPB and NPR's member stations saved the network, which underwent a major restructuring. Today, NPR's funding comes from dues paid by member stations (of which there were more than 550 in 1996), corporate underwriting of network programs, and foundation grants.

NPR's signature programs are *All Things Considered* and *Morning Edition*, produced by the network's news division, based in Washington, D.C., and including correspondents and stringers throughout the world. In its early days, goes an inside joke, the understaffed network covered breaking news a day late and "called it analysis." But today, NPR is a primary source of news for millions of listeners. NPR in the 1990s capitalized on the popularity of talk radio by adding several call-in programs, enabling member stations to broadcast a consistent news/talk format in public radio's in-depth style.

NPR's Cultural Programming Division offers stations a range of programs from the high culture *Performance Today* to the pop culture *Car Talk*, ostensibly an auto-advice show but noted for its wry humor. In 1996, the network was developing a music program entitled *Anthem*, targeted at listeners aged 25 to 35, a demographic in which public radio was traditionally weak.

According to NPR research data, 17 million people listen to NPR member stations each week. Although NPR's dominance in public radio has been eroded somewhat by the rise of other programmers, notably Public Radio International, the NPR "brand" has come to represent public radio for many listeners. This has also made the network a lightning rod for criticism from both conservatives and liberals. Critics on the right have claimed there was a liberal bias in NPR news programming. Listeners on the left complained that the network has lost its alternative edge and meandered into the media mainstream.

NPR's hiring of a telecommunications company executive with strong corporate connections, Delano Lewis, as its president in 1994 reflected the network's view of the economic and technological challenges it faces. However, liberal critics were troubled by the network's talks with commercial media conglomerates over potential partnerships; a 1996 op-ed commentary in the *New York Times* was headlined "Must NPR Sell Itself?"

Buzenberg, William E. "Growing NPR." In *Radio: The Forgotten Medium*, edited by Edward C. Pease and Everette E. Dennis (pp. 185–192). New Brunswick, N.J.: Transaction Publishers, 1995.

Looker, Thomas. *The Sound and the Story: NPR and the Art of Radio*. Boston: Houghton Mifflin, 1995.

Stavitsky, Alan G. "The Changing Conception of Localism in U.S. Public Radio." *Journal of Broadcasting & Electronic Media* 38 (1) (winter 1994): 19–33.

Stavitsky, Alan G., and Timothy W. Gleason. "Alternative Things Considered: A Comparison of National Public Radio and Pacifica Radio News Coverage." *Journalism Quarterly* 71 (4) (winter 1994): 775–786.

National Public Radio. http://www.npr.org

Alan G. Stavitsky

NATIONAL RADIO BROADCASTERS ASSOCIATION (NRBA), a splinter organization of the National Association of Broadcasters (NAB), formed in 1959. The NRBA had 2,000 members, 15 regional groups, and organizations in all 50 states. It grew out of the FM Development Association and gave a voice to smaller radio broadcasters in an era when the rapid growth in popularity of television was widely seen as a threat to the future of radio.

The NRBA promoted sales and listenership of radio, lobbied on behalf of radio, encouraged technical development, gave out the annual Golden Radio Award and Gabbert Award for Leadership, and produced several weekly and monthly publications for members. It also held a yearly convention. In 1986, the NRBA was subsumed into the NAB, merging with its radio division.

John R. Broholm

NATIONAL RADIO CONFERENCES. Four National Radio Conferences convened by the Department of Commerce in the 1920s had as their purpose voluntary cooperation from members of the broadcasting industry.

Principles adopted at the first conference laid the foundations of present broadcasting.

1. Broadcasting channels should be public property.
2. Broadcasting should be conducted as a private enterprise.
3. There should be no monopoly in broadcasting.
4. There must be regulation of the traffic to prevent interference.
5. There should be no person-to-person use of wavelengths except by the military and licensed amateurs.
6. And the then-known wave band was divided into three parts among the broadcaster, the amateurs, and the military authorities.

At the Second National Radio Conference, the Commerce Department abandoned the policy of two-channel allocation of broadcasting stations with the cooperation of the Navy Department and assigned a discrete frequency from a predetermined wave band to each broadcast station. During 1923 and 1924, Congress still couldn't pass a new radio bill. Hoover called the Third National Radio Conference in October 1924 in an effort to stem the tide of interference.

A year later, the fourth and largest National Radio Conference was held on November 9, 1925. Its 400 delegates considered limiting the number of stations, granting licenses on the basis of "public interest." The conference decided that advertising was a proper means of support for broadcasting if it was indirect or institutional. Matters discussed at earlier conferences were again raised. The already tenuous authority of the secretary of commerce disintegrated shortly after the Fourth National Radio Conference due to the Zenith-WJAZ case.

Archer, Gleason L. *History of Radio to 1926.* New York: American Historical Society, Inc., 1938.
Garvey, Daniel E. "Secretary Hoover and the Quest for Broadcast Regulation." *Journalism History* 3 (3) (autumn 1976): 66.

Jansky, C. M., Jr. "The Contributions of Herbert Hoover to Broadcasting." *Journal of Broadcasting* 1 (3) (summer 1957): 249.

Marvin R. Bensman

NATIONAL RELIGIOUS BROADCASTERS (NRB), founded in 1944, is a collective voice of religious broadcasters protecting access to broadcast airwaves, both paid and free, and observing excellent standards in programming the Gospel of Jesus Christ to the world. NRB is governed by a 90-member board of directors elected annually by the voting members. Each year the board establishes an executive committee of five elected officers and five members-at-large elected by the board. Standing committees represent the special interests of religious broadcasters. The NRB also has a full-time professional staff. Legal representation in Washington, D.C. gives NRB members access to federal, state, and local agencies and governments. The NRB supported the *Cable Act of 1992,* which benefited religious television stations, and has consistently fought against reinstatement of the Fairness Doctrine. Current issues include music licensing and spectrum auctions. The NRB represents 800 member organizations and over 1,400 radio and 100 television stations from its Manassas, Virginia, headquarters.

NRB works with the Evangelical Council for Financial Accountability (ECFA) on issues of financial integrity. The NRB publishes a monthly periodical, *Religious Broadcasting,* which includes in-depth articles developed around a theme of importance to the religious broadcasting industry. Feature article authors include well-known industry professionals who offer knowledge, experience, and insight into how the magazine's readers can best impact the religious broadcasting community. *Religious Broadcasting* carries monthly departments informing readers of events and trends in the industry, concentrating on news related to specific areas of interest among broadcasters. Column topics include updates on the Federal Communications Commission (FCC), radio and television programming, selling airtime, and raising funds. The NRB also publishes an annual *Directory of Religious Media* listing all known religious radio and television stations, program producers, agencies, consultants, and book and music publishers. Each listing provides key personnel, addresses, telephone, and fax (when available) numbers, as well as brief descriptions of the station, program, or company. The directory listings may be purchased on diskette by specific listings (i.e., radio stations only, suppliers only). Mailing labels are also available. The membership department publishes a bimonthly newsletter. NRB also maintains an active web site with a Web Directory, Classifieds, Staff Directory, and updates on issues and the annual convention. Members can obtain a comprehensive medical and life insurance plan for employees and a liability insurance plan designed for broadcasters.

The NRB sponsors the Intercollegiate Religious Broadcasters (IRB) for faculty and students at colleges and universities. IRB members receive reduced convention and membership rates. Scholarships and cash awards for student productions are also provided. The black NRB, Hispanic NRB, and international groups are also served through NRB. An international convention/exposition and six regional chapter conventions are held each year, providing inspirational speakers, seminars, and workshops. These gatherings are used to exchange ideas and technology beneficial to the religious broadcasting industry. U.S. presidents, members of Congress, and FCC commissioners and staff are regular speakers and panelists at the conventions. NRB members subscribe to a Statement of Faith and Code of Ethics.

Directory of Religious Media. Manassas, Va.: National Religious Broadcasters. Annual.
Ward, Mark. *Air of Salvation: The Story of Christian Broadcasting.* Grand Rapids, Mich.:
    Baker Books, 1994.
National Religious Broadcasters. http://www.nrb.com/nrb

Linwood A. Hagin

NATIVE-AMERICAN RADIO stations are licensed to Indian tribes and, for the most part, broadcast their signals from reservations. There are approximately 30 indigenous stations operating in the continental United States and Alaska, and this number is growing. The majority serve rural audiences, and of these stations, only four (CKON, WASG, WYRU, WOJB) broadcast east of the Mississippi.

Native-American radio stations debuted in the early 1970s, inspired by a need to preserve their languages and cultures, which were threatened with extinction due to overassimilation into Anglo and mainstream society. As part of the civil rights movement of the 1960s, Native Americans began to question their treatment by the dominant culture. This resulted in greater Indian activism and the creation of groups, such as the American Indian Movement (AIM), whose objectives include calling attention to human rights violations against indigenous peoples, ensuring that Indian history would not be exterminated, and creating a feeling of unity and solidarity among Native Americans. Developing reservation broadcast outlets was perceived as one very important means of accomplishing these objectives.

Construction of Native-owned radio stations began in 1971 at the height of the Indian rights movement. From their inception, Native stations have mostly broadcast noncommercially; only a couple presently sell commercial airtime, but more are planned. Navajo station KTDB in Pine Hill, New Mexico, went on the air in April 1972 and fully directed its signal to Native listeners. Therefore, it claims to be the country's premier Indian-only broadcast operation.

The money to put Native signals on the air and keep them there comes from a variety of sources. Most of them are governmental (either federal or tribal), since all but a handful of Indian-operated stations are public and noncommercial. Lack of funding is the biggest problem confronting Native stations. A key source of funding, the Corporation for Public Broadcasting, has been plagued by congressional cutbacks, which seriously threaten future subsidies from this entity.

Most of these stations employ Native Americans, yet only one or two are exclusively indigenous personnel, and at some Native-licensed stations, non-Indians outnumber Indians. Programming at Native radio stations is very diverse and often eclectic. Music is the primary programming ingredient with a host of genres— country, rock, folk, jazz, and so forth. Most Native stations air traditional tribal music and language programs. Some do so nearly exclusively, while others work the other end of the spectrum and are even National Public Radio (NPR) and Public Radio International (PRI) programming affiliates.

Native media are not a recent manifestation. The first Indian newspaper, the *Cherokee Phoenix,* appeared in 1828, nearly a century and a half ahead of the first Native-operated radio station. Yet while Native press proliferated in various forms in the United States, the birth of indigenous electronic media was belated. Their evolution has been slow, especially in contrast to Canada, where government support has been far more substantial.

Nonetheless, Native Americans have harnessed the airwaves. The past two decades have witnessed the growth of a truly unique medium, one that now employs satellite technology to beam Native programming to the indigenous U.S. stations and the world.

Deloria, Vine, Jr. *Custer Died for Your Sins.* Norman:University of Oklahoma Press, 1969.
Keith, Michael C. *Signals in the Air: Native Broadcasting in America.* Westport, Conn.:
Praeger Publishing, 1995.

Michael C. Keith

NBC NEWS. News coverage by NBC Radio dates to the 1928 presidential election when NBC covered both national conventions and the vote count on election day. A. A. "Abe" Schechter joined NBC in 1932 and was instrumental in pouring the foundation for NBC News. NBC competed vigorously with CBS during World War II. After the war, it developed a solid, permanent news organization around some of its wartime managers and correspondents.

Even as network television was eclipsing radio as a source of entertainment, NBC introduced *Monitor* in 1955. It was a mix of news, music, interviews, and even dramatic sketches. *Monitor* lasted until 1975. Many of its ideas were adopted by the network TV morning programs and by National Public Radio. Another attempt at innovation was less successful when, in 1975, NBC created the News and Information Service (NIS), a nationwide all-news network. Subscribing stations could choose how much of an hour's programming they carried. Two years later, NIS was closed down, having secured only 62 of an anticipated 150 affiliates. NIS did leave a legacy in the form of affiliated news and news/talk stations that continued to broadcast the format after NIS shut down. The all-news radio network was resurrected in the 1980s by CNN and in the 1990s by the Associated Press. In 1987, during corporate cost-cutting by NBC's new owner, General Electric, the NBC Radio Networks were sold to Westwood One, but they were allowed to keep their name.

Bliss, Edward, Jr. *Now the News: The Story of Broadcast Journalism.* New York: Columbia
University Press, 1991.
Frank, Reuven. *Out of Thin Air.* New York: Simon & Schuster, 1991.

Phillip O. Keirstead

NBC SYMPHONY. From 1937 until 1954, millions of Americans regularly heard live orchestral concerts conducted by the legendary Arturo Toscanini, with an orchestra specially assembled for him. The NBC Symphony emerged from discussions between David Sarnoff, NBC president, and Samuel Chotzinoff, a critic for the New York *Post* whom Sarnoff hired as the network's music director. The goal was to induce Toscanini, who had left the New York Philharmonic in 1936, to return to the United States. Sarnoff agreed to assemble an orchestra of the finest available musicians, give Toscanini authority over personnel and repertoire, present programs without commercial sponsorship, and pay the conductor $40,000 net for 10 concerts. Toscanini accepted. Artur Rodzinski was engaged as assistant conductor, and he and Chotzinoff proceeded to assemble the first orchestra expressly formed for radio. After test concerts led by Pierre Monteux and Rodzinski, Toscanini and the NBC Symphony gave their first performance on Christmas night of 1937: works by Brahms, Mozart, and Vivaldi, broadcast from Studio 8-H in New York's RCA Building. The association quickly became legendary. After the contracted 10 concerts, Toscanini regularly renewed his contract, for a total of 18 seasons.

Although Sarnoff's commitment to the arts in American culture was genuine, the NBC Symphony was also an astute business enterprise. The 92 players were signed on to NBC's staff orchestra and regularly used for other musical purposes. Although NBC Symphony concerts were free (even to studio audiences), Toscanini's recordings with the orchestra brought in considerable revenue, along with the prestige Sarnoff sought. The negative aspect of the business arrangement became clear in 1954, when a combination of Toscanini's failing powers and NBC's move into television caused the abrupt disbanding of one of the country's finest artistic institutions. Its members formed the Symphony of the Air, which struggled financially and died in 1963.

Lyons, Eugene. *David Sarnoff: A Biography.* New York: Harper & Row, 1966.
Sachs, Harvey. *Toscanini.* Philadelphia: J. B. Lippincott Company, 1978.

Glen M. Johnson

NETWORK AFFILIATION, a contractual agreement by which individual stations receive programming from a central source. During the formative years of radio networks, the 1930s, a station joined a network to give itself hookups to national events and programs that supplemented local productions.

Network programs may either be commercially sponsored or *sustaining,* meaning they have no commercial sponsor. Stations either buy the programming from the network, or the network pays the stations to run the programming, depending on the affiliation agreement.

For many years, most stations affiliated with one network, but satellite distribution of programming and a proliferation of networks have led to stations affiliating with several networks for different types of news, information, and entertainment programs.

John R. Broholm

NEW AGE, a radio format that is primarily instrumental but does include some carefully selected vocals. The music style is jazz based with such artists as Spyro Gyra, Kenny G, Acoustic Alchemy, and Steely Dan. Also known as adult alternative, jazz, and new adult contemporary, the format targets adults, ages 35 to 44.

Carroll, Raymond L., and Donald M. Davis. *Electronic Media Programming: Strategies and Decision Making.* New York: McGraw-Hill, 1993.

Frederic A. Leigh

NEW ROCK, a radio format that focuses primarily on music by new rock artists not heard on mainstream formats such as top-40 or contemporary hit radio; also known as alternative or modern rock.

Frederic A. Leigh

NEWS PROGRAMMING CRITICISM, the evaluation of the selection, content, or presentation of news programs for error, expression of opinion, or political bias. Criticism of radio news has centered around expressing opinion as commentary, and the degree to which outside institutions have exerted pressure on news organizations. News programming developed slowly in the 1930s, with advertisers preferring to sponsor entertainment programs. Both NBC and CBS began substantial newscasts in 1933, but CBS ran into a problems. Newspapers, apparently threatened by the competition from CBS, began withholding publicity from sponsors of CBS programs. In response, the networks set up a Press-Radio Bureau to supply stations with news but put stringent restrictions on the length of the stories. Local stations' newscasts, however, were not under those restrictions and attracted the attention of advertisers because they were drawing considerable audiences. Radio's growth as a news medium followed in spite of the newspaper pressure.

Outside pressure on radio news continued through the 1930s. In 1935, newspaper publishers attacked the very notion of radio news programming, on the grounds that Federal Communications Commission (FCC) licensing made free gathering and dissemination of the news impossible. They initially forced radio networks to limit the length of newscasts and schedule them so as not to interfere with newspaper sales. The Associated Press withheld its wire services to NBC and CBS from 1933 to 1940.

Foreign news was lacking on radio until the Munich crisis of 1938, which brought reports from European bureaus to the forefront. After that, news was subjected to government scrutiny and criticism, such as President Roosevelt's warning against the broadcast of "false news," a term he did not define. In that environment, the president of NBC told the FCC that there was no such thing as freedom of speech over the air.

Advertisers sometimes canceled sponsorships if a news commentator made remarks with which they did not agree, which happened to H. V. Kaltenborn and Cecil Brown at CBS (Brown later resigned). CBS commentator Boake Carter's strident attacks on the Roosevelt administration's policies resulted in a government investigation into whether he could be deported. His attacks on organized labor caused the Congress of Industrial Organizations (CIO) to boycott one of his sponsors.

Nervousness over commentators' expression of their own opinions led CBS to generate a policy against news commentary and for news analysis that did not promote a point of view. Kaltenborn subsequently left CBS for NBC, but all of the networks soon had policies similar to CBS's. Still, conflicts over the opinions expressed by commentators continued.

Criticism of news programming largely shifted to television as it grew in popularity and influence. Radio news again came in for criticism following the 1981 deregulation of radio, which lessened the requirements for stations to present news and public affairs programming. It was feared that many stations would drop their newscasts in favor of less expensive entertainment programming and that radio news would decline in quality and importance as a result.

The number of radio news jobs dropped sharply, as did the number of all-news radio stations. FM stations especially cut back on hourly newscasts, and overall the amount of news on music stations declined. On the other hand, there was a large increase in the number of stations doing a combination of news and talk formats. Some critics charged that the function of informing the talk show audience was largely handed over to people who were not news professionals but primarily entertainers, such as Rush Limbaugh and Larry King. The revocation of the Fairness Doctrine in 1987 left talk shows (as well as newscasts) free of any regulatory restriction to balance the expression of opinions on controversial topics, which was seen as further eroding the quality of information available on radio. Broadcasters themselves, however, vigorously fought for the end of the doctrine as necessary for extending to broadcasters the same freedom of speech protection enjoyed by other media.

Following radio deregulation, newscast-story selection also came in for criticism on the grounds that the stories' target and format resulted in a skew toward entertainment news and softer "lifestyle" reporting. Smaller news staffs meant less on-the-scene reporting, it was charged, and thus a greater degree of error in stories.

Connors, Edward. "They Still Call It Radio News." *Washington Journalism Review* 13 (4) (May 1, 1991): 39–42.
Culbert, David H. *News for Everyman: Radio and Foreign Affairs in Thirties America.* Westport, Conn.: Greenwood, 1976.

John R. Broholm

NEWS SERVICES are press agencies and wire services that gather, rewrite, edit, and distribute world, national, regional, and state news using their own staff and submissions by subscribers or cooperating news services. Most agencies focus on ready-for-printing articles for newspapers. Some distribute broadcast news scripts ready for reading on the air. Distribution began by telegraph wire but now combines telephone and satellite technology. Some agencies distribute audio news features or provide short- or continuous-audio news feeds to subscribers. The Associated Press, United Press International, and Reuters are the primary new services distributing in the United States.

Phillip O. Keirstead

NEWS-TALK FORMATS. *See* **allocations and classes; AM; information formats; all-talk format.**

NICHE, a small but discernible portion of the radio audience that is served by a format that offers an alternative to mainstream or popular radio stations.

Frederic A. Leigh

NIELSEN Media Research, the sole supplier of national TV network ratings, is virtually the only company providing local TV audience measurements. The company was formerly called A. C. Nielsen and was a subsidiary of Dow Jones (see **A. C. Nielsen Company; Audimeter**).

Lawrence W. Lichty

NOBLE, EDWARD J. (1882–1958), purchased the NBC Blue Network in July 1943 for $8 million and renamed it the American Broadcasting Company (ABC). The purchase also included a radio network of 116 affiliates and ownership of three stations. ABC was the weakest radio network, and Noble decided to invest in television. He built five television stations in a short period of time and realized it was an expensive investment for one man. ABC was losing money and he was short of cash, so he sought a partner. In May 1951, ABC announced that United Paramount Theaters would exchange stock and merge. Noble would become the chairman of the board, Leonard Goldstone would become president. The merger was approved in February of 1953, and Noble received $25 million in stock.

Edward Noble earned his money as the manufacturer of Life Savers candy and had a reputation as a shrewd businessman and world-class tightwad. In 1938, he became the first chairman of the Civil Aeronautics Authority and was later appointed undersecretary of commerce but resigned in 1940 to campaign for Wendell Willkie. In his later years, he gave generously to worthy causes through the Edward Noble Foundation. He died in 1958.

Goldstone, Leonard. *Beating the Odds: The Untold Story Behind the Rise of ABC.* New York: Charles Scribner's Sons, 1991.

Mary E. Beadle

NORELCO is one marketing branch of the Philips electrical and electronics conglomerate of Holland. In 1964, Norelco was the North American marketer responsible for introducing the now-familiar "compact cassette" format, which offered up to 120 minutes of recording on ⅛-inch-wide tape. The term *compact cassette* differentiated the Philips version from an earlier cassette format marketed in 1959 by RCA that used full-sized ¼-inch tape. Among the reasons the RCA format failed were the cassettes' bulkiness, mono and stereo incompatibility, and marginal fidelity.

The original Norelco (Philips) cassette recorders were monaural and were intended primarily for speech dictation, capturing lectures, and so forth. Philips soon developed a compatible stereo format, which allowed tapes made on a mono machine to be played on a stereo deck, and vice versa. Tight control of the physical and electronic characteristics of the machines and tapes offered by Philips' licensees assured that a tape made on any compact cassette recorder would play on any other.

Transport mechanisms gradually improved to reduce the problems of wow and flutter associated with tape moving at only 1⅞ inches per second, and tape formulations were enhanced to achieve better high-frequency response. The near universal adoption of the Dolby B noise reduction system for minimizing tape hiss made possible the mass duplication of prerecorded cassettes having fidelity rivaling that of the best vinyl records. Car radios increasingly offered a cassette player as an option, and devices such as the Sony Walkman (1979) made cassette playback as personal and portable as radio listening. In 1982, sales of prerecorded cassettes surged past sales of LP (long-playing) records, making cassettes one of radio's prime competitors for out-of-home listening.

David T. MacFarland

NOSTALGIA FORMAT features music from big bands and vocalists of the 1940s and early 1950s and is also known as Big Band.

Frederic A. Leigh

O

OBOLER, ARCH (1909–1987). Arch Oboler, Archibald MacLeish, and Norman Corwin were probably the three preeminent writers for radio in the 1930s and 1940s. Many considered Oboler the most prolific of the three, having written well over 800 radio scripts. In addition to radio dramas, he wrote films and stage plays. His first radio drama was accepted by NBC in 1934. If there were any doubts as to his interest, it need only be noted that when he was married in the 1930s, the honeymoon was spent touring haunted houses in New England. He is best remembered for the radio series *Lights Out!*—one of the earliest series to deal with the macabre. With its famous opening lines "It . . . is . . . later . . . than . . . you . . . think!" it terrorized NBC audiences tuned in on Wednesday evenings. He also wrote for *Grand Hotel, Arch Oboler's Plays, Everyman's Theater, First Nighter,* and *The Edgar Bergen–Charlie McCarthy Show.* He is credited with creating stream-of-consciousness monologues in his dramas. Many critics noted his effectiveness in radio through the use of sound effects. In 1940 he wrote his first screen play, *Escape,* and then a dozen years later he wrote and created the first three-dimensional movie, *Bwana Devil.* He frequently took issue with those in radio management and, as a result, became somewhat disaffected from radio following World War II. However, in 1945, in an article in *Variety,* he warned that radio would be succeeded by television just as sound films had succeeded the silents.

Blair, William G. "Arch Oboler, Wrote Thrillers for Radio in 1930's and 40's." *New York Times,* March 22, 1987, p. 36.

MacDonald, J. Fred. *Don't Touch That Dial!: Radio Programming in American Life from 1920 to 1960.* Chicago: Nelson-Hall, 1979.

Moritz, Charles, ed. *Current Biography, 1987.* New York: H. W. Nelson Co., 1987.

Lee E. Scanlon

OBSCENITY is one of the few speech categories that has absolutely no First Amendment protection. Therefore, anything that is deemed to be "obscene" and communicated through any medium, including radio, is subject not only to successful prosecution but also to censorship prior to its broadcast or publication.

The current definition of obscenity stems from a 1973 U.S. Supreme Court ruling, *Miller v. California*. The Court ruled that material is obscene when: (1) an average person, applying contemporary community standards, finds that the work, taken as a whole, appeals to prurient interest, (2) the work depicts in a patently offensive way sexual conduct specifically defined by applicable state law, and (3) the work in question lacks serious literary, artistic, political, or scientific value. This definition was the culmination of more than a century of evolution of obscenity law in the United States and represented an effort to provide objective rather than subjective standards. The subjectivity of defining obscenity was perhaps best represented by Supreme Court Justice Potter Stewart's remark, "I know it when I see it." But even with the Miller standards, defining obscenity remains an imprecise science.

Obscenity is to be distinguished from pornography, indecent speech, and offensive expression. These do not rise to the same level as obscenity and therefore qualify for at least some First Amendment protection. The key in making the distinction often lies in the first prong of the Miller test. The entire work in question must be evaluated, not merely some part of it. Only when the work, taken as a whole, meets the remaining standards of the Miller test may it be considered to be obscene.

Conversely, however, offensive, indecent, or pornographic material may sometimes also qualify as obscene, provided that it meets the Miller test. For example, in the early 1990s, an album by the rap group 2 Live Crew entitled *As Nasty as They Wanna Be* was the subject of years of legal wrangling. A judge in Florida ruled that the album's lyrics were legally obscene because, he said, they appealed to prurient interests, were patently offensive to the community, and were lacking any serious artistic merit. This was the first time in U.S. history such a ruling had been made. Subsequently, a record store owner was prosecuted for selling the album, and three members of the band were arrested for performing the lyrics live. All parties, however, were ultimately acquitted or their convictions in lower courts were overturned on appeal. If nothing else, these incidents illustrate the difficulty in determining whether a particular work is obscene.

What does this mean for the radio broadcaster? Given broadcasting's "pervasive presence" and other unique properties as outlined by the Supreme Court (see, for example, *Pacifica* and *Red Lion*), it is subject to standards much more stringent than those that govern obscenity. That is, the regulations that govern radio broadcasters cast a much wider net than the law that governs obscenity. Well before material rises to the level of obscenity it can violate rules established by the Federal Communications Commission for broadcast licensees. In short, because the rules and regulations that govern material aired by broadcasters is subject to standards much more restrictive than obscenity, it is unlikely that broadcasters need to be directly concerned with obscenity law. Merely adhering to the rules applicable to indecent speech, for example, will generally steer the broadcaster clear of obscenity.

Brockwell, P. Heath. "Grappling with *Miller v. California*: A Search to an Alternative Approach to Regulating Obscenity." *Cumberland Law Review* 24 (winter 1994): 131–144.

Burke, Debra D. "Cybersmut and the First Amendment: A Call for a New Obscenity Standard." *Harvard Journal of Law and Technology* 9 (winter 1996): 87–145.

Clarke, Anne L. "As Nasty As They Wanna Be: Popular Music on Trial." *New York University Law Review* 65 (1990): 1481–1531.

de Grazia, Edward. *Girls Back Everywhere: The Law of Obscenity and the Assault of Genesis.* New York: Random House, 1992.

Saunders, Kevin W. *Violence as Obscenity: Limiting the Media's First Amendment Protection.* Durham, N.C.: Duke University Press, 1966.

Joseph A. Russomanno

OLDIES. Music from the start of the rock 'n' roll era of the 1950s and 1960s is programmed on oldies stations in today's radio markets. Most of the stations also use music from the 1970s.

Robert Hilliard, in *Radio Broadcasting: An Introduction to the Sound Medium,* points out that the oldies are middle-of-the-road (MOR) songs from the early rock 'n' roll period. Michael Keith, in *Radio Production: Art and Science,* gives an example of a station located in the Midwest that promotes its sound as playing the hits "from Chuck Berry to the Beatles."

Hilliard's look at the golden oldies format traces its beginnings to MOR formats that began to incorporate oldies in the late 1960s and early 1970s to supplement and maintain the ups and downs of the format sound.

The early top-40 stations played golden oldies as part of their format offering. According to Hurricane Heeran of *Radio & Records,* two of the earliest oldies stations were WCBS in New York City and WMMS in Cleveland, Ohio, switching to the format in about 1969. KRTH in Los Angeles is another successful major market oldies station. Hausman, Benoit, and O'Donnell, in *Modern Radio Production,* indicate that identifying what an oldie is, is not easy. Some stations program music two to three years old and call them oldies. "You'll find that most rotations . . . in oldie formats center on an identifiable five- or ten-year period."

Oldies formats claim an audience from 25 to 54, but the demographic can extend to age 64. WMXJ-FM, Majic 102.7, an oldies station, targets baby boomers and claims that 74 percent of its listeners are 25 to 54 and 78 percent are 35 to 64. In the spring 1995 *Arbitron,* the station shows a market position of 2 for adults 25 to 54, Monday through Sunday, 6 A.M. to 12 midnight, nonethnic. WGRR in Cincinnati, has a market share average of 5.5 (5.8 in morning-drive time) based on 1995 *Arbitron* ratings. The station claims a very loyal audience as does WKIO in central Illinois. WKIO promotes "[g]reat music, great memories, great people on the air, great prizes to win." FM oldies stations promote the higher-quality sound that FM offers. The early rock 'n' roll sounds better now, they might say, than it did when you were young.

Hausman, Carl, Philip Benoit, and Lewis B. O'Donnell. *Modern Radio Production.* Belmont, Calif.: Wadsworth, 1996.

Hilliard, Robert L. *Radio Broadcasting: An Introduction to the Sound Medium.* 3rd ed. New York: Longman, 1985.

Keith, Michael C. *Radio Production: Art and Science.* Boston: Focal Press, 1990.

Oldies. WGRR-FM Oldies 103.5, Cincinnati, Ohio. http://www.wgrr1035.com/

Oldies. WKIO-FM Oldies 92, Central Illinois. http://www.wkio.com/
Oldies. WMXJ-FM Majic 102.7, South Florida. http://www.wmxj.com/index.html

Arthur Thomas Challis, Jr.

OLD-TIME RADIO (OTR) generally refers to a club, an association, or an old-time radio interest group. There are a growing number of these private radio clubs and program archives throughout the world. The clubs comprise pioneers and interest parties who often have extensive collections, knowledge, and information networks. Many of them publish newsletters and are active in promoting the cause of preserving radio's past. A few of the primary OTR organizations at this writing include: SPERDVAC (Society to Preserve and Encourage Radio Drama, Variety and Comedy); ARSC (Association for Recorded Sound Collectors); Golden Radio Buffs; Indiana Recording Club; Metropolitan Washington OTR Club; Milwaukee Area Radio Enthusiasts; Old-Time Radio Club of Buffalo; Radio Historical Association of Colorado; and the Radio Collectors of America (see **archives, radio**).

Godfrey, Donald G. *Reruns on File: A Guide to Electronic Media Archives.* Hillsdale, N.J.: Lawrence Erlbaum Associates, 1992.

Donald G. Godfrey

OPERATING LOG is a form that shows schedules for facilities, personnel, programs, advertising, and announcements. Usually handled by someone in the traffic department, the log is maintained to examine the day's business. At one time, the operating log demonstrated the station's compliance with Federal Communications Commission regulations for programming and public service, but today the operating log reflects sign-on and sign-off, music titles played, advertisements presented, and public service announcements broadcast. At most stations, the operating log is computerized.

Ginger Rudeseal Carter

OVERNIGHT TIME PERIOD, generally considered as the hours of 12 midnight until 6 A.M., although in some markets overnights are considered the 2 A.M. to 6 A.M. airshift. In the three decades since 24-hour broadcasting became a competitive necessity, programming strategies for this time period have ranged from all-night trucker's shows to talk to formats identical to other dayparts. Overnights have always been a bit problematic due to the unusual audience mix of graveyard-shift workers, late-night revelers, insomniacs, and other people of the night.

Michael Taylor

OWENS, GARY (1936–), began in the 1950s at 16 on KORN, Mitchell, South Dakota, then went to Omaha and Denver before McLendon (a major 1950s chain) hired him to increase ratings in Dallas, Houston, New Orleans, San Antonio, and San Francisco. He moved to Hollywood's KFWB and within a year left for a 20-year stint at KMPC. Hollywood TV producers and directors hired him for parts in movies, TV shows, and cartoons. He has done over 1,000 shows on camera, not counting voice-overs. Owens spent five years on NBC TV's *Rowan and Martin's Laugh-In*. Owens presently hosts the syndicated *Music of Your Life*.

W. A. Kelly Huff

OWNED-AND-OPERATED (O&O) STATION, a radio or television station that is licensed to and managed by a company that also controls a broadcast network. O&O stations carry the company's network programming and become an important part of the network's delivery system. National networks will usually acquire these stations because O&Os provide more control over clearance of network programs to individual markets. In markets where a network does not own a station, the network must rely on affiliated stations, which could preempt network programming at any time. Because the Federal Communications Commission licenses all stations to serve the "public interest," even O&O stations will carry some locally originated and syndicated programming that is separate from the network schedule. Historically, the Federal Communications Commission had set limits on how many stations could be licensed to one company; so networks acquired their own stations in the largest U.S. markets, such as New York, Los Angeles, and Chicago. The practice of building networks around O&Os can be traced back to the 1920s, the earliest period of networking. At this time, AT&T built the most prominent early radio network around its New York–licensed station WEAF, while RCA competed with a radio network anchored by its New York station WJZ. These chains became the NBC Red and NBC Blue Networks in 1926.

Eastman, Susan Tyler, Sydney W. Head, and Lewis Klein. *Broadcast/Cable Programming: Strategies and Practices*. 3rd ed. Belmont, Calif.: Wadsworth Publishing, 1989.

Randall L. Vogt

OWNERSHIP of a radio license, and thereby a radio station, has always been predicated upon meeting the public interest, convenience, and necessity (PICON, criterion written into the 1927 Federal Radio Commission's policies, incorporated into the *Communications Act of 1934,* and kept in the *Telecommunications Reform Act of 1996).* A potential radio station owner must show that this criterion will be met for the community of license before a license will be granted. Once this criterion and the criteria of character and financial stability are met, rarely will the Federal Communications Commission (FCC) deny renewal of the license to the original owner. Transfer of ownership typically occurs by filing FCC Form 314. The station license is assigned to the new owner after FCC approval. Two other forms of license transfers include transfers of control of the licensee (FCC Form 315) and internal corporate restructurings (FCC Form 316).

Before 1982, station owners were required to hold their licenses for a minimum of three years. First-time buyers of radio stations flooded the industry when this antitrafficking rule was repealed. Many entered with highly leveraged buyouts of stations designed to increase the bottom line of the owner's profit-and-loss statement and not necessarily to increase the quality of service to the public. This trend moved radio license holders into positions of responsibility that reported to entities beyond the public. Management and programming decisions were made with corporate executives or public stockholders in mind as well as the public in the community of license.

Ditingo, Vincent M. *The Remaking of Radio*. Boston: Focal Press, 1994.

Keith, Michael C., and Joseph M. Krause. *The Radio Station*. 3rd ed. Boston: Focal Press, 1993.

Linwood A. Hagin

P

PACIFICA FOUNDATION owned the first listener-sponsored radio station; KPFA went on the air in 1949 in Berkeley, California. The Pacifica Foundation was created by Lewis Hill, whose radio theories addressed listener-driven programming. Pacifica offered alternative programming that included "minority viewpoints" since it began broadcasting. One of the first issues dealt with varying opinions concerning the Korean War.

In 1951, Pacifica was given its "first major foundation grant (Ford Foundation) for the support of a noncommercial broadcast operation." Pacifica added a second station in Los Angeles in 1959, KPFK-FM. In 1974, the Symbionese Liberation Army gave tape recordings of Patty Hearst to the two Pacifica stations, and Will Lewis of KPFK was jailed for not yielding the tapes to the Federal Bureau of Investigation (FBI).

In 1960, WBAI, in New York joined the Pacifica stations when philanthropist Louis Schweitzer gave the property to the foundation. KPFT in Houston, Texas, began as a Pacifica station in 1970, and in 1977, WPFW, in Washington, D.C., began broadcasting after Pacifica won "the last available frequency in the nation's capital."

Pacifica is well known for its license renewal fight in the early 1960s. The Federal Communications Commission (FCC) refused to grant license renewals to the three Pacifica stations "pending its investigation into 'communist affiliations.'" Between 1960 and 1963 the House Un-American Activities Committee and the Senate Internal Security Subcommittee undertook an investigation of "Pacifica programming for 'subversion.'" The licenses were granted by the FCC in 1964.

Kahn, in his *Documents of American Broadcasting,* notes that the renewals were granted despite public complaints and were seen as the free-speech principles applied to broadcasting. The FCC reviewed several programs aired on Pacifica stations including a broadcast by the poet Lawrence Ferlinghetti in December 1959 and *The Zoo Story* broadcast, a play by Edward Albee on KPFK in 1963, and several other taped programs.

Robert R. Pauley, president of ABC Radio, said of the FCC's decision (as quoted in *Broadcasting* magazine), "Without commenting on the details of the Pacifica case per se, let me applaud the position of the FCC in granting the broadcaster the privilege of self-determining in programming without undue censure" (p. 66).

Perhaps the U.S. Supreme Court case involving Pacifica's broadcast of the comedian George Carlin's routine "dirty words you can't say on television" on WBAI/New York in 1973 gives Pacifica its greatest notoriety. The 12-minute monologue was heard by a listener who complained to the FCC that the content was indecent and was heard by the listener's 15-year-old son. The FCC ruling dealt with indecency especially as it applies to channeling "the exposure of children to language that describes, in terms patently offensive as measured by contemporary-community standards for the broadcast medium, sexual or excretory activities and organs, at times of the day when there is a reasonable risk that children may be in the audience" (*Pacifica Foundation,* 56 FCC 2d 94 [1975]). As the *History of Pacifica Radio* states, "[N]o sanctions are imposed, but the Carlin Case sets the limits of broadcasting [indecency] for over a decade."

In 1993, Pacifica won its third Court of Appeals ruling thus changing the FCC definitions of "indecent" programming. The Pacifica Foundation has won numerous news and programming awards and in 1969 reported Seymour Hersh's account of the My Lai massacre in Vietnam. Hersh later won a Pulitzer Prize for his reporting. Pacifica also broadcast complete coverage of the Senate Watergate hearings in 1973.

Federal Communications Commission v. Pacifica Foundation, 438 U.S. 726 (July 3, 1978).
Kahn, Frank J. *Documents of American Broadcasting.* 4th ed. Englewood Cliffs, N.J.: Prentice-Hall, 1984.
"A Loosening of Controls on Programs?" *Broadcasting* (January 27, 1964): 66.
Pacifica Foundation, 56 FCC 2d 94 (1975).
Pacifica Foundation. http://www.dorsai.org/~wbai/pacifica/theory.html
Pacifica Radio, History of. http://www.dorsai.org/~wbai/pacifica/history.html

Arthur Thomas Challis, Jr.

PALEY, WILLIAM S. (1901–1990), chairman of CBS Inc., along with NBC's David Sarnoff played a key role in shaping network broadcasting and the U.S. broadcasting industry. Paley lived the great American success story. His parents were Russian Jews from the Ukraine. In the 1890s, Paley's father, Sam, made and sold cigars in Chicago. The senior Paley developed a popular cigar blend and became a moderately successful cigarmaker. The firm eventually moved to Philadelphia, where Bill worked for his father and graduated from the University of Pennsylvania.

Paley understudied as a salesman and his father's assistant on tobacco buying trips for the Congress Cigar Company. He traveled widely and acquired sophisticated tastes that were his lifetime trademark. In 1927, Sam Paley contracted with WCAU in Philadelphia to broadcast a program promoting Congress Cigars. William S. Paley was put in charge and soon revamped the program's format. Cigar sales, which had slumped, began to soar. Paley, through family connections, learned United Independent Broadcasters and its Columbia Network were for sale. Bill and Sam Paley took control of United Independent on September 25, 1928, and at age 26, William S. Paley moved to New York to be president of the company.

Paley developed the concept of free-sustaining programs, which gave Columbia Broadcasting affiliates the programming they desperately needed and kept the network's expenses low. He had a flair for developing talent and refining program concepts that appealed to mass audiences. His Columbia Broadcasting System grew stubbornly in spite of lusty competition from the larger and richer National Broadcasting Company.

Paley found good people to lead his enterprise, including Dr. Frank Stanton, who started in research and rose to lead the company. During World War II, the CBS Network enhanced its news coverage, and Paley went to the European theater, first as a civilian adviser and later as an army colonel working in psychological warfare. One of his jobs was to de-Nazify all German media. Years later, he would vividly recall his visit to the Dachau concentration camp shortly after it was liberated.

Paley returned from the war filled with ideas for his media investment. One priority was to wrest control of programs from the advertising agencies, which dictated their content and production. Another was to become competitive with NBC. In 1948 Paley led a "raid," luring NBC's top talent (including *Amos 'n' Andy, Jack Benny,* and Bing Crosby) to CBS. Ratings rose and CBS achieved equal footing with NBC. Paley became fabulously rich but lowered his percentage of ownership of CBS.

Paley left much of the running of the company to others, allowing himself time for travel, government service, and extravagant social engagements. Paley was removed as chairman in a 1983 palace coup by CBS president Tom Wyman and the corporation's board. By 1985 CBS was slipping in ratings and profits, just as Laurence Tisch, the wealthy chairman of Loews Corporation, developed an interest in the media business. Tisch bought up CBS stock until he had effective control of the firm, now called CBS Inc. William Paley died in 1990.

Auletta, Ken. *Three Blind Mice.* New York: Random House, 1991.

Paley, William S. *As It Happened: A Memoir.* Garden City, N.Y.: Doubleday, 1979.

Paper, Lewis J. *Empire: William S. Paley and the Making of CBS.* New York: St. Martin's Press, 1987.

Smith, Sally Bedell. *In All His Glory.* New York: Simon & Schuster, 1990.

Phillip O. Keirstead

PATENTS POOLS. By 1917, the fact that essential patents in the radio field were in many different hands made it impossible to construct most apparatus legally. For example, British Marconi owned the patent for the first two vacuum-tube elements (the "Fleming valve" or diode), and Lee de Forest controlled the necessary third element of the "audion" or triode, although AT&T had connived to purchase some rights to use it for telephony.

When the United States geared up for World War I, the navy realized that there was no way legally to obtain modern transmitters and receivers. Accordingly, the navy offered to indemnify all manufacturers of radio apparatus for the armed forces against patent infringement suits. In other words, the navy would pay any fines or damages. This pooling of all patents enabled many manufacturers to produce "state-of-the-art" equipment without fear of lawsuits.

At the end of the war, the navy announced that it would no longer indemnify manufacturers for infringement, and the pool dissolved. The situation was worse then ever. This and other problems (i.e., British Marconi's attempt to control American overseas radio communication by purchasing sole rights to use General Electric's [GE's] Alexanderson alternator transmitter; the desire to find products to interest potential buyers and put closed-down war factories to work) led to the establishment of the Radio Corporation of America (RCA) as the "chosen instrument" of American overseas communication. A new patents pool was organized through corporate contractual agreements. Two naval officers (Admiral Bullard and Commander Hooper) and GE's Owen D. Young acted as midwives. Among the pool's members were GE, RCA (which more or less was given the facilities and other assets of American Marconi as a birthday present), AT&T, Westinghouse, United Fruit, Federal Telegraph of California (which had been owned by the navy during WWI), and others. Patents controlled by the navy, including German patents controlled by the Alien Enemy Property Custodian, were now available on a nonexclusive basis. Because GE (which had purchased the assets of American Marconi after the government made it clear that foreign corporations would not be allowed to control American overseas communications) and AT&T were included in the pool, the triode could now be manufactured legally.

Essentially, this series of agreements divided up the field of radio. Each member of the pool could use any patents for its own use and could sell equipment and use radio for specified other purposes. For example, RCA administered the patents pool, now containing nearly 2,000 patents, and took over maritime and transatlantic communication from Marconi. AT&T built broadcast transmitters and believed it had sole rights to radiotelephony (including broadcasting) for hire. GE (60 percent) and Westinghouse (which had tried, unsuccessfully, to "go it alone") (40 percent) later started building radio broadcasting receivers, to be sold by RCA under the "Radiola" label as their agent. Other manufacturers had to pay royalties—as much as 7 percent of the total value of a radio receiver, including the cabinet—to RCA in order to make parts, vacuum tubes, or sets legally.

The stresses on the patents pool were enormous, particularly after radio broadcasting became a major industry. In 1922, RCA started to operate some Westinghouse broadcasting stations. AT&T lost the battle for control of "radio telephony for hire" and sold its stations and fledgling network to RCA for $1 million in 1926, which then established NBC to operate them. GE and Westinghouse moved their receiver manufacturing divisions (including research and development in television) to RCA in 1930.

However, almost immediately, in May 1930, the Justice Department filed a major antitrust suit, and the pool was dissolved, although major aspects remain in force today. AT&T pulled out, and by November 1932, when a consent decree was signed, RCA was independent of GE and Westinghouse, which would be allowed to manufacture and sell radio receivers under their own names after two years of not competing with RCA in this arena. Most important, exclusive patent license agreements made in the 1919–1921 period now became nonexclusive although still administered by RCA.

John Michael Kittross

PATTIZ, NORMAN J. (1943–), is the founder of the Westwood One Companies. He started in 1975 with a small radio syndication company and a rented one-room office in the Westwood section of Los Angeles. He began syndicating special interest programs to a small group of stations. Today, Westwood One owns NBC, Mutual Broadcasting, Unistar Radio Networks, Westwood One Radio Networks, and Westwood One Entertainment.

Westwood One is the largest producer and distributor of radio programming in the United States. It serves over 6,000 radio station affiliates around the globe. The entertainment division produces musical events and concert specials—for example, Barbra Streisand, The Rolling Stones, The Eagles, Paul McCartney, and U2. The Unistar system is a major supplier of music featuring 24-hour satellite service in differing music formats. The Westwood One networks feature personalities with household names—Larry King, Casey Kasem, and Don Imus. New and special events originate from NBC, Mutual, and CNN radio news. Sports coverage includes the National Football League, National Collegiate Athletics Association football, Summer Olympic Games, the Stanley Cup, and major college bowl games.

USA Today described Norm Pattiz as the "Ted Turner of Radio," and *Broadcast Magazine* declared Westwood One as the "radio success story of the 1980s." Pattiz is active in the professional community. He was the 1996–1997 president of the Broadcast Education Association and a trustee of the Museum of Television and Radio. He serves on the Communications Board of the Associated Students at the University of California, Los Angeles, and the board of directors for the Earth Communications Office. He has served with the Radio Network Advertising Bureau and is a recipient of numerous professional and leadership awards.

Donald G. Godfrey

PAYOLA-PLUGOLA. *Payola* is accepting money or another type of valuable consideration in return for including the payer's material in a broadcast without disclosing that fact to the audience. The most common form of payola is where a disc jockey accepts payment from a record distributor in return for playing and/or promoting that distributor's record on the air. Payment may be either in cash or in another form, such as an all-expenses-paid trip to the Super Bowl. *Plugola* is mentioning on the air any commercial product or service that the station owner or any employee has a financial interest in and stands to gain from such mention. For example, a newscaster cannot "plug" a ski resort that the station manager owns. Payola and plugola are illegal practices in the radio industry.

The Federal Communications Commission (FCC) has adopted several rules that govern payola and plugola. Section 317 of the *Communications Act of 1934*, as amended, states, "All matter broadcast by any radio station for which money, service or other valuable consideration is paid, . . . shall be announced as paid for by [the sponsor]." Section 508 requires employees, program producers, and suppliers to notify station management of any payments received in return for the promise of broadcasting specific material. Failure to notify management of such instances and failure to identify sponsorship can result in the station being fined up to $10,000 by the FCC. The disc jockey, newscaster, station manager, or other employee who is found culpable for payola or plugola also may be fined up to $10,000, in addition to being subject to incarceration for up to one year.

The stiffness of these punishments grew out of the television quiz show scandals in the late 1950s and other evidence that many radio program directors and disc jockeys were accepting bribes to play specific records on their stations. In 1980, following lengthy proceedings, the FCC concluded that plugola would be handled on a case-by-case basis. In 1988, following four payola indictments, the FCC issued a reminder to broadcasters that payola could result in both criminal charges and administrative sanctions against the stations involved. This meant that radio stations could jeopardize their FCC licenses to operate.

Carter, T. Barton, Marc A. Franklin, and Jay B. Wright. *The First Amendment and the Fifth Estate: Regulation of Electronic Mass Media.* 4th ed. Westbury, N.Y.: Foundation Press, 1996.

Smith, F. Leslie, Milan Meeske, and John W. Wright II. *Electronic Media and Government: The Regulation of Wireless and Wired Mass Communication in the United States.* White Plains, N.Y.: Longman, 1995.

Robert G. Finney

PEARL HARBOR BROADCAST. December 7, 1941, a somewhat ordinary, quiet Sunday afternoon, quickly became a day to remember for radio listeners across the country. For most Americans, Sunday radio brought music and public affairs programming. On this Sunday, however, radio brought Americans the realization that war had begun. The Japanese attack of Pearl Harbor began at 7:55 A.M. Hawaii time (1:55 P.M. EST). It was not announced to the country until 2:30 P.M. EST. NBC Red had just finished *Sammy Kaye's Sunday Serenade* and was preparing to start the *University of Chicago Roundtable.* Newsman John Daly interrupted: "From the NBC newsroom in New York. President Roosevelt said in a statement today, that the Japanese have attacked Pearl Harbor, Hawaii, from the air. I repeat that President Roosevelt says that the Japanese have attacked Pearl Harbor, in Hawaii, from the air. This bulletin came to you from the NBC newsroom in New York." CBS and NBC Blue quickly followed NBC Red's lead. About 10 minutes later, a second announcement came: Manila was being attacked. During the next several hours, bulletins interrupted regular programming as new details on the bombing became available.

Radio Days. http://www.otr.com/news.html (sound recording).

Mark A. Tolstedt

PEARSON, DREW (1897–1969), was a leading, albeit flamboyant, U.S. print journalist and a pioneer radio commentator. For 40 years, up until his death in 1969, Pearson exerted a great deal of influence in the nation's capital and remained a thorn to many leading politicians. Pearson was a chief critic of Congress and was the first broadcast figure to tangle with Senator Joseph McCarthy. By articulating an enduring public concern that those who served in Congress were opportunists and out of touch with the people they represented, Pearson won millions of followers.

Pearson was born in Evanston, Illinois, and after his schooling in the Chicago area in the 1920s, during the era of Al Capone, embarked on a career as a print reporter. Before taking his first full-time reporting position, Pearson scraped together money from odd-job labor and traveled around the world, believing this odyssey would sharpen his skills in journalism. Finally in 1926, Pearson accepted an offer at the *Baltimore Sun* newspaper. Starting as a street reporter, Pearson advanced as a columnist. The biting tone of Pearson's early writings caught the attention of a newspaper syndicate called United Features, based in Washington, D.C. In 1932, with another figure named Robert S. Allen, Pearson began the column that came to be known as *Washington Merry-Go-Round*. This venture had been inspired by Pearson's 1931 book also called *Washington Merry-Go-Round*, a peppery assault on President Herbert Hoover and Congress.

Eventually seen in hundreds of newspapers across the country, and by the late 1930s Pearson's springboard into radio, *Washington Merry-Go-Round* sought to expose the corruption and sordid affairs of politicians. Often his columns featured sensational exposés of government figures, including senators and U.S. representatives who had come to Washington to represent constituents hundreds and thousands of miles away. Pearson's column was a daily record of the underside of life in the nation's capital.

In 1939, Pearson began as a radio commentator for the NBC Blue chain and remained at this network after it became the American Broadcasting Company in 1943. Heard on Sunday nights, Pearson had ratings that were second only to those of Walter Winchell. Nevertheless, Pearson was at odds with his sponsors constantly. Pearson's best-known target beginning in 1952 was Senator Joseph McCarthy, singled out because of his anticommunist "red-baiting" campaigns in Congress. In 1953, Pearson's sponsor, the Adam Hat company, dropped Pearson allegedly because of pressure McCarthy had applied. Nevertheless, Pearson's exposés galvanized public contempt for the Wisconsin senator and cleared the way for his condemnation in the U.S. Senate.

Pearson continued in radio through the 1950s and 1960s and groomed a figure named Jack Anderson as his successor as writer of the *Merry-Go-Round* column. Pearson wrote two books, *The Case against Congress* and *The Senator,* in 1968. He died the following year. Pearson is the namesake of the Drew Pearson Foundation, which annually confers journalism's top award for investigative reporting.

Anderson, Douglas A. *A "Washington Merry-Go-Round" of Libel Actions.* Chicago: Nelson Hall, 1980.

Anderson, Jack. *Confessions of a Muckraker.* New York: Random House, 1979.

Kluckhohn, Frank. *The Drew Pearson Story.* Chicago: C. Halberg, 1967.

Pearson, Drew. *The Case against Congress.* New York: Simon and Schuster, 1968.

Craig M. Allen

PERSONS USING RADIO (PUR) is an indication of how many people are listening to radio at a given time within a particular market. PUR can be provided as a raw number of people or as a percentage of the population within the metropolitan statistical area (MSA) or total survey area (TSA). PUR will usually be at its highest during the morning-drive period.

Webster, James G., and Lawrence W. Lichty, eds. *Ratings Analysis: Theory and Practice.* Hillsdale, N.J.: Lawrence Erlbaum Associates, 1991.

Ronald Razovsky

PHILCO CORPORATION, one of the nation's leading radio manufacturers. Headquartered in Philadelphia, Pennsylvania, its history begins in 1892 with Thomas Spencer, who formed a company to produce carbon arc lamps. Initially called the Spencer Company, a few months after its organization it became known as the Helios Electric Company; then in 1906, it was reorganized as the Philadelphia Storage Battery Company when it made batteries. It was a modest business until the advent of gasoline automobiles, which needed storage batteries and electric lighting. The company grew slowly until the 1920s. In 1923, the first signs of commercial radio were becoming evident, and Philco advertised "Philco Drynamic A & B Radio Batteries."

Ironically, Philco's best year-to-date sales were in 1927—the same year RCA began producing a radio set that would operate on alternating current (AC) power where batteries were no longer needed. Facing the challenge and producing radio receivers, the years 1928 to 1937 transformed the Philadelphia Storage Battery Company into Philco—the nation's leading radio set manufacturers.

Douglas, Alan. *Radio Manufacturers of the 1920's.* (2: 231–238). New York: Vestal Press, Ltd., 1991.
Wolkonowicz, John Paul. "The Philco Corporation: Historical Review and Strategic Analysis, 1892–1961." Master's thesis, Massachusetts Institute of Technology, 1981.

Donald G. Godfrey

PHILCO RADIO PLAYHOUSE was a radio anthology that began on ABC in 1953 and consisted of plays adapted for radio. Joseph Cotton was the host for the program. Stars from Hollywood performed leading roles in each play, along with some radio and television actors. Philco was the sponsor for both the radio and television versions.

Philco sponsored another national network show, one it inherited from the Kraft products company, the *Philco Radio Time* starring Bing Crosby. Glenn Riggs was the show's announcer, and the orchestra was led by John Scott Trotter. This program was the first "recorded" program, and its first broadcast was in 1946.

Dunning, John. *Tune in Yesterday: The Ultimate Encyclopedia of Radio Programs: 1930–1976.* Englewood Cliffs, N.J.: Prentice-Hall, 1976.

ElDean Bennett

PHILLIPS, IRNA (1901–1973), is recognized as the originator of the genre of soap opera as it became successful on radio and, later, television. Though serialized stories existed on radio before her, it was Phillips who packaged the programs and invested in them the qualities that made them successful. Phillips's innovations included focusing stories on families (as opposed to neighborhoods or workplaces), incorporating professional characters (doctors, lawyers), and using cliff-hanger endings. Phillips was also the first to utilize such soap staples as organ music to bridge scenes and the slowly paced storyline so her (predominantly) housewife audience could continue their housework without missing much. Additionally, Phillips was enthusiastic in using her shows as educational tools, creating plots that educated listeners about the war effort and other causes.

A former radio actress, Phillips created and wrote her first soap, *Painted Dreams*, for WGN/Chicago in 1930. *Dreams* proved successful, and Phillips followed it with other long-lasting dramas, all of them for network broadcast: *Today's Children, Road of Life, The Guiding Light*, and *The Right to Happiness*. By 1943, Phillips had a total of five programs on the air. Her writing output was estimated at over 2 million words per year.

Phillips moved her talents and most of her series to television in the 1950s. Eventually, the radio installments of the series were ceased once the TV adaptions took off. Phillips found even greater success on TV, creating *Another World, Days of Our Lives,* and *As the World Turns.* Her show *Guiding Light* is now the longest-running series in broadcasting history.

O'Dell, Cary. *Women Pioneers in Television: Biographies of Fifteen Industry Leaders.* Jefferson, N.C.: McFarland, 1996.
Phillips, Irna. "Every Woman's Life Is a Soap Opera." *McCall's* (March 1965): 116+.
Wyden, Peter. "Madame Soap Opera." *Saturday Evening Post* (June 25, 1960): 129+.

Cary O'Dell

PICKARD, SAM, born December 1, 1895, was a pioneer educational and farm broadcaster. As extension director at Kansas State Agricultural College, Manhattan, in 1922, he sent Kansas State professors to Kansas City for WDAF's *School of the Air.* The next year he produced Kansas State's *College of the Air,* offering credit courses broadcast remote from the campus on KFKB, Milford. It continued on Kansas State's own KSAC, beginning in December 1924. Students in 39 states and Canada enrolled.

Pickard also produced and announced KSAC's *Rural School Program, House-wives Half-Hour,* and *Farm Hour,* a daily noon program that lasted nearly 50 years with programs on agriculture, sewing, cooking, and child care. When Kansas State president William Jardine became U.S. secretary of agriculture in 1925, Pickard was hired as radio division chief to initiate U.S. Department of Agriculture (USDA) broadcasting.

Pickard became acting secretary of the first Federal Radio Commission (FRC) and permanent secretary, April 20, 1927. He was appointed Fourth Zone commissioner on November 1, 1927. He dealt with license regulations for early experimental TV and high-frequency radio. Pickard resigned from the FRC in 1929 and joined Columbia Broadcasting System as vice president for station relations. As Columbia expanded westward, in 1931 Pickard joined with radio pioneer Arthur Church (KBMC) and Joe Porter to form First National Television (FNT) school in Kansas City, Missouri. With CBS assistance, FNT trained radio engineers and built and operated mechanical TV station W9XAL (1932) and experimental high-frequency radio station W9XBY (1934), heard nationwide.

Baker, John C. *Farm Broadcasting: The First Sixty Years.* Ames: Iowa State University Press, 1981.

U.S. Federal Radio Commission. *First Annual Report.* Washington, D.C.: Government Printing Office, 1927.

U.S. Federal Radio Commission. *Third Annual Report.* Washington, D.C.: Government Printing Office, 1929.

William James Ryan

PIRATE RADIO is a collective term for unlicensed radio stations that broadcast to the general public. They are also called "free-radio" stations. These illegal broadcasters present many types of music and information but can be broadly characterized as having an idiosyncratic "underground" flavor. Pirates operate independently, taking to the airwaves to offer an alternative to legitimate radio or to command public attention for some personal reason. Pirates can be found on FM, AM, and shortwave bands but are usually difficult to pick up because of unsophisticated equipment and/or technical knowledge. They rarely broadcast on regular schedules and often switch frequencies and locations to avoid being detected and fined by the Federal Communications Commission (FCC).

For as long as there has been federal regulation of radio, there have been pirates. Early pirates were mostly indistinguishable from commercial and public service stations except that they did not have licenses. Regulation was not very strict before the *Communications Act of 1934* created the FCC, so pirates flourished in the 1920s. After 1934, the FCC found and forced many off the air. Tighter controls during World War II eliminated pirates almost completely.

Pirate radio did not make a significant showing again until the late 1960s, when members of the youth counterculture adopted it to spread their ideals. These were the first of the modern, iconoclastic pirates. Through the 1970s, 1980s, and 1990s, pirates of varied musical tastes and extreme ideologies appeared and disappeared, to the fascination of many radio hobbyists.

Yoder, Andrew. *Pirate Radio: The Incredible Saga of America's Underground, Illegal Broadcasters.* Solana Beach, Calif.: HighText Publications, 1996.

Kathleen M. O'Malley

PLAYLISTS. Radio stations' use of playlists is as old as radio itself. Originally used simply to document the records played, stations' use of playlists took on a much more active programming role as the industry turned to differing music formats in the 1950s. In format radio, the programmer's goal is to provide a consistent, homogenous sound, pursuing a target audience. Based in part on Todd Storz and Gordon McClendon's theory of hit rotation, predetermined playlists allow the station to define its sound very precisely. Programmers use a number of sources when determining songs for their playlists, including national and local sales charts, airplay charts from stations nationwide, and the popularity of songs from years past.

Keith, Michael C. *The Radio Station.* 4th. ed. Boston: Focal Press, 1997.

Mark A. Tolstedt

POLITICS AND MEDIA. From radio's earliest days, politics and broadcasting intersected at the point of presidential elections. In Detroit, experimenter Thomas E. Clark built transmitters and radio receivers for steamers in the Great Lakes and contracted with them to transmit news of the election of 1906. Ten years later, Lee de Forest broadcast presidential returns provided by the New York *American* and mistakenly proclaimed Charles Evans Hughes as the next president. The results of the 1920 race between Warren G. Harding and James M. Cox, both of Ohio, were broadcast from the experimental wireless desk of 8MK at the *Detroit News,* and KDKA in East Pittsburgh, Pennsylvania, where Westinghouse's publicist Leo Rosenberg announced news of Harding's victory.

In 1924, both parties employed radio to promote presidential candidates. Democrat John W. Davis spent $40,000 to broadcast his speeches, and GOP opponent Calvin Coolidge spent three times that amount to win the election. Four years later, a type of political spot was born when Republicans organized "Minute Men" all over the country to buy time on local radio stations and give brief talks in support of the GOP ticket.

The politics of talk radio provoked the nation in the 1930s with *America's Town Meeting of the Air* on NBC featuring live, political debates from New York's Town Hall. Mutual Broadcasting System answered with its *American Forum of the Air* and *The People's Rally.* CBS in 1938 hired Lyman Bryson to host *The People's Platform.* Bryson earlier had assisted George V. Denny in producing *America's Town Meeting of the Air.* The radio talk shows of this era were sustaining programs (without commercial sponsorship), and two of them, *The People's Platform* and *America's Town Meeting of the Air,* maintained audiences through the 1950s.

Political demagoguery found a voice in radio during the depression when Detroit priest Father Charles Coughlin took to the air to promote social justice and the silver standard. His rolling "Rs" and mellifluous delivery won him an audience on network radio, but his volatile attacks on "Franklin Doublecrossing Roosevelt" and anti-Semitic overtones prompted CBS executives to relinquish his radio podium. A string of stations sold time to Father Coughlin for his sermons broadcast during the Great Depression.

No less charismatic was the radio style of Senator Huey P. Long (D–La.), who began broadcasting speeches as the governor in the 1920s and spoke to the nation on NBC in the early 1930s. The folksy storyteller would begin by inviting listeners to telephone their friends and tell them Huey was on the air. By 1935, Long and Coughlin had attracted large followings to their political causes, and some believed if the two radio performers consolidated forces, Long would win the White House. That prospect was eliminated when an assassin's bullet struck down the "Kingfish" in the state capital of Baton Rouge in October 1935.

President Roosevelt's radio talent was demonstrated in both his public speeches and *Fireside Chats,* the first of which aired on March 12, 1933. Over the next 11 years, the president used his fireside forum 28 times to reassure Americans they had nothing to fear from perils at home or abroad. FDR also found radio an ally in his campaign speeches. Roosevelt chose to conduct one audience in a refrain chiding his opponent's isolationist supporters in Congress. The president would begin with one Congressman's name, "Martin," to which the audience rejoined, "Barton and Fish!" After hearing the enthusiasm generated by the president on radio, Republican Wendell Wilkie said he knew he would not win on election day.

NBC Radio alerted Americans to a dispatch from KGU in Hawaii on December 7, 1941: "We have witnessed this morning the attack on Pearl Harbor and the severe bombing of Pearl Harbor by army planes that are undoubtedly Japanese . . . It's no joke it's a real war." Seventy-nine percent of American homes heard, on radio, the president ask Congress for a declaration of war as he spoke of a day that would "live in infamy." The next week, 60 million Americans were engrossed in a radio performance of *We Hold These Truths* with Corporal James Stewart introducing FDR. On December 16, 1941, an Office of Censorship was created by the U.S. government, but it was to be on a voluntary basis. There were no forced measures of compliance with government officials requiring radio scripts or banning radio programs. Nonetheless, a number of quiz and entertainment shows left the air during the war years.

A type of voluntary censorship was undertaken by the radio networks during the prewar years when CBS announced it would no longer use network commentators, only news analysts. In a joint statement on war coverage, NBC and CBS agreed to refrain from airing editorial judgments. That same year, the Federal Communications Commission (FCC) made it a public policy by reprimanding WAAB in Boston for indulging in one-sidedness, adding that a "truly free radio cannot be used to advocate the causes of the licensee . . . the broadcaster cannot be an advocate."

That proclamation, known as the Mayflower Doctrine, after the company challenging WAAB's license, eventually produced the Fairness Doctrine in 1949. As a result of the outcry from broadcasters claiming their First Amendment rights had been abridged, the FCC held a series of hearings and issued its *Report on Editorializing by Broadcast Licensees,* which held that radio editorials were acceptable so long as opposing viewpoints were aired. After more than three decades of trying to enforce the Fairness Doctrine, the FCC backed away from most of its provisions in 1987, rescinding all but the personal attack rule.

The political tactics of Sen. Joseph McCarthy (R–Wisc.) and his followers cost some broadcasters their careers in the 1950s, destroyed by the fears of anticommunist organizations. John Henry Faulk, a WCBS announcer, was elected vice president of the New York chapter of the American Federation of Television and Radio Artists, and he repudiated the tactics of Aware, Inc., an anticommunist group backed by Syracuse supermarket executive Laurence Johnson and headed by Vincent Hartnett. Faulk had not been blacklisted before, but he became the target of an Aware bulletin accusing him of communist activities. He countered with a libel suit against Johnson and Hartnett, and his attorney Louis Nizer won the case in 1963.

The equal opportunities provision, Section 315 of the *Communications Act of 1934,* became a subject of concern to Congress in 1959. The rule was not difficult to interpret for candidate speeches but became muddled on other occasions, especially at news events. When the FCC gave equal time to the opponents of Mayor Richard Daley, who had appeared on television at a March of Dimes rally, Congress stepped in with exemptions to Section 315 for bona fide news coverage, documentaries, and debates.

Without network stars and prime-time programming, radio reinvented itself in the 1950s and began to play a different role in political campaigns. Candidates reached out to targeted, local audiences. In 1972, President Nixon's campaign strategists placed $85,000 in radio ads on stations near military bases and defense plants to attack George McGovern's proposed cuts to the U.S. Defense budget. In 1976, presidential-hopeful Jimmy Carter took advantage of radio's niche formats, emphasizing his civil rights record on urban stations while highlighting his southern heritage on country music stations.

The rise of talk shows in the 1990s demonstrated renewed political strength for radio. Conservative talk-show hosts mobilized American public opinion against federal health care, the Fairness Doctrine, congressional pay raises, Democrats in Congress, and the "liberal" media, among others. In 1992, talk shows were considered to be the second most important source of information for American voters next to the presidential debates. In the election of 1994, talk radio was credited with changing the balance of power in Congress for the first time in 40 years from Democrat to Republican. The GOP in 1996 set up a talk-show row at its national party convention, and candidates of both parties booked time on radio talk shows as part of their campaign strategy.

Diamond, Edwin, and Stephen Bates. *The Spot: The Rise of Political Advertising on Television.* 3rd ed. Cambridge: MIT Press, 1992.

William R. Davie

POLLING, PUBLIC OPINION, the use of surveys to describe public attitudes toward current issues, especially voting preferences during election campaigns. From the 1820s, efforts to track public opinion depended on "straw polls," in which readers of newspapers and magazines used reply coupons to express their preferences. In the 1930s, pollsters including George Gallup and Elmo Roper began using scientifically selected samples of the voting population, with news organizations as their major clients. They adapted their methods from the sphere of advertising and marketing research and came to prominence in 1936. The *Literary Digest* mistakenly predicted an Alf Landon landslide defeat of Franklin D. Roosevelt, based on a mail-in survey of automobile owners and households with telephones. Gallup, Roper, and Archibald Crossley used more representative samples in correctly predicting Roosevelt's election. However, in 1948, all three organizations predicted that Thomas Dewey would beat Harry Truman; Roper conducted no polls after the middle of September, and they all failed to account for shifts in opinion late in the campaign. Truman won a famous come-from-behind victory.

Pollsters generally use randomly selected respondents, often chosen from clusters of randomly selected precincts or geographic areas. Random cluster samples can achieve high mathematical accuracy, called sampling error, but pollsters still must contend with errors introduced by the wording of survey questions and the practices of poll-takers.

Political campaigns rely heavily on polls to guide the shaping of campaign strategy and rhetoric. Private polling on behalf of candidates has become a major campaign expense.

The use of exit polls, which survey voters just after they have voted, has introduced another level of predictive accuracy into public opinion and voting surveys. News organizations use exit polls to project winners in elections long before all of the states have stopped voting in national elections. The practice has attracted criticism and legislative attention, although evidence that such projections have a significant effect on voting is inconclusive, and no legislation has resulted to date.

Gawiser, Sheldon R., and G. Evans Witt. *A Journalist's Guide to Public Opinion Polls.* Westport, Conn.: Praeger, 1994.

Lavrakas, Paul J., and Jack K. Holley, eds. *Polling and Presidential Election Coverage.* Newbury Park, Calif.: Sage, 1991.

John R. Broholm

POPOFF, ALEXANDER STEPANOVITCH (1859–1905), Russian wireless inventor. Born in a small mining village in the Urals region of Russia, son of a priest, Popoff finished schooling at Perm and entered the University of St. Petersburg in 1877, graduating in 1882. A decade after its formation, he joined the physics faculty of the Torpedo School located at Kronstadt and remained there from 1883 to 1901.

Popoff first applied wireless research to concerns about predicting thunderstorms when he modified Branly coherers to detect atmospheric electricity lightning charges at a distance. Popoff has long been revered in Russia as *the* inventor of radio, based on a public demonstration in St. Petersburg involving wireless signaling over 600 yards of letters (to spell out Heinrich Hertz's name) on May 7, 1895, but there is no available documentation of this event.

He installed his wireless apparatus on a Russian cruiser two years later and embarked on a series of wireless ship-to-shore experiments including one 1900 event where some fishermen's lives were saved. He was later a professor at St. Petersburg's Electrotechnical Institute, of which he was elected director just before his death.

Dunlap, Orrin E., Jr., ed. "Alexander Stepanovitch Popoff: Russia's Marconi." In *Radio's 100 Men of Science* (pp. 127–128). New York: Harper, 1944.

Radovsky, M. *Alexander Popov: Inventor of Radio.* Translated by G. Yankovsky. Moscow: Foreign Languages Publishing House, 1957.

Christopher H. Sterling

POSITIONING "is what you do to the mind of the prospect." Successful positioning involves considering not only a product's strengths and weaknesses but also the strengths and weaknesses of its competitors. The strategy is increasingly applied by radio and television stations as well as radio and television program producers and distributors to carve a place for themselves in a very crowded marketplace. Ries and Trout outlined four key principles to keep in mind when attempting to position a product or service: (1) Don't attack the market leader head on. (2) The mind only accepts information that matches its prior knowledge or experience. Therefore, if there is a market leader, other companies must position themselves relative to it in the consumer's mind. (3) Just because a company is well known in one field doesn't mean it can transfer that recognition to another. (4) Confusion is the enemy of successful positioning. If positioning the product in one place in the prospect's mind worked, don't try to reposition it. Also, when a lot of change is taking place, don't add to the confusion by repositioning your product. *If it ain't broke, don't fix it.* One of the most critical aspects of "positioning" is being able to evaluate objectively products and services and how they are viewed by customers and "prospects."

Ries, Al, and Jack Trout. *Positioning: The Battle for Your Mind.* New York: McGraw-Hill, 1981.

Marianne Barrett

POULSEN, VALDEMAR (1869–1942), Danish scientist and inventor of continuous wave arc transmitter. Son of a judge in Denmark's highest court, Poulsen studied for a natural science degree at the University of Copenhagen (1889–1893) and entered the technical department of the Copenhagen Telephone Company. He developed a means of recording telephone conversations on steel wire, dubbed the *telegrafonen.* It was a predecessor of modern recording methods.

In 1903, Poulsen developed his direct-current arc-based radiotelephony system that generated continuous waves and allowed transmission of voice signals. However, the system also transmitted considerable harmonics and noise, and the heat thrown off (an indicator of inefficiency) required fans or water cooling. When combined with the Pederson "tikker" for reception, the "Poulsen system" created the best means of voice telephony until the later development of alternator and vacuum-tube transmitter.

The arc principal was widely known (Reginald Fessenden used one for his early transmissions from Roanoke Island in North Carolina, and Lee de Forest's early shipboard installations on the "Great White Fleet" of 1907 were also arcs). The Poulsen system was licensed for use in the United States to Cyril F. Elwell in 1909, and early Poulson arcs were used to demonstrate wireless possibilities in central California. Soon, improved and increased in capacity and manufactured in California, arc transmitters became the core of the Poulsen Wireless Telephone and Telegraph Company, with transmitters in San Francisco, Stockton, and Sacramento. Under different management and with an infusion of funds, more and higher-powered stations—13 by 1912—were built by what was now known as the Federal Telegraph Company for wireless service to Hawaii and on to the Orient, in competition with cables. French and British government stations also operated with Poulsen arcs during World War I.

Aitken, Hugh G. J., ed. "Elwell, Fuller, and the Arc." In *The Continuous Wave: Technology and American Radio, 1900–1932* (pp. 87–161). Princeton, N.J.: Princeton University Press, 1985.

Dunlap, Orrin E., Jr., ed. "Valdemar Poulsen: Harnessed the Arc to Wireless." In *Radio's 100 Men of Science* (pp. 153–155). New York: Harper, 1944.

Elwell, C. F. *The Poulsen Arc Generator.* New York: Van Nostrand, 1923.

Elwell, C. F. "The Poulsen System of Radiotelegraphy: History of Development of Arc Methods." *Electrician* (May 28, 1920): 596–599.

Christopher H. Sterling

POWER ROTATION AND TOP 40. *Power rotation* refers to a category of recorded music intended for the highest frequency of airplay. The songs in this category are sometimes called *powers*. Records are placed in a power rotation because of some combination of strong sales, star quality of the artist, effective promotion, heavy adoption by other stations, or frequent telephone requests. Trade newspapers such as *Radio & Records* reproduce the rotation level of current hit music at certain key reporting stations, with the result that many other stations in the country follow the featured stations' lead.

Power rotations are one of the legacies of the music presentation systems developed in the top-40 format. Early top-40 stations limited their playlist to the 40 or so most popular records of the day, but it soon became apparent that the songs at the bottom of the chart were not as attractive to listeners as those at the top. As a result, many top 40s began playing the dozen or so hottest records much more frequently, in effect, putting them into a power rotation where a given title might be heard every two or three hours. By contrast, each of the 20 to 30 current records in medium rotation might be heard only once in a daypart, while the titles in light rotation might only be aired a couple of times a day.

Over the years, the music rotation systems developed for the top-40 format have been adopted by other hit-oriented formats such as country, urban, and adult contemporary. The number of songs in each rotation category varies by format, by city, by station practice, and by time of day.

David T. MacFarland

PRESS-RADIO BUREAU (PRB) (1934–1938), a news "clearinghouse" created under the Biltmore Agreement (see **Biltmore Agreement; Press-Radio War**) to rewrite wire service news bulletins into brief newscasts for radio news operations. PRB began operation on March 1, 1934, in New York City. The director was James W. Barnett, a former editor of the *New York World*. Under the Biltmore Agreement, the PRB would take Associated Press, United Press International, and International News Service reports and create two five-minute newscasts to be used by the network radio stations. There were usually about 20 bulletins available for each newscast, and the bulletins generally consisted of about 30 words each. There were a number of specific restrictions placed on the material made available to radio news operations that were designed to maximize the importance of the newspapers. Specifically, the morning bulletins could not air before 9:30 A.M., and the evening bulletins could air after 9 P.M. to protect the two main newspaper editions. The bulletins and PRB-prepared newscasts could not be sponsored, and the broadcasters were responsible for funding PRB operations. In the case of major breaking news, the PRB could issue special bulletins covering the general highlights of the story, but the bulletins had to refer the listening audience to the newspaper for the full story. The significance of the PRB was that it marked the beginning of the end of the Press-Radio War. On the surface, it seemed that the print media had won in that it severely restricted network radio's news operation. But as pioneer broadcaster Paul White noted, radio had given up income, some integrity, and a glorious opportunity, but the formation of the network radio news departments had forced the newspapers to withdraw their pressure on the wire services, and a supply of news for radio was assured (White, p. 42).

Two key factors also emerged with regard to the PRB. Both Jackaway and White note that the guidelines, carefully crafted to benefit the print media, were either ignored or sidestepped. The second key reason for the demise of the PRB was that only the network stations participated. The 600-plus independent stations, under the leadership of the National Association of Broadcasters (NAB), never subscribed to the Biltmore Agreement and began to seek alternative sources of news. These alternative sources quickly became available through broadcast news services such as the Yankee Network in Boston and Transradio Press. This caused the PRB to ease its own release restrictions in order to remain competitive. Another key factor in the eventual dissolution of the informal Biltmore Agreement and the PRB was a strong enemy in Washington. Gwenyth Jackaway describes how Senator Clarence Dill, coauthor of the *1927 Radio Act* and the *Communications Act of 1934,* believed the Biltmore Agreement was one-sided and constituted a monopolistic control over the news by the print media. Dill even accused the print media of abusing press freedom (Jackaway, p. 30). Dill threatened to create a government-run news service, but the PRB had been disbanded before Dill's proposal got beyond the planning stages.

Jackaway, Gwenyth L. *Media at War: Radio's Challenge to the Newspapers, 1924–1939.* Westport, Conn.: Praeger, 1995.
White, Paul W. *News on the Air.* New York: Harcourt, Brace & Co., 1947.

Michael D. Casavantes

PRESS-RADIO WAR (1924–1939) was a concerted effort by the print-media establishment to prevent or limit the continued growth of the news-gathering and dissemination capability of radio. The post–World War I period was a time of growth for the United States in both new technology and consumerism. The fledgling medium of radio also experienced a tremendous growth surge during the 1920s, with some 1,400 stations on the air by the middle of the decade. Radio news during this period generally was limited to special-event coverage such as national elections, political conventions, and the Lindbergh kidnaping and subsequent trial of Bruno Hauptmann. However, as radio began to realize the profit potential from news, it began to increase its coverage of spot news events. This led many advertisers to view the new medium as a relatively inexpensive way to reach current and potential customers. Gwenyth Jackaway notes that the print media saw the rise of radio news as a direct threat to its institutional identity, structure, and function (Jackaway, p. 4). To counter this threat to its advertising monopoly and status as the nation's premier news source, the print media and wire services began a concerted effort to restrict radio's access to news gathered by the wire services and print sources. The American Newspapers Publishers Association's (ANPA's) radio committee, headed by Ed Harris of the Richmond (Indiana) *Palladium,* began pressuring the wire services to restrict radio access to wire news copy. At one point, all three wire services refused to sell their product to radio stations. In response, the fledgling radio networks created their own news-gathering capabilities.

In December 1933, representatives from the wire services, newspapers, and radio networks met at the Hotel Biltmore in New York City and negotiated the Press-Radio agreement. The general terms of the Biltmore Agreement called for network radio to dismantle its news organizations in return for access to wire service bulletins filtered through the Press Radio Bureau (PRB). The rules of the Biltmore Agreement were extremely restrictive for radio—including provisions prohibiting bulletins over five minutes in length; bulletins could not air until after the morning and evening newspaper editions were on the newsstand; and in the case of major breaking stories, the bulletins were to refer listeners to the newspaper for more information.

The restrictions placed on radio news were modified in 1934 and 1935, due primarily to competition from independent news services created specifically to provide news to radio. In April 1935, both United Press and the International News Service decided to sell their product to independent stations. The following year, the long-running feud between the print and broadcast media ended. The PRB was discontinued in 1938. In May 1939 the Associated Press lifted its ban on sponsored newscasts of its services and created a separate Press Association to provide broadcast-style rewrites of its print wire to radio stations.

Bliss, Edward, Jr. *Now the News: The Story of Broadcast Journalism.* New York: Columbia University Press, 1991.

Chester, Giraud. "The Press Radio War: 1933–1935." *Public Opinion Quarterly* 13 (summer 1949): 263.

Jackaway, Gwenyth L. *Media at War: Radio's Challenge to the Newspapers, 1924–1939.* Westport, Conn.: Praeger, 1995.

White, Paul W. *News on the Air.* New York: Harcourt, Brace & Co., 1947.

Michael D. Casavantes

PROGRAMMING means two things: first, the content or substance of material scheduled on the air; and second, the decision-making process about the sequence and composition of the material that is broadcast. A program director orchestrates the elements together. In earlier periods of radio, a director actually worked with actors in reading their scripts. As radio moved from the era of drama to that of music, news, and sports, the program director determined which music was played at what time of the day (dayparts), in which sequences various kinds of music were played, or what kinds of nonmusic materials and talents were heard on the station. Indeed, the design of these combinations could make a station successful or be its undoing.

A radio station's identity is determined by its programming. Some of the most common radio programming formats include: soft hits, contemporary hits radio, album-oriented rock or classic rock, country, black/urban, jazz, classical, and news/talk. Often listeners will adhere to a single programming format or listen to a single station. Building a faithful listenership is an important selling point to advertisers, particularly if a station's listenership has specific demographic characteristics of interest to advertisers.

Programming—Advertiser Control. Earlier in radio's history, many programs' production and distribution costs were fully paid by a sponsor, an advertiser who oversaw the program's production. With such close sponsorship identity, there was opportunity for the advertiser to unduly influence or control the program's contents. Some were benign: Soap manufacturers wanted uplifting messages directed toward housewives. These melodramas became known as "soap operas," because of the close association with a few manufacturers of soap and household products. Other sponsors became final judges of what the program would contain. For example, in 1935, Cream of Wheat cereal sponsored a Sunday evening series, *The Town Crier,* that examined current issues. When its narrator and critic, Alexander Woollcott, derided Hitler, the sponsor asked him to refrain. When Woollcott would not promise that, the series was canceled. For years to come, other sponsor influences were felt on programming content.

Programming—Codes. Early broadcasting codes covered the possible effects programs containing any element of crime, mystery or horror, obscenity or profanity, or derision of the disabled could have on all family members. Moreover, children's programs were to "contribute to the healthy development of character and personality." In 1982, the code was dropped (see **codes of ethics**), but in 1990 the National Association of Broadcasters created a new Statement of Principles dealing specifically with violence, drugs, substance abuse, and sexually oriented material. Two special responsibilities were identified as well: responsibly exercised artistic freedom and responsibility in children's programming.

Programming—Delivery Systems. In the early days, programs were distributed through a "network" linking of stations, with telephone lines the most common delivery form. Linking stations together by land lines created the first networks, and later some programs used packaged delivery. Though land distribution eventually included microwave relays, such distribution was subject to technical problems that affected sound quality. Plus, there was the continuing expense for line leasing. When satellites became a viable delivery system, radio was among the first to use dish antennae to receive clear-stereo transmission. Even stations whose programming had come mostly from their own music library were able to use preprogrammed series of satellite-delivered music hits, often with nationally known disc jockey personalities. Today, most U.S. radio stations own at least one satellite dish, often more to bring in both network and individually purchased program packages "live-by-satellite."

Programming—Developments. Radio programming moved from primarily local to mostly network, back to local with emphasis on programming for casual listeners. It then became a listener's "constant companion," practically omnipresent with the mobility made possible by transistors and miniaturized circuitry. Indeed, technology seems to have driven many developments in radio programming. Television had profound impact on both program types and when listeners tuned in. Now developments seem to be focused on delivery—mostly by satellite, with programs produced away from the local stations that carry them. Technology has also made it possible for more radio stations to exist due to finer splintering of the listening audience. For example, it's not just talk radio now—it's talk radio with specific political leanings; not just a sports station—but one specializing in specific sports or sports of only certain teams. Moreover, satellites could deliver many channels of specialized programs directly to listeners who had home-satellite dishes. Developing specialized and segmented programming seems likely to continue and lead to further success of radio.

Programming—FCC Control Effort. Since the *Communications Act of 1934* mandated that stations serve in the "public interest, convenience, and necessity," the Federal Communications Commission (FCC) gauged how well a station did by the programming it carried. To make this clear and legal, in 1945 the FCC created its Blue Book. After warning stations about breech of promise in living up to its commitment, it outlined that stations carry sustaining programming, that is, not paid for by advertisers but sustained by the station's own income. Stations were also to reflect "programs of local interests, activities and talent," to discuss public issues, and finally, to avoid advertising excesses. Later, the FCC issued its *1960 Programming Policy Statement,* replacing the Blue Book. With the deregulation the 1980s, the FCC held stations to virtually no programming requirements except to adhere to the federal codes that disallowed airing "obscene, profane or indecent language." The FCC imposed heavy fines, and their right to do so was upheld by the courts in the mid-1990s, revealing that the FCC control of programming was not totally dead.

Programming—Moral Issues. As radio programming attempted to pierce through all the "sound clutter," controversial programs or those taking issue with conventional moral issues or social values were aired. In the 1970s, these were referred to as "topless radio," referencing the social taboo of public nudity. Although the FCC penalized stations based on federal codes, the trend continued using double entendres that could legitimately be interpreted with innocent meanings. During the 1980s, some disc jockeys exhibited their talent with the outrageous and the outlandish: "shock jocks." One such personality was Howard Stern whose humor attracted large numbers of mostly young, white, male listeners. His irreverent themes repeated stories of sex, nudity, masturbation, bestiality, and misogyny. The FCC charged the station that aired his program on several counts, with fine after fine, eventually mounting well past a million dollars. The parent corporation, Infinity Broadcasting, fought the fines but eventually paid most of them to be eligible to purchase more stations with the FCC's approval. Moral issues will continue to be a programming issue for both radio and television.

Programming—National versus Local. The basic concept in establishing frequency allocation was for stations to be assigned to a locale or region that they were to serve. For many years, the FCC looked at programming to ensure it reflected some local interests. This was especially critical during the golden age when radio's popularity could be attributed to network programming, though most stations still maintained local programming.

More recently, with satellite delivery of a wide programming variety and the ability such delivery systems have to give unique character to program selections, the issue of localism has resurfaced. Although regulations directing stations toward local programming have been deregulated, many of the more successful stations maintain local programming to satisfy their mostly local advertisers.

Programming—Network Control. Because networks have traditionally had relatively large audiences, compared to local stations, they have had the resources to create well-developed programs, often with well-known talents. During radio's heyday, the most envied programs (such as *Amos 'n' Andy, Jack Benny, Fibber McGee & Molly*) were on the networks. Stations carrying network programs by contractual agreement (affiliates) gladly carried these more popular programs, being almost subservient to the networks' wishes. There was concern that such linking gave too much control over stations to the networks. With the advent of television, such concern diminished together with the regulations that were built to control the networks.

Programming—Research. Most research today is for two express purposes: to determine ratings—how many people are listening from a survey of area listeners—and to determine a commercial's effectiveness. Sampling research has been done in written (diary) form, by telephone, with electronic devices detecting the tuned-in frequencies, with direct instantaneous lines or devices, and combinations of these methods. Major rating services included Hooper, Nielsen Arbitron, Birch, and regional services, such as Wilhight. Research for advertising effectiveness isolated ads for specific items, then measured their sales and correlated them to the advertising. As research continued to develop, more specific information about the demographics of listeners has been uncovered, allowing advertising to be ever more exact and focused.

Programming—Spin-offs. When a program spins off another, the result is an imitation. Usually success is the reason for the imitation, and the spin-off is an attempt to have success rub off, too. Imitations can occur in the form of plot, character, or themes. There are many famous spin-offs in the history of radio programming. After the first daytime mellow drama proved to be successful, other successful spin-offs came along. After the first radio mysteries held listeners entranced and frightened, others managed to do the same. As with many aspects of life, success breeds imitation.

Programming—Syndicated. A syndicated program refers to the system of distribution where a program "package" is marketed on a station-to-station basis. These receiving stations need have no association with each other, as would be the case with network affiliates carrying a network program. Once on the network, programs can be syndicated "off network" in a special series of reruns. New programs, or "first-run syndication," packaged together and sold to stations individually, can also be considered a kind of syndicated program.

Val E. Limburg

PROGRESSIVE COUNTRY blends aspects of country and western, bluegrass, and folk with the insurgent sounds of southern rock and blues. It is also known as "outlaw country," "redneck rock," "alternative country," and even "twang core." Progressive country in the 1970s featured artists such as Waylon Jennings, Willie Nelson, Emmylou Harris, Asleep at the Wheel, Jerry Jeff Walker, and the Nitty Gritty Dirt Band. The active Austin, Texas, music scene yielded many progressive country acts during this time. In the 1990s, progressive country has evolved into the Americana-radio format, a term coined by Rob Bleetstein of *Gavin* magazine in January 1995. Top Americana artists in the 1990s include Lyle Lovett, Nanci

Griffith, Alison Krauss & Union Station, Steve Earle, Iris DeMent, and Bruce Springsteen. While the Americana charts often include mainstream country artists such as Dwight Yoakam, The Mavericks, and Mary Chapin Carpenter, they are more likely to incorporate an eclectic mix of music that includes bluegrass, folk, Texas swing, rockabilly and zydeco, and other "roots" music that may be considered too country and/or too adventurous for modern corporate Nashville. Americana, like its predecessor progressive country, represents a no-holds-barred type of music genre that emphasizes both diversity and quality.

Bleetstein, Rob. "One Year down the Americana Highway." *Gavin* (January 19, 1996): 33.
Endres, Clifford. *Austin City Limits*. Austin: University of Texas Press, 1987.

Carla E. Gesell

PROGRESSIVE JAZZ. *See* **jazz formats on radio.**

PROGRESSIVE ROCK FORMAT, the stage between the "freeform" and the fully developed "album-oriented rock" that carried the underground into mainstream ratings success. Progressive rock format formalized the freeform approach that allowed each air personality nearly absolute programming control. As Scott Muni, WNEW, noted in an interview, "Where many of the free forms went wrong was in their selection of programmers. In free-form, instead of there being only one PD, each person on the air is a programmer. If they think that they are experts in their own minds, they'll kill the station" ("The AOR Story," p. 38). To prevent this, progressive rock programmers established formatic structures allowing great latitude in song choice and "creative-set building," while assuring order and consistency in the station's total air sound. Specific categories had to be played at certain points within the format rotation. Linear rotations tended to be more favored by progressive rock programmers since they withstood counterprogramming better and eliminated time as a factor in music programming. Linear rotations moved fully through the format's structure, allowing greater latitude for tracks that did not fit the restrictions imposed by a hot clock. Progressive rock format's development and growth alongside the success of many of the freeform stations, most notably Metromedia's powerhouses, led to some very intense ratings battles in almost every large market and many small markets around the country.

"The AOR Story." *Radio & Records* (1978): 38.

Michael Taylor

PROMOTION, ON-AIR, includes all of the elements that form a radio station's market position, image, attitude, and identity: tune-in promos for programs, personalities, dayparts, and special events; contests, slogans, bumpers, jingles, teases, and station identifications (IDs).

Scheduled around programming but not entirely separate from it, it's designed to support marketing and branding efforts and is an instrument of quarter-hour audience maintenance and increased listener sampling. In competitive markets, promotion also performs an important function distinguishing like-formatted radio stations from each other.

Joseph R. Piasek

PROPAGANDA, the systematic propagation of a doctrine, cause, or information reflecting the views and interests of the advocates, applies to American radio in two important ways. In the first and most specific sense, the Federal Radio Commission (FRC) established a sharp contrast between what it termed a *general public service station,* which delivered a well-rounded program of interest to the entire listening public, and a *propaganda station,* where the licensee was more interested in spreading a particular viewpoint. This distinction first was made in the context of the FRC's 1928 plan of spectrum reallocation where general public service stations were favored by the commission during the all-important processes of frequency reallocation and license renewal. For example, the FRC found in favor of the Chicago Tribune''s WGN and against the Chicago Federation of Labor's WCFL ("the Voice of Labor"), holding that there is no place for a station catering to any group and that all stations should "serve public interest against group or class interest." The underlying principle, that stations were licensed to serve "listeners" rather than "users," would be repeated at several crucial junctures in the history of broadcast regulation, including by the U.S. Supreme Court in its 1969 *Red Lion* decision upholding the Fairness Doctrine. As a consequence of the distinction between general public service and propaganda stations, the FRC reduced the hours or eliminated the frequencies of numerous nonprofit broadcasters, typically in favor of stations affiliated with a major network. Over time, commercial advertising became the primary form of financial support, and commercial sponsorship continues having important influences upon the content of programming.

In its second and most general sense, propaganda, as symbolic action intended to influence behavior, is at the heart of any discussion of the relation between radio and political power. Radio-based propaganda is most often conceived in the context of European fascist propaganda of the 1930s. In the United States, however, Father C. E. Coughlin ("the radio priest") was one of the most successful practitioners of radio propaganda, delivering his first radio sermon in the mid-1920s. At the height of his popularity in the 1930s, it was estimated he reached a national audience of 40 million. In an age of mass democracy, government-by-opinion propaganda's relevance is perhaps greater than ever. It is not limited to the authoritarian dissemination of falsehoods by the state. Many techniques of modern public relations and advertising, often well financed and scientifically based, draw upon principles of propaganda in their attempts to secure public understanding and support for a variety of private causes. In the contemporary age, it would make little sense to attempt to distinguish between the propagandist and the advertising executive. Moreover, the modern propagandist does not assume that its subjects are malleable victims who easily fall prey to the techniques of mediated discourse. Instead, propaganda draws upon each individual's willingness to become emotionally involved and base his or her actions on other than strictly rational grounds. Therefore, a sophisticated view of propaganda describes a complex and interactive process where the media acts as merely one of many agents of socialization and belief formation.

McChesney, Robert W. *Telecommunications, Mass Media, and Democracy: The Battle for the Control of U.S. Broadcasting, 1928–1935.* New York: Oxford University Press, 1993.

Edward M. Lenert

PUBLIC AFFAIRS PROGRAMMING. The *Communications Act of 1934* requires radio stations to serve the "public interest, convenience, and necessity." This phrase, which has been carried over into the new *Telecommunications Act,* historically implies that stations offer a certain amount of informational programming in addition to music and entertainment features. One of the ways broadcasters have attempted to fulfill this responsibility is through regularly scheduled public affairs programs. While similar to newscasts in that they are designed to inform listeners about current events, public affairs shows last much longer and usually cover one issue but with greater detail. A typical public affairs program might feature an interview with the chief of police and a city council member discussing ways to lower the local crime rate. Depending on a station's format, a public affairs show might be as short as 15 minutes or as lengthy as three hours. Each station's public affairs shows—taken as a whole—should equitably represent different perspectives on the various issues. Each broadcaster is also responsible for regularly surveying the community in order to know what issues should be covered on these shows. Each station is required to keep a yearly record in its public file of issues important to the local community and the dates and times of the different public affairs shows that discussed those issues. By the nature of the format, news/talk stations offer plenty of public affairs/discussion programs; however, music stations historically program public affairs shows during hours when few people are listening (such as early Sunday mornings). This is done to avoid receiving low audience ratings during times attractive to advertisers.

Today, the Federal Communications Commission's (FCC's) interpretation of public affairs programming has considerable lenience. As stations target a specified audience, the question of pubic interest becomes one of service to the listeners of the station. Abbreviated news, community billboards, all sorts of community involvement, and entertainment are considered under this broader marketplace interpretation of public interest and public affairs programming.

Kenneth D. Loomis

PUBLIC BROADCASTING ACT OF 1967 was signed into law by President Lyndon B. Johnson on November 7 to firmly establish a mechanism for the preservation and development of an alternative, noncommercial, educational radio and television system in the United States. An outgrowth of recommendations by the Carnegie Commission on Educational Television, the act authorized creation of a Corporation for Public Broadcasting, to be headed by a 15-member board appointed by the president and approved by the Senate. The act also authorized $9 million to finance the first year of the corporation's operation and extended through fiscal 1970 the educational television (ETV) construction program authorized under the *Educational Television Facilities Act of 1962.*

Virtually all the momentum that led up to creating public broadcasting legislation focused on the medium of television. The conference that proposed the Carnegie Commission was sponsored by educational television representatives, and the commission's mandate was clearly television. Within the commission's recommendations was establishing a Corporation for Public Television, as it was with President Johnson's message to Congress and the subsequent companion bills to come out of the House and Senate. The pervasive opinion within the educational television community was that the spotty educational track record would only serve to weaken chances for federal appropriations if radio were included. Standing against the political strength of educational television factions at the National Association of Educational Broadcasters (NAEB), Jerrold Sandler, executive director of NAEB's national educational radio division, mounted the effort to have radio included in the language of the act. Sandler's campaign involved a conference at the Johnson Foundation's Wingspread Center in Racine, Wisconsin, and commissioning a report outlining the accomplishments of educational radio. That report, *The Hidden Medium,* was distributed to Washington policy makers after the Senate and House bills had been scheduled for hearings, but it made a significant impact. Jerrold Sandler's impassioned testimony during the Senate hearings prompted Senator Griffin of Michigan to propose that the bill be broadened to include radio and the name of the oversight agency be changed to the Corporation for Public Broadcasting. Public radio was born.

Burke, John E. *An Historical-Analytical Study of the Legislative and Political Origins of the Public Broadcasting Act of 1967.* New York: Arno Press, 1979.
Herman W. Land Associates, Inc. *The Hidden Medium: A Status Report on Educational Radio in the United States.* New York: Herman W. Land Associates, Inc., 1967.
Witherspoon, John, and Roselle Kovitz. *The History of Public Broadcasting.* Washington, D.C.: Current Publishing, 1987.

Robert K. Avery

PUBLIC FILE is maintained to meet the Federal Communications Commission (FCC) requirement that each broadcast station maintain and make accessible to the public those documents related to that station's federal license. The public can review how the station portrays itself in FCC correspondence, then make judgments about the station's effectiveness in meeting its federal public interest requirements. Stations report that public demand to inspect the file is minimal, though interest sometimes increases when a station is applying for license renewal. Station personnel must make the file available to any member of the public during normal business hours. FCC personnel are allowed access to the file for inspection whenever the station is in operation.

Public file documents include license applications to the FCC, ownership reports, political broadcasting records, employment reports, and the FCC procedure manual. The public file must also include letters from the public that deal with programming. A key component of the public file is the issues/programs list. It covers 5 to 10 issues the station has determined are of significant interest to the community and the programs aired that helped the community engage those issues. This is the primary way for the public and the FCC to determine if the station meets its obligation to serve the public interest. The file must be kept within the city of license, and the FCC can fine stations for failure to maintain and make a complete public file available.

FCC Rules and Regulations. Section 73.3527.

Jeffrey M. McCall

PUBLIC INTEREST, CONVENIENCE, AND NECESSITY, the legal standard by which broadcast stations' performance in the United States is judged. The Federal Communications Commission (FCC) is charged with regulating broadcast stations according to this standard.

When Congress adopted the *Radio Act of 1927,* it borrowed this regulatory standard from the transportation law term that applied primarily to questions about authorizing new or abandoning old train routes. Congress retained the public interest standard when it passed the *Communications Act of 1934.* However, Congress did not define the phrase in either piece of legislation, instead leaving definition and implementation initially to the Federal Radio Commission (FRC) and then to the FCC. This lack of definition by Congress has given the FCC great flexibility in fashioning regulatory programs and requirements. It has also led to extensive litigation from participants in the policy-making process who disagree with the commission's determinations.

Several variations of the public interest phrase are found throughout the *Communications Act,* and the courts have declared that the public interest, convenience, and necessity should be read collectively, not disjunctively—no policies serve only the public interest with others serving the public convenience and still others the public necessity.

From the beginning of broadcast regulation under the 1927 and later the 1934 acts, it was clear that the public interest standard included technical regulation. Cleaning up the crowded airwaves was the purpose of the 1927 act, and engineering standards established by the commissions generally were not significantly challenged. However, when the FRC and then the FCC began adopting content or structural regulations based on their promoting public interest, broadcasters began to question the limits of the standard. In *National Broadcasting Company v. United States* (1943), NBC challenged the FCC's chain broadcasting rules on a number of fronts, including the notion that the requirements were outside the FCC's authority under the public interest standard. The Supreme Court disagreed, ruling that the FCC's power to promulgate rules under the public interest standard was "expansive and not niggardly." Twenty-six years later, the Supreme Court upheld the commission's Fairness Doctrine and personal attack rules—rules that required broadcast stations to provide access to particular persons or points of view against a constitutional challenge, finding that the public's interest in hearing diverse viewpoints outweighed the broadcast station's ability to control content.

The number and complexity of broadcast regulations under the public interest standard inexorably increased throughout the 1950s, 1960s, and early 1970s.

Beginning with the FCC chairmanship of Charles Ferris during the Carter administration, however, a new concept of public interest deregulation began to find adherents at the commission. Instead of the FCC defining the public interest through its regulations, the promoters of deregulation argued that the public interest was better served by economic, marketplace forces exemplified by consumer choices. According to a later chairman of the commission, Mark Fowler (himself a champion of deregulation), "the public interest is what interests the public."

Arguments about whether government or the economic marketplace should determine public interest abound today. Presently, broadcasting regulation is a mixture of government oversight and marketplace regulation, all presumably working together to serve the public interest, convenience, and necessity.

Fowler, Mark S., and Daniel L. Brenner. "A Marketplace Approach to Broadcast Regulation." *Texas Law Review* 60 (1982): 207.

Michael A. McGregor

PUBLIC RADIO describes a class of nonprofit broadcasting stations, noncommercial by law, allocated a set of designated FM frequencies. They are generally characterized by their dedication to social and cultural goals, in contrast to profit and audience maximization.

Though many of the earliest U.S. radio stations were based at educational institutions, the model of a privately controlled, entertainment-driven, commercial broadcasting system quickly took hold during the medium's formative years. Contemporary public radio owes its existence to a group of educators and activists who worked during the 1920s, 1930s, and 1940s to establish a presence for public service broadcasting in the model of most other industrialized, democratic nations. Though they were unsuccessful in lobbying for reserved frequencies on the then-dominant AM band, their legacy is the spectrum set aside on the FM band in 1945 for *noncommercial educational* radio. With passage of the *Public Broadcasting Act of 1967,* public radio stations began to receive federal funding, dispersed through the Corporation for Public Broadcasting. However, despite major growth in audience and funding since then, public radio remains ancillary to the dominant commercial system.

There are almost 1,500 U.S. radio stations licensed by the Federal Communications Commission (FCC) as "noncommercial educational." In general usage, however, the term *public radio* has come to stand for those stations that provide regular, public service–oriented programs intended for a general audience. (This categorization excludes noncommercial religious broadcasters and stations that exist primarily to train students for broadcasting careers.) Most public radio stations are found in the allocated spectrum between 88 and 92 megahertz on the FM band; about 30 noncommercial stations, which predate the allocation, operate on AM. The *Communications Act* bans noncommercial stations from broadcasting advertisements. They may carry "underwriting" credits, funded by businesses, governed by FCC guidelines designed to limit their commercial nature. Funding is a mix of support from institutional licensees, often colleges and universities; underwriting and foundation grants; tax-based support from federal, state, and local governments; and contributions from listeners.

A robust programming marketplace exists in public radio. There are two major public radio networks in the United States, though neither own stations in the manner of commercial broadcast networks. Public radio stations affiliate with National Public Radio (NPR) and Public Radio International (PRI), paying dues for the right to carry news and cultural programs distributed by NPR and PRI; stations may affiliate with either network, or with both. In addition, regional networks, individual stations, and independent producers make their programs available via public radio's satellite interconnection to supplement local production.

Comprehensive news and public affairs coverage distinguishes public radio programming. NPR is noted for its daily "newsmagazines," *Morning Edition* and, its afternoon counterpart, *All Things Considered,* which have garnered a loyal following through their blend of hard news, analysis, and puckish wit. Well-known public radio news programs distributed by PRI include *Monitor Radio,* produced by the *Christian Science Monitor, Marketplace,* for economic news; and *The World,* for international affairs. Other network offerings include news of the Latino- and Native-American communities, as well as journalism from the British Broadcasting Corporation (BBC), Canadian Broadcasting Corporation (CBC), and Germany's Deutsche Welle. Public radio journalism is characterized by its depth, use of sound to create a sense of place, and commitment to reflecting the national diversity. Yet public radio has also attracted criticism from all quarters for its news programming. Conservatives allege that public radio has a liberal bias, while the left claims public radio emulates commercial media and no longer provides a fresh alternative.

While classical music has been a programming staple since the educational radio era, jazz and other musical genres have established themselves on the public radio airwaves. Some public radio stations broadcast "world beat" formats heavy in reggae and salsa, while others carry folk, ethnic music, and even progressive rock.

In addition to news and cultural programs, public radio has bred some unique and popular hybrids. Garrison Keillor's *A Prairie Home Companion,* modeled after the variety programs of old-time live radio, and *Car Talk,* featuring two philosophical Boston auto mechanics who dispense more jokes than auto-repair advice, became surprise hits.

While public radio-program schedules were often eclectic, encompassing a variety of musical genres on a single station, public radio stations in the 1990s increasingly focused their formats into consistent streams of programming. Some stations abandoned music in favor of all-news/all-talk programs, while still others jettisoned news and went to all-music formats, often motivated by audience research findings. Such research became central to public radio decision making during the 1980s, when declining levels of tax-based support forced stations to look to listeners and underwriters for larger shares of their operating budgets. Nonetheless, the use of audience research became a lightning rod for controversy: some critics charged it represented the ascendance of market considerations over the social and cultural imperatives of public radio.

Community radio stations have largely resisted this trend. Community stations generally broadcast many different kinds of programs, often hosted by volunteers. Many carry programming distributed by the Pacifica Foundation's chain of avowedly leftist stations. However, most community stations have smaller audiences and budgets than their traditional public radio counterparts.

The future of public radio remains uncertain. Continued federal funding was in doubt in the mid-1990s as a result of deficit reduction imperatives and the antipathy of congressional Republicans toward public broadcasting in general. New audio-delivery systems such as direct-to-home satellite, cable, and the Internet threatened terrestrial broadcasting. The demographics of public radio listeners as well educated and affluent attracted commercial ventures interested in forming partnerships but raised fears that public radio would have to "sell its soul" to survive.

Avery, Robert K., and Robert Pepper. "Balancing the Equation: Public Radio Comes of Age." *Public Telecommunications Review* 7 (November–December 1979): 19–30.

Rowland, Willard D. "Public Service Broadcasting in the United States: Its Mandate, Institutions and Conflicts." In *Public Service Broadcasting in a Multichannel Environment: The History and Survival of an Ideal,* edited by Robert K. Avery (pp. 157–194). White Plains, N.Y.: Longman, 1993.

Stavitsky, Alan G. "'Guys in Suits with Charts': Audience Research in U.S. Public Radio." *Journal of Broadcasting and Electronic Media* 39 (2) (spring 1995): 177–189.

Current. http://www.current.org/ (a trade newspaper covering public broadcasting).

Alan G. Stavitsky

PUBLIC RADIO INTERNATIONAL (PRI) is a public radio network, based in Minneapolis, that acquires, commissions, and distributes programming to public radio stations. PRI was created in response to National Public Radio's (NPR's) near-monopoly over public radio's programming marketplace in the early 1980s. As manager of public radio's interconnection system as well as the industry's leading producer, NPR wielded considerable influence over public radio programming. Many of the nation's public radio stations were unhappy with NPR's decisions on what to distribute, often denying national access to local broadcasters. One noteworthy case involved Minnesota Public Radio's request to distribute Garrison Keillor's *A Prairie Home Companion,* NPR refused, believing the program's appeal was too regional.

In 1982, five public radio stations formed American Public Radio (APR) Associates, as a subsidiary of Minnesota Public Radio, to distribute locally produced public radio programs over the system's satellite interconnection. The following year, the founders dropped "Associates" from the title and incorporated APR. The organization was renamed Public Radio International in 1994.

Today, more than 550 public radio stations are affiliated with PRI, which distributes more than 300 hours of programming per week. Many public radio stations affiliate with both PRI and NPR. Unlike NPR, which produces much of the programming it distributes, PRI acquires and commissions programs from stations and independent producers, then distributes the finished shows.

Well-known PRI programs include *A Prairie Home Companion, Marketplace, The World,* and *Monitor Radio,* in addition to classical music offerings such as *Saint*

Paul Sunday Morning. PRI has also increased the international presence on the U.S. airwaves by distributing programming from the British Broadcasting Corporation (BBC), Canadian Broadcasting Corporation (CBC), and Germany's Deutsche Welle.

Salyer, Steven A. "Monopoly to Marketplace Competition Comes to Public Radio." In *Radio: The Forgotten Medium,* edited by Edward C. Pease and Everette E. Dennis (pp. 185–192). New Brunswick, N.J.: Transaction Publishers, 1995.
Stavitsky, Alan G. "The Changing Conception of Localism in U.S. Public Radio." *Journal of Broadcasting and Electronic Media* 38 (1) (winter 1994): 19–33.
Public Radio International. http://www.pri.org

Alan G. Stavitsky

PUBLIC SERVICE ANNOUNCEMENTS (PSAs), free-of-charge messages devoted to a nonprofit cause, they run a variety of lengths and have been used to promote the sale of war bonds, announce legal deadlines, give health/safety advisories, and serve as a community bulletin board announcing upcoming events. Although the station does not receive any remuneration for airing them, stations use them to promote themselves and their concern for their community and also to fill unsold airtime. More PSAs are aired during the month of January, a slow sales time, than any other month.

Eastman, Susan Tyler, and Douglas A. Ferguson. *Broadcast/Cable Programming: Strategies and Practices.* 5th ed. Belmont, Calif: Wadsworth, 1997.
Gross, Lynne Schafer. *Telecommunications: An Introduction to Electronic Media.* 6th ed. Guilford, Conn.: Brown & Benchmark, 1997.

Margot Hardenbergh

PUNK was a musical and cultural movement that began in the mid-1970s. Acerbic punk lyrics targeted everything from the government to schools to the progressive rock popular at the time. The songs were short, loud, fast, and sloppy. Many punk bands took pride in their limited musical skills and relatively simple songs.

The Ramones, the Patti Smith Group, Talking Heads, Television and Richard Hell, and the Voidoids were among the seminal New York punk bands usually credited with launching the movement, which gathered little media notice outside of the underground press in 1974–1975. It was not until 1976 that London bands, led by the Clash and the Sex Pistols, attracted international attention.

Sensational articles on the confrontational music and style usually did not translate into record sales. Punk groups failed to dent the American top 40, and had only limited success on the British charts. By 1979, college radio was the music's primary broadcast venue in America. As their music became more polished and complex, however, a handful of artists initially associated with punk, such as the Clash, Blondie, and Talking Heads, garnered commercial radio airplay.

With the release of *Nevermind* in September 1991, Nirvana refocused mainstream interest on punk rock. Despite limited initial promotion, the album sold a surprising 200,000 copies in its first three weeks. Bolstered by heavy rotation on MTV, *Nevermind* knocked Michael Jackson's *Dangerous* off the top of the *Billboard* albums chart in January 1992. *Nevermind* proved to the music industry that punk could be popular and profitable. After its release, major record companies put more money into signing and marketing bands like Green Day, Soundgarden, and Soul Asylum, who had previously recorded in relative obscurity on smaller, punk-oriented labels. Radio stations played more alternative and "modern rock" music, marked by the punk sound that they had rejected 15 years before.

Arnold, Gina. *Route 666: On the Road to Nirvana.* New York: St. Martin's Press, 1993.
Henry, Tricia. *Break All the Rules: Punk Rock and the Making of a Style.* Ann Arbor, Mich.: UMI Research Press, 1989.
Savage, Jon. *England's Dreaming: Anarchy, Sex Pistols, Punk Rock and Beyond.* New York: St. Martin's Press, 1992.

David Weinstein

PUR. *See* **persons using radio (PUR).**

PYNE, JOE (1925–1970), host of one of radio's early talk programs. He was known especially for his confrontational approach. Mr. "Fist-in-your-Face" had his program on KTTV, Los Angeles, and made no pretense at being a nice guy. Ex-marine and an amputee, Pyne always seemed to be against the whole world, snarling at his guests and the studio audience—calling them "morons" or "meatheads."

Pyne's national attention can be centered on one program. On August 4, 1965, at the height of the riot activity in the Watts section of Los Angeles, a black guest warned that a "race war" was at hand. Pyne pulled a gun from his belt and yelled, "Let 'em come! I'm ready for 'em!" It was a serious enough incident for the Federal Communications Commission (FCC) to threaten to pull KTTV's license—and for the *Joe Pyne* show to enter national syndication through Hartwest. The syndication peaked at 85 markets, years ahead of other controversials such as William Buckley and Alan Burke.

Pyne did a week's worth of shows at one sitting, making the program economical to produce, and it did well in the marketplace.

Bogasian, Eric. *Talk Radio.* New York: Vintage Books, 1988.
Erickson, Hal. *The First Forty Years—1947–1987.* Jefferson, N.C.: McFarland and Company, Inc., Publishers, 1989.
Loufer, Peter. *Inside Talk Radio: American Voices on the Air.* Secaucus, N.J.: Carol Publishing Group, 1995.

ElDean Bennett

Q

QUADRAPHONIC SOUND. When stereo sound finally made it into the home in the late 1950s, it had only two channels, despite existing capabilities for many more channels. As the popularity of home stereo grew, equipment manufacturers tried to expand the stereo system by "surrounding" the audience with sound. In 1967, a method of encoding and decoding sound to squeeze four tracks of information into the existing two-channel stereo system was developed. The method, called quadraphonics, required two additional speakers in the rear corners of the listening room. The failure of quad in the home market had several causes. There were at least three competing and incompatible quad systems being marketed, producers and engineers were not certain how to really use the extra channels, and consumers had a difficult time hearing the difference between quadraphonic and stereo sounds.

Kripalani, Manjeet. "Quad Sound Reincarnated." *Forbes* 146 (12) (November 26, 1990): 270–272.

Home Stereo and Quadraphonic Sound. http://sylfest.hiof.no/~bjornbb/dolby/dspl/ppf-quad.html

Mark A. Tolstedt

QUARTER-HOUR LISTENING. *See* **cume; quarter-hour maintenance.**

QUARTER-HOUR MAINTENANCE, the process of carrying radio listeners over from one quarter-hour to the next. This is done by scheduling popular song sweeps that start in one quarter-hour and end in the next. Radio audiences are measured in 15-minute or quarter-hour segments, so program and music directors attempt to maintain listeners for as many segments as possible.

Carroll, Raymond L., and Donald M. Davis. *Electronic Media Programming: Strategies and Decision Making.* New York: McGraw-Hill, 1993.

Frederic A. Leigh

R

RACIAL ISSUES. In 1968, the Kerner Commission Report stated that the "media report and write from the standpoint of a white man's world." Today, more than 25 years later, minority groups are still underrepresented in employment, programming, and ownership. The roots of racial disparities in American radio began when the medium was in its infancy with the daily broadcasts of *Amos 'n' Andy*. This program's stereotypes portrayed African Americans as lazy, ignorant, and superstitious. In the years since the *Amos 'n' Andy* broadcasts, programming has also stereotyped other minorities on radio as well. Asians, for example, have been portrayed as "shrewd and sly."

On rare occasions, programs such as *Destination Freedom* successfully captured positive themes in African-American family life, social activities, and political protests. Nevertheless, full participation in radio as writers, actors, and reporters has remained a distant goal for minorities. Asian Americans listen to fewer hours of radio programming than other ethnic groups. On the other hand, African Americans and Hispanics listen to three hours of radio on average each day, which is higher usage than other ethnic groups, including whites. Approximately 16 percent of all employees at radio stations are minorities, yet minority population in the United States is nearly 30 percent. In addition, 85 percent of radio stations employ no minorities. Minorities are underrepresented in most employment categories, especially as news reporters and managers.

Spanish-language radio stations reach approximately 2 percent of the U.S. population. Black/urban stations reach 7 percent of the population. Minority radio station ownership, although increasing, is still small, with less than 300 of the 12,000 radio stations in this country owned by minorities. Advertising, or rather the lack of it, plagues minority radio station owners.

Finally, talk-radio shows in the 1990s have often exacerbated racial tensions in American society. Radio talk-show hosts such as G. Gordon Liddy, Rush Limbaugh, Bob Grant, and others have used issues such as affirmative action, welfare, and public education in ways that highlighted racial differences and heightened racial tension.

Hilmes, Michele. "Invisible Men: *Amos 'n' Andy* and the Roots of Broadcast Discourse." *Critical Studies in Mass Communication* 10 (1993): 301–321.

Laufer, Peter. *Inside Talk Radio: America's Voice or Just Hot Air?* Secaucus, N.J.: Carol Publishing Group, 1995.

U.S. Kerner Commission. *Report of the National Advisory Commission on Civil Disorders.* New York: Bantam Books, 1968.

Gilbert A. Williams

RADIATION, the process by which energy is emitted as electromagnetic waves. Radio waves range from very low frequencies (3 kilohertz [kHz]) to extremely high frequencies (300,000 megahertz [MHz]). U.S. radio stations radiate waves in the medium frequency range for AM (535–1,705 kHz) and the very high frequency range for FM (88–108 MHz).

It also refers to the energy radiated in the form of a wave caused by a magnetic field interacting with an electric field. In order of increasing wavelength and decreasing frequency, the types of electromagnetic radiation are cosmic rays, gamma rays, X-rays, ultraviolet radiation, visible light, infrared radiation, and finally, radio waves. The individual quantum of electromagnetic radiation is the photon. Electromagnetic radiation results from the acceleration of a charged particle. It can travel through a vacuum and does not require a material medium. The theory of electromagnetic radiation was developed by James Clerk Maxwell (1865), and the actual existence of radio waves and their radiation was proven by Heinrich Hertz (1887).

Mark J. Braun

RADIO ACT OF 1912 was the first federal congressional legislation that attempted the comprehensive regulation of U.S. radio communication. This act authorized the secretary of commerce and labor to license all U.S. stations, except those operated by the federal government and those involved in intrastate point-to-point communication. According to the act, licensees had to be companies incorporated within, or citizens of the United States or Puerto Rico. Each license document was to contain the act's restrictions under which the license was granted; specify the station's ownership, location, purpose, authorized wavelength, and operating hours; and provide other information as necessary for identification and to estimate the station's range. The act required that while in operation all licensed-station apparatus be under the supervision of personnel licensed by the secretary.

By the early 1920s, with the growth of commercial radio broadcasting, the legislation had proven inadequate, and the secretary's discretionary rights—to issue licenses and determine the operating wavelengths, hours, and power of individual stations meeting the legal qualifications—was virtually eliminated through three legal decisions (*Hoover v. Intercity Radio,* 1923; *United States v. Zenith Radio Corp.,* 1926; and the *Attorney General's Opinion of 8 July 1926*). To correct the limitations of the *Radio Act of 1912* and expand the federal government's power over radio transmissions and communications, on February 23, the *Radio Act of 1927* was signed into law (see also **Commerce and Labor, U.S. Department of**).

Kahn, Frank J., ed. *Documents of American Broadcasting*. Rev. ed. New York: Appleton-Century-Crofts, 1972.

Radio Act of 1912. Public Law 264, 62nd Congress, August 13, 1912.

Steven C. Runyon

RADIO ACT OF 1927 came from the Department of Commerce's regulation of broadcasting from 1922 through 1926. The *Radio Act of 1927* specified that a Federal Radio Commission (FRC) regulate all forms of interstate and foreign radio transmissions and communications within the United States by licensing. Congress settled on the phrase "public interest, convenience, and necessity" as the basis for such regulation.

The FRC, for one year, was to be the original licensing authority, and after that year, the secretary of commerce was to succeed as the licensing authority, with the commission becoming an advisory and appellate body. The *Radio Act of 1927* was extended by Congress to March 6, 1929, then to December 31, 1929, and finally made of indefinite duration in December 1929 until the passage of the *Communication Act of 1934,* which remained essentially the same.

The FRC continued to examine and license radio operators; inspect all transmitting stations; make field-strength measurements; monitor radio stations; investigate violations of radio laws and regulations and reports of interference or unsatisfactory service; undertake engineering surveys of radio stations; furnish technical information; and designate call letters. These functions were transferred, and the other specific powers granted to the FRC by the *Radio Act of 1927* were passed on to the Federal Communications Commission (FCC) in 1934.

Marvin R. Bensman

RADIO & RECORDS MAGAZINE (R&R), since 1973, has provided the radio and recording industries with some of the most detailed business information available. Among all the media trade magazines, *R&R* probably best reflects all aspects of radio. It covers personnel changes, legislation, the business of radio, ratings, music, news, promotions, and airplay information. *R&R* is especially well known for its outstanding playlists, compiled for each of the popular formats. Even with annual subscription rates in excess of $299, most commercial stations subscribe. Issued weekly, individual columns cover the popular radio formats, performers, new music releases, news, sales, and marketing. In addition, *R&R* also publishes the "Marketing & Promotion Guide" and "Program Supplier Guide" annually and the "Ratings Report & Directory" twice a year; it also offers weekly job hotline and fax news service. It serves as an excellent resource on the radio and recording industries and the symbiotic relationship between them.

Radio & Records Online. http://www.rronline.com

Mark A. Tolstedt

RADIO CORPORATION OF AMERICA (RCA) was born in October 1919 from complex post–World War I negotiations among the navy, General Electric (GE), and British Marconi and its subsidiary American Marconi. In March 1919, British Marconi officials approached GE to renew its prewar offer to buy the

Alexanderson alternator. Because this huge machine was the most effective means of long-distance wireless communication at that time, its purchase would give the Marconi companies control over American transatlantic wireless communication, a move neither the navy nor Congress wanted. After several visits with naval officials, Admiral W. H. G. Bullard, Commander Stanford Hooper, and Owen Young (then head of GE's legal department) persuaded GE's board of directors to buy American Marconi. He then convinced British Marconi to sell these assets rather than risk action by a Congress totally opposed to foreign control of American-based international communications. GE established RCA to operate these stations.

The new company's charter mandated that foreigners could hold no more than 20 percent of its stock, that all members of the board be Americans, and that the government have one board representative to present the government's views. Owen Young became the board's chairman, and two former American Marconi officers, Edward J. Nally and David Sarnoff, became, respectively, its new president and commercial manager. GE and RCA signed cross-licensing agreements allowing the other firm to use each other's radio patents.

Within three years, similar cross-licensing agreements were signed with Westinghouse, American Telegraph and Telephone (AT&T), and United Fruit Company, a large firm whose patents to several radio devices it used in long-distance communication among its numerous Central and South American plantations. With nearly 2,000 patents pooled, agreements gave each company part of the radio business as then understood: international, maritime, and amateur. Broadcasting had not been a part of these considerations and, within months, disputes arose among the signatories over which firm controlled radio broadcasting to the general public.

The "Telephone Group" (AT&T and Western Electric) battled the "Radio Group" (RCA, GE, and Westinghouse) for control over broadcasting. Each group maintained it had sole rights to broadcast under the cross-licensing agreements. Complicating matters for the two groups was a congressionally mandated Federal Trade Commission (FTC) investigation of the cross-licensing agreements for monopolistic practices. The FTC report resulted in complaints against the signatories. Consequently, the two groups decided to submit their dispute quietly to binding arbitration. After months of hearings, arbiter Boydon Hull decided in favor of the Radio Group. Not to be outdone, the Telephone Group's attorneys then told the Radio Group the agreements must have been monopolistic to give the Radio Group such control over radio. Unwilling to risk open warfare in the midst of the FTC investigation, both sides moved covertly to resolve the dispute, resulting in the formation of the National Broadcasting Company (NBC) in 1926.

By 1930, RCA had unified GE, Westinghouse, and RCA's radio set–manufacturing industry under its aegis to the consternation of smaller radio-receiver manufacturers. The Department of Justice began to analyze the transactions, claiming a possible restraint of trade in radio apparatus existed and, in May 1930, filed an antitrust suit to break up this consolidation. Over the next two and one-half years, attorneys for the accused companies sought to separate the firms without causing damage to the firms. On November 13, 1932, just a few days before the suit reached the courts, they worked out a compromise with Justice Department attorneys. On November 21, the companies signed a consent decree. GE and Westinghouse agreed to divest themselves of RCA stock and to resign from RCA's board of directors. The two companies could not compete with RCA's set manufacturing for two years. The decree also mandated the license agreements made from 1919 to 1921 be made nonexclusive. Consequently, RCA became totally autonomous. Its new president, David Sarnoff, was to lead it to new heights in broadcasting, international communications, radio-set manufacturing, and television research and development.

During the 1930s, RCA operated NBC's networks, the Red and the Blue. Challenges to network control over broadcasting forced NBC to sell off the Blue Network to candy baron Edward Noble, and that network became the American Broadcasting Company (ABC) in 1945.

RCA's Sarnoff also led the charge to move FM radio from its pre–World War II spectrum assignment of 42 to 50 megahertz (MHz) to make room for television. RCA put is full weight behind the fight, which lasted from 1944 to 1947 and ended with FM's move to 88 to 108 MHz. This relocation made the prewar FM industry obsolete and eclipsed FM's development in favor of television. Television's rapid growth during the postwar era awarded RCA tremendous financial benefits in its control over patents and its sale and manufacture of television sets.

At the beginning of the postwar television era, RCA and CBS battled over standards for color television. While CBS promoted a system that was incompatible with then-existing black and white broadcasting, RCA continued to perfect its compatible system. In 1950, the Federal Communications Commission (FCC) adopted the CBS standards, only to rescind them three years later in favor of RCA's system, favored by the manufacturing industry. Shortly thereafter, RCA demonstrated its videotape recording (VTR) system, but this system was flawed. In 1956, Ampex announced its practical VTR system, and the next year the two companies entered into a patent pool to perfect compatible systems for both color and monochrome television.

In late 1986 GE purchased RCA for $6.28 billion, bringing the company back to its origins. A few months later, in July 1987, Westwood One purchased the NBC Radio Network for $50 million, and the NBC-owned-and-operated stations were also sold. The pioneering radio network was no more, and RCA/GE continued concentrating on the more profitable television business.

Louise Benjamin

RADIO LIBERTY (RL) was established as a private radio station—operated by the Central Intelligence Agency (CIA)–funded American Committee for Liberation of the Peoples of Russia (Radio Liberty, Inc.)—following a 1949 U.S. State Department Cold War broadcasting proposal. RL began in January 1953 from Munich studios, programming in as many as 20 languages of the Soviet republics. Staffed by American intellectuals and Soviet refugees, RL's objective was to provide uncensored news about the USSR. In 1973, Congress established the Board for International Broadcasting to replace the CIA as financial backer and merged RL with Radio Free Europe (RFE) to form RFE/RL, Inc.

Critchlow, James. *Radio Hole-in-the-Head/Radio Liberty: An Insider's Story of Cold War Broadcasting*. Washington, D.C.: American University Press, 1995.
Kalugin, Oleg. *The First Directorate*. New York: St. Martin's Press, 1994.

William James Ryan

RADIO-TELEVISION NEWS DIRECTORS ASSOCIATION (RTNDA) is the principal broadcast news trade organization. From its roots in radio and based in Washington, D.C., the RTNDA grew into a worldwide organization that actively worked to advance the interests of those engaged in radio and television journalism. The RTNDA celebrated its fiftieth anniversary in 1995 with nearly 2,000 active, associate, retired, participating, and student members.

It was called the National Association of Radio News Editors when it was founded in March 1946 because of sentiment (largely expressed in the print news media) that those in broadcasting lacked standards and were not legitimate members of the news profession. The RTNDA was conceived as the broadcast equivalent of the American Society of Newspaper Editors, a print-trade organization with a managerial orientation. Jack Hogan, the founder of RTNDA, was the news director of WCSH in Portland, Maine. His objective was to set standards in news reporting and inspire an exchange of ideas relating to news gathering and news reporting. The first RTNDA executive committee also included Tom Eaton of WTIC in Hartford; Al Gordon of KFWB in Los Angeles; Sig Mickelson of WCCO in Minneapolis; and Soren Munkhoff of WOW in Omaha.

The first RTNDA constitution, approved at the organization's first convention in Cleveland in 1946, established the RTNDA mainly as a public service organization unconcerned with labor problems and the issue of higher wages. Although formed in light of labor-management tensions and the rise of unionization, the RTNDA refrained from involvement in these matters and from advocacy on partisan issues, which remained part of its character. Further, although it later would depend on sizable donations from the major New York–based broadcast networks, the RTNDA took a pro-localism position and became a grassroots entity not beholden to the networks. The name of the organization had been changed to the National Association of Radio News Directors by 1947 and, finally, to Radio-Television News Directors Association in 1953. The latter name change reflected the organization's response to growth of television news in the early 1950s.

Partially because of radio, but largely because of television, the RTNDA grew rapidly during the 1960s. By its twenty-fifth anniversary convention in 1970, the RTNDA listed more than 1,000 members. That same year, David Louie, a student at Northwestern University, received the first Radio Television News Directors Foundation (an arm of the original organization) scholarship. In 1973, the RTNDA began conducting research on salaries, staff sizes, and the employment of women and minorities in radio and television. The RTNDA's scholarship and research programs became important parts of its mission.

As it grew, the RTNDA frequently was at the cusp of some of the controversial issues that steered the evolution of modern broadcast news. In 1974, after considerable disagreement among members throughout the previous year, members passed a resolution clearing the way for research consultants in most of the nation's broadcast newsrooms. Of particular interest to those in radio news was a study commissioned by the RTNDA and performed by one of the consultants, Frank N. Magid Associates, in 1984. This study indicated that television was perceived as matching radio news in immediacy—radio's ostensible advantage—and went on to predict a decline in radio news. It was denounced by some radio managers.

The RTNDA's greatest period of growth came in the 1980s. In 1980, following the death of RTNDA chair Len Allen, the organization named Ernie Schultz as permanent president. David Bartlett succeeded Schultz in 1989 and continued to centralize activities at RTNDA headquarters in Washington. In 1987, the organization began a system of student-affiliate chapters at universities across the United States, which considerably swelled the association's membership. Also during the 1980s, the RTNDA urged political leaders to give broadcasters full First Amendment rights, to repeal the Fairness Doctrine, and to permit photographs obtained by remote-sensing orbiting satellites to be disseminated.

It was during this same period that RTNDA's in-house magazine, *Communicator,* expanded from a small newsletter into an authoritative journal on radio and television news. *Communicator* was spearheaded by Joe Tiernan, its first full-time editor and publisher, who joined the RTNDA in 1984. By 1990, the RTNDA had expanded its role as a clearinghouse for those seeking jobs in broadcast news and established a full-time employment service that, at two-week intervals, circulated lists of job openings to members.

RTNDA celebrated its fiftieth anniversary in 1995 with a budget of $2 million, most defrayed by its members. To help reinstitute interest in radio news, RTNDA formed an alliance with NAB Radio, an arm of the National Association of Broadcasters, in 1994. Although the RTNDA's mission remained wide ranging, one of its major responsibilities was circulating a model code of standards and practices. Hundreds of radio and television newsrooms subscribed to the RTNDA Code following revisions in the 1970s.

The finalized Code stated that radio and television journalists should gather and report information of importance and interest to the public accurately, honestly, and impartially. Further, they should strive to present the news in a way that is balanced, conduct themselves in a way that protects them from conflicts of interest, respect the dignity of news makers, and not rebroadcast others' transmissions without permission. In 1994, RTNDA began circulating its Code on wallet-sized cards.

Through the 1990s, RTNDA continued with a full-time president and a staff based in Washington. The president was assisted by a chair, usually a news director from a local newsroom elected by RTNDA members at the organization's annual conventions. As the major gathering point for RTNDA members and their activities, these RTNDA conventions were planned to alternate between Los Angeles and New Orleans on succeeding years.

RTNDA. "Fifty Years of Electronic Journalism." *Communicator* (September 1995).

Craig M. Allen

RADIO TRUST, sometimes referred to as the "Radio Group," was a group of radio businesses formed in the early 1920s following World War I to facilitate the growth of the radio industry. Patent interference cases were creating an impasse. The companies involved were AT&T, General Electric, Westinghouse, and RCA. These manufacturers created a "trust" when they agreed that to break the patent impasse they should divide the rights: AT&T would manufacture transmitters; GE and Westinghouse would manufacture receivers; and RCA would act as the sales agent for the manufactured receivers. The trust agreement was doomed from the beginning. The first controversy in the trust dealt with the question of who had the rights to broadcast. They all wanted those rights. The second controversy was the enforcement of the "trust agreement and the patent pools." They were basically unenforceable. For example, literally enforced, GE and Westinghouse would have been the only two radio manufacturers. The third controversy was the effect of antitrust laws on the agreement. RCA was at the time a subsidiary of General Electric. The trust agreements began breaking apart in 1923 when patent licenses were distributed widely and again in 1926 when AT&T withdrew from broadcasting. In 1930, the Justice Department brought action against the trust, and it was dissolved in 1932.

Inglis, Andrew F. *Behind the Tube: A History of Broadcasting Technology and Business.* Boston: Focal Press, 1990.

Donald G. Godfrey

RAP MUSIC is an artistic expression that emerged in the early 1970s partly as a reaction to the soul music of Motown and other forms of rhythm and blues. A musical group called the Sugar Hill Gang first popularized the rap music genre. Rap music is also known as hip-hop. As a musical style, rap music blends "rapping" or speaking with African-American musical rhythms.

Rap music uses oral communication culture as its primary means of expression. The rapping style is a form of speech popularized by African Americans in the twentieth century. As rap music developed and evolved during the 1980s and 1990s, it became the music of choice for a new generation of teenagers and young people. For example, in 1990, 8.5 percent of all music sold in the United States was rap music. By 1994, the percentage had dropped slightly to 7.9, but that figure still topped other categories such as classical, gospel, and jazz. Moreover, although the basic form changed little, the themes expressed through rap music did. In the mid- to late 1980s, the genre began to reflect hip-hop culture, a subculture of urban youth. Hence, rap music reflected the environment these youths live in. Drug use, gangs, crime, unemployment, poor education, violence, and unplanned teen pregnancies often characterize this urban environment. Rap artists such as Ice-T, Ice Cube, Snoop Doggy Dogg, Easy-E, NWA, and Tupac Shakur sang songs that embraced hip-hop culture completely, including its attendant values. "Gangsta rap," which this style became known as, celebrated violence, denigrated women, and expressed hatred toward policemen, "the system," and whites.

Rap music has tended to focus on male-oriented themes; however, some female rap artists have emerged. Among the female rap music artists are Salt-N-Pepa, M. C. Lyte, and Queen Latifah. Finally, rap music artists have demonstrated a need for "authenticity"; that is, a desire to live lifestyles that mirror their musical themes. Often, these lifestyles and the resulting behavior are self-destructive.

Baker, Houston A. *Black Studies, Rap and the Academy.* Chicago: University of Chicago Press, 1993.
Fink, Michael. *Inside the Music Industry.* New York: Schirmer Books, 1989.
MEE Productions, Inc. *The MEE Report: Reaching the Hip Hop Generation.* Philadelphia, Pa.: MEE Productions, Inc., 1992.

Gilbert A. Williams

RATE CARD, a grid that shows a radio station's charges for its commercial—the different costs of purchasing commercial time based on the time of day the commercials (spots) will run, how many spots will be purchased, and the length of each spot (i.e., 30 or 60 seconds). The rates can remain in place indefinitely or can change on a daily basis, depending on changes in the station's ratings, the rate card prices of other stations, and the cost of buying advertising on other media in the market.

Kenneth D. Loomis

RATINGS SYSTEMS. *See* **A. C. Nielsen, Company; Arbitron; audience research; Crossley, Archibald Maddock; diary; research.**

RCA RADIOS. The Radio Corporation of America was formed in 1919 by General Electric to operate the newly acquired Marconi company's wireless telegraphy business. Additional stock was purchased by Westinghouse and AT&T. These companies "pooled patents" in order to research, design, and manufacture crystal and, eventually, radio sets. Between 1919 and 1923, the companies developed cross-licensing agreements permitting each to use the others' patents to develop radio sets. RCA acted as the sales agent for these manufacturing firms. This cooperative effort made possible the manufacture of large quantities of sets during the early years of radio between 1920 and 1925, when public demand for radios exceeded manufacturing capabilities. The manufacturing and marketing capabilities of these corporations, in addition to their dominance in the broadcast of radio programming, made them the leaders and predominant factor in radio-receiver development. No salable receivers could be built without licenses from RCA for patents it owned and controlled until RCA relaxed its licensing agreements in the 1930s.

Early crystal sets were battery powered, had three-dial tuning, used earphones or headsets, and were sold as kits without cabinetry. With the advent of radio programming in 1921, the public demanded more sophisticated and easier-to-operate sets. This led to numerous improvements by the engineers at RCA and its manufacturing partners. By 1925, sets were operated by alternating current and had built-in speakers and high-quality cabinetry that permitted radios to be at home in a person's living room. The average price of a set dropped from approximately $125 in 1926 to $40 by 1934.

Douglas, Alan. *Radio Manufacturers of the 1920's.* Vols. 1–3. 3rd ed. Chandler, Ariz.: Sonoran Publishing Inc., 1995.
Harlow, Alvin. *Old Wires and New Waves: The History of the Telegraph, Telephone, and Wireless.* New York: Appleton-Century, 1936. Reprint, Arno Press, 1971.
Sobel, Robert. *RCA.* New York: Stein and Day, 1986.

Bruce W. Russell

REACH/FREQUENCY indicate the success of an advertising campaign. Reach measures the total number of individuals who listen to a commercial, whereas frequency measures the average number of times a typical audience member has heard a particular commercial. Reach is the same figure as a cume. Advertisers plan commercial campaigns using reach and frequency figures as goals.

Warner, Charles. *Broadcast and Cable Selling.* Belmont, Calif.: Wadsworth Publishing Co., 1986.

Ronald Razovsky

RECEIVERS. Radio was first thought to be useful for ships at sea or large businesses. Consumers began buying receivers in the early 1920s when popular programming was "broadcast" by radio stations to a wide and largely unknown audience. Not surprisingly, the earliest programmers were the same businesses who manufactured receivers. Before advertising, programming was designed to sell radio receivers.

The basic function of a radio receiver is to detect and amplify electromagnetic energy to the point that it is useful for human senses. Receivers are the last link in the technical chain that make radio signals functional. Most receivers have four essential parts: (1) an antenna-ground system to collect radio waves; (2) a tuner that selects the frequency to be received and rejects all others; (3) a reproducer changing radio wave energy to a form that the senses can receive; and (4) a detector to change radio wave energy to a form where it can operate the reproducer.

The earliest receivers, spark gap, were only useful for wireless telegraphy. Their range and selectivity were extremely limited and could not transmit voice or audio information. Through the years, radio stations' ranges increased with improved radio receiver sensitivity. Later, the crystal detector was the favorite among experimenters and hobbyists. Lee de Forest's invention of the audion tube and Major Edwin Howard Armstrong's using it as a regenerative circuit made amplification possible and negated the need for headsets.

By the 1920s, development of the tuning coil made selecting specific stations possible by tuning into their specific frequencies. The available frequencies increased through the 1920s but could not keep up with the number of radio stations broadcasting to a growing audience.

The U.S. receivers designs are regulated by the Federal Communications Commission (FCC). The FCC determines allocation of nongovernmental spectrum services; thus, receiver manufacturers must adhere to federal technical standards. Some museums that exhibit consumer receivers are on the World Wide Web.

Marcus, Abraham, and William Marcus. *Elements of Radio.* 5th ed. Englewood Cliffs, N.J.: Prentice-Hall, 1965.

McNicol, Donald. *Radio's Conquest of Space: The Experimental Rise in Radio Communication.* New York: Murray Hill Books, 1946. Reprint, New York: Arno Press, 1974.

Antique Wireless Association. Electronic Communication Museum. http://www.ggw.org/ freenet/a/awa/index.html (1996).

Bellingham Antique Radio Museum. http://www.antique-radio.org/radio.html

Genco, Lou. "Old-time Radio Website." http://www.old-time.com/toc.html (October 1996).

Museum of Radio & Technology. http://www.library.ohiou.edu/MuseumR&T/museum.htm

"Radio Netherlands Antique and Old Time Radio." http://www.rnw.nl/en/pub/antique.html (November 1996).

David Spiceland

RECURRENT-MUSIC CATEGORY are records that are no longer powers or currents on a hit-formatted station but that are too young to be considered gold (oldies). Some stations begin to move recurrents into the gold category in as little as three to six months; others take several years. The number of records at any given time is also highly variable; some stations might have several dozen songs; others well over 100.

Recurrents typically are played less frequently than either powers or currents. A song played frequently, too soon after being in a power rotation, can make listeners "burned out" on the hit switch stations to avoid hearing it.

David T. MacFarland

RED LION BROADCASTING CO., INC. V. FEDERAL COMMUNICATIONS COMMISSION, 395 U.S. 367 (1969), U.S. Supreme Court case that upheld the constitutionality of the Fairness Doctrine and its related rules on personal attacks and political editorials. This case arose when radio station WGCB, owned by the Red Lion Broadcasting Co. in Red Lion, Pennsylvania, broadcast an attack on author Fred Cook by right-wing evangelist Billy James Hargis. Hargis claimed that Cook defended the Alger Hiss spy case, criticized Edgar Hoover, and wrote a book to smear Senator Barry Goldwater. Concluding that the program was a personal attack on him, Cook demanded a free reply time under the personal attack rule of the Fairness Doctrine. The Red Lion Broadcasting Co. declined, Cook then filed a complaint with the Federal Communications Commission (FCC), which ordered Red Lion to grant Cook the opportunity to respond.

The Supreme Court rejected the argument of broadcasters that they be allowed under the First Amendment to use their allocated airwaves to broadcast whatever they chose to broadcast. Drawing a distinction between the broadcasting media and the print media, the Court noted that "differences in the characteristics of news media justify differences in the First Amendment standards applied to them" (395 U.S. at 386–387).

Citing the spectrum scarcity issue facing broadcasters, the Supreme Court warned against the free marketplace of ideas being monopolized by the government or by a private licensee. In this connection, the Court recognized a fiduciary duty of broadcast licensees to serve the public in presenting those views and voices that are representative of the community and that would otherwise be barred from the airwaves. The right of the viewers and listeners should prevail over the right of the broadcasters, the Supreme Court stated, adding that the crucial right of the public to receive suitable access to sociopolitical, aesthetic, moral, and other ideas cannot be constitutionally abridged either by Congress or by the FCC (395 U.S. at 390).

The Supreme Court further dismissed as "at best speculative" the contention of broadcasters that the Fairness Doctrine failed to contribute to the marketplace of ideas because broadcasters tended to avoid coverage of any controversial public issues that might precipitate the doctrine's application. Nevertheless, the Court noted: "[I]f experience with the administration of these doctrines indicates that they have the net effect of reducing rather than enhancing the volume and quality of coverage, there will be time enough to reconsider the constitutional implications" (395 U.S. at 393).

In 1984, the Supreme Court in *FCC v. League of Women Voters of California* (468 U.S. 364 [1984]) indicated its willingness to reconsider the Fairness Doctrine issues in the contexts of technological advances affecting the broadcasting regulatory system. The U.S. Court of Appeals for the District of Columbia Circuit in 1986 held that the Fairness Doctrine had never been intended by Congress as a statutory mandate. In August 1987, the FCC abolished the doctrine but did not eliminate its corollaries the Personal Attack Rule and the Political Editorializing Rule. President Ronald Reagan vetoed a congressional attempt to enact the Fairness Doctrine as a statutory requirement.

Friendly, Fred W. *The Good Guys, the Bad Guys and the First Amendment: Free Speech vs. Fairness in Broadcasting.* New York: Random House, 1975.
Schmidt, Benno C., Jr. *Freedom of the Press vs. Public Access.* New York: Praeger Publishers, 1976.
Simmons, Steven J. *The Fairness Doctrine and the Media.* Berkeley: University of California Press, 1978.

Kyu Ho Youm

REGULATION of radio broadcasting was determined early on, while yet in its infancy. As Americans discovered—during the 1920s—that voiced messages could be heard by means of a radio receiver, imaginations were struck by this new medium for communicating a wide variety of messages. By 1926, the airwaves were full of radio signals interfering with each other. Those who had invested in radio receivers were frustrated because their listening was continually interrupted with overlapping signals. Indeed, the time came to be labeled as the "era of chaos."

The public demanded Congress do something, and the result was the *Radio Act of 1927.* It created a five-person Federal Radio Commission (FRC) with the power to regulate this chaotic medium. The original intent seemed to give the FRC "traffic-cop" functions—keep frequencies apart, regulate their power, and control this all by licensing. By 1934, the idea of regulation seemed to be working well enough so that Congress made the legislation permanent: the *Communications Act of 1934,* which created a seven-person Federal Communications Commission

(FCC). Part of the act's provisions directed that licensees use the valuable resources, frequencies, in "the public interest, convenience and necessity." This was a heavy responsibility placed on the station licensee, and the FCC was directed to enforce that provision.

One enforcement provision was the station's license renewal—at first every three years—requiring stations to indicate how well they had served the public. If enough challenges were filed protesting the station's performance, the FCC held hearings to determine license renewal. More than one station was threatened with loss of its license for a perceived lack of responsibility.

How could the FCC ensure that the station act in the public interest, or give serious stations guidance? One answer seemed to be that the stations go beyond "frivolous" entertainment programs and carry news and public affairs—programs that became significant during World War II. In 1946, the FCC issued its policy statement, *Public Service Responsibility of Broadcast Licensees,* which became known as its Blue Book, and outlined that well-balanced programming must be carried, including local, live programs and discussion of public issues. Later, the FCC determined that "the important local public issues" were to be determined by the station's efforts of "ascertainment of public needs." The Blue Book also directed that advertising carried by the station was not to be excessive or abusive.

The early eras of radio also displayed its social power. The FCC, conscious of this, sought to limit the number of stations or control of a single licensee (corporate or individual). No more than seven radio stations (AM), and later seven FM stations and seven TV stations, could be controlled by one licensee. Moreover, the FCC prohibited what it called "duopoly," which prohibited a licensee from having more than one station of the same kind in the same service area. Later, all such restrictions relating to ownership were liberalized.

There were also deliberate attempts to balance the ideas broadcast on radio. At first, the FCC disallowed editorial or advocacy positions by the station, a decision that came to be known as the Mayflower Decision. Then, the FCC developed a Fairness Doctrine—the stations that allowed one side of a controversial issue to be aired should allow all sides to be put forth. The FCC's power to enforce the doctrine was confirmed by the U.S. Supreme Court in the *Red Lion Broadcasting Co. v. FCC* decision (1969). Later, as the media developed greater diversity and numbers, this doctrine was dropped as part of the deregulatory measures. Still some related regulatory measures, part of the *Communications Act* ("equal time" provisions where a station, if it allows access by a political candidate, must allow access to all other candidates for the same office; and provisions to allow access by political candidates for federal office), are among several related regulations still in force. Other regulatory measures mandated by federal law for the FCC to enforce include the provision against broadcasting any "obscene, indecent or profane language."

More recently, Congress passed the *Telecommunication Act of 1996.* This law lifted many of the restrictions not already deregulated by the FCC during the Reagan administration (see **deregulation**). Some restrictions are more marked in the 1996 act, however (i.e., violence and obscenity). The 1996 act required every TV set sold in the United States be capable of blocking programming based on an electronically encoded rating. This was to be set up from a system where violence, sex, and other indecent materials could be identified on a voluntary basis. Although the newer regulatory legislation lifted many earlier restrictions placed on broadcasters, it increased the fines for broadcasting obscenity. Presumably this would affect radio, as well as TV and cable, but this restriction was challenged in court.

Earlier eras marked regulatory control with an eye to antitrust, insuring that the market remained competitive and was not dominated by any one media corporation. By the 1990s, there were large media conglomerates, but since there were many, no threat of monopolization seemed apparent. In 1996, Congress repealed its earlier ban against allowing telephone companies to provide video programming in their own service area but still would not allow them to buy cable systems (or visa versa), except in sparsely populated nonurban areas.

With the new technology and the potential for intermixing cable and telephone, both in functions and in wiring and audio and video, Congress also preempted state and local regulations that would bar cable operators and others from providing local telephone service. Indeed, any system that became part of effective competition was no longer under the strict regulation that it once was.

The notion of regulation by the government on behalf of the people, protecting its interests in spectrum frequencies, has dramatically changed, allowing the free marketplace and competition to determine regulatory patterns.

Val E. Limburg

REGULATION, SELF-. The broadcast industry is subject to regulations imposed by Congress and by the Federal Communications Commission (FCC). At times, however, restraint of programming or business practices comes not through formal regulation but rather in response to public concerns. In these instances, broadcasters enact self-regulatory measures to avoid further government regulation and respond to the listening public's concerns.

An area that broadcasters have exercised self-regulation concerns advertising. The National Association of Broadcasters (NAB) formalized a code for radio advertising in 1929 that outlined unacceptable commercial practices. In particular, the code identified certain commercial claims and product types that were inappropriate. The code also suggested that radio stations should limit commercial time to no more than 18 minutes per hour. It is important to note, however, that the code was nonbinding and was developed only as a guideline for acceptable broadcast practices. Ultimately, a Justice Department antitrust probe of the NAB's television code led to the dissolution of both the radio and television codes in 1982.

Today, most broadcast stations have formal guidelines that outline content and product types deemed generally unacceptable for their audience. These traditionally include specific personal products and controversial social issues that might offend portions of a station's audience. However, standards are not industry wide, meaning that advertising is screened by each network, broadcast group, or individual radio station for acceptability.

A recent test of this self-regulation focuses on the industry's voluntary ban on advertising distilled liquors. Although there is no federal law banning alcohol advertisement on broadcast stations, the industry has generally refused to air wine and distilled liquor advertising. After a Houston television station accepted a liquor distributor's advertisement, many broadcasters reconsidered this voluntary ban. Broadcasters cited an increasingly competitive advertising market and the common acceptance of beer commercials as a rationale for accepting the liquor advertisements. Although government leaders, including President Bill Clinton, and citizen advocacy groups have appealed to broadcasters to continue the voluntary ban, many have indicated their interest in accepting distilled liquor commercials.

Another example involves public and governmental concerns over explicit music lyrics. Although some lyrics referring to sex, violence, and drug usage do not meet the legal definition of indecency, they may still be judged inappropriate for a broadcast audience. A radio station may choose to edit or alter offensive words or play the song in its original form at hours when it is unlikely that children are in the audience. Yet another option would be to refuse a song altogether, which has been the case recently with some explicit gansta rap.

Franklin, Marc C., and David A. Anderson. *Mass Media Law, Cases and Materials.* Westbury, N.Y.: Foundation Press, Inc., 1993.

Zelezny, John D. *Communications Law, Liberties, Restraints, and the Modern Media.* Belmont, Calif.: Wadsworth Publishing, 1993.

Cynthia A. Cooper

REGULATION OF PROGRAMMING. As the primary administrative agency over broadcasting, the Federal Communications Commission (FCC) is charged with overseeing the regulatory framework guiding this ever-changing industry. Although Section 326 of the *Communications Act* prohibits commission censorship of broadcast programming, the FCC has enforced limited programming restrictions when it has ruled them necessary to protect against potential harm to the audience. Specifically, the FCC has issued regulations regarding indecent programming, broadcast hoaxes, and contests and promotions.

One of the most contested areas of programming regulation is broadcasting indecent material. Although the FCC has held the authority to regulate indecent programming since the 1940s, the lack of a clear standard for indecency led to inconsistent FCC decisions involving suggestive or offensive programs. The popular 1970s radio format known as *topless radio* pushed to the forefront the need for an indecency standard.

In the late 1970s, the FCC articulated a clearly defined legal standard for indecent programming. Responding to a single complaint, the FCC investigated a radio station's afternoon broadcast of a George Carlin monologue entitled "Filthy Words." During the excerpt, Carlin offered his commentary on the meaning of some words in society including seven words that could never be said on the broadcast medium. Although the FCC imposed no formal penalty against the radio station, it did rule that the broadcast was indeed indecent. In addition, it suggested that broadcasting should be held to a higher standard of conduct than other media because of its access to unsupervised children, the lack of a sufficient warning system of upcoming offensive material, and the scarcity of spectrum space, which required broadcasters to operate in the public interest.

Indecent material was defined by the FCC as language that describes, in terms patently offensive as measured by contemporary community standards, sexual and excretory activities and organs. Ten years later, in response to complaints over shock jocks such as Howard Stern, the FCC interpreted this definition to include the context of programming as well.

The FCC's attention to indecent programming generally stemmed from a concern over its potential harm to children, but it also recognized the right of adults to have access to informational and entertainment programming that dealt with mature subjects. Consequently, the FCC created a *safe harbor* zone during which programming that otherwise might be banned as indecent could be broadcast because it was unlikely that children would be in the audience. Despite the simplistic concept of channeling such programming, the exact time-of-day restrictions became the subject of extensive legal proceedings. After nearly a decade of litigation, the courts approved channeling indecent material between 10:00 P.M. and 6:00 A.M.

Another area of concern has been the potential harm caused by broadcast hoaxes. Ever since Orson Welles's 1938 broadcast of *War of the Worlds* caused some listeners to believe an invasion from Mars was actually happening, the government has been concerned with the far-reaching effects of this pervasive medium. As humor and satire are often a part of any broadcast, the FCC has been careful to make a distinction between a station's harmless prank on April Fool's Day and the more deceptive and serious broadcast hoaxes that pose a potential danger to the public.

In November 1991, the FCC announced its intention of instituting a rule specifically addressing broadcast hoaxes. The commission explained that the action was necessary given a recent broadcast hoax that endangered public safety and resulted in the use of substantial public safety resources to respond to events fabricated by on-air talent at radio stations. A fake nuclear war attack, accompanied by the Emergency Broadcast System warning, resulted in a $25,000 fine against St. Louis radio station KSHE. The FCC received numerous complaints about the hoax, and although it had no official rule prohibiting hoaxes at that time, the station received the maximum fine allowed due to the broadcast of a false distress signal.

Another fake announcement that provoked complaints was a fake announcement by WALE (Providence, Rhode Island) that one of its disc jockeys (DJs) had been shot in the head. Within minutes of the announcement, local law enforcement and media were at the station attempting to uncover the facts.

A more serious incident that gained nationwide attention involved a fake murder confession on a call-in show on station KROQ (Los Angeles). During a regularly featured program called *Confess Your Crime,* an anonymous caller claimed to have killed his girlfriend but failed to identify her before hanging up. The confession drew a great deal of publicity from local media as well as the NBC series *Unsolved Mysteries.* The Los Angeles County Sheriff's Department launched a 10-month search for the killer and the victim based on hundreds of leads from across the nation including many relatives of runaway or missing girls. Ultimately, the confession was exposed as a hoax, designed as a publicity stunt by the program's two DJs.

Again, the FCC had no rule against hoaxes at this time, so no formal action was taken against the station. Later, the station did take action against the announcers and reimbursed the Sheriff's Department for expenses involved in its investigation.

After extensive discussion with broadcasters, the FCC (in 1992) instituted a formal rule prohibiting hoaxes that involve broadcasting false information of a crime or catastrophe that actually causes harm or threat to public safety or the diversion of public safety officials. Recognizing the potential chilling effect of such regulation, the FCC exempted fictional and dramatic programming from the hoax ruling.

A concern over public safety has also been a factor in regulation governing broadcast contests and promotions. In general, station-sponsored contests are permitted as long as they do not involve fraudulent or misleading rules and do not endanger public safety. All rules governing eligibility and awarding of prizes must be announced, and the method of winning a contest must not pose a safety hazard to the public. Although the FCC does not give specific examples regarding contests and promotions, it is generally best to avoid any action that could cause personal injury to participants or the involvement of public safety officials.

Creech, Kenneth C. *Electronic Media Law and Regulation.* 2nd ed. Boston: Focal Press, 1996.
Holsinger, Ralph, and Jon Paul Dilts. *Media Law.* 4th ed. New York: McGraw-Hill, 1996.
Cynthia A. Cooper

RELIGIOUS BROADCASTERS. *See* **national religious broadcasters (NRB).**

RELIGIOUS PROGRAMS, the third most prevalent radio format, feature religious music and news, worship services, and sermons. Coincident with radio's 1920s beginnings, religious programming commenced with fundamentalist Christian groups preaching their philosophy. But as radio developed generally into a commercial medium, many religious broadcasters actually chose to run commercial operations.

Early on, policies permitting religious programming or radio ownership were fraught with conflicts and problems. Individualistic religious personalities, such as Aimee Semple McPherson, challenged the government's right to regulate religious program broadcasting. Most often, religious programmers followed the rules but felt drawn to answer to a higher authority in matters of conscience.

Regulation from 1927 to 1956 was both public and private as government agencies silenced offending religious broadcasters by reassigning frequencies, and competition caused some to fail. Major radio networks bent to pressure from mainline, liberal Protestant church groups to stop accepting paid religious programming. Rather, they offered "sustaining time," public service slots for some religious programs, which cut down programming by fundamentalist groups. In the 1940s, National Religious Broadcasters (NRB) fundamentalist groups' lobbying efforts included hiring Washington legal counsel to find ways to stop alleged network discrimination against religious programming.

From 1956 to 1977, radio faced tremendous competition from TV stations, and many radio stations sold time for religious broadcasting. The NRB gained power as liberal Protestants lost ground against strong evangelical radio and TV interests.

During the 1970s and 1980s, technology (i.e., using cable TV instead of major networks) and competition allowed religious programmers to reach more people. Jim Bakker's PTL club, Trinity Broadcast Network (TBN), Pat Robertson's Christian Broadcast Network (CBN), and others built significant followings and financial support with cable and satellite distribution.

But during the late 1980s, several "televangelism" scandals caused losses of audience and financial support upon which broadcast ministries relied. Bakker was imprisoned for financial irregularities; Jimmy Swaggart was discredited on morals charges; Oral Roberts made questionable pleas for financial support. No regulatory backlash occurred despite concerns about fraudulent practices. However, considerable pressure from regulators and from responsible religious broadcasters caused religious programmers to clean up their acts.

Critics have argued for years against government support of or licensing of religious broadcast stations because it violates the establishment clause of the First Amendment. Religious advocates counterargue that prohibiting religious programming violates their equal protection guarantees under the Constitution. Interference with religious programming, whether technical or content regulation, will continue to be controversial.

Yet today religious programming is a popular, powerful force in radio (1995 figures show the religious radio format third with 1,227 stations behind country and adult contemporary formats). Religion programming takes two paths: religious music played all day; and religious talk and information. The phenomenal rise of Christian popular music has made radio stations take note. *Billboard* magazine tracks sales of Christian popular music, and many stations play the most popular in their mix.

Hadden, J. K. "Policing Religious Airwaves: The Case for Marketplace Regulation." *Brigham Young University Journal of Public Law* 8 (1994): 393–416.

Hill, G. H., and Lenwood David. *Religious Broadcasting, 1920–83: A Selectively Annotated Bibliography.* New York and London: Garland Publishing, 1984.

Keith, Michael C. *Radio Programming: Consultancy and Formatics.* Boston: Focal Press, 1987.

                                                                                                    J. R. Rush

REMOTE BROADCASTING came into existence in the very early days of radio. Simply put, these broadcasts originated outside the station's studio facilities. They were more difficult in the early years of radio because of the equipment's weight. As technology brought lighter, more portable equipment, such broadcasts proliferated.

Some of the earliest remote broadcasts were of sporting events. In 1921, KDKA brought prize fights and major league baseball games to listeners. In 1922, WEAF (New York) brought the report of the Chicago-Princeton football game from Stagg Field in Chicago. Election returns became almost mandatory after KDKA's first coverage of the Harding-Cox presidential election.

Following these early experimental years, remote broadcasting became almost commonplace, with stations in small towns broadcasting from a newly opened grocery store or department store. Stations in larger markets covered almost anything that seemed of interest to the public. Newly created mobile equipment made it all possible.

One of the biggest forms were broadcasts of dance bands in the Big Band Era. In the late 1950s, CBS produced its Saturday night dance program, starting at the Steel Pier in New Jersey, on to the Trianon Ballroom, and gradually moving westward with the different time zones. It was one way to produce programming following TV's inroads.

Radio set the stage for television to follow. Many stations broadcast coverage of local sports teams, speeches by important dignitaries, on-site news coverage of interesting stories, and so forth. One of the biggest stories covered by remote broadcast was the 1937 coverage of the German dirigible *Hindenberg*'s arrival. The giant airship's gas bags exploded into flame as it touched down at the New Jersey landing field. The announcer was so overcome that he actually left the scene and his microphone to go inside the building to compose himself.

Today, television has picked up remote broadcasting begun by radio in news and many other areas. Electronic news gathering (ENG) equipment has made remote broadcasting as easy as in-studio broadcasting has been since its beginning.

ElDean Bennett

REPEATER STATION. *See* **translators.**

RESEARCH. *See* **audience research.**

RHYTHM AND BLUES. In 1949, *Billboard* magazine's Jerry Wexler coined the phrase to describe music formerly referred to as "racc" music. Rhythm and blues combined elements of country blues, urban blues, jazz, and gospel. Rhythm and blues is an "ensemble music." It consists of vocals (solo or group), a rhythm section (electric guitar and/or string bass, piano, drums), and a "supplementary unit" (the saxophone or other wind instruments) (Southern, p. 499).

Rhythm and blues structure is similar to that of the blues—for example, the call-and-response patterns. In addition, the 12-bar musical structure is also used. Additionally, rhythm and blues lyrics often are sexually suggestive and contain double entendres, with references to sexual expression (Redd). Performers originated in many U.S. regions and cities; however, the South, Southwest, Kansas City, Chicago, and Memphis produced performers who played key roles in its development. Rhythm and blues artists were widely imitated by whites, who used it to create "rock 'n' roll" music. Individuals who developed and popularized rhythm and blues included Willie Mae Thornton, Ruth Brown, Louis Jordan, Jackie Wilson, Little Richard, Clyde McPhatter, LaVern Baker, Sam Cooke, and BoDiddley—who most directly influenced Elvis Presley.

Gospel quartets of the 1920s had a significant impact on the development of rhythm and blues quartets of the 1950s; groups such as the Ravens and Orioles imitated their singing styles. Other rhythm and blues groups used "doo-wop," "ohh-waa," "ko-ko-boop," "oo-bi-dee," and "sh-boom"—also derived from gospel quartet music.

Floyd, Samuel A. *The Power of Black Music.* New York: Oxford University Press, 1995.
Redd, Lawrence. *Rock Is Rhythm and Blues.* East Lansing: Michigan State University Press, 1974.
Southern, Eileen. *The Music of Black Americans: A History.* New York: W. W. Norton, 1971.

Gilbert A. Williams

RKO (RADIO-KEITH-ORPHEUM) was incorporated in 1928 when Keith-Al-bee-Orpheum (KAO) and Film Booking Office (FBO) merged under the auspices of the Radio Corporation of America. The merger brought together the radio and film industries primarily to compete in the relatively new "talking" motion picture business. RCA had created the technology necessary in its Photophone system of sound-on-film recording. The other two companies, KAO and FBO, brought a chain of motion picture theaters and a film production studio to the merger.

In the 1960s, RKO General owned a group of television stations and was a subsidiary of General Tire. It became involved in a challenge of its station licenses, based on the "questionable" character of the parent company General Tire. A Federal Communications Commission (FCC) hearing and court cases lasted nearly a quarter of a century.

Archer, Gleason L. *Big Business and Radio.* New York: American Historical Company, Inc., 1939.

Frederic A. Leigh

ROCK 'N' ROLL was coined by disc jockey Alan Freed to describe the music being played by stations that would come to be known as top-40 outlets. While today the musical form is known simply as "rock," in the mid-1950s "rock 'n' roll" was actually an amalgam of three genres: traditional Tin Pan Alley pop, black rhythm and blues, and country and western.

In 1954, the pop field and the record charts were almost entirely dominated by traditional music that appealed to adult values and tastes. Disc jockeys such as Freed had discovered that the gritty lyrics and heavy beat of rhythm and blues records, produced largely by small independent labels, appealed strongly to teenagers—a new market segment, with their own spendable income and lifestyle. As network radio shows and stars moved to television and adults abandoned evening radio listening for TV viewing, teenagers gravitated to the stations playing "rebellious" rock 'n' roll music.

In 1954, Bill Haley and His Comets applied their country and western–tinged pop style to Joe Turner's rhythm and blues tune "Shake, Rattle and Roll," turning it into a pop hit. By 1956, Elvis Presley cemented the connection between pop, rhythm and blues, and country and western, paving the way for groups such as the Everly Brothers, whose acoustic guitar–based blend of country and rock 'n' roll was referred to as "rockabilly."

David T. MacFarland

ROGERS, ROY (KING OF THE COWBOYS) AND EVANS, DALE. One of the original "singing cowboys" in the movies, Leonard Frank Sly (1911–) was born in Cincinnati, Ohio, on November 5, 1911. He was proud of his Indian heritage (he had the Choctaw Indian eyes) all his life. In 1930, Leonard (Len, who had always wanted to sing) and his father packed the family car and headed to California. The 1923 Dodge broke down in New Mexico and then again in Arizona. It was the era of the movie *Grapes of Wrath,* and the Slys looked like they came right out of Steinbeck's story. Len worked at numerous jobs but finally got a small group of musicians together. In June 1933 the group, known at the time as the International Cowboys Band, played Warner Brothers Theater in Los Angeles and sang "Tumbling Tumbleweeds." Over the years, they played under a number of different names. Finally a radio announcer, intentionally or not, introduced them as the Sons of the Pioneers, and the name stuck. In 1937, Len heard about a screen test at Republic Studios for "singing cowboys." He had to sneak into the studio lot where he met Sol C. Siegel, who knew him from the Sons of the Pioneers. He sang "Hadie Brown" for his audition because of the yodeling part and also sang "Tumbling Tumbleweeds."

On October 13, after getting a release from his contract at Columbia Pictures, he signed with Republic Studios and was given the name Dick Weston. Republic star Gene Autry was threatening to leave the studio if he didn't get a new contract, and Republic used Dick Weston as leverage against Autry. The studio kept him on, and during an Autry absence, he moved up quickly. The studio decided they didn't like the name Dick Weston and after some thought came up with Roy Rogers. The golden Palomino (whose name was changed from "Golden Cloud" to Trigger, which they said was more western) entered Roy's life in 1938. His first feature film was *Washington Cowboy,* which had been slated for Autry. When the studio put Roy in, they changed the title to *Under Western Stars* and used Trigger. The ensuing years saw Roy tour around the country and change films from the "Old West" image to the good Samaritan cowboy in the modern West.

Roy had met Lucille Wood Smith (Dale, 1912–) when they were touring the circuits, mostly one-night stands. In 1944, when she was married to R. Evans and Roy was married to his second wife (Arline), Dale was teamed as Roy's leading lady in *The Cowboy and the Señorita.* She went on to become a part of Roy's road, radio, and TV shows. In 1944, Roy also was introduced in a new medium, Roy Rogers Comic books.

Roy Rogers's career in radio began with the *Tommy Riggs and Betty Lou Show* on NBC when he and Trigger guest starred in 1943. In 1944, he had his own show, *The Roy Rogers Show,* each Tuesday at 8:30 P.M. on Mutual, with Goodyear Tire and Rubber Co. as the sponsor. Other shows followed on both NBC and Mutual Radio Networks, and he used the Sons of the Pioneers as much as he could on the shows. He eventually got into some dramatic shows, such as in 1949 with "Horse Thieves of Paradise Valley" and "Ghost Town Men." With the Sons of the Pioneers, he often performed over KTRH. A contest, sponsored by longtime sponsor Quaker Oats, offered the winner a chance to perform in a movie with Roy, Dale, and Gabby Hayes, a longtime sidekick.

Roy Rogers and Dale Evans, with their nearly-as-famous horses, provided entertainment that was fit for families or children alone. They appeared for many years, in films and on radio and television, always maintaining a high level of entertainment. The theme song, which Roy chose as his own but which both came to sing at the end of performances, was "Happy Trails." Trigger, when he died of old age, was stuffed and mounted and is kept in the Roy Rogers Museum. There were other Triggers, the son of the original being the first replacement.

ElDean Bennett

ROGERS, WILL (1879–1935), Oklahoma cowboy comedian, political satirist, author, columnist, and Hollywood star, helped inaugurate NBC on November 15, 1926—recounting his recent European trip and a visit with President Calvin Coolidge—live from Independence, Kansas. In January 1928 as master of ceremonies for a nationwide radio jubilee, he "introduced" Coolidge, then imitated the president, saying, "The nation is prosperous on the whole, but how much prosperity is there in a hole?" In 1930 he began a regular 14-part, 15-minute radio series for $72,000, which he gave to charity. Rogers refused network censorship and even satirized NBC on its 1934 anniversary.

William James Ryan

ROOSEVELT, FRANKLIN D. (FDR) (1882–1945), the thirty-second president of the United States, served in that office between 1933 and 1945. FDR made important contributions to radio by finalizing the regulatory environment and pioneering the use of radio for political purposes.

Educated at Harvard and the Columbia University School of Law, Roosevelt entered politics as a New York state senator in 1910. He served as secretary of the navy between 1913 and 1920 and was the unsuccessful Democratic vice presidential candidate in 1920. The defeat of Roosevelt and his running mate, James Cox, was the substance of the first major radio broadcast on pioneer station KDKA in Pittsburgh. After serving as New York governor following the election of 1928, Roosevelt became president in a landslide victory over incumbent Herbert Hoover in 1932. Americans were frustrated by Hoover's failure to come to grips with the Great Depression, which Roosevelt promised to end.

A key component of what became the New Deal was Roosevelt's application of radio in rallying public support for relief and recovery programs. As part of his "Hundred Days," Roosevelt in March 1933 introduced the *Fireside Chat,* a major development in radio communication as for the first time a prominent political leader had broken from the tradition of formal speeches and provided an appeal in a personalized manner. Roosevelt's off-the-cuff and informal style was illustrated in the first *Fireside Chat,* in which Roosevelt opened by telling listeners, "I have come to you tonight to talk about banking." *Fireside Chats* by that name appeared on radio throughout 1933. Roosevelt would apply the same calming technique on radio following Japan's invasion of Pearl Harbor in 1941, which led to America's entry into World War II.

It was also during the New Deal that Congress approved legislation, spearheaded by the Roosevelt administration, that created the Federal Communications Commission (FCC) in 1934. Key to the passage of the *Communications Act of 1934* was a measure approved by Roosevelt prohibiting the FCC from censoring broadcast fare. Roosevelt appointed E. O. Sykes as the first FCC chair.

At the outbreak of World War II, the Roosevelt administration formed and coordinated an agency called the Office of War Information (OWI). Headed by Gardner Cowles, a prominent radio broadcaster and publisher, OWI sought to involve the media in decisions relating to disseminating information from the war front, including censorship, and to avoid the propaganda seen during World War I. Although riddled by disagreements, Roosevelt's OWI wound up harmonizing the otherwise differing objectives of government and the media, and this helped rally a unified home-front response to the war.

Although his initiatives were far-reaching, Roosevelt often was accused of swing with the two largest broadcast enterprises, NBC and CBS. While just a few years old, Roosevelt's FCC was confronted by allegations it had permitted a monopolization of radio. Finally in 1943, Roosevelt had the Justice Department investigate potential antitrust violations by the big network. That year the *Report on Chain Broadcasting* ordered the breakup of what had been two dominant NBC radio networks. The smaller of these two chains, the NBC Blue Network, was the foundation of what became ABC.

Shortly after winning an unprecedented fourth term as president and just months before the end of World War II, Roosevelt died of a cerebral hemorrhage in April 1945. His funeral was heard on radio throughout the United States and in many other parts of the world.

Burns, James MacGregor. *Roosevelt: The Lion and the Fox.* New York: Harcourt Brace, 1956.
Schlesinger, Arthur. *The Age of Roosevelt.* 3 vols. Boston: Houghton Mifflin, 1957, 1959, 1960.
Winfield, Betty Houchin. *FDR and the News Media.* Urbana: University of Illinois Press, 1990.

Craig M. Allen

ROPER, ELMO BURNS, JR. (1900–1971). A noted pioneer in marketing research and political polling, Roper was born in Hebron, Nebraska. His polling methods came from his background in market research, which he first developed in the jewelry business in Iowa, then as a clock salesman, where he made a habit of questioning customers about what kinds of clocks they liked. He moved to New York in 1933 and started his own company. In 1935, *Fortune* magazine hired him to conduct public opinion surveys.

Roper came to national prominence in the 1936 presidential election. One of the nation's leading publications, *Literary Digest,* using mailed-in replies from subscribers as well as telephone households and automobile owners, predicted an Alf Landon landslide victory. But Roper and other pollsters, such as George Gallup and Archibald Crossley, were using far more sophisticated methods of sampling the voting population. Their samples were comparatively small but far more representative of voters as a whole. Roper's prediction of an election win by Franklin D. Roosevelt was within 1 percent of the actual popular vote.

Roper's predictions of the presidential races in 1940 and 1944 were very accurate, but his methods failed in the 1948 election. Roper found Roosevelt's popularity to be very stable throughout his campaigns; when Thomas Dewey opened a large, early lead in the race, Roper mistakenly assumed there would be no major shifts. Roper published his last results in September, based on data that were already a month old. The result was a famous come-from-behind victory by Harry Truman in spite of predictions by most major polling organizations that Dewey's lead was safe. Roper's prediction missed Truman's actual support by 12 percent, and the discrepancy led to a postelection reexamination of polling techniques by pollsters in general.

Roper wrote a syndicated column, *What People Are Thinking,* featuring the results of his polls of public opinion on current events. He did public opinion research for *Fortune* for 15 years and served as editor-at-large for *Saturday Review.* He also authored *You and Your Leaders,* in which he wrote that he felt the polls had helped defeat Dewey. He was also critical of politicians who conducted their own polls and then released only the results that were favorable to them. Roper said he had come to see simple predictions of election outcomes as useless, and he developed an interest in finding out how much average citizens knew about public policy issues to see where more information was needed. Roper stayed active in public opinion measurement until his retirement in 1966.

John R. Broholm

ROTATION, MUSIC. *See* **power rotation and top 40.**

S

SAERCHINGER, CESAR, a radio journalist and one of the "Murrow boys" (see **CBS News**).

SARNOFF, DAVID (1891–1971), radio and television pioneer, was an immigrant who, by his death, had climbed the rungs of corporate America to head the Radio Corporation of America (RCA). Born on February 27, 1891, in Russia, Sarnoff spent his early years studying to be a rabbi. After immigrating to the United States in 1900, he had to work to feed his mother, ailing father, and siblings, first, by selling Yiddish-language newspapers and, second by seeking a full-time job.

After a few months working for the Commercial Cable Company, the American subsidiary of a British firm that controlled undersea cable communication, he was lured to the American Marconi Company. Once there, he began his corporate rise, including being Marconi's personal messenger when the inventor was in town. With Marconi's endorsement, Sarnoff became a junior wireless telegraph operator and, at age 17, volunteered for wireless duty at one of the company's remote stations. There he studied the station's technical library and took correspondence courses. Eighteen months later, he became Marconi's youngest manager when appointed manager of the Sea Gate, New York, station. After volunteering as a wireless operator for an Arctic sealing expedition, he became operator of the Marconi wireless purchased by the John Wanamaker department stores. At night he continued his studies.

Then, on April 14, 1912, he heard the faint reports of the *Titanic* disaster. One of a number of wireless operators reporting the tragedy, Sarnoff would later claim he was the only one remaining on air after President Howard Taft ordered others to remain silent. Another likely erroneous claim was Sarnoff's assertion he wrote his famous "Radio Music Box Memo" predicting broadcasting in 1915. The version so often cited was actually written in 1920, when others were also investigating and predicting broadcasting.

As his career thrived, Sarnoff's personal life also grew. On July 4, 1917, he married Lizette Hermant following a closely supervised courtship. They had three sons: Robert (who succeeded his father as RCA's president), Edward, and Thomas.

In 1919, when British Marconi sold its American Marconi assets to General Electric (GE) to form RCA, Sarnoff came on board as commercial manager. Under the tutelage of Owen D. Young, RCA's chairman, Sarnoff was soon in charge of broadcasting as general manager of RCA and was integral in forming NBC in 1926. Under Young's guidance, he negotiated the secret contracts with AT&T that led to NBC's development.

In 1927 Sarnoff was elected to RCA's board, and during the summer of 1928, he became RCA's acting president when then-president General James G. Harbord took a leave of absence to campaign for Herbert Hoover. His eventual succession to that position was assured. During the end of the decade, Sarnoff negotiated successful contracts to form Radio-Keith-Orpheum (RKO) motion pictures, to introduce radios as a permanent fixture in automobiles, and to consolidate all radio manufacturing by the Victor company under RCA's banner. On January 3, 1930, the 39-year-old Sarnoff became RCA's president.

The next two years were pivotal in Sarnoff's life as the Department of Justice sued GE and RCA for monopoly and restraint of trade. Sarnoff led industry efforts to combat the government's efforts that would have destroyed RCA. The result was a consent decree in 1932 calling for RCA's divestiture from GE and licensing of RCA's patents to competitors. When GE freed RCA, Sarnoff was at the helm and, for nearly three decades, would oversee numerous communications developments, including television, radar, sonar, satellites, rocketry, and computers.

Of the industry controversies in which Sarnoff was a part, three stand out: adoption of black-and-white television standards in the 1930s, adoption of color television standards in the 1950s, and battles with Edwin Howard Armstrong over FM radio's development and patents.

In the 1930s, other manufacturers, especially Philco, Dumont, and Zenith, fought Sarnoff's push for adoption of RCA's monochrome television standards as the industry norm. In 1936, the Radio Manufacturers Association (RMA) set up a technical committee to seek agreement on industry standards, an action blessed actively by Sarnoff and silently by the Federal Communications Commission (FCC). For over five years the committee fought over standards. Meanwhile, Sarnoff told the RMA, standards or not, he would initiate television service at the opening of the New York World's Fair on April 20, 1939. Skirmishes continued for the next two years over standards, but finally in May 1941 the FCC's National Television System Committee (NTSC) set standards at 525 lines, interlaced, and 30 frames per second.

During the 1950s, Sarnoff battled CBS over color television and eventually won. In 1951, the FCC approved CBS's system, but that system was not compatible with existing monochromatic television. Sarnoff capitalized on this problem and pushed RCA's development of a compatible system. Eventually, CBS gave up its color television system as "economically foolish," and the FCC adopted RCA's compatible system.

At the same time Sarnoff was battling CBS, his feud over FM with his once-close friend Armstrong consumed numerous court appearances in the 1940s and early 1950s. The feud ended in 1954 with Armstrong's regrettable suicide, but Armstrong's widow, Marion, went on to win all of his suits, even though it took her 15 years to do so.

Sarnoff died in his sleep on December 12, 1971, of cardiac arrest. At his funeral he was eulogized as a visionary who had the capacity to see into tomorrow and to make it work. His obituary began on page one and ran nearly one full page in the *New York Times* and aptly summed up his career in these words: "He was not an inventor, nor was he a scientist. But he was a man of astounding vision who was able to see with remarkable clarity the possibilities of harnessing the electron."

Bilby, Kenneth. *The General: David Sarnoff and the Rise of the Communications Industry.* New York: Harper & Row, 1986.

"David Sarnoff of RCA Is Dead: Visionary Broadcast Pioneer." *New York Times,* December 13, 1971, obituary, pp. 1, 43.

Louise Benjamin

SARNOFF, ROBERT WILLIAM (1918–), was the son of General David and Lizette Sarnoff. He was a graduate of Harvard University and served in the armed forces during World War II. At the end of the war he took a job with Gardner Cowles, a Des Moines, Iowa, newspaper and magazine publisher. In 1948, he was hired at NBC as an assistant to executive vice president Frank Mullen. By 1952, he was head of the NBC Film Division—the division that produced *Victory at Sea.* In 1955 he was appointed president of NBC, and in 1965, president and chief operating officer of RCA. He became active head following his father's death in 1971. He was fired from RCA in 1975 following the economic reverses of the 1960s and 1970s.

Bilby, Kenneth. *The General: David Sarnoff and the Rise of the Communications Industry.* New York: Harper & Row Publishers, 1986.

Donald G. Godfrey

SATELLITES, electronic retransmission devices launched by rocket or transported on NASA (National Aeronautics and Space Administration) shuttle craft to geosynchronous orbital positions 22,300 miles over the earth's equator. The satellite's transponders receive signals from uplink stations on earth and retransmit the signals to downlink receivers. The satellite has a relatively long life because it uses solar energy to recharge its batteries. Satellites initially provided wide coverage for radio networks by overcoming barriers that limited terrestrial wireless signals and beating high costs and lower quality associated with wired networks. Cost-effective retransmission and distribution by satellite spawned dozens of specialized radio networks and program services.

Most satellites cover wide geographic areas, described as the satellite's "footprint." Some are capable of sending focused "spot-beam" signals aimed at limited geographic targets. The United States and the Soviet Union launched the first satellites, the Soviet *Sputnik* and the U.S. *Explorer,* in the late 1950s. The early satellites were used for military communication and observation purposes. By 1964 the United Nations had formed INTELSAT (International Telecommunications Satellite Consortium), which promoted the use of satellites for telephone and data relay. In the late 1970s, National Public Radio (NPR) led the way for radio networks when NPR switched from telephone lines to satellite distribution of its network.

New satellite technology called direct broadcast by satellite (DBS) relays compressed digital audio signals. It is expected to fuel a proliferation of satellite radio program services (DARS, digital audio radio service) and to focus on providing audio programming directly to automobiles without having the signal pass through a terrestrial transmitter.

Satellite technology plays an important role in distributing news, sports, and special events. Press agencies and networks depend on satellite technology to transport news items to their central newsrooms. After they are edited, the news items are frequently distributed to subscribers by satellite. Satellite technology plays an important role in distributing sports events such as the Superbowl or World Cup Soccer and is essential in distributing special events such as coronations and concerts.

Satellites have many functions. They carry a great deal of the domestic U.S. and international telephone and data traffic. Ship captains, airplane pilots, and explorers rely on the satellite-based global-positioning system (GPS). Businesses, governments, and educational institutions distribute and collect data and transmit audio and video programming for training and distance learning via inexpensive satellite-based very small aperture terminal (VSAT) systems.

Other satellites help scientists map the earth's resources, and intelligence organizations spy on potential threats to national security. Low-earth-orbit satellites will soon be introduced to make cellular-telephone service widely available across the United States and, eventually, around the world.

Gross, Lynne S. *Telecommunications: An Introduction to Electronic Media.* Dubuque, Iowa: Wm. C. Brown, 1988.
Keirstead, Phillip O., and Sonia-Kay Keirstead. *The World of Telecommunication: Introduction to Broadcasting, Cable, and New Technologies.* Boston: Focal Press, 1990.

Phillip O. Keirstead

SATELLITE STATIONS were originally used by radio networks to provide programming to affiliated local stations. Formalizing direct-satellite service to individual radios began in 1990, when a petition was filed with the Federal Communications Commission (FCC) for rule making to allocate spectrum space for a satellite digital audio radio service (DARS). FCC envisioned that satellite DARS would be a multichannel national service competing with and complementing traditional local radio. This service would reach underserved areas and provide specialized programming not otherwise easily available. On April 1, 1997, the FCC awarded a portion of the available spectrum space to each of two winning auction bidders for a national DARS service.

Hudson, Heather. *Communication Satellites: Their Development and Impact.* New York: Free Press, 1990.

Steven C. Runyon

SAUDEK, ROBERT first appeared in radio broadcasting as one of the choir boys singing from the Pittsburgh Calvary Episcopal Church on KDKA on January 2, 1921. He became vice president of ABC, where he created "high-minded radio documentaries" on such issues as urbanization, education, public education, and American consumerism. In 1951 he moved to direct the Ford Foundation's radio and television workshop. He is noted for his work on *Omnibus,* a television program that ran on Sunday afternoons and was described by Erik Barnouw as "often touching brilliance." Saudek was in charge of the program from November 9, 1952, to April 16, 1961. The Wesleyan University Cinema Archive houses the collection. Saudek was instrumental in establishing the New York Museum of TV & Radio in 1974. He was later appointed chief of the Motion Picture, Broadcasting and Recorded Sound Division at the Library of Congress. He passed away on March 17, 1997 at the age of 85.

Saudek, Robert. (Obituary). *New York Times,* March 17, 1997.

Donald G. Godfrey

SCHECHTER, A[BLE] A[LAN] (1908–1989), first head of NBC news and special events, was born in Central Falls, Rhode Island. He graduated in journalism from Boston University and then served as a reporter for the *Providence Journal* and *New York World* before joining the Associated Press (AP) and later the International News Service (INS) as an editor in New York. He moved to radio when he was hired in 1932 by NBC as a publicity specialist and soon moved to the fledgling news and special events department for NBC.

Schechter had to work around the Biltmore Agreement limitations on network reporting and grew to depend on the telephone to acquire reluctant interviewees. Most broadcasts were human interest features or stunts (singing-mouse contests, for example) rather than hard news. Schechter became head of news and special events in 1938. He left NBC in October 1941 (just after publishing his book, which details highlights of his NBC years) to join the new Office of War Information. He was later a public affairs officer for the War Department, helping arrange coverage of Pacific island-hopping campaigns. He served as a Mutual Network vice president in charge of news from 1945 to 1950, then returned to NBC and, among other things, helped to create the *Today* show and served as its first executive producer. He formed his own public relations firm in 1952, which was acquired by Hill and Knowlton in 1973. Schechter was killed in a car accident in 1989.

Bliss, Edward, Jr. *Now the News: The Story of Broadcast Journalism.* New York: Columbia University Press, 1992.
Schechter, A. A., with Edward Anthony. *I Live on Air.* New York: Frederick Stokes, 1941.

Christopher H. Sterling

SCHULKE, JAMES ALLEN [JIM] (1922–), broadcasting executive and FM programming pioneer. He was born in Cleveland, Ohio, and reared in suburban Lakewood. He did undergraduate work at Denison University and received an M.B.A. from Harvard. Widely recognized for his efforts in advancing FM recognition, Jim Schulke began his professional career in graduate school as advertising director for the *Harvard Business Review.* Between 1950 and 1962, Schulke held several positions in the entertainment industry, working first for the advertising agency Young & Rubicam and, later, for Paramount Television, where he managed KTLA-TV in Los Angeles.

Schulke's involvement with the development of FM escalated with his election in 1963 as president of the National Association of FM Broadcasters (NAFMB). Following a one-year term there, Schulke teamed with Bob Richer to create Quality Media Inc. (QMI), whose focus was directed exclusively toward FM advertising sales. When the Federal Communications Commission (FCC) imposed restrictions on duplicate AM-FM programming in the mid-1960s, he founded Schulke Radio Productions (SRP) to service the programming needs of FM broadcasters. SRP focused solely on the syndication of its beautiful music format, which consisted of an extensive library of lush instrumental and vocal recordings.

This meticulously researched and programmed format succeeded because of Schulke's attention to detail. He carefully scrutinized both the aesthetic and technical aspects of the format's execution. Stations adhering to the Schulke regimen were rewarded with unprecedented ratings successes.

During the peak popularity of the format in the late 1970s and early 1980s, SRP-programmed stations in the major markets typically finished in first or second place overall in the ratings. Cox Broadcasting purchased 90 percent interest in SRP in 1979. Now retired, Schulke currently resides in Florida.

Lanza, Joseph. *Elevator Music: A Surreal History of Muzak, Easy-Listening, and Other Moodsong.* New York: St. Martin's Press, 1994.
"Our Respects to . . . James Allen Schulke." *Broadcasting* 88 (November 2, 1959): 121.

Bruce Mims

SCOPES TRIAL. The "Monkey Trial" in Dayton, Tennessee in July 1925 convicted John T. Scopes of teaching Darwinian evolution to high school students. The case was set up by the American Civil Liberties Union to test on appeal anti-Darwinian state laws. But the trial became a media circus when William Jennings Bryan, three-time Democratic nominee for president, and free-thinking liberal lawyer Clarence Darrow joined the prosecution and defense, respectively. The dramatic climax of the trial came on July 20, when Darrow questioned Bryan as an expert witness on biblical inerrancy.

Although media coverage of the Scopes trial was primarily by newspapers, notably H. L. Mencken's writing for the Baltimore *Sun,* it is also important in radio history. The Chicago *Tribune* negotiated an arrangement with the Dayton court, allowing live broadcasting of the proceedings on the newpaper's radio station, WGN. Reporter Philip Kinsley coordinated the newspaper's coverage, and announcer Quin Ryan manned the microphone in Dayton. The proceedings were relayed over long-distance telephone lines and cost the *Tribune* $1,000 per day. Defendant Scopes remembered Ryan sitting with his microphone in a corner on the defense side of the courtroom. Ryan presumably followed the court when the proceedings were moved outside due to heat.

Scopes's conviction was overturned on a technicality, although Tennessee's antievolution law remained in effect until 1968. The Scopes trial became the basis of the play and movie *Inherit the Wind.*

Scopes, John T., and James Presley. *Center of the Storm: Memoirs of John T. Scopes.* New York: Holt, Rinehart and Winston, 1967.

Wendt, Lloyd. *Chicago Tribune: The Rise of a Great American Newspaper.* Chicago: Rand McNally, 1979.

Glen M. Johnson

SEGMENTATION, AUDIENCE. Most radio stations try to gain as many listeners between the ages of 25 and 54 years old as possible because people in this age demographic are attractive to advertisers. To gain listener loyalty and good ratings in this demographic, stations have found it necessary to target specific niche audiences within that larger age group. The result is that different segments of the general 25–54 audience may be targeted by different stations. Assume there is a community with five radio stations all seeking to gain the largest number of listeners between 25 and 54 years old. Currently one of the stations is playing oldies, one is playing a wide range of old and new country music, one is an adult contemporary station playing a mix of more recent pop hits, one is formatting news/talk, and one is playing easy-listening music. From this array, assume the country station is the number-one station in the market. Its younger listeners don't like the older songs but listen only because they can't hear country on any other station. Also, assume the easy-listening station has the least number of listeners 25 to 54 because its programming appeals primarily to people over the age of 55. In this scenario the easy-listening station might decide to change to country but to program only new "hot" country songs appealing to younger country listeners. With this strategy the new country station would hope to win over an attractive segment of the first country station's audience and might even hope to gain some of the younger members of the adult contemporary station's 25–54 audience. If this strategy were successful, the "hot" country station would have resegmented the local audience in such a way that its ratings would be more appealing to advertisers. This type of audience fragmentation occurs in most markets through different format combinations. Because there are many radio stations all seeking audience shares within the same 25–54 age demographic, this large age group is viewed as a complex array of various age "segments." Each station hopes that its segment will be the largest and will therefore attract the most advertising.

Kenneth D. Loomis

SELF-REGULATION. *See* **regulation, self-.**

SENATE COMMERCE COMMITTEE derives its power over broadcasting from Article 1, Section 8 (3) of the U.S. Constitution, giving Congress the power to regulate interstate commerce. Congress established independent regulatory agencies to oversee such areas, and the Federal Radio Commission was born in 1927 following a series of hearings before the Senate Commerce Committee. Senator Clarence C. Dill of Washington and Representative Wallace White of Maine sponsored the bill that gave licensing authority over broadcasting to an independent bipartisan commission appointed by the president. Among the Senate Commerce Committee members, the chairman has power over its activities, but the groundwork for telecommunications policy is laid at the subcommittee level.

Having set basic policy through rewrites of the enabling act in 1927, 1934, and 1996, Congress generally does not influence policy or administration through amending bills or new legislation. Members use informal controls over the commissioners appointed to the Federal Communications Commission (FCC); they exercise power over the FCC budget, give advice and consent to all FCC appointees, and control matters by legislative inaction. Committee members maintain a delicate relationship with the broadcasting industry, having to rely on stations and networks for generating support in political campaigns while at the same time protecting the public interest in broadcasting.

Krasnow, Erwin G., Lawrence D. Longley, and Herbert A. Terry. *The Politics of Broadcast Regulation.* 3rd ed. New York: St. Martin's Press, 1982.

William R. Davie

SEQUENCING refers to the order in which airplay music is presented. At stations that follow a hit-oriented format and use a music rotation system, which record is played next is at least partly determined by the rotation level of that song. But even stations with unlimited playlists need a reason for choosing what to play next. Among the most common reasons for either maintaining or changing from one record to the next are: to continue/vary the tempo; to maintain/alter the instrumentation; and to sustain/alter the mood. Layered on top of those decisions is the desire to provide variety in presentation. As a result, there are often also such changes as: from a group vocal to a solo; from vocals to instrumentals; or from one gender of vocalist to the other.

David T. MacFarland

SEVAREID, ARNOLD ERIC (1912–1992), a veteran newsman and commentator, is best known for his 13 years of television commentary on the *CBS Evening News.* He wrote for the University of Minnesota school paper while attending university and became the copy boy for the *Minneapolis Journal* after his graduation in 1935. Hired by E. R. Murrow in 1939, he became one of the Murrow boys. He covered World War II, reporting on the Battle of Britain, the London Blitz, from behind the Russian lines, and D-Day. He was the CBS News Bureau Chief in Washington, D.C. He retired from CBS in 1977 and died in 1992.

Sevareid, Eric. *Not So Wild a Dream.* New York: Atheneum, 1976.

Donald G. Godfrey

SHIPPING AND WIRELESS. Marine communication was the first major market for wireless technology at the beginning of the twentieth century. Radio inventor Guglielmo Marconi was the first to install shipboard stations, followed by Slaby-Arco of Germany and several others. Although seen as a novelty at first by many, the importance of wireless to both commercial and military ships became more evident as wireless was seen to save lives following ship disasters at sea.

The first ships to carry wireless as a permanent installation were British lightships outfitted and operated by Marconi beginning in 1898. Between 1900 and 1901, both the British and Italian navies contracted with Marconi to install wireless apparatus and operators on their ships. At the same time, the large shipping companies of Europe, Great Britain, and America began to install wireless sets on selected ships in their merchant and passenger fleets. The Cunard White Star Line, the Lloyd Steamship Company, the Belgian Mail Packet, and the American Line were among the early users. The United Fruit Company also took an early interest in wireless, seeing the advantage of using radio to coordinate its banana trade between Central and North America. By 1906 it had contracted with de Forest to install wireless on all of its steamships.

In the United States, commercial shipboard radio installations began to increase sharply after the *Titanic* disaster of 1912, rising from 300 to 600 ship stations. Naval installations did not increase much until preparations for U.S. entry into World War I caused the number to rise from 300 to 1,400. Early regulation of radio reflected the mostly marine applications of the technology. The *Wireless Ship Act of 1910* required all steamers with 50 or more persons to have wireless aboard. This act was amended in 1912 to require at least two operators aboard each ship after 1,500 lives were lost on the *Titanic*.

Hancock, Harry E. *Wireless at Sea.* London: Marconi International Marine Communication Company, 1950. Reprint. New York: Arno Press, 1974.

Mayes, Thorn L. *Wireless Communication in the United States: The Early Development of American Radio Operating Companies.* East Greenwich, R.I.: New England Wireless and Steam Museum, Inc., 1989.

Christina S. Drale

SHIRER, WILLIAM L. (1904–1993), reporter for CBS Radio, author of numerous books, both fiction and fact, with emphasis on World War II Germany. One of "Murrow's Boys," William L. Shirer was born in Chicago. He moved into the world of reporting following his schooling at Coe College in Iowa. He went to Germany in 1925 and spent 35 years as a reporter, commentator, and historian. He worked for Hearst's Universal News Service in Europe. When Edward R. Murrow was assigned by Paul White to head CBS News—to put together a radio news team to cover the events occurring in Europe—he drew people from other media. When Hearst shut down Universal Service, Shirer was let go and Murrow grabbed him immediately. With his extensive experience and background and already 10 years in Germany, he was a natural choice. It was Shirer's change of jobs that enabled him to be in Vienna on the night of March 11–12, 1938, when Austria ceased to exist as Chancellor Kurt von Schuschnigg bowed out before Hitler's threats and violence, and ill-prepared Nazi armies poured across the Austrian border to complete the *Anschluss*. Shirer fought his way through singing Nazi crowds to the unofficial headquarters for foreign correspondents, the Café Louvre. There he learned that the Nazi's had taken over the foreign ministry. Nothing but controlled news could be sent out of Vienna, it was clear. Shirer phoned Murrow, who was in

Warsaw that night, and was told to go to London to prepare for a broadcast the following night. He continued covering Germany and other parts of the European theater throughout World War II.

He kept diaries throughout his experience, and it was from these notes on the history of the times and ultimate access to both Nazi and Allied documents that he was able to write his books, most of them concerning Germany and the events of the war. Prime among them was the book *The Rise and Fall of the Third Reich,* a history of Nazi Germany, published in 1959. Other books were *Berlin Diary,* published in 1941, *End of a Berlin Diary, Midcentury Journey, The Challenge of Scandinavia,* and three works of fiction, *The Traitor, Stranger Come Home,* and *The Consul's Wife.* He spent five and a half years sifting through documents of the Third Reich and the Allied countries to compile his history of the Nazi regime as well as using his personal notes. He continued some broadcasting for CBS, mostly commentary, following the end of the war in Europe. He split most of his later years between New York and a country home in Connecticut and lectured.

Hohenberg, John. *Foreign Correspondence: The Great Reporters and Their Times.* New York: Columbia University Press, 1964.
Shirer, William L. *Berlin Diary: The Journal of a Foreign Correspondent, 1934–1941.* New York: Knopf, 1940, 1941. Reprint, New York: Galahad Books, 1995.
Shirer, William L. *The Rise and Fall of the Third Reich.* New York: Simon and Schuster, 1960.

ElDean Bennett

SHORTWAVE. The discovery that short waves (a combination of waves' nature plus their refraction by the ionosphere), from 15 to 60 meters, could be received over long distances was a great step forward for intercontinental communication. During the 1920s, shortwave came into its own along with radio broadcasting in general. Transmitters became more powerful and stable, and AT&T and RCA were seriously involved in shortwave.

During World War II shortwave thrived with both propaganda and more objective information. The British Broadcasting Corporation (BBC) had started broadcasts in 1932 to reach all areas of the vast British empire. By the end of the war the BBC World Service was broadcasting in 45 languages. Today the estimated audience is 140 million. In the United States the Voice of America, founded in 1942, broadcasts around the world as an agency of the United States Information Agency, providing most familiar radio formats.

William F. Lyon

SIMULCASTING, the *simul*taneous broad*casting* of program material via similar or dissimilar transmission channels. The term most commonly applies to duplicating AM radio programming by colocated FM stations. AM-FM simulcasting was widely implemented by duopoly licensees in the 1950s and 1960s when independently programmed FM stations failed to achieve profitability. Experiments in stereophonic transmission via AM-FM and FM-TV simulcasting were conducted in the 1950s prior to the introduction of FM multiplex in 1962. Similarly, FM stations occasionally were utilized to simulcast stereo audio for television prior to the development of two-channel sound for that medium.

"Broadcasting for Both Ears." *Business Week* (February 28, 1959): 27.

Federal Communications Commission. *Report and Order in the Matter of Amendment of Part 73 of the Commission's Rules, Regarding AM Station Assignment and the Relationship between the AM and FM Services.* Washington, D.C.: 45 FCC Reports 1515, 1964.

Bruce Mims

SIXTH REPORT AND ORDER, the 1952 Order of the Federal Communications Commission (FCC) that lifted the television licensing freeze in effect since 1948, assigned television channels to specific communities throughout the country, and reserved certain channels for noncommercial educational use.

Although legally authorized since 1939, television in the United States did not generate much interest until after the end of World War II. By 1948 there were 108 television stations on the air, and many more applications for stations were on file at the commission. At that time, only 12 VHF frequencies (channels 2–13) were assigned to the television broadcast service, and the FCC soon realized that additional spectrum would be needed to fill the growing demand for television stations. Accordingly, in 1948, the FCC "froze" all television licensing while determining what additional spectrum to allocate to television and how to assign individual channels.

After four years of study, the commission adopted its *Sixth Report and Order* in this proceeding. It not only lifted the television licensing freeze, but also, in order to meet the need for additional spectrum, allocated the UHF band (channels 14–83) to the television service. Instead of assigning television channels on an ad hoc basis based on individual interference studies (as is done with AM radio assignments), the FCC chose to create a table of assignments in which specific channels were assigned to specific communities based on standard mileage separation criteria. This assignment scheme allowed for predictable and fair distribution of television channels across the country. In the *Sixth Report and Order,* 2,053 channels were assigned to 1,291 different communities. Assignments were made according to the following set of priorities: (1) provide at least one television service to all parts of the United States; (2) provide each community with at least one television station; (3) provide a choice of at least two television services to all parts of the country; (4) provide each community with at least two television stations; and (5) assign additional channels to various communities depending on their size, geographical location, and number of television services available in those communities. This Table of Allocations, while amended many times, is still in effect today. FM radio channel assignments are handled in the same way.

In order to facilitate the growth of noncommercial educational broadcasting, the FCC reserved 242 of the assigned channels for use only by noncommercial, educational licensees. Some observers view this action as crucial to the ultimate survival of noncommercial television in the United States.

Although the *Sixth Report and Order* promoted orderly distribution of television channels across the country, there were negative effects. The FCC chose to "intermix" VHF and UHF channels in many markets. Because UHF transmission quality was inferior to VHF, this put UHF broadcasters at a serious competitive disadvantage in those markets. Also, the commission's assignment of VHF frequencies very nearly guaranteed that only three national networks would prosper; not enough markets were assigned a fourth VHF frequency to support a fourth national network. This factor is often cited as a contributing cause of the demise of the Dumont Television Network.

Besen, Stanley M., Thomas G. Krattenmaker, A. Richard Metzger, and John R. Woodbury. *Misregulating Television: Network Dominance and the FCC.* Chicago: University of Chicago Press, 1984.

Sixth Report and Order in Docket 8736, 41 F.C.C. 148, 17 Fed. Reg. 3905 (1952).

Michael A. McGregor

SKIP PHENOMENON. *See* **sky wave.**

SKLAR, RICK (1930–1992), refined the controlled playlist programming strategy of top-40 radio into the tight playlist tactics of "all-hits radio" format. His mechanistic approach to programming reduced the role of the disk jockey to that of an announcer and set the precedent for much of today's tightly formatted music radio programming. As program director at WABC-AM (New York), his innovative programming (combined with intense local promotion tied to local schools) led WABC-AM to the top of New York radio for much of the 1960s, claiming one quarter of the listeners in the largest radio market.

Fornatale, Peter, and Joshua Mills. *Radio in the Television Age.* Woodstock, N.Y.: Overlook Press, 1980.

Sklar, Rick. *Rocking America: An Insider's Story.* New York: St. Martin's Press, 1984.

Smith, Wes. *The Pied Pipers of Rock 'n' Roll.* Marietta, Ga.: Longstreet Press, 1989.

Jonathan David Tankel

SKY WAVE, clear channel AM broadcast signals transmitted at 50,000 watts that reflect off the Kennelly-Heavyside layer (a portion of the ionosphere cooled and therefore more dense at night from lack of sunlight) and returned to earth hundreds of miles away from the station. This is called the skip phenomenon. Sky waves make it possible to hear distant AM stations late at night. Sky waves fade and intensify, so reception does, too. In the early days of radio, listeners "dial-twisted" at night to receive distant broadcasts. This exciting radio adventure is still possible. Try tuning to Class 1-A clear channel frequencies that include 640 KFI (Los Angeles), 650 WSM (Nashville), 710 KIRO (Seattle), 720 WGN (Chicago), 750 WSB (Atlanta), 760 WJR (Detroit), 770 WABC (New York), 820 WBAP (Ft. Worth), 830 WCCO (Minneapolis), 840 WHAS (Louisville), 870 WWl (New Orleans), 880 WCBS (New York), 890 WLS (Chicago), 1020 KDKA (Pittsburgh), 1030 WBZ (Boston), 1040 WHO (Des Moines), 1100 WWWE (Cleveland), 1120 KMOX (St. Louis), 1160 KSL (Salt Lake City), 1180 WHAM (Rochester, New York), 1190 WOWO (Ft. Wayne, Indiana), 1200 WOAI (San Antonio), 1210 WGMP (Philadelphia), and 1530 WCKY (Cincinnati).

Charles F. Aust

SLANDER. *See* **libel and slander.**

SMITH, ALFRED EMANUEL (1873–1944), governor of New York and Democratic Party presidential candidate in 1928, was born on December 30, 1873, in New York City. Smith was elected to the state assembly in 1903 and became speaker of the assembly in 1913. He helped write new labor codes protecting factory workers, earning a reputation as a social reformer. In 1918 Smith was elected governor. After losing reelection in 1920, he won again in 1922, 1924, and 1926.

Smith was a candidate for the Democratic Party presidential nomination in 1924 but lost to John W. Davis. In 1928 he won the nomination but lost the election to Herbert Hoover. Smith's loss was blamed on his opposition to prohibition, his Roman Catholicism, and the nation's general economic prosperity.

Although Smith campaigned with the new medium of radio, he was hurt politically by his unwillingness or inability to speak to broadcast audiences with a less affected New York accent. For example, he pronounced "radio" as "raddio" and "hospital" as "horspital." Smith sought the Democratic Party nomination in 1932, but lost it to Franklin Roosevelt. He campaigned for Roosevelt but opposed the New Deal. In 1936 Smith supported Republican Party candidate Alf Landon and, in 1940, GOP nominee Wendell Willkie.

Smith oversaw construction of the Empire State Building and served as its corporation president. In his final years he also was heavily involved in fund raising for charities, including the American Red Cross, United Services Organization, and Catholic Charities. Smith died on October 4, 1944.

Handlin, Oscar. *Al Smith and His America.* Boston: Little, Brown and Company, 1958.
Smith, Alfred E. *Up to Now: An Autobiography.* New York: Viking Press, 1929.
Warner, Emily Smith, with Hawthorne Daniel. *The Happy Warrior: A Biography of My Father, Alfred E. Smith.* Garden City, N.Y.: Doubleday and Company, Inc., 1956.

Robert C. Fordan

SMITH, HOWARD KINGSBURY, JR. (1914–), was a pioneering newsman and commentator. He was born in Ferriday, Louisiana, but his family moved to New Orleans, where he spent his growing years. He was a 1936 honors graduate of Tulane University. Fluent in both German and French, Smith studied in Europe and was enrolled at Oxford until World War II broke out, when he took a job with United Press in London. He was one of the Murrow boys who gained his reputation as a reporter during World War II. His 20-year career with CBS came to an end in 1961, when he and William Paley disagreed over the handling of editorial matters. *Howard K. Smith—News and Comment* debuted on February 14, 1962, on ABC, where he remained until 1979. He retired to his home in Maryland on the Potomac River.

Cloud, Stanley, and Lynne Olsen. *The Murrow Boys: Pioneers on the Front Lines of Broadcast Journalism.* New York: Houghton Mifflin, 1996.

Donald G. Godfrey

SOAP OPERA. *See* **advertising, history of; Berg, Gertrude; Golden Age of Radio; Hummert, Anne and Frank; Phillips, Irna; programming; World War II and radio.**

SOCIETY OF PROFESSIONAL JOURNALISTS. *See* **SPJ.**

SOFT ROCK, the precursor to adult contemporary or contemporary adult, the soft-rock radio format featured quiet rock tunes popular within the past few years. Soft rock became popular during the 1970s, when FM stations were on the rise. According to Michael Keith, soft rock finds its origins in the "chicken rock" stations of the 1960s, so named because they were too "chicken" to play rock 'n' roll, instead only playing softer tunes from the pop rock genre. "Chicken rock," a product of AM, served as the forerunner of mellow rock, an alternative to heavier rock formats, which developed on FM stations. Young adult listeners looked to mellow rock as an alternative to the increasing number of heavier rock stations. According to Keith, as the term *mellow,* a throwback to the psychedelic culture of the late 1960s, became outdated, this type of music became known as soft rock during the mid-1970s. Unlike mellow rock, the soft-rock format included more mainstream standards. With the late 1970s came disco and the renewed popularity of hit music formats and the decline of soft-rock audiences. Eventually, soft rock evolved into the adult contemporary format of the 1980s and 1990s.

Howard, Herbert H., Michael S. Kievman, and Barbara Moore. *Radio, TV, and Cable Programming.* 2nd ed. Ames: Iowa State University Press, 1994.
Keith, Michael C. *Radio Programming: Consultancy and Formatics.* Boston: Focal Press, 1987.

Erika Engstrom

SOS. *See* **World War I and radio.**

SOUL MUSIC is a derivative of rhythm and blues. The term *soul music* originated with jazz musicians of the mid-1950s, who coined the phrase to explain their return to their musical roots. Singer Ray Charles, however, is often credited with popularizing this unique blend of rhythm and blues and gospel music that became known as soul. Charles's recordings of "I Gotta Woman," which was based on the black religious tune "My Jesus Is All the World to Me," and his "What'd I Say" used gospel and rhythm and blues to create these hit songs. For example, in the latter song, Charles used moans, screams, sexual innuendo, and the piano as it's played in church to attract listeners. Moreover, "What'd I Say" used the religious fervor of call and response and combined it with the sexual expressionism of rhythm and blues.

Soul music became immensely popular among audiences all over the world. Singers such as James Brown, Aretha Franklin, The Supremes, Issac Hayes, Stevie Wonder, The Temptations, Teddy Pendergrass, Smokey Robinson, and Gladys Knight all produced best-selling albums and singles that combined elements of blues, rhythm and blues, and gospel to create soul music. The Motown sound, Stax

Records in Memphis, and Philadelphia International Records (PIR) all used tambourines, hand clapping, the "backbeat," call-and-response phrasings, and "rhythmic repetition" to create soul music.

In addition, soul music differed from blues as it placed emphasis on the first-person plural rather than singular. Vocalists have dominated soul music. Soul music performers demanded audience involvement, in much the same way as gospel singers. The vocal call-and-responses replaced the "brass riffs" of blues and rhythm and blues, which are used to produce countermelodies.

Finally, soul music employed falsetto screams and melisma, testifying, and the emotional preaching style of many African-American ministers.

Floyd, Samuel A. *The Power of Black Music.* New York: Oxford University Press, 1995.

Haralambos, Michael. *Right on: From Blues to Soul in Black America.* New York: Drake Publishers, 1975.

Shaw, Arnold. *The World of Soul; Black America's Contribution to the Pop Music Scene.* New York: Cowles Book Co., 1970.

Gilbert A. Williams

SPECTRUM, sometimes called the electromagnetic spectrum or the radio spectrum, refers to the frequencies used for the transmission of a signal from one point to another. The abstract concept of the spectrum was first introduced in 1822 by Jean-Baptiste Fourier. It was decades before James Clerk Maxwell published an article suggesting that a signal could be sent electromagnetically using the spectrum. It was not until 1888 that Heinrich Hertz physically tested and proved Fourier's and Maxwell's theories. In 1895, Guglielmo Marconi began his experiments in "wireless" communication, which led to the use of the spectrum as a means of communication for ship-to-shore telegraph and later to "radiotelephony," or sending voice messages by wireless.

The use of spectrum is regulated by international agreement. The International Telecommunications Union (ITU) oversees the allocation of the spectrum worldwide. The ITU conducts radio conferences periodically to discuss allocation and reassignment of frequencies. World Administrative Radio Conferences used to be conducted every four years but have recently moved to a two-year cycle. In addition, there are Regional Administrative Radio Conferences, involving only nations in a particular region—the United States belongs to Region II (essentially the Western Hemisphere).

The allocation of spectrum for nongovernmental uses in the United States has been handled by the Federal Communications Commission (FCC) since its creation in 1934. Prior to that, the secretary of commerce was responsible for assigning frequencies. When radio stations were first licensed in 1920, a single frequency was authorized. In 1921, the number of applications had risen to warrant a second frequency. In 1922, a third frequency was made available. Finally in 1923, Commerce Secretary Herbert Hoover stated the need for a new allocation system with more frequencies for broadcasting. After years of deliberations, Congress finally responded with the *Radio Act of 1927,* followed by the *Communications Act in 1934.*

Since 1927, the allocation of spectrum for AM radio broadcasting has remained essentially unchanged. The band (535 kilohertz to 1605 kilohertz) allows for 107 different channels, which the FCC has assigned to more than 4,000 different stations. In 1979, the AM band was expanded up to 1,705 kilohertz, allowing for another 10 channels.

On the other hand, FM allocations were radically changed. In 1940, the FCC established 42 to 50 megahertz as the band for FM broadcasting. In 1945, the FCC shifted FM's allocations to its current assignment at 88 to 108 megahertz. While this more than doubled the channels available (from 40 to 100), it also made every existing FM receiver obsolete and required retuning every existing transmitter.

Television spectrum was designed for 19 VHF channels as early as 1937. By the end of the freeze in 1952, the FCC had taken back Channel 1 (currently used for amateur radio), relocated many of the VHF frequencies, and assigned channels 14 to 83 as UHF television frequencies. The most significant reassignment of television spectrum since 1952 came in 1983, when the FCC removed UHF Channels 70 to 83 and reassigned that spectrum for landmobile use.

Dom Caristi

SPERDVAC. *See* **old-time radio (OTR).**

SPJ (SOCIETY OF PROFESSIONAL JOURNALISTS) is the largest journalism professional organization in the United States. SPJ has approximately 14,000 members. The organization was founded in 1909 as Sigma Delta Chi by 10 students at DePauw University. The organization was created as a college journalism honorary society, but soon professional chapters developed around the nation. SPJ is a not-for-profit organization. It promotes First Amendment rights of the free press and high standards of ethical conduct in journalism. The society provides career services and sponsors a national awards program. It publishes the *QUILL,* a magazine that addresses current issues in journalism.

Society of Professional Journalists. http://www.SPJ.org/

Jeffrey M. McCall

SPORTS RADIO FORMAT. One of radio's talk formats, sports is a major subset of general talk radio, handled by telephone with the listeners playing a large part in the programming of a station. Sports broadcasting began with two major forms of programs: first, news reporting as a special topic, either as part of a regular newscast or as a sports news program; second, direct sporting events broadcasting from their venue. KDKA in Pittsburgh included sports among the first programs in its first year of operation. Baseball and boxing were among the earliest sports covered by direct broadcast; NBC and David Sarnoff used the Dempsey-Carpentier match to lure people to the network. A number of outstanding sports voices were developed (i.e., Mel Allen, Red Barber, and Harry Carey). Most early reporters had not been participants in sports but were sports enthusiasts who turned to radio. Eventually, "ex-jocks," retired sports figures, got into the business but, without any radio background, left much to be desired. They became more successful when television arrived, and they could be recognized as "stars" in a sport rather than as broadcasters. One radio figure was "old number 98" Tom Harmon, who had been a football star at the University of Michigan and a World War II aviator hero. But he was largely limited to sports news reporting. Major sports news broadcasts included CBS's *Sports Time,* a five-minute report that covered the country and was one of the most concise and best produced.

Networks vie each year for rights to the big sporting events: the World Series, Super Bowl, New Year's Day Bowl games and others. Even television has not really diminished the radio coverage of such events. But most sports play-by-play is now done on a local station basis, with a station covering a local team.

In the 1960s, talk radio began across the country, using a telephone and making the audience a part of the show through participation via telephone calls. Sports quickly became one of the most popular subjects. Soon, special programs for talk radio were created around sports. On-air personalities fielded questions and engaged in discussion of sports with the public who were on the telephone. On given days, a topic will be established for the discussions. Other times, it is anything goes, with the caller able to choose the topic and ask the question.

The listener is rarely allowed much time to give opinions on the topic under discussion. The format is structured to allow the on-air person to display his or her knowledge and background in sports history, records, anecdotes, and so on. Occasional guests from the world of sports frequently sit in, joining in the talk, usually on their sport.

One of the early "talk" markets was Boston, and sports talk got a strong beginning there with the strong professional lineup of sports: the Celtics, the Bruins, the Red Sox, and the many colleges located in the greater Boston area. CBS's station WEEI was one of the pioneers of this form of broadcasting. The format consists of a producer who fields calls, screening out the nonacceptable callers, and the specialist who performs in the studio, on air. It is a relatively inexpensive form of programming, and the dialogue is at once interesting, and compelling, attracting listeners in large numbers.

Bergreen, Laurence. *Look Now, Pay Later. The Rise of Network Broadcasting.* Garden City, N.Y.: Doubleday, 1980.

ElDean Bennett

SPOT LOAD, the number of commercials played in a given hour, evolved slowly from loads calculated in minutes of airtime to the number of actual commercials (units) played. Throughout the 1950s and into the mid-1960s, little concern was given to spot loads as stations opted for selling and airing as many commercials as possible. This attitude altered in the latter half of the 1960s as in-format competition intensified, music lists began to shorten, and ratings pressure led to concerns over quarter-hour maintenance. The general acceptance of the concept of "inventory control" allowed programmers and managers to develop unit limits rather than time limits.

Eastman, Susan Tyler, and Douglas A. Ferguson. *Broadcast/Cable Programming: Strategies and Practices.* 2nd ed. Belmont, Calif.: Wadsworth, 1985.

Michael Taylor

SPOT RATE, the price charged per commercial aired. Setting spot rates involves careful calculation of the station's total costs, the market's tolerance for pricing, and the station's available inventory. The simple formula for initial rate development is dividing total costs by inventory to determine the required average unit rate to maintain station profitability. This simple formula assumes all inventory being sold out so adjustments are made for: (1) the desirability of inventory; (2) the historical success rate of the station's sales team; (3) a factor for projected success required for break-even operations; and (4) the competitive nature of the market regarding advertising revenue.

O'Donnell, Lewis B., Carl Hausman, and Philip Benoit. *Radio Station Operations: Management and Employee Perspectives.* Belmont, Calif.: Wadsworth, 1989.

Michael Taylor

SPOT SETS, the organization of commercial units into clusters, were common for good-music formatted stations during the 1950s, and their adoption by other mass appeal formats such as top 40 began in the early 1960s with the rise of formatting using hot clocks to control song placement. The idea of placing commercials into preordered points within the sound hour also took hold and led to prioritizing spot sets for load order within the hour. Breaks one and three would fill before breaks two and six, and so on. This load priority system also led to the refinement of making certain breaks "stop sets," which would stop the music regardless of commercial loading while the remaining sets would be music stops only if filled with commercial content.

Michael Taylor

STANDARD AM/FM BROADCAST BANDS. AM is a range of frequencies from 535 to 1,705 kilohertz (kHz), and FM includes all frequencies between 88.0 and 108.0 megahertz (MHz). AM includes 117 channels, each with a 10-kHz bandwidth, beginning at 540 and continuing through 1,700 kHz. By 1997 there were approximately 4,854 stations in America operating on channels within this band of frequencies. FM includes 100 channels, each with a 200-kHz bandwidth, beginning at 88.1 MHz and continuing through 107.9 MHz. The portion of the FM band between 88.0 and 92.0 MHz is reserved for noncommercial broadcasting. By 1997 there were approximately 5,429 commercial stations and 1,868 noncommercial stations on the FM band.

Steven C. Runyon

STANTON, FRANK (1908–), was the president of the CBS network from 1946 to 1973. He began his career in the Office of Radio Research at Princeton University. There Stanton worked with Paul F. Lazersfield and Hadley Cantril organizing some of the first major publications regarding audience research. He was fundamentally an academic, with his Ph.D. from Ohio State. His specialization was social psychology.

At CBS, Stanton was the number-two figure; William Paley made the policy decisions, and Stanton executed them. Research and polling remained important to his administration. Stanton was an outspoken proponent of the broadcast industry during his tenure at CBS. He retired in 1973, to head the American Red Cross.

Donald G. Godfrey

STATION REPRESENTATIVE (REP), the advertising firm that represents radio stations in the sale of commercial time to national and geographic advertisers. Station reps may also advise stations on programming and audience research (see **advertising**).

Frederic A. Leigh

STATIONS are Federal Communications Commission (FCC)–licensed facilities operated to broadcast radio signals over the air on an assigned frequency. Stations are identified as either AM, FM, or shortwave and are distinguished in part by the specific modulation techniques employed (amplitude or frequency modulation) and the allocated frequency band (medium, high, or very high). The assigned bandwidth as well as signal propagation characteristics associated with the frequency band further characterize each service in terms of coverage range and signal quality. Stations are also defined as commercial (carrying commercial messages for compensation) and noncommercial.

There are approximately 12,000 radio stations in the United States. Experimental AM radio stations first appeared before the 1920s, with the first official radio license being issued to WBZ, Springfield, Massachusetts, on September 15, 1921. FM emerged from its experimental stage before World War II. The number of stations has generally increased over the years, with a slight downtrend for AM in the 1930s and a downtrend for FM in the 1950s as it struggled with becoming established. AM experienced rapid growth from the late 1940s to the early 1970s. FM has grown steadily since the late 1950s. Noncommercial stations have shown moderate, yet steady, growth since the early 1940s.

By the end of 1992, the number of commercial FM stations had grown to equal the number of commercial AM stations at over 5,000 stations each. An increase in the AM band from 1,605 kilohertz (kHz) to 1,705 kHz became effective in the early 1990s but did little to increase the number of AM stations since the frequencies were assigned to existing stations and were initially simulcast. During 1993, the total number of stations dropped, but by 1995, the number of commercial FM stations and noncommercial stations had again increased, while the number of commercial AM stations continued to decline. By 1996, there were slightly more than 1,800 noncommercial stations, 5,200 FM stations, and 4,900 AM stations. There are very few shortwave operations in the United States, limited primarily to evangelistic-religious outlets broadcasting to foreign audiences.

The 1990s is marked as a period of station consolidations. The early 1990s were difficult economically, and many stations turned to LMAs (local marketing agreements), while the FCC struck down its station ownership duopoly rule. Later, deregulation under the *Telecommunications Act of 1996* spurred a radio station–buying spree, stimulating the market along with a considerable boost in advertising revenues. The act eliminated the national ownership limit and raised the limits on ownership within a market. In markets with 45 or more stations, there is an eight-station ownership limit, with a maximum of five being either FM or AM; in markets with 30 to 44 stations, a seven-station limit with only four FMs or AMs; in markets with 15 to 29 stations, six, with only four FMs or AMs; and in markets with 14 or less, five, and no more than three FMs or AMs. The 1990s has also seen a marked increase in the number of news, talk, and news/talk stations. The number of Spanish-language stations has also increased dramatically.

Broadcasting & Cable Yearbook. New Providence, N.J.: Reed Reference, 1996.

Laurie Thomas Lee

STEREOPHONIC SOUND is three-dimensional, allowing a listener to note the spatial extent of sound. Stereo was sought for electronic communication quite simply because human beings hear with two ears. The first attempt to broadcast in stereo took place in 1925 at WPAY-AM in New Haven, Connecticut. One channel of the station's audio was broadcast on one AM frequency, and another channel was broadcast over a separate frequency, or AM-AM. Other similar unsuccessful attempts at stereocasting were tried using the two-frequency, transmitter, or station approach: AM-FM, FM-FM, TV-AM. The stereo popularity boom began in earnest in the 1950s, when stereo tape and stereo discs (records) were introduced for public consumption. The tremendous popularity of stereo records gave rise to consumer demand and the motivation to move toward stereo broadcasting.

The Federal Communications Commission (FCC) approved FM stereo in 1961 but did not allow AM stereo until 1982. However, the AM stereo decision was a historic departure from the FCC's 50-year tradition of standard setting. For the first time ever, the FCC decided not to set a system standard, opting only to police technical parameters. In other words, any system could be employed as long as it met certain operating requirements. Without a standard system around which stations, manufacturers, and consumers could rally, the AM stereo marketplace created confusion, uncertainty, and chaos. Ultimately, AM stereo lost most of its industry and consumer support. The FCC finally made Motorola's C-QUAM system the AM stereo system standard in 1993 but only after a congressional mandate.

Grant, August E. *Communications Technology Update.* 3rd ed. Boston: Focal Press, 1994.
Sunier, John. *The Story of Stereo: 1881–.* New York: Gernsback Library, Inc., 1960.
Talbot-Smith, Michael. *Broadcast Sound Technology.* Boston: Focal Press, 1990.

W. A. Kelly Huff

STERN, HOWARD (1954–), "shock-jock" whose syndicated morning radio program has caused controversy due to his use of "indecent" language. Stern is the son of Ben and Ray Stern and was born in Queens, New York. Ben Stern worked as a radio engineer at WHOM, which later became WKTU. Howard's first interest in radio was spawned at an early age. He attended Roosevelt High School in Long Island, New York. Howard attended the Boston University School of Communication, where he graduated with honors in 1976. His first appearance on the radio was at the college station. His first job in radio was at WNTN-AM Boston, where he worked as the daytime host in a progressive rock format. Stern moved from station to station working at WCCC, Hartford, Connecticut; DC-101FM, Washington, D.C.; and WNBC, New York. He and his wife Alison have three daughters. His autobiography *Howard Stern: Private Parts* was a best seller in 1994 and was turned into the successful movie *Private Parts* in 1997.

Stern's style as a "shock jock" combines profanity, sexual references, and an argumentative uncooperative narrative style with a "nothing is sacred, no holds barred" approach to talk radio. It is a style that has him at continual odds with the Federal Communications Commission (FCC). Stern and his syndication company, Infinity, have been fined nearly $2 million by the FCC for indecency on the radio (see also **indecency**). In 1996, CBS/Westinghouse purchased Infinity and Stern's radio program. While the program has been highly rated in the 39 radio markets, where it was sold as of 1997, expansion into other markets has been slow due to concerns about high cost and controversial content. Still, Howard Stern has proclaimed himself to be the "King of All Media."

Broadcasting & Cable 127 (9) (March 3, 1997), p. 39.
Broadcasting & Cable 127 (24) (June 9, 1997), p. 23.
Stern, Howard. *Howard Stern: Private Parts*. New York: Pocket Books, 1994.

Frederic A. Leigh

STOP SET, a break in radio programming allowing for the broadcast of commercials and other station-related announcements.

Frederic A. Leigh

STORZ, TODD (1924–1964), was one of the pioneers of top-40 radio. He first implemented the format at station KOWH-AM in Omaha, which he purchased in 1949. Twenty-five years old at the time, Storz converted the independent station from a polyglot format to one concentrating strictly on popular music. Within two years, the station rose from sixth place to first in the market's ratings. Storz's Mid-Continent Broadcasting Company used the Omaha formula at stations it purchased in New Orleans (WTIX), Kansas City (WHB), Minneapolis (WDGY), Miami (WQAM), St. Louis (KXOK), and Oklahoma City (KOMA).

The basis for Storz's radio programming strategy was repetition of the country's top-40 tunes. Storz used local jukeboxes, sheet music, record sales, and trade journals to determine popularity. He explained in a 1957 interview, "The programming of music is out of our hands. It is controlled entirely by the choice of the public. If the public suddenly showed a preference for Chinese music, we would play it" (Land, p. 86). Storz's stations supplemented the music with short news reports and frequent station identifications. In addition, they hired personable disc jockeys who actively promoted the station and its music.

In 1956, *Time* magazine dubbed Storz "The King of Giveaway" because of his aggressive promotions. Storz's stations staged citywide buried treasure hunts, awarding over $100,000 to the winners. The Federal Communications Commission (FCC) criticized Mid-Continent Broadcasting for attempting to purchase the listening audience, but it did not formally regulate the giveaways. Mid-Continent stations also ran Lucky House Number contests, in which a street address was announced on the air, and if the occupant called the station within minutes, he or she won a prize. In 1957, Storz was earning $600 a week from other broadcasters who had taken out licenses to use his copyrighted promotion.

By the time Storz died in 1964, there were hundreds of top-40 stations, modeled on the formula established by Storz, Gordon McLendon, and a handful of other broadcasters.

"King of Giveaway." *Time* (June 4, 1956): 100–102.
Land, Herman. "The Storz Bombshell." *Television* (May 1957): 85–92.
MacFarland, David T. *The Development of the Top 40 Radio Format.* New York: Arno Press, 1979.

David Weinstein

SUBLIMINAL AUDIO, any sound listened to below the conscious level. Commonly referred to as radio's "background" dimension, it is received without the listener being fully aware of the reception. The sound may have been initially received as conscious sound, then moved without deliberation to subliminal reception. Such is the case when a person wakes up to the radio on the alarm clock, then proceeds to get dressed. Initially lying in bed, that person may listen intently to the deejay, the music, the weather, or the news. But as that person gets out of bed to search for clothes to put on and thinks about upcoming events for the day, the sounds of the radio may become subliminal, moved to the background of the person's attention. What is notable about the shift between foreground audio and background, or subliminal audio, is that the volume of the audio can remain constant while the shift takes place. There is some debate about whether subliminal audio information is received and stored in a listener's memory to the same extent as foreground audio. However, subliminal audio does not cease to exist in the listener's mind; it simply operates at a level below the listener's foreground attention. While music formats tend to operate more consistently as subliminal audio, nonmusic formats (news, talk, sports) tend to operate more consistently as foreground audio. Advertisements sometimes are heard by listeners as foreground audio and other times are received as background audio.

McKenzie, Robert. "Are We Really Giving Today's Aural Age the Hearing It Deserves?" *Feedback* 36 (4) (1996): 25–28.
Shane, Ed. "Radio and Subliminal Timekeeping." *Feedback* 35 (1) (winter 1994): 1–3.

Robert McKenzie

SUBSIDIARY COMMUNICATIONS AUTHORIZATIONS (SCAs), officially changed to Subsidiary Communications Services, are ancillary services available on radio and television allocations or frequencies. These signals are part of the bandwidth assigned to stations but carry inaudible signals to special receivers. AM stations may multiplex services such as automatic commands from central locations to turn off appliances. Television stations can offer additional services on their vertical blanking interval (VBI). Television subcarrier rules were liberalized in 1984. Originally, FM stations could only offer SCAs, or subcarriers, for broadcast services like Muzak. These services were expanded by the Federal Communications Commission (FCC) in 1983 to allow FM stations to offer additional services, and the FM base band was expanded to 99 kilohertz (KHz) from 67 KHz. One subcarrier is used for stereo broadcasting; the other two can be used for paging or other services. Specifically, noncommercial FM stations could use their SCAs for remunerative services (BC Docket 82–1), a decision by the FCC to assist noncommercial stations to be self-supporting. One concern expressed at the time was the impact such provisions would have on the delivery of reading services by noncommercial stations. The ability of these services to compete with profit-oriented options was expressed. Additional modifications were made in the rules to affect commercial FM stations in 1984. One problem with this service is its limitation for targeted signals only. Other services also authorized in 1983 included a set aside for three channels dedicated to long-distance paging.

Bolter, Walter G., ed. *Telecommunications Policy for the 1980s: The Transition to Competition.* Englewood Cliffs, N.J.: Prentice-Hall, 1984.

Eastman, S. "Policy Issues Raised by the FCC's 1983 and 1984 Subcarrier Decisions." *Journal of Broadcasting* 28 (3) (summer 1984): 289–303.

Ginsburg, D. H., M. H. Botein, and M. D. Director. *Regulation of the Electronic Mass Media.* St. Paul: West Publishing Co., 1991.

Head, Sydney W. *Broadcasting in America.* 3rd ed. Boston: Houghton Mifflin, 1976.

Wenmouth Williams, Jr.

SUPERHETERODYNE RECEIVER uses a combination of regeneration and heterodyne principles to produce a sensitive tuner of weak signals. The superheterodyne was invented by Edwin Armstrong in 1918. The principle of regeneration, developed by Armstrong in 1912, provides the vacuum-tube receiver with a more powerful means of amplification. The signal from the plate circuit is fed back into the grid via an oscillating wing circuit; this causes the signal to be amplified continuously. The heterodyne principle was first developed by Reginald Fessenden in 1901. A high-frequency radio wave can be mixed with another wave of a slightly lower frequency, producing a third "beat" wave oscillating at a frequency that is the difference of the two and that can be made audible. Armstrong combined these two ideas to produce a receiver that heterodyned ultrahigh frequencies to produce a beat wave and then used a regenerative circuit to amplify the new wave signal before feeding it to an audio circuit and loudspeaker.

Lewis, Thomas S. W. *Empire of the Air: The Men Who Made Radio.* New York: HarperCollins Publishers, 1991.

Christina S. Drale

SUPREME COURT, UNITED STATES, has played a vital role in the development of radio as well as other media. While the Court can exercise both original and appellate jurisdiction, it is primarily an appellate court. Under this jurisdiction, the Court reviews cases from lower federal courts and from state supreme courts when those cases relate to questions of federal law.

While the number of its members has varied over its history, the U.S. Supreme Court now consists of nine justices, one of whom is the Chief Justice of the United

States. Considered "first among equals," the opinion of the Chief Justice carries no more weight than those of any of the eight associate justices. Any added power that the Chief Justice has is primarily in the administrative realm—leading deliberations and, to some extent, assigning which justice will write case opinions.

When vacancies occur on the Court, the president nominates a replacement, who then requires approval of the U.S. Senate. Although it has occurred three times in history—most recently with William Rehnquist in 1986—associate justices are not typically elevated to Chief Justice. Instead, individuals from outside the Court are nominated. The nominating and approval processes have the potential to be politically charged.

Cases come to the Supreme Court as direct appeals through a "writ of certiorari" filed by an attorney representing one side or the other. Only when at least four justices vote to hear a case—granting the petition of certiorari—is it heard. Fewer than 5 percent of all petitions are granted. When a petition is denied, the most recent lower court ruling stands. While justices rarely disclose the reasons for a petition being granted or denied, it is generally thought that the circumstances of a case must encompass significant constitutional issues before acceptance is considered.

Once a case is granted review, it is scheduled for written and oral arguments. Attorneys are expected to submit legal briefs to the Court so the justices can study them prior to hearing the case. The attorneys for each side are provided 30 minutes each to present their case publicly before the justices in the Supreme Court's courtroom in Washington, D.C. These "oral arguments" often contain "give and take" between the justices and the lawyer. Usually within a few days, the justices hold closed conferences to discuss the merits of each case, to further review the written briefs, then to vote on the case. No one but the justices themselves are permitted in the discussion room. The discussion is directed by the Chief Justice, with the order of discussion determined by seniority. Afterward, a preliminary vote is taken, occurring in the inverse order of seniority, with the Chief Justice going last. Whichever side of a case has the most votes is considered the majority. The Court's opinion is written by one justice. Other justices may write their own concurring opinions or may simply concur with another opinion. Similarly, dissenting opinions—those by justices in the minority of the case vote—are typically written. Those, too, may be joined by other justices, or separate dissenting opinions may be authored. Occasionally, the Court issues "per curiam" opinions. These are unattributed opinions written by one or more justices in the majority and published merely as the Court's opinion.

In addition to ruling on the specifics of a case, Supreme Court opinions are known for how they interpret the Constitution, sometimes establishing standards to the extent of making new law, sometimes merely clarifying constitutional principles. Opinions often rely on precedent—previous rulings whose circumstances or principles can be similarly applied. Justices, however, are not bound by precedent and may, in fact, break with tradition. It is under those circumstances that, critics say, the Court or factions of it erroneously embark on making new law rather than merely interpreting the Constitution. Conversely, defenders of this practice believe that rulings—and the Constitution—should evolve as society itself changes.

Given its nature and role, the ramifications of the Supreme Court's rulings have permeated most, if not all, American institutions, including radio broadcasting. Several of the Court's most important rulings in broadcasting stem from circumstances involving radio and its unique properties. While these cases are explored elsewhere in depth, they are mentioned briefly here to illustrate the reach, power, and integral role the Supreme Court has played in the regulatory evolution of American radio. In a 1943 ruling, *National Broadcasting Co. v. United States,* the Court upheld the constitutionality of the broadcast regulatory system. Both NBC and CBS had attacked broadcast regulation as an infringement on their First Amendment rights. Specifically, the Federal Communications Commission (FCC) had adopted "chain broadcasting regulations" to curb the power of the networks and enhance the development of new networks. The existing networks believed this was a violation of the First Amendment and used the opportunity to attack broadcast regulation generally. The Supreme Court ruled the FCC's power extended beyond merely supervising airwave traffic, that it also has the burden of determining the composition of that traffic. The Court said the FCC was charged with encouraging the "effective use of radio in the public interest, if need be, by making special regulations applicable to radio stations engaged in chain broadcasting." Perhaps most significant, the ruling singled out broadcasting and its unique and finite properties, saying that those subject it to regulation not found in other media: "Freedom of utterance is abridged to many who wish to use the limited facilities of radio. Unlike other modes of expression, it is subject to governmental regulation. Because it cannot be used by all, some who wish to use it must be denied."

Slightly more than a quarter century later, the Supreme Court revisited similar issues. In *Red Lion Broadcasting Co. v. Federal Communications Commission,* the Court was once again confronted by a radio broadcaster seeking freedom from FCC-imposed regulation. A radio station owned by Red Lion Broadcasting Co. challenged the Fairness Doctrine, a requirement that broadcasters present issues of public importance and that all sides of such issues be discussed. Moreover, the station challenged the FCC's regulatory authority. Not only did the Supreme Court uphold the Fairness Doctrine (although it was subsequently determined that the rule was unnecessary), it sustained FCC power, once again basing its rationale on the "differences in the characteristics of new media." Those differences, the Court said, "justify differences in the First Amendment standards applied to them." Specifically, because broadcasting is perceived as operating within an arena of limited spectrum space, the Supreme Court has ruled that regulations such as those designed to institute fairness are constitutional. In spite of First Amendment–based challenges to the contrary, the Court said in *Red Lion:* "There is nothing in the First Amendment which prevents the Government from requiring a licensee to share his frequency with others. . . . It is the right of the viewers and listeners, not the right of the broadcasters, which is paramount."

The uniqueness of broadcasting and radio was also integral to another noteworthy Supreme Court ruling. In *FCC v. Pacifica Foundation* (1978), the Supreme

Court not only created a new category of expression, indecent speech; it also based its ruling on broadcasting's "uniquely pervasive presence." Accordingly, the Court ruled that the ability to thwart the possibility of certain material—patently offensive, indecent material—from entering our homes plainly outweighs the First Amendment rights of an intruder, that is, broadcaster. Thus, the specifics of another major ruling originated with the unique characteristics of radio broadcasting. In short, the Supreme Court has consistently maintained that because of those properties—scarcity of spectrum and pervasive presence, for example—a different, less stringent level of First Amendment protection is justified.

Cox, Archibald. *The Court and the Constitution.* Boston: Houghton Mifflin Company, 1987.
Lewis, Anthony. *Make No Law: The Sullivan Case and the First Amendment.* New York: Random House, 1991.
Rehnquist, William H. *The Supreme Court: How It Was, How It Is.* New York: Morrow, 1987.
Smolla, Rodney A., ed. *A Year in the Life of the Supreme Court.* Durham, N.C.: Duke University Press, 1995.

Joseph A. Russomanno

SUSPENSE was a weekly, dramatic, anthology series first heard on CBS in 1942. As its title suggests, the program featured stories in which characters found themselves in unanticipated, deadly situations, often the result of their own greed and ambitions. It was sponsored originally by Roma Wines and later by Autorite spark plugs. Unity among the narrative and commercial segments was provided by an announcer who both represented the sponsor and introduced the story. Under Autorite sponsorship, commercials were dramatized in a witty, self-reflexive manner, featuring actors who portrayed audience members listening to the *Suspense* episode being broadcast.

The blurring of textual frames was not limited to the interplay between commercials and narrative. In one way or another, merging and blending of textual elements was the signature motif of the entire series. Most significantly, *Suspense* explored the boundary between objective reality and subjective delusion when stories centered upon amnesiacs, psychotics, and other mentally unbalanced characters, although the "real" reality was usually disclosed in the dramatic climax.

Socioeconomic class formed another boundary surveyed regularly by the series, although that boundary was less permeable than those between reality and fantasy or between commercials and narrative. Jeopardy to middle-class stability was a regular, though subliminal, theme used by *Suspense* writers. Typical stories centered on average, middle-class individuals whose placid lives were ruptured by mistaken identity, horrifying nightmares, or kidnap by murderers on the run. Middle-class stability was also often disrupted by characters who committed murder in order to rise above their social position. Despite their predictable return to the status quo, however, *Suspense* episodes carried listeners through many unexpected twists and curves along the way.

Most stories were narrated in the first person, many times from the villain's perspective. As such, listeners could explore the machinations of a murderer's mind, following the steps from the planning stage to the evil deed to ultimate foil. In other cases, listeners subjectively witnessed benign protagonists' scramble to reestablish tranquil normalcy.

Suspense was a rare opportunity for major film actors to play against type, as once more the series toyed with listeners' expectations, in this case, crossing the line of celebrities' carefully constructed radio and screen personas. Jim and Marian Jordan (of radio's *Fibber McGee & Molly* fame), for example, played a retired husband and wife whose car was hijacked by a crazed killer in a tense drama requiring considerable acting skill, especially by Marian. Ozzie and Harriet Nelson portrayed a couple who would rather kill an aging uncle than wait for their inheritance. Similarly, Danny Kaye was a killer utterly lacking in conscience, while Lucille Ball played a con artist posing as a sexy high-school student. Other guest stars included Cary Grant, James Mason, Orson Welles, Ray Milland, Ronald Reagan, and James Stewart.

Besides being a showcase for actors' otherwise untapped ranges of dramatic talent, *Suspense* was also a means of promoting guest stars' newest films, a common practice on prime-time radio. Usually, a fleeting plug was read by the series announcer ("Mr. Stewart can currently be seen in Universal Studio's production of . . .") following a few moments of scripted chitchat between the announcer and the star. If the featured actor had no current or upcoming releases, a plug was given for some other film produced by that actor's studio.

Although *Suspense* was rarely among the highest-rated programs, it consistently earned a respectable Hooper rating, averaging in the teens. Its most notable program was "Sorry, Wrong Number," starring Agnes Moorehead; "Sorry, Wrong Number" was produced several times on *Suspense,* sold as a record in the late 1940s, and made into a successful film.

From 1949 to 1954, the popular *Suspense* formula was transferred to live television, influencing the content and style of that medium in its early years. It was also reprised briefly on television in 1964. The radio version continued until 1962 as one of network radio's last dramatic series. Like many radio programs, *Suspense* has been commercially available on cassettes for many years. Most recently, in the early 1990s, 40 episodes were released in two boxed sets by Minnesota Public Radio, complete with commercials. The program's continued success, decades after its initial run, suggests that it, along with a relatively few other series such as *The Shadow* and *The Lone Ranger,* will strongly influence how radio drama is imagined by generations who grew up during the television era.

Van Horne, H. "Radio's Most Perfect Script." *Saturday Review of Literature* 30 (September 27, 1947): 51.

Warren Bareiss

SUSTAINING PROGRAMS. From the earliest days of commercial broadcasting, stations and later networks continually worked to fill all time slots with sponsored programming (i.e., programming that not only featured commercials but also were produced by advertising agencies on behalf of sponsors). Not all programming segments could be sold all the time, so networks and individual stations filled the gaps with unsponsored programs on a sustaining basis. By "sustaining," broadcasters meant that they would sustain the costs of these programs until a sponsor could be found to either assume the production responsibilities and costs of the shows (and thus turn a profit for the broadcaster) or fill the respective slot with their own program. Broadcasters' commitment to sustaining shows was partial at best; sustaining shows were principally a short-term solution to ongoing scheduling problems.

While individual sustaining features were stop-gap measures to temporarily address advertising shortages, sustaining programs overall served crucial functions for the commercial broadcasting system. From time to time in network radio history, citizen groups and government regulators challenged networks' control of the airwaves, charging that the foundations of democratic society were undermined when communication systems were controlled by a few organizations whose fundamental concern was profit rather than social welfare. Church groups, educators, and labor unions, for example, argued that advertising determined a conservative bias in programming, while some independent stations—notably those controlled by labor and educational institutions—claimed that affiliates had an unfair advantage due to monopolistic power wielded by their networks. In answer to such protests, government regulators on occasion investigated the extent to which networks carried out their functions as stewards of the public airwaves. For example, a 1941 Federal Communications Commission (FCC) probe was strongly supported by the Roosevelt administration, which conducted several other antimonopoly investigations at the time.

In such cases, sustaining programs provided the solution commercial broadcasters needed to thwart citizens' groups and regulators. Sustaining shows kept federal regulators at bay, because networks and affiliates could emphasize the public service they performed by broadcasting sustaining programs of a cultural or educational nature. The commercial system, it was thus argued, was not solely concerned with the bottom line.

Indeed, programming produced and funded by networks often was qualitatively different from commercial shows. Programs featuring "serious" (i.e., light, classical) music, discussion programs, and dramatizations of classic literature were typical sustaining fare. Series such as *Columbia's School of the Air* (featuring lessons on art, civics, and history) continued to function as fillers in the unsold portion of network schedules, yet they also provided an air of credibility to commercial broadcasters.

At the same time, sustaining programs were a means of experimentally tapping possible audience interests and building those interests into profitable markets. For example, *The Mercury Theatre on the Air* (which broadcast the infamous "War of the Worlds") began as a sustaining venture that dramatized famous literary works. It was later picked up by the Campbell's Soup company and broadcast as the *Campbell's Playhouse.*

There was, however, truth to the argument that sustaining programs in some cases were venues through which political perspectives effectively censored by the commercial broadcasting system were presented. Advertising agencies who produced programs on behalf of sponsors were careful to maintain conservative tones so as not to offend potential consumers; however, unsponsored programs were less restrictive in that regard—a fact that made such shows "pet projects" for many creative network personnel despite the low pay involved. As a result, sustaining broadcasts sometimes bore a socially critical edge. Archibald MacLeish's 1939 "The Fall of the City" (heard on the *Columbia Workshop*) was a case in point; the program took a fiercely anti-Nazi position even while such feelings were still highly controversial.

During World War II, sustaining programs as means of rallying the home front further solidified commercial broadcasters' legitimacy. Sustaining productions by radio writers such as Norman Corwin and Arch Oboler boosted American moral and defiance against Axis powers. Such programs were stirring evocations of the democratic spirit, equating the monumental struggle against fascism with the efforts of the average man and woman on the street.

Sustaining programs were also directly linked with the war effort when producers of *Columbia's School of the Air* worked closely with the Office of War Information, using the series as a means of conveying important news, information, and instructions to civilian listeners. Furthermore, sustaining programs were central to CBS's expansion into Latin America during the war. All of the network's initial broadcasts in Latin America were on a sustaining basis, with network president William S. Paley claiming that CBS would use its sustaining programming to fight fascism in that part of the world.

After the war, progressive radio producers such as Norman Corwin were forced out of radio due to the political climate of the Cold War; however, sustaining programs continued to be broadcast, sometimes maintaining their critical edge despite the political dangers involved. NBC's *Dimension X* and *X Minus One,* for example, took on McCarthyism, capitalism, and American expansionism on more than one occasion, albeit indirectly via a science fiction format.

Sustaining broadcasts of the late 1940s and early 1950s also gave networks early experience with a new sponsorship arrangement. As increasing numbers of advertisers moved their productions to television, networks began to offer sustaining programs for limited sponsorship. No longer would advertisers have to take responsibility for entire series; rather, they could sponsor a series for a limited time at a much reduced cost. As a result, some control over programming content and the broadcast schedule shifted away from sponsors to that of the networks—an arrangement that networks would actively pursue in early television. Even so, like sponsors, networks eventually abandoned national productions (with the exception of news), so that by the late 1950s, sustaining series faded from the airwaves.

"CBS to S.A." *Time* (June 1, 1942): 62.

"Chains Unchained?" *Time* (May 12, 1941): 69–70.

McChesney, Robert W. *Telecommunications, Mass Media and Democracy: The Battle for the Control of U.S. Broadcasting.* New York: Oxford University Press, 1993.

Miller, N. "Self-regulation in American Radio." *Annals of the American Academy of Political & Social Science* 213 (1940): 93–96.

"The Networks Present More and Better Unsponsored Programs." *Newsweek* (November 8, 1937): 20–21.

Paley, W. S. "Broadcasting in American Society." *Annals of the American Academy of Political & Social Science* 213 (1940): 63–68.

"The 'School of the Air' (CBS) to Be an Official Channel for War News." *School and Society* (September 26, 1942): 263–264.

Warren Bareiss

SWEEP, MUSIC, is an uninterrupted period of music on music radio. Two early radio programming syndicators, Schulke Radio Productions and Bonneville International Corporation, began the strategy of employing music sweeps. These "commercial-free" segments of programming serve to attract and hold listeners who generally dislike commercial interruptions and who may otherwise tune away at a commercial. Programmers will typically sweep music across the quarter hour for ratings purposes. Music sweeps can, however, convey and perpetuate a negative attitude toward advertising messages. Programmers try to compromise between the length of music sweeps and the number and length of necessary commercial spot breaks and other stop sets.

Eastman, Susan Tyler, and Douglas A. Ferguson. *Broadcast/Cable Programming: Strategies and Practices.* 5th ed. Belmont, Calif.: Wadsworth, 1997.

Keith, Michael C. *Radio Programming: Consultancy and Formatics.* Boston: Focal Press, 1987.

Laurie Thomas Lee

SWING, ERA OF. Swing is a form of jazz music with a strong rhythmic essence, frequently performed by big bands and associated with dancing, which reached its peak of popularity between 1935 and 1945. This music combines the spirit of free expression and improvisation characteristics of jazz, with written arrangements for ensemble presentation. Swing attracted its largest audience, especially teens and young adults, through radio broadcasts, recordings, films, and live performances. The big bands of Benny Goodman, Glenn Miller, Tommy Dorsey, Artie Shaw, Count Basie, and many others gathered tremendous followings through national exposure on network radio. This helped to ensure well-attended personal engagements for the bands, often in hotels and ballrooms. Names of ballrooms such as the Meadowbrook, Glen Island Casino, the Trianon, the Aragon, and the Palomar became part of the national vocabulary. These, too, were sites of remote broadcasts, expanding swing's reach and popularity still further. Some of these programs were sustaining, but as swing and individual bands became more well known, sponsors were increasingly willing to provide support. Swing music became part of the war effort, aimed at heightening morale for the military in various world locations and for civilians at home. By the mid-1940s, public affection for swing waned, giving way to the rising prominence of vocalists as featured performers. Some bands turned to a bebop style, which never gained swing's widespread acceptance. Economics also played a role in swing's lessened popularity, as expenses and costs for the relatively large groups of 12 or so musicians became increasingly prohibitive.

Deffaa, Chip. *Swing Legacy.* Metuchen, N.J.: Scarecrow Press, 1989.

Schuller, Gunther. *The Swing Era: The Development of Jazz 1930–1945.* New York: Oxford University Press, 1989.

Simon, George. *The Big Bands.* New York: Schirmer Books, 1967.

B. R. Smith

SWING, RAYMOND "GRAM" (1887–1968), began his journalism career with the *Cleveland Press.* In World War I, he was foreign correspondent for the *Chicago Daily News.* In the 1930s Swing began broadcasting with the BBC and then with CBS, Mutual, and NBC. As many as 5 million listeners (estimated) tuned in to his news analysis. He concluded his career with the Voice of America. He came under attack in 1953 from Senator Joseph McCarthy. Swing felt his only reply to the McCarthy attacks was to resign, sending a copy of his resignation to the *New York Times.* His was one of the first voices to fight back against McCarthyism. He returned to the Voice, where he stayed until his death.

Scanlon, Lee E. Personal interviews. Washington, D.C., 1962–1963.
Swing, Raymond "Gram." *Good Evening!* London: Bodley Head Ltd., 1964.

Lee E. Scanlon

SYNDICATION is the process of marketing programs on a station-by-station basis, rather than through a network, for a specified number of plays. Programs are provided by syndicators—companies that hold the rights to distribute the programs nationally or internationally.

Radio syndication began in the 1950s when radio networks lost revenue and audiences to television and cut back to mostly news and sports programs. Syndicators provided features and short musical programs for local stations, usually on tape or disc. Later, the development of satellite delivery and compact discs revolutionized the industry, somewhat blurring the distinction between syndicators and networks.

There are two forms of radio syndication: (1) syndicated formats, which provide stations with a continuous music format, and (2) syndicated features, which supplement a station's programming with primarily news and entertainment features. Unlike networks, format syndicators typically provide only music and rarely sell commercial time. Format syndicators include Broadcast Programming Inc. (BPI) and TM Century Inc. Feature syndicators include Westwood One (*The Casey Kasem Countdown*) and EFM Media (*Rush Limbaugh Show*). Unlike networks, syndicators usually charge for their programs. Payments involve cash, barter, or cash-plus-barter. About 50 major syndicators and hundreds of regional suppliers exist. About half of all commercial radio stations use syndicated programming.

Demand for syndicated programming has increased in the 1990s due to station ownership consolidation and the rising popularity of national radio personalities. Syndicated programming is seen as a cost-effective way to program across several stations and establish identity. Competition among syndication companies has also increased.

Eastman, Susan Tyler, and Douglas A. Ferguson. *Broadcast/Cable Programming: Strategies and Practices.* 5th ed. Belmont, Calif.: Wadsworth, 1997.

Laurie Thomas Lee

T

TALK PROGRAMS. *See* **all-talk format.**

TAPE RECORDING, until the recent development of digital recording, was the major means of preserving radio program material for broadcast at a later time. Tape recording eventually offered improved fidelity and greater reliability compared to both transcription discs and wire recording, an earlier magnetic technique.

Singer Bing Crosby backed efforts by Ampex to achieve high-fidelity tape recording based on the German "Magnetophon" design captured at the end of WWII. He moved his popular show from NBC to ABC in 1946 when ABC broke the major networks' prohibition against airing recorded programs. Tape recorders began to be used in local stations by 1947, but short segments such as commercials, promos, and jingles were hard to thread and cue quickly. That was solved in 1959 when the endless-loop tape cartridge came into wide use in broadcasting.

David T. MacFarland

TARGET MARKET/AUDIENCE is the desired audience defined demographically or psychographically at which programming and advertising is aimed. Faced with a growing number of program services, stations began deliberately limiting their appeal to specific audience segments—a practice referred to as "narrowcasting." Advertisers influenced the trend by seeking to reach only those people with money and an interest in their product. Noncommercial stations try to target specific audience groups most likely to pay membership fees or provide other support. Radio further employs "segmentation," whereby extremely narrow subsets are defined based on both demographic and psychographic characteristics.

Laurie Thomas Lee

TECHNICAL STANDARDS, more accurately called *standardized technical specifications* for broadcast transmission and reception apparatus, was the mechanism for establishing technical standards in the United States in the early days of broadcasting. Recognizing that regulatory commissions could provide greater expertise in technical areas, Section 4 [e] of the *Radio Act of 1927* gave the Federal Radio Commission (FRC) the authority to regulate technical aspects of broadcasting. This charge was continued when the Federal Communications Commission (FCC) was established under Title III, Section 303 [g] of the *Communications Act of 1934.*

The main reasons for standardizing broadcast technical specifications are to provide for a uniform minimum level of audio quality—such as to prevent spectrum interference—and to ensure equipment interchangeability, so that all types of transmitters will emit a signal that is decodable by all brands of radios. An advantage of standardization is that it gives a measure of "insurance" to both manufacturers and consumers of broadcast apparatus, in that technical standards guarantee that a device will operate within established electronic parameters. The short-term effects of clear standards can include lower research and development (R&D) and production costs, accelerated diffusion and adoption of new products, and decreased chance of product obsolescence. Clear technical standards can also aid in establishing an industry and thus can be used as an economic development tool. One risk associated with setting technical standards is selecting a "wrong" standard and, in the long run, freezing obsolete technologies in the marketplace, thereby discouraging future technological refinement and innovation.

For decades, the broadcast and consumer electronics industries developed competitive proposals for broadcast apparatus, then tested them under a competitive process supervised by the FCC. The FCC would finally decide which proposed standard best served the pubic interest in terms of balancing cost and quality, and then set a technical standard. In the early 1980s, the FCC questioned its role as arbiter of technical standards and in a string of decisions (AM stereo, low power television [LPTV], direct broadcast by satellite [DBS], teletext) sharply curtailed its previous role as standard setter in favor of a laissez-faire "marketplace" approach. Under this deregulatory model, the FCC set only minimum technical standards and allowed competition in the marketplace to select a de facto standard. By the mid-1980s the FCC seemed to favor an approach that "protected" technical standards selected by industry (as in the case of TV stereo). While the future of technical standard-setting activity by the FCC is not yet settled, it is worth noting that in the early 1990s Congress mandated that the FCC set a standard for AM stereo. The FCC appeared to be considering accepting high-definition television (HDTV) technical standards proposed by an industry "grand alliance" and recommended by an industry advisory committee to the FCC.

On an international level, the International Telecommunication Union (ITU) was established in 1865 and its International Consultative Committee for Radio enables 166 member nations to standardize and coordinate international telecommunications, including the allotment of radio frequencies. The ITU is located in Geneva and became affiliated with the United Nations in 1947.

Braun, Mark. *AM Stereo and the FCC: Case Study of a Marketplace "Shibboleth."* Norwood, N.J.: Ablex, 1994.

Sterling, Christopher H. "The 'New Technology': The FCC and Changing Technological Standards." *Journal of Communication* 32 (1) (1982): 138.

Mark J. Braun

TELECOMMUNICATIONS ACT OF 1996 (Public Law No. 104–104, 110 Stat. 56 [1996]) is the first major rewrite of American communications law since passage of the *Communications Act of 1934.* According to the Federal Communications Commission (FCC), the goal of the act is to let anyone enter the communications business and allow communications businesses to compete against one another. The act relaxes many of the rules that prohibit telephone companies, cable systems, and broadcasters from providing similar services. It also modifies the multiple owner-ship rules and directs the FCC to implement rules requiring television receivers to contain V-Chip technology. The V-Chip will allow electronic in-home blocking of violent or sexually explicit programming.

Title V of the act is known as the *Communications Decency Act (CDA).* The *CDA* would apply broadcastlike indecency standards to the Internet. The *CDA* would prohibit intentional transmission of indecent or "patently offensive" materi-als to minors over the Internet. The American Civil Liberties Union filed suit against the Justice Department on grounds that the *CDA* violated the First Amendment. Pending the outcome of the case, the Justice Department did not enforce the provisions of *CDA. ACLU v. Reno* (1996) was heard by a three-judge panel. The three-judge panel found the Internet-indecency ban unconstitutional, noting that the Internet deserves the broadest possible constitutional protections. Judge Stewart Dalzell likened the Internet to newspapers and magazines, as opposed to "more tightly regulated broadcast transmissions." The Supreme Court upheld *CLU v. Reno U.S. Dist. Ct. E. Pa.* in 1997.

The major provisions of the act affecting radio, television, and cable are:

Broadcast Ownership. The FCC's long-standing policy on diversity of broad-cast ownership has been relaxed. The radio duopoly rules have been expanded from a maximum of three stations, and the national ownership limits for radio have been repealed. Before passage of the act, one entity could own 20 AM and 20 FM stations, for a total of 40. The new rules modify the duopoly and radio ownership rules as follows: markets with 45 or more stations, one entity can own eight, five of which may be of the same service (AM or FM); with 30 to 44 stations, the limit is seven, with a maximum of four in the same service; with 15 to 29, the limit is six, with no more than four of the same service; and with 14 or fewer stations, five is the limit, with no more than three of the same service.

The act also directs the FCC to waive the "one-to-a-customer" rule in the top-50 markets and repeal the 12-station national ownership cap for television. Under the act, one entity may own an unlimited number of television stations, provided those stations do not reach more than 35 percent of the national audience. The FCC will also reconsider the television duopoly rules.

The act repeals the dual network rule for television; however, it prohibits ABC, CBS, and NBC from merging. It also does away with the network cable cross-ownership rule, allowing the major networks to own cable systems. Finally, the act allows cable/MMDSs (multichannel, multipoint distribution systems, also called "wireless cable") cross ownership in areas where existing cable systems face effective competition.

Broadcast Licensing Changes. Although the act leaves the public interest standard intact, it eliminates comparative license renewal proceedings. The FCC will not accept competing applications unless it has already decided a license won't be renewed. The act also increases radio and television license terms to eight years instead of a television license five years and seven years for radio stations.

Advanced Television (ATV). The act addresses the transition from the National Television Systems Committee (NTSC) standard to digital television transmission (ATV) and limits ATV eligibility to holders of existing full-power television broadcast licenses. In addition to providing programming on a main channel, ATV licensees will be allowed to offer "ancillary and supplemental services," such as data transmission. Existing NTSC TV frequencies will be returned to the FCC at the end of an unspecified transition period from NTSC to ATV. The FCC will collect fees from broadcasters for use of the newly created ATV channels.

Violence on TV. The act directed the industry to devise a rating code for video containing "sexual, violent or other indecent material about which parents should be informed." It also requires all TV sets larger than 13 inches manufactured one year after the act to include a V-Chip, capable of blocking out material judged by the viewer as offensive or undesirable. The V-Chip provision of the act is subject to expedited review by a three-judge district court with direct appeal to the Supreme Court.

Telephone Company Entry into Video Distribution. Under the act, telephone companies are allowed to provide video in their service areas as common carriers, cable system, or as "open video systems." Must Carry, Retransmission Consent, Syndicated Exclusivity, Network Nonduplication, and Sports Exclusivity rules apply to telephone companies who choose to provide video services.

Other Provisions. The FCC is directed to mandate closed captioning; it has adopted rules barring zoning restrictions on the use of television receiver antennas; rates for small cable systems will be deregulated, which makes it more difficult for customers to contest cable rates; cable companies will be allowed to provide local telephone service; the Regional Bell Operating Companies (RBOCs—Baby Bells) will be allowed to provide long-distance service.

The *Telecommunications Act of 1996* generated a great deal of controversy. In addition to the concerns over the *Communications Decency Act* provisions, the V-Chip provision raised constitutional questions. Telephone companies, concerned over the potential of cable television's entry into the long-distance business, persuaded a U.S. court of appeals to temporarily issue a stay on implementing rules.

The 1996 Telecommunications Act: Law & Legislative History. Bethesda, Md.: Pike & Fischer Inc., 1996.

Telecommunications Act of 1996. http://www.fcc.gov/telecom.html (October 4, 1996).

Kenneth C. Creech

TELECOMMUNICATIONS POLICY, OFFICE OF (OTP), was established in 1970 by President Richard Nixon to serve as the president's adviser on all matters dealing with the electronic media. As stated in the president's reorganization plan submitted to Congress, the agency was to "enable the executive branch to speak with a clearer voice and to act as a more effective partner in the discussions of communications policy with both the Congress and the Federal Communications Commission [FCC]." OTP was reorganized out of existence with the creation of the National Telecommunications and Information Administration under President Jimmy Carter.

Most broadcasters in the 1970s saw OTP as an administrative attempt to have greater control over electronic communications. The agency's first director, Clay Whitehead, spoke out against network domination of local stations. He stated that local stations were responsible for whatever they aired, despite who produced it. His implication was that local stations needed to be sure that the news they received from their networks was not biased—this at a time when the Nixon administration was already vocal in criticizing network news. OTP expanded its assault on networks by claiming that television reruns resulted in unemployment in the entertainment industry. Although no regulation or action resulted, networks were attentive to the OTP. OTP also negotiated a compromise between the National Association of Broadcasters and the National Cable Television Association, which led to a 1972 cable television rule making by the FCC.

Dom Caristi

TELEPHONE SURVEY of radio audiences by random telephone calls to potential listeners. Telephone researchers generally utilize the coincidental method, in which respondents are asked if they are listening to a station at the time of the call; or the recall method, in which respondents are asked to recall station listening patterns over a period of time such as the past week.

Frederic A. Leigh

THOMAS, LOWELL JACKSON (1892–1981), was born in Woodington, Ohio. He was raised in the Colorado gold fields of Cripple Creek, Colorado, and attended Valpariaso University; University of Denver; Kent College of Law, Chicago; and Princeton University, where he earned several degrees studying law and public speaking.

His journalistic career began with the Cripple Creek *Times*. From there he moved to Victor, Colorado, working at the *Daily Record* and the *Daily News*. Later in Denver, he worked for the newspapers in that city while attending the university. In Chicago, he reported for the Chicago *Journal*, where he associated with Carl Sandburg and Floyd Gibbons.

Thomas reported on World War I from Cario, Egypt. These experiences produced his first published book, *With Lawrence in Arabia*, which was a best-seller. He came to radio in 1923, at first appearing casually, describing his travels and experiences. His first newscast was on September 19, 1930. It was a 15-minute newscast, broadcast on the NBC Blue Network five nights per week. The 1930s reflect the peak of his radio career. The audience reported for his 1936 broadcasts was estimated at 20 million. He wrote and edited his own material with a small staff—Prosper Buranelli and Louis Sherwin.

Thomas was known for his conversational style. He told people the story. He was the narrator for the Fox Movietone newreels, which appeared in the movie theaters for 17 years. He loved to travel and was constantly on the move. From his personal adventures, books, television series, and news reports continued to flow. Among them were television series such as *The World of Lowell Thomas* and *Lowell Thomas Remembers*. At the age of 84, Thomas retired from radio in 1976.

Fang, Irving E. *Those Radio Commentators!* Ames: Iowa State University Press, 1977.

Donald G. Godfrey

THOMPSON, DOROTHY (1894–1961), a renowned and controversial journalist, was also a frequent radio commentator whose broadcasts not only added to her influence but ultimately enhanced her legend. She was born in Lancaster, New York, and graduated from Syracuse. She eventually fled to Europe and was soon filing stories for the International News Service. In 1925 she was appointed head of the New York *Evening Post*'s Berlin office, the first American woman ever to head a foreign news outpost. A 1931 interview with Hitler and the book Thompson wrote about it made her famous and resulted in her expulsion from Germany.

Back in America, Thompson began writing her column *On the Record,* which at its height was in over 200 newspapers. Thompson made the first of her regular radio appearances in 1937 as a news commentator for NBC. Over the next few years until the end of World War II, Thompson was seldom off the airwaves, and her omnipresence solidified her place as the "First Lady of American Journalism." In 1939, *Time* labeled Thompson and Eleanor Roosevelt as the two most influential women in America.

Thompson's forceful speeches and reports, mostly on the war in Europe, on her series *The General Electric Hour,* regularly reached over 5 million listeners. Later, on radio, Thompson was heard for 15 consecutive days and nights in 1939 reporting on Poland's invasion. Her broadcasts to England during the Blitz endeared her to that nation until the end of her life. And in 1942, over CBS, Thompson broadcast a weekly series of anti-Nazi reports via shortwave into Germany.

"Cartwheel Girl." *Time* (June 12, 1939): 47–51.

Kurth, Peter. *American Cassandra: The Life of Dorothy Thompson.* Boston: Little, Brown and Company, 1990.

Sanders, Marion K. *Dorothy Thompson: A Legend in Her Time.* Boston: Houghton Mifflin Company, 1973.

Cary O'Dell

TIME SPENT LISTENING (TSL) measures the average amount of time a typical listener spends listening to a particular station within a daypart. TSL is a general indicator of listener satisfaction for a station. TSL figures will vary depending upon the daypart and the format of a radio station. Contemporary hit radio stations, for example, may expect lower TSL numbers than a classic rock station.

Webster, James G., and Lawrence W. Lichty, eds. *Ratings Analysis: Theory and Practice.* Hillsdale, N.J.: Lawrence Erlbaum Associates, 1991.

Ronald Razovsky

TIP SHEETS in the radio industry are informational services providing music, news, or industry tips to stations and others, typically on a subscription basis. There are many specialized tip sheets, which may be distributed as newsletters (*The Gavin Report,* well-known American radio tip sheet), E-mail services (Wireless Flash News Service), web sites (Radio On-Line), fax (Industry R&D, Inside Radio), or 900-number telephone services (Radio Hotline). National radio tip sheets include station summaries, market analyses, audience requests, job openings, listings of new singles, sales and airplay charts, interviews, trends, and gossip.

Laurie Thomas Lee

TITANIC **DISASTER.** The *Wireless Ship Act of 1910* required ships with more than 50 passengers to carry wireless sets. When, in one of the best-known mishaps of the century, the RMS *Titanic* rammed an iceberg on April 14, 1912, and sank, hundreds of passengers were saved because of the ship's wireless distress signals. Sadly, 1,517 lives were lost. Interference caused by the many amateur wireless operators who went on the air after the disaster seriously hindered rescue operations. This helped make clear the need for radio guidelines. The *Radio Act of 1912* required transmitting stations to be licensed by the secretary of commerce, who could assign wavelengths and time limits; and ship, amateur, and government transmissions were assigned distinct places in the spectrum.

The *Titanic* disaster also played a role, albeit a questionable one, in the personal myth surrounding General David Sarnoff, longtime president of the Radio Corporation of America and founder of NBC. Radio legend places him on duty as a wireless operator for Wanamaker's Department Store in New York the night the *Titanic* sank. Sarnoff reportedly received the ship's distress message, alerted the press, and then went without food and sleep for the next three days while he heroically manned his post as the only link between the tragedy in the North Atlantic and the mainland. Although this makes for a great story, recent research suggests Sarnoff's role was far from central and considerably less heroic.

Archer, Gleason L. *History of Radio to 1926.* New York: American Historical Society, Inc., 1938.

Benjamin, Louise M. "In Search of the Sarnoff 'Radio Music Box' Memo." *Journal of Broadcasting and Electronic Media* 37 (3) (summer 1993): 325.

Bilby, Kenneth. *The General: David Sarnoff and the Rise of the Communications Industry.* New York: Harper & Row, 1986.

Michael Woal

TOKYO ROSE (1916–) never called herself "Tokyo Rose." She was an American, a graduate of the University of California at Los Angeles, and a victim of injustice. Born on July 4, 1916, in Los Angeles, Iva Ikuko Toguri majored in zoology because she wanted to be a doctor. Her father operated a small business as a grocer and importer. She was a *nisei*—"second generation." After graduating in 1941 she went to Japan for the summer to care for her mother's ill sister. Apparently because of the U.S. oil embargo against Japan, she found it difficult to get a ship back at the end of the summer. She was still there when the Japanese attacked Pearl Harbor. Now U.S. immigration officers delayed her. The Japanese secret police demanded she renounce her U.S. citizenship. When she refused, they denied her a ration card for food and declared her an enemy alien. Meanwhile in the United States, her family was "relocated" to an internment camp. She did not know the whereabouts of her family for three years. She finally got a job at a newspaper monitoring and transcribing U.S. broadcasts. She took a second job as a secretary at Radio Tokyo.

In early 1943, NHK (Japanese Broadcasting Corporation) was ordered by the government to create "strategic broadcasts." The result was a program call the *Zero Hour,* usually Monday through Saturday from 6:00 P.M. to about 7:15 P.M. The title was apparently chosen since it was to be received across the Pacific with many different time zones, or possibly after the name of the Japanese fighter planes. The scripts were written by an Australian major, Charles Cousens, who was an announcer and former writer, being held as a prisoner of war (POW). The first English-speaking announcers on the show were also from a nearby POW camp, and Miss Toguri smuggled food to them.

Typist Toguri was asked to audition as an announcer and probably began in the middle of November 1943. Her part on the program was usually about a quarter of an hour introducing American jazz and light classical phonographs. She read Cousens's script without ad-libbing or change. He told her to "consider yourself a soldier under orders, I will not let you do anything against your country." The other parts of the program included messages to GIs, news, other music including military marches, and a commentary.

Miss Toguri at first called herself "Ann"—for announcer—on the air. Later she was "Orphan Ann"—a supposed reference to American soldiers who were orphans in the Pacific (forgotten and much lonelier than those fighting in Europe?). She never called herself "Tokyo Rose." No one else, at or on the air at NHK, ever called her Tokyo Rose. There never was a Tokyo Rose. There might have been as many as 20 different female announcers on the air from Japan probably as early as the summer of 1942. One who played classical music was called "Dutchie." Apparently the use of female and fairly husky voices were to add to the feeling of loneliness and alienation. The basic idea of the International Section of NHK was to instill war weariness among the GIs. NHK was said to reject the more blatant, strident propaganda of "Lord Haw Haw" and other Germany broadcasters.

By the summer of 1943, many GIs were talking about "Tokyo Rose." Apparently the name was coined by one of them, maybe based on the Germany propagandist "Axis Sally." Here is a transcript of a broadcasting of August 14, 1944:

> Hello you fighting orphans of the Pacific. How's tricks? This is after her weekend Ann back on the air [???] Reception OK? Well, it better be because this is all-request night and I've got a pretty nice program for my favorite little family [??] Marines of the pacific islands. (National Archives)

Other announcers, not Orphan Ann, on this program talked about rumors in Honolulu, strikes in the United States, Australian war brides of American soldiers arriving in San Francisco, and:

> How'd you like to be back in Los Angeles tonight, dancing at Coconut Grove with your best girl? . . . parked with her in Griffith Park listening to the radio? I wonder who your wives and girl friends are out with tonight? Maybe with a 4F or a war plant worker making big money while you are out here fighting and knowing you can't succeed. Wouldn't you California boys like to be at Coconut Grove tonight with your best girl? You have plenty of Coconut Groves, but no girls. (National Archives)

Most experts agree that these broadcasts had no effect on the morale of American troops. Many were said to tune in for the music. On one occasion a woman announcer complained that newer jazz records were not available. Soon, on a bomb run, new phonographs were parachuted—the package was addressed to "Tokyo Rose" (NHK).

By 1945 Miss Toguri had married Philip D'Aquino, a pacifist, Portuguese citizen living in Japan. He tried to get her to accept Portuguese citizenship, but she refused to renounce her American citizenship. When Japan surrendered, many American journalists wanted to interview Tokyo Rose. In several press accounts, she seemed to admit to being Tokyo Rose in a kidding way and agreed to appear in an army film. She was taken to prison where she learned for the first time that her mother had died in a relocation camp. Her family had moved to Chicago.

When she became pregnant, she and her husband applied to reenter the United States. Radio commentator and columnist Walter Winchell attacked her, saying she should be tried for treason. Attorney General Tom Clark was asked, by President Roosevelt, to investigate. She was charged with treason, her baby died at birth, and she was brought back to the United States on a troop ship.

A song at the time went:

> I bet you're sorry Tokyo Rose . . .
> You stuck a knife into the U.S.A.
> You forgot what they taught you at good ol' UCLA.

In July 1949 her trial began in San Francisco, and while electrical transcriptions were displayed on a table, they were never played. She was found guilty and sentenced to 10 years in prison and a fine of $10,000. But several witnesses against her seemed to recant, and her husband agreed to leave and never return to the United States.

On January 28, 1956, Mrs. D'Aquino, after seven years in jail, was released for "good behavior." She move to Chicago where her father operated a mercantile business, but almost immediately the U. S. Immigration Service initiated deportation proceedings. She had to return to San Francisco, but she and her attorney, Wayne Collins, won the case. Twenty years later President Gerald Ford was interested in the case. On his last day in office, January 19, 1977, he signed a full pardon for the first woman ever convicted of treason in the United States.

Howe, Russell Warren. *The Hunt for "Tokyo Rose."* New York: Madison Books, 1990.

Kutler, Stanley I. *The American Inquisition: Justice and Injustice in the Cold War.* New York: Hill and Wang, 1982.

National Archives. *Sounds of History, World War II.* Washington, D.C.: National Archives Trust Fund Board, 1980.

NHK (Nippon Hosa Kyokai). *50 Years of Japanese Broadcasting.* Tokyo: NHK, 1977.

Tokyo Rose: Victim of Propaganda. Greystone Productions, 1995. (A&E cable network, August 9, 1995).

Lawrence W. Lichty

TOP 40, initially referred to the 40 most popular records played by a station, often in a "countdown" format. Top 40 became the widely imitated music format used by radio, in the late 1950s, to regain audiences from television. Today, the industry has replaced the term with "CHR" (for "contemporary hits radio"), but the public still refers to many hit-oriented music stations as top 40s.

The pioneers of the format, Todd Storz and Gordon McLendon, developed top 40 on their stations in Omaha and Dallas, respectively. As it succeeded, they added other stations in middle-sized markets. The major markets were the last to get a top-40 station. Top 40 was a refinement of an earlier format called "music and news," which demanded little concentration from the audience and was very inexpensive to produce. New York's WNEW had been successful with this record-based format since the 1930s, but both the music and the announcing were oriented toward adults. In contrast, early top 40 was associated with rock 'n' roll music and teenagers, in part because in the mid-1950s, adult radio listeners had switched over to TV viewing. Teens were a growing and otherwise unserved audience that was rapidly embraced by both the radio and record industries.

Music selection was the most important factor in the success of the format. Rather than playing all the popular records of the day, top 40s offered a limited playlist. By 1956, the leaders in the format were also repeating the hottest songs more often than the less popular tunes—the earliest "power" rotation system. Format clocks were developed to determine which songs should be played at any given point in the hour, in any daypart.

Many other elements were also a part of the formula. Disc jockeys had to be energetic and upbeat to match the music. Brief weather, traffic, and sports reports were always introduced with singing jingles, and station identification jingles were sprinkled liberally throughout each hour to keep the call letters in the listeners' consciousness in case they were contacted by a ratings company. Some stations paid bonuses to the jocks who crammed the most call letter mentions into their shows and levied fines against those who allowed a few seconds of "dead air."

Promotion was another important part of the mix. Top-40 stations were usually not the well-known "powerhouse" stations at the low end of the AM dial; because they had no history to trade on, they decided to make instant history by giving away huge sums of money, sponsoring treasure hunts, throwing cash from tall buildings, and so on. Even the gaudy "news cruisers" that reported on fender-benders were part of the promotional plan.

The success of the top-40 format, in gathering large audiences even as television was decimating the traditional radio listening audience, encouraged other types of specialization and format experimentation. Country, oldies, classic rock, adult contemporary, and urban are just some of the formats that evolved from the original top-40 model.

David T. MacFarland

TOPLESS RADIO. *See* **all-talk radio; indecency; programming; regulation of programming.**

TOTAL SURVEY AREA (TSA) consists of the metropolitan statistical area (MSA) and other adjacent counties where a significant number of people listen to radio stations broadcasting from the MSA. Counties comprising the TSA are based upon historical listening patterns and are revised biennially. Arbitron provides most of its ratings measures for the TSA as well as the MSA.

Fletcher, James E., ed. *Broadcast Research Definitions.* Washington, D.C.: National Association of Broadcasters, 1988.

Ronald Razovsky

TRAFFIC DIRECTOR is responsible for scheduling everything that airs. Working under the direction of station management—program directors and news directors—these individuals schedule programs, program elements, commercials, promotion spots, public service announcements, emergency broadcast alerts, station identifications, sign-ons, and sign-offs.

The radio traffic director also creates a system to organize the station's program elements, commercials, and promotional spots (promos), deciding when these elements are broadcast. The daily log, a system used at most radio stations, includes all programming elements broadcast and further serves as a record of what aired. In addition, the broadcast log is a record for billing advertising for commercials played over the air.

The ideal traffic director is precise, with a keen eye for detail. This individual should handle pressure easily, as it is part of the job. In addition, the traffic manager should have good working relationships with others at the radio station, especially employees in the programming, promotion, and sales departments—the three departments that work most closely with the traffic department.

Each time a sales order is written, a copy of it goes to the traffic director. The traffic director usually then enters that information into a computer. He or she records all pertinent data related to the commercial such as start and end date, time, length, and advertising rate. Additionally, traffic directors track promotional spots in the same manner, and both commercials and promos use airtime (inventory) to sell time and build or maintain audiences.

Keith, Michael C., and Joseph M. Krause. *The Radio Station.* 3rd ed. Boston: Focal Press, 1993.

Warner, Charles, and Joseph Buchman. *Broadcast and Cable Selling.* Belmont, Calif.: Wadsworth, 1991.

Gilbert A. Williams

TRANSISTORS are devices utilizing semiconductor materials (crystalline solids) such as silicon and germanium. They were the first-generation replacement for vacuum tubes in most applications. Transistors required less power to operate, thereby creating less heat, were smaller and lighter, less susceptible to physical damage, and had a significantly longer service life. By the early 1950s their use in radio allowed smaller and more portable receivers, which increased radio listening at a time when radio was losing its traditional audience to television. By the late 1960s, transistors were being superseded by the integrated circuit.

Steven C. Runyon

TRANSLATORS are low-power, unattended repeater stations used to receive a weak broadcast signal, amplify it, and rebroadcast it on a different frequency by means of a transmitter. The translator permits a station's broadcast signal to be picked up by a sensitive receiver and be rebroadcast to reach an audience in remote sites who are unable to receive the signal due to physical barriers such as mountainous terrain. Translators are usually located at the highest available elevation to achieve maximum coverage.

Bruce W. Russell

TRENDLE, GEORGE WASHINGTON (1884–1972), was born in Norwalk, Ohio, on July 4, 1884, to German immigrant parents. He had initially planned to be a minister, but after his family moved to Detroit, he graduated from law school and became a bookkeeper. He and his partner, John H. King (Kunsky), eventually owned a number of theaters in Michigan. When Trendle saw the promise of radio, he bought a struggling Detroit radio station and changed the call letters to WXYZ.

In early 1933, without a network and having to develop their own programming, Trendle and Buffalo, New York, writer Fran Striker came up with a western hero. He was independently wealthy (he owned a silver mine), wore a mask, and was a symbol of justice, a righter of wrongs. The hero, Dan Reid, was one of six Texas Rangers ambushed by Butch Cavendish and his gang. All the Rangers were killed except Reid, who was nursed back to health by Tonto, an Indian Reid had rescued when they were both boys. *The Lone Ranger* was to be a positive example for children and garnered a large audience in Detroit and eventually on the Mutual Radio Network. Trendle later said, "You don't need a lot of bloodshed. My programs always stressed good American principles." He also said he "wanted a good, clean show to keep the Parent-Teacher Association off our neck." (*New York Times,* p. 1,097).

The formula was advanced by several additional radio shows, including *The Green Hornet, Sgt. Preston of the Yukon,* and *The American Agent.* Several of these shows were filmed for television and picked up an entirely new audience. Trendle died of a heart attack on May 10, 1972, in Grosse Pointe, Michigan. His private papers are at the Detroit Public Library.

Bickel, Mary E. *George W. Trendle, Creator and Producer of The Lone Ranger, The Green Hornet, Sgt. Preston of the Yukon, The American Agent and Other Successes.* New York: Exposition Press, 1971.

Dunning, John. *Tune in Yesterday: The Ultimate Encyclopedia of Old-time Radio 1925–1976.* Englewood Cliffs, N.J.: Prentice-Hall, 1976.

New York Times Biographical Service. *A Compilation of Current Biographical Information of General Interest* 3 (5) (May 1972, George Washington Trendle). New York: Arno Press.

"Sounds from the History of Radio. *The Lone Ranger.*" Bellingham Antique Radio Museum Web Page. http://www.antique-radio.org/sounds/shows/lonerange/lranger.html

David Spiceland

TROUT, ROBERT (1908–), was the first CBS anchorperson. He was brought to CBS during the mid-1930s and worked under Paul White with what was a small CBS staff at the time; it consisted only of White, his assistant H. V. Kaltenborn, and Trout. Trout was known for his baritone voice. He read the news as well as did the station breaks for *Jack Armstrong, the All-American Boy.*

William L. Shirer and Edward R. Murrow were the two largely responsible for the first radio *CBS News Roundup,* March 13, 1939, but it was the voice of Robert Trout who anchored the newscasts from New York. It was a historic program as Trout called for reports from correspondents from Europe. This first *CBS News Roundup* not only set the stage for CBS News, but the patterns established are evident today. "And now back to Robert Trout in New York" became a familiar out cue to listeners during World War II.

Following the war, CBS began a program with correspondents from around the globe and Robert Trout as anchor. *Robert Trout with the News Till Now* was the focus of the CBS News programming. In 1947, Trout was replaced as anchor by Murrow.

Cloud, Stanley, and Lynne Olsen. *The Murrow Boys: Pioneers on the Front Lines of Broadcast Journalism.* New York: Houghton Mifflin, 1996.

Donald G. Godfrey

TRUMAN, HARRY S. (1884–1972), the thirty-third president of the United States, was best known in a radio context for his speeches announcing the end of World War II and the beginning of postwar reconversion; his use of radio in his political campaigns; and for marshaling radio to confront Senator Joseph McCarthy, whose anticommunist campaigns were dominating headlines at the close of the Truman presidency.

Truman was a native of Independence, Missouri, and had been a local politician prior to his election to the U.S. Senate in 1934. Truman was Franklin Roosevelt's vice presidential candidate in 1944 and had served as vice president for only a few weeks prior to FDR's death and his succession to the presidency in April 1945.

Although not considered a pioneer in the medium, nor, with a shrill voice, particularly effective in it, Truman used radio regularly. Following series of radio speeches at the conclusion of World War II, including a broadcast announcing the dropping of the first atomic bomb, Truman turned to radio as a means of responding to his political opponents, largely members of the 1946 Congress, whom Truman branded as "do nothings." During his uphill 1948 defeat of Thomas Dewey, after Truman had further lambasted his political opponents on radio, well-wishers urged him to "Give 'em hell."

That Truman was not as astute in radio as his predecessor, FDR, was illustrated in Truman's failure to rally support for American involvement in the Korean War, beginning in 1950, and in his veto of the *McCarran Act,* which provided for the registration of communists. Although later rated as one of the greatest presidents, Truman chose not to run for reelection in 1952 and left office in 1953 with a public approval rating of around 30 percent, one of the lowest ever recorded.

Hamby, Alonzo L. *Man of the People: A Life of Harry S. Truman.* New York: Oxford University Press, 1995.

McCullough, David. *Truman.* New York: Simon and Schuster, 1992.

Williams, Herbert Lee. *The Newspaperman's President: Harry S. Truman.* Chicago: Nelson Hall, 1984.

Craig M. Allen

U

UNDERGROUND, COMMERCIAL RADIO, also referred to as progressive, freeform, and alternative, debuted in 1966 on station WOR-FM in New York City. It offered listeners an eclectic mix of rock, folk, jazz, classical, and blues. By broadcasting such a unique blend of recordings, it defied the conventional approach to radio programming, which invariably prescribed a single or primary music genre, such as that featured by top 40, beautiful music, country, and other popular formats of the day.

Although WOR-FM's underground presentation was short-lived (lasting but a few months), another station soon undertook the challenge of countering the established norm in radio music programming. KMPX-FM in San Francisco went on the air with its freewheeling, unstructured sound in 1967.

Many of the individuals who played a central role in developing the commercial underground format were from mainstream stations, which strictly adhered to rigid programming guidelines. These individuals were eager to break from the predictable playlists in order to provide audiences with music that commercial radio seldom aired. This discontent resonated with the rebellious nature of an era that gave rise to significant counterculture behavior, especially among young people, many of whom embraced the new gestalt that loudly trumpeted the cosmic virtues of peace and freedom.

Deejays in underground radio abandoned the high-intensity and affected styles found in pop chart formats for a more conversational sound. The emphasis was on being real and natural. Underground jocks were themselves first and foremost. Among the preeminent pioneers of the format are Tom Donahue, Larry Miller, Scott Muni, Larry Yurdin, Thom O'Hair, Dusty Street, and Bob Fass. Other early commercial underground stations include WNEW-FM (New York), KSAN-FM (San Francisco), WBCN-FM (Boston), WABX-FM (Detroit), WEBN-FM (Cincinnati), and KSHE-FM (St. Louis).

The format came to a premature end in the 1970s as big business and owners reasserted their control and reimposed strictures that proved antithetical to the nature of the underground programming approach.

Keith, Michael C. *Voices in the Purple Haze: Underground Radio in the Sixties.* Westport, Conn.: Praeger, 1997.

Ladd, Jim. *Radio Waves: Life and Revolution on the FM Dial.* New York: St. Martin's Press, 1991.

Post, Steve. *Playing in the FM Band: A Personal Account of Free Radio.* New York: Viking Press, 1974.

Michael C. Keith

UNIONS, in the radio industry, describes labor organizations that represent technical personnel at stations, networks, and production companies. These unions are referred to as below-the-line unions, which comes from a budget term that divides fixed (below-the-line) and variable (above-the-line) costs. Above-the-line unions that represent creative/artistic radio personnel are called *guilds.* The degree of unionization varies considerably by geographic region, but almost all major urban markets are unionized. The largest broadcasting union representing engineers, production personnel, and other technical positions at ABC and NBC Networks and their owned-and-operated stations is the National Association of Broadcast Employees and Technicians (NABET). Below-the-line technical personnel at CBS and its owned-and-operated stations are represented by the International Brotherhood of Electrical Workers (IBEW). Above-the-line personnel such as announcers, disc jockeys, newscasters, and other performers are represented by the American Federation of Television and Radio Artists (AFTRA). Writers who prepare written scripts or other copy such as news reports are represented by the Writers' Guild of America (WGA). Other below-the-line unions involved in the radio industry in some markets include: the International Alliance of Theatrical and Stage Employees (IATSE), the Communication Workers of America (CWA), and the Teamsters. Other above-the-line unions include the Directors' Guild of America (DGA), and the American Federation of Musicians (AFofM).

Pringle, Peter K., Michael F. Starr, and William E. McCavitt. *Electronic Media Management.* 3rd ed. Boston: Focal Press, 1995.

Sherman, Barry L. *Telecommunications Management.* 2nd ed. New York: McGraw-Hill, 1995.

Robert G. Finney

UNISTAR RADIO NETWORKS was a company that produced and distributed news and music programming during the 1980s and early 1990s. In the early 1980s, the company was formed from a merger of the United Stations and Transtar Radio Networks—hence, the name Unistar. It quickly grew into one of the nation's most successful format syndicators. With the arrival of affordable satellite-distribution technologies and the tight economic environment of the mid- and late 1980s, radio stations found it increasingly attractive to replace local air staffs with less expensive, well-researched, and well-formatted national programming. Unistar was able to capitalize on this environment by providing stations with a wide array of continuous, long-form music and news programming distributed by satellite. Unistar offered two CNN news formats, CNBC Business Radio, and numerous music formats within the broad groups of country, oldies, standards, and adult contemporary.

In 1993, Unistar entered into a management agreement with Infinity Broadcasting Corporation whereby the business affairs of Unistar would be handled by Infinity's management team. Infinity owned a number of radio stations across the country but, at the time, had not involved itself in programming syndication. Mel Karmazin, president and chief executive officer (CEO) of Infinity, became the CEO of Unistar. Unistar's former CEO, Nick Verbitsky, resigned but was retained as a consultant. In 1994, Unistar was purchased by Westwood One, itself a producer and distributor of syndicated radio formats and also under a management agreement with Infinity. Westwood One had primarily specialized in distributing singular, short-form programs such as the Don Imus morning show, Larry King, Bruce Williams, Casey Kasem, and other features designed to be inserted into radio stations' local formats. The acquisition of Unistar enabled Westwood One to become the United States' largest radio program syndicator, distributing both short-form and long-form programming. With the purchase by Westwood One, the Unistar name disappeared as its operations simply became part of the larger company. Westwood One reorganized itself into two main divisions: the Entertainment Division—which contained most of the short-form features—and the Radio Networks Division—which included most of the long-form formats established previously by Unistar. The result was Infinity—the owner of more radio stations than any other company—also controlled the management of the country's largest radio-programming syndication organization.

Kenneth D. Loomis

UNITED FRUIT COMPANY, one of five companies to join the radio patents pool in the early 1920s giving American commercial interests control over the American radio industry. United Fruit developed an interest in radio technology in an effort to better coordinate its international banana trade. Using de Forest's equipment and later Fessenden's heterodyne alternator, United Fruit set up shore stations in Central America and the Caribbean basin and outfitted its large fleet of refrigerated steamships. It acquired the Wireless Specialty Apparatus Company in 1912, giving it control of the Pickard and Dunwoody patents for crystal detectors and thereby positioning it for participation in the cross-licensing agreements with General Electric, RCA, AT&T, and Westinghouse.

Kepner, Charles David, Jr., and Jay Henry Soothill. *The Banana Empire: A Case Study of Economic Imperialism.* New York: Vanguard Press, 1935.
Wilson, Charles Morrow. *Empire in Green and Gold: The Story of the American Banana Trade.* New York: Greenwood Press, 1968.

Christina S. Drale

UNITED INDEPENDENT BROADCASTERS. *See* **Coats, George A.; Columbia Broadcasting System (CBS).**

UNITED STATES COURTS. *See* specific court listing.

UNIVERSITY OF CHICAGO ROUNDTABLE, innovative early educational radio program produced by the University of Chicago for NBC. Two university professors and an invited guest expert discussing current affairs for 30 minutes each week does not sound like the makings of a successful network radio program. Yet for more than 20 years, the *University of Chicago Roundtable,* heard each Sunday over the NBC Red Radio Network, was among the most popular public service programs in American radio. Inspired by the freewheeling discussions common at the roundtable in the University of Chicago cafeteria, the program was created by Chicago alumnus Judith Waller, who held the post of educational (later public service) director for NBC's Central Region. After several years on Chicago NBC station WMAQ, the program went national in 1933. For many years, production was subsidized by a grant from the Sloan Foundation.

In its early years, the *Roundtable* was virtually the only network program that was neither scripted nor rehearsed, exhibiting an uncommon spontaneity that was likely the key to its success. More than a week of planning and research went into each *Roundtable* broadcast, and the leader of each week's discussion attempted to keep the participants within the bounds of a prearranged outline. However, panelists, particularly the faculty members, resisted suggestions that they work from scripts.

Panelists were chosen for their outspoken nature, and controversy was a *Roundtable* staple. Several programs prompted the network to offer free reply-time to someone criticized during the discussion. Network officials threatened more than once to cancel the series over particularly controversial programs, but it stayed on the air until the mid-1950s. The program's first moderator, Professor T. V. Smith, became a U.S. congressman.

Heistad, Mark J. "Radio without Sponsors: Public Service Programming in Network Sustaining Time, 1928–1952." Ph. D. dissertation, University of Minnesota, 1997.
Waller, Judith C. *Radio: The Fifth Estate.* Boston: Houghton Mifflin Company, 1946.

Mark J. Heistad

URBAN CONTEMPORARY FORMAT developed as a consequence of the disco music phenomenon of the late 1970s. The format's roots are in dance music, which often features the best African-American performers mixed with other popular music. The format has been especially popular in America's urban areas—thus its name.

Another characteristic of the urban contemporary format is the use of a "hot clock," which is a means of controlling music selections, commercial placement, and announcer comments. In addition, disc jockeys are also a prominent feature of this format. Urban contemporary disc jockeys tend to be friendly, energetic, and upbeat. Moreover, they are expected to have knowledge about the music they play and express an affinity for it.

Musical selections on urban contemporary radio stations includes rhythm and blues, rap, and some top-40 tunes. Artists such as Mary J. Blige, Boyz II Men, En Vogue, Madonna, and All-4-One are often heard on these stations. Urban contemporary formats attract listeners from a variety of ethnic backgrounds, including African Americans, Caucasians, Hispanics, and Asian Americans. Moreover, the format tends to attract teenagers and young adults, especially females. Urban contemporary formats include news as well; however, it is not a prominent feature. Live-remote broadcasts, community service programming, and public service announcements are common aspects of the urban contemporary format. Approximately 7 percent of radio stations nationwide use it.

Dominick, Joseph R., Barry L. Sherman, and Gary A. Copeland. *Broadcasting/Cable and Beyond: An Introduction to Modern Electronic Media.* 3rd ed. New York: McGraw-Hill, 1996.

Keith, Michael C. *Radio Programming: Consultancy and Formatics.* Boston: Focal Press, 1987.

Gilbert A. Williams

USIA (UNITED STATES INFORMATION AGENCY) was established on August 1, 1953, to operate the U.S. Voice of America (VOA) and print, film, and television propaganda but independent from the State Department. The USIA was a direct result of President Harry Truman's "Campaign of Truth" begun in 1950 at the start of the Korean War. The programming it provided was intended to influence foreign audiences and was not intended for American audiences.

In 1981, a government television network was established linking 60 overseas television systems to the USIA headquarters in Washington, which provides satellite links for two-way news conferences. President George Bush used this system to address foreign publics during the Persian Gulf Crisis. In 1983, USIA created "Worldnet" as a daily television service distributed worldwide by satellite. Most of Worldnet's programming is news and general information. *Dialogue* is an hour-long live program in which journalists, politicians, and people from around the world debate U.S. experts on various subjects. Other programming is supplied by commercial, cable, or public broadcasting such as *The News Hour* with Jim Lehrer (PBS) or *This Week with David Brinkley* (ABC). Surveys show very small audiences, which lead to budget cuts and limit the ability to provide original programming.

Fortner, Robert S. *International Communication.* Belmont, Calif.: Wadsworth, 1993.

Gross, Lynne, ed. *The International World of Electronic Media.* New York: McGraw-Hill, 1995.

"USIA Publishes Guide to TV in Eastern Europe." *Broadcasting* 18 (March 5, 1990): 16–17.

Mary E. Beadle

V

VAN DYKE, CHARLIE, one of the legendary voices in broadcasting. He has worked as an on-air personality in some of the major radio markets in the country. Van Dyke worked as morning personality and program director at KLIF in Dallas, a Gordon McLendon station. He also worked on air at KHJ, Los Angeles; KFRC, San Francisco; and WLS, Chicago. Charlie Van Dyke currently is an independent voice talent working out of Phoenix, Arizona.

Routt, Edd, James B. McGrath, and Fredric A. Weiss. *The Radio Format Conundrum.* New York: Hastings House, 1978.

Frederic A. Leigh

VARIETY MAGAZINE, an authoritative trade paper focusing on the entertainment business, is published weekly for international distribution by Cahners Publications. *Variety* has been covering radio since the early 1920s when the then-new medium was recognized for its growing importance in American culture. *Variety* was the first, in July 1941, to use the term *disc jockey* to describe those who presented recorded music on radio. Also, *Variety*'s reporting has often served as a gauge indicating the relative popularity of radio performers and music. The magazine, with a circulation of 35,000, is based at 154 West 46th Street, New York City.

Fornatale, Peter, and Joshua E. Mills. *Radio in the Television Age.* Woodstock, N.Y.: Overlook Press, 1980.

Tim England

VICTOR TALKING MACHINE COMPANY, the leading manufacturer of "talking machines" during the first 30 years of the twentieth century, at first produced phonographs and recordings of military bands, recitations, and comedies. The company grew rapidly, expanding its manufacturing and recording line. In 1925, Victor recognized the popularity of a new talking machine, the radio, by producing a radio/phonograph set consisting of an RCA Radiola in combination with a Victrola. When purchased by RCA for $154 million in 1929, Victor had manufactured over 8 million instruments and produced records in more than 40 languages. Victor's trademark, Nipper, was the most famous dog in the world.

Barnum, Frederick O., III. *"His Master's Voice" in America*. Camden, N.J.: General Electric, 1991.

Bergonzi, Benet. *Old Gramaphones & Other Talking Machines*. New York: State Mutual Book & Periodical Service, 1989.

Wolverine Antique Music Society. http://www.teleport.com/~rfrederi/

Sandra L. Ellis

VOICE OF AMERICA (VOA) is the external broadcasting voice of the United States and is a function of the United States Information Agency (USIA). The VOA is prohibited by law from broadcasting to domestic audiences; however, anyone with a shortwave receiver may pick up the signals.

The VOA was established shortly after the United States' entry into World War II as a function of the Office of War Information headed by Elmer Davis (a popular radio commentator appointed to the position by President Franklin Roosevelt). The VOA's first broadcast was on February 23, 1942.

After World War II, the VOA was transferred to the State Department and became part of the Cold War arsenal. The VOA increased its foreign-language presentations and transmitted news, music, and other programming to most parts of the world.

In 1955 the United States Information Agency was established to operate the VOA as well as other information functions of the State Department that dealt with print, film, and, television propaganda.

The VOA broadcasts in 30 to 50 languages (the number of languages in use varies with needs) and averages over 2,200 hours of programming per week. VOA programming originates in Washington, D.C., and is relayed to satellites and transmitters in domestic and foreign locations. The VOA broadcasts on shortwave frequencies and to Central America and the Caribbean on AM frequencies.

Mange, Lawrence, ed. *Passport to World Band Radio*. 10th ed. Penn's Park: International Broadcasting Services, Ltd., 1994.

Regis Tucci

W

WABC-AM (New York, 770 kilohertz [KHz]) has often been a bellwether of changes in the radio industry. In September 1921, Westinghouse put WJZ on the air in Newark, New Jersey. WJZ became the flagship station of the Radio Group network (see **Radio Corporation of America [RCA]**). In 1926, as a result of the merger the radio stations divested from AT&T, and RCA established WJZ as the base for the Blue Network, which by 1932 was under the auspices of the National Broadcasting Company (NBC). As such, WJZ was an exemplar of the network era of radio broadcasting. In 1943, the Blue Network was sold to Edward F. Noble as a result of the Federal Communications Commission (FCC) duopoly rules. In 1945, the network was renamed the American Broadcasting Company, and WJZ took the call letters WABC. As radio became more localized, WABC moved from full-service to music programming. By the early 1960s, WABC-AM was one of the leading rock 'n' roll stations in the country. In 1961, WABC-FM went on the air to simulcast programming. In 1967, under FCC regulations, the two stations separated programming (the latter eventually becoming WPLJ-FM). As "All-Hits Radio," WABC-AM was New York's top radio station in the 1960s but began to lose audience share to the FM music stations of which ironically WPLJ-FM was a pioneer. In 1983, Musicradio WABC changed to Talkradio WABC. Today, the station still programs primarily call-in talk and sports, carrying local and syndicated programs including Rush Limbaugh, who broadcasts from their studios.

Sklar, Rick. *Rocking America: An Insider's Story.* New York: St. Martin's Press, 1984.
WABC-AM. http://members.gnn.com/thebighump/wabc.htm

Jonathan David Tankel

WAGNER-HATFIELD AMENDMENT, unsuccessful amendment to the *Communications Act of 1934* that would have allocated one quarter of all broadcast frequencies to nonprofit stations. In 1934, U.S. Senators Robert Wagner (D–N.Y.) and Henry Hatfield (R–W.Va.) offered an amendment calling for a federal set-aside of 25 percent of all broadcast frequencies for educational, religious, agricultural, labor, cooperative, and similar nonprofit broadcasters. The amendment was the brainchild of John B. Harney of the Paulist Fathers and enjoyed wide support among labor, education, religious, and other noncommercial broadcasters who had seen their "rights to the air" diminish since the establishment of the Federal Radio Commission in 1927.

The trade magazine *Variety* at one point gave the amendment a "better than 50–50 chance" of passage. *Broadcasting* warned its readers that "self-seeking reformers" threatened the entire commercial radio structure. Coordinated and relentless lobbying against the measure by commercial radio interests resulted in a compromise, Section 307(c), which called for a Federal Communications Commission (FCC) study of noncommercial broadcasting. FCC hearings on the issue featured confusing and, at times, contradictory testimony from noncommercial broadcasters and promises from commercial broadcasters that the educators and others could have all the free time they wished on commercial stations. The FCC concluded that noncommercial broadcasters needed no special protection from Washington.

Following defeat of the Wagner-Hatfield Amendment, commercial broadcasters and nonprofit groups entered into a short-lived "era of cooperation." Commercial stations and networks quickly appointed public service directors who coordinated the production of new public service programming broadcast in unsold or sustaining time. However, just three years after the FCC hearings, one of the most important cooperative producers of educational programming, the Committee on Civic Education by Radio, concluded that nonprofit groups were treated so poorly by commercial broadcasters that it was useless to "attempt systematic education" via commercial radio.

Committee on Civic Education by Radio of the National Advisory Council on Radio in Education and the American Political Science Association. *Four Years of Network Broadcasting.* Chicago: University of Chicago Press, 1937.

Leach, Eugene E. *Tuning Out Education: The Cooperation Doctrine in Radio, 1922–1938.* Washington, D.C.: Current, 1983.

McChesney, Robert W. *Telecommunications, Mass Media and Democracy: The Battle for the Control of U.S. Broadcasting, 1928–1935.* New York: Oxford University Press, 1993.

Tyler, Tracy F., ed. *Radio as a Cultural Agency: Proceedings of a National Conference on the Use of Radio as a Cultural Agency.* Washington, D.C.: National Committee on Education by Radio, 1934.

Mark J. Heistad

WALLER, JUDITH CARY(1889–1973), a pioneer broadcaster, was one of the first managers of a radio station, WMAQ, Chicago. Waller was born on February 19, 1889, in Oak Park, Illinois. After graduation from the Oak Park High School in 1908 and a year's tour of Europe, Waller went to business college and worked in advertising and publishing in Chicago and New York.

In 1922, the business manager of the *Chicago Daily News* asked Waller to run the radio station the paper had just purchased. Although she had never heard of radio and was not confident she could manage it, Waller became an expert in programming as noted by her credits. She was the first to broadcast play-by-play baseball games from a home ballpark, with the Chicago Cubs in 1925. She brought the *Amos 'n' Andy* creators to the station in 1928 and helped make them a national hit for NBC. She was the originator of the *University of Chicago Roundtable* for WMAQ in 1931. Later carried by the NBC Network, it became the standard for public service programming for two decades. She continued promoting educational programming for television, developing the award-winning preschool program *Ding-Dong School.*

Waller became vice president and general manager of WMAQ in 1929, and when the NBC Network purchased the station in 1931 she became the network's public service director. She participated in all four national radio conferences called by Secretary of Commerce Herbert Hoover in the 1920s, helped form the National Association of Broadcasters, served on the University Association for Professional Radio Education, and wrote the classic text *Radio, the Fifth Estate* in 1946. After her retirement from NBC in 1957, she led television workshops at Purdue University and lectured at Northwestern. She died of a heart attack on October 28, 1973, in Evanston, Illinois.

Benjamin, Louise. "Judith Cary Waller." In *Women in Communication: A Biographical Sourcebook,* edited by Nancy Signorielli (pp. 415–418). Westport, Conn.: Greenwood, 1996.

Williamson, Mary E. "Judith Cary Waller: Chicago Broadcasting Pioneer." *Journalism History* 3 (4) (1976–1977): 111–115.

Margot Hardenbergh

WAR INFORMATION, OFFICE OF (OWI). Created by President Roosevelt by Executive Order 9182 on June 13, 1942, the OWI was charged with utilizing America's mass media to inform U.S. citizens both home and abroad about U.S. government programs and policies during World War II. Former reporter Elmer Davis was appointed OWI director. Named to head the OWI's domestic and international branches were William B. Lewis and Robert Sherwood, respectively. A Committee on War Information Policy, chaired by OWI Director Davis, was created to set basic OWI policy and to approve OWI plans.

OWI's most important responsibility was coordinating and prioritizing informational programming produced by some 40 government agencies. It did not produce radio programs itself but solicited assistance from civilian organizations like the Advertising Council and the National Association of Broadcasters to produce and schedule programs and public service announcements with war-related themes. Particular themes that broadcasters were asked to emphasize included the "nature of the enemy," "fighting forces, their jobs, training, morale," and "home forces, and [the] need for all-out civilian participation."

The OWI also took advantage of U.S. shortwave radio stations and the facilities of the Armed Forces Radio Network to air programming meant to boost the morale of international civilian listeners and troops stationed abroad. President Truman's Executive Order 9608 terminated the OWI on August 31, 1945. The OWI's wartime responsibilities were transferred to an interim agency that in time would become the U.S. Information Agency.

Dryer, Sherman. *Radio in Wartime.* New York: Greenburg, 1942.
Landry, Robert. *This Fascinating Radio Business.* New York: Bobbs-Merrill, 1946.
Siepmann, Charles. *Radio in Wartime.* America Faces the War, No. 13. New York: Oxford University Press, 1942.

Ronald Garay

WEAF (NEW YORK CITY) was established and operated by the American Telephone and Telegraph Company (AT&T) from August 1922 until November 1, 1926, when the station was sold to NBC. During that four-year period, the station was used for an experiment AT&T termed "toll telephony."

Toll telephony was seen by AT&T as an outgrowth and logical extension of the telephone business. Until and for some time after the experiment, money in broadcasting was made from the manufacture and sale of radio sets to the public. The costs of broadcasting were borne by those who purchased components to build radios or factory-assembled receivers. AT&T, not a manufacturer of radios, had the corporate experience of the telephone business and decided that WEAF would be a broadcast facility available to anyone desiring to address the public. AT&T applied the principle of the common carrier to broadcasting as that principle was applied to the corner pay phone; the equipment and resources of AT&T, in this case WEAF, could be leased by anyone who wished to pay the price. WEAF became America's first broadcasting pay station (Banning).

WEAF was noted for a number of firsts in broadcasting. The first simultaneous broadcast from two stations, WEAF, New York and WN8C, Boston, took place on January 23, 1925; in May of 1925 WEAF hired Graham McNamee, who became one of the most popular announcers of the 1920s; the first broadcast involving transcontinental telephone circuits was accomplished on February 8, 1924; and during the summer of 1924, WEAF broadcast to 12 cities the activities of the Republican and Democratic national conventions.

Of all the firsts in which WEAF was involved, the one to have the most lasting effect on American broadcasting took place on August 28, 1922, when the first "commercial" was aired. On that Monday afternoon at 5:15, the Queensboro Corporation aired the first of a series of 15-minute announcements concerning apartment houses at Jackson Heights, New York. The last of the announcements aired in September, and the Queensboro Corporation reported several thousand dollars in sales. The Tidewater Oil Company and the American Express Company began experimental announcements that month also. WEAF prohibited any mention of price since that was considered direct advertising.

That first commercial on WEAF was an indicator of a great change to come. The cost of broadcasting was being removed from the buyers of radios and component parts and being placed on those who wished to reach the listeners with commercial messages. Manufacturers would still sell receivers, but a new method of "sponsorship" would allow radio and later television to grow beyond the wildest dreams of early broadcasters.

Banning, William Peck. *Commercial Broadcasting Pioneer: The WEAF Experiment 1922– 1926.* Cambridge: Harvard University Press, 1945.

Lackmann, Ronald W. *Same Time—Same Station: An A–Z Guide to Radio from Jack Benny to Howard Stern.* New York: Facts on File, Inc., 1996.

Regis Tucci

WEATHER BROADCASTING is vital to agricultural and maritime economies, as well as to sea, land, and air travelers. In 1847, Smithsonian Secretary Joseph Henry proposed the first organized use of electronic technology to issue public storm warnings. The Smithsonian gathered telegraphed reports to produce a daily weather map. In 1902, the Marconi company began wireless weather reports to ships at sea. In 1904, President Theodore Roosevelt assigned experimental wireless weather reports to the U.S. Navy and Coast Guard; on July 15, 1913, daily radiotelegraph weather bulletins began from naval stations in Virginia and Florida.

The University of North Dakota radiotelegraph station in 1914 sent Weather Bureau reports to a network of wireless operators who relayed forecasts to farmers. On January 3, 1921, the University of Wisconsin began probably the first systematic, weather radio broadcasts. By June 1922, 20 of the nation's 36 commercial licensees carried weather reports; all licensees did by 1923. During World War II, radio stations avoided weather forecasts for security reasons.

In 1959, Congress established a pilot project in agricultural weather reporting in Stoneville, Mississippi; its daily, regional weather reports for mass media were so successful in saving crops and boosting the economy that, as Environmental Studies Service Centers, this began in other states. The National Weather Service has developed a nationwide broadcasting system, available on special FM receivers, above 162 megahertz (MHz). The Emegency Broadcast System (EBS) (now, Emergency Alert System [EAS]) is available for any threat to life or property, including severe weather. All commercial licensees are equipped for EBS/EAS notification, but participation is voluntary.

Baker, John C. *Farm Broadcasting: The First Sixty Years.* Ames: Iowa State University Press, 1981.
Hughers, Patrick. *A Century of Weather Service, 1870–1970.* New York: Gordon and Breach, 1970.

William James Ryan

WELLES, ORSON [GEORGE] (1915–1985). Celebrated as one of radio's most innovative personalities, Welles's "War of the Worlds" 1938 drama caused a national panic. Welles's radio career falls into four periods.

Between 1935 and 1937, he emerged on radio, appearing as McGafferty, the scheming banker, in Archibald McLeish's "Panic," aired as part of the 1935 *March of Time* series. In 1936 he played Lamont Cranston, the invisible character on *The Shadow* mystery program. His splendid voice and popularity with the cultural elite won him opportunities in classical roles. During 1937, he appeared on the CBS *Summer Shakespeare* series, NBC's Civil War program *Roses and Drums,* and Mutual's *Les Miserables,* a series adapted from Victor Hugo's novel.

On the *Columbia Workshop,* he received the principal role in McLeish's "The Fall of the City," the first American verse play for radio. Welles appeared as a reporter, a format he later used to make the "War of the Worlds" broadcast believable. Welles's success gained him so many radio appearances he hired an ambulance to get through traffic between studios. In May 1938, his picture appeared on the cover of *Time* magazine, confirming his national popularity.

Welles's second period, the Mercury era, is highlighted by the "War of the Worlds" broadcast, bringing him international notoriety. In 1938, CBS approached Welles with the idea of a weekly one-hour series of classic dramas. Actors from Welles's existing stage group, the Mercury Theatre, were hired. The series began as the *First Person Singular* and was later renamed the *Mercury Theatre on the Air.* The original title referred to an innovative narration approach used by Welles in which he acted as the narrator while building himself directly into the drama.

Among the broadcasts were "Dracula" and "Treasure Island." On Halloween eve, an adaption by Howard Koch of H. G. Welles's *The War of the Worlds* was aired. Presented in the format of a news broadcast, the program's early minutes were deliberately dull. Events slowly emerged into an excited pace as the aliens killed their first victims. Listeners tuning in late panicked after hearing the announcer reporting news of a hostile attack. Because the broadcast occurred in the midst of fear of an invasion or involvement in war, the drama unleashed hidden paranoia. The next morning, the *New York Times* headline claimed "Radio Listeners in Panic, Taking War Drama as Fact." Welles had demonstrated the power of radio. Overnight, he became part of American folklore. The series ended in 1940.

In a third phase, the war years, he engaged in many political and propaganda programs supporting the war effort, President Roosevelt, and the New Deal policies. Most notable were his *Ceiling Unlimited,* patriotic dramas about bombers and flyers (1942–1944); *Orson Welles Almanac,* humor and political commentary (1943–1944); *Orson Welles Commentaries,* social-political commentary on literature (1945–1946); and his appearances on *The Cavalcade of America,* a series dealing with political and historical subjects.

Finally, in the 1950s, he appeared in radio productions, mostly in London, including *The Adventures of Harry Lime* and *The Black Museum.* The *Harry Lime* show represented the only time he played the main character throughout an entire series.

Brady, Frank. *Citizen Welles.* New York: Charles Scribner's Sons, 1989.

Callow, Simon. *Orson Welles: The Road to Xanadu.* New York: Viking Press, 1996.

Koch, Howard. *The Panic Broadcast.* New York: Avon Books, 1971.

Leaming, Barbara. *Orson Welles.* New York: Viking Press, 1985.

Orson Welles on the Air: The Radio Years. Monograph. New York: Museum of Broadcasting, 1988.

Shepard, Richard F. "Master of Radio: Welles on the Air." *New York Times,* November 30, 1988, p. C26.

Tavares, Frank. *A Critical Analysis of Selected Dramatic Elements in the Radio Series "The Lives of Harry Lime," with Orson Welles.* Ann Arbor, Mich.: University Microfilms International, 1976.

Wood, Bert. *Orson Welles: A Bio-Bibliography.* New York: Greenwood Press, 1990.

Frank Chorba

WESTERN ELECTRIC began in 1869 as a small, electrical-manufacturing firm called Gray and Barton. It eventually became a subsidiary of AT&T, manufacturing radio transmitters as well as telephone apparatus.

Enos Barton had been a telegraph operator, and Elisha Gray was an inventor and former physics professor. They teamed up with Western Union executive General Anson Stager to establish Gray and Barton on November 18, 1869, in Cleveland, Ohio. In 1872, the company was reorganized and renamed Western Electric Manufacturing Company. In 1876, Gray and Barton attended the Philadelphia Exhibition and witnessed Alexander Graham Bell's demonstration of the telephone. Shortly thereafter, Western Electric began to work on telephone technology. Five years later, Bell's American Bell Telephone Company bought a controlling interest in Western Electric for the purpose of using it as a manufacturer of telephone apparatus. AT&T took over American Bell Telephone in 1899 and became the parent company to Western Electric.

Western Electric and AT&T became involved in the radio field by virtue of their interest in de Forest's audion as a telephone-line amplifier. AT&T bought the line amplifier rights from de Forest in 1913, and Western Electric began to manufacture the audion for telephone use. During this time, Western Electric engineers worked on improving de Forest's design and eventually produced radio tubes as well, particularly transmitting tubes. AT&T bought radiotelephone rights to the audion in 1915, and by the time the United States entered World War I, Western Electric, like General Electric and Westinghouse, was producing radio tubes for the military. Western Electric introduced the first mass-produced transmitting tube, the five-watt VT-2 "baseball" in 1918.

After the war, Western Electric and AT&T entered into the patents pooling agreement with General Electric, RCA, and the other radio patent allies. Under this agreement, Western Electric had exclusive rights to manufacture radio tube transmitters. When AT&T entered the radio broadcasting business in 1922 with station WEAF, it was a 5,000-watt Western Electric transmitter, model 1A, that was installed. Soon after, Western Electric appeared to restrict the sale of its transmitters in the New York area in order to effectively force the use of the WEAF "toll" station and protect it from interference. When threat of antitrust action convinced AT&T to withdraw from the radio business in the mid-1920s, Western Electric continued to manufacture radio apparatus, but now did so nonexclusively.

In 1925, the combined engineering departments of AT&T and Western Electric were formed into Bell Laboratories, the research and development subsidiary of AT&T. Western Electric remained as AT&T's manufacturing subsidiary until 1984, when as a result of an antitrust settlement, AT&T spun off its local telephone companies and restructured its remaining assets. Western Electric was absorbed into a new subsidiary called AT&T Technologies, which consolidated its development and manufacturing divisions. In 1995, AT&T restructured again, forming Lucent Technologies, which includes six divisions encompassing research and development (Bell Laboratories), service, and manufacturing. Four of the six new divisions—business communications systems, consumer products, microelectronics, and multimedia ventures and technologies—include manufacturing functions formerly handled by Western Electric.

Gorman, Paul A. *Century One . . . A Prologue*. New York: Newcomen Society in North America, 1969.

Lucent Technologies. *Fact Book*. http://www.att.com/lucent/

Christina S. Drale

WESTINGHOUSE Electric and Manufacturing Company, Pittsburgh, Pennsylvania. The Westinghouse interest in radio began with Frank Conrad, an engineer who started experimenting with radio in 1912. World War I produced lucrative radio manufacturing contracts, but at the war's end, there was a transition to commercial radio. Conrad put radio station 8XK on the air, which later became KDKA and was known for the first U.S. commercial broadcast on November 2, 1920. Westinghouse became a part of the radio trust in 1921. It held patents to Fessenden's earlier radio work and Edwin Armstrong's regenerative detector and oscillator. Within the trust, it had the rights to manufacture radio receivers. In 1921–1922, during radio's first boom, Westinghouse sold thousands of sets. It was also in the early 1920s when Westinghouse hired Vladimir K. Zworykin, a Russian immigrant and engineer, who would contribute to the history of television.

Douglas, Alan. *Radio Manufacturers of the 1920's*. Vols. 1–3. New York: Vestal Press, Ltd., 1991. 3rd ed., reprint, Chandler, Ariz.: Sonoran Publishing Inc. 1995.

Donald G. Godfrey

WESTINGHOUSE RADIOS. The Westinghouse Electric and Manufacturing Company entered radio broadcasting as a manufacturer of vacuum tubes due to its electric lamp-bulb manufacturing capabilities. In 1920 Westinghouse purchased a patent from Edwin H. Armstrong for a "superheterodyne" circuit that greatly increased radio amplification capabilities. Through a "patent pooling" arrangement between Westinghouse, General Electric, and AT&T, these companies were leaders in developing and manufacturing crystal and radio sets that were marketed by the Radio Corporation of America (RCA) in the 1920s. A cross-licensing agreement between these and several smaller companies facilitated manufacturing and distributing early radio sets to the public. Without these early agreements, no one company had sufficient patents to manufacture radio sets effectively. As a result of major technical research by Westinghouse and GE, numerous improvements were made to the radio sets, making them more reliable and more affordable. These improvements helped radio to penetrate the home market during the lean years of the depression era—the 1930s. An antitrust suit in 1932 caused Westinghouse to sell its stock in RCA and operate independently in manufacturing and distributing radio sets.

Westinghouse began radio broadcasting in Pittsburgh in 1920 to establish a station to stimulate sales of their radio receivers and to increase publicity for the company name. In the first year, they produced the Aeriola, Jr., a crystal set that sold for $25; the Aeriola Sr., the first home receiver with a vacuum tube, which sold for $60; and the Aeriola Grand, with a built-in loudspeaker and multiple vacuum tubes, which sold for $175. Public demand and acceptance of radio and broadcasting led to demand surpassing supply. In two years, 1920–1922, the nation went from a handful of amateur experimenters to 2 million homes with radios. Demand was high for both small, inexpensive table-top models as well as full console models, which commanded a place as a formal piece of furniture in many households. By 1925, the demand for battery-operated radios had shifted to sets powered by alternating current. Sets that used to contain three tuning dials and only a headset had evolved to sets with single-dial tuning and built-in speakers. Additional features promoted the radio set as an "audio center" containing a phonograph, push-button tuning, and shortwave band selection as America fell in love with radio and broadcast programming.

Bruce W. Russell

WESTINGHOUSE STRATOVISION, in 1945 a new method introduced by Westinghouse for transmitting FM radio and television signals—a forerunner of satellite broadcasting. The idea was to use an airplane, equipped to broadcast four channels for television and five for FM, as a transmitter rather than a ground transmitter, thus eliminating ground-relay stations and cable. With an airplane flying in a circular pattern at 30,000 feet over a broadcast site, a signal relayed from the ground could be distributed to an area 422 miles in diameter. This was the equivalent of the size of the states of New York, New Jersey, and Pennsylvania. This was an enormous increase in area over the current line-of-sight transmission, which could only reach 50 miles. The plan called for 7 airplanes to be airborne across the United States at the same time so a signal could be broadcast from coast to coast. With 14 airplanes airborne at the same time and strategically located across the United States, television could reach 78 percent of the population. Westinghouse believed that Stratovision would make existing land-line networks obsolete because it was considerably cheaper to operate each airplane than any system in operation at the time. In 1948, test flights that broadcast television and radio broadcasts were conducted over western Pennsylvania and met with success. The first public test of Stratovision broadcast the Republican National Convention in Philadelphia on June 23 and a boxing match. A B-29 flying over western Pennsylvania picked up a signal from Baltimore and rebroadcast it. The success of this effort led Westinghouse to file a petition in August 1948 with the Federal Communications Commission (FCC) requesting permission to allow KDKA-TV in Pittsburgh, Pennsylvania, to use Stratovision as its transmitter.

In September 1948, the FCC froze all new permits, thus stalling the efforts of Stratovision. Concern from smaller stations that they would be unable to compete with Westinghouse's Stratovision coupled with AT&T's development of a cable system to connect large sections of the country led Westinghouse to abandon the project.

Hinds, Lynn B. *Broadcasting the Local News: The Early Years of Pittsburgh's KDKA-TV.* University Park: Pennsylvania State University Press, 1995.

Bruce W. Russell

WESTWOOD ONE, a major company that innovated satellite-linked, radio broadcast networks during the 1970s and two decades later became part of the largest radio company in history. Named for a Los Angeles neighborhood by founder Norman J. Pattiz in 1974, the company took off when Pattiz hired local disc jockey Casey Kasem to host a countdown pop music program that Pattiz sold to hundreds of radio stations across the United States. Pattiz relied upon barter syndication whereby he produced the music show, found national advertisers to buy time, and then put together an ad hoc network. In return, the stations got to sell the remaining advertising slots to local sponsors and take on no costs in the process. By the early 1990s, the five Westwood One radio networks—Westwood One, NBC's The Source, NBC Talknet, NBC Radio Network, and Mutual—offered such feeds as *MTV News, Bright AC, The Oldies Channel, Country Countdown, Money Magazine Business Report, Science Update,* and the regular broadcasts of Dr. Joyce Brothers, Don Criqui, and Larry King.

Westwood One's growth accelerated in the 1980s with takeovers of two of the most important radio networks in the history of the U.S. radio medium. For example, Mutual was an important radio network in the 1930s ands 1940s of low-power, small-town stations. For $37 million in December of 1985 Westwood One acquired Mutual from Amway Corporation. Two years later General Electric sold the NBC Radio Network to Westwood One for $50 million. During the 1990s, Westwood One kept pace by distributing programming from such leading new networks as CNN and CNBC.

The corporate history of Westwood One took a major turn in October 1993 when the company purchased yet another network, Unistar, and then tendered day-to-day management control to Infinity Broadcasting. Infinity, the largest owner and operator of radio stations in the United States, added "shock jocks" Don Imus and Howard Stern to the Westwood One offerings. Infinity's Mel Karmazin became the chief executive officer of Westwood One, replacing founder Norm Pattiz. With this vertical integration Infinity + Westwood One became the key player in radio. In June 1996, Infinity sold out to Westinghouse, parent company of CBS, for nearly $5 billion. This new colossus now operated more than 80 radio stations across the United States, dominating listening in two dozen cities including 7 stations in New York City, 6 in Los Angeles, 10 in Chicago, 8 in San Francisco, and 4 in Washington, D.C. It also meant that only the ABC Radio Network was not under Infinity control. A small part of the deal, the monopoly of radio networks from NBC to CBS to Mutual to Westwood One, caught the eye of regulators; as of November 1996, what will happen to Westwood One awaits decisions by the Department of Justice, the Federal Communications Commission, and the Federal Trade Commission. The deal could go through as its stands or some or all of the networks might be required to be spun off.

Douglas Gomery

WHA, a radio station founded about 1915 at the University of Wisconsin, is the oldest educational, noncommercial outlet. The station began with experimentation in the physics department in Madison, which started as early as 1909. Voice transmissions were begun in 1917, and while all other "amateur" stations in the United States were silenced during World War II, the station, now licensed at 9XM, was used by the navy to communicate with ships associated with the Great Lakes Training Center.

Records are incomplete, and unclear, but apparently regular radio services from the university did not resume until January 1, 1921, with weather and market reports. The call letters were assigned on January 13, 1922, and to this day, the station has broadcast talks, lectures, entertainment, music, formal courses for credit, and in-school programs for students from elementary to high school. More than anything else, the station, and now a statewide network of FM stations, has sought to extend the borders of the university to the borders of the state—The Wisconsin Idea.

Smith, R. Franklin. "Oldest Station in the Nation?" *Journal of Broadcasting* 4 (1) (winter 1959–1960): 40–55.

Lawrence W. Lichty

WHITE, PAUL (1902–1956), organizer of the first CBS news operation, was CBS news chief during World War II. According to William Paley, "Radio news grew up with World War II," and it was White who managed and organized the growth. Beginning with a small staff, White's job during the mid-1930s was to work with the correspondents arranging events for broadcast. However, as the war unfolded, these correspondents evolved into reporters who names were recognized in every household: Robert Trout, Edward R. Murrow, William L. Shirer, Elmer Davis, H. V. Kaltenborn, Larry LeSueur, Eric Sevareid, and Howard K. Smith.

In 1938 CBS launched the first *CBS News Roundup*. It was a news program that, under White's supervision, called for correspondents throughout Europe to report via shortwave back to the studios in New York where Robert Trout was the anchor. The *CBS News Roundup* set patterns of news that are still apparent in today's news programming. White remained with CBS until 1947, when he moved to San Diego to work as a commentator for the CBS affiliate KFMB. He passed away in 1956 at age 52.

White, Paul W. *News on the Air.* New York: Harcourt, Brace & Co., 1947.

Donald G. Godfrey

WHITE, WALLACE HUMPHRY, JR.(1887–1952), was a major influence in drafting the *Radio Act of 1927* and the *Communications Act of 1934.* A lawyer by profession, White was a Republican from Lewiston, Maine. He worked on radio legislation from its inception. After Secretary of Commerce Hubert Hoover called the First Radio Conference on February 27, 1922, it was Representative White who proceeded to draft proposed legislation from the recommendations of the conferees. His first radio bills fell on a disinterested House of Representatives, but he hammered away at legislation until 1927.

In his legislative work, White was an outspoken proponent of the people's right to enjoy radio as a means of communication. He was not a well-known orator but was highly respected because of his knowledge and expertise. Later, in his Senate career, he was known as a "quiet, back stage negotiator." Representative White served in the House of Representatives from 1917 to 1931; and as a senator from Maine, he served from 1931 to 1939.

Donald G. Godfrey

WILEY, RICHARD (1934–), was a commissioner (1972–1977) and chair (1974–1977) of the Federal Communications Commission. Deregulation began during his tenure (see **deregulation; Federal Communications Commission [FCC]**).

Donald G. Godfrey

WINCHELL, WALTER (1897–1972), Broadway columnist for the New York *Mirror* from 1929 until 1963. He pioneered modern celebrity journalism, a mixture of reporting, gossip, and commentary served up in a slangy, neologistic, staccato style. Originally a vaudevillian, as a journalist Winchell became a celebrity in his own right, known for his gray fedora and his rapid-fire, wisecracking speech. His subject matter, his style, and his persona played well on radio. He began hosting programs on WABC, New York, in 1930 and between 1932 and 1955, his highly rated Sunday night broadcasts were heard over the NBC Blue Network (eventually ABC). Aspiring to be known as a serious journalist, Winchell aggressively covered the investigation of the kidnapping and murder (1932) of the Lindbergh baby and the subsequent trial of Bruno Richard Hauptmann. He claimed partial credit for Hauptmann's arrest after urging bank tellers on the air to check serial numbers for traces of ransom money. In 1939, the gangster Lewis "Lepke" Buchalter surrendered to Winchell personally after a broadcast. In 1944, Winchell engaged in a radio debate (from separate studios) with Representative Martin Dies, chair of the House Un-American Activities Committee, whom Winchell had charged with insufficient zeal against American fascists. Following World War II, Winchell himself became increasingly zealous as an anticommunist, strongly supporting Senator Joseph McCarthy. Winchell's popularity declined through the 1950s, and his television ventures failed (except for voice-over narration of *The Untouchables*). After four years on the Mutual network, his radio program ended in 1959; his syndicated newspaper column was canceled in 1967.

Gabler, Neal. *Winchell: Gossip, Power and the Culture of Celebrity.* New York: Knopf, 1994.
Klurfelt, Herman. *Winchell: His Life and Times.* New York: Praeger, 1976.

Glen M. Johnson

WIRELESS SHIP ACT OF 1910. Congress enacted this law, its first radio regulation, to enhance safety at sea, not only on luxury liners but also on ships carrying immigrants or passengers in steerage. Inspired by the rescue of 1,200 people after the *Republic* and the *Florida* collided off New York in January 1909, Congress required oceangoing passenger ships to have "an efficient apparatus for radio-communication, in good working order, in charge of a person skilled in the use of such apparatus." Radios had to have a 100-mile range and had to be compatible with other maritime radios.

John P. Ferré

WIRE SERVICES: AP AND UPI, the major American news-gathering organizations providing global coverage of news events to print and broadcast news organizations. The Associated Press (AP) is the oldest wire service, founded in 1848 by six New York City newspapers as a news-gathering cooperative. With more than 230 bureaus worldwide, AP serves more than 1,700 newspapers and 6,000 broadcast operations nationally as well as providing service to 110 foreign countries. The United Press (UP) was formed in 1907 by Edward W. Scripps as a competitor for the AP. The United Press was merged with William Randolph Hearst's International News Service (INS) in 1958 to form United Press International (UPI).

Emery, Edwin, and Michael Emery. *The Press and America: An Interpretive History of the Mass Media.* 5th ed. Englewood Cliffs, N.J.: Prentice-Hall, 1984.

Michael D. Casavantes

WLW, Cincinnati, was the most powerful station ever to operate in the United States. Calling itself "The Nation's Station," it broadcast local programming to a huge coverage area in Ohio, Indiana, and Kentucky, but with listeners in Michigan, West Virginia, Illinois, and Tennessee—and in many more states at night. A number of important radio stars began their careers at WLW, and the station developed programs later carried on the national networks.

Powel Crosley, Jr., got interested in radio in 1921 when his son asked for a "radio toy" as a birthday present. After building a set for his boy, the father was hooked on radio. He started his own amateur station and, in about a year, was the largest manufacturer of radio sets and parts in the world (see **Crosley, Powel, Jr.**).

Crosley built his first station in his home, which was licensed as 8XAA in July 1921. In March 1922 his company—Crosley Manufacturing Corporation, Cincinnati, Ohio—was assigned the call sign WLW for a "land-radio station" of 50 watts on 360 meters. Such a station could have had a range of about 100 miles, but it shared that frequency with hundreds of other stations. In April 1923 the power was increased to 500 watts, and to 1,000 watts a year later, and the Commerce Department announced it might use 5 kilowatts (kW) on a "strictly experimental" basis.

As the manufacturer of smaller, inexpensive, and thus less sensitive radio receivers, Crosley was much more interested than many other radio broadcasters in higher power. The station was operated primarily to provide programming for purchasers of Crosley sets "as a medium of advertising and publicity." The company's weekly magazine, distributed to radio retailers and purchasers of new sets, asked listeners to fill out a questionnaire to "vote on programs" listed in a variety of music, talk, and drama categories "they would like to hear."

The earliest programs on the station were musical variety using amateur talent, talks, and a number of soloists who were invited to the station. In August 1922, Fred Smith was hired as station director; he was the first employee. He inaugurated a regular daytime schedule of market reports, financial news, weather, and phonograph records. He arranged for many musical variety and live-music remotes during the evening hours. He wrote original radio dramas as well—the first on December

22, 1922. On April 3, 1923, the station broadcast *When Love Wakens,* an original play written by Smith especially for radio—probably the first in history.

In 1923, Smith wrote: "The nature of radio programs eventually will follow the demands of economic conditions, which in other words is but the demand of the public . . . that it be a joy bringer. The basis of radio programs has established itself: it is music. . . . Music is audible sunshine." But Smith tried many other formats at the station including programs for children, lectures to teach swimming, and re-creation of a boxing match based on telephone reports he got from a staff member at the arena; and he read news items interspersed with "appropriate musical selections" played on an organ. He would revive and revise this idea as the basis for the news drama program *The March of Time,* which he invented (see **The March of Time**).

WLW was designated a class "B" station by the Commerce Department in June 1923, one of only about 39 (of 500) U.S. stations that could use higher power. When the Federal Radio Commission (FRC) set about "cleaning up the broadcast situation" and announced frequency assignment for 694 stations beginning on June 1, 1927, WLW was assigned 700 kilocycles (now kHz), the only U.S. station using that frequency. Thus, it became a "clear channel" station. It was one of only ten stations using 5 kW of power and on May 25, 1928, the FRC authorized WLW to begin construction of facilities for 50 kW again one of only ten stations with that output. But Crosley wanted more.

By now WLW was affiliated with both NBC Red and Blue Networks but originating more expensive and high-quality local programming than most other stations in the country. Only the network-owned stations had such large staffs. In June 1929, a hookup was arranged connecting WLS, Chicago, WOR, New York, and WLW. Called the Quality Radio Group, the stations carried each other's programs, making a huge audience in most of the Northeast available to advertisers. In 1934, WLW, along with WOR, WGN in Chicago, and WXYZ in Detroit with its prize *The Lone Ranger,* established the Mutual Broadcasting System (see **Mutual Broadcasting System [MBS]**).

In June 1932, the FRC authorized WLW to construct a 500,000-watt experimental station and to conduct tests from 1 A.M. to 6 A.M. On May 2, 1934, the station began using this "superpower" all hours after a dedication by President Franklin Roosevelt, who pushed a gold key on his White House desk to turn on the new water-cooled transmitter. Thus, WLW transmitted with 10 times more power than any other AM station—then or now—until March 1, 1939, when the Federal Communications Commission (FCC) refused to continue the higher-power "experimental" license. The decision to end the experiment was controversial, complex, and political but stemmed in large part from complaints by other stations who resented WLW's enormous economic advantage. The station had proved that higher power was possible, did not cause more-than-normal interference with adjacent stations, and did not blanket out other stations for nearby listeners. Many other AM stations of the world soon began using this much, and even more, power. WLW enjoyed much higher ratings than even the hometown station in many, many cities in its huge coverage area. While the bulk of the listening audience was in a circle around Cincinnati stretching to Chicago, Detroit, Pittsburgh, and Nashville, a fund-raising appeal during floods on the Ohio River brought donations from 48 states.

The company also began a shortwave service and relayed WLW programs to the world until the facility was taken over during World War II to provide government propaganda broadcasts. In 1942 six new transmitters installed at that facility became the largest installation for Voice of America.

During the 1930s, WLW had a staff of about 350, including about 200 working directly in programming. The station carried programs from both NBC networks, CBS, and MBS. The station also liked to call itself "The Cradle of the Stars" for those who worked there early in their careers including: Virginia Payne (who created the serial heroine Ma Perkins), The Mills Brothers, Andy Williams, writer Rod Serling, Betty and Rosemary Clooney (younger brother Nick was later a news anchor at the TV station), The McGuire Sisters, actor Frank Lovejoy, Red Skelton, Durward Kirby, Eddie Albert, Thomas W. "Fats" Waller, Red Barber, The Ink Spots, Norman Corwin (who quit after only a few weeks when the station refused to broadcast news about labor strikes), and Erik Barnouw. Some liked to joke that the call letters stood for World's Lowest Wages.

In the 1930s about 50 percent of all WLW programming was local, 40 percent in evening hours. The station's staff originated programming carried on NBC, especially variety and country music, and many Mutual programs. It also did original drama—some destined for the network included *Ma Perkins* (soap opera) and *Mr. District Attorney* (crime), for example. In the late 1930s it added a great deal of agriculture programming, even starting its own experimental farm, as part of an attempt to retained the 500-kW superpower.

The station produced popular early morning hillbilly-variety programs, as well as educational series for in-school listening (in cooperation with The Ohio State University and the state's department of education). WLW was a "regional" service—nearly a network unto itself. The same can be said of other important clear channel stations—WGN, WCCO, WSM—but none had so much originally produced local programming as "The Nation's Station."

From 1949 to April 1953, WLW's programming was broadcasting simultaneously on FM stations in Cincinnati, Dayton, and Columbus, Ohio—as the station sought to duplicate the huge WLW-AM coverage in the new medium. But the growth of FM listening was slow. The company concentrated on TV with new stations in Indianapolis and Atlanta. WLW-T, the Crosley TV station founded in 1949 in Cincinnati, was the first NBC affiliate outside of New York state and one of the earliest stations to go to color. Many WLW radio programs were first simulcast on, then moved solely to, the TV outlet. In 1955 it was the first radio station to provide weather forecasts based on radar—which was shared with the TV station. In 1958 it was one of the first stations with helicopter traffic reports. From the 1960s to date it often ranked only third or fourth in local ratings (losing out to "top-40" formats) in Cincinnati but had the largest cumulative audience of any station in the city because of its larger coverage area—1961, for example, Nielsen reported listeners in 184 counties in four states. In the 1990s it still has the largest total audience of any Cincinnati station.

As network programming declined, WLW became a middle-of-the-road station in the 1950s, producing "magazine" programs of news, information, talks, and some music during the most important morning and afternoon hours. Other types of music, classical all-night long, filled most of the rest of the hours. The format was "adult contemporary" in the 1970s and 1980s. It now concentrates on news, talk, and sports, as do many of the most powerful AM radio stations. It is one of the key stations of Jacor Communications, which operates (1997) more than 130 other stations in 28 markets, including 7 others in Cincinnati.

Lichty, Lawrence W. "'The Nation's Station': A History of Radio Station WLW." Ph.D. dissertation, Ohio State University, 1964.

Lawrence W. Lichty

WOLFMAN JACK(1938–1996) was born Robert Weston Smith in Brooklyn, New York, on January 21, 1938. He was a radio pioneer influenced by Alan Freed and taught the trade by Nashville's John Richbourg. After minor gigs as Daddy Jules at Newport News, Virginia's WYOU-AM and as Big Smith at Shreveport, Louisiana's KCIJ-AM, he took his most important position at 250,000-watt XERF in Ciudad Acuna, Mexico, just below Del Rio, Texas, and became Wolfman Jack. He blasted a rock and blues blend into North America and as far as the USSR and sold plastic Jesus figurines, pills, coffins, and inspirational literature. In 1965, he purchased XERB and later XEG and XELO.

In 1970 he began a 16-year association with Armed Forces Radio and worked in Louisiana for KDAY. Immortalized in the Guess Who's 1972 song "Clap for the Wolfman," he played himself in 1973's *American Graffiti,* where he was first seen. Fans who assumed he was black were surprised. In 1973 he started a 9-year stint as host of NBC-TV's concert show *The Midnight Special.* He spent most of the 1980s appearing as a nostalgia act at oldies concerts and car shows. He hosted an unsuccessful oldies revival on the Nashville Network in 1989. He moved to Belvidere, North Carolina, and hosted a live weekly radio show from Washington, D.C.'s *Planet Hollywood.* On July 1, 1995, he died at home, having just returned from a 20-city promotional tour for his book. He was posthumously inducted into the Radio Hall of Fame on October 27, 1996.

Wolfman Jack. *Have Mercy! Confessions of the Original Rock 'n' Roll Animal.* New York: Warner Books, 1995.

W. A. Kelly Huff

WOR, New York, the fourteenth oldest standard-broadcasting (AM) radio station still operating in the nation and probably the forty-nineth to be licensed, serves a potential audience of tens of millions located more than 100 miles up and down the East Coast from a well-situated transmitter site and directional antenna array in the marshes of the New Jersey Meadowlands.

At one time the flagship station for the Mutual network, WOR produced many programs in its studios at 1440 Broadway, in New York City, which have been in use for almost 70 years. Today its programming is largely talk oriented, with telephone-in shows on health, finance, and personal advice.

WOR was first licensed on February 20, 1922, reportedly had its license picked up at the Department of Commerce just before the Washington's Birthday holiday by engineer Jack Poppele, and began broadcasting two days later using 250 watts of power on 833 kilohertz (kHz) (360 meters, the wavelength then used by most broadcasting stations) with the airing of Al Jolson's *April Showers*. It soon increased power to 500 watts and moved to 740 kHz. On June 15, 1927, WOR moved to the clear channel frequency of 710 kHz, on which it still broadcasts.

Its original owner was the L. Bamberger Department Store in Newark, NJ. When taken over by the R. H. Macy store in 1929, the licensee name changed to the Bamberger Broadcasting Service. In 1948, it became part of General Teleradio, was purchased by Don Lee Broadcasting System (a West Coast company) in 1952, and bought by RKO Pictures (later RKO General) at the end of 1955.

It was one of the original CBS stations in 1927 and became one of the four founding stations of the Mutual Broadcasting Service (with WLW [Cincinnati], WGN [Chicago], and WXYZ [Detroit]) in 1934, remaining with Mutual until August 1961.

Known for its newscasts as early as 1934, WOR was the home of many well-known broadcasters such as John B. Gambling (whose *Rambling with Gambling* program is now in its third generation of "John Gambling" hosts) and "Uncle Don" Carney (whose children's program was taken away after he was accused of saying, before his mike was turned off, "That'll hold the little bastards for tonight"; probably a bum rap, although Carney had a reputation as a lush and a womanizer). During the 1940s, WOR originated many 15-minute children's serials, soap operas, and other programming such as *The Shadow* for Mutual.

WOR, noted for engineering experimentation, was an early 50-kW licensee (1935), used a directional antenna as early as 1939, was a rejected applicant for 500 kW in June 1942, and experimented with facsimile in 1937.

John Michael Kittross

WORLD WAR I AND RADIO. There was no radio broadcasting during World War I. In the United States, all "amateur" (including most experimenters') stations were ordered off the air. The only "commercial" stations were for communicating with ships at sea, and other transmitters were reserved for the military. However, there were occasional "broadcasts": Using Morse code, every SOS was a "to whom it may concern" broadcast; President Woodrow Wilson's "14 Points" message was transmitted to Germany so that anyone could listen in; the station that became WHA, Madison, Wisconsin, sent regular weather reports to shipping on the Great Lakes; and some transmitters were tested in such a way as to provide entertainment to listeners.

Nevertheless, many technological and operational advances were made that led to broadcasting's innovation in the 1920s, as can easily happen during wartime—the armed forces were lavish with research and development money, thousands of servicemen became aware of and trained in radio, and the idea of transmissions without using wires took firm hold of the national psyche.

Several nonbroadcast milestones of wireless communication were passed during WWI. In 1915 (before the United States entered the war), AT&T had made an experimental radiotelephony transmission to Paris, using 500 vacuum tubes in parallel and a navy antenna; General Electric's Alexanderson alternator made it possible for there to be reliable transatlantic radio communication for the first time; the Zimmermann Telegram, a German offer to Mexico of U.S. territory if it allied itself to Germany, was intercepted and decoded by the British and supplied to the United States, showing once again that "secrecy" and "radio" were incompatible concepts; radio was used worldwide for propaganda by the Russian Bolsheviks; and improvements were made in both ship-to-shore and continent-to-continent communication—improvements that could not be interrupted by the simple act of physically cutting through transatlantic cables (as the British did to the Germans at the start of the war).

In April 1917, as the United States entered the war, all amateur stations were closed down by the government as part of an antiespionage effort. At the same time, wired telegraph and telephone were placed under Post Office supervision. Most commercial stations were taken over in the name of national security (through purchase or lease in the case of non-German stations, or confiscation in the case of German stations on American soil) by the navy, which had a desperate need to reach its ships across the Atlantic and Pacific, leaving only a few army stations not under navy control. All other transmitters were shut down and disassembled, which meant that experimenters in the field of broadcasting, such as "Doc" Herrold in San Jose, went off the air.

At the same time, the navy established a patents pool by offering to indemnify manufacturers making equipment for the armed forces against patent infringement suits, leading to a rapid increase in the rate of wireless invention and innovation. The armed forces, particularly the navy, rapidly adopted radio telegraphy. The army started placing radios in its units, commonly six to a division of 20,000 men: one to each of four regiments, one to division artillery, and one at headquarters. Lightweight vacuum-tube transceivers (transmitter/receiver) units were developed to the point where Signal Corps Major Edwin Armstrong (later the inventor of FM) designed one that could be used in an airplane.

At the start of WWI, radio was used mostly for the safety of life and property at sea. By its end, it was a communications utility that was in competition with submarine cables and even land-based telegraph lines. With all of its technical drawbacks, radio was more than one industry ready to happen at the end of WWI. Thousands had been trained during the war, and the interest and financial backing were there. One of these postwar developments was broadcasting, which developed into a major mass medium from an amalgam of public interest in wireless and desire for entertainment that radio might bring to everyone, technological improvements including vacuum-tube radiotelephony and Armstrong's "feedback" circuit, money that couldn't be spent while goods were being diverted to the military, factories that no longer had customers, and a general desire for new markets to prevent the economic depression that had followed all previous wars.

John Michael Kittross

WORLD WAR II AND RADIO. American radio listeners were introduced to war-related news reports by the intense coverage given the so-called "Munich crisis" in September 1938. CBS Radio Network reporters William L. Shirer and H. V. Kaltenborn devoted nearly 48 hours of airtime to the crisis. Subsequent reporting about wartime conditions in Europe by London-based CBS reporter Edward R. Murrow was said to have reversed the isolationist views of many listeners regarding America's participation in the war.

The quality and quantity of the networks' war-related coverage once America entered World War II was such that radio quickly became the preferred news medium. In addition, many of the radio programs that listeners were accustomed to hearing as well as hundreds of specially produced programs incorporated a "win-the-war" theme.

Radio personalities like Fibber McGee and Molly, Eddie Cantor, and Kate Smith fashioned programs that catered to listeners' patriotism. Children's programs, dramatic series, and documentaries with titles like *Don Winslow of the Navy, Counter Spy,* and *This Is War* carried similar patriotic themes. Characters in popular soap operas were forced by creative writers to deal with a variety of wartime situations. Even advertisers played a key wartime role by encouraging radio listeners to conserve scarce commodities.

U.S. government agencies such as the Office of War Information used radio to alert listeners to wartime mobilization needs. And special government units like the Office of Censorship and the Foreign Broadcast Intelligence Service were established to monitor both domestic and international radio broadcasts for subversive program content.

Kirby, Edward, and Jack Harris. *Star-Spangled Radio.* Chicago: Ziff-Davis, 1948.
MacDonald, J. Fred. *Don't Touch That Dial!: Radio Programming in American Life, 1920–1960.* Chicago: Nelson-Hall, 1979.

Ronald Garay

WWJ began on August 31, 1920, as 8MK and was owned by the *Detroit News* (Michigan). It broadcast election returns from local, state, and congressional primaries more than two months before KDKA, known as 8XK, broadcast the national election returns on November 2, 1920. Although most accept KDKA as the first broadcast station, WWJ claims several radio programming firsts in addition to the first news and election returns: first sports program, first sports play-by-play from the scene, first complete symphony broadcast, and the first radio appearances by Fanny Brice and Will Rogers. Owned and operated for many years by the *Detroit News,* the station is now owned by CBS, Inc., which proclaims it "America's First Commercial Radio Station" (see also **8MK**).

Willis, Edgar. *Foundations in Broadcasting: Radio and Television.* Oxford: Oxford University Press, 1951.

AWWJ 950: Newsradio. http://www.wwj.com (November 26, 1996).

Larry L. Jurney

X, Y

YOUNG, OWEN (1874–1962), was born on an upstate New York farm on October 27, 1874. Ultimately he rose through the ranks of corporate America to head both the Radio Corporation of America (RCA) and General Electric (GE) in radio's pivotal decade of the 1920s. Young's college education at St. Lawrence University and law degree from Boston University prepared him for work in the expanding utilities industries. His early career success brought him to the attention of GE, which he joined in 1913 as vice president and general counsel. In 1919 at the urging of the navy, Young realized the possibilities of wireless for worldwide communication and created RCA. He became the new corporation's chairman and, in 1922, assumed the chairmanship of GE. Throughout the 1920s, as head of these communication titans, Young played a key role in guiding the fledgling radio industry's growth and development.

Among the radio institutions Young helped develop was the National Broadcasting Company (NBC). As early as 1922, Young and his protegé David Sarnoff had envisioned a separate broadcasting company. During the mid-1920s, a protracted patent controversy evolved over who owned rights to broadcasting, the "Radio Group" of GE, RCA, and Westinghouse or the "Telephone Group" of AT&T and Western Electric. NBC was born out of complicated negotiations between the two groups and went on the air in November 1926.

As chief executive officer of RCA, Young oversaw much of NBC's early network evolution, but his career in radio came to an end with the 1932 consent decree breaking up RCA and GE. Young was also known as an international statesman through his attempts to devise workable solutions to Germany's post–World War I reparations and his work with Franklin Roosevelt's administration. He died on July 11, 1962, in St. Augustine, Florida.

Louise Benjamin

YOUR HIT PARADE, which debuted in 1935 on NBC Radio, featured America's most popular songs, as determined by a national survey of record and sheet-music sales. The program often booked major artists of the day, including Frank Sinatra,

Doris Day, and Dinah Shore, to perform the hit songs. Sponsor of the program during its entire run was Lucky Strike cigarettes, manufactured by the American Tobacco Company. Each program ended in a climactic fashion with the week's most popular song being performed. In the 1950s, *Your Hit Parade* was simulcast on radio and television until its cancellation in April 1959.

DeLong, Thomas A. *The Mighty Music Box: The Golden Age of Musical Radio.* Los Angeles, Calif.: Amber Crest Books, 1980.

Swartz, Jon D., and Robert C. Reinehr. *Handbook of Old-time Radio: A Comprehensive Guide to Golden Age Radio Listening and Collecting.* Metuchen, N.J.: Scarecrow Press, 1993.

Williams, John R. *This Was "Your Hit Parade."* Camden, Maine: Courier-Gazette, 1973.

Tim England

Z

ZENITH RADIO CORPORATION, late in 1924, manufactured receivers, applied for a permit, built a station, and in due course, received a license for 930 kilohertz (kHz), which it had to share with several other stations. Zenith soon wanted more than the two hours a week it had originally requested and asked for permission to broadcast longer hours on an unused wavelength at 910 kHz, which the United States had agreed to reserve for Canadian stations. Permission was refused. When Zenith defiantly jumped to 910 kHz, other stations announced their intention to arbitrarily take any frequency they desired. The Commerce Department took Zenith to court, but an Illinois Federal District Court decided on April 26, 1926, that there was no express grant of power in the act to the secretary of commerce to establish regulations. Finally, the Commerce Department tried to get the pending Dill-White radio bill through Congress, but it was too late in the session. The attorney general, in a requested opinion issued on July 8, 1926, supported the position that the secretary did not have adequate legal power to deal with the situation. The department then had no choice but to continue processing applications, and in a period of seven months in 1926, more than 200 new stations went on the air, creating intolerable interference in major urban areas. Eugene F. McDonald, president of Zenith, subsequently became the first president of the National Association of Broadcasters.

Bensman, Marvin. "The Zenith-WJAZ Case and the Chaos of 1926–27." *Journal of Broadcasting* 14 (4) (fall 1970): 423.

Marvin R. Bensman

ZOO FORMAT is an archetype of contemporary top-40 radio. Primarily employed in morning drive, the zoo includes cohosts, sidekicks, telephone calls, sound effects, sarcasm, malcontent, and an abundance of behavior not unlike a bunch of wild animals.

Juvenile by design and appeal, the zoo format throws put-ons, celebrity interviews, pop culture references, contests, rim shots, talk-ups, hot hits, and pimple cream spots up in the air, to form a tightly structured, timing-intensive, playlist-driven, apparently spontaneous, live entertainment program, characterized by a cacophonous, yet euphonious, on-air environment.

Joseph R. Piasek

Select Bibliography

Abramson, Albert. *Zworykin: Pioneer of Television.* Chicago: University of Illinois Press, 1995.

Adams, Michael. *Broadcasting's Forgotten Father: The Charles Herrold Story.* San Jose: Perham Foundation, 1994. 60 min. VHS videotape.

Adams, Michael, and Kimberly Massey. *Introduction to Radio: Programming and Production.* Dubuque: Wm. C. Brown Communications, Inc., 1994.

Adams, Mike. "The Race for Radiotelephone." *AWA Review* 10 (1996): 79–149.

"Adviser Becomes Boss: Drake Signs with RKO." *Broadcasting* (October 16, 1972): 61–62.

Aitken, Hugh. G. J. *The Continuous Wave: Technology and American Radio, 1900–1932.* Princeton, N.J.: Princeton University Press, 1985.

Aitken, Hugh G. J., ed. "Hertz." In *Symphony and Spark: The Origins of Radio* (pp. 40–79). New York: Wiley, 1976.

Alexander, Alison, James Owers, and Rod Carveth. *Media Economics: Theory and Practice.* Hillsdale, N.J.: Lawrence Erlbaum Associates, 1993.

Alexander, Shawn. "What Is the State of the Format?" *R & R: The Industries Newspaper,* January 19, 1996, p. 80.

Alford, W. Wayne. *NAEB History, 1954–1965.* Washington, D.C.: National Association of Educational Broadcasters, 1966.

Allen, Craig. *Eisenhower and the Mass Media.* Chapel Hill: University of North Carolina Press, 1993.

Allen, Fred. *Much Ado about Me.* Boston: Little, Brown, 1956.

Allen, Fred. *Treadmill to Oblivion.* Boston: Little, Brown, 1954.

Allen, Mel. Obituary. *The Phoenix Gazette,* June 18, 1996.

Alten, Stanley L. *Audio in Media.* 2nd ed. Belmont, Calif.: Wadsworth, 1986.

Ambrose, Stephen. *Eisenhower.* 2 vols. New York: Simon and Schuster, 1983, 1984.

American Radio Relay League, Inc. *The ARRL Handbook for the Radio Amateur.* Newington, Conn.: American Radio Relay League. Annual.

Anderson, Douglas A. *A "Washington Merry-Go-Round" of Libel Actions.* Chicago: Nelson Hall, 1980.

Anderson, Jack. *Confessions of a Muckraker.* New York: Random House, 1979.

Anderson, J. T., and Tony Sanders. *LMA Handbook.* Alexandria, Va.: Radio Business Report, 1992.

Andrews, Bart, and Ahrgus Juilliard. *Holy MacKeral: The Amos 'n' Andy Story!* New York: E. P. Dutton, 1986.

Antitrust. Code of Federal Regulations. Title 47, Part 73, Section 3555. Washington, D.C.: U.S. Government Printing Office, 1996. Published by the Office of the Federal Register, National Archives and Records Administration as a special edition of the Federal Register.

Antitrust. USCA 47 Section 533 (a) 70 RR 2d 903. *In re* Revision of Radio Rules and Policies. 1992.

Archer, Gleason L. *Big Business and Radio*. New York: American Historical Company, Inc., 1939.

Archer, Gleason L. *History of Radio to 1926*. New York: American Historical Society, Inc., 1938. Reprint, New York: Arno Press, 1971.

Archibald, Sam. "The Revised F.O.I. Law and How to Use It." *Columbia Journalism Review* (July–August 1977): 54.

Arnold, Gina. *Route 666: On the Road to Nirvana*. New York: St. Martin's Press, 1993.

Article 19. *Information, Freedom and Censorship: World Report 1991*. Chicago: American Library Association, 1991.

Arts Censorship Project. *Popular Music under Siege*. New York: American Civil Liberties Union, 1996.

Ashley, Paul. *Say It Safely*. Seattle: University of Washington Press, 1972.

Atherton, Ray, prod., and Lee Scott, dir. *Mr. Entertainment: Milton Berle, a Biography*. Omnivision Films, Inc., 1995. Distributed by Simitar Entertainment, Plymouth, Minn.

Auletta, Ken. *Three Blind Mice*. New York: Random House, 1991.

Autry, Gene, with Mickey Herskowitz. *Back in the Saddle Again*. Garden City, N.Y.: Doubleday & Company, Inc., 1978.

Avery, Robert K. "Talk Radio: The Private-Public Catharsis." In *Talking to Strangers: Mediated Therapeutic Communication*, edited by Gary Gumpert and Sandra L. Fish (pp. 87–97). Norwood, N.J.: Ablex Publishing, 1990.

Avery, Robert K., Paul E. Burrows, and Clara J. Pincus. *Research Index for NAEB Journals*. Washington, D.C.: Public Telecommunications Press, 1980.

Avery, Robert K., Donald G. Ellis, and Thomas W. Glover. "Patterns of Communication on Talk Radio." *Journal of Broadcasting* 22 (1) (winter 1978): 5–17.

Avery, Robert K., and Robert Pepper. "Balancing the Equation: Public Radio Comes of Age." *Public Telecommunications Review* 7 (November–December 1979): 19–30.

Aylesworth, Merlin Hall. "What Broadcasting Means to Business," "Who Pays for Broadcasting," and "The Listener Rules Broadcasting." *Little Books on Broadcasting*. Nos. 1, 5, 11. New York: National Broadcasting Co., 1927–1929.

Baida, Peter. "Breaking the Connection." *American Heritage* 36 (5) (June–July 1985): 65–80.

Baker, Houston A. *Black Studies, Rap and the Academy*. Chicago: University of Chicago Press, 1993.

Baker, John C. *Farm Broadcasting: The First Sixty Years*. Ames: Iowa State University Press, 1981.

Baker, LeGrand, Kelly D. Christensen, Darren Bell, and Thomas E. Patterson, eds. *Register of the Rosel H. Hyde Collection*. Provo: Brigham Young University, 1992.

Baker, W. J. *A History of the Marconi Company*. London: Methuen & Co. Ltd., 1970.

Bannerman, R. Leroy. *Norman Corwin and Radio: The Golden Years*. Tuscaloosa: University of Alabama Press, 1986.

Banning, William Peck. *Commercial Broadcasting Pioneer: The WEAF Experiment 1922–1926*. Cambridge: Harvard University Press, 1945.

Barabas, SuzAnne, and Gabor Barabas. *Gunsmoke: The Complete History and Analysis of the Legendary Broadcast Series with a Comprehensive Episode-by-Episode Guide to Both the Radio and Television Programs*. Jefferson, N.C.: McFarland & Company, 1990.

Barnouw, Erik. *The Golden Web: A History of Broadcasting in the United States, 1933–1953*. Oxford: Oxford University Press, 1968.

Barnouw, Erik. *Radio Drama in Action: Twenty-five Plays of a Changing World*. New York: Rinehart & Company, 1945.

Barnouw, Erik. *A Tower in Babel: A History of Broadcasting in the United States to 1933*. New York: Oxford University Press, 1966.

Barnouw, Erik. *Tube of Plenty: The Evolution of American Television*. New York: Oxford University Press, 1975.

Barnum, Frederick O., III. *"His Master's Voice" in America*. Camden, N.J.: General Electric, 1991.

Barrett, Margreth. *Intellectual Property: Cases and Materials*. St. Paul: West Publishing Co., 1995.

Barron, James. "So What to Do with Souvenirs of Camelot?" *New York Times,* April 24, 1996, p. A1.

Barron, Jerome A., and C. Thomas Dienes. *First Amendment Law in a Nutshell*. St. Paul: West Publishing Co., 1993.

Basie, Count, as told to Albert Murray. *Good Morning Blues*. New York: Random House, 1985.

Baskerville, David. *Music Business Handbook & Career Guide*. 6th ed. Thousand Oaks, Calif.: Sage, 1996.

Baudino, Joseph E., and John M. Kittross. "Broadcasting's Oldest Stations: An Examination of Four Claimants." *Journal of Broadcasting* 21 (1) (winter 1977): 61–83.

Beasley, Maurine H., and Sheila Gibbons. *Taking Their Place: A Documentary History of Women and Journalism*. Washington, D.C.: American University Press in cooperation with the Women's Institute for Freedom of the Press, 1993.

Bell, Alexander Graham. "Upon the Production of Sound by Radiant Energy." *American Journal of Science* 21 (1884): 463–490.

Bell, Douglas. *Years of the Electric Ear: Norman Corwin (an interview)*. Metuchen, N.J.: Scarecrow Press, Inc., 1994.

Benjamin, Louise. "Judith Cary Waller." In *Women in Communication: A Biographical Sourcebook,* edited by Nancy Signorielli (pp. 415–418). Westport, Conn.: Greenwood, 1996.

Benjamin, Louise M. "In Search of the Sarnoff 'Radio Music Box' Memo." *Journal of Broadcasting and Electronic Media* 37 (3) (summer 1993): 325–335.

Bensman, Marvin. "Regulation of Broadcasting by the Department of Commerce, 1921–1927." In *American Broadcasting: A Source Book on the History of Radio and Television,* edited by Lawrence Lichty and Malachi Topping. New York: Hastings House, 1975.

Bensman, Marvin. "The Zenith-WJAZ Case and the Chaos of 1926–27." *Journal of Broadcasting* 14 (4) (fall 1970): 423–440.

Berg, Gertrude. *Molly and Me*. New York: McGraw-Hill, 1961.

Bergonzi, Benet. *Old Gramaphones & Other Talking Machines*. New York: State Mutual Book & Periodical Service, 1989.

Bergreen, Laurence. *Look Now, Pay Later. The Rise of Network Broadcasting*. Garden City, N.Y.: Doubleday, 1980.

Bernstein, Jeremy. *Three Degrees above Zero: Bell Labs in the Information Age*. New York: Charles Scribner, 1984.

Besen, Stanley M., Thomas G. Krattenmaker, A. Richard Metzger, and John R. Woodbury. *Misregulating Television: Network Dominance and the FCC.* Chicago: University of Chicago Press, 1984.

Beville, Hugh Malcolm, Jr. *Audience Ratings: Radio, Television, and Cable.* Rev. ed. Hillsdale, N.J.: Lawrence Erlbaum Associates, 1987.

Bickel, Mary E. *George W. Trendle, Creator and Producer of The Lone Ranger, The Green Hornet, Sgt. Preston of the Yukon, The American Agent and Other Successes.* New York: Exposition Press, 1971.

Bilby, Kenneth. *The General: David Sarnoff and the Rise of the Communications Industry.* New York: Harper & Row, 1986.

"Bill Seeks to Curb Door-to-Door Fakers." *New York Times,* December 19, 1949.

"Biographical Notes: Alfred N. Goldsmith." *Journal of the SMPTE* (November 1972): 869–870.

Black Radio: Telling It Like It Was. A 13-part radio documentary series with Lou Rawls. Washington, D.C.: Radio Smithsonian, Smithsonian Productions, 1996. (Series tapes are available for research at the Archives of African American Music and Culture, Indiana University, Bloomington; and the Museums of Radio and Television in Los Angeles and New York.)

Blair, William G. "Arch Oboler, Wrote Thrillers for Radio in 1930's and 40's." *New York Times,* March 22, 1987, p. 36.

Blau, Eleanor. "Pauline Frederick, 84, Network News Pioneer, Dies." *New York Times,* May 11, 1990, p. D18.

Bleetstein, Rob. "One Year down the Americana Highway." *Gavin* (January 19, 1996): 33.

Bliss, Edward, Jr. *Now the News: The Story of Broadcast Journalism.* New York: Columbia University Press, 1991.

Bliss, Edward, Jr., ed. *In Search of Light: The Broadcasts of Edward R. Murrow, 1938–1961.* New York: Alfred A. Knopf, 1967.

Blythe, Cheryl, and Susan Sackett. *Say Goodnight, Gracie!* New York: E. P. Dutton, 1986.

Boemer, Marilyn. *The Children's Hour: Radio Programs for Children, 1929–1956.* Metuchen, N.J.: Scarecrow Press, 1989.

Bogasian, Eric. *Talk Radio.* New York: Vintage Books, 1988.

Bohn, Thomas W., and Lawrence W. Lichty. *"The March of Time:* News as Drama." *Journal of Popular Film* 2 (4) (fall 1973): 373–387.

Bolter, Walter G., ed. *Telecommunications Policy for the 1980s: The Transition to Competition.* Englewood Cliffs, N.J.: Prentice-Hall, 1984.

"Bonneville International Corporation." *Encyclopedia of Mormonism.* Vol. 1. New York: Macmillan Publishing Company, 1992.

Bonneville International Oral History Series. Conducted by Heritage Associates, W. Dee Halverson. Salt Lake City: Bonneville International Corporation, 1992.

Bormann, Ernest. "This Is Huey P. Long Talking." *Journal of Broadcasting* 2 (2) (spring 1958): 111–122.

Borzillo, Carrie. "Women Consultants Hard to Find." *Billboard* (January 23, 1993): 75–76.

Boskin, Joseph. *SAMBO: The Rise and Demise of an American Jester.* New York: Oxford University Press, 1986.

Boyer, Peter J. *Who Killed CBS? The Undoing of America's Number One News Network.* New York: Random House, 1988.

Brady, Frank. *Citizen Welles.* New York: Charles Scribner's Sons, 1989.

Brady, Rodney H. *Bonneville International Corporation: A Values-Driven Company Composed of Values-Driven People.* New York: Newcomen Society of the U.S., 1994.

Braun, Mark. *AM Stereo and the FCC: Case Study of a Marketplace "Shibboleth."*
Norwood, N.J.: Ablex, 1994.

Brightbill, George D. *Communications and the United States Congress, a Selectively
Annotated Bibliography of Committee Hearings, 1870–1976.* Washington, D.C.: Broadcast Education Association, 1978.

Brinkley, Alan. *Voices of Protest: Huey Long, Father Coughlin & The Great Depression.*
New York: Vintage Books, 1982.

Brittain, James E. *Alexanderson: Pioneer in American Electrical Engineering.* Baltimore:
Johns Hopkins University Press, 1992.

Broadcasting & Cable 127 (9) (March 3, 1997), p. 39.

Broadcasting & Cable 127 (24) (June 9, 1997), p. 23.

"Broadcasting for Both Ears." *Business Week* (February 28, 1959): 27.

Brockwell, P. Heath. "Grappling with *Miller v. California:* A Search to an Alternative
Approach to Regulating Obscenity." *Cumberland Law Review* 24 (winter 1994): 131–144.

Brooks, Tim, and Earle Marsh. *The Complete Directory to Prime Time Network TV Shows,
1946–Present.* New York: Ballantine Books, 1979.

Brown, R. "Time Warner Takes Stake in Cable Radio." *Broadcasting* 123 (6) (February 8,
1993): 31.

Buckwalter, Len. *ABC's of Citizen Band Radio.* Indianapolis: Howard W. Sams & Co., Inc.,
1966.

"Bullard, Radio Chief, Faces a Difficult Task." *New York Times,* April 17, 1927, sec. VIII, p.
22:1.

Bunis, Marty, and Sue Bunis. *The Collector's Guide to Antique Radios.* Paducah, Ky.:
Collector Books, 1996.

Bunzell, Reed. "Filling the Magic Box." *Broadcasting* 121 (supp.) (December 1, 1991): 28.

Burke, Debra D. "Cybersmut and the First Amendment: A Call for a New Obscenity
Standard." *Harvard Journal of Law and Technology* 9 (winter 1996): 87–145.

Burke, John E. *An Historical-Analytical Study of the Legislative and Political Origins of the
Public Broadcasting Act of 1967.* New York: Arno Press, 1979.

Burke, John E. "The *Public Broadcasting Act of 1967:* Part I: Historical Origins and the
Carnegie Commission." *Educational Broadcasting Review* 6 (April 1972): 105–119.

Burkum, Larry G. "'This is a Test': The Evolution of the Emergency Broadcast System."
Journal of Radio Studies 2 (1993–1994): 141–150.

Burns, George, with David Fisher. *Gracie: A Love Story.* New York: G. P. Putnam's Sons,
1988.

Burns, James MacGregor. *Roosevelt: The Lion and the Fox.* New York: Harcourt Brace, 1956.

Butters, Pat. "The Last Vaudevillian: Burns' Not-Always-Funny 100 Years." *Washington
Times,* January 28, 1996, sec. B, p. 87.

Buxton, Frank, and Bill Owen. *The Big Broadcast 1920–50.* New York: Viking Press, 1972.

Buxton, Frank, and Bill Owen. *Radio's Golden Age: The Programs and the Personalities.*
New York: Easton Valley Press, 1966.

Buzenberg, William E. "Growing NPR." In *Radio: The Forgotten Medium,* edited by Edward
C. Pease and Everette E. Dennis (pp. 185–192). New Brunswick, N.J.: Transaction
Publishers, 1995.

Buzzard, Karen S. *Chains of Gold: Marketing the Ratings and Rating the Markets.*
Metuchen, N.J.: Scarecrow Press, 1990.

Callow, Simon. *Orson Welles: The Road to Xanadu.* New York: Viking Press, 1996.

Campbell, Lewis, and William Garnett. *The Life of James Clerk Maxwell.* London: Macmillan and Co., 1882. (Reprinted in 1969 by Johnson Reprint Corporation, New York and London, as No. 85 in *The Sources of Science* series.)

Cantor, Louis. *Wheeling on Beale: How WDIA-Memphis Became the Nation's First All-Black Radio Station and Created the Sound that Changed America.* New York: Pharos, 1992.

Cantril, Hadley. *The Invasion from Mars: A Study in the Psychology of Panic.* Princeton, N.J.: Princeton University Press, 1940.

Cantril, Hadley, and Gordon W. Allport. *The Psychology of Radio.* New York: Harper & Brothers, 1935. Reprint, New York: Arno Press, 1971.

Carlin, John C. "The Rise and Fall of Topless Radio." *Journal of Communication* 26 (winter 1976): 31–37.

Carnegie Commission on Educational Television. *Public Television: A Program for Action.* New York: Bantam Books, 1967.

Carroll, Raymond L., and Donald M. Davis. *Electronic Media Programming: Strategies and Decision Making.* New York: McGraw-Hill, 1993.

Carson, Gerald. *The Roguish World of Doctor Brinkley.* New York: Holt, Rinehart & Winston, 1960.

Carter, T. Barton, Marc A. Franklin, and Jay B. Wright. *The First Amendment and the Fifth Estate: Regulation of Electronic Mass Media.* 4th ed. Westbury, N.Y.: Foundation Press, 1996.

"Cartwheel Girl." *Time* (June 12, 1939): 47–51.

"CBS to S.A." *Time* (June 1, 1942): 62.

"Chains Unchained?" *Time* (May 12, 1941): 69–70.

Chandler v. Florida, 449 U.S. 560 (1981).

Channan, Michael. *Repeated Takes: A Short History of Recording and Its Effects on Music.* London: Verso, 1995.

Charnley, Mitchell V. "Should Courtroom Proceedings Be Broadcast?" *Journal of the Federal Bar Association* 11 (1950): 64.

Chase, Francis, Jr. *Sound and Fury. An Informal History of Broadcasting.* New York: Harper & Brothers Publishers, 1942.

Chester, Giraud. "The Press Radio War: 1933–1935." *Public Opinion Quarterly* 13 (summer 1949): 263.

Chester, Giraud, Garnet R. Garrison, and Edgar E. Willis. *Television and Radio.* 3rd ed. New York: Appleton-Century-Crofts, 1963.

CIS/Index and *CIS/Annual.* Washington, D.C.: Congressional Information Service.

Clark, Charles. "Sex, Violence and the Media." *CQ Researcher* 17 (November 1995): 1019–1036.

Clark, Dick, and Richard Robinson. *Rock, Roll & Remember.* New York: Crowell, 1976.

Clarke, Anne L. "As Nasty as They Wanna Be: Popular Music on Trial." *New York University Law Review* 65 (1990): 1481–1531.

Cloud, Stanley, and Lynne Olsen. *The Murrow Boys: Pioneers on the Front Lines of Broadcast Journalism.* Boston: Houghton Mifflin, 1996.

CMJ New Music Report. Great Neck, N.Y.: College Media, Inc., 1996.

Cole, Wayne S. *Charles A. Lindbergh and the Battle against American Intervention in World War II.* New York: Harcourt Brace Jovanovich, 1974.

Colford, Paul. *The Rush Limbaugh Story: Talent on Loan from God: An Unauthorized Biography.* New York: St. Martin's Press, 1993.

Collins, T. A. "The Local Service Concept in Broadcasting." *Iowa Law Review* 65 (1980): 553.

Committee on Civic Education by Radio of the National Advisory Council on Radio in Education and the American Political Science Association. *Four Years of Network Broadcasting.* Chicago: University of Chicago Press, 1937.

Communications Act of 1934. Title II Common Carriers (47 U.S.C. 201–228).

Compaine, Benjamin M. "The Impact of Ownership on Content: Does It Matter?" *Cardozo Arts & Entertainment Law Journal* 13 (1995): 755.

"Concert by Wireless." *London Times,* May 20, 1920, p. 14.

Connors, Edward. "They Still Call It Radio News." *Washington Journalism Review* 13 (4) (May 1, 1991): 39–42.

Conot, Robert. *A Streak of Luck.* New York: Seaview Books, 1979.

"Contemporary Hits Radio." *Radio & Records* (July 5, 1996): 35–41.

"Controlling Press and Radio Influence on Trials." *Harvard Law Review* 63 (1950): 840.

Cooper, Roger. "The Status and Future of Audience Duplication Research: An Assessment of Ratings-Based Theories of Audience Behavior." *Journal of Broadcasting and Electronic Media* 40 (1) (winter 1996): 96–116.

Correll, Charles, and Freeman Gosden. *All about Amos 'n' Andy.* New York: Rand McNally, 1929.

Corwin, Norman. *Thirteen by Corwin.* New York: Henry Holt and Company, 1942.

Cox, Archibald. *The Court and the Constitution.* Boston: Houghton Mifflin, 1987.

"Creating the Craft of Tape Recording." *Hi Fidelity* (April 1976): x.

Creech, Kenneth C. *Electronic Media Law and Regulation.* 2nd ed. Boston: Focal Press, 1995.

Critchlow, James. *Radio Hole-in-the-Head/Radio Liberty: An Insider's Story of Cold War Broadcasting.* Washington, D.C.: American University Press, 1995.

Cronkite, Walter L. *A Reporter's Life.* New York: Alfred A. Knopf, 1996.

Crosby, Bing. *Call Me Lucky.* New York: Simon & Schuster, 1953.

Culbert, David H. "Boake Carter: Columbia's Voice of Doom." In *News for Everyman: Radio and Foreign Affairs in Thirties America* (pp. 34–66). Westport, Conn.: Greenwood, 1976.

Dates, Janette L., and William Barlow, eds. *Split Image: African Americans in the Mass Media.* 2nd ed. Washington, D.C.: Howard University Press, 1993.

"David Sarnoff of RCA Is Dead: Visionary Broadcast Pioneer." *New York Times,* December 13, 1971, obituary, pp. 1, 43.

Day, Jennifer Cheeseman. *Population Projections of the United States, by Age, Sex and Hispanic Origin: 1993–2050.* Washington, D.C.: U.S. Department of Commerce, Economics and Statistics, Bureau of the Census, 1993.

Dearling, Robert, and Celia Dearling. *The Guinness Book of Recorded Sound.* Enfield, England: Guinness Books, 1984.

Deffaa, Chip. *Swing Legacy.* Metuchen, N.J.: Scarecrow Press, 1989.

de Forest, Lee. *Father of Radio: The Autobiography of Lee de Forest.* Chicago: Wilcox and Follett, 1950.

de Grazia, Edward. *Girls Back Everywhere: The Law of Obscenity and the Assault of Genesis.* New York: Random House, 1992.

DeLong, Thomas A. *The Mighty Music Box: The Golden Age of Musical Radio.* Los Angeles, Calif.: Amber Crest Books, 1980.

Deloria, Vine, Jr. *Custer Died for Your Sins.* Norman:University of Oklahoma Press, 1969.

DeMaw, Doug. *QRP Notebook.* Newington, Conn.: American Radio Relay League, 1989.

DeMers Dispatch (Exton, Penn.). October 1996, pp. 1–4.

Denisoff, R. Serge. *Inside MTV.* New Brunswick, N.J.: Transaction Publishers, 1988.

de Tunselmann, G. W. "Hertz's Researches on Electrical Oscillations." In *Annual Report of the Board of Regents of the Smithsonian Institution* (pp. 145–203). Washington, D.C.: U.S. Government Printing Office, 1890.

Diamond, Edwin, and Stephen Bates. *The Spot: The Rise of Political Advertising on Television.* 3rd ed. Cambridge: MIT Press, 1992.

Dill, C. C. "Traffic Cop for the Air." *American Review of Reviews* 75 (February 1927): 191.

Dill, Clarence C. *Where Water Falls.* Spokane: C. W. Printing, 1970.

Directory of Religious Media. Manassas, Va.: National Religious Broadcasters. Annual.

Ditingo, Vincent M. *The Remaking of Radio.* Boston: Focal Press, 1994.

Documents in American Broadcasting. FCC Docket 5060 (May 1941).

Dominick, Joseph R., Barry L. Sherman, and Gary A. Copeland. *Broadcasting/Cable and Beyond: An Introduction to Modern Electronic Media.* 3rd ed. New York: McGraw-Hill, 1996.

Douglas, Alan. *Radio Manufacturers of the 1920's.* Vols. 1–3. New York: Vestal Press, Ltd., 1991. 3rd ed., reprint, Chandler, Ariz.: Sonoran Publishing Inc. 1995.

Douglas, George. *The Early Days of Radio Broadcasting.* Jefferson, N.C.: McFarland, 1987.

Douglas, Susan J. *Inventing American Broadcasting 1899–1922.* Baltimore: Johns Hopkins University Press, 1987.

"Dr. Conrad and His Work." Unauthored Westinghouse Press Release. Mass Communication History Center, Wisconsin Historical Society, Madison, 1942.

Dreher, Carl. "His Colleagues Remember 'The Doctor.'" *IEEE Spectrum* (August 1974): 32–36; same issue, obituary, pp. 114–115.

Dryer, Sherman. *Radio in Wartime.* New York: Greenburg, 1942.

Duffy, Dennis. *Marshall McLuhan.* Toronto: McClelland and Stewart, 1969.

Dunlap, Orrin E., Jr., ed. *Radio's 100 Men of Science.* New York: Harper, 1944.

Dunning, John. *Tune in Yesterday: The Ultimate Encyclopedia of Old-time Radio 1925–1976.* Englewood Cliffs, N.J.: Prentice-Hall, 1976.

Dupree, Sherry Sherod, and Herbert Clarence Dupree. *From Natural Music to Contemporary Gospel: Field Songs, Rock 'n' Roll, Rap, and Film.* Institute of Black Culture. Found online at http://www.ufsa.ufl.edu/oss/IBC/choirlinenotes.html

EAS Primer. Indianapolis: Society of Broadcast Engineers, 1997.

Eastland, Terry. "Rush Limbaugh's Revolution." *American Spectator* (September 1992): 22–27.

Eastman, S. "Policy Issues Raised by the FCC's 1983 and 1984 Subcarrier Decisions." *Journal of Broadcasting* 28 (3) (1984): 289–303.

Eastman, Susan Tyler, and Douglas A. Ferguson. *Broadcast/Cable Programming: Strategies and Practices.* 5th ed. Belmont, Calif.: Wadsworth, 1997.

Eberly, Philip, K. *Music in the Air.* New York: Hastings House, 1982.

Elwell, C. F. *The Poulsen Arc Generator.* New York: Van Nostrand, 1923.

Elwell, C. F. "The Poulsen System of Radiotelegraphy: History of Development of Arc Methods." *Electrician* (May 28, 1920): 596–599.

Elwell, Cyril. "[Unpublished] Autobiography." Clark Radiana Collection, Clark Papers, Smithsonian, 1943.

Ely, Melvin Patrick. *The Adventures of Amos 'n' Andy: A Social History of an American Phenomenon.* New York: Free Press, 1991.

Emergency Alert System (EAS). Code of Federal Regulations. Title 47, Part 11. Washington, D.C.: U.S. Government Printing Office, 1996. Published by the Office of the Federal

Register, National Archives and Records Administration as a special edition of the Federal Register.

Emery, Edwin, and Michael Emery. *The Press and America: An Interpretive History of the Mass Media.* 5th ed. Englewood Cliffs, N.J.: Prentice-Hall, 1984.

Empire of the Air: The Men Who Made Radio. PBS Documentary. Producer, Ken Burns. Narrator, Jason Robards. Air date, January 28, 1992.

Endres, Clifford. *Austin City Limits.* Austin: University of Texas Press, 1987.

Engelman, Ralph. *Public Radio and Television in America.* Thousand Oaks, Calif.: Sage Publications, 1996.

Ennis, Philip H. *The Seventh Stream: The Emergence of Rocknroll in American Popular Music.* Hanover, N.H.: University Press of New England, 1992.

Erickson, Hal. *The First Forty Years—1947–1987.* Jefferson, N.C.: McFarland and Company, Inc., Publishers, 1989.

Estes v. Texas, 381 U.S. 532 (1965).

Everson, George. *The Story of Television: The Life of Philo T. Farnsworth.* New York: W. W. Norton, 1949.

Fagen, M. D., ed. *A History of Engineering and Science in the Bell System: The Early Years (1875–1925).* New York: Bell Telephone Laboratories, 1975.

Fahie, John J. *A History of Wireless Telegraphy, Including Some Barewire Proposals for Subaqueous Telegraphs.* Edinburgh: Blackwood, 1899. Reprint, New York: Arno Press, 1971.

Fang, Irving E. *Those Radio Commentators!* Ames: Iowa State University Press, 1977.

Farnsworth, Elma G. *Distant Vision: Romance and Discovery on an Invisible Frontier.* Salt Lake City: Pemberly-Kent Publishers, 1989.

FCC Rules and Regulations. Section 73.3527.

Federal Communications Commission. *Report and Order in the Matter of Amendment of Part 73 of the Commission's Rules, Regarding AM Station Assignment and the Relationship between the AM and FM Services.* Washington, D.C.: 45 FCC Reports 1515, 1964.

Federal Communications Commission. *Report on Chain Broadcasting.* Washington, D.C.: U.S. Government Printing Office, 1941. Reprint, New York: Arno Press, 1974.

Federal Communications Commission v. Pacifica Foundation, 438 U.S. 726 (July 3, 1978).

Federal Radio Commission. *Annual Report of the Federal Radio Commission to the Congress of the United States.* Washington, D.C.: U.S. Government Printing Office, 1927.

Federal Radio Commission. *Second Annual Report of the Federal Radio Commission to the Congress of the United States, 1928.* Washington, D.C.: U.S. Government Printing Office, 1928.

Federal Radio Commission. *Third Annual Report of the Federal Radio Commission to the Congress of the United States, 1929.* Washington, D.C.: U.S. Government Printing Office, 1929.

Federal Theater Project Records. National Archives, Record Group 69: Records of the WPA.

Fessenden, Helen M. *Fessenden: Builder of Tomorrows.* New York: Coward-McCann, 1940. Reprint, with a new index, New York: Arno Press, 1974.

Fessenden, Reginald A. "Wireless Telephony." In *The Development of Wireless to 1920,* edited by George Shiers. New York: Arno Press, 1977.

"Fibber & Co." *Time* (April 20, 1940): 41.

Fife, Marilyn D. "Regulatory Processes in Broadcasting." Ph.D. dissertation, Stanford University, 1983.

Fink, Michael. *Inside the Music Industry.* 2nd ed. New York: Schirmer Books, 1996.

Finkelstein, Sidney. *Sense and Nonsense of McLuhan*. New York: International Publishers, 1968.

Flannery, Gerald, ed. *Commissioners of the FCC: 1927–1994*. Lanham, Md.: University Press of America, 1995.

Flannigan, Hallie. *Arena*. New York: Duell, Sloan and Pearce, 1940.

Fletcher, James E., ed. *Broadcast Research Definitions*. Washington, D.C.: National Association of Broadcasters, 1988.

Floyd, Samuel A. *The Power of Black Music*. New York: Oxford University Press, 1995.

FM Allocations. Code of Federal Regulations. Title 47, Part 73, Sections 201–211 (FM Broadcast Stations) and 501–513 (Noncommercial Educational FM Broadcast Stations). Washington, D.C.: U.S. Government Printing Office, 1996. Published by the Office of the Federal Register, National Archives and Records Administration as a special edition of the Federal Register.

"FM's Drag Feet on Program Split." *Broadcasting* 88 (June 21, 1965): 40–42, 44.

Fornatale, Peter, and Joshua E. Mills. *Radio in the Television Age*. Woodstock, N.Y.: Overlook Press, 1980.

Fortner, Robert S. *International Communication*. Belmont, Calif.: Wadsworth, 1993.

Fowler, Mark S., and Daniel L. Brenner. "A Marketplace Approach to Broadcast Regulation." *Texas Law Review* 60 (1982): 207.

Fox, Stephen. *The Mirror Makers: A History of Advertising and Its Creators*. New York: Random House, 1984.

Frank, Reuven. *Out of Thin Air*. New York: Simon & Schuster, 1991.

Franklin, Marc C., and David A. Anderson. *Mass Media Law, Cases and Materials*. Westbury, N.Y.: Foundation Press, Inc., 1993.

Friendly, Fred W. *The Good Guys, the Bad Guys and the First Amendment: Free Speech vs. Fairness in Broadcasting*. New York: Random House, 1975.

Frost, S. E., Jr. *Education's Own Stations*. Chicago: University of Chicago Press, 1937.

Gabler, Neal. *Winchell: Gossip, Power and the Culture of Celebrity*. New York: Knopf, 1994.

Garay, Ronald. *Gordon McLendon: The Maverick of Radio*. New York: Greenwood, 1992.

Garvey, Daniel E. "Secretary Hoover and the Quest for Broadcast Regulation." *Journalism History* 3 (3) (autumn 1976): 66.

Gawiser, Sheldon R., and G. Evans Witt. *A Journalist's Guide to Public Opinion Polls*. Westport, Conn.: Praeger, 1994.

Gebbels, Tim. "The BBC World Service." *Contemporary Review* 267 (1556) (September 1995): 139 (3).

Gellhorn, Ernest. *Antitrust Law and Economics in a Nutshell*. 3rd ed. St. Paul: West Publishing, 1986.

George, Nelson. *The Death of Rhythm & Blues*. New York: Plume, 1988.

Gernsback, Hugo. *Radio for the Beginner*. New York: Radio Publications, 1938.

Gibbons, Edward. *Floyd Gibbons: Your Headline Hunter*. New York: Exposition, 1953.

Gilbert, Douglas. *Floyd Gibbons: Knight of the Air*. New York: Robert McBride, 1930.

Ginsburg, D. H., M. H. Botein, and M. D. Director. *Regulation of the Electronic Mass Media*. St. Paul: West Publishing Co., 1991.

Glick, Edwin L. "The Life and Death of the Liberty Broadcasting System." *Journal of Broadcasting* 23 (2) (spring 1979): 117–135.

Godfrey, Donald G. "Canadian Marconi: CFCF the Forgotten First." *Canadian Journal of Communication* 8 (4) (1982): 56–71.

Godfrey, Donald G. "CBS World News Roundup: Setting the Stage for the Next Half Century." *American Journalism* 7 (3) (summer 1990): 164–172.

Godfrey, Donald G. *Reruns on File: A Guide to Electronic Media Archives.* Hillsdale, N.J.: Lawrence Erlbaum Associates, 1992.

Godfrey, Donald G. "Senator Dill and the *1927 Radio Act.*" *Journal of Broadcasting* 23 (4) (fall 1979): 477–489.

Godfrey, Donald G., Val Limburg, and Heber G. Wolsey. "KSL Salt Lake: 'At the Crossroads of the West.'" In *Television in America: Local Station History from Across the Nation,* edited by Michael D. Murray and Donald G. Godfrey (pp. 338–352). Ames: Iowa State University Press, 1997.

Goldberg, Robert, and Gerald Jay Goldberg. *Anchors: Brokaw, Jennings, Rather and the Evening News.* New York: Birch Lane Press, 1990.

Goldman, Martin. *The Demon in the Aether: The Story of James Clerk Maxwell.* Edinburgh, Scotland: Paul Harris Publishers in association with Adam Hilger Ltd., 1983.

Goldstone, Leonard. *Beating the Odds: The Untold Story behind the Rise of ABC.* New York: Charles Scribner's Sons, 1991.

Gorman, Paul A. *Century One . . . A Prologue.* New York: Newcomen Society in North America, 1969.

Gottfried, Martin. *George Burns: The Hundred-Year Dash.* New York: Simon & Schuster, 1996.

Graf, Rudolf F. *Modern Dictionary of Electronics.* Indianapolis, Ind.: Howard W. Sams & Co., Inc., 1984.

Grant, August E. *Communications Technology Update.* 3rd ed. Boston: Focal Press, 1994.

Greb, Gordon L. "The Golden Anniversary of Broadcasting." *Journal of Broadcasting* 3 (1) (winter 1958–1959): 3–13.

Greenfield, Thomas A. *Radio: A Reference Guide.* Westport, Conn.: Greenwood, 1989.

Gregg, Robert L. *America's Town Meeting of the Air 1935–1950.* London: University Microfilms International, 1961.

Gross, Lynne S. *Telecommunications: An Introduction to Electronic Media.* Dubuque, Iowa: Wm. C. Brown, 1988.

Gross, Lynne Schafer. *Telecommunications: An Introduction to Electronic Media.* 6th ed. Guilford, Conn.: Brown & Benchmark, 1997.

Gross, Lynne, ed. *The International World of Electronic Media.* New York: McGraw-Hill, 1995.

The Story of Gunsmoke. Produced by John Hickman. Washington, D.C.: WAMU, 1976. An audio history with interviews. 5 hours.

Hackett, David. A., trans. *The Buchenwald Report.* San Francisco: Westview Press, 1995.

Hadden, J. K. "Policing Religious Airwaves: The Case for Marketplace Regulation." *Brigham Young University Journal of Public Law* 8 (1994): 393–416.

Hagen, Chet. *Grand Ole Opry.* New York: Henry Holt, 1989.

Hagin, Linwood A. "U.S. Radio Consolidation: The Structures and Strategies of Selected Duopolies." Ph.D. dissertation, University of Tennessee, 1994.

Haight, Timothy R., ed. *Telecommunications Policy and the Citizen.* New York: Praeger Publishers, 1979.

Halloran, Mark, ed. *The Musician's Business and Legal Guide.* 4th ed. Englewood Cliffs, N.J.: Prentice-Hall, 1991.

Hamburg, Morton I., and Stuart N. Brotman. *Communications Law and Practice.* New York: Law Journal Seminars Press, 1995.

Hamby, Alonzo L. *Man of the People: A Life of Harry S. Truman.* New York: Oxford University Press, 1995.

Hammer, Peter. "Jack Mullin: The Man and His Machines." *Journal of the Audio Engineering Society* 37 (6) (June 1989): 490–504.

Hammer, Peter, and Don Ososke. "The Birth of the German Magnetophon Tape Recorder 1928–1945." *db* (March 1982): 47–52.

Hammond, John Winthrop. *Men and Volts: The Story of General Electric.* New York: J. B. Lippincott Company, 1941.

Hancock, Harry E. *Wireless at Sea.* London: Marconi International Marine Communication Company, 1950. Reprint, New York: Arno Press, 1974.

Handlin, Oscar. *Al Smith and His America.* Boston: Little, Brown and Company, 1958.

Haralambos, Michael. *Right on: From Blues to Soul in Black America.* New York: Drake Publishers, 1975.

"Hard Times for Easy Listening." *Broadcasting* 116 (November 28, 1988): 122.

Harlow, Alvin. *Old Wires and New Waves: The History of the Telegraph, Telephone, and Wireless.* New York: Appleton-Century, 1936. Reprint, Arno Press, 1971.

Harmon, Jim. *Radio Mystery and Adventure and Its Appearances in Film, Television and Other Media.* Jefferson, N.C.: McFarland, 1992.

Harper, Jim. "Gordon McLendon: Pioneer Baseball Broadcaster." *Baseball History* (spring 1986): 42–51.

Harwood, Kenneth. "Competition and Content in Communication Research." *Journal of Broadcasting and Electronic Media* 35 (1) (winter 1991): 95–99.

Hausman, Carl, Philip Benoit, and Lewis B. O'Donnell. *Modern Radio Production.* Belmont, Calif.: Wadsworth, 1996.

Havig, A. *Fred Allen's Radio Comedy.* Philadelphia: Temple University Press, 1990.

Hawks, Ellison. *Pioneers of Wireless.* London: Methuen and Co., 1927. Reprint, New York: Arno Press, 1974.

Head, Sydney W. *Broadcasting in America.* 3rd ed. Boston: Houghton Mifflin, 1976.

Head, Sydney W., and Christopher H. Sterling. *Broadcasting in America: A Survey of Electronic Media.* Boston: Houghton Mifflin, 1990.

Head, Sydney W., Christopher H. Sterling, and Lemuel Schofield. *Broadcasting in America: A Survey of Electronic Media.* 7th ed. Boston: Houghton Mifflin, 1994.

Head, Sydney W., Christopher H. Sterling, Lemuel Schofield, Thomas Spann, and Michael McGregor. *Broadcasting in America: A Survey of Electronic Media.* 8th ed. Boston: Houghton Mifflin, 1998.

Heistad, Mark J. "Radio Without Sponsors: Public Service Programming in Network Sustaining Time, 1928–1952." Ph. D. dissertation, University of Minnesota, 1997.

Helms, Harry L. *All about Ham Radio: How to Get a License and Talk to the World.* Solana Beach, Calif.: HighText Publications, 1992.

Hench, Bill, and Vincent Lynch. *The Golden Jukebox Age.* Berkeley: Lancaster-Miller, 1981.

Henry, Tricia. *Break All the Rules: Punk Rock and the Making of a Style.* Ann Arbor, Mich.: UMI Research Press, 1989.

Herman W. Land Associates, Inc. *The Hidden Medium: A Status Report on Educational Radio in the United States.* New York: Herman W. Land Associates, Inc., 1967.

Heuton, Cheryl. "Radio Formats Now Total More than 50." *Mediaweek* 5 (43) (November 13, 1995): 12 (1).

Hickerson, Jay. *Hello Again Newsletter;* and *What You Always Wanted to Know About Circulating Old-time Radio Shows,* 1986. (Box 4321, Hamden, Conn. 06514).

Hill, Frank E. *Listen and Learn.* New York: American Association for Adult Education, 1937.

Hill, Frank Ernest. *Tune in for Education.* New York: National Committee for Education by Radio, 1942.

Hill, G. H., and Lenwood David. *Religious Broadcasting, 1920–83: A Selectively Annotated Bibliography*. New York and London: Garland Publishing, 1984.

Hill, Harold E. *NAEB History, 1925–1954*. Washington, D.C.: National Association of Educational Broadcasters, 1954.

Hilliard, Robert L. *Radio Broadcasting: An Introduction to the Sound Medium*. 3rd ed. New York: Longman, 1985.

Hilmes, Michele. "Invisible Men: *Amos 'n' Andy* and the Roots of Broadcast Discourse." *Critical Studies in Mass Communication* 10 (1993): 301–321.

Hinds, Lynn B. *Broadcasting the Local News: The Early Years of Pittsburgh's KDKA-TV*. University Park: Pennsylvania State University Press, 1995.

"History of the American Marconi Company." *Old Timer's Bulletin* 13 (1) (June 1972): 11–18.

Hogan, J. V. L. *The Outline of Radio*. Boston: Little, Brown, 1923, 1925, 1928.

Hohenberg, John. *Foreign Correspondence: The Great Reporters and Their Times*. New York: Columbia University Press, 1964.

Holder, Dennis. "Mixing Public Radio with Private Enterprise: Minnesota Public Radio Cashes In," *Washington Journalism Review* 6 (5) (June 1984): 42–47.

Holsinger, Ralph, and Jon Paul Dilts. *Media Law*. 4th ed. New York: McGraw-Hill, 1996.

Hoover, Herbert. *Memoirs*. Vols. I–II. New York: Macmillan Company, 1951–1952.

Hoover, Herbert. *The Memoirs of Herbert Hoover: The Cabinet and the Presidency, 1920–1933*. New York: Macmillan, 1951.

Hoover's Handbook of American Business. 2 vols. Austin: Hoover's Business Press, Inc., 1996.

Hoover v. Intercity Radio Company, 52 App. D.C. 339, 286 F. 1003, writ of error dismissed as moot, 266 U.S. 636 (1924).

Hosley, David H., and Gayle K. Yamada. *Hard News: Women in Broadcast Journalism*. New York: Greenwood, 1987.

Howard, Herbert H., Michael S. Kievman, and Barbara Moore. *Radio, TV, and Cable Programming*. 2nd ed. Ames: Iowa State University Press, 1994.

Howard, Jay. "Contemporary Christian Music: Where Rock Meets Religion." *Journal of Popular Culture* 26 (1992): 123–130.

Howe, Russell Warren. *The Hunt for "Tokyo Rose."* New York: Madison Books, 1990.

Howeth, Captain L. S. *History of Communications—Electronics in the United States Navy*. Washington, D.C.: U.S. Government Printing Office, 1963.

How to Use the Federal FOI Act. 6th ed. Washington, D.C.: FOI Service Center, 1987.

Hudson, Heather. *Communication Satellites: Their Development and Impact*. New York: Free Press, 1990.

Hughers, Patrick. *A Century of Weather Service, 1870–1970*. New York: Gordon and Breach, 1970.

Hughes, Emmet. *The Ordeal of Power*. New York: Atheneum, 1963.

Hyde, Stuart. *Television and Radio Announcing*. 7th ed. Boston: Houghton Mifflin, 1995.

Hyman, Sydney. *The Lives of William Benton*. Chicago: University of Chicago Press, 1969.

Imus, Don. *God's Other Son: A Novel*. New York: Simon & Schuster, 1994.

Imus, Don. *Imus in the Morning: One Sacred Chicken to Go*. RCA Records, 1973. LSP-4819.

Imus, Don, and Fred Imus. *Two Guys Four Corners*. New York: Villard, 1997. Photographs.

Inglis, Andrew F. *Behind the Tube: A History of Broadcasting Technology and Business*. Boston: Focal Press, 1990.

In the Matter of Amendment of Section 73.3555 [formerly Sections 73.35, 73.240, and 73.636] of the Commission's Rules Relating to Multiple Ownership of AM, FM and Television Broadcast Stations, 56 RR 2d, 859, 1984.

In the Matter of Editorializing by Broadcast Licensees, 13 FCC 1246, 1949.

"Irrelevant Justification." *Cash Box* (January 11, 1969): 3.

Jackaway, Gwenyth L. *Media at War: Radio's Challenge to the Newspapers, 1924–1939.* Westport, Conn.: Praeger, 1995.

Jackson, Paul. *Saturday Afternoons at the Old Met: The Metropolitan Opera Broadcasts, 1931–1950.* Portland, Oreg.: Amadeus-Timber, 1992.

Jansky, C. M., Jr. "The Contributions of Herbert Hoover to Broadcasting." *Journal of Broadcasting* 1 (3) (summer 1957): 249.

Johnson, Nicholas. *Broadcasting in America: The Performance of Network Affiliates in the Top 50 Markets.* 42 FCC 2nd 1, 1973.

Jolley, W. P. *Marconi.* New York: Stein and Day/Publishers, 1972.

Jordan, Robert Oakes, and James Cunningham. *The Sound of High Fidelity.* Chicago: Windsor Press, 1958.

Josephson, Matthew. *Edison.* New York: McGraw-Hill, 1959.

Josiah, W. J., Jr. "The Superstation and the Doctrine of Localism." *Communications and the Law* 3 (fall 1981): 3.

Kahn, Frank J., ed. *Documents of American Broadcasting.* New York: Appleton-Century-Crofts, 1968.

Kahn, Frank J., ed. *Documents of American Broadcasting.* 4th ed. Englewood Cliffs, N.J.: Prentice-Hall, 1984.

Kaltenborn, H. V. *Fifty Fabulous Years.* New York: G. P. Putnam's Sons, 1950.

Kalugin, Oleg. *The First Directorate.* New York: St. Martin's Press, 1994.

Keillor, Garrison. *WLT: A Radio Romance.* New York: Penguin Books, 1991.

Keirstead, Phillip O., and Sonia-Kay Keirstead. *The World of Telecommunication: Introduction to Broadcasting, Cable, and New Technologies.* Boston: Focal Press, 1990.

Keith, Michael C. *Radio Production: Art and Science.* Boston: Focal Press, 1990.

Keith, Michael C. *Radio Programming: Consultancy and Formatics.* Boston: Focal Press, 1987.

Keith, Michael C. *The Radio Station.* 4th ed. Boston: Focal Press, 1997.

Keith, Michael C. *Signals in the Air: Native Broadcasting in America.* Westport, Conn.: Praeger Publishing, 1995.

Keith, Michael C. *Voices in the Purple Haze: Underground Radio in the Sixties.* Westport, Conn.: Praeger Publishing, 1997.

Keith, Michael C., and Joseph M. Krause. *The Radio Station.* 3rd ed. Boston: Focal Press, 1993.

Kendrick, Alexander. *Prime Time: The Life of Edward R. Murrow.* Boston: Little, Brown, 1969.

Kepner, Charles David, Jr., and Jay Henry Soothill. *The Banana Empire: A Case Study of Economic Imperialism.* New York: Vanguard Press, 1935.

King, Larry. *Larry King.* New York: Simon and Schuster, 1982.

"King of Giveaway." *Time* (June 4, 1956): 100–102.

Kinsbury, Paul. *The Grand Ole Opry History of Country Music.* New York: Villard, 1995.

Kirby, Edward, and Jack Harris. *Star-Spangled Radio.* Chicago: Ziff-Davis, 1948.

Kirby, Kathleen Ann. "Shouldn't the Constitution Be Color Blind? *Metro Broadcasting, Inc. v. FCC* Transmits a Surprising Message on Racial Preferences." *Catholic University Law Review* 40 (1991): 403.

Kittross, John M. "The *Journal* and Communication Scholarship." *Journal of Broadcasting and Electronic Media* 35 (1) (winter 1991): 101–104.

Kleinfield, Sonny. *The Biggest Company on Earth.* New York: Holt, Rinehart and Winston, 1981.

Kluckhohn, Frank. *The Drew Pearson Story.* Chicago: C. Halberg, 1967.

Klurfelt, Herman. *Winchell: His Life and Times.* New York: Praeger, 1976.

Koch, Howard. *The Panic Broadcast.* New York: Avon Books, 1971.

Koop, Theodore. *Weapon of Silence.* Chicago: University of Chicago Press, 1946.

Krasnow, Erwin G., Lawrence D. Longley, and Herbert A. Terry. *The Politics of Broadcast Regulation.* 3rd ed. New York: St. Martin's Press, 1982.

Kraueter, David W., ed. "Alfred N. Goldsmith (1888–1974)." In *Radio and Television Pioneers: A Patent Bibliography* (pp. 158–170). Metuchen, N.J.: Scarecrow Press, 1992.

Kripalani, Manjeet. "Quad Sound Reincarnated." *Forbes* 146 (12) (November 26, 1990): 270–272.

Kurth, Peter. *American Cassandra: The Life of Dorothy Thompson.* Boston: Little, Brown and Company, 1990.

Kutler, Stanley I. *The American Inquisition: Justice and Injustice in the Cold War.* New York: Hill and Wang, 1982.

Lackmann, Ronald W. *Same Time—Same Station: An A-Z Guide to Radio from Jack Benny to Howard Stern.* New York: Facts on File, Inc., 1996.

Ladd, Jim. *Radio Waves: Life and Revolution on the FM Dial.* New York: St. Martin's Press, 1991.

Land, Herman. "The Storz Bombshell." *Television* (May 1957): 85–92.

Landry, Robert. *This Fascinating Radio Business.* New York: Bobbs-Merrill, 1946.

Langguth, A. J. *Norman Corwin's Letters.* New York: Barricade Books, 1994.

Lanza, Joseph. *Elevator Music: A Surreal History of Muzak, Easy-Listening and Other Moodsong.* New York: St. Martin's Press, 1994.

Lashner, Marilyn A. "The Role of Foundations in Public Broadcasting, II: The Ford Foundation." *Journal of Broadcasting* 21 (2) (spring 1977): 235–254.

The Latin American Market Planning Report. Miami: Strategy Research Corporation, 1996.

Laufer, Peter. *Inside Talk Radio: America's Voice or Just Hot Air?* Secaucus, N.J.: Carol Publishing Group, 1995.

Lavrakas, Paul J., and Jack K. Holley, eds. *Polling and Presidential Election Coverage.* Newbury Park, Calif.: Sage, 1991.

Leach, Eugene E. *Tuning Out Education: The Cooperation Doctrine in Radio, 1922–1938.* Washington, D.C.: Current, 1983.

Leaming, Barbara. *Orson Welles.* New York: Viking Press, 1985.

Lessing, Lawrence. *Man of High Fidelity: Edwin Howard Armstrong.* Philadelphia: J. B. Lippincott, 1956.

Lewis, Anthony. *Make No Law: The Sullivan Case and the First Amendment.* New York: Random House, 1991.

Lewis, George H., ed. *All That Glitters: Country Music in America.* Bowling Green, Ohio: Bowling Green Popular University Press, 1993.

Lewis, Thomas S. W. *Empire of the Air: The Men Who Made Radio.* New York: Harper-Collins Publishers, 1991.

Lichty, Lawrence W. "'The Nation's Station': A History of Radio Station WLW." Ph.D. dissertation, Ohio State University, 1964.

Lichty, Lawrence W., and Thomas W. Bohn. "Radio's *March of Time:* Dramatized News." *Journalism Quarterly* 51 (3) (autumn 1974): 458–62.

Lichty, Lawrence W., and Malachi C. Topping. *American Broadcasting: A Source Book on the History of Radio and Television.* New York: Hastings House Publishers Inc., 1975.

Limburg, Val E. *Electronic Media Ethics.* Boston: Focal Press, 1994.

Lindbergh, Charles A. *The Spirit of St. Louis.* New York: Charles Scribner's Sons, 1953.

Lindlof, Thomas R., ed. *Natural Audiences.* Norwood, N.J.: Ablex Publishing Company, 1987.

Lodge, Oliver. *Signaling Through Space without Wires: The Work of Hertz and His Successors.* New York: Van Nostrand, 1894, 1898, 1900. Latter edition reprint, New York: Arno Press, 1974.

Looker, Thomas. *The Sound and the Story: NPR and the Art of Radio.* Boston: Houghton Mifflin, 1995.

"A Loosening of Controls on Programs?" *Broadcasting* (January 27, 1964): 66.

Lott, George E. "The Press-Radio War of the 1930s." *Journal of Broadcasting* 14 (3) (summer 1970): 275–286.

Loufer, Peter. *Inside Talk Radio: American Voices on the Air.* Secaucus, N.J.: Carol Publishing Group, 1995.

Lull, J. T., L. M. Johnson, and C. E. Sweeney. "Audiences for Contemporary Radio Formats." *Journal of Broadcasting* 22 (4) (fall 1978): 439.

Lyons, Eugene. *David Sarnoff: A Biography.* New York: Harper & Row, 1966.

Mabee, Carlton. *The American Leonardo: A Life of Samuel F. B. Morse.* New York: Alfred A. Knopf, 1944.

Macaulay, David. *The Way Things Work.* Boston: Houghton Mifflin, 1988.

MacDonald, J. Fred. *Don't Touch That Dial!: Radio Programming in American Life, 1920–1960.* Chicago: Nelson-Hall, 1979.

MacDonald, J. Fred, ed. *Richard Durham's Destination Freedom: Scripts from Radio's Black Legacy, 1948–50.* New York: Praeger Publishers, 1989.

MacFarland, David T. *The Development of the Top 40 Radio Format.* New York: Arno Press, 1979.

MacFarland, David T. "Up from Middle America: The Development of Top-40." In *American Broadcasting: A Source Book on the History of Radio and Television,* edited by Lawrence W. Lichty and Malachi C. Topping (pp. 399–403). New York: Hastings House Publishers Inc., 1975.

MacLaurin, W. Rupert. *Invention and Innovation in the Radio Industry.* New York: Arno Press and the *New York Times,* 1971.

Malone, Bill C. *Country Music U.S.A.* Austin: University of Texas Press, 1985.

Management and Operation of Armed Forces Radio and Television Service. DOD 5120.20-R. Washington, D.C.: Office of the Assistant Secretary of Defense (Public Affairs), February 1988.

Mange, Lawrence, ed. *Passport to World Band Radio.* 10th ed. Penn's Park: International Broadcasting Services, Ltd., 1994.

Marchand, Philip. *Marshall McLuhan: The Medium and the Messenger.* New York: Ticknor & Fields, 1989.

Marconi, Degna. *My Father, Marconi.* New York: McGraw-Hill, 1962.

Marcus, Abraham, and William Marcus. *Elements of Radio.* 5th ed. Englewood Cliffs, N.J.: Prentice-Hall, 1965.

Marsh, Dave, and Kevin Stein. *The Book of Rock Lists.* New York: Dell Publishing, 1981.

Marzolf, Marion. *Up from the Footnote: A History of Women Journalists.* New York: Hastings House, 1977.

Mason, Elizabeth B., and Louis M. Starr, eds. *The Oral History Collection of Columbia University*. New York: Columbia University, Oral History Research Office, 1979.

Mayes, Thorn L. *Wireless Communication in the United States: The Early Development of American Radio Operating Companies*. East Greenwich, R.I.: New England Wireless and Steam Museum, Inc., 1989.

Mayflower Decision. 8 FCC 333, 338.

McAdams, Katherine. "Minorities." In *The Handbook on Mass Media in the United States*, edited by Erwin K. Thomas and Brown H. Carpenter (pp. 191–206). Westport, Conn.: Greenwood, 1994.

McBride, Mary Margaret. *Out of the Air*. New York: Doubleday, 1960.

McBride, Mary Margaret. "Secrets." *Good Housekeeping* 129 (March 1950): 41.

McChesney, Robert W. *Telecommunications, Mass Media and Democracy: The Battle for the Control of U.S. Broadcasting 1928–1935*. New York: Oxford University Press, 1993.

McCullough, David. *Truman*. New York: Simon and Schuster, 1992.

McGrath, Tom. *MTV: The Making of a Revolution*. Philadelphia: Running Press, 1996.

McKenzie, Robert. "Are We Really Giving Today's Aural Age the Hearing It Deserves?" *Feedback* 36 (4) (1996): 25–28.

McLaughlin, John. "The Wider World of Sport." *Sky: The Magazine of International Culture* (November 1996): 21–26.

McNicol, Donald. *Radio's Conquest of Space: The Experimental Rise in Radio Communication*. New York: Murray Hill Books, 1946. Reprint, New York: Arno Press, 1974.

MEE Productions, Inc. *The MEE Report: Reaching the Hip Hop Generation*. Philadelphia, Pa.: MEE Productions, Inc., 1992.

Middleton, Kent, and Bill Chamberlain. *The Law of Public Communication*. New York: Longman, 1994.

Milam, Lorenzo W. *The Radio Papers: From KRAB to KCHU*. San Diego: MHO & MHO Works, 1986.

Miller, Arthur R., and Michael H. Davis. *Intellectual Property: Patents, Trademarks and Copyright in a Nutshell*. 2nd ed. St. Paul: West Publishing, 1990.

Miller, Jonathon. *McLuhan*. London: William Collins, 1971.

Miller, N. "Self-regulation in American Radio." *Annals of the American Academy of Political & Social Science* 213 (1940): 93–96.

Miller, Robert M. *Harry Emerson Fosdick: Preacher, Pastor, Prophet*. New York: Oxford University Press, 1985.

Milton, Joyce. *Loss of Eden: A Biography of Charles and Anne Morrow Lindbergh*. New York: HarperCollins, 1993.

Minow, Newton N. *How Vast the Wasteland Now?* New York: Gannett Foundation Media Center, Columbia University, May 9, 1991.

Minow, Newton N., and Craig Lamay. *Abandoned in the Wasteland*. New York: Hill and Wang. 1995.

Mirabile, Lisa, ed. "Capital Cities/ABC Inc." In *International Directory of Company Histories*. Vol. 2. Chicago: St. James Press, 1990.

Mirabito, Michael M. A. *The New Communications Technologies*. 2nd ed. Boston: Focal Press, 1994.

Mitchell, Curtis. *Cavalcade of Broadcasting*. Chicago: Follett Publishing Company, 1970.

Montell, William Lynwood. *Singing the Glory Down: Amateur Gospel Music in South Central Kentucky 1900–1990*. Lexington: University Press of Kentucky, 1991.

Moritz, Charles, ed. *Current Biography, 1987*. New York: H. W. Nelson Co., 1987.

"Mormon Tabernacle Choir." In *Encyclopedia of Mormonism* (2: 950–952). New York: Macmillan Publishing Company, 1992.

Morris, William, ed. *American Heritage Dictionary of the English Language.* Boston: Houghton Mifflin, 1981.

Morrow, Bruce, and Laura Baudo. *Cousin Brucie! My Life in Rock 'n' Roll Radio.* New York: Beech Tree Books, 1987.

Morse, Edward Lind, ed. *Samuel F. B. Morse: His Letters and Journals.* Boston: Houghton Mifflin, 1914.

Muller, Helen M. *Education by Radio.* New York: H. W. Wilson Company, 1932.

Mullin, John T. "The Birth of the Recording Industry." *Billboard* (November 18, 1972).

"The Networks Present More and Better Unsponsored Programs." *Newsweek* (November 8, 1937): 20–21.

Newman, Mark. *Entrepreneurs of Profit and Pride: From Black-Appeal to Radio Soul.* New York: Praeger Publishers, 1988.

New York Times Biographical Service. *A Compilation of Current Biographical Information of General Interest* 3 (5) (May 1972, George Washington Trendle). New York: Arno Press.

New York Times Biographical Service. *A Compilation of Current Biographical Information of General Interest* 11 (2) (February 1980, Chester Lauck). New York: Arno Press.

NHK (Nippon Hosa Kyokai). *50 Years of Japanese Broadcasting.* Tokyo: NHK, 1977.

The 1996 Telecommunications Act: Law & Legislative History. Bethesda, Md.: Pike & Fischer Inc., 1996.

Occhiogrosso, Peter. *Tell It to the King.* New York: Putnam, 1988.

O'Connor, John J. "A National Institution." *New York Times* Biographical Service (December 1974): 1672–1673.

O'Dell, Cary. *Women Pioneers in Television: Biographies of Fifteen Industry Leaders.* Jefferson, N.C.: McFarland, 1996.

O'Donnell, Lewis B., Carl Hausman, and Philip Benoit. *Announcing: Broadcast Communicating Today.* Belmont, Calif.: Wadsworth, 1996.

O'Donnell, Lewis B., Carl Hausman, and Philip Benoit. *Radio Station Operations: Management and Employee Perspectives.* Belmont, Calif.: Wadsworth, 1989.

Office of Censorship. *Code of Wartime Practices for American Broadcasters.* Washington, D.C.: U.S. Government Printing Office, June 15, 1942 (and subsequent editions).

Office of Censorship. *A Report on the Office of Censorship.* Historical Reports on War Administration. Series 1. Washington, D.C.: U.S. Government Printing Office, 1945.

O'Hara, J. G., and W. Pricha. *Hertz and the Maxwellians.* London: Peter Peregrinus, 1987.

"Orleck, Joseph P." *New York Times,* February 6, 1997, sec. B, paid death notices, col. 1, p. 13.

Orson Welles on the Air: The Radio Years. Monograph. New York: Museum of Broadcasting, 1988.

Oslin, George P. *The Story of Telecommunications.* Macon, Ga.: Mercer University Press, 1992.

"Our Respects to . . . James Allen Schulke." *Broadcasting* 88 (November 2, 1959): 121.

Owen, Billy. *The Big Broadcast: 1920–1950.* New York: Viking Press, 1972.

Pacifica Foundation, 56 FCC 2d 94 (1975).

Paley, William S. *As It Happened: A Memoir.* Garden City, N.Y.: Doubleday, 1979.

Paley, W. S. "Broadcasting in American Society." *Annals of the American Academy of Political & Social Science* 213 (1940): 63–68.

Paper, Lewis J. *Empire: William S. Paley and the Making of CBS.* New York: St. Martin's Press, 1987.

Pareles, Jon, and Patricia Reminisce, eds. *The Rolling Stone Encyclopedia of Rock & Roll.* New York: Summit Books, 1983.

Patoski, Joe Nick. "Rock 'n' Roll's Wizard of Oz." *Texas Monthly* (February 1980): 101–104, 167–171.

Pearce, Christopher. *Jukebox Art.* London: H. C. Blossom, 1991.

Pearson, Drew. *The Case against Congress.* New York: Simon and Schuster, 1968.

Pember, Don R. *Mass Media Law.* Dubuque, Iowa: Brown & Benchmark, 1996.

Persico, Joseph E. *Edward R. Murrow, an American Original.* New York: McGraw-Hill, 1988.

Peterson, Alan. "WILD, WAKY, KRZY Call Letter Combos." *Radio World* (December 27, 1995): 34.

Phillips, Irna. "Every Woman's Life Is a Soap Opera." *McCall's* (March 1965): 116+.

Phillips, V. J. *Early Radio Wave Detectors.* London: Peter Peregrinus, 1980.

Pickett, William B. *Homer E. Capehart: A Senator's Life.* Indianapolis: Indiana Historical Society, 1990.

Poindexter, Ray. *Golden Throats and Silver Tongues: The Radio Announcers.* Conway, Ark.: River Road Press, 1978.

Polskin, Howard. "MTV at 10: The Beat Goes On." *TV Guide* 3 (August 1991): 4–8.

Post, Steve. *Playing in the FM Band: A Personal Account of Free Radio.* New York: Viking Press, 1974.

Price, Byron. "Governmental Censorship in War-Time." *American Political Science Review* 36 (October 1942): 837–849.

Price, Deborah Evans. "Country and Christian Pubs Love Their Neighbors." *Billboard* (April 20, 1996): 44–47.

Pringle, Peter K., Michael F. Starr, and William E. McCavitt. *Electronic Media Management.* 3rd ed. Boston: Focal Press, 1995.

"The Problems of Radio Reallocation." *Congressional Digest* 7 (10) (October 1928): 255–286.

"Programming: The Executioner." *Time* (August 23, 1968): 48.

Prowitt, Marsha. *Guide to Citizen Action in Radio and Television.* New York: Office of Communication, United Church of Christ, 1971.

"Putting FM in Its Place in the Top 50." *Broadcasting* (January 22, 1979): 40, 42, 45, 48–49.

Quinlan, Sterling. *Inside ABC: American Broadcasting Company's Rise to Power.* New York: Hastings House, 1979.

Radio Act of 1912. Public Law 264, 62nd Congress, August 13, 1912.

"Radio Formats." *Mediaweek* 5 (33) (September 4, 1995): 95 (1).

Radio Today. New York: Arbitron, 1995.

Radovsky, M. *Alexander Popov: Inventor of Radio.* Translated by G. Yankovsky. Moscow: Foreign Languages Publishing House, 1957.

Ray, William. *FCC: The Ups and Downs of Radio-TV Regulation.* Ames: Iowa State University Press, 1990.

RCA Receiving Tube Manual. Harrison, N.J.: Radio Corporation of America, Electron Tube Division, 1961.

Redd, Lawrence. *Rock Is Rhythm and Blues.* East Lansing: Michigan State University Press, 1974.

Rehnquist, William H. *The Supreme Court: How It Was, How It Is.* New York: Morrow, 1987.

"Riding Gain." *Broadcasting and Cable* 127 (3) (January 20, 1997): 46.

Ries, Al, and Jack Trout. *Positioning: The Battle for Your Mind.* New York: McGraw-Hill, 1981.

Riley, Donald W. "The History of American Radio Drama." Ph.D. dissertation, Ohio State University, 1945.

"'Rock and Roll Muzak.'" *Newsweek* (March 9, 1970): 85.

Rose, Ernest D. "How the U.S. Heard about Pearl Harbor." *Journal of Broadcasting* 5 (4) (fall 1961): 285–298.

Rosen, Philip T. *The Modern Stentors: Radio Broadcasters and the Federal Government, 1920–1934.* Westport, Conn.: Greenwood Press, 1980.

Rosenberg, Neil V. *Bluegrass: A History.* Urbana: University of Illinois Press, 1985.

Rosenthal, Raymond, ed. *McLuhan: Pro and Con.* Baltimore: Penguin, 1968.

Routt, Edd, James B. McGrath, and Fredric A. Weiss. *The Radio Format Conundrum.* New York: Hastings House, 1978.

Rowland, Willard D. "Public Service Broadcasting in the United States: Its Mandate, Institutions and Conflicts." In *Public Service Broadcasting in a Multichannel Environment: The History and Survival of an Ideal,* edited by Robert K. Avery (pp. 157–194). White Plains, N.Y.: Longman, 1993.

RTNDA. "Fifty Years of Electronic Journalism." *Communicator* (September 1995).

Rumsey, Francis. *Digital Audio Operations.* Boston: Focal Press, 1991.

Ryan, Halford R. *Harry Emerson Fosdick: Persuasive Preacher.* Westport, Conn.: Greenwood Press, 1989.

Ryan, Milo. *History in Sound.* Seattle: University of Washington Press, 1963.

Sachs, Harvey. *Toscanini.* Philadelphia: J. B. Lippincott Company, 1978.

Sack, Robert D., and Sandra S. Baron. *Libel, Slander, and Related Problems.* 2nd ed. New York: Practising Law Institute, 1994.

Sadie, Stanley, with Alison Latham, eds. *Brief Guide to Music.* 2nd ed. Englewood Cliffs, N.J.: Prentice-Hall, 1990.

Salyer, Steven A. "Monopoly to Marketplace Competition Comes to Public Radio." In *Radio: The Forgotten Medium,* edited by Edward C. Pease and Everette E. Dennis (pp. 185–192). New Brunswick, N.J.: Transaction Publishers, 1995.

Sanders, Marion K. *Dorothy Thompson: A Legend in Her Time.* Boston: Houghton Mifflin, 1973.

Sanford, Bruce W. *Libel and Privacy.* 2nd ed. Englewood Cliffs, N.J.: Prentice-Hall Law & Business, 1996.

Sanger, Elliott M. *Rebel in Radio: The Story of WQXR.* New York: Hastings House, 1973.

Sarno, Edward. "The National Radio Conferences." *Journal of Broadcasting* 13 (1969): 189–202.

Saunders, Kevin W. *Violence as Obscenity: Limiting the Media's First Amendment Protection.* Durham, N.C.: Duke University Press, 1966.

Savage, Jon. *England's Dreaming: Anarchy, Sex Pistols, Punk Rock and Beyond.* New York: St. Martin's Press, 1992.

Scanlon, Lee E. Personal interviews. Washington, D.C., 1962–1963.

Schaden, Chuck. "Speaking of Radio: Chuck Schaden's Conversation with Jim Jordan." *Nostalgia Digest* (December–January 1985): 33–40.

Schechter, A. A., with Edward Anthony. *I Live on Air.* New York: Frederick Stokes, 1941.

Schillmoeller, Edward A. "National Television Measurement Quality Priorities." *Journal of Advertising Research* 33 (3) (May–June 1993): RC10(3).

Schlesinger, Arthur. *The Age of Roosevelt.* 3 vols. Boston: Houghton Mifflin, 1957, 1959, 1960.

Schmeckbeier, Laurence F. *The Federal Radio Commission: Its History, Activities and Organization.* Washington, D.C.: Brookings Institution, 1932.

Schmidt, Benno C., Jr. *Freedom of the Press vs. Public Access.* New York: Praeger Publishers, 1976.

Scholl, Peter. *Garrison Keillor.* New York: Macmillan, 1993.

"The 'School of the Air' (CBS) to Be an Official Channel for War News." *School and Society* (September 26, 1942): 263–264.

Schuller, Gunther. *The Swing Era: The Development of Jazz 1930–1945.* New York: Oxford University Press, 1989.

Scopes, John T., and James Presley. *Center of the Storm: Memoirs of John T. Scopes.* New York: Holt, Rinehart and Winston, 1967.

Seib, Philip M. *Rush Hour: Talk Radio, Politics and the Rise of Rush Limbaugh.* Ft. Worth, Tex.: Summit Group, 1993.

Seldes, Gilbert. "The Great Gildersleeve." *Saturday Review* (June 2, 1956): 26.

Settel, Irving. *A Pictorial History of Radio.* New York: Grosset & Dunlap, 1967.

Sevareid, Eric. *Not So Wild a Dream.* New York: Atheneum, 1976.

Shane, Ed. "Radio and Subliminal Timekeeping." *Feedback* 35 (1) (winter 1994): 1–3.

Shapiro, Nat, and Nat Henthoff, eds. *Hear Me Talkin' to Ya'.* New York: Rinehart, 1955.

Shaw, Arnold. *The World of Soul: Black America's Contribution to the Pop Music Scene.* New York: Cowles Book Co., 1970.

Sheml, Sidney, and M. William Krasilovsky. *This Business of Music.* 2nd ed. New York: Billboard Books, 1990.

Shepard, Richard F. "Jack Benny, 80, Dies of Cancer on Coast." *New York Times* Biographical Service (December 1974): 1670–1672.

Shepard, Richard F. "Master of Radio: Welles on the Air." *New York Times,* November 30, 1988, p. C26.

Sherman, Barry L. *Telecommunications Management.* 2nd ed. New York: McGraw-Hill, 1995.

Sherman, Stratford P. "Capital Cities' Capital Coup." *Fortune* 112 (1) (April 15, 1985): 51–52.

Shiers, George, ed. *Technical Development of Television.* New York: Arno Press, 1977. (Reprint of articles published between 1911 and 1970 by various publishers.)

Shirer, William L. *Berlin Diary: The Journal of a Foreign Correspondent, 1934–1941.* New York: Knopf, 1940, 1941. Reprint, New York: Galahad Books, 1995.

Shirer, William L. *The Rise and Fall of the Third Reich.* New York: Simon and Schuster, 1960.

Shurick, E. P. J. *The First Quarter-Century of American Broadcasting.* Kansas City: Midland Publishing Co., 1946.

Siepmann, Charles. *Radio in Wartime.* America Faces the War, No. 13. New York: Oxford University Press, 1942.

Simmons, Steven J. *The Fairness Doctrine and the Media.* Berkeley: University of California Press, 1978.

Simon, George. *The Big Bands.* New York: Schirmer Books, 1967.

Sivowitch, Elliot N. "A Technological Survey of Broadcasting's Pre-History, 1876–1920." *Journal of Broadcasting* 15 (1) (winter 1970–1971): 1–20.

Sixth Report and Order in Docket 8736, 41 F.C.C. 148, 17 Fed. Reg. 3905 (1952).

Sklar, Rick. *Rocking America: An Insider's Story.* New York: St. Martin's Press, 1984.

Smith, Alfred E. *Up to Now: An Autobiography.* New York: Viking Press, 1929.

Smith, F. Leslie, Milan Meeske, and John W. Wright II. *Electronic Media and Government: The Regulation of Wireless and Wired Mass Communication in the United States.* White Plains, N.Y.: Longman, 1995.

Smith, R. Franklin. "Oldest Station in the Nation?" *Journal of Broadcasting* 4 (1) (winter 1959–1960): 40–55.

Smith, Richard D. *Bluegrass*. Chicago: Cappella, 1995.

Smith, Richard N. *Thomas E. Dewey and His Times*. New York: Simon and Schuster, 1982.

Smith, Sally Bedell. *In All His Glory*. New York: Simon & Schuster, 1990.

Smith, Wes. *The Pied Pipers of Rock 'n' Roll*. Marietta, Ga.: Longstreet Press, 1989.

Smolla, Rodney A. *Law of Defamation*. New York: Clark Boardman Callaghan, 1996.

Smolla, Rodney A., ed. *A Year in the Life of the Supreme Court*. Durham, N.C.: Duke University Press, 1995.

Sobel, Robert. *RCA*. New York: Stein and Day, 1986.

Southern, Eileen. *The Music of Black Americans: A History*. New York: W. W. Norton, 1971.

Sperber, A. M. *Murrow: His Life and Times*. New York: Freundlich Books, 1986.

Spiceland, David, ed. "Multiplexing." In *McGraw-Hill Encyclopedia of Science and Technology*. 7th ed. New York : McGraw-Hill, 1992.

Stark, Phyllis. "Consultancy Alliances Prosper." *Billboard* (June 10, 1995): 75–76.

Stavitsky, Alan G. "The Changing Conception of Localism in U.S. Public Radio." *Journal of Broadcasting and Electronic Media* 38 (1) (winter 1994): 19–33.

Stavitsky, Alan G. "'Guys in Suits with Charts': Audience Research in U.S. Public Radio." *Journal of Broadcasting and Electronic Media* 39 (2) (spring 1995): 177–189.

Stavitsky, Alan G., and Timothy W. Gleason. "Alternative Things Considered: A Comparison of National Public Radio and Pacifica Radio News Coverage." *Journalism Quarterly* 71 (4) (winter 1994): 775–786.

Stearn, Gerald Emanuel, ed. *McLuhan: Hot and Cool*. New York: Dial, 1967.

Sterling, Christopher H. "A Critique of the Changing Role of the *Journal*." *Journal of Broadcasting and Electronic Media* 35 (1) (winter 1991): 105–107.

Sterling, Christopher. "Decade of Development: FM Radio in the 1960s." *Journalism Quarterly* 48 (1971): 222–230.

Sterling, Christopher H. "The 'New Technology': The FCC and Changing Technological Standards." *Journal of Communication* 32 (1) (1982): 138.

Sterling, Christopher H., and John M. Kittross. *Stay Tuned: A Concise History of American Broadcasting*. Belmont, Calif.: Wadsworth, 1990.

Stern, Howard. *Howard Stern: Private Parts*. New York: Pocket Books, 1994.

Stix, Harriet. "Sincerity Is 'Secret' Behind Her Success." *New York Herald Tribune*, November 28, 1960.

Stone, Alan. *Economic Regulation and the Public Interest: The Federal Trade Commission in Theory and Practice*. Ithaca, N.Y.: Cornell University Press, 1977.

Strak, Phyllis. "Stations Spell Out Tradition." *Billboard* (March 13, 1993): 14+.

Straub, Duane G. "The Role of Secretary of Commerce Herbert Hoover in the Development of Early Radio Regulation." Master's thesis, Michigan State University, 1964.

Streeter, Thomas. *Selling the Air*. Chicago: University of Chicago Press, 1996.

Stuessy, Joe. *Rock & Roll: Its History and Stylistic Development*. Englewood Cliffs, N.J.: Prentice-Hall, 1990.

Stumf, Charles, and Tom Price. *Heavenly Days! The Story of Fibber McGee & Molly*. Wayneville, N.C.: World of Yesterday Press, 1987.

Sullivan, R. Lee. "Radio Free Internet." *Forbes* (April 22, 1996): 44–45.

Summers, Robert. *Wartime Censorship of Press and Radio*. Vol. 15, No. 8. New York: H. W. Wilson, 1942.

Sunier, John. *The Story of Stereo: 1881–*. New York: Gernsback Library, Inc., 1960.

Sussman, Leonard R. *Power, the Press and the Technology of Freedom: The Coming Age of ISDN.* New York: Freedom House, 1989.

Swartz, Jon D., and Robert C. Reinehr. *Handbook of Old-time Radio: A Comprehensive Guide to Golden Age Radio Listening and Collecting.* Metuchen, N.J.: Scarecrow Press, 1993.

Swing, Raymond "Gram." *Good Evening!* London: Bodley Head Ltd., 1964.

Talbot-Smith, Michael. *Broadcast Sound Technology.* Boston: Focal Press, 1990.

Tavares, Frank. *A Critical Analysis of Selected Dramatic Elements in the Radio Series "The Lives of Harry Lime," with Orson Welles.* Ann Arbor, Mich.: University Microfilms International, 1976.

"Tennis Starts Act in New Television." *New York Times,* August 25, 1934, sec. 14, p. 4.

Terrace, Vincent. *Radio's Golden Years: The Encyclopedia of Radio Programs: 1930–1960.* San Diego: A. S. Barnes and Company, Inc., 1981.

Theall, Donald F. *The Media Is the Rear View Mirror: Understanding McLuhan.* Montreal: McGill-Queen's University Press, 1971.

Thomas, Robert McG. "Anne Hummert, 91, Dies: Creator of Soap Operas." *New York Times,* July 21, 1996, p. 27.

"Thoughts from Lake Wobegon on the Superhighway." *Broadcasting & Cable* (January 10, 1994): 56–58.

Tokyo Rose: Victim of Propaganda. Greystone Productions, 1995. (A&E cable network, August 9, 1995).

Tricker, R. A. R. *The Contributions of Farraday and Maxwell to Electrical Science.* New York: Pergamon Press, 1966.

Trigg, S. Jenell. "The Federal Communications Commission's Equal Opportunity Employment Program and the Effect of *Adarand Constructors, Inc. v. Pena." CommLaw Conspectus* 4 (1996): 237.

Tull, Charles J. *Father Coughlin and the New Deal.* Syracuse: Syracuse University Press, 1965.

Tunstall, Jeremy. *The Media in Britain.* London: Constable, 1983.

"TV's First Star and Favorite Uncle." *Broadcasting & Cable* (October 28, 1996): 108.

Tyler, Tracy F., ed. *Radio as a Cultural Agency: Proceedings of a National Conference on the Use of Radio as a Cultural Agency.* Washington, D.C.: National Committee on Education by Radio, 1934.

USCA 47 Section 533 (a) 65 RR 2d 1676. *Amendment of Section 73.3555 of the Commission's Rules,* The Broadcast Multiple Ownership Rules, 1989.

The U.S. Consumer Electronics Industry in Review. Arlington, Va.: Electronic Industries Association, 1958. Annual.

The U.S. Hispanic Market. Miami: Strategy Research Corporation, 1996.

The U.S. Hispanic Population Book. Miami: Strategy Research Corporation, 1997.

"USIA Publishes Guide to TV in Eastern Europe." *Broadcasting* 18 (March 5, 1990): 16–17.

U.S. Kerner Commission. *Report of the National Advisory Commission on Civil Disorders.* New York: Bantam Books, 1968.

Van Horne, H. "Radio's Most Perfect Script." *Saturday Review of Literature* 30 (September 27, 1947): 51.

Veciana-Suarez, Ana. *Hispanic Media, USA.* Washington, D.C.: Media Institute, 1987.

Vizard, Frank. "Good Morning, Cable Radio." *Popular Mechanics* 170 (5) (May 1993): 118–119.

Vizard, Frank. "The Return of Digital Radio on Cable." *Broadcasting* 118 (26) (June 25, 1990): 50–52.

Walker, Stanley. *Dewey: An American of This Century.* New York: Whitlesey House, a division of the McGraw-Hill Book Company, 1944.

Waller, Don. *The Motown Story.* New York: Charles Scribner's Sons, 1985.

Waller, Judith C. *Radio: The Fifth Estate.* Boston: Houghton Mifflin, 1946.

Ward, Ed, Geoffrey Stokes, and Ken Tucker. *Rock of Ages: The Rolling Stone History of Rock & Roll.* New York: Summit Books, 1986.

Ward, Mark. *Air of Salvation: The Story of Christian Broadcasting.* Grand Rapids, Mich.: Baker Books, 1994.

Warner, Charles, and Joseph Buchman. *Broadcast and Cable Selling.* 2nd ed. Belmont, Calif.: Wadsworth Publishing Company, 1993.

Warner, Emily Smith, with Hawthorne Daniel. *The Happy Warrior: A Biography of My Father, Alfred E. Smith.* Garden City, N.Y.: Doubleday and Company, Inc., 1956.

Warren, Donald. *Radio Priest: Charles Coughlin, the Father of Hate Radio.* New York: Free Press, 1996.

Waterman, David. "Narrowcasting and Broadcasting on Non-broadcast Media." *Communication Research* 19 (February 1992): 3.

Watkins, Mel. *On the Real Side: Laughing, Lying and Signifying the Underground Tradition of African American Humor that Transformed American Culture, from Slavery to Richard Pryor.* New York: Touchstone, 1994.

Watkinson, John. *An Introduction to Digital Audio.* Oxford: Focal Press, 1994.

Webster, James G., and Lawrence W. Lichty. *Ratings Analysis: Theory and Practice.* Hillsdale, N.J.: Lawrence Erlbaum Associates, 1991.

Wendt, Lloyd. *Chicago Tribune: The Rise of a Great American Newspaper.* Chicago: Rand McNally, 1979.

Wertheim, Arthur Frank. *Radio Comedy.* New York: Oxford University Press, 1979.

Whitcomb, Dan. "Friends and Family Bid George Burns Farewell." Reuters, March 12, 1996, Newsbank CD.

White, Llewellyn. *History of Broadcasting: Radio to Television.* New York: Arno Press, 1971.

White, Paul W. *News on the Air.* New York: Harcourt, Brace & Co., 1947.

"Why Own One of the Wonders of the World." *Economist* (July 13, 1991): 87–88.

Wienberg, Jonathan. "Broadcasting and Speech." *California Law Review* 81 (1993): 1103.

Wiener, Leonard. "Tinkering with Radio on the Web." *U.S. News & World Report* (April 1, 1996): 72.

Willey, George A. "End of an Era: The Daytime Radio Serial." *Journal of Broadcasting* 5 (2) (spring 1961): 97–115.

Williams, Herbert Lee. *The Newspaperman's President: Harry S. Truman.* Chicago: Nelson Hall, 1984.

Williams, John R. *This Was "Your Hit Parade."* Camden, Maine: Courier-Gazette, 1973.

Williams, T. Harry. *Huey Long.* New York: Alfred A. Knopf, 1969.

Williamson, Mary E. "Judith Cary Waller: Chicago Broadcasting Pioneer." *Journalism History* 3 (4) (1976–1977): 111–115.

Willis, Edgar. *Foundations in Broadcasting: Radio and Television.* Oxford: Oxford University Press, 1951.

Wilson, Charles Morrow. *Empire in Green and Gold: The Story of the American Banana Trade.* New York: Greenwood Press, 1968.

Winfield, Betty Houchin. *FDR and the News Media.* Urbana: University of Illinois Press, 1990.

Witherspoon, John, and Roselle Kovitz. *The History of Public Broadcasting.* Washington, D.C.: Current Publishing, 1987.

Wolfe, Harold. *Herbert Hoover: Public Servant and Leader of the Loyal Opposition.* New York: Exposition Press, 1956.

Wolfman Jack. *Have Mercy! Confessions of the Original Rock 'n' Roll Animal.* New York: Warner Books, 1995.

Wolkonowicz, John Paul. "The Philco Corporation: Historical Review and Strategic Analysis, 1892-1961." Master's thesis, Massachusetts Institute of Technology, 1981.

Wolsey, Heber G. "The History of Radio Station KSL from 1922 to Television." Ph.D. dissertation, Michigan State University, 1967.

Wood, Bert. *Orson Welles: A Bio-Bibliography.* New York: Greenwood, 1990.

Wood, Clement. *The Life of a Man, a Biography of John R. Brinkley.* Kansas City: Goshorn Publishing Co., 1934.

"World Market–1960." *Cash Box* (January 9, 1960).

Worsham, James. "End of the Line for the ICC." *Nation's Business* 84 (3) (March 1996): 32.

Wyden, Peter. "Madame Soap Opera." *Saturday Evening Post* (June 25, 1960): 129+.

Yoder, Andrew. *Pirate Radio: The Incredible Saga of America's Underground, Illegal Broadcasters.* Solana Beach, Calif.: HighText Publications, 1996.

Zapoleon, Guy. "Jeremy's Spoken . . . 'The New Rock Revolution Is Here.'" *Radio Ink* (August 21–September 3, 1995): 30–31.

Zelezny, John D. *Communications Law, Liberties, Restraints, and the Modern Media.* Belmont, Calif.: Wadsworth Publishing, 1993.

Web Sites

Caution should be given to these citations as they are dynamic and constantly changing. Please note that we have updated this list as of February 12, 1998 so some citations may not be as they appear in the original entry.

ASCAP. http://www.ascap.com

Allen, Steve. http://www.dove.org/whoswho/allenbio.htm

Antique Radios Online. http://www.antiqueradios.com/

Antique Wireless Association. Electronic Communication Museum. http://www.ggw.org/freenet/a/awa/index.html

"AudioNet: The Broadcast Network on the Internet." http://www.audionet.com/

Bellingham Antique Radio Museum.http://www.antique-radio.org/

Bell Laboratories.
    Home Page. http://www.bell-labs.com/
    "Over 70 Years of Innovation: 1925 to Today." http://www.lucent.com/timeline/

Big Band. http://www.jazzhall.org/jazz.cgi?$BIGBAND

Big Bands Database. http://cnct.com/home/mlp/bigbands.html

Billboard Online. http://www.billboard.com

Billboard Music Charts. http://la.yahoo.com/external/bpi/music_chart/

BMI.Com. http://bmi.com/index.html (a searchable database for and about songwriting and music licensing)

The Broadcast Archive. http://www.oldradio.com/

Broadcasting's Forgotten Father: The Charles Herrold Story. http://www.kteh.org/prod/docs/docherrold.html (60 min., VHS videotape, 1994)

Cash Box. http://www.accessnashville.com/cashbox/

Charts, Music. http://www.yahoo.com/entertainment/music/charts (list of links to various music charts)

Copyright Basics Circular 1. ftp://ftp.loc.gov/pub/copyright/circs/circ01.html

Current. http://www.current.org/ (a trade newspaper covering public broadcasting)

Dees, Rick. http://www.rick.com

de Forest, Lee. http://ishmael.nmh.northfield.ma.us/lee/deforest.html

Diode. http://www.antique-radio.org/terms/diode.html

Drive Time. http://www.whjt.com/drive_clock.html

Duopoly. http://www.fedele.com/website/fcc/telecom.htm

Elwell, Cyril F. http://www.sfmuseum.org/hist/elwell.html

Farnsworth Chronicles. http://songs.com/noma/philo/index.html

Federal Communications Commission (FCC). http://www.fcc.gov/

Freeform Radio. WFMU-FM Radio 91.1, New York City. http://www.wfmu.org

Genco, Lou. "Old-Time Radio." http://www.old-time.com/

Gospel Music. http://www.ufsa.ufl.edu/oss/IBC/Gospelchoir.html

History of Radio Transmission. http://www.penstock.avnet.com/radio.htm

Home Stereo and Quadraphonic Sound. http://sylfest.hiof.no/~bjornbb/dolby/dspl/ppf-quad.html

Hypertext FCC Rules Project. http://www.hallikainen.com/FccRules/

International Radio. http://guide-p.infoseek.com/International_radio_stations?tid'2881

Internet Jazz Hall of Fame. http://www.jazzhall.org/

Johnson, Nicholas. http://soli.inav.net/~njohnson/

Jukebox from Hell©. http://www.discjockey.com/jukebox

Library of American Broadcasting. http://www.lib.umd.edu/UMCP/LAB/

The Lone Ranger. "Sounds from the History of Radio." Bellingham Antique Radio Museum. http://www.antique-radio.org/sounds/shows/lonerange/lranger.html

Lucent Technologies. *Fact Book*. http://www.lucent.com/news/factbook/factbook.html

"*Lum & Abner* Episode Guide." Compiled by Virgil A. Stewart, 1995. http://www.old-time.com/logs2.html (select *Lum & Abner* from the list provided and then display the log).

Motown. "Welcome to Motown 40.com." http://www.motown.com

Museum of Radio & Technology. http://ouvaxa.cats.ohiou.edu/~post/MRT/

Musicradio WABC-AM 77. http://musicradio.computer.net/index.html

National Public Radio Online. http://www.npr.org

National Religious Broadcasters. http://www.nrb.com/

Oldies.

    WGRR-FM Oldies 103.5, Cincinnati, Ohio. http://www.wgrr1035.com/

    WKIO-FM Oldies 92, Central Illinois. http://www.wkio.com/

    WMXJ-FM Majic 102.7, South Florida. http://www.wmxj.com/index.html

Pacifica Foundation. http://www.pacifica.org/

Pacifica Radio. WBAI 99.5 FM. http://www.wbai.org/

PRI, Public Radio International. http://www.pri.org

Radio and Records, Inc. "R&R, the Industries Newspaper." http://www.rronline.com

Radio Broadcast Rules. 47 CFR Part 73. http://www.fcc.gov/mmb/asd/bickel/amfmrule.html

Radio Days. http://www.otr.com/main.html

Radio News. http://www.otr.com/news.html (sound recording).

Radio History Society. http://www.radiohistory.org/links.htm

Radio Netherland's "Antique and Old Time Radio." http://www.rnw.nl/realradio/antique_index.html

Radio Papers Repository. http://www.broadcast.net/HyperNews/get/forums//radio.html

Real Audio Web Site." http://www.realaudio.com/

Rock and Roll Hall of Fame and Museum, Cleveland, Ohio. http://www.rockhall.com

Society of Professional Journalists. http://www.SPJ.org/

Telecommunications Act of 1996.

    http://www.fcc.gov/telecom.html

    http://www.fedele.com/website/ fcc/telecom.htm

Texaco-Metropolitan Opera International Radio Network. http://www.texaco.com/arts/arts. htm

Wolverine Antique Music Society. http://www.teleport.com/~rfrederi/

WWJ Newsradio 950. http://www.wwj.com/history.html

Yahoo!: Internet Radio Sites. http://www.yahoo.com/Computers_and_Internet/Internet/ Entertainment/Internet_Broadcasting/Radio/Stations/

Index

Page numbers for main entries in the Dictionary are set in boldfaced type.

About the Contributors

Mike Adams is professor of radio, television, and film (RTVF) at San Jose State University where he coordinates the RTVF program and serves as faculty adviser to the FM station. Adams has written two textbooks, authored numerous articles on radio history, and has written and produced a PBS documentary on historical broadcasting.

Craig M. Allen is an associate professor in the Walter Cronkite School of Journalism and Telecommunication at Arizona State University. His research interests include broadcast news and the political media.

Steven D. Anderson is on the faculty at the University of Oklahoma in the School of Journalism and Mass Communication. His teaching and research interests are in multimedia, new technologies, and broadcast journalism. Before entering academe, he was the environmental reporter and weekend weathercaster for KCNC-TV, Denver, Colorado, between 1982 and 1989. He also worked as a news photographer, weathercaster, and news reporter at stations in Fresno, California, and Fargo, North Dakota.

Charles F. Aust is assistant professor of mass communication in the Department of Communication at Kennesaw State University, Kennesaw, Georgia.

Robert K. Avery is professor of communication at the University of Utah. A former radio announcer and broadcast administrator, he serves as a consultant to public radio and television stations. His principal research interests include public broadcasting, telecommunications policy, and the study of mediated encounters.

Warren Bareiss teaches communication at Shorter College in Rome, Georgia. His interests include the history of mass media, the practices and philosophies of "alternative" media institutions, and how concepts of space and culture influence media content.

Erik Barnouw is professor emeritus of dramatic arts at Columbia University. He is the author of the three-volume *History of Broadcasting in the United States*, as well as a *Tube of Plenty* and *Media Marathon*. He is one of the industry's most respected historians.

Marianne Barrett is an assistant professor in the Walter Cronkite School of Journalism and Telecommunication at Arizona State University. Her teaching and research interests are broadcasting and cable programming, management, and economics.

Mary E. Beadle is an associate professor of communications at John Carroll University. She teaches undergraduate courses in broadcasting and film. She has published articles on using the Internet in communication classes and media history. Her interest in international media has led to her presenting workshops in Russia, Paraguay, and Argentina. Her current research projects include several in media history and a study of the influence of American television on Argentine students.

Louise Benjamin is the associate director of the Peabody Awards and an assistant professor in the Department of Telecommunications at the University of Georgia, Athens, Georgia. She teaches communication history and law and policy. Her research has appeared in numerous journals, including *Journal of Broadcasting and Electronic Media, Journalism Quarterly,* and *The Historical Journal of Film, Radio, and Television.* She worked as a TV writer/producer/director for five years.

ElDean Bennett is professor emeritus of the Walter Cronkite School of Journalism and Telecommunication at Arizona State University. His research and teaching interests are in international media.

Marvin R. Bensman is a professor in the Department of Communication at the University of Memphis. His research emphasis is on broadcast history and media and entertainment law.

Edward Bliss, Jr., was educated at Yale and worked on Ohio newspapers before joining CBS in New York. For 25 years he was an editor at CBS News, working as writer-producer for Edward R. Murrow and news editor for the *CBS Evening News with Walter Cronkite.* In 1968, he founded the broadcast journalism program at American University. His published works include *Now the News,* a history of broadcast journalism in the United States.

Mark J. Braun is associate professor and chair of the Department of Communication Studies at Gustavus Adolphus College. He teaches courses in mass communication, broadcasting, and the regulation of electronic media and is former chair of the Law and Policy Division of the Broadcast Education Association.

John R. Broholm is an associate professor of journalism at the William Allen White School of Journalism and Mass Communications of the University of Kansas. He is a former television news and executive producer.

Dom Caristi is assistant professor and coordinator of electronic media studies in the Journalism and Mass Communication Department at Iowa State University. His research is primarily in electronic media policy and regulation.

Ginger Rudeseal Carter is an assistant professor of journalism at Georgia College and State University. Her research interests include media and the space program and oral history.

Michael D. Casavantes is a senior lecturer at the Walter Cronkite School of Journalism and Telecommunication at Arizona State University. Casavantes worked 15 years in radio and television news, including a nine-year tenure as a radio news director.

Arthur Thomas Challis, Jr. is an assistant professor of communication at Southern Utah University (SUU). He is also president and general manager of Kolob Broadcast Radio Enterprises, Inc. The corporation has owned and operated KBRE-AM-FM in Cedar City, Utah, since 1993. He has been the sports play-by-play voice of SUU since the fall of 1974.

Frank J. Chorba is professor of mass communications at Washington University. His research interests include radio studies, critical television viewing skills, and the effects of mass media. He is the founding editor of the *Journal of Radio Studies*.

Cynthia A. Cooper is an assistant professor and director of graduate studies in the Department of Mass Communications at Southern Illinois University at Edwardsville. Her research and publications involve mass media law and regulation of violence on television.

Kenneth C. Creech is Fairbanks Professor of Communication and head of the Telecommunication Arts Department at Butler University. He is also general manager of WTBU-TV, Indianapolis, and author of *Electronic Media Law & Regulation*.

William R. Davie is an assistant professor and broadcasting coordinator in the Department of Communication at the University of Southwestern Louisiana. His research interests include television news, politics, and media.

Donald Diefenbach is assistant professor of mass communication at the University of North Carolina at Asheville. He teaches video production, research methods, and media effects courses. His research examines television content and public health issues.

Christina S. Drale is an associate dean of Arts and Letters and a faculty member in the Department of Communication and Mass Media at Southwest Missouri University. Her teaching and research interests include broadcast history, media ethics, mass communication theory, and new technologies.

Sandra L. Ellis teaches courses in radio and television journalism and mass media history at the University of Wisconsin at River Falls. She is interested in the history of communications technology and collects old radios, TVs, telephones, and photographic equipment.

Tim England is an assistant professor in the Department of Mass Communication at Southwest Texas State University at San Marcos. Prior to teaching, England worked for 18 years in radio broadcasting in Kentucky, Indiana, Virginia, and Tennessee.

Erika Engstrom is an assistant professor in the Greenspun School of Communication at the University of Nevada at Las Vegas. Her research interests include broadcast news, children's TV programming, and intercultural communication.

John P. Ferré is an associate professor of communication at the University of Louisville. He studies ethical, religious, and historical dimensions of mass media in the United States.

Robert G. Finney is a professor at California State University, Long Beach.

Robert C. Fordan is an assistant professor of communication at Central Washington University. His research and publications surround media history, politics, and pedagogical issues.

Ronald Garay is a professor and associate dean for undergraduate studies and administration in the Manship School of Mass Communication at Louisiana State University at Baton Rouge. His research and publications pertain to broadcast history, cable television operations, and electronic media regulation.

Carla E. Gesell is an instructor at the University of Tennessee at Martin. Her research interests include talk radio, computer-mediated communication, and new technologies.

Donald G. Godfrey is a professor in the Walter Cronkite School of Journalism and Telecommunication at Arizona State University. His publications include *Television in America: Local Station History from across the Nation, Reruns on File: A Guide to Electronic Media Archives,* and numerous journal publications. His teaching and professional interests are news, corporate communications, programming, and history.

Douglas Gomery is professor in the College of Journalism at the University of Maryland. He is the author of nine books and many articles on the economics and history of the mass media. His column on broadcasting business is a regular feature of the *American Journalism Review.*

Linwood A. Hagin is an assistant professor of telecommunication studies in the Department of Communication & Theater at Youngstown State University. His research interests include media ownership, management, public policy, and history.

Margot Hardenbergh is on the faculty of Marist College. Her research interests include history of the media, the social impact of changing media technologies, public access, and news values.

Kenneth Harwood is a professor emeritus and the founding director of the School of Communication at the University of Houston. He studies economics of media.

Mark J. Heistad is assistant professor in the College of Communications at the Pennsylvania State University. Formerly a public radio news producer and documentarian, his research interests include broadcasting law and policy, the history of public service broadcasting, and First Amendment theory.

Robert A. Heverly, Esq. is assistant director of the Government Law Center of Albany Law School, where he has been employed since 1992. In addition, he teaches graduate and undergraduate courses, including courses and seminars in communications law, as an adjunct faculty member at the College of Saint Rose and various law-related courses at Siena College and the State University of New York at Albany.

Gloria G. Horning is an assistant professor of broadcast journalism at Florida A&M University. Her credentials include 12 years as a television news producer and director. Currently she is working on her third documentary surrounding the issues of environmental racism.

W. A. Kelly Huff is associate professor of mass communication at Savannah State University in Savannah, Georgia. His research and publications surround electronic media technologies, management, policy and regulation, radio-TV journalism, and media history. He is also a media consultant.

Glen M. Johnson is professor of English at the Catholic University of America in Washington, D.C., where he directs the Communication Studies Program.

Larry L. Jurney is a professor of mass communication at Oklahoma Christian University in Oklahoma City. His research has focused on local religious use of American cable systems.

Phillip O. Keirstead is professor and sequence coordinator for broadcast journalism at Florida A&M University in Tallahassee. He is the author of seven books on journalism and technology, and a veteran of CBS News, the Associated Press, and local broadcast news.

Michael C. Keith is a professor of communication at Boston College. He is the author of more than a dozen books and was a former professional broadcaster. He served as chair of education at the Museum of Broadcast Communications. His research and publications deal with all aspects of the electronic media.

John Michael Kittross served on the faculties of the University of Southern California, Temple University, and Emerson College for 35 years. For more than a dozen years he edited the *Journal of Broadcasting*. Kittross is coauthor of *Stay Tuned: A Concise History of American Broadcasting* and has authored or edited numerous other books, articles, reviews, and reports. He currently is editor of *Media Ethics* magazine and managing director of K\E\G Associates, an academic consulting firm.

Laurie Thomas Lee is an assistant professor in the Department of Broadcasting at the University of Nebraska at Lincoln. Her research and publications are in the areas of new technology, privacy policy, and telecommunications law.

Frederic A. Leigh is associate director of the Walter Cronkite School of Journalism and Telecommunication at Arizona State University. His research interests include radio history, programming, and management.

Edward M. Lenert is an assistant professor in the Department of Communication at Trinity University. He is a licensed attorney, and his research focuses on issues related to the interaction of technology and society in the context of law and policy.

Lawrence W. Lichty is professor of radio/television/film at Northwestern University.

Val E. Limburg is an associate professor of the Edward R. Murrow School of Communications, Washington State University, Pullman, Washington. His research and teaching interests are in law, ethics, and media history. He is the author of *Electronic Media Ethics* and *Mass Media Literacy*.

Robert H. Lochte is an associate professor and director of television studios at Murray State University. His research interests include nineteenth-century American wireless inventions and interactive television.

Kenneth D. Loomis is an assistant professor in the Department of Communication/Journalism at the University of Wisconsin at Eau Claire. His broadcasting background spans 22 years, 11 of those years at three radio stations in Dallas, Texas. This experience is complemented by his ongoing research, study, and teaching in the field of mass communication.

William F. Lyon is assistant professor of communication arts at Taylor University. Prior to his present position, he was television producer-director with SUNY College at Cortland, New York, and a director at ABC affiliate WIXT-Television in Syracuse, New York.

David T. MacFarland is an associate professor of radio-TV-multimedia in the A. Q. Miller School of Journalism and Mass Communications at Kansas State University. He is the author of *The Development of the Top 40 Radio Format* and *Contemporary Radio Programming Strategies,* now in its second edition with a new title: *Future Radio Programming Strategies.*

Fran R. Matera is an associate professor in the Walter Cronkite School of Journalism and Telecommunication at Arizona State University. Her research and publications include Hispanic audiences, media coverage of ethnic groups, televised presidential debates, and media ethics.

Peter E. Mayeux is a professor in the Broadcasting Department, College of Journalism and Mass Communications, at the University of Nebraska at Lincoln. His research and publications involve mass media history and writing-technique projects.

Jeffrey M. McCall is an associate professor and chair of the Department of Communication Arts and Sciences at DePauw University. His research interests are in broadcast journalism and media pedagogy.

Michael A. McGregor is associate professor of telecommunications at Indiana University. His research and teaching interests are in telecommunications law and policy.

Robert McKenzie is an associate professor of communication studies at East Stroudsburg University, where he is also the faculty adviser to WESS (90.3 FM), a 1,000-watt, student-run radio station with a diversified program format. He teaches classes primarily in broadcasting, including radio practicum, broadcast journalism, voice for broadcasting, ethical and legal issues in broadcasting, and comparative media. His research has resulted in the publication of several journal articles and two book chapters on subjects ranging from news analysis to international mass communication to college radio.

Beverly G. Merrick is an assistant professor at New Mexico State University, where she does historical research on radio and women journalists, more particularly on Mary Margaret McBride, pioneer talk-show host. Her research includes in-depth articles on members of the Newswomen's Club of New York.

Fritz Messere is an associate professor at the State University of New York at Oswego. Research and publication areas include telecommunications policy, broadcast law, new technologies, and multimedia utilization.

Bruce Mims is an assistant professor of mass communication at Southeast Missouri State University. He holds memberships in the Broadcast Education Association and the Popular Culture Association. His research interests are in radio programming history, regulation of broadcasting, and audio technologies.

Barbara Moore is a professor and head of the Department of Broadcasting at the University of Tennessee, Knoxville. She is coauthor of *Radio, TV and Cable Programming* and editor of Horton Foote's *Three Trips to Bountiful*. Her interest is in broadcast programming, and she has written several articles on that subject.

Michael D. Murray is professor and chairman, Department of Communication, University of Missouri at St. Louis. He specializes in the history of broadcast news. Murray is widely published in the field and has also received a number of awards for teaching excellence, including a Frank Stanton Fellowship from the International Radio and Television Society and the Missouri Governor's Award, the highest teaching recognition in that state.

Cary O'Dell is the former archives director for the Museum of Broadcast Communications in Chicago and is the author of the book *Women Pioneers in Television: Biographies of Fifteen Industry Pioneers*. He is currently with the Wolfgang Bayer/"Best of Nature" Stock Footage Library at the Discovery Channel in Bethesda, Maryland. His research and writing are focused on radio and television history.

Kathleen M. O'Malley is a writer and editor interested in mass media, popular culture, counterculture, and psychology. She graduated from Rutgers University and has worked in book publishing ever since. She is a native and tireless defender of New Jersey.

Lindsey E. Pack is assistant professor of Communications and Theatre Arts at Frostburg State University in Frostburg, Maryland.

Joseph R. Piasek is a professor of mass communications at Quinnipiac College and a producer and consultant for Nickelodeon, the children's cable TV network, as well as its Nick at Nite/ TV Land unit. He also has two decades of radio programming and promotion under his headphones.

Ronald Razovsky is an assistant professor in the Speech Communication and Theatre Department at SUNY at Oneonta. His research interests include audience analysis and television visualization.

David E. Reese is director of WUJU and an assistant professor in the Department of Communications at John Carroll University. His research interests include radio station operations, audio production, and digital technology.

Steven C. Runyon has been director of media studies and general manager of KUSF at the University of San Francisco since 1974. He is a published mass media historian whose other specialties include broadcast production and management. In addition, he has significant professional experience in San Francisco broadcasting.

J. R. Rush is an associate professor in the Department of Communications, Brigham Young University, Provo, Utah where he teaches communications law, introduction to electronic media, and the impact of new media technology. His research interests include communications technology and law.

Bruce W. Russell has been assistant chair, Department of Communication, Slippery Rock University since 1983. He teaches public speaking, introduction to audio and video production, studio television production, electronic field production, mass media and society, and communication research methods.

Joseph A. Russomanno is an assistant professor in the Walter Cronkite School of Journalism and Telecommunication at Arizona State University. His broadcasting experience includes ten years in radio and television news as a reporter, producer, and executive producer. His research interests include broadcasting and the political process, media law, and the First Amendment and freedom of expression–related issues.

William James Ryan is associate professor of communication at Rockhurst College and director of the Kansas City Broadcasting Oral History Project.

Lee E. Scanlon teaches at Eastern New Mexico University, Portales, New Mexico.

B. William Silcock teaches broadcast journalism at the University of Missouri's School of Journalism, where he serves as executive producer for KOMU-TV (NBC). A former Fulbright Scholar to Ireland, his research interests include transnational television news, media ethics, and cultural studies.

B. R. Smith is an associate professor in the Broadcast and Cinematic Arts Department at Central Michigan University. His research interests include media history and criticism.

Tom Spann is an associate professor in the Department of Broadcasting, College of Journalism and Mass Communications, University of Nebraska. His primary area of emphasis is audio and video production.

David Spiceland is an assistant professor in the Communication Department at Appalachian State University. His research interests include broadcast editorializing, the Fairness Doctrine, broadcast journalism, early broadcast history, emerging electronic media, and FM radio development.

Alan G. Stavitsky is associate professor of journalism and communication at the University of Oregon. A former journalist in both public and commercial radio and television, he also serves as a consultant to national and local public radio organizations.

Christopher H. Sterling is an associate dean for graduate affairs in the arts and sciences at George Washington University (GWU). He is the author or coauthor of more than a dozen books including *Stay Tuned: A Concise History of American Broadcasting*. He edited the *Journal of Broadcasting* from 1972 to 1977 and taught at the University of Utah and Temple University before moving to the Federal Communications Commission (1980–1982) and GWU where he's been on the faculty since 1982.

Mary Kay Switzer is an associate professor in the Communication Department, California State Polytechnic University at Pomona. Her research and publications focus on multimedia, distance learning, and television in the courtroom.

Jonathan David Tankel is an associate professor in the Department of Communication at Indiana University–Purdue University, Fort Wayne. His work examines the intersection of media production, technology, economics, and popular culture.

Michael Taylor is currently an instructor at Valdosta State University. He has an extensive background in the radio broadcast industry in all levels of station operations, 1966–1995. His teaching areas include mass media, electronic media regulation, electronic media ethics, radio programming, audience analysis and research, broadcast management, and radio production. His research interests are radio history—from 1948 to the present—and broadcast economics.

Mark A. Tolstedt is an associate professor in the Division of Communication at the University of Wisconsin at Stevens Point.

Regis Tucci is currently a professor at Mississippi Valley State University where his teaching interests are in broadcast communication and history. His research interests are in history and military broadcast.

Max Utsler has been an associate professor of journalism at the University of Kansas since 1984. Prior to that, he served as assistant news director of KSDK-TV in St. Louis. He was a member of the faculty at the University of Missouri at Columbia from 1973 to 1983. His research and creative interests include corporate television and TV news-interviewing techniques.

Randall L. Vogt is an assistant professor in the Department of Mass Communication at Shaw University. His research interest is in broadcast history.

David Weinstein teaches in the American Studies Department at the University of Maryland at College Park. His teaching and publications concern media history, pop culture, and American history.

Gilbert A. Williams is an associate professor in the Department of Telecommunication at Michigan State University. His research interests are in broadcast and cable programming, communications history, and representation of minorities in the mass media.

Sonja Williams teaches scriptwriting and radio production courses as an assistant professor in the Department of Radio, Television and Film at Howard University. Williams also is an award-winning radio documentary producer, who has been actively involved in noncommercial and commercial radio for the past 20 years. She has managed and programmed radio stations in various parts of the United States, and she has served as a public relations consultant for various community-based organizations.

Wenmouth Williams, Jr. is a professor in the Roy H. Park School of Communications at Ithaca College. His research interests are public policy and media effects.

Michael Woal is an assistant professor at the University of New Mexico at Gallup. His research focuses on broadcasting history and film/video aesthetics.

Kyu Ho Youm is a professor of journalism at Arizona State University's Walter Cronkite School of Journalism and Telecommunication. He has published extensively in communications law in both U.S. and foreign journals since 1985.

William H. Young has taught English, American studies, and communication studies at Lynchburg College since 1964. His primary teaching emphases are popular culture and mass media. He has written extensively on American popular culture.

ISBN 0-313-29636-7

90000>

EAN

9 780313 296369

HARDCOVER BAR CODE